W9-AEP-898

Sheldon Natenberg

OPTION VOLATILITY & PRICING

Advanced Trading Strategies and Techniques

McGraw-Hill
New York San Francisco Washington, D.C. Auckland Bogotá Caracas Lisbon London Madrid Mexico City Milan Montreal New Delhi San Juan Singapore Sydney Tokyo Toronto

ISBN 1-55738-486-X

Printed in the United States of America

BB

20 19 18 17 16 15 14 13 12 11

CB/TAQ/BJS

McGraw-Hill
A Division of The McGraw-Hill Companies

To Paul, *for convincing me to become an options trader;*

To Hen and Jerry, *for their financial help when I needed it;*

To Eddie, *who encouraged me to finish the book and get off the computer so he could do his homework;*

And most of all to Leona, *for her support and encouragement.*

❖ Table of Contents ❖

Preface to the First Edition **xi**
Preface to the Second Edition **xiii**

❖ 1 ❖
The Language of Options 1
Contract Specifications 1
Exercise and Assignment 4
Market Integrity 8
Margin Requirements 9
Settlement Procedures 10

❖ 2 ❖
Elementary Strategies 13
Simple Buy and Sell Strategies 13
Risk/Reward Characteristics 16
Combination Strategies 19
Constructing an Expiration Graph 23

❖ 3 ❖
Introduction to Theoretical Pricing Models 35
Expected Return 36
Theoretical Value 37
A Word on Models 39
A Simple Approach 40
Exercise Price 46
Time to Expiration 46
Price of the Underlying 47
Interest Rates 47
Dividends 48
Volatility 49

❖ 4 ❖
Volatility **51**
Random Walks and Normal Distributions 51
Mean and Standard Deviation 56
Underlying Price as the Mean of a Distribution 60
Volatility as a Standard Deviation 60
Lognormal Distributions 61
Daily and Weekly Standard Deviations 65
Volatility and Observed Price Changes 67
A Note on Interest Rate Products 68
Types of Volatilities 69

❖ 5 ❖
Using an Option's Theoretical Value **81**

❖ 6 ❖
Option Values and Changing Market Conditions **95**
The Delta 99
The Gamma 103
The Theta 111
The Vega or Kappa 113
The Rho 116
Summary 118

❖ 7 ❖
Introduction to Spreading **127**
What Is a Spread? 127
Why Spread? 132
Spreading as a Risk Management Tool 133

❖ 8 ❖
Volatility Spreads **137**
Backspread (also referred to as a *ratio backspread* or *long ratio spread)* 138
Ratio Vertical Spread (also referred to as a *ratio spread, short ratio spread, vertical spread,* or *front spread)* 139
Straddle 141
Strangle 143

Butterfly 145
Time Spread (also referred to as a *calendar spread* or *horizontal spread)* 148
The Effect of Changing Interest Rates and Dividends 154
Diagonal Spreads 157
Other Variations 157
Spread Sensitivities 159
Choosing an Appropriate Strategy 161
Adjustments 168
Entering a Spread Order 169

❖ 9 ❖
Risk Considerations **173**
Choosing the Best Spread 173
Practical Considerations 181
How Much Margin for Error? 187
Dividends and Interest 188
What Is a Good Spread? 192
Adjustments 193
A Question of Style 195
Liquidity 196

❖ 10 ❖
Bull and Bear Spreads **199**
Naked Positions 199
Bull and Bear Ratio Spreads 199
Bull and Bear Butterflies and Time Spreads 201
Vertical Spreads 202

❖ 11 ❖
Option Arbitrage **213**
Synthetic Positions 213
Conversions and Reversals 217
Arbitrage Risk 223
Boxes 228
Jelly Rolls 231
Using Synthetics in Volatility Spreads 233
Trading without Theoretical Values 235

❖ 12 ❖
Early Exercise of American Options **241**
Futures Options 241
Stock Options 243
The Effect of Early Exercise on Trading Strategies 250

❖ 13 ❖
Hedging with Options **257**
Protective Calls and Puts 258
Covered Writes 260
Fences 263
Complex Hedging Strategies 265
Portfolio Insurance 268

❖ 14 ❖
Volatility Revisited **273**
Some Volatility Characteristics 273
Volatility Forecasting 279
A Practical Approach 282
Some Thoughts on Implied Volatility 290

❖ 15 ❖
Stock Index Futures and Options **301**
What Is an Index? 301
Calculating an Index 302
Replicating an Index 304
Stock Index Futures 305
Index Arbitrage 309
Index Options 313
Biases in the Index Market 326

❖ 16 ❖
Intermarket Spreading **331**
An Intermarket Hedge 335
Volatility Relationships 336
Intermarket Volatility Spreads 339
Options on Spreads 351

❖ 17 ❖
Position Analysis 353

Some Simple Examples 353
Graphing a Position 358
A Complex Position 367
Futures Option Positions 372

❖ 18 ❖
Models and the Real World 385

Markets Are Frictionless 386
Interest Rates Are Constant over the Life of an Option 388
Volatility Is Constant over the Life of the Option 390
Trading Is Continuous 394
Volatility Is Independent of the Price of the Underlying Contract 399
Over small periods of time the percent price changes in an underlying contract are normally distributed, resulting in a lognormal distribution of underlying prices at expiration 400
Skewness and Kurtosis 402
Volatility Skews 405
A Final Thought 416

❖ Appendix A ❖
A Glossary of Option and Related Terminology 419

❖ Appendix B ❖
The Mathematics of Option Pricing 431

Option Pricing Models 431
Normal Distributions 439
Volatility Calculations 442
The Extreme Value Method 443
The Exponential and Natural Logarithm Functions 446

❖ Appendix C ❖
Characteristics of Volatility Spreads 449

❖ Appendix D ❖
What's the Right Strategy? 451

❖ Appendix E ❖
Synthetic and Arbitrage Relationships **453**
Arbitrage Values for European Options (no early exercise permitted) 455
Other Useful Relationships: 456

❖ Appendix F ❖
Recommended Reading **457**
Elementary Books 457
Intermediate Books 459
Advanced Books 461

❖ **Index** ❖ **463**

❖ Preface to the First Edition ❖

Within the last decade trading options has increased at an explosive rate. Not only have traditional market participants, speculators, hedgers, and arbitrageurs all become actively involved in option markets, but the number of individual floor traders willing to risk their own capital in these markets has grown dramatically. Yet the trader entering an option market for the first time may find that his initial efforts are less than totally successful. Indeed, the learning period in options during which a trader gains full confidence in his ability to survive and thrive under all types of market conditions may require many months or even years of trading experience. Unfortunately, the great majority of traders do not survive this learning period. The usual characteristics of options, the subleties of the marketplace, and the unforseen risks, all seem to conspire against the inexperienced trader and eventually lead to his demise.

Much of the pain experienced by a new trader could be avoided if the trader were better prepared for the realities of option trading. Unfortunately, existing option literature has tended to take either a highly theoretical approach best suited to an academic environment, or a simplistic approach presenting options as just another way of trading stocks or commodities. Neither approach is likely to meet the needs of the serious trader. The former approach is not only mathematically beyond the capabilities of most traders, but relies heavily on theoretical assumptions which are too often violated in the real world. The latter approach cannot possibly prepare a serious trader for the wide variety of strategies with which he must be familiar, nor with the very real risks to which he will be exposed.

This book was written with the hope of filling the void in the traditional option literature by combining theory and real-world practice. Moreover, it was written primarily with the serious trader in mind. This includes traders whose firms are actively involved in option markets, either by choice or by necessity, or individual traders who wish to make the most of the opportunities offered by options. This is not meant to discourage those who are casually or peripherally involved in options markets from reading this book. Additional insight into any subject is always worthwhile. But understanding options requires substantial effort. The serious trader, because his livelihood often depends on this understanding, will usually be more willing to invest the time and energy required to attain this goal.

In preparing the reader for the option marketplace, the author has tried to combine an intuitive approach to option theory with a discussion of the real-life problems with which he will be confronted. Of course, the reader who is comfortable with mathematics is in no way discouraged from delving more deeply into the theory of option pricing in many of the excellent academic presentations of the subject. But the important point is that such a rigorous opproach is not necessary for success in option trading. Indeed, the great majority of successful option traders have never even looked at a mathematical presentation of option theory. Nor would many of them be capable of understanding the complex mathematics if they did.

Much of the presentation in this book will necessarily be colored by the author's personal experiences as a floor trader. Sophisticated hedging strategies, such as portfolio insurance, and complex intermarket spreading strategies are touched upon only briefly, if at all. Yet the principles of option evaluation which enable a floor trader to successfully participate in an option market are the same principles which will enable any participant to make the best use of options, regardless of the reasons for entering the market. Additionally, the author is able to place special emphasis on a lesson which floor traders quickly learn but which casual traders too often forget. Without a very healthy respect for the risks of option trading and a full understanding of risk management techniques, today's profits can quickly turn into tomorrow's losses.

Because of the more recent introduction of listed options on futures contracts and the increased interest in these markets, the author has tended to concentrate the examples in the text on these options. However, the principles which lead to success in futures options are equally valid in commodity, stock, and index option markets.

The core material in this book was developed in classes taught by the author to traders at the Chicago Board of Trade. In expanding the material into book form the author has tried to draw on a wide variety of other sources. Foremost among these are the many floor traders who offered their comments and criticisms. In addition, special thanks go to Greg Monroe of the Chicago Board of Trade Education Department and Mark Rzepczynski of the Chicago Mercantile Exchange Research Department for their comments on the text, and to David Isbister of Monetary Investments International for preparation of some of the values used in the tables.

Finally, my thanks to the staff at Probus Publishing for their encouragement, patience, and assistance in dealing with a first time author.

Sheldon Natenberg
Chicago

❖ Preface to the Second Edition ❖

In 1986, when I first discussed with Probus Publishing the idea of an option book for professional traders, there was considerable doubt as to whether there would be sufficient interest to justify publication of such a book. After all, how many professional option traders are there? To everyone's (pleasant) surprise, when the book came out not only did it turn out that a large number of professionals were purchasing the book, but many non-professionals also seemed to be very interested in this approach.

The revised edition is no different in its focus. The new material is likely to be of greatest interest to the serious option trader. While the material may also be of interest to the non-professional, it is the professional, whose livelihood depends on a complete understanding of options, who will be most willing to spend the time required to master the material.

In the new edition I have tried to incorporate the comments and suggestions which traders have made concerning the first edition. Some of the more important additions:

Expanded coverage of stock options—When I sat down to write the first edition the emphasis was on commodity options. This was primarily a marketing decision. At the time there were several books available on stock options, but hardly any commodity options. However, with the success of the first edition, and at the suggestion of many friends at the CBOE, I felt it would be worthwhile giving stock options equal emphasis.

More on volatility—Given its importance, a second chapter on volatility has been added with more detailed discussion of volatility characteristics and considerations.

A chapter on stock index futures and options—These markets have become so important, and are so interconnected, that some discussion is mandatory in any book on options. While one chapter cannot possibly cover every aspect of index markets, I have tried to touch on how these markets differ from traditional option markets, and the effect of these differences on trading strategies.

A discussion of intermarket spreading—Much of the most sophisticated trading involves spreading options in one underlying market against options in a different underlying market. I have included a discussion on the relationship between similar underlying markets, and the methods traders use to construct spreads when a relationship appears to be mispriced.

A more detailed discussion of volatility skews—This is probably the one area about which I am most often asked, the tendency of different exercise prices to trade at different implied volatilities. I have tried to include a discussion of this phenomenon, and several methods by which traders deal with this problem.

I have also deleted two appendicies:

A guide to software—New software is being introduced so quickly that it did not seem practical to include a list of vendors and products as I did in the first edition. Nor am I familiar with every piece of software available, so it would be unfair to those vendors who have good products but whom I might inadvertantly omit. The best way for traders to choose software is to talk to other traders and to read some of the industry periodicals to find out what programs are being used to evaluate options.

Historical volatilities—When the first edition came out I suspected that some new traders might not have access to any volatility data, so I included some historical volatility graphs for selected futures contracts. Now, however, volatility data in some form is available to almost all option traders so I did not feel that volatility charts, which would quickly become outdated, would be worth including.

As in the first edition, I make no claims to being a theoretician, and this book is not intended to take the place of a good book on option theory. But theory is only important as a means to an end—the actual trading of options in the marketplace. Whatever theory is in the book, I have tried to present in non-technical language. For a more complete discussion of option pricing theory, the reader can consult any of the advanced books to be found in Appendix F.

Nor is it my intention to make decisions for the reader or to tell the reader how to trade. There are many ways to trade successfully in an option market. Regardless of a trader's own style, without a complete familiarity with the necessary tools, and a proficiency in their use, it is almost impossible to be successful in options. I have tried to explain what these tools are, how they work, and the variety of ways in which traders use them to make decisions that fit their own individual needs and trading styles. In doing so, I have attempted, as much as possible, to avoid contaminating the reader with my own personal preferences and prejudices.

In a sense, nothing in either this or the first edition of *Option Volatility and Pricing Strategies* is new. All the theory, trading strategies, and risk management considerations, are familiar to experienced traders in one form or another. My goal has been to put all this material together and present it in an orderly, easily understandable format which I hope will form a solid foundation upon which an aspiring option trader can build a successful career.

This book is a result not only of my efforts, but of the efforts of the many traders who were kind enough to read this material and offer their comments and suggestions. Without their help I could not hope to cover all the important aspects of options. To all of them, and to the editors at Probus Publishing Company, who displayed patience above and beyond the call of duty, I offer my thanks and enduring gratitude.

Sheldon Natenberg
Chicago
June 1994

❖ 1 ❖

The Language of Options

Every option market brings together traders and investors with different expectations and goals. Some enter the market with an opinion on which direction prices will move. Some intend to use options to protect existing positions against adverse price movement. Some hope to take advantage of price discrepancies between similar or related products. Some act as middlemen, buying and selling as an accommodation to other market participants and hoping to profit from the difference between the bid and ask price.

Even though expectations and goals differ, every trader's education must begin with an introduction to the terminology of option trading, and to the rules and regulations which govern trading activity. Without a facility in the language of options, a trader will find it impossible to communicate his desire to buy or sell in the marketplace. Without a clear understanding of the terms of an option contract, and his rights and responsibilities under that contract, a trader cannot hope to make the best use of options, nor will he be prepared for the very real risks of trading.

CONTRACT SPECIFICATIONS

Options are of two *types*. A *call option* is the right to buy or take a *long* position in a given asset (typically a security, commodity, index, or futures contract) at a fixed price on or before a specified date. A *put option* is the right to sell or take a *short* position in a given asset.

Note the difference between an option and a futures contract. A futures contract requires delivery at a fixed price. The buyer and seller of a futures contract both have obligations which they must meet. The seller must make delivery and the buyer must take delivery of the asset. The buyer of an option, however, has a choice. He can choose to take delivery (a call) or make delivery (a put). If the buyer of an option chooses to either make or take delivery, the seller of the option is obligated to take the other side. In option trading all rights lie with the buyer and all obligations with the seller.

The asset to be bought or sold under the terms of the option is the *underlying* asset or, more simply, the underlying. The *exercise price,* or *strike price,* is the price at which the underlying will be delivered should the holder of an option choose to exercise his right to buy or sell. The date after which the option may no longer be exercised is the *expiration date.*

If an option is purchased directly from a bank or other dealer, the quantity of the underlying to be delivered, the exercise price, and the expiration date can all be tailored to meet the buyer's individual requirements. If the option is purchased on an exchange, the quantity of the underlying to be delivered, as well as the exercise price and expiration date, are predetermined by the exchange.[1]

As an example of an exchange traded option, the buyer of a crude oil October 21 call on the New York Mercantile Exchange has the right to take a long position in one October crude oil futures contract for 1,000 barrels of crude oil (the underlying), at a price of $21 per barrel (the exercise price), on or before October expiration (the expiration date). The buyer of a General Electric March 80 put on the Chicago Board Options Exchange has the right to take a short position in 100 shares of General Electric stock (the underlying) at a price of $80 per share (the exercise price), on or before March expiration (the expiration date).

Since stock has no expiration date, the underlying asset for a stock option is simply some number of shares in the underlying stock. In the case of futures options, however, the situation can be somewhat confusing, since a futures contract has a limited life span. The underlying asset for an option on a futures contract is usually the futures month identical to the expiration month of the option. The underlying asset for a crude oil October 21 call on the NYMEX is one October crude oil futures contract. The underlying asset for a Treasury Bond June 96 put on the Chicago Board of Trade is one June Treasury Bond futures contract.

Some futures exchanges also list *serial options*, whereby options with different expiration dates have identical underlying futures contracts. When there is no futures contract with the same expiration month as the option, the underlying contract for that option is the nearest futures contract after the expiration of the option. For example, the underlying for a December Deutschemark option on the Chicago Mercantile Exchange is one December Deutschemark futures contract. With no October or November futures contract available, the underlying for an October or November Deutschemark option is also one December futures contract. December is the nearest futures month after the expiration of October and November options.

Expiration dates for exchange traded contracts are not uniform, but are set by each individual exchange. The expiration date for stock options in the United States is usually the third Saturday after the third Friday of the expiration month. For options on futures contracts, however, the expiration need not coincide with the delivery month specified in the option contract. In some cases the exact expiration date for a futures option can predate the delivery month of the underlying futures contract by several weeks. A crude oil option on the NYMEX will typically expire the first Saturday of the preceding month, so that an October option will actually expire the first Saturday in September.

---

1. Several exchanges have recently introduced *flex options*, which permit the buyer and seller to negotiate both the exercise price and expiration date. These are still considered exchange traded options since the contracts are guaranteed by the exchange.

Figure 1-1: Contract Specifications

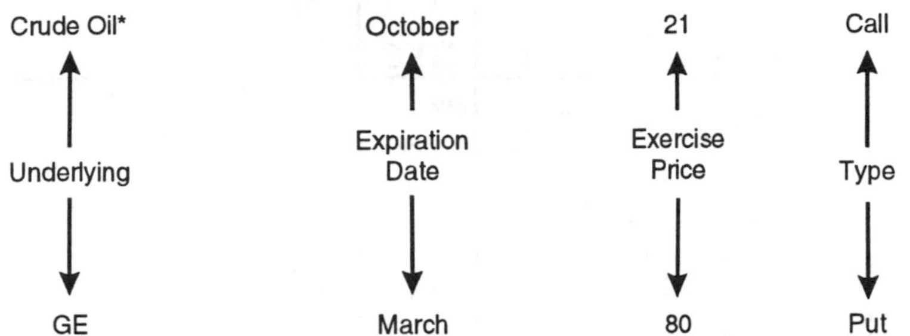

*If this is a futures option, the underlying is a futures contract rather than the physical commodity.

Figure 1-2: An Option Buy Order

BUY	C (P)	GTC			
10 VOL	GE STOCK	JAN FEB (MAR)	APR MAY JUN	70 EXPX	3½ PREM
CON CXL		JUL AUG SEP	OCT NOV DEC		

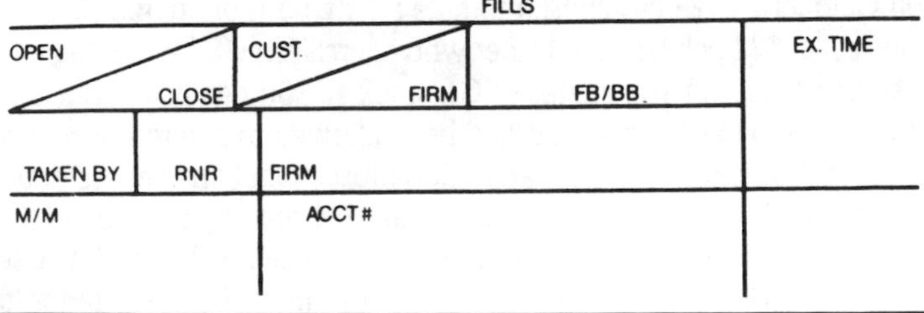

Figure 1-3: An Option Sell Order

SELL | (C) | P | GTC

25 VOL | OEX STOCK | JAN FEB MAR | APR MAY JUN | 425 EXPX | 7¼ PREM

CON | CXL | JUL AUG SEP | OCT (NOV) DEC

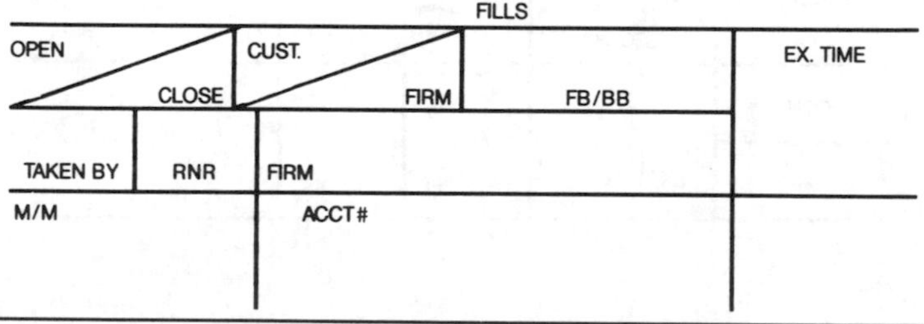

EXERCISE AND ASSIGNMENT

A trader who owns a call or a put option has the right to *exercise* that option prior to its expiration date, thereby converting the option into a long underlying position, in the case of a call, or a short underlying position, in the case of a put. A trader who exercises a crude oil October 21 call has chosen to take a long position in one October crude oil futures contract at $21 per barrel. A trader who exercises a GE March 80 put has chosen to take a short position in 100 shares of GE stock at $80 per share. Once an option is exercised it ceases to exist, just as if it had been allowed to expire unexercised.

A trader who intends to exercise an option must submit an exercise notice to either the seller of the option, if purchased from a dealer, or to the guarantor of the option, if purchased on an exchange. When a valid exercise notice is submitted, the seller of the option is *assigned.* Depending on the type of option, he will be required to take a long or short position in the underlying contract at the specified exercise price.

In addition to its underlying contract, exercise price, expiration date, and type, an option is further identified by the conditions of exercise. An option is either *American,*

Figure 1-4: The Exercise and Assignment Process

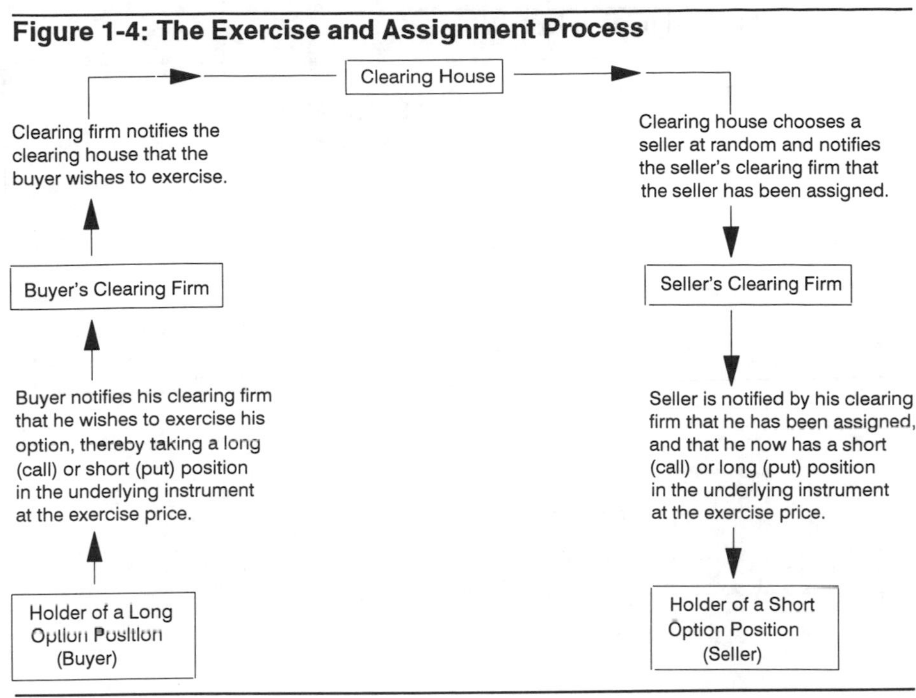
Clearing House
Clearing firm notifies the clearing house that the buyer wishes to exercise.
Clearing house chooses a seller at random and notifies the seller's clearing firm that the seller has been assigned.
Buyer's Clearing Firm
Seller's Clearing Firm
Buyer notifies his clearing firm that he wishes to exercise his option, thereby taking a long (call) or short (put) position in the underlying instrument at the exercise price.
Seller is notified by his clearing firm that he has been assigned, and that he now has a short (call) or long (put) position in the underlying instrument at the exercise price.
Holder of a Long Option Position (Buyer)
Holder of a Short Option Position (Seller)

Figure 1-5: An Exercise Notice

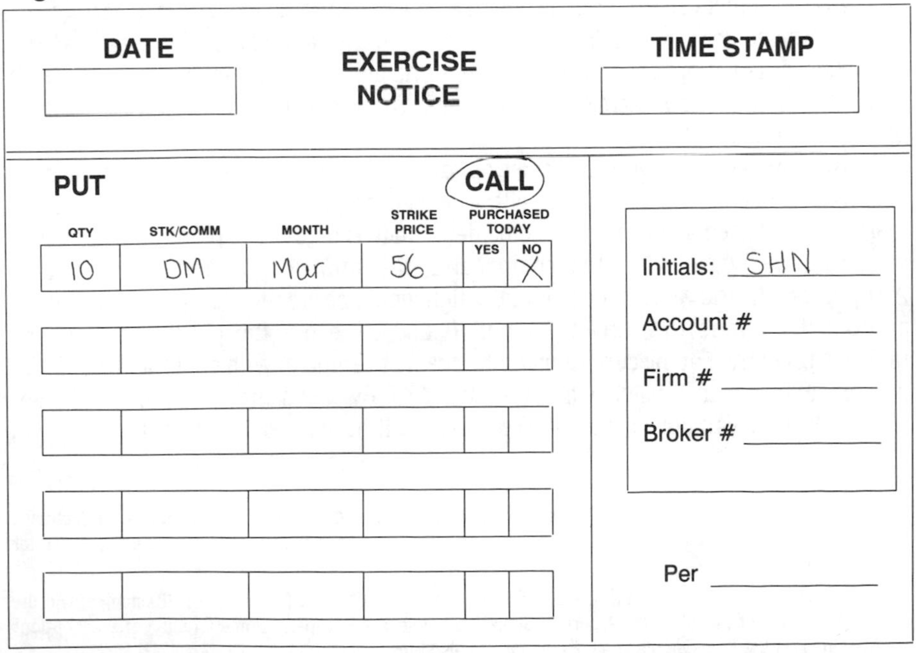

DATE

EXERCISE NOTICE

TIME STAMP

PUT

CALL (circled)

QTY	STK/COMM	MONTH	STRIKE PRICE	PURCHASED TODAY YES	PURCHASED TODAY NO
10	DM	Mar	56		X

Initials: SHN

Account # ________

Firm # ________

Broker # ________

Per ________

Figure 1-6: An Assignment Notice

DATE

ASSIGNMENT NOTICE

QTY	STK/COMM	MONTH	STRIKE PRICE	PUT	CALL
15	Crude Oil	Oct.	18		X
5	T-Bonds	Dec.	108	X	

Initials: RJN

Account # ________

Firm # ________

whereby the holder can exercise the option at any time prior to expiration, or *European*, whereby the holder can exercise the option only on expiration day.[2] The great majority of exchange traded options throughout the world are American options, carrying with them the right of early exercise. Indeed, all U.S. exchange traded stock and futures options are American.[3]

As in any competitive market, an option's price, or *premium*, is determined by supply and demand. Buyers and sellers make competitive bids and offers in the marketplace. When a bid and offer coincide, a trade is made. The premium paid for an option can be separated into two components, the *intrinsic value* and the *time value*. An option's intrinsic value is the amount which would be credited to the option holder's account if he were to exercise the option and close out the position against the underlying contract at the current market price. For example, with gold trading at $435 per ounce, the intrinsic value of a $400 call is $35. By exercising his option, the holder of the $400 call can buy gold at $400 per ounce. If he sells gold at the market price of

2. Since exchanges need time to process exercise and assignment notices, the holder of an exchange traded option must usually submit an exercise notice no later than the close of business on the day prior to expiration.

3. Certain index options, such as the S&P 500 traded on the Chicago Board Options Exchange, and the Major Market traded on the American Stock Exchange, are European. Some foreign currency options traded on the Philadelphia Stock Exchange are also European.

$435 per ounce, $35 per ounce will be credited to his account. With a certain stock trading at $62, the intrinsic value of a $70 put is $8. By exercising his option, the holder of the put can sell the stock at $70 per share. If he then buys the stock back at the market price of $62, he will show a total credit of $8.

A call will only have intrinsic value if its exercise price is less than the current market price of the underlying contract. A put will only have intrinsic value if its exercise price is greater than the current market price of the underlying contract. The amount of intrinsic value is the amount by which the call's exercise price is less than the current underlying price, or the amount by which the put's exercise price is greater than the current underlying price. No option can have an intrinsic value less than zero.

Usually an option's price in the marketplace will be greater than its intrinsic value. The additional amount of premium beyond the intrinsic value which traders are willing to pay for an option is the time value, sometimes also referred to as the option's *time premium* or *extrinsic value.* As we shall see, market participants are willing to pay this additional amount because of the protective characteristics afforded by an option over an outright long or short position in the underlying contract.

An option's premium is always composed of precisely its intrinsic value and its time value. If a $400 gold call is trading at $50 with gold at $435 per ounce, the time value of the call must be $15, since the intrinsic value is $35. The two components must add up to the option's total premium of $50. If a $70 put on a stock is trading for $9 with the stock at $62, the time value of the put must be $1, since the intrinsic value is $8. The intrinsic value and the time value must add up to the option's premium of $9.

Even though an option's premium is always composed of its intrinsic value and its time value, it is possible for one or both of these components to be zero. If the option has no intrinsic value, its price in the marketplace will consist solely of time value. If the option has no time value, its price will consist solely of intrinsic value. In the latter case, we say that the option is trading at *parity.*

While an option's intrinsic value can never be less than zero, it is possible for an option, if it is European, to have a negative time value. (More about this when we look at early exercise in Chapter 12.) When this happens the option can trade for less than parity. Usually, however, an option's premium will reflect some non-negative amount of intrinsic and time value.

Any option which has a positive intrinsic value is said to be *in-the-money* by the amount of the intrinsic value. With a stock at $44, a $40 call is $4 in-the-money. With Deutschemarks at 57.75, a 59 put is 1.25 in-the-money. An option which has no intrinsic value is said to be *out-of-the-money.* The price of an out-of-the-money option consists solely of time value. In order to be in-the-money, a call (put) must have an exercise price lower (higher) than the current price of the underlying contract. Note that if a call is in-the-money, a put with the same exercise price and underlying contract must be out-of-the-money. Conversely, if the put is in-the-money, a call with the same exercise price must be out-of-the-money.

Finally, an option whose exercise price is identical to the current price of the underlying contract is said to be *at-the-money.* Technically, such an option is also out-of-the-money since it has no intrinsic value. We make the distinction between an

Figure 1-7: In- and Out-of-the-Money Options

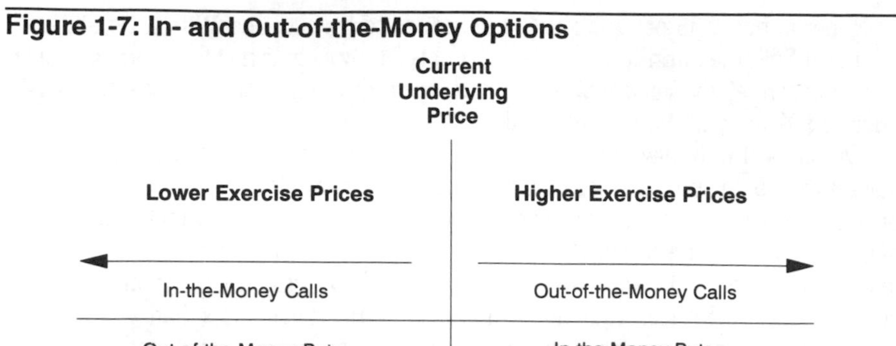

at-the-money and out-of-the-money option because an at-the-money option has the greatest amount of time premium and is usually traded very actively.

If we want to be very precise, the exercise price of an option must be identical to the current price of the underlying contract for the option to be at-the-money. However, for exchange-traded options, the term is commonly applied to the call and put whose exercise price is closest to the current price of the underlying contract. With a stock at $74 and $5 between exercise prices ($65, $70, $75, $80, etc.), the $75 call and the $75 put would be considered the at-the-money options. These are the call and put options with exercise prices closest to the current price of the underlying contract.

MARKET INTEGRITY

An important consideration for every market participant is the integrity of the market. No trader will want to trade in a market where there is a chance that the opposing trader will default on a contract. If a trader purchases an option, he wants to be certain that the seller will fulfill the terms of the contract if the option is exercised.

In order to guarantee that the integrity of the market will be maintained, each options exchange has established a progression of responsibility for the fulfillment of the terms of an option. The primary responsibility falls to the individual trader. If the seller of an option is assigned, he must be prepared to take the required long or short position in the underlying contract at the specified exercise price. In practical terms, this means a trader must have access to capital at least equal to the option's intrinsic value.

If an individual trader is unable to fulfill the terms of the contract, the responsibility falls to the trader's clearing firm. A clearing firm is a member firm of the exchange which processes trades made by an individual, and which agrees to fulfill any financial obligation arising from those trades. No individual may trade on an exchange without first becoming associated with a clearing firm.

If the clearing firm cannot fulfill the terms of the contract, the final responsibility rests with the clearing house. Each exchange has established, or has become a member of, a clearing house which guarantees the integrity of all trades. Once an option trade has been made, the connection between the buyer and seller is severed, with the clearing house assuming the role of buyer from every seller, and seller to every buyer. If there were no central clearing house, the buyer of an option would be totally dependent on the good faith of the seller or the seller's clearing firm to fulfill the terms of the option in the event of exercise. Because the clearing house guarantees every trade, all buyers can be certain there will be an opposing party prepared to make or take delivery if an option is exercised. The clearing process is shown in Figure 1-8.

This system of guarantees has proven effective in ensuring the integrity of options exchanges. While individual traders and clearing firms occasionally fail, a clearing house has never failed in the United States.

MARGIN REQUIREMENTS

When a trader makes an opening trade on an exchange, the exchange may require the trader to deposit with the clearing house some amount of *margin*, or good faith capital.[4] Such deposits ensure that if the market moves adversely, the trader will still be able to fulfill any future financial obligations resulting from the trade.

In lieu of cash, margin requirements may often be met by depositing government treasury instruments or, less commonly, commercial securities. Clearing firms collect these margin requirements from their traders and forward the funds to the clearing

Figure 1-8: The Clearing Process

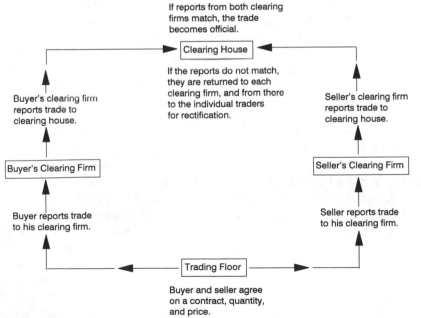

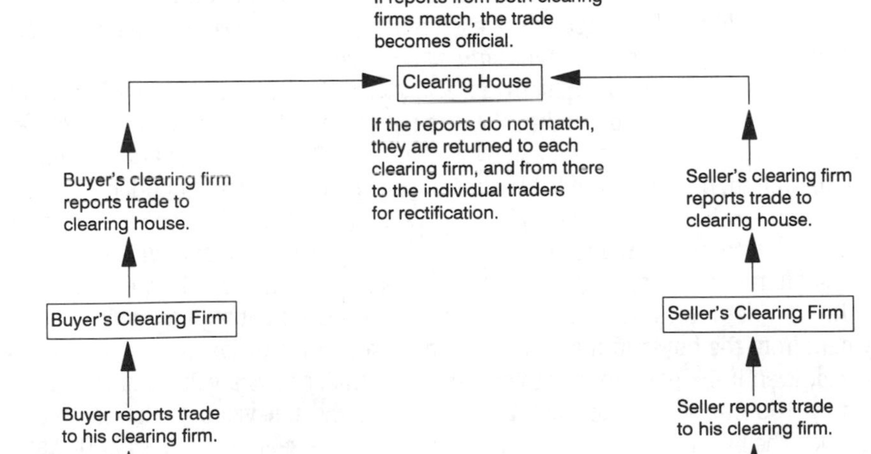
If reports from both clearing firms match, the trade becomes official.
Clearing House
If the reports do not match, they are returned to each clearing firm, and from there to the individual traders for rectification.
Buyer's clearing firm reports trade to clearing house.
Seller's clearing firm reports trade to clearing house.
Buyer's Clearing Firm
Seller's Clearing Firm
Buyer reports trade to his clearing firm.
Seller reports trade to his clearing firm.
Trading Floor
Buyer and seller agree on a contract, quantity, and price.

4. Margin requirements for a professional trader in an equity option market are referred to as a *haircut*.

house. In theory, margin deposits at the clearing house still belong to the individual trader and, as such, any interest or dividends accruing to the margin deposit also belongs to the trader. Some clearing firms, however, do not return this interest to the trader, claiming that it is part of the fee paid by the trader for the clearing services of the member firm. This can occasionally become a sensitive point between trader and clearing firm, and should be settled before an individual begins to trade.

Margin requirements for both options and underlying contracts are set by the clearing house, using as guidelines the current value of the position as well as the potential risk. While an underlying position, particularly if it is a futures contract, usually has a fixed margin requirement, the margin for an option position can change over time since the margin for an option often depends on the amount by which it is in- or out-of-the-money. Positions consisting of a combination of options, or options and underlying instruments, may have reduced margin requirements because the risk to one contract may be partially offset by the value of another contract. Additionally, traders who are exchange members may receive professional consideration in the form of reduced margin requirements. Every trader should become familiar with the margin requirements for the market in which he is trading. Doing so will ensure that he has sufficient capital to initiate and hold positions as long as he deems necessary.

SETTLEMENT PROCEDURES

New option traders are often confused because settlement procedures may vary from one exchange to another. Indeed, settlement procedures for an option and its underlying contract may differ. Two methods are commonly used to settle exchange-traded contracts—*stock-type settlement* and *futures-type settlement.*

Suppose a trader buys 100 shares of a $50 stock. The value of the stock is $5,000, and the buyer is required to pay the seller the full amount. If the stock rises to $60 per share, the owner of the stock will show a profit of $10 per share, or a total profit of $1,000. Even so, he won't be able to actually spend this $1,000 profit until he formally liquidates the position by selling his 100 shares at $60 per share. This type of settlement procedure, where purchase requires full and immediate payment, and where profits or losses are unrealized until the position is liquidated, is known as stock-type settlement.

In contrast to stock-type settlement, futures-type settlement requires no initial cash payment from the buyer to the seller. Moreover, all profits or losses are immediately realized, even if the position is not liquidated. If a trader buys a gold futures contract covering 100 ounces of gold for $450 per ounce, the full value of the contract is $45,000. The buyer, however, is not required to pay the seller the full $45,000 value of the contract. The buyer does not have to pay any money at all. He is only required to deposit with the clearing house some amount of good-faith margin. At the end of each trading day both the buyer and the seller will immediately realize any profits or losses resulting from movement in the price of the gold futures contract. If gold rises from $450 to $470 per ounce, $2,000 ($20 × 100) will be credited to the buyer's account, and he will have immediate use of these funds even if he does not liquidate the position. Of course, if the price of gold drops to $430 per ounce, he will realize an immediate loss of $2,000. If he does not have sufficient funds in his account to cover this loss, the clearing house will issue a *variation* call.

There is an important distinction between a margin call and a variation call. A margin call is issued by the clearing house to ensure that a trader can fulfill future financial obligations should the market move against him. Margin calls can be met with funds which, even though deposited at the clearing house, still belong to the trader and consequently can earn interest for the trader. A variation call is issued in order to fulfill current financial obligations in the form of realized losses. A variation call must be met with a cash payment which is immediately deducted from a trader's account. If a trader has deposited securities with the clearing house as margin and receives a variation call, he must either deposit the additional variation amount in cash, or the clearing house will sell the securities in his account to generate enough cash to meet the variation call. If the remaining securities and cash in the account is not sufficient to meet the current margin requirements, the trader may be forced to liquidate his position.

We make this very important distinction between stock- and futures-type settlement because some options are settled like stock and some options are settled like futures. It is important for a trader to know which he is trading. Currently all exchange-traded options in the United States, whether options on stock, futures, indices, or foreign currencies, are settled like stock. Options must be paid for immediately and in full, and profits or losses are unrealized until the position is liquidated. In stock option markets this is both logical and consistent, since both the underlying contract and options on that contract are settled using identical procedures. However, on U.S. futures options markets, the underlying contract is settled one way (futures-type settlement) while the options are settled in a different way (stock-type settlement). This can sometimes cause problems when a trader has bought or sold an option to hedge a futures position. Even if the profits from the option position exactly offset the losses from the futures position, the profits from the option position, because the options are settled like stock, are only paper profits. On the other hand, the losses from the futures position will require an immediate cash outlay to cover a variation call. If a trader is unaware of the different settlement procedures, he can occasionally find himself with unexpected cash flow problems.

The settlement situation on many exchanges outside the U.S. has been simplified by making option and underlying settlement procedures identical. If the underlying is subject to stock-type settlement, then so are the options on the underlying. If the underlying is subject to futures-type settlement, then so are the options. Under this method a trader is unlikely to get a surprise variation call on a position which he thinks is well hedged.

Before concluding this chapter, it will be useful to define the terms *long* and *short* as they are used in option trading versus their use in trading an underlying contract. In a long underlying position a trader will profit if prices rise and lose if prices fall. In a short underlying position a trader will profit if prices fall and lose if prices rise. There is a tendency to carry this terminology over into the option market by referring to any position which will profit from a rise in the price of the underlying contract as a long position, and any position which will profit from a fall in price as a short position.

More generally, however, the terms long and short refer to the purchase or sale of a contract, and this is the sense in which we apply these terms to option trading. A trader who has purchased an option is long the option, and a trader who has sold the option is short. There is no confusion when we refer to a long call position because the trader who is long a call also has a *long market position.* Calls will, in theory, rise in value if the underlying market rises. But a long put position is a *short market position.* A trader who has purchased a put wants the underlying market to decline because a put will theoretically increase in value as the market declines. Throughout the text, whenever there is the possibility of confusion, an attempt will be made to distinguish between a long or short market position versus a long or short option position.

❖ 2 ❖

Elementary Strategies

The trader who enters an option market for the first time may find himself subjected to a form of "contract shock." Unlike a trader in equities or futures, whose choices are limited to a small number of instruments, an option trader must often deal with a bewildering assortment of contracts. With at least three different expiration months, with each month having several different exercise prices, and with both calls and puts available at each exercise price, it is not unusual for an option trader to be faced with as many as 40 different contracts.

Even if we eliminate the inactively traded options, a new trader may still have to deal with 15 or 20 different options. With so many choices available, a trader needs some logical method of deciding which options actually represent profit opportunities. Which should he buy? Which should he sell? Which should he avoid altogether? The choices are so numerous that many prospective option traders give up in frustration.

For the trader who does persevere, a certain logic in the pricing of options begins to emerge. As he becomes familiar with this logic, he can begin to formulate potentially profitable strategies. Initially he will concentrate on the purchase or sale of individual options. From there he will go on to combination strategies. Eventually he will become comfortable with complex strategies involving several different contracts.

How might a beginning trader assess an option's value? One simple method depends on guessing where the underlying contract will be at expiration. If an option position is held to expiration, the option will be worth either zero, if it is at- or out-of-the-money, or intrinsic value (parity), if it is in-the-money. The purchase of an option will be profitable if its trade price is less than its value at expiration. The sale of an option will be profitable if its trade price is greater than its value at expiration.

SIMPLE BUY AND SELL STRATEGIES

For example, suppose the following options are available with two months remaining to expiration, and the underlying contract trading at 99.00:

	85	90	95	100	105	110	115
Calls	14.05	9.35	5.50	2.70	1.15	.45	.20
Puts	.10	.45	1.55	3.70	7.10	11.35	16.10

Suppose we believe that the underlying contract will rise to at least 108 by expiration. We might then purchase a 100 call for 2.70. If we are correct, and the contract does in fact end at 108, our profit at expiration will be the option's intrinsic value of 8.00 less the 2.70 we originally paid, or 5.30. Given the above prices, if the underlying market rises to 108 by expiration we will show a profit if we purchase any call with an exercise price less than 110. The intrinsic value of each of these options at expiration will be greater than its current price in the marketplace.

What about the 110 and 115 calls? If we believe that 108.00 is a reasonable upside goal for the underlying contract, but consider it unlikely that the price will rise above 110, then we will prefer to be sellers of the 110 and 115 calls. If we sell the 110 call for .45 and the underlying contract never rises above 110.00, the 110 call will expire worthless and we will get to keep the full premium of .45. We can also sell the 115 call for .20, giving us an additional 5 point margin for error. If the underlying contract never rises above 115.00, the 115 call will expire worthless and we will get to keep the full premium of .20.

We can use the same approach to assess the potential profit from the purchase or sale of a put. As with a call, a put's intrinsic value at expiration must be greater than its trade price in order for the purchase of a put to be profitable. If the underlying contract rises to 108.00 by expiration, any put with an exercise price of 105 or less will be worthless. If we sell any of these puts, we will profit by the full amount of the premium. If we sell the 110 or 115 puts, they will not be totally worthless at expiration because, with the underlying contract at 108.00, they will have intrinsic values of 2.00 and 7.00, respectively. However, this will still be less than their trade prices of 11.35 and 16.10. We will show a profit of 9.35 from the sale of the 110 put and 9.10 from the sale of the 115 put.

As we change our assumptions about the likely price of the underlying contract at expiration, we alter the likely profit or loss from any option position. If, instead of rising to 108.00, the underlying contract actually rises to 120.00, the purchase of the 100 call for 2.70 will result in a profit of 17.30 rather than 5.30. On the other hand, if the underlying contract falls to 90.00, the purchase of the 100 call will result in the loss of the full premium of 2.70. In the latter case, if we sell the 110 put for 11.35, instead of making 9.35 as we would with the underlying contract at 108.00, we will actually lose 8.65.

Using a value for an option of either zero or intrinsic value, we can graph the profit or loss at expiration from any option trade which we might make today. Such graphs not only enable the new trader to assess the likely profitability of an option trade, but also help him to understand some of the unusual characteristics of options. However, before looking at graphs of various option positions, we ought to look at the profit and loss graph of an underlying contract. Because it is a derivative instrument, an option's value is always dependent on the price of the underlying instrument. At expiration an option's value is totally dependent on the price of the underlying contract. Indeed, if we have an opinion on the likely price of the underlying contract at some date in the future, we don't need to trade options at all. We can simply buy or sell the underlying contract.

Figure 2-1 shows the value at expiration of both a long and a short position in our example underlying contract taken at the current price of 99.00. The horizontal (x) axis represents the price of the underlying futures contract, and the vertical (y) axis represents the profit or loss from our position. Note that each graph is a straight 45° line

Figure 2-1

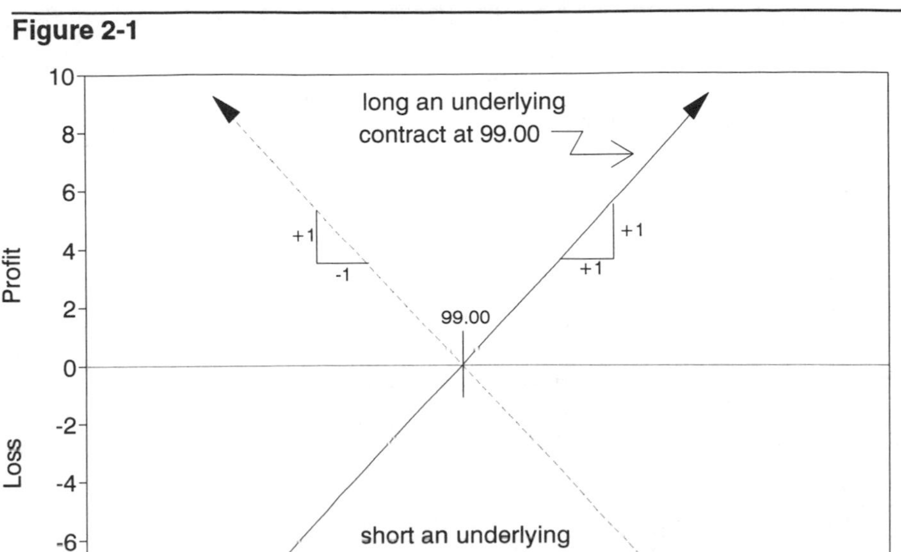

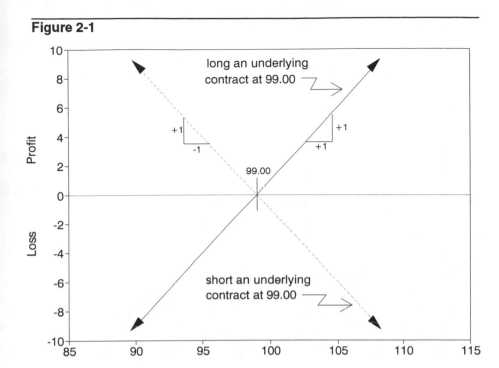

extending infinitely far in either direction.[1] The potential profit or loss to each position is therefore unlimited. Note also that there is a continuous one-to-one relationship between movement in the underlying contract and the value of the position. If we take a long position, for each point the underlying contract rises, we make a point; for each point the underlying contract falls, we lose a point. If we take a short position the situation is just reversed. For each point the underlying contract rises, we lose a point; for each point the underlying contract falls, we make a point.

Using the same evaluation method, Figure 2-2 shows the profit or loss at expiration from the purchase of a 100 call at 2.70. Note that in this case the graph is no longer a straight line. If the underlying contract falls below 100 at expiration the 100 call will be out-of-the-money and therefore worthless, and we will lose the full 2.70 we paid for the call. Above 100, the call will be in-the-money, and will increase in value at the same rate as the underlying contract; the position will gain one point in value for each point rise in the value of the underlying contract. If the underlying contract finishes at 102.70, the 100 call will be worth its intrinsic value of 2.70, and we will break exactly even. Above 102.70, the profit from the purchase of the 100 call is potentially unlimited, just like a long position in the underlying contract.

---

1. Of course, an underlying price cannot fall below zero, so the downside profit or loss is in theory limited. However, if the price of an underlying contract should go to zero, it will probably seem like an unlimited profit or loss to most traders.

Figure 2-2

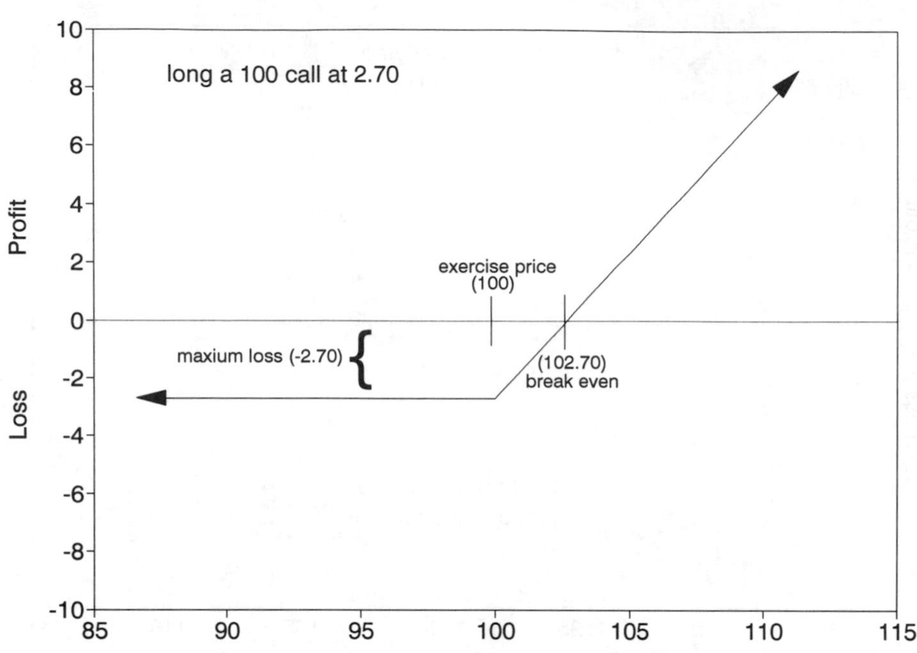

RISK/REWARD CHARACTERISTICS

The profit and loss graph of a long call position at expiration will always have the same general shape as the graph in Figure 2-2. The position will always have limited downside risk and unlimited upside profit potential. The exact point at which the maximum loss will occur is determined by the exercise price (the point at which the graph bends) and the price of the option. Graphs of long positions in the 95, 100, and 105 calls are shown in Figure 2-3.

Figure 2-4 represents the profit and loss from a short position in the 95, 100, and 105 calls. These are simply inversions of the long call graphs. The positions now have profit potential limited to the amount of the premium for which they were sold, and unlimited upside risk similar to a short position in the underlying contract.

Figure 2-5 represents long positions in the 95, 100, and 105 puts. The risk/reward characteristics of these positions are similar to long call positions, but now the limited risk is on the upside and the unlimited profit potential is on the downside. The position will break even if the underlying contract falls below the exercise price by exactly the amount of the option's trade price. Below that break-even price the potential profit to the position is unlimited, increasing by one point for each point drop in the price of the underlying contract.

Figure 2-3

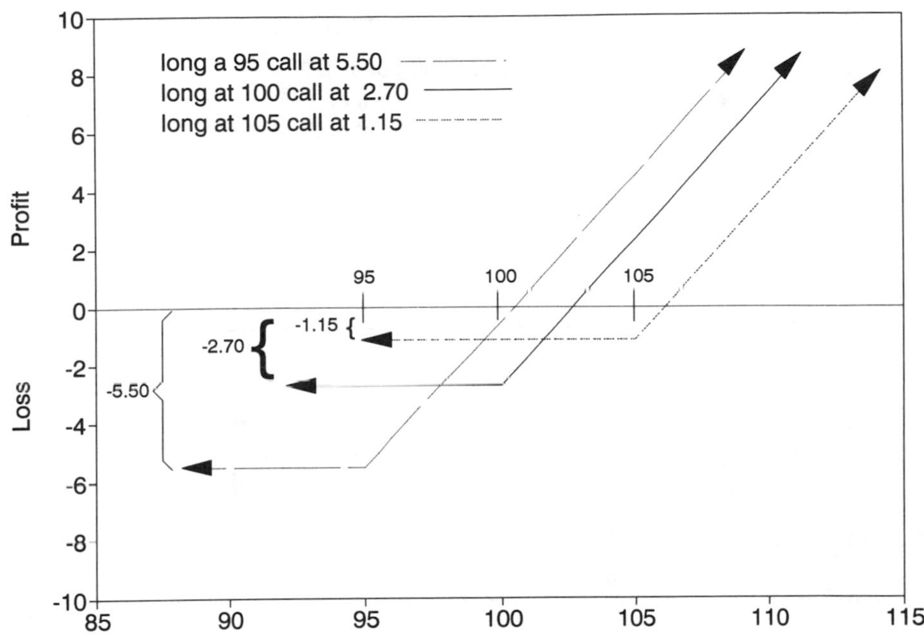

Figure 2-4

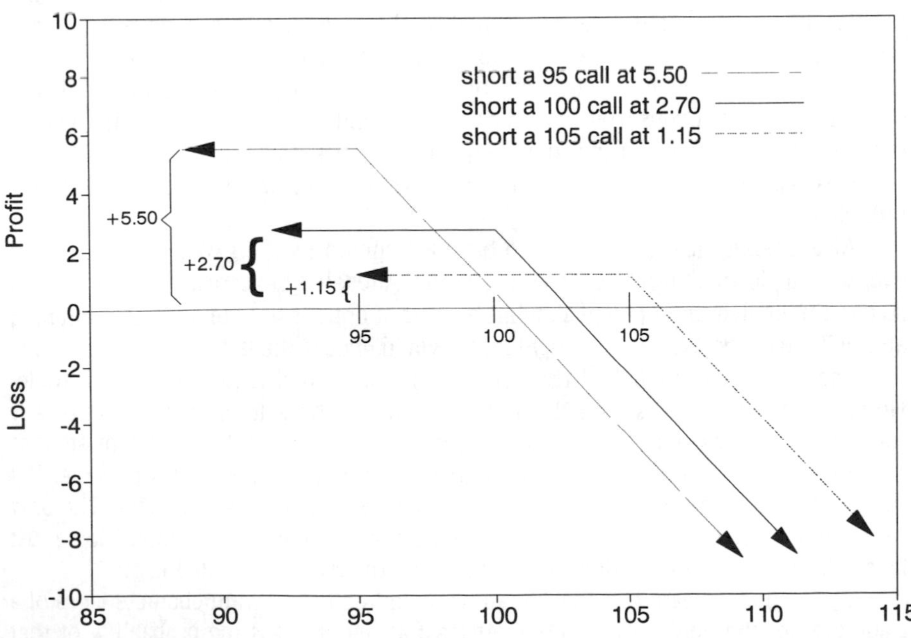

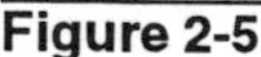
Figure 2-5

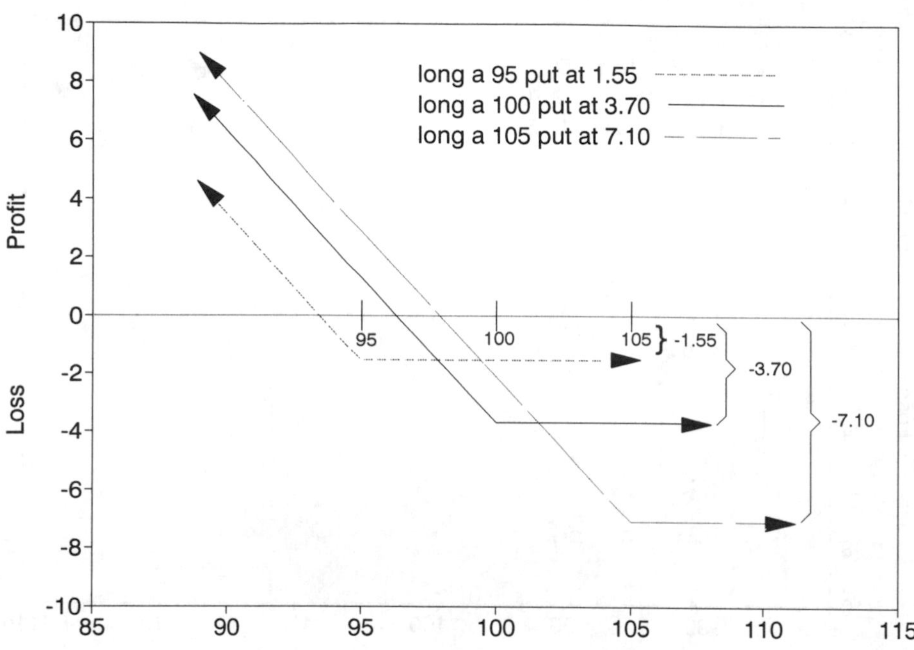

The short put positions in Figure 2-6 are inversions of the graphs in Figure 2-5. Each position has upside profit potential limited to the amount of the trade price, and a potentially unlimited loss similar to a long position in the underlying contract.

Figures 2-3 through 2-6 illustrate two of the most important characteristics of options: buyers of options have limited risk and potentially unlimited reward; sellers of options have limited reward and potentially unlimited risk. More specifically, net buyers (sellers) of calls have unlimited upside reward (risk), and net buyers (sellers) of puts have unlimited downside reward (risk).

At this point, new traders tend to have a common reaction. Why would anyone ever want to do anything other than buy options? After all, a buyer of options has limited risk and unlimited profit potential, while a seller of options has limited profit potential and unlimited risk. Who in their right mind would choose the latter over the former?

The prospect of unlimited risk certainly seems a good reason to avoid a trade. However, if a trader gives some thought to the matter, he will realize that almost any trade in a stock or commodity market carries with it unlimited risk. A violent adverse move which does not give a trader time to cover his position is always possible. Yet traders take long and short positions in stocks and commodities all the time. The only explanation must be that they believe the chances of sustaining a catastrophic loss must be small, so small that the potential profit justifies the risk of unlimited loss.

Option traders learn that the limited or unlimited risk/reward characteristics of a trade are not the only considerations. At least as important is the probability of that

Figure 2-6

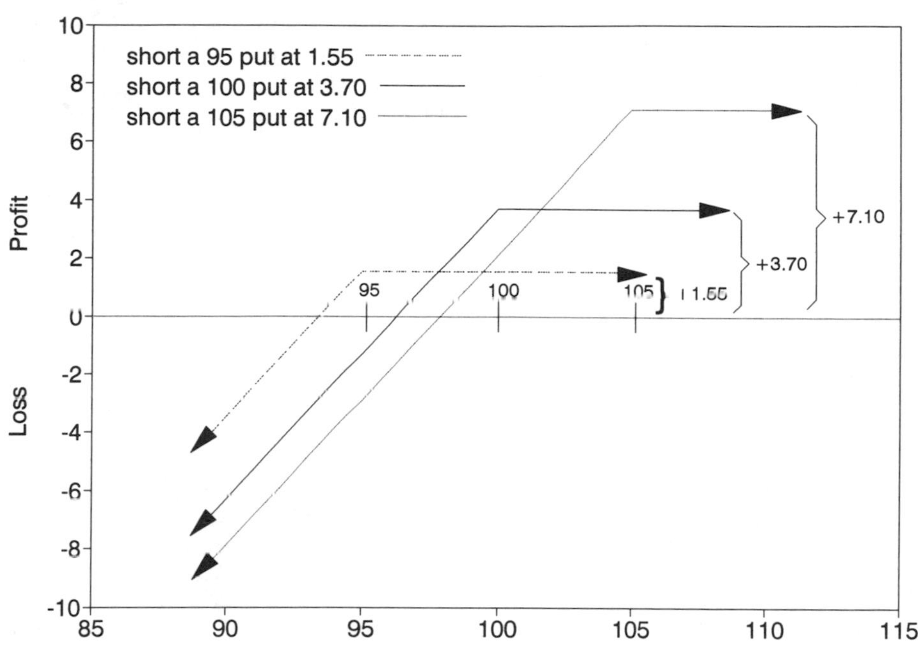

unlimited profit or loss. As an example, suppose a trader is considering a trade which has only two possible outcomes. In one case the trader will double his money; in the other case he will go broke. It may seem that a rational trader will avoid such a trade because the reward does not appear to justify the risk. But suppose the probability of the second outcome is only one chance in a million. Suppose in fact that the exact circumstances which will cause the trader to go broke have never before occurred. Now how does the trade look? The reward is still limited and the risk unlimited. Yet most traders would probably make the trade in spite of the potentially disastrous results.

In addition to the potential risk and reward associated with any trade, a trader must also consider the likelihood of the various outcomes. Is the reward, even a limited one, sufficient to offset the risk, albeit an unlimited one? Sometimes it is; sometimes it isn't.

COMBINATION STRATEGIES

When considering an option trade we need not restrict ourselves to the purchase or sale of individual options. We can also combine option positions to form new positions with their own unique characteristics. Figure 2-7 shows the profit and loss at expiration from the combined purchase of a 100 call for 2.70, and a 100 put for 3.70. Here we have paid a total of 6.40, which will be our maximum loss if both options expire worthless. This will happen only if the underlying contract is right at 100 at expiration. If the underlying contract is above 100 at expiration the put will be worthless, but the call

Figure 2-7

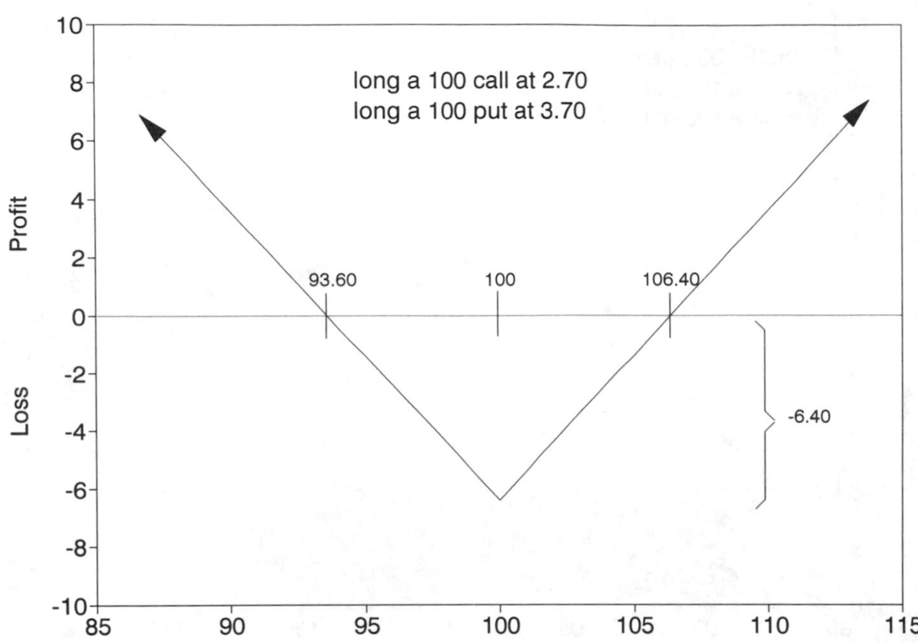

will act like a long underlying position, gaining one point in value for each point the underlying contract rises. If the underlying contract is below 100 the call will be worthless, but the put will act like a short underlying position, gaining one point in value for each point the underlying contract falls. In order for the position to do no worse than break even, it must be worth at least the 6.40 we originally paid. This will occur if either the 100 call or the 100 put turns out to be worth 6.40. At expiration, the underlying contract must be at or above 106.40, or at or below 93.60. Outside of this range, the potential profit is unlimited.

Under what conditions might we initiate the position in Figure 2-7? Such a position might be sensible if we thought a large move in the underlying contract would take place in the near future, but were uncertain as to the direction of that move. If the move were sufficiently large (above 106.40 or below 93.60) the position would be profitable. Of course we might also take the opposite view, that the underlying contract was unlikely to either fall below 93.60 or rise above 106.40. Under these conditions we might prefer to sell both the 100 call and 100 put (Figure 2-8). Now our profit is limited to the total premium of 6.40, while our risk in either direction is unlimited. But if we feel strongly that the underlying contract is likely to stay in the 93.60–106.40 range through expiration, the risk might be worth taking.

Suppose we take a view similar to that in Figure 2-8, that the underlying contract is unlikely to make a big move in either direction. But because there is always a chance

Figure 2-8

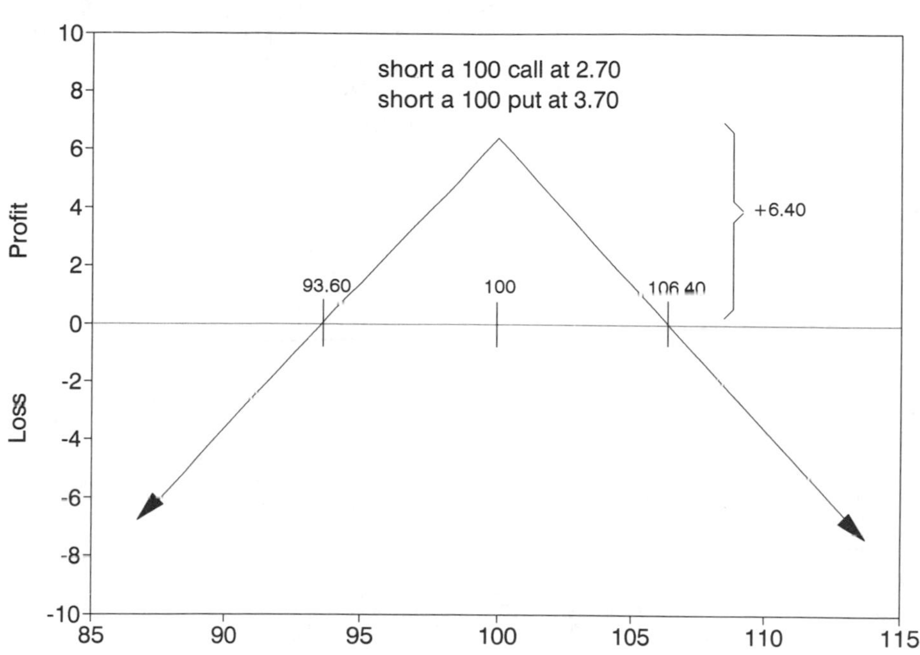

we could be wrong, we might want to increase our margin for error by increasing our range of profitability beyond the 93.60–106.40 range. Instead of selling a 100 call and a 100 put, we might sell a 95 put for 1.55 and a 105 call for 1.15. This position (Figure 2-9) will realize its maximum profit of 2.70 anywhere within the 95–105 range, where both options will expire worthless. We won't lose money unless the underlying contract finishes below 92.30 or above 107.70 at expiration. In the former case the 95 put will be worth at least 2.70, and in the latter case the 105 call will be worth at least 2.70. There is, as always, a tradeoff for this increased range of profitability. Our maximum profit now is only 2.70, whereas in Figure 2-8 it was 6.40. In return for a reduced risk, we must be satisfied with a reduced profit potential. Option traders are constantly required to make these types of tradeoffs between risk and reward. If a potential reward is big enough, it may be worth taking a big risk. But if the potential reward is small, the accompanying risk should also be small.

The positions in Figures 2-7, 2-8, and 2-9 all have either unlimited reward or unlimited risk because they are either net long or net short options. If we purchase and sell equal numbers of options of the same type, we can create positions which have both limited risk and limited reward. For example, we might buy a 90 call for 9.35 and sell a 100 call for 2.70, for a total debit of 6.65 (Figure 2-10). If the underlying contract finishes below 90.00 both options will expire worthless and we will lose our total investment of 6.65. If the underlying contract finishes above 100, the 90 call, which

Figure 2-9

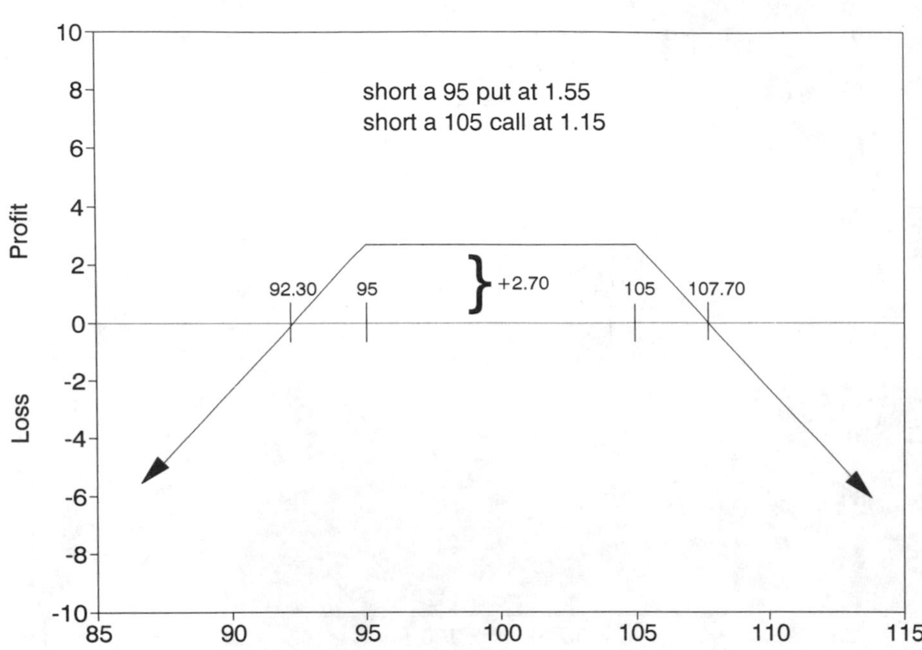

we own, will be worth exactly 10 points more than the 100 call, and we will realize the maximum profit of 3.35. Between 90 and 100 the position will be worth some amount between zero and 10 points. In order to do no worse than break even we must recoup our original investment of 6.65. We will be able to do this if the underlying contract is at 96.65 or higher at expiration. The 90 call will then be worth at least 6.65. Like the outright purchase of a call, this position wants the market to rise so that we will realize our maximum profit of 3.35. Here, however, we are willing to give up the unlimited upside profit potential associated with the outright purchase of a 90 call, in return for the partial downside protection afforded by the sale of the 100 call. The position is bullish, but with both limited risk and limited reward.

If we are bearish on the market we might create a position with limited risk and limited reward by inverting the position in Figure 2-10. That is, we might sell the 90 call and purchase the 100 call. Now our potential profit is limited to 6.65 if the market finishes below 90, and our potential loss is limited to 3.35 if the market finishes above 100.

We can also create a bearish position with both limited risk and limited reward by purchasing a put with a higher exercise price and selling a put with a lower exercise price. For example, we might buy a 105 put for 7.10 and sell a 100 put for 3.70, for a total debit of 3.40 (Figure 2-11). If the underlying contract is below 100 at expiration,

Figure 2-10

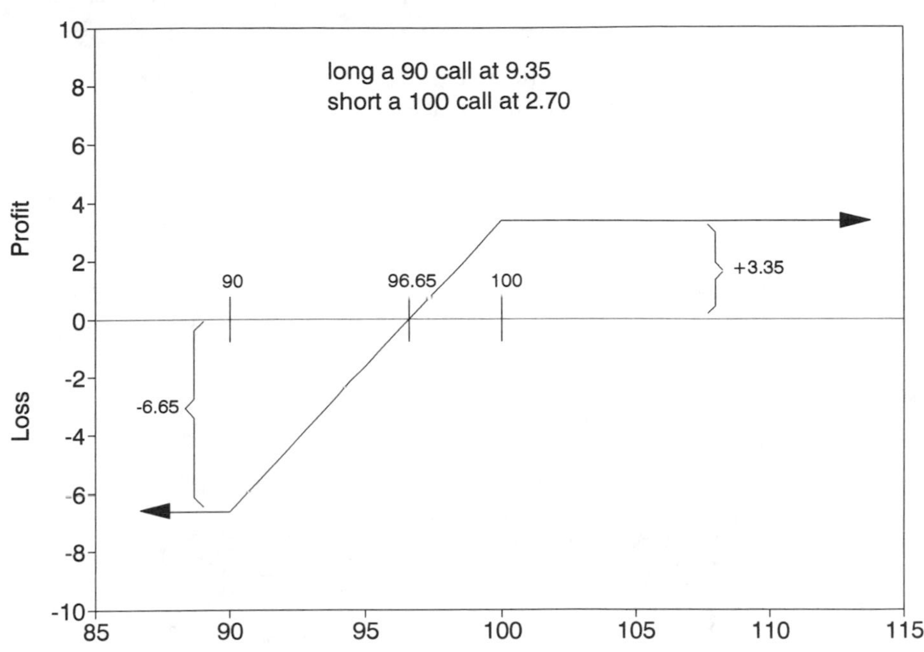

the 105 put will be worth exactly 5 points more than the 100 put, and we will realize our maximum profit of 1.60. If the underlying contract is above 105 at expiration, both options will be worthless and we will lose our entire investment of 3.40. The position will do no worse than break even if the underlying contract is at or below 101.60, for then the 105 put will be worth at least 3.40. Like the outright purchase of a put, this position is bearish. However, we have chosen to give up the unlimited downside profit potential associated with the outright purchase of the 105 put in return for the partial upside protection afforded by the sale of the 100 put.

CONSTRUCTING AN EXPIRATION GRAPH

From the foregoing examples, we can formulate some simple rules for drawing expiration profit and loss graphs:

1. If the graph bends, it will do so at an exercise price. Therefore, we can calculate the profit or loss at each exercise price involved and simply connect these points with straight lines.

2. If the position is long and short equal numbers of calls (puts), the potential downside (upside) risk or reward will be equal to the total debit or credit required to establish the position.

Figure 2-11

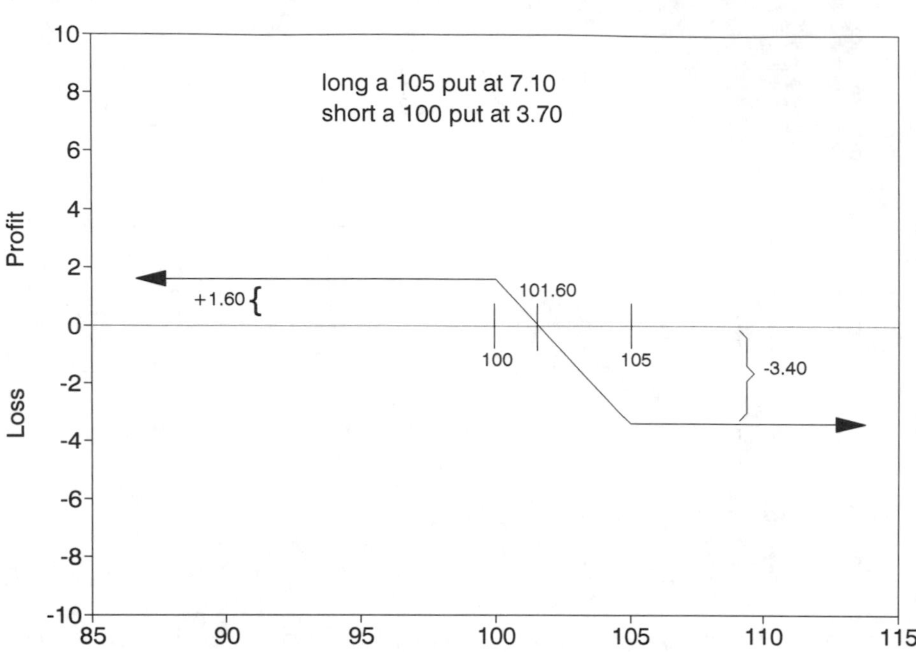

3. Above the highest exercise price all calls will go into-the-money, so the entire position will act like an underlying position which is either long or short underlying contracts equal to the number of net long or short calls. Below the lowest exercise price all puts will go into-the-money, so the entire position will act like an underlying position which is either long or short underlying contracts equal to the number of net long or short puts.

To see how we can use these rules to construct an expiration graph, consider the following position:

long one 95 call at 5.50
short three 105 calls at 1.15

The first step is to determine the profit or loss at each exercise price (95 and 105). If the underlying contract finishes at 95, both the 95 and 105 calls will be worthless. Since the entire position was established for a debit of 2.05 (-5.50 + 3 × 1.15), at 95 the position will show a loss of 2.05. If the underlying contract finishes at 105, the 95 call will be worth 10.00 and the 105 calls will be worthless. Since we own the 95 call, the position will be worth 10 points less the initial debit of 2.05, or 7.95. We can plot and connect these two points on a graph (Figure 2-12a).

Figure 2-12a

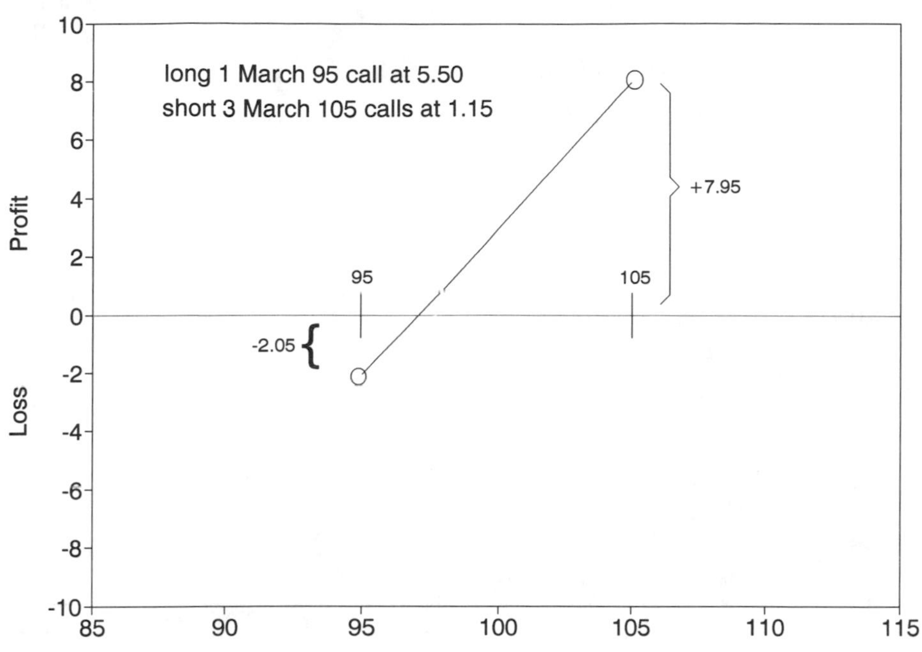

Next, we note that there are no puts involved in this position, so the maximum downside loss we can incur is the 2.05 debit required to establish the position. This loss will occur anywhere below 95 (Figure 2-12b).

Finally, above 105 both the 95 and 105 calls will go into-the-money, so that all options will begin to act like long underlying contracts. We will be long one underlying contract in the form of a 95 call, and short three underlying contracts in the form of three 105 calls. The net result is that above 105 we have a position which is equivalent to being short two underlying contracts. For each point increase in the price of the underlying contract, our position will lose two points (Figure 2-12c).

Applying this method to a more complex example, what would be the expiration graph of the following position?

short one 90 call at 9.35
long two 100 calls at 2.70
short four 95 puts at 1.55
long two 100 puts at 3.70

Figure 2-12b

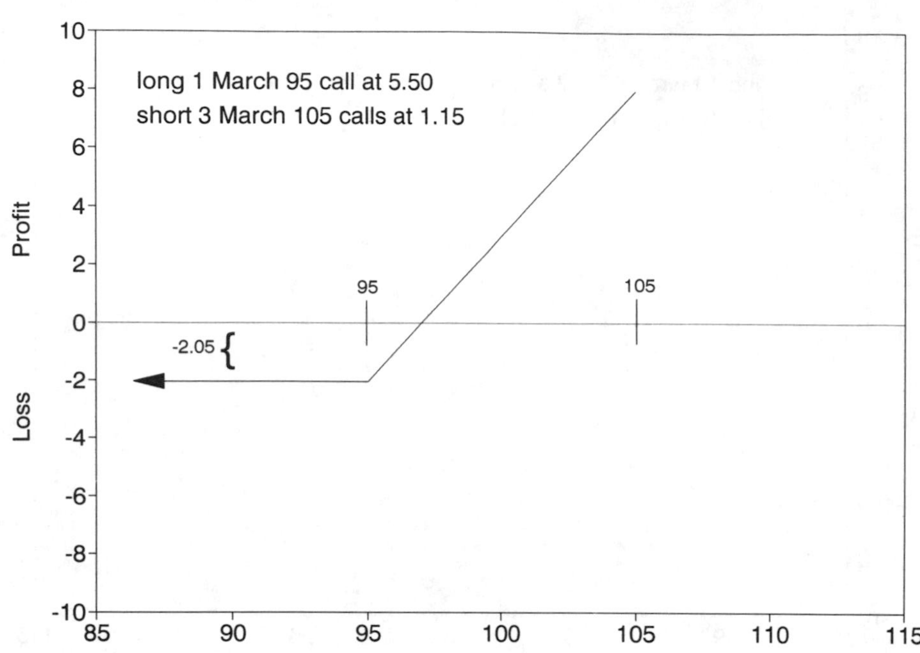

Figure 2-12c

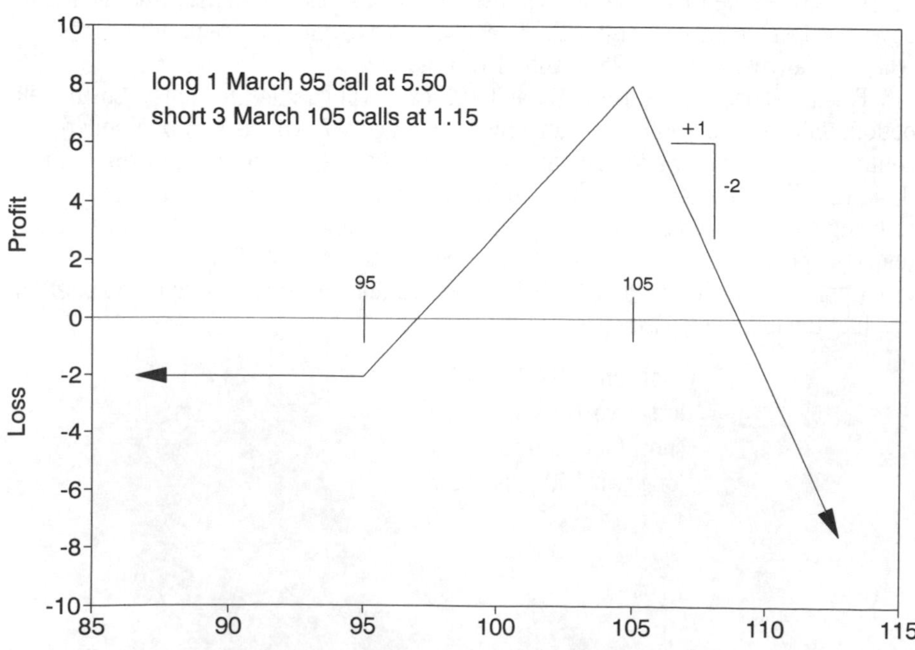

First, what happens at the three exercise prices involved? At 90 we have:

90 call	+9.35
100 calls	–2 × 2.70
95 puts	–4 × 3.45
100 puts	+2 × 6.30
Total	+2.75

At 95 we have:

90 call	+4.35
100 calls	–2 × 2.70
95 puts	+4 × 1.55
100 puts	+2 ×1.30
Total	+7.75

And at 100 we have:

90 call	–.65
100 calls	–2 × 2.70
95 puts	+4 × 1.55
100 puts	–2 × 3.70
Total	–7.25

We can plot and connect these profit and loss points at each of the exercise prices (Figure 2-13a).

Next, below 90 all calls will be worthless and all puts will act like short underlying contracts. Since the position is net short two puts, the graph will act like a position which is long two underlying contracts. For each point that the underlying contract falls below 90, the position will lose two points (Figure 2-13b).

Finally, above 100 all puts will be worthless and all calls will act like long underlying contracts. Since the position is net long one call, above 100 it will act like a position which is long one underlying contract. For each point rise in the underlying contract, the position will gain one point in value (Figure 2-13c).

Using this method we can draw the expiration profit and loss graph of any position, no matter how complex. The position may consist of underlying contracts, and calls and puts at various exercise prices. But as long as all options expire at the same time, the value of the position at expiration will be fully determined by the price of the underlying contract.

Using options and underlying contracts it is also possible to create positions which mimic other option and underlying positions. For example, what are the characteristics of the following position?

long one 100 call at 2.70
short one 100 put at 3.70

Figure 2-13a

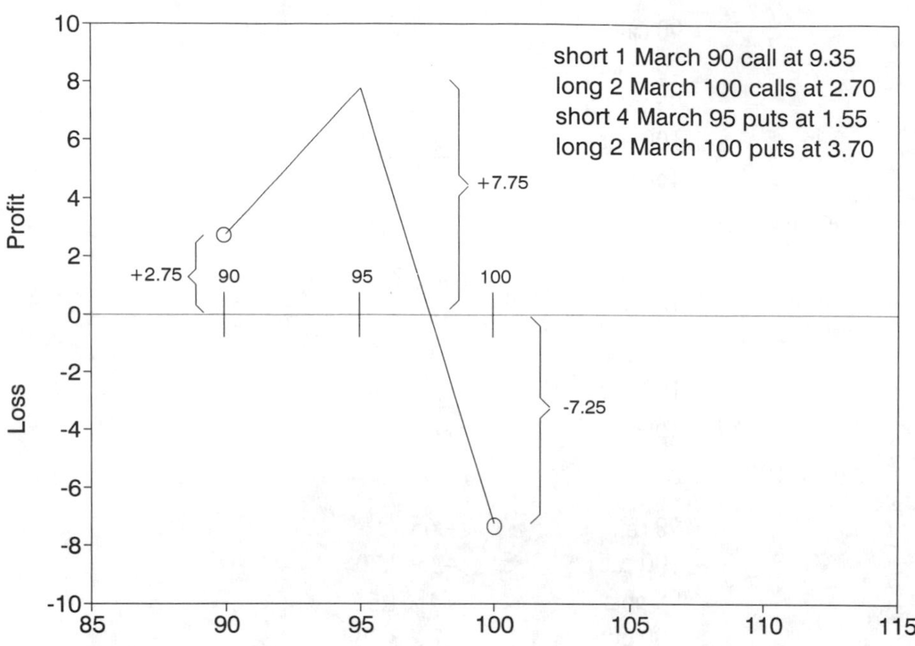
short 1 March 90 call at 9.35
long 2 March 100 calls at 2.70
short 4 March 95 puts at 1.55
long 2 March 100 puts at 3.70
+7.75
+2.75
-7.25
Profit
Loss
90
95
100
10
8
6
4
2
0
-2
-4
-6
-8
-10
85
90
95
100
105
110
115

Figure 2-13b

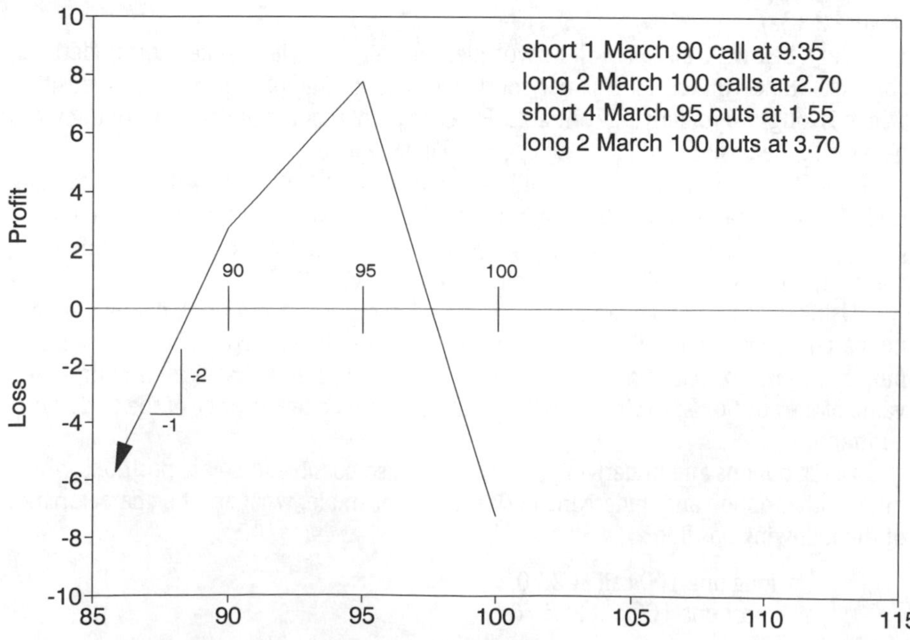
short 1 March 90 call at 9.35
long 2 March 100 calls at 2.70
short 4 March 95 puts at 1.55
long 2 March 100 puts at 3.70
-2
-1
Profit
Loss
90
95
100
10
8
6
4
2
0
-2
-4
-6
-8
-10
85
90
95
100
105
110
115

Figure 2-13c

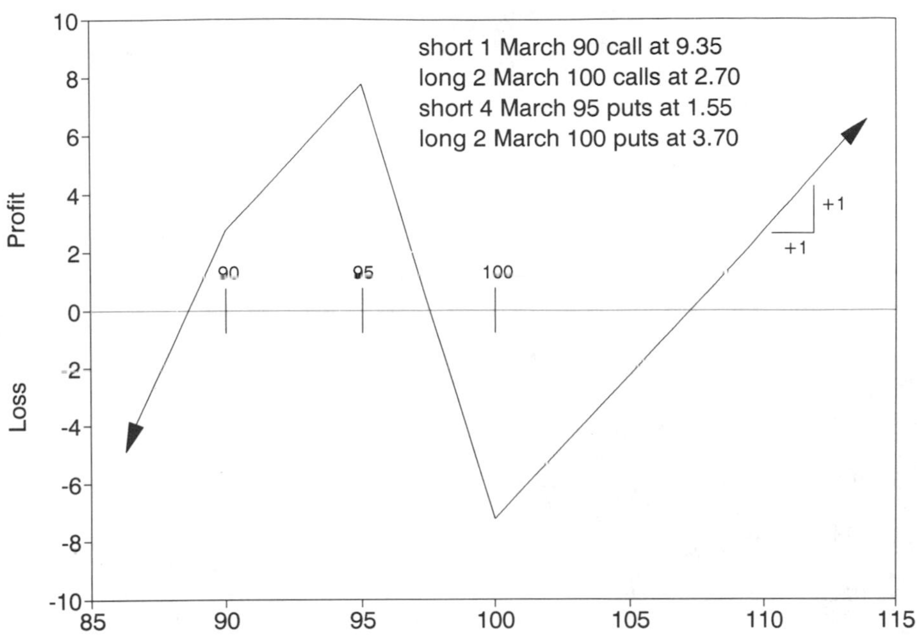

With the underlying contract above 100 at expiration, the 100 put will be worthless and the 100 call will act like a long underlying contract. With the underlying contract below 100 at expiration, the 100 call will be worthless and the 100 put will act like a short underlying contract. However, since the position is *short* the 100 put, when the 100 put is in the money it will act like a long underlying contract. In other words, this position will mimic a long underlying position regardless of where the underlying contract is at expiration (Figure 2-14). The only real difference between the option position and a long position in the underlying contract is that the option position will create a credit of one point.

Or consider the following position:

long one 90 put at .45
short one 100 call at 2.70
long one underlying contract at 99.00

The value of this position at expiration is given in Figure 2-15. Note the similarity between this position and the one in Figure 2-10. The only difference appears to be that we replaced the long 90 call with the combination of a long 90 put and a long underlying contract. Therefore, a long 90 put and a long underlying contract together must mimic a long 90 call. As proof, the reader should draw the expiration profit and loss graph of the following two positions:

Figure 2-14

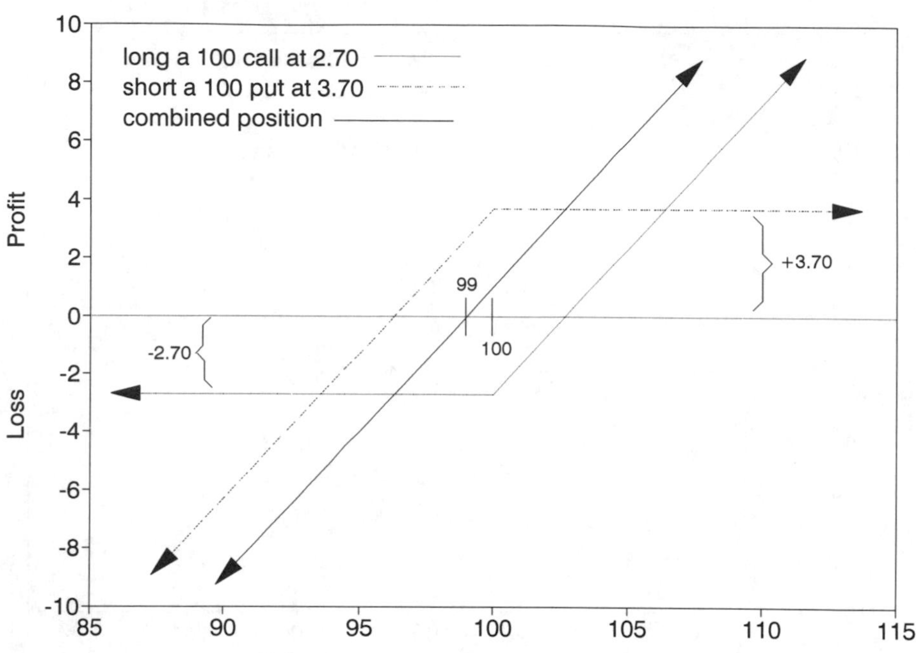

Figure 2-15

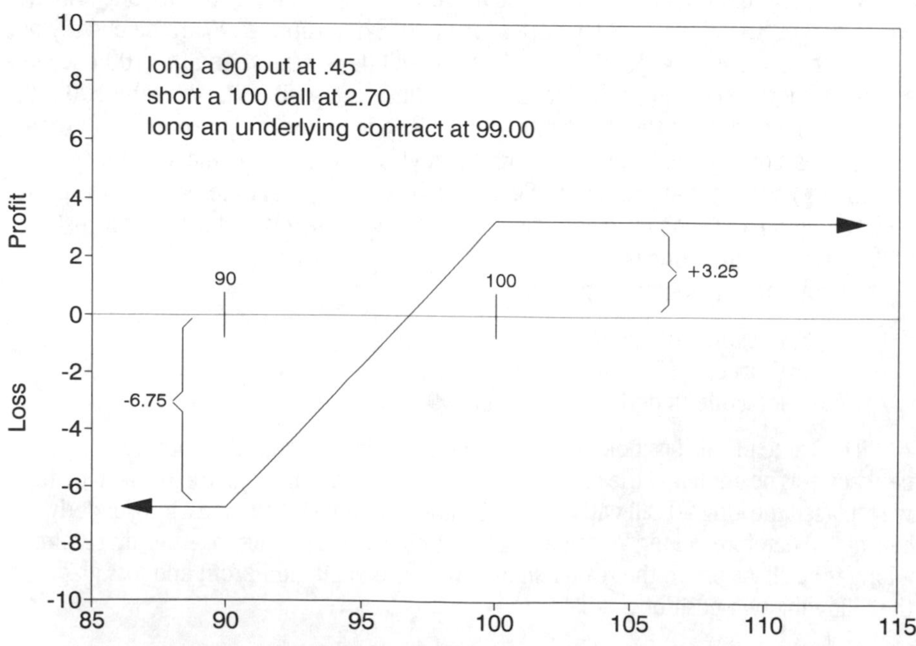

1. long a 90 call at 9.35
2. long a 90 put at .45 and long an underlying contract at 99.00

Although there will be a small difference in the profit and loss to each position, both positions will have graphs with the same general shape.

The reader who is new to options may find it useful to sit down with the business section of a newspaper and create and graph a variety of option and underlying positions.[2] This will enable him to become comfortable with many of the concepts introduced in the first two chapters, and will make the subsequent material that much easier to understand. Typical newspaper listings for futures options and stock options are shown in Figure 2-16.

While elementary strategies such as the ones discussed in this chapter are a convenient method of introducing the new trader to basic option characteristics, in actual practice it is very unlikely that a trader will put on a position and let it go to expiration. Even if he were to initiate a position with such an intent, he would be foolish indeed to simply walk away from the position and come back at expiration to find out whether he had made or lost money. As market conditions change, a position which seemed sensible yesterday may not seem quite so sensible today. Based on new conditions the trader may want to—indeed, may have to—alter his strategy. This is true for all traders, not just for option traders. A trader who buys stock in the belief that it will rise would be foolish not to reassess his position if the stock were to unexpectedly drop several points. An option trader who sells 105 calls in the belief that the underlying contract will never rise above 105 would likewise be foolish not to reassess the situation if the underlying contract were to make a rapid upward move from 99 to 104. He may still believe that the underlying contract will not rise above 105, but he is unlikely to have the same degree of confidence. *Every trader reserves the right to make a more intelligent decision today than he made yesterday.*

The serious trader must be able to identify potentially profitable strategies given current market conditions. But he must also be able to adjust to changing market conditions and to take protective measures when the market moves adversely. In the next chapter we will begin our investigation of basic option pricing theory, and show how this theory can be used to help a trader achieve these goals.

2. In the United States, *Investor's Business Daily*, the *New York Times*, and *The Wall Street Journal* all carry extensive listings of exchange traded futures options and stock options.

Figure 2-16

Futures and Futures Options

FRIDAY, OCTOBER 22, 1993

Futures

Month	Open	High	Low	Settle	Change	-Lifetime- High	Low
CORN (CBT); 5,000 bushels; ¢ per bushel (1 = $50.00)							
Dec	$255^{1}/_{4}$	256	$253^{1}/_{4}$	$253^{1}/_{2}$	$-2^{1}/_{4}$	$268^{1}/_{2}$	$225^{1}/_{4}$
Mar94	263	$264^{1}/_{4}$	$261^{1}/_{4}$	$261^{1}/_{2}$	$-2^{1}/_{2}$	$266^{1}/_{2}$	$232^{3}/_{4}$
May	$267^{1}/_{4}$	$268^{1}/_{2}$	265	$265^{1}/_{4}$	-3	$270^{1}/_{2}$	$238^{1}/_{2}$
Jul	$268^{1}/_{2}$	270	$266^{1}/_{4}$	$266^{1}/_{2}$	$-3^{1}/_{2}$	$270^{1}/_{2}$	241
Sep	260	$260^{1}/_{2}$	$257^{1}/_{4}$	$257^{1}/_{2}$	$-3^{1}/_{4}$	$261^{1}/_{2}$	$240^{1}/_{2}$
Dec	$251^{3}/_{4}$	253	249	$249^{1}/_{4}$	$-3^{3}/_{4}$	255	$236^{1}/_{2}$
EURODOLLARS (CME); $1,000,000; points of 100% (.01 = $25.00)							
Dec	96.50	96.52	96.48	96.49	-.02	96.61	90.22
Mar94	96.50	96.52	96.46	96.47	-.04	96.62	90.28
Jun	96.30	96.31	96.24	96.25	-.05	96.75	90.40
Sep	96.08	96.10	96.02	96.03	-.06	96.24	90.36
Dec	95.70	95.73	95.65	95.66	-.05	95.87	90.71
Mar95	95.62	95.65	95.57	95.58	-.05	95.80	95.24
Jun	95.42	95.44	95.37	95.37	-.05	95.60	95.71
Sep	95.25	95.27	95.20	95.20	-.05	95.43	91.31
Dec	94.97	94.98	94.91	94.91	-.06	95.81	91.18
GERMAN BONDS (LIFFE); DM 250,000; points of 100% (.01 = DM 25.00)							
Dec	100.13	100.50	100.03	100.46	+.29	100.58	94.25
Mar94	100.26	100.55	100.21	100.56	+.30	100.66	97.30
Jun	.....	.....	.....	100.46	+.27	100.49	98.94
CRUDE OIL (NYMEX); 1,000 barrels; $ per barrel (.01 = $10.00)							
Dec	18.37	18.43	18.02	18.07	-.28	23.00	17.14
Jan94	18.47	18.57	18.18	18.22	-.28	21.15	17.40
Feb	....	18.64	18.36	18.37	-.25	20.81	17.64
Mar	18.71	18.74	18.48	18.50	-.22	21.10	17.86
Apr	18.78	18.83	18.58	18.61	-.21	20.88	18.05
May	18.90	18.91	18.72	18.72	-.20	21.07	18.20
Jun	19.01	19.02	18.80	18.82	-.19	21.35	18.31
Jul	19.07	19.08	18.89	18.89	-.18	20.78	18.50
Aug	.....	.....	.....	18.96	-.17	20.78	18.72

Figure 2-16 (continued)

Futures and Futures Options

FRIDAY, OCTOBER 22, 1993

Futures Options

Strike Price	Calls-Settle			Puts-Settle		
CORN OPTIONS (CBT)						
	Dec	Mar	May	Dec	Mar	May
230	23 1/2	31 1/2	35 1/4	1/8	1/4	5/8
240	14 1/8	22 3/4	25 1/2	5/8	1	1 1/4
250	6 1/2	14 3/4	18 1/2	3	3 1/4	3 3/4
260	2 1/4	9 1/8	12 3/4	8 1/2	7 1/2	7 1/4
270	5/8	5 1/2	8 3/4	17	13 1/2	13
280	1/8	3 1/4	5 1/4	26 1/2	.....	.....
290	1/8	1 1/2	3 1/2	36 1/2	.....	.....
300	1/8	7/8	2	.....	.....	.....
EURODOLLAR OPTIONS (CME)						
	Dec	Mar	Jun	Dec	Mar	Jun
95.25	1.26	1.26	1.07	cab	cab	.04
95.50	1.01	1.01	.84	cab	.01	.05
95.75	.75	.77	.62	cab	.02	.09
96.00	.51	.54	.43	.01	.04	.15
96.25	.27	.30	.26	.02	.08	.24
96.50	.08	.13	.13	.08	.17	.37
96.75	.01	.03	.05	.25	.32	.50
97.00	cab	.01	.01	.49	.50	.....
GERMAN BOND OPTIONS (LIFFE)						
	Dec	Mar	Jun	Dec	Mar	Jun
98.50	1.99	2.33	.....	.03	.27	.....
99.00	1.52	1.94	.....	.06	.38	.....
99.50	1.11	1.58	.....	.15	.52	.....
100.00	.72	1.28	.....	.26	.72	.....
100.50	.44	1.01	.....	.48	.95	.....
101.00	.24	.79	.....	.78	1.23	.....
101.50	.13	.57	.....	1.17	1.51	.....
102.00	.07	.41	.....	1.61	1.85	.....
CRUDE OIL OPTIONS (NYMEX)						
	Dec	Jan	Feb	Dec	Jan	Feb
15.00	3.08	.....	.....	.01	.03	.06
16.00	2.09	.....	.....	.02	.08	.13
17.00	1.14	1.39	.....	.07	.18	.27
18.00	.35	.65	.92	.28	.43	.55
19.00	.06	.24	.44	.99	1.02	1.07
20.00	.02	.09	.20	1.95	1.86	1.82
21.00	.01	.03	.07	2.94	2.80	....
22.00	.01	.01	.04	3.93	....	....

Figure 2-16 (continued)

Equity Options

FRIDAY, OCTOBER 22, 1993

S&P 100 INDEX - OEX 424.15 (CBOE)

Strike	Calls-Last			Puts-Last		
Price	Nov	Dec	Jan	Nov	Dec	Jan
390	.....	.....	.....	7/16	1 3/16	2
395	29 7/8	30	.....	9/16	1 1/2	2 1/2
400	28 1/4	29 1/8	31	3/4	1 15/16	3 1/8
405	21 3/8	.....	26 3/8	1 1/16	2 5/8	3 3/8
410	18	18	20 3/8	1 7/16	3 1/4	5
415	11 1/2	13 1/2	.....	2 3/16	4 1/8	6 1/4
420	7 1/8	9 3/4	12 3/4	3 1/4	5 5/8	7 7/8
425	4	6 5/8	10 7/8	5	7 1/2	9 1/4
430	1 3/4	4 1/8	6 3/8	8	10	11 3/4
435	3/4	2 3/8	5 3/4	12	13	14 1/4
440	5/16	1 3/16	2 3/4	16 1/2	16 1/2	16
445	1/8	1/2	2 1/8	.....	17 1/4	19 1/2
450	1/16	1/4	1 1/16	23 3/4	26	24
455	1/16	1/8	1/2	.....	.....	.....

IBM 44 1/4 (CBOE)

Strike	Calls-Last			Puts-Last		
Price	Nov	Jan	Apr	Nov	Jan	Apr
35	....	.....	10 7/8	1/16	5/16	9/16
40	4 3/4	5 3/4	7 1/4	5/16	1	1 5/8
45	1 1/4	2 9/16	3 5/8	1 7/8	2 15/16	3 3/4
50	3/16	15/16	1 13/16	.....	5 5/8	6 3/4
55	1/16	3/8	7/8	.....	11	.....

MOTOROLA 103 1/4 (AMEX)

Strike	Calls-Last			Puts-Last		
Price	Nov	Dec	Jan	Nov	Dec	Jan
90	13 3/8	13 7/8	.....	1/2	1 1/8	.....
95	9 1/4	10 1/4	11 1/4	3/4	1 3/4	2 15/16
100	5 3/8	7	8	2 1/8	3 1/2	5 3/8
105	2 3/4	4 1/4	5 1/4	4 1/4	6 1/2	7
110	1	2 3/8	3	.....	.....	10 1/8
115	1/4	1	2 1/8	14	.....	.....

❖ 3 ❖

Introduction to Theoretical Pricing Models

In the last chapter we looked at some of the simple option strategies a trader might initiate given an opinion on an underlying contract's likely price movement. Whatever the basis for the opinion, it will probably be expressed with terms such as "good chance," "highly likely," "possible," "improbable," etc. The problem with this approach is that opinions cannot easily be expressed in numerical terms. What do we really mean by "good chance"? Or by "highly unlikely"? If we want to approach option markets logically we will need some method of quantifying our opinions about price movements.

From the elementary strategies discussed in the previous chapter it is clear that the direction in which the underlying market moves can have a significant effect on the profitability of an option strategy. Consequently, option traders are sensitive to the direction in which the underlying market moves. But an option trader has an additional problem: the speed of the market. A commodity trader who believes a commodity will rise in price within a specified period can be reasonably certain of making a profit if he is right. He simply buys the commodity, waits for it to reach his target price, then sells the commodity for a profit.

The situation is not quite so simple for an option trader. Suppose a trader believes a commodity will rise in price from $100, its present price, to $120 within the next five months. Suppose also that a $110 call expiring in three months is available at a price of $4. If the commodity rises to $120 by expiration, the purchase of the $110 will result in a profit of $6 ($10 intrinsic value less the $4 cost of the option). But is this profit a certainty? What will happen if the price of the commodity remains below $110 for the next three months and only reaches $120 after the option expires? Then the option will expire worthless and the trader will lose his $4 investment.

Perhaps the trader would do better to purchase a $110 call which expires in six months rather than three months. Now he can be certain that when the commodity reaches $120, the call will be worth at least $10 in intrinsic value. But what if the price of the six-month option is $12? In that case the trader might still show a loss. Even though the underlying commodity reaches the target price of $120, there is no guarantee that the $110 call will ever be worth more than its $10 intrinsic value.

A trader in an underlying market is almost exclusively interested in the direction in which the market will move. While the option trader is also sensitive to directional considerations, he must also give careful consideration to how fast the market is likely to move. If a futures trader and an option trader take long market positions in their respective instruments, and the market does in fact move higher, the futures trader is assured of a profit while the option trader may show a loss. If the market fails to move sufficiently fast, the favorable directional move may not be enough to offset the option's loss in time value. This is the primary reason speculators generally lose in option markets. A speculator usually buys options for their seemingly favorable risk/reward characteristics (limited risk/unlimited reward). But if he purchases options, not only must he be right about market direction, he must also be right about market speed. Only if he is right on both counts can he expect to make a profit. If predicting the correct market direction is difficult, correctly predicting direction and speed is probably beyond most traders' capabilities.

The concept of speed is vital in trading options. It is so important that there are many option strategies which depend only on the speed of the underlying market and not at all on its direction. Indeed, if a trader is highly proficient at predicting directional moves in the underlying market, he is probably better advised to stick to the underlying instrument. It is only when he has some feel for the speed component that a trader can hope to intelligently enter the option market.

The option trader who wants to intelligently evaluate the potential profitability of an option trade is faced with the task of analyzing several different factors. At a minimum he must consider:

1. The price of the underlying contract
2. The exercise price
3. The amount of time remaining to expiration
4. The direction in which he expects the underlying market to move
5. The speed at which he expects the underlying market to move

Ideally, he would like to express each of these factors numerically, feed the numbers into a formula, and derive a value for the option. By comparing the value to its price in the marketplace, the trader would then know whether the purchase or sale of the option was likely to be profitable. This is essentially the goal of option evaluation: to analyze an option based on the terms of the option contract, as well as current market conditions and future expectations.

EXPECTED RETURN

Suppose we are given the opportunity to roll a six-sided die, and each time we roll we will receive a dollar amount equal to the number which comes up. If we roll a one, we get $1; if we roll a two, we get $2; and so on up to six, in which case we get $6. If we were to roll the die an infinite number of times, on average, how much would we expect to receive per roll?

We can calculate the answer using some simple arithmetic. There are six numbers which can come up, each with equal probability. If we add up the six possible outcomes

1+2+3+4+5+6=21 and divide this by the six faces of the die we get 21/6 = 3½. That is, on average we can expect to get back $3½ each time we roll the die. This is the average, or *expected*, return. If someone were to charge us for the privilege of rolling the die, what might we be willing to pay? If we purchased the chance to roll the die for less than $3½, in the long run we would expect to be winners. If we paid more than $3½, in the long run we would expect to be losers. And if we paid exactly $3½, we would expect to break even. Note the qualifying phrase "in the long run." The expected return of $3½ is a realistic goal only if we are allowed to roll the die many, many times. If we are allowed to roll only once, we cannot count on getting back $3½. Indeed, on any one roll it is impossible to get back $3½ since no face of the die has exactly 3½ spots. Nevertheless, if we pay less than $3½ for even one roll of the die, the laws of probability are on our side because we have paid less than the expected return.

In a similar vein, consider a roulette bet. A roulette wheel has 38 slots, numbered 1 through 36, 0 and 00.[1] Suppose a casino allows a player to choose a number. If the player's number comes up, he receives $36; if any other number comes up, he receives nothing. What is the expected return from this proposition? There are 38 slots on the roulette wheel, each with equal probability, but only one slot will return $36 to the player. If we divide the one way to win $36 by the 38 slots on the wheel, the result is $36/38 = $.9474, or about 95¢. A player who pays 95¢ for the privilege of picking a number at the roulette table can expect to break about even in the long run.

Of course, no casino will let a player buy such a bet for 95¢. Under those conditions the casino would make no profit. In the real world, a player who wants to purchase such a bet will have to pay more than the expected return, typically $1. The 5¢ difference between the $1 price of the bet and the 95¢ expected return represents the profit potential, or *edge*, to the casino. In the long run, for every dollar bet at the roulette table, the casino can expect to keep about 5¢.

Given the above conditions, any player interested in making a profit would rather switch places with the casino so that he could be the house. Then he would have a 5¢ edge on his side by selling bets worth 95¢ for $1. Alternatively, the player would like to find a casino where he could purchase the bet for less than its expected return of 95¢, perhaps 88¢. Then the player would have a 7¢ edge over the casino.

THEORETICAL VALUE

The theoretical value of a proposition is the price one would expect to pay in order to just break even in the long run. Thus far the only factor we have considered in determining the value of a proposition is the expected return. We used this concept to calculate the 95¢ fair price for the roulette bet. There may, however, be other considerations.

Suppose that in our roulette example the casino decides to change the conditions of the bet slightly. The player may now purchase the roulette bet for its expected return

1. As is customary in the U.S., we assume a roulette wheel with 38 slots. In some parts of the world the roulette wheel may have no slot 00. This of course changes the odds.

of 95¢ and, as before, if he loses the casino will immediately collect his 95¢. Under the new conditions, however, if the player wins the casino will send him his $36 winnings in two months. Will both the player and the casino still break even on the proposition?

Where did the player get the 95¢ he used to place his bet at the roulette wheel? In the immediate sense he may have taken it out of his pocket. But a closer examination may reveal that he withdrew the money from his savings account prior to visiting the casino. Since he won't receive his winnings for two months, he will have to take into consideration the two months interest he would have earned had he left the 95¢ in his savings account. If interest rates are 12% annually (1% per month), the interest loss is 2% × 95¢, or about 2¢. If the player purchases the bet for its expected return of 95¢, he will still be a 2¢ loser because of the cost of carrying a 95¢ debit for two months. The casino, on the other hand, will take the 95¢, put it in an interest-bearing account, and at the end of two months collect 2¢ in interest.

Under these new conditions the theoretical value of the bet is the expected return of 95¢ less the 2¢ carrying cost on the bet, or about 93¢. If a player pays 93¢ for the roulette bet today and collects his winnings in two months, neither he nor the casino can expect to make any profit in the long run.

The two most common considerations in a financial investment are the expected return and carrying costs. There may, however, be other considerations. For example, suppose the casino decided to send the player a 1¢ bonus over the next two months. He could then add this additional payment to the previous theoretical value of 93¢ to get a new theoretical value of 94¢. This is similar to the dividend paid to owners of stock in a company. And, in fact, dividends are an additional consideration in evaluating options on stock.

Exchanges will perhaps object to the casino analogy. They prefer that option trading not be thought of as gambling. There is certainly no desire here to assess the moral implications of either gambling or option trading. The fact remains that the same laws of probability which enable a casino to set the odds for different games of chance are the same laws of probability which enable a trader to evaluate an option.

The concept of theoretical value based on probability is common in many aspects of business. For those uncomfortable with the gambling analogy, one can go back to the original justification for options and think of them as insurance policies which require the payment of a premium. Through the use of statistical data and probability theory, an actuary at an insurance company will attempt to calculate the likelihood that the insurance company will have to make good on an insurance policy. He can then factor into the equation what the insurance company expects to earn on premium payments, and thereby arrive at a theoretical value for the insurance policy. The policy can then be offered to prospective customers at an additional cost, which represents the theoretical edge to the insurance company.

In the same way, the goal of option evaluation is to determine, through the use of theoretical pricing models, the theoretical value of an option. The trader can then make an intelligent decision whether the option is overpriced or underpriced in the marketplace, and whether the theoretical edge is sufficient to justify going into the marketplace and making a trade.

A WORD ON MODELS

Before continuing, a few observations on models in general will be worthwhile.

A model is a scaled down or more easily managed representation of the real world. The model may be a physical one, such as a model airplane or building, or it may be a mathematical one, such as a formula. In each case, the model is constructed to help us better understand the world in which we live. *However, it is unwise, and sometimes dangerous, to assume that the model and the real world which it represents are identical in every way.* They may be very similar, but the model is unlikely to exactly duplicate every feature of the real world.

All models, if they are to be effective, require us to make certain prior assumptions about the real world. Mathematical models require the input of numbers which quantify these assumptions. If we feed incorrect data into the model, we can expect an incorrect representation of the real world. Every model user must be aware: garbage in, garbage out.

These general observations about models are no less true for option pricing models. An option model is only someone's idea of how options might be evaluated under certain conditions. Since either the model itself, or the data which we feed into the model, might be incorrect, there is no guarantee that model-generated values will be accurate, nor can we be sure that these values will bear any logical resemblance to actual prices in the marketplace.

There is in fact a great deal of disagreement among traders as to the usefulness of option pricing models. Some traders feel that models are so much hocus-pocus, and have no relationship to what goes on in the real world. Other traders feel that once they have a sheet of theoretical values in hand all their problems are solved. The reality lies somewhere in between.

A new option trader is like someone entering a dark room for the first time. Without any guidance he will grope in the dark and may eventually find what he is looking for. The trader who is armed with a basic understanding of theoretical pricing models enters the same room with a small candle. He can make out the general layout of the room, but the dimness of the candle prevents him from distinguishing every detail. Moreover, some of what he does see may be distorted by the flickering candle. In spite of these limitations, a trader is more likely to find what he is looking for with a small candle than with no illumination at all.

The real problems with theoretical pricing models arise after the trader has acquired some sophistication. As he gains confidence he may begin to increase the size of his trades. When this happens, his inability to make out every detail in the room, as well as the distortions caused by the flickering candle flame, take on increased importance. Now a misinterpretation of what he thinks he sees can lead to financial disaster, since any error in judgement will be greatly magnified.

The sensible approach is to make use of a model, but with a full awareness of what it can and cannot do. Option traders will find that theoretical pricing models are invaluable tools to understanding the pricing of options. Because of the insights gained from a model, the great majority of successful option traders rely on some type of theoretical pricing model. However, an option trader, if he is to make the best use of a theoretical pricing model, must be aware of its limitations as well as its strengths. Otherwise he may be no better off than the trader groping in the dark.[2]

A SIMPLE APPROACH

How might we adapt the concepts of expected return and theoretical value to the pricing of options? We might begin by calculating the expected return for an option. Let's take a simple example.

Suppose an underlying contract is trading at $100 and that on a certain date in the future, which we will call expiration, the contract can take on one of five different prices: $80, $90, $100, $110, or $120. Assume, moreover, that each of the five prices is equally likely with 20% probability. The prices and probabilities might be represented by the line in Figure 3-1.

If we take a long position in the underlying contract at today's price of $100, what will be the expected return from this position at expiration? 20% of the time we will lose $20 when the contract ends up at $80. 20% of the time we will lose $10 when the contract ends up at $90. 20% of the time we will break even when the contract ends up at $100. 20% of the time we will make $10 when the contract ends up at $110. And 20% of the time we will make $20 when the contract ends up at $120. We can write the arithmetic:

$$-(20\% \times \$20) - (20\% \times \$10) + (20\% \times 0) + (20\% \times \$10) + (20\% \times \$20) = 0$$

Since the profits and losses exactly offset each other, the expected return to the long position is zero. The same reasoning will show that the expected return to a short position taken at the current price of $100 is also zero. Given the prices and probabilities, if we take either a long or short position we can expect to just break even in the long run.

Now suppose that we take a long position in a $100 call. Forgetting for a moment about what we might pay for the call, what will be the expected return given the prices and probabilities in Figure 3-1? If the underlying contract finishes at $80, $90, or $100 the call will expire worthless. If the underlying contract finishes at $110 or $120 the call will be worth $10 and $20, respectively. The arithmetic is:

$$(20\% \times 0) + (20\% \times 0) + (20\% \times 0) + (20\% \times \$10) + (20\% \times \$20) = +\$6$$

Figure 3-1

$80	$90	$100	$110	$120
20%	20%	20%	20%	20%

2. Two interesting articles discuss these limitations:
Figlewski, Stephen; "What Does an Option Pricing Model Tell Us about Option Prices?," *Financial Analysts Journal,* September/October 1989, pages 12-15.
Black, Fischer; "Living Up to the Model," *Risk,* Vol. 3, No. 3., March 1990, pages 11-13.

The call can never be worth less than zero, so the expected return from the call position is always a non-negative number, in this case $6.

If we want to develop a theoretical pricing model using this approach, we might propose a series of possible prices and probabilities for the underlying contract at expiration. Then, given an exercise price, we can calculate the value of the option at each price outcome, multiply the value by its associated probability, add up all these numbers, and thereby obtain an expected return for the option.

In the foregoing example we took a very simple situation with only five possible price outcomes, each with identical probability. What changes might we make in order to develop a more realistic model? For one thing, we would have to know the settlement procedure for the option. In the United States, all options are subject to stock-type settlement, which requires full payment for the option. If the $100 call will have an expected return of $6 at expiration, we will have to deduct the carrying costs to get its value today. If interest rates are 12% annually (1% per month) and the option will expire in two months, we will have to discount the $6 expected return by the 2% carrying cost, or about 12¢. The theoretical value of the option will then be $5.88.

What other factors might we have to consider? We assumed that all five price outcomes were equally likely. Is this a realistic assumption? Suppose you were told that only two possible prices were possible at expiration, $110 and $250. With the underlying contract at $100 today, which do you think is more likely? Based on experience, most traders would probably agree that extreme price changes which are far away from today's price are less likely than small changes which remain close to today's price. For this reason, $110 is more likely than $250. To take this into consideration, perhaps our price outcomes, in terms of probability, ought to be concentrated around the present price of the underlying contract. Such a distribution is shown in Figure 3-2. Now the expected return from a $100 call is:

$$(10\% \times 0) + (20\% \times 0) + (40\% \times 0) + (20\% \times \$10) + (10\% \times \$20) = \$4.00$$

If, as before, the option is subject to stock-type settlement and carrying costs are 2%, the theoretical value of the option will now be $3.92.

Note that in Figure 3-2 all outcomes and probabilities are arranged symmetrically. Even though the new probabilities altered the expected return for the $100 call, the expected return from any position taken in the underlying contract is still zero. For each upward price move, there is a downward move of equal magnitude and probability. We might, however, believe that the expected return to an underlying contract is not zero, that there is a greater chance that the contract will move one direction rather than another. Look at the price outcomes and probabilities in Figure 3-3. Using these new probabilities, the expected return from a long position in the underlying contract is:

$$-(10\% \times \$20) - (20\% \times \$10) + (30\% \times 0) + (25\% \times \$10) + (15\% \times \$20) = +\$1.50$$

and the expected return for the $100 call is:

$$(10\% \times 0) + (20\% \times 0) + (30\% \times 0) + (25\% \times \$10) + (15\% \times \$20) = +\$5.50$$

Figure 3-2

$80	$90	$100	$110	$120
10%	20%	40%	20%	10%

Figure 3-3

$80	$90	$100	$110	$120
10%	20%	30%	25%	15%

Note that the underlying contract now has a positive expected return, so it may seem that there is money to be made simply by purchasing the underlying contract. This would be true if there were no other considerations. But suppose the underlying contract is a stock, and therefore subject to stock-type settlement. If we purchase the stock at today's price of $100 and hold it for some period, there is a carrying cost associated with the investment. If the carrying cost is exactly equal to the expected return of $1.50, we will just break even. For a long stock position to be profitable, the stock must appreciate by at least the amount of carrying costs over the holding period. Therefore, the expected return from the stock must be some positive number. If we assume that any stock trade will just break even, the expected return must be equal to the carrying costs.

Some stocks also pay dividends. If the dividend is paid during the holding period, it will affect the expected return. A trader who buys stock will have to pay out carrying costs, but he will receive the dividends. If we again assume that a stock trade will break even, the expected return at the end of the holding period must be identical to the carrying costs less the dividend. If the carrying cost for the stock over some period is $3.50, and a $1.00 dividend is expected during this period, the expected return at the end of the period must be $2.50. A trader who purchases the stock today will incur an interest debit of $3.50 at the end of the holding period, but this will be exactly offset by the $1.00 dividend which he receives during the holding period,[3] as well as the $2.50 expected return at the end of the period.

In an *arbitrage-free* market, where no profit can be made by either buying or selling a contract, all credits and debits, including the expected return, must exactly cancel out. If we assume an arbitrage-free market, we must necessarily assume that the *forward price*, the average price of the contract at the end of the holding period, is the current price, plus an expected return which will exactly offset all other credits and debits. If the holding costs on a $100 stock over some period are $4, the forward price must be $104. If the stock also pays a $1 dividend, the forward price must be $103. In both cases the credits and debits will exactly cancel out.

The calculation of a forward price depends on the characteristics of the contract as well as market conditions. In the case of a stock, the considerations are the price of the

3. The trader can also earn interest on the dividend from the time he receives it until the end of the holding period. Since this will usually be a very small amount in relation to the other factors, we will ignore it.

stock, the length of the holding period, interest rates, and dividends. In the case of a futures contract, the situation is much simpler. A futures contract requires no initial cash outlay, since it is subject to futures-type settlement. Moreover, a futures contract does not pay dividends. This means that the forward price of a futures contract in an arbitrage-free market is simply the current price of the futures contract. If a trader buys a futures contract at $100, the break even price for the contract at the end of the holding period is $100.

Going back to our very simple pricing model, we might make the assumption that the underlying market is arbitrage-free,[4] that there is no money to be made from trading the underlying contract. The expected return must then be equal to the difference between the current price of the underlying market and its forward price. In the case of stock, the expected return will be carrying costs less dividends. In the case of futures, the expected return will be zero.

Even if we assume an arbitrage-free market in the underlying, with appropriate probabilities associated with each price outcome, we still have one major problem. In our simplified model there were only five possible price outcomes, while in the real world there are an infinite number of possibilities. To enable our model to more closely approximate real world conditions we will have to construct a probability line with every possible price outcome and its associated probability. This may seem an impossible task, but it is the basis for all theoretical pricing models.

We can now summarize the necessary steps in developing a model:

1. Propose a series of possible prices at expiration for the underlying contract
2. Assign an appropriate probability to each possible price
3. Maintain an arbitrage-free underlying market
4. From the prices and probabilities in steps 1, 2, and 3, calculate the expected return for the option
5. From the option's expected return, deduct the carrying cost

If we can accomplish all this, we will finally have a theoretical value from which we can begin to trade.

Prior to 1973, evaluation of options required the solution of complex mathematical equations. Since such methods were slow and tedious, a trader who tried to use them quickly found that profit opportunities disappeared faster than the evaluation methods could identify them. In 1973, concurrent with the opening of the Chicago Board Options Exchange, Fischer Black and Myron Scholes introduced the first practical theoretical pricing model for options. The Black-Scholes Model, with its relatively simple arithmetic and limited number of inputs, most of which were easily observable, proved an ideal tool for traders in the newly opened U.S. option market. Although other models have since been introduced to overcome some of its original deficiencies, the Black-Scholes Model remains the most widely used of all option pricing models.

---

4. We need not necessarily assume an arbitrage-free underlying market. But we shall see that this is an important assumption in most theoretical pricing models.

In its original form, the Black-Scholes Model was intended to evaluate European options (no early exercise permitted) on non-dividend paying stocks. Shortly after its introduction, realizing that most stocks do pay dividends, Black and Scholes added a dividend component. In 1976, Fischer Black made slight modifications to the model to allow for the evaluation of options on futures contracts. And in 1983, Mark Garman and Steven Kohlhagen made several other modifications to allow for the evaluation of options on foreign currencies.[5] The futures version and the foreign currency version are known officially as the Black Model and the Garman-Kohlhagen Model, respectively. But the evaluation method in each version, whether the original Black-Scholes Model for stock options, the Black Model for futures options, or the Garman-Kohlhagen Model for foreign currency options, is so similar that they have all come to be known as simply the Black-Scholes Model. The various forms of the model differ primarily in how they calculate the forward price of the underlying contract, and an option trader will simply choose the form appropriate to the underlying instrument.

The great majority of options currently traded are American options, carrying with them the right of early exercise. For this reason, it may seem that the Black-Scholes model, with its assumption of no early exercise, is poorly suited for use in most markets. However, the Black-Scholes Model has proven so easy to use that many traders do not believe the more accurate values derived from an American option pricing model, which allows for the possibility of early exercise, is worth the additional effort. In some markets, particularly futures options markets, the additional early exercise value is so small that there is virtually no difference between values obtained from the Black-Scholes model and values obtained from an American pricing model.

Due to its widespread use and its importance in the development of other pricing models, we will for the moment restrict ourselves to a discussion of the Black-Scholes model and its various forms. In later chapters we will consider the question of early exercise. We will also look at alternative methods for pricing options when we question some of the basic assumptions in the Black-Scholes Model.

The reasoning which led to the development of the Black-Scholes Model depends on the five steps we listed earlier in this chapter when we proposed a simple method for evaluating options. Black and Scholes worked originally with call values, but put values can be derived in much the same way. Alternatively, we will see in Chapter 11 that in an arbitrage-free market there is a unique relationship between an underlying contract, and a call and put with the same exercise price and expiration date. This relationship enables us to derive a put value simply by knowing the associated call value.

In order to calculate an option's theoretical value using the Black-Scholes Model, we need to know at a minimum five characteristics of the option and its underlying contract. These are:

1. The option's exercise price
2. The amount of time remaining to expiration

5. We are speaking here of options on a physical foreign currency, rather than options on a foreign currency futures contract. The latter may be evaluated using the Black Model for futures options.

3. The current price of the underlying contract
4. The risk-free interest rate over the life of the option
5. The volatility of the underlying contract

The last input, volatility, may be unfamiliar to the new trader. While we will put off a detailed discussion of this input to the next chapter, from our previous discussion one can reasonably infer that volatility is related to the speed of the market.

If we know each of the required inputs, we can feed them into the theoretical pricing model and thereby generate a theoretical value.

Black and Scholes also incorporated into their model the concept of the *riskless hedge.* For every option position there is a theoretically equivalent position in the underlying contract such that, for small price changes in the underlying contract, the option position will gain or lose value at exactly the same rate as the underlying position. To take advantage of a theoretically mispriced option, it is necessary to establish a hedge by offsetting the option position with this theoretically equivalent underlying position. That is, whatever option position we take, we must take an opposing market position in the underlying contract. The correct proportion of underlying contracts needed to establish this riskless hedge is known as the *hedge ratio.*

Why is it necessary to establish a riskless hedge? Recall that in our simplified approach an option's theoretical value depended on the probability of various price outcomes for the underlying contract. As the underlying contract changes in price, the probability of each outcome will also change. If the underlying price is currently $100 and we assign a 25% probability to $120, we might drop the probability for $120 to 10% if the price of the underlying contract falls to $80. By initially establishing a riskless hedge, and then by adjusting this hedge as market conditions change, we are taking into consideration these changing probabilities.

In this sense an option can be thought of as a substitute for a similar position in the underlying contract. A call is a substitute for a long position; a put is a substitute for a short position. Whether it is better to take the position in the option or in the underlying

Figure 3-4

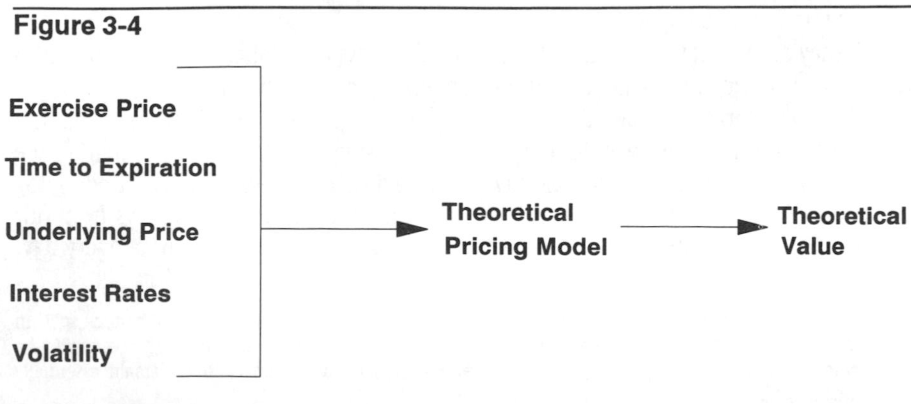

contract depends on the theoretical value of the option and its price in the marketplace. If a call can be purchased (sold) for less (more) than its theoretical value, it will, in the long run, be more profitable to take a long (short) market position by purchasing (selling) calls than by purchasing (selling) the underlying contract. In the same way, if a put can be purchased (sold) for less (more) than its theoretical value, it will, in the long run, be more profitable to take a short (long) market position by purchasing (selling) puts than by selling (buying) the underlying contract.

Since the theoretical value obtained from a theoretical pricing model is no better than the inputs into the model, a few comments on each of the inputs will be worthwhile.

EXERCISE PRICE

There ought never be any doubt about the exercise price of an option, since it is fixed in the terms of the contract and does not vary over the life of the contract.[6] A Deutschemark March 58 call traded on the Chicago Mercantile Exchange cannot suddenly turn into March 59 call or a March 57 call. An IBM July 55 put traded on the Chicago Board Options Exchange cannot turn into a July 50 put or a July 60 put.

TIME TO EXPIRATION

Like the exercise price, the option's expiration date is fixed and will not vary. Our DM March 58 call will not suddenly turn into an April 58 call, nor will our IBM July 55 put turn into a June 55 put. Of course, each day that passes brings us closer to expiration, so in that sense the time to expiration is constantly growing shorter. However, the expiration date, like the exercise price, is fixed by the exchange and will not change.

Time to expiration, like all inputs in the Black-Scholes Model, is entered as an annualized number. If we are entering raw data directly into the model we must make the appropriate annualization. With 91 days remaining to expiration, we would enter an input of .25 ($91/365 \approx .25$). With 36 days remaining, we would enter .10 ($36/365 \approx .10$). However, most option evaluation computer programs already have this transformation incorporated into the software so that we need only enter the correct number of days remaining to expiration.

It may seem that we have a problem in deciding what number of days to enter into the model. We need the amount of time remaining to expiration for two purposes, to calculate the interest considerations and to calculate the likelihood of movement in the underlying contract. For volatility purposes in assessing the "speed" of the market we are only interested in trading days. Only on those days can the price of the underlying contract actually change. This might lead us to drop weekends and holidays from our calculations. On the other hand, for interest rate purposes we must include every day.

---

6. It is true that an exchange may adjust the exercise price of a stock option if there is a stock split. In practical terms this is not really a change in the exercise price because the exercise price retains the same relationship to the stock price. The characteristics of the option contract remain essentially unchanged.

If we borrow or lend money we expect the interest to accrue every day, no matter that some of the days are not business days.

It turns out that this is not really a problem. In calculating the "speed" of the market we observe only the price changes that occur on business days. But we can make slight changes to this observed value and annualize the number before feeding it into the theoretical pricing model. The result is that we can feed into our model the actual number of days remaining to expiration knowing that the model will interpret the number correctly.

PRICE OF THE UNDERLYING

Unlike the exercise price and time to expiration, the correct price of the underlying is not always obvious. At any one time there is usually a bid price and an asked price, and it may not be clear whether we ought to use one or the other of these prices, or perhaps some price in between.

We have noted that the correct use of an option's theoretical value requires us to hedge the option position with an opposing trade in the underlying contract. Therefore the underlying price we feed into our theoretical pricing model ought to be the price at which we believe we can make the opposing trade. If we intend to purchase calls or sell puts, both of which are long market positions, we will have to hedge by selling the underlying contract. In that case we ought to use the bid price since that is the price at which we can sell the underlying. On the other hand, if we intend to sell calls or buy puts, both of which are short market positions, we will have to hedge by purchasing the underlying contract. Now we ought to use the asked price since that is the price at which we can buy the underlying.

In practice, the bid and offer are constantly changing, and many traders will simply use the last trade price as the basis for theoretical evaluation. But the last trade price may not always reflect the present market. Even the settlement price quoted in a newspaper may not accurately reflect the market at the close of business. The last trade price may show 75¼ for a contract, but the market at the close may have been 75¼ bid, 75½ offered. A trader who hoped to buy at 75¼ would have very little chance of being filled because of the difficulty of buying at the bid price. Even a purchase at some middle price, say 75⅜, may be unlikely if the market is very unbalanced with many more contracts being bid for at 75¼ than offered at 75½. For all of these reasons, an experienced trader will rarely enter an option market without knowing the exact bid and offer in the underlying market.

INTEREST RATES

Since an option trade may result in either a cash credit or debit to a trader's account, the interest considerations resulting from this cash flow must also play a role in option evaluation. This is a function of interest rates over the life of the option.

The interest rate component plays two roles in the theoretical evaluation of options. First, it may affect the forward price of the underlying contract. If the underlying contract is subject to stock-type settlement, as we raise interest rates we raise the forward price, increasing the value of calls and decreasing the value of puts. Secondly, the interest rate may affect the cost of carrying the option. If the option is subject to stock-type settlement, as we raise interest rates we decrease the value of the option. In spite of the fact that the interest rate plays two roles, in most cases the same rate is applicable and we need only input one interest rate into the model. If, however, different rates are applicable, such as would be the case with foreign currency options (the foreign currency interest rate plays one role, the domestic currency interest rate plays a different role) the model will require the input of two interest rates. This is the case with the Garman-Kohlhagen version of the Black-Scholes Model.

The fact that interest rates play a dual role also means that the relative importance of interest rates will vary, depending on the type of underlying instrument and the settlement procedure. For example, interest rates have a much greater impact on the value of stock options than on futures options. As we raise interest rates, we increase the forward price of stock, but leave the forward price of a futures contract unchanged. At the same time, assuming stock-type settlement, as we raise interest rates we decrease the value of options. The option price, however, is usually very small in relation to the price of the underlying contract.

What interest rate should a trader use when evaluating options? Most traders cannot borrow and lend at the same rate, so the correct interest rate will, in theory, depend on whether the trade will create a debit or a credit. In the former case the trader will be interested in the borrowing rate, while in the latter case he will be interested in the lending rate. In practice, however, the most common solution is to use the *risk-free* interest rate, i.e., the most secure rate. In the United States, the government is usually considered the most secure borrower of funds, so that the yield on a government security with a term equivalent to the life of the option is the general benchmark. For a 60-day option, use the yield on a 60-day treasury bill; for a 180-day option, use the yield on a 180-day treasury bill.

DIVIDENDS

We did not list dividends as an input in Figure 3-4 since they are only a factor in the theoretical evaluation of stock options, and then only if the stock is expected to pay a dividend over the life of the option.

In order to accurately evaluate a stock option, a trader must know both the amount of the dividend which the stock will pay and the *ex-dividend* date, the date on which a trader must own the stock in order to receive the dividend. The emphasis here is on ownership of the stock. A deeply in-the-money option may have many of the same characteristics as stock, but only ownership of the stock carries with it the right to collect the dividend.

In the absence of other information, most traders tend to assume that a company will continue the same dividend policy it has had in the past. If the company has been paying a 75¢ dividend each quarter, it will probably continue to do so. However, this is not always a certainty. Companies sometimes increase or decrease dividends, and occasionally omit them completely. If there is the possibility of a change in a company's dividend policy, a trader has to consider its impact on option values. Additionally, if the ex-dividend date is expected just prior to expiration, there is the danger that a delay of several days will cause the ex-dividend date to fall after expiration. For purposes of option evaluation, this is the same as eliminating the dividend completely. In such a situation a trader ought to make a special effort to ascertain the exact ex-dividend date.

VOLATILITY

Of all the inputs required for option evaluation, volatility is the most difficult for traders to understand. At the same time, volatility often plays the most important role in actual trading situations. Changes in our assumptions about volatility can have a dramatic effect on an option's value, and the manner in which the marketplace assesses volatility can have an equally dramatic effect on an option's price. For these reasons, we will devote the next chapter to a detailed discussion of volatility.

❖ 4 ❖
Volatility

What is volatility and why is it so important to an option trader? The option trader, like a trader in the underlying instrument, is interested in the direction of the market. But unlike the trader in the underlying, an option trader is also extremely sensitive to the speed of the market. If the market for an underlying contract fails to move at a sufficient speed, options on that contract will have less value because of the reduced likelihood of the market going through an option's exercise price. In a sense, volatility is a measure of the speed of the market. Markets which move slowly are low-volatility markets; markets which move quickly are high-volatility markets.

One might guess intuitively that some markets are more volatile than others. Between 1980 and 1982, the price of gold moved from $300 per ounce to $800 per ounce, more than doubling its price. Yet few traders would predict that the S&P 500 Index might more than double in a similar period. A commodity trader knows that precious metals are generally more volatile than interest rate instruments. In the same way, a stock trader knows that high-technology stocks tend to be more volatile than utility stocks.

If we knew whether a market was likely to be relatively volatile, or relatively quiet, and could convey this information to a theoretical pricing model, any evaluation of options on that market would be more accurate than if we simply ignored volatility. Since option models are based on mathematical formulae, we will need some method of quantifying this volatility component so that we can feed it into the model in numerical form.

RANDOM WALKS AND NORMAL DISTRIBUTIONS

Consider for a moment the pinball maze pictured in Figure 4-1. When a ball is dropped into the maze at the top it moves downward, pulled by gravity, through a series of nails. When the ball encounters each nail there is a 50% chance the ball will move to the right, and a 50% chance it will move left. The ball then falls down to a new level where it encounters another nail. Finally, at the bottom of the maze the ball falls into one of the troughs.

The path the ball follows as it moves downward through the maze of nails is known as a *random walk*. Once the ball enters the maze nothing can be done to artificially alter its course, nor can one predict ahead of time the path the ball will take through the maze.

Figure 4-1: Random Walk

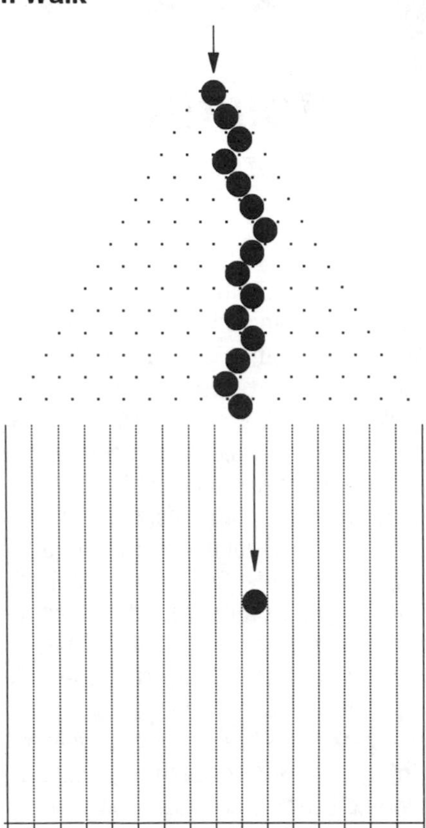

If enough balls are dropped into the maze, we might begin to get a distribution of balls similar to that in Figure 4-2. Most of the balls tend to congregate near the center of the maze, with a decreasing number of balls ending up in troughs further away from the center. The distribution which results from dropping many balls into our maze is referred to as a *normal*, or bell-shaped, *distribution.*

If we were to drop an infinite number of balls into the maze we might approximate the distribution with a *normal*, or bell-shaped, *curve* such as the one overlaid on the distribution in Figure 4-2. Such a curve is symmetrical (if we flipped it from right to left it would look the same), it has its peak in the center, and its tails always flare down and away from the center.

Normal distribution curves are used to describe the likely outcomes of random events. For example, the curve in Figure 4-2 might also represent the results of flipping a coin 15 times. Each outcome, or trough, would represent the number of heads which occurred after each 15 flips. An outcome in trough zero would represent zero heads and 15 tails; an outcome in trough 15 would represent 15 heads and zero tails. Of course, we would be surprised to flip a coin 15 times and get all heads or all tails. Assuming the

Figure 4-2: Normal Distribution

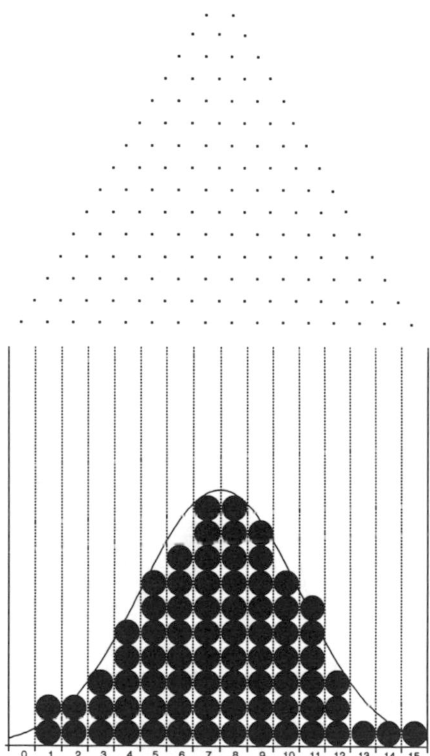

coin is perfectly balanced; some outcome in between, perhaps 8 heads and 7 tails, or 9 heads and 6 tails, seems more likely.

Suppose we change our maze slightly by closing off a row of nails so that each time a ball encounters a nail and goes either left or right, it must drop down two levels before it encounters another nail. If we drop enough balls into the maze we may end up with a distribution represented by the curve in Figure 4-3. Since the sideways movement of the balls is restricted, the curve will have a higher peak and narrower tails than the curve in Figure 4-2. In spite of its altered shape, this curve still represents a normal distribution, although one with slightly different characteristics.

Finally, we might block off some of the spaces between nails so that each time a ball drops down a level it must move two nails left or right before it can drop down to a new level. Again, if we drop enough balls into the maze we may get a distribution which resembles the curve in Figure 4-4. This curve, while still a normal distribution curve, will have a much lower peak and its tails will spread out much more quickly than the curves in either Figure 4-2 or 4-3.

Figure 4-3: Low Volatility Distribution

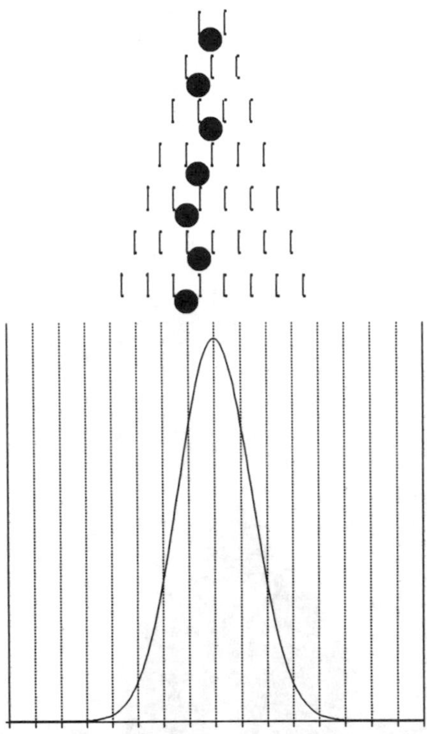

Suppose we now think of the ball's sideways movement as the up and down price movement of an underlying contract, and the ball's downward movement as the passage of time. If we assume that each day the underlying contract can move up or down $1, the price distribution after 15 days might be represented by the curve in Figure 4-2. If we assume the price can move up or down $1 every two days, the price distribution after 15 days might be represented by the curve in Figure 4-3. And if we assume that each day the price can move up or down $2, the price distribution might be represented by the curve in Figure 4-4.

With the underlying contract presently at $100 and 15 days to expiration, how might we evaluate a $105 call? One way is to assume that prices follow a random walk through time and that one of the curves in Figures 4-2, 4-3, or 4-4 represents the likely distribution after 15 days. The comparative value of the $105 call under these three scenarios is shown in Figure 4-5. If we assume a distribution similar to Figure 4-3, we can see that the underlying contract has very little chance of reaching $105. Consequently, the value of the $105 call will be low. If we assume a distribution similar to Figure 4-2, there is an increased probability of the underlying reaching $105, and this will increase the value of the $105 call. Finally, if we assume a distribution similar to

Figure 4-4: High Volatility Distribution

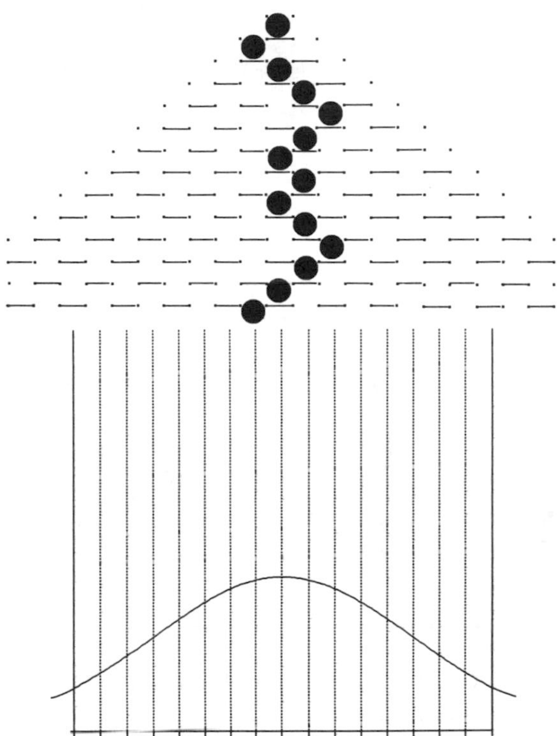

Figure 4-4, there is a very real likelihood that the $105 call could finish in-the-money. As a result, the value of the option will increase dramatically.

If we assume only that the price movement of an underlying contract follows a random walk, and nothing about the likely direction of movement, the curves in Figures 4-2, 4-3, and 4-4 might represent possible price distributions in a moderate-volatility, low-volatility, and high-volatility market, respectively. In a low-volatility market, price movement is severely restricted, and consequently options will command relatively low premiums. In a high-volatility market the chances for extreme price movement is greatly increased, and options will command high premiums.

Since the different price distributions in Figure 4-5 are symmetrical, it may seem that increased volatility should have no effect on an option's value. After all, increased volatility may increase the likelihood of large upward movement, but this should be offset by the equally greater likelihood of large downward movement. Here, however, there is an important distinction between an option position and an underlying position. Unlike an underlying contract, an option's potential loss is limited. No matter how far the market drops, a call option can only go to zero. In our example, whether the market finishes at $80 or $104 at expiration, the $105 call will be worthless. However, if we buy the underlying contract at $100, there is a tremendous difference between the

Figure 4-5: Price Distribution at Expiration

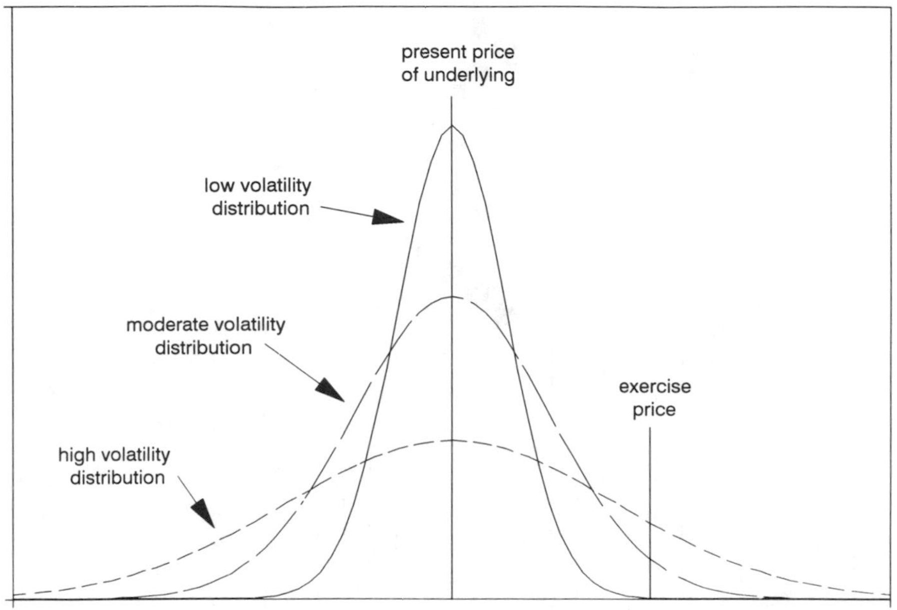

market finishing at $80 or $104. With an underlying contract all outcomes are important; with an option, only those outcomes which result in the option finishing in-the-money are important. In Figure 4-5, we are only concerned with price outcomes to the right of the exercise price. Everything else is zero.

This leads to an important distinction between evaluation of an underlying contract and evaluation of an option. If we assume that prices are distributed along a normal distribution curve, the value of an underlying contract depends on where the peak of the curve is located, while the value of an option depends on how fast the curve spreads out.

MEAN AND STANDARD DEVIATION

Suppose we want to use the concept of price movement based on normal distribution curves in a theoretical pricing model. To do this we need a method of describing the characteristics of the curve to the model. Since the model is based on mathematics, we need to describe the curve in numerical terms so that we can feed the numbers into the model.

Fortunately, a normal distribution curve can be fully described with two numbers, the *mean* and the *standard deviation.* If we know that a distribution is normal, and we also know these two numbers, then we know all the characteristics of the distribution.

Graphically, we can interpret the mean as the location of the peak of the curve, and the standard deviation as a measure of how fast the curve spreads out. Curves which spread out very quickly, such as Figure 4-4, have a high standard deviation; curves which spread out very slowly, such as Figure 4-3, have a low standard deviation.

While the mean is nothing more than the average outcome, and therefore a familiar concept for many traders, the standard deviation may not be quite so familiar. Indeed, one need not know how either of these numbers are calculated in order to successfully trade options. (For those who are interested, a more detailed discussion appears in Appendix B.) What is important to an option trader is the interpretation of these numbers, in particular what a mean and standard deviation suggest in terms of likely price movement.

Let's go back to Figure 4-2 and consider the troughs numbered 0 to 15 at the bottom. We suggested that these numbers might represent the number of heads resulting from 15 flips of a coin. Alternatively, they might also represent the number of times a ball went right at each nail as it dropped down through the maze. The first trough is assigned zero since any ball which ends there must have gone left at every nail. The last trough is assigned 15 since any ball which ends there must have gone right at every nail.

Suppose we are told that the mean and standard deviation in Figure 4-2 are 7.50 and 3.00, respectively. What does this tell us about the distribution? (The actual mean and standard deviation of 7.51 and 2.99 are calculated in Appendix B. Here, for simplicity, we will round to 7.50 and 3.00.) The mean tells us the average outcome. If we add up all the outcomes and divide by the number of occurrences, the result will be 7.50. In terms of the troughs, the average result will fall half-way between troughs 7 and 8. (Of course this is not an actual possibility. However, we noted in Chapter 3 that the average outcome does not have to be an actual possibility for any one outcome.)

The standard deviation not only describes how fast the distribution spreads out; it also tells us something about the likelihood of a ball ending up in a specific trough or group of troughs. In particular, the standard deviation tells us the probability of a ball ending up in a trough which is a specified distance from the mean. For example, we may want to know the likelihood of a ball falling down through the maze and ending up in a trough lower than 5 or higher than 10. We can answer the question by asking how many standard deviations the ball must move away from the mean, and then determine the probability associated with that number of standard deviations.

The exact probability associated with any specific number of standard deviations can be found in mathematical tables in most books on statistics. Alternatively, such probabilities can be closely approximated using an appropriate formula (see Appendix B). For option traders the following approximations will be useful:

±1 standard deviation takes in approximately 68.3% (about 2/3) of all occurrences

±2 standard deviations takes in approximately 95.4% (about 19/20) of all occurrences

±3 standard deviations takes in approximately 99.7% (about 369/370) of all occurrences

Note that each number of standard deviations is preceded by a plus or minus sign. Because normal distributions are symmetrical, the likelihood of up movement and down movement is identical.

Now let's try to answer our question about the likelihood of getting a ball in a trough lower than 5 or higher than 10. We can designate the divider between troughs 7 and 8 as the mean of 7½. If the standard deviation is 3, what troughs are within one standard deviation of the mean? One standard deviation from the mean is 7½ ± 3 = 4½ to 10½. Again interpreting ½ as the divider between troughs, we can see that troughs 5 through 10 fall within one standard deviation of the mean. We know that one standard deviation takes in about 2/3 of all occurrences, so we can conclude that out of every three balls we drop into the maze, two should end up in troughs 5 through 10. What is left over, one out of every three balls, will end up in one of the remaining troughs, 0-4 and 11-15. Hence, the answer to our original question about the likelihood of getting a ball in a trough lower than 5 or higher than 10 is about 1 chance in 3, or about 33%. (The exact answer is 100% – 68.3%, or 31.7%.) This is shown in Figure 4-6.

Let's try another calculation, but this time we can think of the problem as a wager. Suppose someone offers us 30 to 1 odds that we can't drop a ball into the maze and get it specifically in troughs 14 or 15. Is this bet worth making? One characteristic of standard deviations is that they are additive. In our example, if one standard deviation is 3, then two standard deviations are 6. Two standard deviations from the mean is therefore 7½ ± 6 = 1½ to 13½. We can see in Figure 4-6 that troughs 14 and 15 lie outside two standard deviations. Since the probability of getting a result within two standard deviations is approximately 19 out of 20, the probability of getting a result beyond two standard deviations is 1 chance in 20. Therefore 30 to 1 odds may seem very favorable. Recall, however, that beyond two standard deviations also includes troughs 0 and 1. Since normal distributions are symmetrical, the chances of getting a ball specifically in troughs 14 or 15 must be half of 1 chance in 20, or about 1 chance in 40. At 30 to 1 odds the bet must be a bad one since the odds do not sufficiently compensate us for the risk involved.

In Chapter 3 we said that one logical approach to option evaluation is to assign a probability to an infinite number of possible price outcomes for an underlying contract. Then, if we multiply each possible price outcome by its associated probability we can use the results to calculate an option's theoretical value. The problem is in dealing with an infinite number of price outcomes and probabilities, since an infinite number of anything is not easy to work with. Fortunately, the characteristics of normal distributions have been so closely studied that formulas have been developed which facilitate the computation of both the probabilities associated with every point along a normal distribution curve, as well as the area under various portions of the curve. If we assume that prices of an underlying instrument are normally distributed, these formulas represent a unique set of tools with which we can solve for an option's theoretical value. This is one of the reasons Black and Scholes adopted the normal distribution assumption as part of their model.

Figure 4-6

Mean = 7.50

Standard Deviation = 3.00

±1 standard deviation = 68.3% (2/3)

±2 standard deviations = 95.4% (19/20)

±3 standard deviations = 99.7% (369/370)

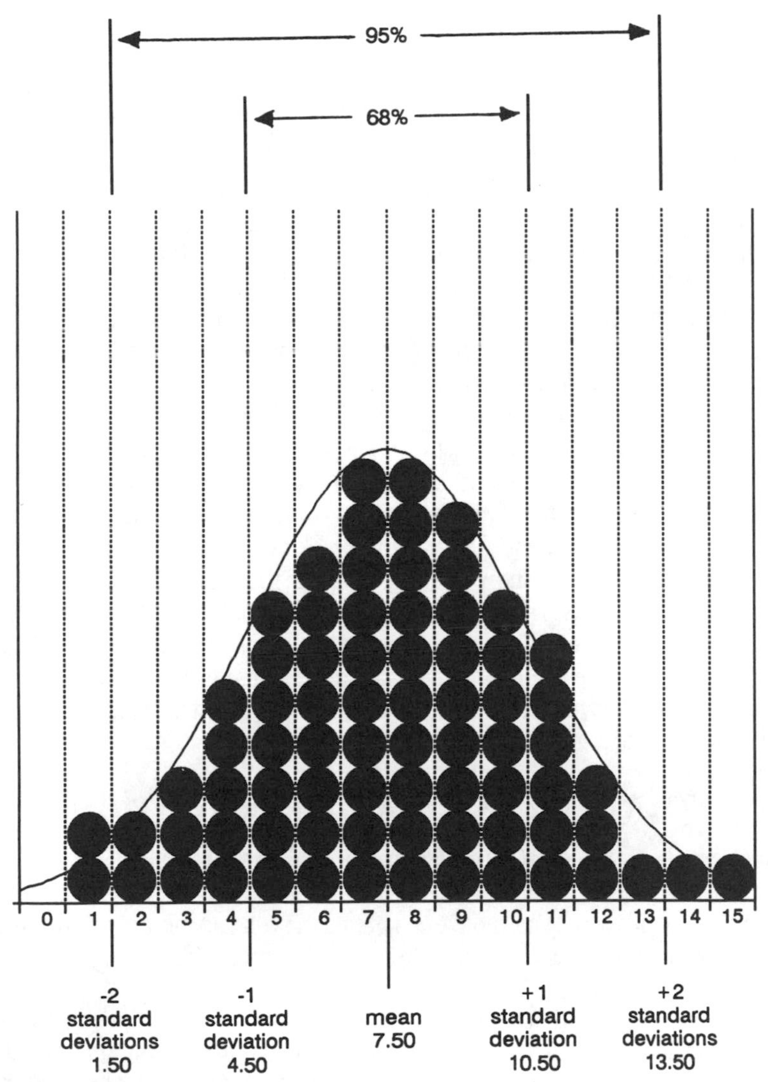

UNDERLYING PRICE AS THE MEAN OF A DISTRIBUTION

Now that we have decided to describe prices in terms of a normal distribution, how do we feed this distribution into a theoretical pricing model? Since all normal distributions can be described by a mean and the standard deviation, in some way we must feed these two numbers into our pricing model.

When we enter the present price of an underlying instrument we are actually entering the mean of a normal distribution curve. An important assumption in the Black-Scholes Model is that, in the long run, a trade in the underlying instrument will just break even. It will neither make money nor lose money. Given this assumption, the mean of the normal distribution curve assumed in the model must be the price at which a trade in the underlying instrument, either a purchase or a sale, would just break even. What is that price? The answer depends on the type of underlying instrument.

Suppose a trader purchases a futures contract at 100 and holds the position for three months. Where does the price of the futures contract have to be at the end of three months for the trader to break even? Since futures contracts entail no carrying costs, nor do they pay dividends, the break even price three months from now is exactly the original trade price of 100.

Now suppose that a trader purchases a $100 stock and holds it for three months. Where does the stock price have to be at the end of the holding period for the trader to break even? Since the purchase of stock requires immediate payment, the break even price will have to include the cost of carrying a $100 debit for three months. If interest rates are 8% annually the carrying cost on $100 for three months is $\frac{3}{12} \times 8\% \times \$100 = \$2$. Therefore, the stock price must be $102 at the end of three months for the trade to break even. If the stock will pay a dividend of $1 during the holding period, then the stock price need only be $101 for the trade to break even.

Note that this is exactly how we calculated the forward price of a contract in Chapter 3. And indeed this is exactly the type of calculation built into the various forms of the Black-Scholes Model. When we enter an underlying price into the Black-Scholes model, based on the type of underlying instrument, interest rates, and dividends, the model calculates the forward price of the underlying instrument at expiration and makes this price the mean of a normal distribution curve.

VOLATILITY AS A STANDARD DEVIATION

In addition to the mean, we also need a standard deviation to fully describe a normal distribution curve. This is entered in the form of a volatility. With some slight modifications, which we will discuss shortly, we can define the volatility number associated with an underlying instrument as a one standard deviation price change, in percent, at the end of a one-year period.

For example, suppose that an underlying futures contract is currently trading at 100 and has a volatility of 20%. Since this represents a one standard deviation price change, one year from now we expect the same futures contract to be trading between 80 and 120 ($100 \pm 20\%$) approximately 68% of the time, between 60 and 140 ($100 \pm (2 \times 20\%)$)

approximately 95% of the time, and between 40 and 160 (100 ± (3 × 20%)) approximately 99.7% of the time.

If the underlying contract is a stock currently trading at $100, then the 20% volatility will have to be based on the forward price of the stock at the end of one year. If interest rates are 8% and the stock pays no dividends, the one-year forward price will be $108. Now a one standard deviation price change is 20% × $108 = $21.60. So one year from now we would expect the same stock to be trading between $86.40 and $129.60 ($108 ± $21.60) approximately 68% of the time, between $64.80 and $151.30 ($108 ± (2 × $21.60)) approximately 95% of the time, and between $43.20 and $172.90 ($108 ± (3 × $21.60)) approximately 99.7% of the time.

Suppose we come back at the end of one year and find our futures contract, which we thought had a volatility of 20%, trading at 35. Does this mean our volatility of 20% was wrong? A price change of more than three standard deviations may be unlikely, but one shouldn't confuse unlikely and impossible. Flipping a perfectly balanced coin 15 times may result in 15 heads, even though the odds against it are more than 32,000 to 1. If 20% was the right volatility, the odds of the futures price going from 100 to 35 one year later is more than 1,500 to 1. But one chance in 1,500 is not impossible, and perhaps this was the one time in 1,500 when the price would indeed end up at 35. Of course, it is also possible that we had the wrong volatility. But we wouldn't know this without looking at price changes of the futures contract over many years so that we have a representative price distribution.

LOGNORMAL DISTRIBUTIONS

Is it reasonable to assume that the prices of an underlying instrument are normally distributed? Beyond the question of the exact distribution of prices in the real world, the normal distribution assumption has one serious flaw. A normal distribution curve is symmetrical. Under a normal distribution assumption, for every possible upward move in the price of an underlying instrument there must be the possibility of a downward move of equal magnitude. If we allow for the possibility of a $50 instrument rising $75 to $125, we must also allow for the possibility of the instrument dropping $75 to a price of –$25. Since it is impossible for traditional stocks and commodities to take on negative prices, the normal distribution assumption is clearly flawed. What can we do about this?

Up to now we have defined volatility in terms of the percent changes in the price of an underlying instrument. In this sense an interest rate and volatility are similar in that they both represent a *rate of return*. The primary difference between interest and volatility is that interest generally accrues at a positive rate, while volatility represents a combination of positive and negative rates of return. If one invests money at a fixed interest rate, the value of the principal will always grow. But if one invests in an underlying instrument with a volatility other than zero, the instrument may go either up or down in price. Volatility, which is a standard deviation, says nothing about the direction of movement.

Since volatility represents a rate of return, an important consideration is the manner in which the rate of return is calculated. For example, suppose we were to invest $1,000 for one year at an annual interest rate of 12%. How much would we have at the end of one year? The answer depends on how the 12% interest on our investment is paid out.

Rate of Payment	Value after One Year	Total Yield
12% once a year	$1,120.00	12%
6% twice a year	$1,123.60	12.36%
3% every three months	$1,125.51	12.55%
1% every month	$1,126.83	12.68%
12%/52 every week	$1,127.34	12.73%
12%/365 every day	$1,127.47	12.75%
12% compounded continuously	$1,127.50	12.75%

As interest is paid more often, even though it is paid at the same rate of 12% per year, the total yield on the investment increases. The yield is greatest when interest is paid continuously. In this case it is just as if interest were paid at every possible moment in time.

Although less common, we can do the same type of calculation using a negative interest rate. For example, suppose we were to lose 12 percent annually on our $1,000 investment (interest rate = –12%). How much would we have at the end of a year? The answer depends on the frequency at which our losses accrue.

Rate of Loss	Value after One Year	Total Yield
–12% once a year	$880.00	–12%
–6% twice a year	$883.60	–11.64%
–3% every three months	$885.29	–11.47%
–1% every month	$886.38	–11.36%
–12%/52 every week	$886.80	–11.32%
–12%/365 every day	$886.90	–11.31%
–12% compounded continuously	$886.92	–11.31%

In the case of a negative interest rate, as losses are compounded more frequently, even though at the same rate of –12% per year, the loss becomes smaller, and so does the negative yield.

In the same way that interest can be compounded at different intervals, volatility can also be compounded at different intervals. For purposes of theoretical pricing of options, volatility is assumed to compound continuously, just as if the price changes in the underlying instrument, either up or down, were taking place continuously but at an annual rate corresponding to the volatility number associated with the underlying instrument.

What would happen if at every moment in time the price of an underlying could go up or down a given percent, and that these up and down movements were normally distributed? When price changes are assumed to be normally distributed, the continuous compounding of these price changes will cause the prices at maturity to be *lognormally* distributed. Such a distribution is skewed toward the upside because upside prices resulting from a positive rate of return will be greater, in absolute terms, than downside prices resulting from a negative rate of return (Figure 4-7). In our interest rate example, a continuously compounded rate of return of +12% yields a profit of $127.50 after one year, while a continuously compounded rate of return of −12% yields a loss of only $113.08. If the 12% were a volatility, then a one standard deviation upward price change at the end of one year would be +$127.50, while a one standard deviation downward price change would be −$113.08. Even though the rate of return was a constant 12%, the continuous compounding of the 12% yielded different upward and downward moves.

The Black-Scholes Model is a *continuous time* model. It assumes that the volatility of an underlying instrument is constant over the life of the option, but that this volatility is continuously compounded. These two assumptions mean that the possible prices of the underlying instrument at expiration of the option are lognormally distributed. It also explains why options with higher exercise prices carry more value than options with lower exercise prices, where both exercise prices appear to be an identical amount away from the price of the underlying instrument. For example, suppose a certain underlying contract is trading at exactly 100. If there are no interest considerations and we assume

Figure 4-7: Lognormal Distribution

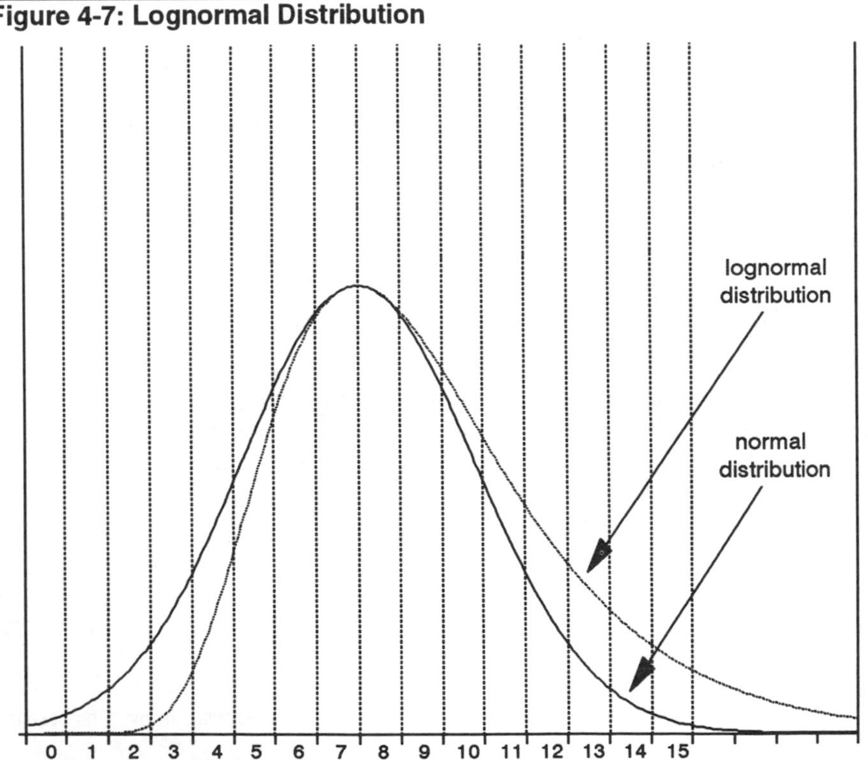

a normal distribution of possible prices, then the 110 call and the 90 put, both being 10% out-of-the-money, ought to have identical theoretical values. But under the lognormal assumption in the Black-Scholes Model, the 110 call will always have a greater value than the 90 put. In absolute terms, the lognormal distribution assumption allows for greater upside price movement than downside price movement. Consequently, the 110 call will have a greater possibility of price appreciation than the 90 put.[1]

Finally, the lognormal assumption built into the Black-Scholes Model overcomes the logical problem we initially posed. If we were to allow for the possibility of unlimited upside price movement of an underlying instrument, a normal distribution assumption would force us to allow for unlimited downside movement. This would require us to accept the possibility of negative prices for the underlying instrument, clearly not a possibility for most optionable instruments. A lognormal distribution, however, does allow for open ended upside prices (the logarithm of $+\infty$ is $+\infty$), while bounding downside prices by zero (the logarithm of $-\infty$ is zero). This is a more realistic representation of how prices are actually distributed in the real world.

A more complete discussion of logarithmic price changes and probability calculations can be found in Appendix B.

We can now summarize the most important assumptions governing price movement in the Black-Scholes Model:

1. Changes in the price of an underlying instrument are random and cannot be artificially manipulated, nor is it possible to predict beforehand the direction in which prices will move.

2. The percent changes in the price of an underlying instrument are normally distributed.

3. Because the percent changes in the price of the underlying instrument are assumed to be continuously compounded, the prices of the underlying instrument at expiration will be lognormally distributed.

4. The mean of the lognormal distribution will be located at the forward price of the underlying contract.

The first of these assumptions may meet with resistance from some traders. Technical analysts believe that by looking at past price activity it is possible to predict the future direction of prices. One can chart support and resistance points, double tops and bottoms, head and shoulders, and many similar formations which are believed to predict future price trends. We leave debate on this question to others. The important point here is that the Black-Scholes Model makes the assumption that price changes are random and that their direction cannot be predicted. This does not mean that there is no predictive requirement in using the Black-Scholes Model. However, price prediction

---

1. Of course, this is only theory. There is no law that says the price of the 90 put in the marketplace cannot be greater than the price of the 110 call.

will focus on the magnitude of the price changes, rather than on the direction of changes.

As we shall see later, there is also good reason to question the third assumption, that prices are lognormally distributed at expiration. This may be a reasonable assumption for some markets, but a very poor assumption for other markets. Again, the important point here is for the trader who uses a theoretical pricing model to understand the assumptions on which the theoretical values are based. He can then make his own decision, based on his knowledge of a particular market, as to whether these assumptions, and hence the theoretical values generated by the model, are likely to be accurate.

DAILY AND WEEKLY STANDARD DEVIATIONS

As an annual standard deviation, we know what the volatility tells us about the likely price movement of a contract over a one-year period. However, this is a period of time longer than the life of most listed options. We might want to know what a volatility tells us about price changes over a shorter period of time, for example over a month, or a week, or a day.

An important characteristic of volatility is that it is proportional to the square root of time. As a result of this, we can approximate a volatility over some period of time shorter than a year by dividing the annual volatility by the square root of the number of trading periods in a year.

Suppose we are interested in a daily volatility. While it would take a logarithmic calculation to give us an exact daily volatility, if we ignore the relatively minor effect of continuous compounding over such a short period of time, it is possible to make an estimate of daily volatility. First we must determine the number of daily trading periods in a year. That is, if we look at prices at the end of every day, how many times a year can prices change? If we restrict ourselves to exchange traded options, even though there are 365 days in a year, prices cannot really change on weekends or holidays. This leaves us with about 256 trading days during the year.[2] Since the square root of 256 is 16, to approximate a daily volatility we can divide the annual volatility by 16.

Going back to our futures contract trading at 100 with a volatility of 20%, what is a one standard deviation price change over a day's time? 20%/16 = 1¼%, so a one standard deviation daily price change is 1¼% × 100 = 1.25. We expect to see a price change of 1.25 or less approximately two trading days out of every three, and a price change of 2.50 or less approximately 19 trading days out of every 20. Only one day in 20 would we expect to see a price change of more than 2.50.

We can do the same type of calculation for a weekly standard deviation. Now we must ask how many times per year prices can change if we look at prices once a week. Unlike trading days, we don't have "holiday" weeks, so we must make our calculations using all 52 trading weeks in a year. Dividing our annual volatility of 20% by the square root of 52, or approximately 7.2, we get 20%/7.2 ≈ 2¾. For our futures contract

2. Depending on holidays, the number of trading days is usually somewhere between 250 and 255. We use 256 as a reasonable approximation since its square root is a whole number and therefore easier to work with.

trading at 100, we would expect to see a price change of 2.75 or less two weeks out of every three, a price change of 5.50 or less 19 weeks out of every 20, and only one week in twenty would we expect to see a price change of more than 5.50.

Since we assume that the price of a stock will appreciate by the carrying cost, it may seem that we cannot use the same method (divide by 16 for daily volatility; divide by 7.2 for weekly volatility) to approximate expected movement in an underlying stock. However, over a short period of time, the carrying cost component, like the effect of continuous compounding of volatility, will be relatively small. Therefore, we can use the same method as a reasonable estimate of daily and weekly volatility. For example, suppose a stock is trading at $45 per share and has an annual volatility of 28%. What is an approximate one standard deviation price change over a day's time and over a week's time?

For a daily volatility we calculate:

$$28\%/16 \times \$45 = 1.75\% \times \$45 = \$.79$$

For a weekly volatility we calculate:

$$28\%/7.2 \times \$45 = 3.89\% \times \$45 = \$1.75$$

We expect to see a price change of approximately ¾ point or less two days out of every three, 1½ points or less 19 days out of every 20, and only one day in 20 would we expect to see a price change of more than 1½ points. On a weekly basis, we would expect to see a price change of 1¾ points or less two weeks out of every three, a price change of 3½ points or less 19 weeks out of every 20, and only one week in 20 would we expect to see a price change of more than 3½ points.

We have used the phrase "price change" in conjunction with our volatility estimates. Exactly what do we mean by this? Do we mean the high/low during some period? Do we mean open to close price changes? Or is there another interpretation? While various methods have been suggested to estimate volatility,[3] the traditional method has been to calculate volatility based on settlement-to-settlement price changes. Using this approach, when we say a one standard deviation daily price change is ¾ point, we mean a ¾ point price change from one day's settlement price to the next day's settlement price. The high/low or open/close price change may have been either more or less than ¾ point, but it is the settlement-to-settlement price change on which we focus.

---

3. See:
Parkinson, Michael, "The Extreme Value Method of Estimating the Variance of the Rate of Return," *Journal of Business,* 1980, vol. 53, no. 1, pp. 61–64.
Garman, Mark B. and Klass, Michael J., "On the Estimation of Security Price Volatilities from Historical Data," *Journal of Business,* 1980, vol. 53, no. 1, pp. 67–78.
Beckers, Stan, "Variance of Security Price Returns Based on High, Low, and Closing Prices," *Journal of Business,* 1983, vol. 56, no. 1, pp. 97–112.

VOLATILITY AND OBSERVED PRICE CHANGES

Why is it important for a trader to be able to estimate daily or weekly price changes from an annual volatility? Volatility is the one input into a theoretical pricing model which cannot be directly observed. Yet many option strategies, if they are to be successful, require an accurate assessment of volatility. Therefore, an option trader needs some method of determining whether his expectations about volatility are indeed being realized in the marketplace. Unlike directional strategies, whose success or failure can be immediately observed from posted prices, there is no posting of volatilities. A trader must determine for himself whether he is using a reasonable volatility input into the theoretical pricing model.

For example, suppose a certain underlying contract is trading at 40 and a trader is using a 30% volatility for theoretical evaluation. A one standard deviation daily price change is approximately 30%/16 × 40 = .75. Over five days of trading a trader notes the following five settlement-to-settlement price changes:

+.43, –.06, –.61, +.50, –.28

Are these five price changes consistent with a 30% volatility?

The trader expects to see a price change of more than .75 (one standard deviation) about one day in three, or between one and two times over a five-day period. Yet during this five-day period he did not see a price change of this magnitude even once. What conclusions can be drawn from this?[4] One thing is certain: these five price changes are not consistent with 30% volatility. The trader might explain the discrepancy in one of two ways. On the one hand, perhaps this was expected to be an abnormally quiet week (perhaps it was a holiday week); and next week when trading returns to normal the market will go right back to making moves which are more consistent with a 30% volatility. If the trader comes to this conclusion, perhaps he ought to continue to use a 30% volatility for his calculations. On the other hand, perhaps there is no apparent reason for the market being less volatile than predicted by a 30% volatility. He may simply be using the wrong volatility. If the trader comes to this conclusion, perhaps he ought to consider using a new volatility input which is more consistent with the observed price changes. If he continues to use a 30% volatility in the face of price changes which are significantly less than predicted by that number, he will be assigning the wrong probabilities to the possible price outcomes for the underlying contract. Consequently, he will generate incorrect theoretical values, defeating the purpose of using a theoretical pricing model in the first place.

Exactly what volatility is associated with the five price changes in the foregoing example? Without some rather involved calculations it is difficult to say. (The answer is actually 18.8%.) However, if a trader has some idea beforehand of what price changes he expects, he can easily see that the changes over the five-day period are not consistent with a 30% volatility.

---

4. Five days is admittedly a very small sample from which to draw a meaningful conclusion about volatility. The method and reasoning, however, are still valid.

Let's look at another example. Now the underlying contract is trading at 332½ and a trader notes the following five daily price changes:

$$-5,\ +2\tfrac{1}{2},\ +1,\ -7\tfrac{3}{4},\ -4\tfrac{1}{4}$$

Are these price changes consistent with an 18% volatility? At 18% a one standard deviation price change is approximately 18%/16 × 332½ = 3¾. Over five days we expect to see a price change of more than 3¾ between one and two times. Yet here we have a price change of more than 3¾ three days out of five. And once the price change was 7¾ (more than two standard deviations) which we expect to see only one day in twenty. Again, unless the trader believes that the five price changes occurred during an extraordinary week, then perhaps he ought to consider changing his volatility figure so that it is more consistent with the observed price changes.

A NOTE ON INTEREST RATE PRODUCTS

Suppose Eurodollars are at 93.00 and we assume a volatility of 16 percent. We can apply the method previously described to calculate an approximate one standard deviation daily price change: 16%/16 × 93.00 = .93. As any trader familiar with the Eurodollar market will attest, a daily price change of .93 is wildly unlikely. How can we account for this seemingly illogical answer? One might conclude that we simply have the wrong volatility, and some lower number is more accurate. In fact, the 16% volatility is not at all unusual for Eurodollars, so the explanation must lie elsewhere.

Eurodollars, like many other interest rate contracts (U.S. Treasury Bills, Short Sterling, Euromarks, Euroyen) are indexed from 100. This means that the interest rate associated with a Eurodollar contract is 100 less the value of the contract. It also means that, barring the unlikely advent of negative interest rates, the contract cannot take on a value greater than 100. In this respect, 100 acts as a limiting value for Eurodollars in the same way that zero acts as a limiting value for traditional underlying contracts such as stocks and commodities. We can integrate this characteristic into our calculations by assuming that the value of a Eurodollar contract is actually 100 less its listed price. If the listed price is 93.00, for theoretical evaluation purposes we must use a value of 100 – 93.00, or 7.00, in our pricing model. If we define the value of the contract as 7.00, a one standard deviation price change is 16%/16 × 7.00 = .07. This is certainly a more realistic result than .93.

To be consistent, if we index Eurodollar prices from 100 we must also index exercise prices from 100. Therefore, a 93.50 exercise price in our pricing model is really a 6.50 (100 – 93.50) exercise price. This also requires us to reverse the type of option, changing calls to puts and puts to calls. To see why, consider a 93.50 call. For this call to go into-the-money, the underlying contract must rise above 93.50. But this requires that interest rates fall below 6.50 percent. Therefore, a 93.50 call in listed terms is the same as a 6.50 put in interest rate terms. A model which is correctly set up to evaluate options on Eurodollar or other types of indexed interest rate contracts automatically makes this transformation. The price of the underlying contract and the exercise price are subtracted from 100, while listed calls are treated as puts and listed puts are treated as calls.

Note that this type of transformation is not required for most bonds and notes. Depending on the coupon rate, the prices of these products may range freely without upper limit, often exceeding 100. They are therefore most often evaluated using a traditional pricing model, although interest rate products present other problems that may require specialized pricing models.

It is possible to take an instrument such as a bond and calculate the current yield based on its price in the marketplace. If we were to take a series of prices and from these calculate a series of yields, we could also calculate the *yield* volatility, i.e., the volatility based on the change in yield. We might then use this number to evaluate the theoretical value of an option on the bond, although to be consistent we would also have to specify the exercise price in terms of yield. Because it is possible to calculate the volatility of an interest rate product using these two different methods, interest rate traders sometimes refer to yield volatility (the volatility calculated from the current yield on the instrument) versus price volatility (the volatility calculated from the price of the instrument in the marketplace).

TYPES OF VOLATILITIES

When traders discuss volatility, even experienced traders may find that they are not always talking about the same thing. When a trader makes the comment that the volatility of XYZ is 25%, this statement may take on a variety of meanings. We can avoid confusion in subsequent discussions if we first define the various ways in which traders interpret volatility.

Future Volatility

Future volatility is what every trader would like to know, the volatility that best describes the future distribution of prices for an underlying contract. In theory it is this number to which we are referring when we speak of the volatility input into a theoretical pricing model. If a trader knows the future volatility, he knows the right "odds." When he feeds this number into a theoretical pricing model, he can generate accurate theoretical values because he has the right probabilities. Like the casino, he may occasionally lose because of short-term bad luck. But in the long run, with the odds on his side, a trader can be fairly certain of making a profit.

Of course, traders rarely talk about the future volatility since it is impossible to know what the future holds.

Historical Volatility

Even though one cannot know the future, if a trader intends to use a theoretical pricing model he must try to make an intelligent guess about the future volatility. In option evaluation, as in other disciplines, a good starting point is historical data. What typically has been the volatility of this contract over some period in the past? If, over the past ten years the volatility of a contract has never been less than 10% nor greater than 30%, a guess for the future volatility of either 5% or 40% hardly makes sense. This does not mean that either of these extremes is impossible (in option trading the impossible always seems to happen sooner or later), but based on past performance, and in the absence of any extraordinary circumstances, a guess within the historical limits of 10% and 30% is probably more realistic than a guess outside these limits. Of course, 10% to 30% is still a huge range, but at least the historical data offers a starting point. Additional information may further narrow the estimate.

Note that there are a variety of ways to calculate historical volatility, but most methods depend on choosing two parameters, the historical period over which the volatility is to be calculated, and the time interval between successive price changes. The historical period may be ten days, six months, five years, or any period the trader chooses. Longer periods tend to yield an average or characteristic volatility, while shorter periods may reveal unusual extremes in volatility. To become fully familiar with the volatility characteristics of a contract, a trader may have to examine a wide variety of historical time periods.

Next, the trader must decide what intervals to use between price changes. Should he use daily price changes? Weekly changes? Monthly changes? Or perhaps he ought to consider some unusual interval, perhaps every other day, or every week and a half. Surprisingly, the interval which is chosen does not seem to greatly affect the result. Although a contract may make large daily moves, yet finish a week unchanged, this is by far the exception. A contract which is volatile from day to day is likely to be equally volatile from week to week, or month to month. This is typified by the graphs in Figure 4-8. The data points on the three graphs represent the volatility of the S&P 500 index over successive 50-day periods. For the solid line daily price changes were used, for the dotted line price changes every two days were used, and for the broken line price changes every 5 days were used. Even though the graphs occasionally diverge, for the most part they exhibit the same general volatility levels and trends.

As a general rule, services which supply historical volatility data base their calculations on daily settlement-to-settlement price changes. If this is not the case, an explanation of how the volatility was calculated will usually accompany the data. If, for example, a service gave the volatility of a contract for the month of August as 21.6%, it can be assumed that the calculations were made using the daily settlement-to-settlement price changes for all the business days during that month.

Historical and future volatility are sometimes referred to as *realized* volatility.

Forecast Volatility

Just as there are services which will attempt to forecast future directional moves in the price of a contract, there are also services which will attempt to forecast the future volatility of a contract. Forecasts may be for any period, but most commonly cover periods identical to the remaining life of options on the underlying contract. For an underlying contract with three months between expirations, a service might forecast volatilities for the next three, six, and nine months. For an underlying with monthly expirations, a service might forecast volatilities for the next one, two, and three months. Due to the relatively recent introduction of options, volatility forecasting is still in its infancy, and must be considered an inexact science at best. Nonetheless, a trader's guess

Figure 4-8: S&P 500 Index 50-Day Historical Volatility

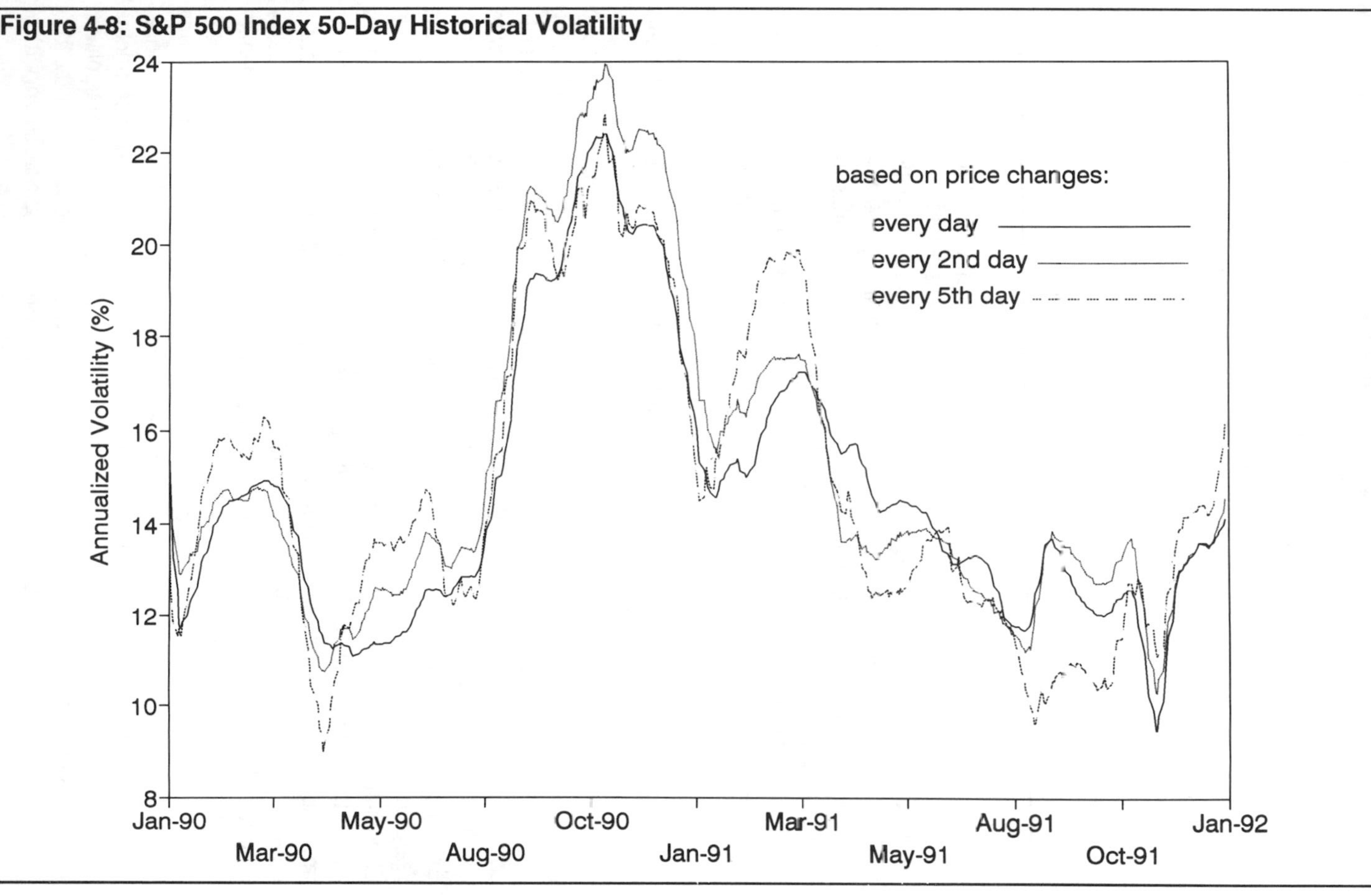

about the future volatility of a contract might very well take into consideration any volatility forecast to which he has access.

Implied Volatility

Generally speaking, future, historical, and forecast volatility are associated with an underlying contract. We can talk about the future volatility of the S&P 500 index, or the historical volatility of U.S. Treasury Bonds, or a forecast volatility for IBM stock. In each case we are referring to the volatility of the underlying contract. There is, however, a different interpretation of volatility which is associated with an option rather than with the underlying contract.

Suppose a certain futures contract is trading at 98.50 with interest rates at 8%. Suppose also that a 105 call with three months to expiration is available on this contract, and that our best guess about the volatility over the next three months is 16%. If we want to know the theoretical value of the 105 call we might feed all these inputs into a theoretical pricing model. Using the Black-Scholes Model, we find that the option has a theoretical value of .96. Having done this we might compare the option's theoretical value to its price in the marketplace. To our surprise, we find that the option is trading for 1.34. How can we account for the fact that we think the option is worth .96, while the marketplace seems to believe it is worth 1.34?

One way to answer the question is to assume that everyone in the marketplace is using the same theoretical pricing model that we are, in this case the Black-Scholes Model. If we make this assumption, then the discrepancy between our value of .96 and the marketplace's value of 1.34 must be due to a difference of opinion concerning one or more of the inputs into the model. We can therefore start going down the list of inputs and try to identify the culprits.

We know that it can't be either the amount of time to expiration or the exercise price, since these inputs are fixed in the option contract. What about the underlying price of 98.50? Perhaps we think the price of the underlying is at 98.50, but it is really trading at some higher price, say 99.00. Indeed, in such circumstances it is always wise to double check the inputs. But suppose we still find that the underlying is at 98.50. Even given that there is a spread between the bid and ask price, if the market is reasonably liquid it is unlikely that the spread would be wide enough to cause a discrepancy of .38 in the value of the option. Perhaps our problem is the interest rate of 8%. But, as we noted in the last chapter, the interest rate component is usually the least important of the inputs into a theoretical pricing model. And in the case of futures options, the interest rate component is often trivial. This leaves us with only one likely culprit, and that is volatility. In some sense, the marketplace must be using a volatility other than 16% to evaluate the 105 call.

What volatility is the marketplace using? To find out, we can ask the following question: If we hold all other inputs constant (time to expiration, exercise price, underlying price, interest rates), what volatility must we feed into our theoretical pricing model to yield a theoretical value identical to the price of the option in the marketplace? In our example, we want to know what volatility will yield a value of 1.34 for the 105 call. Clearly the volatility has to be higher than 16%, so we might sit down with a computer programmed with the Black-Scholes Model and start to raise the volatility. If we do, we will find that at a volatility of 18.5% the 105 call has a theoretical value of 1.34. We refer to this volatility as the *implied volatility* of the 105 call. It is the volatility we must feed into our theoretical pricing model to yield a theoretical value identical to the price of the option in the marketplace. We can also think of it as the volatility being implied to the underlying contract through the pricing of the option in the marketplace.

When we solve for the implied volatility of an option we are assuming that the theoretical value (the option's price) is known, but that the volatility is unknown. In effect, we are running the theoretical pricing model backwards to solve for this unknown, as shown in Figure 4-9. In fact, this is easier said than done since most theoretical pricing models cannot be reversed. However, a number of computer programs have been written which can quickly solve for the implied volatility when all other inputs are known.

Note that the implied volatility depends on the theoretical pricing model being used. For some options, a different model can yield a significantly different implied volatility. The accuracy of an implied volatility also depends on the accuracy of inputs into the model. This not only includes the price of the option, but the other inputs as well. In particular, problems can occur when an option has not traded for some time, but market conditions have changed significantly. Suppose in our example the price of 1.34 for the 105 call reflected the last trade, but that trade took place two hours ago when the underlying futures contract was actually at 99.25. If the price of the underlying contract is 99.25, the implied volatility of the option at a price of 1.34 is actually 17.3%. This is a significant difference, and underscores the importance of accurate and timely inputs when calculating implied volatilities.

Services which supply theoretical analysis of options usually include implied volatilities. The implied volatilities may be for each option on an underlying contract, or there may be one implied volatility which is representative of all options on the same

Figure 4-9

Using the Model to Solve for a Theoretical Value

Knowns	**Unknowns**
Exercise Price (105)	Theoretical Value
Time to Expiration (3 months)	(?? = .96)
Underlying Futures Price (98.50)	
Interest Rates (8%)	
Volatility (16%)	

Using the Model to Solve for an Implied Volatility

Knowns	**Unknowns**
Exercise Price (105)	Implied Volatility
Time to Expiration (3 months)	(?? = 18.5%)
Underlying Futures Price (98.50)	
Interest Rates (8%)	
Option Price (1.34)	

underlying. In the latter case, the figure will usually represent an average of all the individual implied volatilities. The single implied volatility is weighted according to some criteria, such as volume of options traded, open interest, or, as is most common, by assigning the greatest weight to the at-the-money options.

The implied volatility in the marketplace is constantly changing because option prices, as well as other market conditions, are constantly changing. It is as if the marketplace were continuously polling all participants to come up with a consensus volatility for the underlying contract. This is not a poll in the true sense, since all traders do not huddle together and eventually vote on the correct volatility. However, as bids and offers are made, the trade price of an option will represent the equilibrium between supply and demand. This equilibrium can be translated into an implied volatility.

Even though the term premium really refers to an option's price, it is common among traders to refer to the implied volatility as the *premium* or *premium level*. If the current implied volatility is high by historical standards, or high relative to the recent historical volatility of the underlying contract, a trader might say that premium levels are high; if implied volatility is unusually low, he might say that premium levels are low.

Assuming a trader had a reliable theoretical pricing model, if he could look into a crystal ball and determine the future volatility of an underlying contract he would be able to accurately evaluate options on that contract. He might then look at the difference between each option's theoretical value and its price in the marketplace, selling any options which were overpriced relative to the theoretical value, and buying any options which were underpriced. If given the choice between selling one of two overpriced options, he might simply sell the one which was most overpriced in total dollars. However, a trader who has access to implied volatilities might use a different yardstick for comparison. He might compare the implied volatility of an option to either a volatility forecast, or to the implied volatility of other options on the same underlying contract. Going back to our example of the 105 call, we might say that with a theoretical value of .96 and a price of 1.34, the 105 call is .38 overpriced. But in volatility terms it is 2.5% overpriced since its theoretical value is based on a volatility of 16% (the trader's volatility estimate) while its price is based on a volatility of 18.5% (the implied volatility). Due to the unusual characteristics of options, it is often more useful for the serious trader to consider an option's price in terms of implied volatility rather than in terms of its total dollar price.

For example, suppose a Treasury Bond 98 call is trading for 3-32 ($3,500) with a corresponding implied volatility of 10.5%. Suppose also that a 102 call with the same expiration date is trading for 1-16 ($1,250) with an implied volatility of 11.5%. In total dollar terms the 102 call is $2,250 cheaper than the 98 call. Yet an experienced trader will probably conclude that in theoretical terms the 98 call is actually less expensive than the 102 call because the implied volatility of the 98 call is a full percentage point less than the implied volatility of the 102 call. Does this mean that one ought to buy the 98 call and sell the 102 call? Not necessarily. If the future volatility of the Treasury Bonds turns out to be 8%, then both options are overpriced; while if volatility turns out to be 14%, both options are underpriced. Moreover, the leverage values of the options may not be the same so that their sensitivity to changes in market conditions may, under some circumstances, make several 102 calls a more desirable purchase than one 98 call. If we ignore these considerations, in relative terms the 98 call is a better value because its implied volatility is lower.

While option traders may at times refer to any of the four types of volatilities, two of these stand out in importance, the future volatility and the implied volatility. The future volatility of an underlying contract determines the *value* of options on that contract. The implied volatility is a reflection of each option's *price*. These two numbers, value and price, are what all traders, not just option traders, are concerned with. If a contract has a high value and a low price, then a trader will want to be a buyer. If a contract has a low value and a high price, then a trader will want to be a seller. For an option trader this usually means comparing the future volatility with the implied volatility. If implied volatility is low with respect to the expected future volatility, a trader will prefer to buy options; if implied volatility is high, a trader will prefer to sell options. Of course, future volatility is an unknown, so we tend to look at the historical and forecast volatilities to help us make an intelligent guess about the future. But in the final analysis, it is the future volatility which determines an option's value.

To help the new trader understand the various types of volatility, consider the following analogy to weather forecasting. Suppose a trader living in Chicago gets up on a July morning and must decide what clothes to wear that day. Do you think he will consider putting on a parka? This is not a logical choice because he knows that *historically* it is not sufficiently cold in Chicago in July to warrant wearing a winter coat. Next, he might turn on the radio or television to listen to the weather *forecast*. The forecaster is predicting clear skies with temperatures around 90° (32°C). Based on this information, our trader has reached a decision: he will wear a short sleeve shirt with no sweater or jacket, and he certainly won't need an umbrella. However, just to be sure, he decides to take a look out the window to see what the people outside are wearing. To his surprise, everyone is wearing a coat and carrying an umbrella. The people outside, through their clothing, are *implying* completely different weather. What clothes should the trader then wear? He must make some decision, but whom should he believe, the weather forecaster or the people in the street? There can be no certain answer because the trader will not know the *future* weather until the end of the day.

Much depends on the trader's knowledge of local conditions. Perhaps the trader lives in an area far removed from where the weather forecaster is located. Then he must give added weight to local conditions. On the other hand, perhaps the people in the street all listened to a weather forecaster who has a history of playing practical jokes.

The decision on what clothes to wear, just like every trading decision, depends on a great many factors. Not only must the decision be made on the basis of the best available information, but the decision must also be made with consideration for the possibility of error. What are the benefits of being right? What are the consequences of being wrong? If a trader fails to take an umbrella and it rains, that may be of little consequence if the bus picks him up right outside his residence and drops him off right outside his place of work. On the other hand, if he must walk several blocks in the rain, he might catch the flu and be away from work for a week. The choices are never easy, and one can only hope to make the decision that will turn out best in the long run.

Seasonal Volatility

There is one other type of volatility with which a commodity trader may have to deal. Certain agricultural commodities, such as corn, soybeans, and wheat, are very sensitive to volatility factors arising from severe seasonal weather conditions. Such conditions occur especially in the summer months when drought can destroy major portions of a crop and cause prices to fluctuate wildly. For this reason, grains show a significant increase in volatility during the months of June, July, and August. Conversely, they show a significant decrease during the early spring months, before American planting has begun but after the South American crop has been harvested. Given these factors, one must automatically assign a higher volatility to an option contract which extends through the summer months. If, in February, a trader has assigned a volatility of 18% to a May soybean contract, he will certainly choose some higher volatility, perhaps 22%, for a November contract. He knows that the November contract includes the summer months, while the May contract does not. The effect of seasonal volatility on soybeans is shown in Figure 4-10.

A trader who is new to options might initially question whether volatility is really that important. He has probably been pursuing directional strategies where volatility was not a consideration. It is also possible to pursue a variety of directional strategies in the option market. But if a trader has a thorough understanding of volatility, he has an additional variable with which to work. He can, in effect, approach the market from two directions instead of one. Many traders find it easier to work exclusively with

Figure 4-10: Monthly Soybean Volatility (1980–1992)

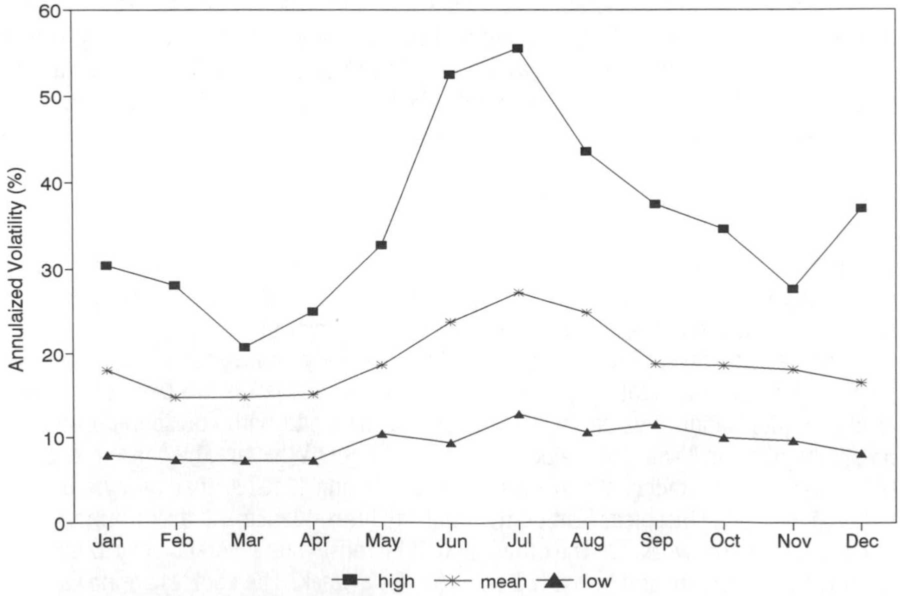

Courtesy of the Chicago Board of Trade.

volatility, rather than try to guess market direction. Moreover, volatility strategies can be extremely profitable and, when chosen intelligently, can even reduce a trader's risk exposure. These two variables, market direction and volatility, enable an option trader to pursue many strategies not available to the pure stock or futures trader.

Changing our assumptions about future volatility can have a dramatic effect on the value of options. To see this, look at the prices, theoretical values, and implied volatilities for ten-week gold options in Figure 4-11. Note the change in theoretical values as volatility is increased from 11% to 14% to 17%. The 360 call and put, which are essentially at-the-money, change by approximately 1.85 ($185) for each three-percentage-point increase in volatility. While out-of-the-money options do not show as great a dollar change in value, in percent terms their sensitivity to a change in volatility is even greater. As volatility increases from 11% to 14%, the 390 call and 330 put more than double in value, and double again as volatility increases from 14% to 17%. A three-percentage-point change in volatility over ten weeks is not at all uncommon. Indeed, the volatility of gold can show swings of six or seven percentage points in a relatively short period of time. This is evident from the historical volatility of gold shown in Figure 4-12.

Given its importance, it is not surprising that the serious option trader spends a considerable amount of time thinking about volatility. Using his knowledge of historical, forecast, implied, and, in the case of agricultural commodities, seasonal volatility, he

Figure 4-11

3 May 1991
August Gold Futures at 358.30
Time to expiration = 10 weeks
Interest rate = 5.50%

Exercise Price	Settlement Price	Implied Volatility	Theoretical Value If . . .		
			Vol. = 11%	Vol. = 14%	Vol. = 17%
Calls					
330	29.20	15.36	28.27	28.84	29.69
340	20.60	14.48	19.26	20.40	21.73
350	13.20	13.86	11.61	13.28	15.01
360	7.80	13.89	6.02	7.87	9.73
370	4.20	14.00	2.62	4.20	5.88
380	2.40	14.93	.94	2.01	3.32
390	1.40	15.93	.28	.86	1.75
Puts					
330	1.20	15.28	.29	.87	1.72
340	2.60	14.69	1.17	2.31	3.64
350	5.10	14.04	3.41	5.08	6.80
360	9.50	13.92	7.70	9.55	11.41
370	15.70	13.88	14.18	15.77	17.45
380	23.70	14.57	22.40	23.47	24.78
390	32.50	15.13	31.62	32.20	33.08

Figure 4-12: 10-Week Gold Volatility

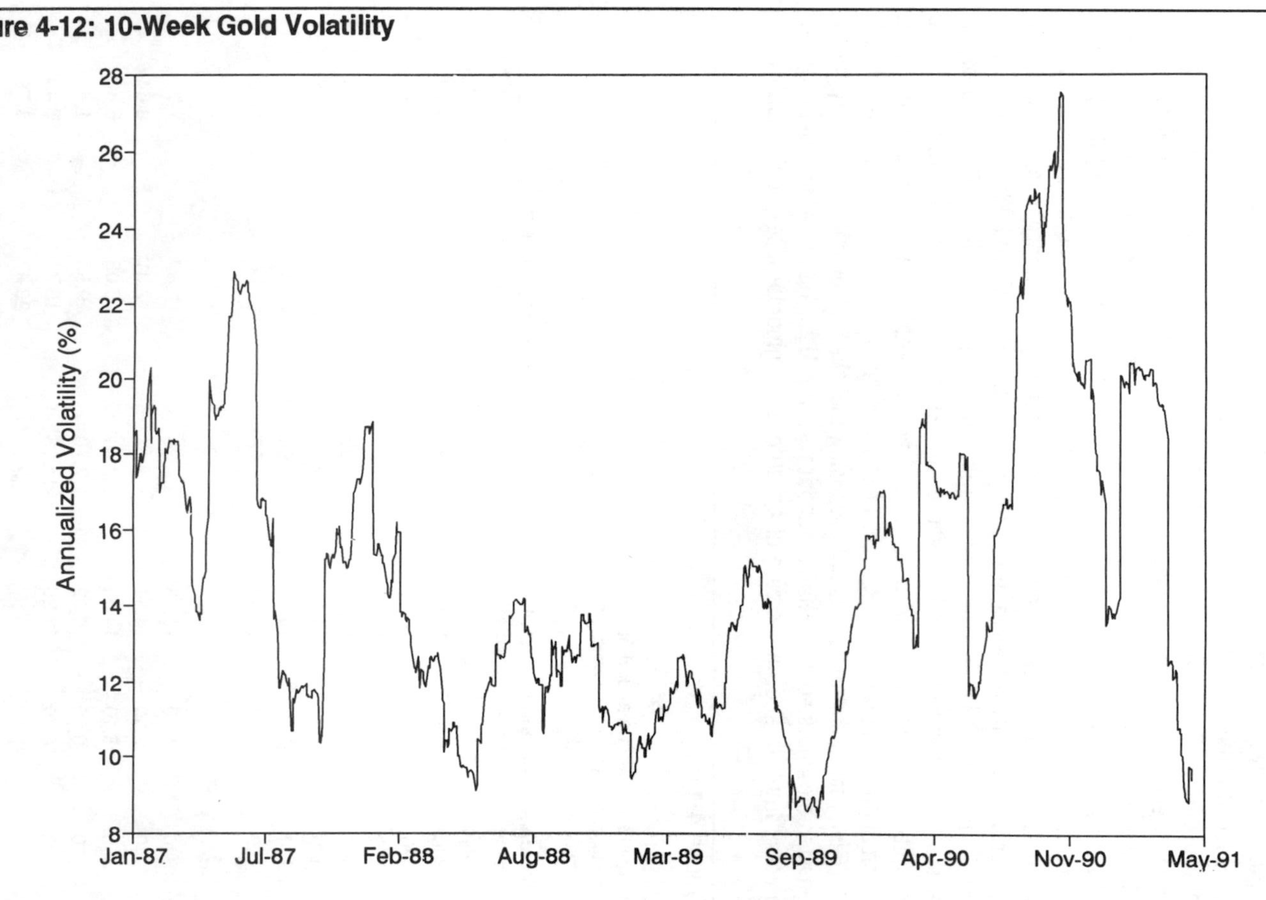

must try to make an intelligent decision about future volatility. From this, he will look for option strategies which will be profitable when he is right, but which will not result in a disastrous loss when he is wrong. Because of the difficulty in predicting volatility, a trader must always look for strategies which will leave the greatest margin for error. No trader will survive very long pursuing strategies based on a future volatility estimate of 15% if such a strategy results in a loss when volatility actually turns out to be 16%. Given the shifts that occur in volatility, a one-percentage-point margin for error is no margin for error at all.

We have not yet concluded our discussion of volatility. But before continuing, it will be useful to look at option characteristics, trading strategies, and risk considerations. We will then be in a better position to examine volatility in greater detail.

❖ 5 ❖

Using an Option's Theoretical Value

From a theoretician's point of view, the Black-Scholes Model represents a novel solution to a complex problem. The model requires a limited number of inputs and relatively simple mathematical calculations. These factors have made the Black-Scholes Model the most popular of all option pricing methods.

While a trader might appreciate the elegance of the mathematics, it is still the actual performance of the model in the marketplace which is his primary consideration. Is it really possible to profit from price discrepancies between model-generated values and the market prices of options?

To see how the model is intended to function, let us make two assumptions:

1. The price distribution of an underlying contract is accurately represented by a lognormal distribution.
2. We actually know the future volatility of an underlying contract.

Clearly, the second assumption is not very realistic since we obviously don't know the future. As we shall see later, the first assumption is also highly questionable. But for the time being, rather than focus on the assumptions in the model, we want to focus on its use by a trader. If we make these assumptions, and the Black-Scholes Model does indeed work, then we ought to be able to turn any difference between an option's price and its theoretical value into a profit. How should we go about doing this?

Suppose that a series of options are available on a certain futures contract with the following conditions:

June futures price	= 101.35
Interest rate	= 8.00%
Time to June expiration	= 10 weeks

Suppose also that the options are subject to stock-type settlement, requiring full payment of the premium, as they currently are on U.S. markets.

Given that we can choose any exercise price we want, and that we can choose the type of option we want (call or put), the only input we still need for accurate evaluation of options on this futures contract is volatility. Since we have made the assumption that we actually know the future volatility of the underlying futures contract, let's imagine that we have a crystal ball which will tell us the future volatility. When we look into the crystal ball we see a volatility figure of 18.3% over the next 10 weeks. Now we have all the necessary inputs for theoretical evaluation, and it only remains to choose a specific option.

The June 100 call, being close to at-the-money, is likely to be actively traded, so let's focus on that option. Feeding our inputs into the Black Model (the futures variation of the Black-Scholes Model), we find that the June 100 call has a theoretical value of 3.88. When we check its price in the marketplace, we find that it is being offered at 3.25. How can we profit from this discrepancy?

Clearly, our first move will be to purchase options since they are underpriced by .63. Can we now walk away from the position and come back at expiration to collect our money?

We noted in Chapter 3 that the purchase or sale of a theoretically mispriced option requires us to establish a hedge by taking an opposing position in the underlying contract. When this is done correctly, for small changes in the price of the underlying, the increase (decrease) in the value of the option position will exactly offset the decrease (increase) in the value of the opposing position in the underlying contract. Such a hedge is unbiased, or *neutral*, as to the direction of the underlying contract.

The number which enables us to establish a neutral hedge under current market conditions is a by-product of the theoretical pricing model and is known as the *hedge ratio* or, more commonly, the *delta*. We will discuss the delta in greater detail in the next chapter, but certain characteristics will be important in our present example:

1. The delta of a call option is always somewhere between 0 and 1.00.
2. The delta of an option can change as market conditions change.
3. An underlying contract always has a delta of 1.00.

Option traders commonly drop the decimal point when discussing deltas, a convention which we will also follow. Therefore, the delta of a call will fall in the range of 0 to 100, and an underlying contract will always have a delta of 100.[1]

Going back to our example, in order to make correct use of the option's theoretical value, we also need to know the delta, in this case 57 (.57). This means that for each option which we purchase we must sell 57% of an underlying contract to establish an unbiased or neutral hedge. Since the purchase or sale of fractional futures contracts is not permitted, we intend to purchase 100 June 100 calls and sell 57 June futures contracts. This maintains the proper neutral ratio but allows us to deal in whole numbers of contracts. We have established the following position:

Contract	Contract Delta	Delta Position
Buy 100 June 100 calls	57	+5700
Sell 57 June futures	100	–5700

1. This convention originated in the U.S. stock option market where an underlying contract typically consisted of 100 shares of stock. It became common to equate one delta with each share of stock.

Note that the delta position on each side of the hedge is the number of contracts multiplied by the contract delta, keeping in mind that the purchase of a contract is represented by a positive sign and the sale of a contract is represented by a negative sign. The option delta position is therefore +100 × 57 = +5700 and the futures position is –57 × 100 = –5700. When we add these two numbers together, +5700 and –5700, the total delta position is zero, and we say that the position is *delta neutral.* Within a small range, a delta neutral position has no particular preference for either upward or downward movement in the underlying market. If the total delta position is a positive number, this indicates an upward bias; if the total delta position is a negative number, this indicates a downward bias.

Having established a delta neutral hedge we must still deal with the fact that a theoretical value is based on probability. The roulette player who is able to purchase a roulette bet for less than its theoretical value can only expect to show a profit if he is allowed to play many, many times. On any one bet he will most likely lose, since there is only one way for him to win but 37 ways for him to lose. The same is true of our hedge. The odds may be on our side because we have purchased undervalued options. But in the short run our hedge might very well result in a loss. Is there anything we can do to offset the possibility of short-term bad luck?

We know that in the long run the laws of probability are on our side. We can be fairly certain of making a profit if we are given the chance to make many bets at the same favorable odds. The more bets we make, the better our chances of making a profit identical to that predicted by the theoretical pricing model. One way to accomplish this is to approach the initial hedge as a continuing series of small bets. We can replicate the long-term probability by reassessing our position at regular intervals, and then making appropriate changes in the position so that each new interval represents a new bet.

Suppose that one week later the price of the June futures contract has moved up to 102.26. At this point we can feed the new market conditions into our theoretical pricing model:

June futures price	= 102.26
Interest rate	= 8.00%
Time to June expiration	= 9 weeks
Volatility	= 18.3%

Note that we have made no change in the interest rate or volatility. The theoretical pricing model we are using, the Black model, assumes that these two inputs remain constant over the life of the option. Based on the new inputs we can calculate the new delta for the 100 call, in this case 62. The delta position is now:

Contract	Contract Delta	Delta Position
Long 100 June 100 calls	62	+6200
Short 57 June futures	100	–5700

Our total delta position is now +500. This is the end of one bet, with another about to begin.

Whenever we begin a new bet we are required to return to a delta neutral position. In our example it will be necessary to reduce our position by 500 deltas. As we shall see later, there are a number of different ways to do this. But to keep our present calculations as simple as possible we will make the necessary trades in the underlying futures market, since an underlying contract always has a delta of 100.

Here we wish to sell off 500 deltas, and we can do this by selling 5 futures contracts. Our delta position is now:

Contract	Contract Delta	Delta Position
Long 100 June 100 calls	62	+6200
Short 62 June futures	100	–6200

We are again delta neutral and about to begin a new bet. As before, our new bet depends only on the volatility of the underlying futures contract, and not on its direction.

The extra five futures contracts we sold were an *adjustment* to our position. Adjustments are trades which are not necessarily made for the purpose of adding to the theoretical edge, although they may also have that effect. Rather, they are made primarily to ensure that a position remains delta neutral. In our case, the sale of the five extra futures contracts has no effect on our theoretical edge since futures contracts have no theoretical value.[2] The trade was made solely for the purpose of adjusting our hedge to remain delta neutral.

The steps we have thus far taken illustrate the correct procedure in using an option's theoretical value:

1. Purchase (sell) undervalued (overvalued) options.
2. Establish a delta neutral hedge against the underlying contract.
3. Adjust the hedge at regular intervals to remain delta neutral.

Since volatility is assumed to compound continuously, theoretical pricing models assume that adjustments are also made continuously, and that the hedge is being adjusted at every moment in time. Such continuous adjustments are not possible in the real world, since a trader can only trade at discrete intervals. By making adjustments at regular intervals, we are conforming as best we can to the principles of the theoretical pricing model.

Using the proper procedure, how would the adjustment process look if we were to carry the hedge to expiration? The results are shown in Figure 5-1. In our example adjustments were made at weekly intervals. At the end of each interval the delta of the June 100 call was recalculated from the time remaining to expiration, the current price of the underlying futures contract, the fixed interest rate of 8.00%, and the known volatility of 18.3%. Note that we have not changed the volatility, even though other market conditions may have changed. Volatility, like interest rates, are assumed to be

2. While a futures trader might talk about the theoretical value of a futures contract, from an option trader's point of view the underlying contract has no theoretical value. The theoretical value is whatever price the trader thinks he can trade the contract at.

constant over the life of the option. In practice, a trader may, and often does, change his opinion about volatility.

What will we do with our position at the end of ten weeks when the options expire? At that time we plan to close out the position by:

1. Letting any out-of-the-money options expire worthless.
2. Selling any in-the-money options at parity (intrinsic value) or, equivalently, exercising them and offsetting them against the underlying futures contract.
3. Liquidating any outstanding futures contracts at the market price.

Let's go through this procedure step by step and see what the complete results of our hedge were.

Original Hedge: At June expiration (week 10) we can liquidate our June 100 calls by either selling them at 2.54, or by selling futures at 102.54 and exercising the calls. Either method will result in a credit of 2.54 to our account. Since we originally paid 3.25 for each option, we have effectively lost .71 per option, and our total loss on the options is 100 × –.71 = –71.00.

As part of our original hedge we also sold 57 June futures at 101.35. At expiration we had to buy them back at 102.54, for a loss of 1.19 per contract. Our total loss on the futures is therefore 57 × –1.19 = –67.83. Adding this to our option loss, the total loss on the original hedge is –71.00 –67.83 = –138.83. This certainly does not appear to have been successful. We expected to make money on the hedge, and yet we have a sizable loss.

Adjustments: The original hedge was not our only transaction. In order to remain delta neutral, we were forced to buy and sell futures contracts over the ten-week life of the option. At the end of week one we were 500 deltas long, so we had to sell 5 futures at

Figure 5-1

Week	Futures Price	Delta of 100 Call	Total Delta Position	Adjustment in Futures	Total Futures Adjustment	Variation	Interest on Variation
0	101.35	57	0	0	0	0	0
1	102.26	62	+500	sell 5	–5	–51.87	–.72
2	99.07	46	–1,600	buy 16	+11	+197.78	+2.43
3	100.39	53	+700	sell 7	+4	–60.72	–.65
4	100.76	56	+300	sell 3	+1	–19.61	–.18
5	103.59	74	+1,800	sell 18	–17	–158.48	–1.22
6	99.26	45	–2,900	buy 29	+12	+320.42	+1.97
7	98.28	35	–1,000	buy 10	+22	+44.10	+.20
8	99.98	50	+1,500	sell 15	+7	–59.50	–.18
9	103.78	93	+4,300	sell 43	–36	–190.00	–.29
10	102.54			buy 36			

102.26. At the end of week two we were 1600 deltas short, so we had to buy 16 futures at 99.07; and so on each week until the end of week ten. At expiration we were short an extra 36 futures contracts, and we bought these in at the closing price of 102.54. Note that each time the futures price rose our delta position became positive, so that we were forced to sell futures; and each time the futures price fell our delta position became negative, so that we were forced to buy futures. Because our adjustments depended on the delta position, we were forced to do what every trader wants to do: buy low and sell high.

What was the result of all the adjustments required to maintain a delta neutral position? In fact the result was a profit of 205.27. (The reader may wish to confirm this by adding up the cash flow from all the trades in the adjustment column in Figure 5-1.) This profit more than offset the losses incurred from the original hedge.

Carrying Costs: What else will effect our final profit or loss? Originally we bought calls and sold futures. While futures are subject to futures-type settlement and require no initial cash outlay, the options are subject to stock-type settlement and require full payment. We bought 100 calls for 3.25 each, for a total outlay of 325.00. Based on our assumed 8.00% interest rate, the carrying cost on 325.00 for 10 weeks is .08 x 70/365 × 325.00 = 4.99. We will have to include this debit of 4.99 in our final calculations.

Variation Costs: Finally, we must take into consideration the variation costs required to maintain our futures position. As futures move up or down in price, cash is either credited to, or debited from, a trader's account. In theory, a trader can earn interest on a cash credit, but must pay interest on a cash debit. For example, we initially sold 57 futures contracts at 101.35. One week later the futures price rose to 102.26, so our account was debited 57 × (101.35 – 102.26) = –51.87. Financing this debit for nine weeks at 8.00% cost us –51.87 × .08 × 63/365 = –.72. In order to remain delta neutral at the end of week one we sold an additional five futures contracts, for a new total of short 62 futures. One week later (week 2) the futures price fell to 99.07, so our account was credited 62 × (102.26 – 99.07) = +197.78. The amount of interest we were able to earn on this credit for 8 weeks at 8.00% was +197.78 × .08 × 56/365 = +2.43. The cash flow resulting from futures variation is shown in Figure 5-1 under the "variation" column, and the resulting interest is shown under the "interest on variation" column. The total interest is +1.36.

We can now summarize all the profit and loss components resulting from our position:

Original Hedge	Adjustments	Option Carrying Costs	Variation Costs
–138.83	+205.27	–4.99	+1.36

The total profit is –138.83 +205.27 –4.99 +1.36 = +62.81. How much did the theoretical pricing model predict we would make? We bought 100 calls worth 3.88 for 3.25 each, for a total theoretical edge of 100 × (3.88 – 3.25) = 100 × .63 = +63.00. In other words, the theoretical model came very close to predicting the actual profit from the position.

In our example, the profit and loss was made up of four components. Two of these were profitable (the adjustments and the variation costs) while two were unprofitable (the original hedge and the option carrying costs). Is this always the case? It is impossible to determine beforehand which components will be profitable and which will not. One could just as easily construct an example where the original hedge was profitable and the adjustments were not. The important point here is that if a trader's inputs are correct, in some combination he can expect to show a profit (or loss) approximately equal to that predicted by the theoretical pricing model.

Of all the inputs, volatility is the only one which is not directly observable. Where did our volatility figure of 18.3% come from? Obviously, one can't know the future volatility, but in this case the author took the ten price changes in Figure 5-1 and calculated the annualized standard deviation of the logarithmic changes (the volatility). Hence, the volatility of 18.3% was the correct volatility for this series of price changes. The complete calculations are given in Appendix B.

In the foregoing example we assumed that the market was *frictionless*, that no external factors affected the total profit or loss. This assumption is basic to many economic models, including the Black-Scholes Model. In a frictionless market we assume that:

1. Traders can freely buy or sell the underlying contract without restriction
2. All traders can borrow and lend money at the same rate.
3. Transaction costs are zero.
4. There are no tax considerations.

A trader will immediately realize that option markets are not frictionless, since each of the above assumptions is violated to a greater or lesser degree in the real world. For example, in certain futures markets there is a daily limit on the amount of allowable price movement. When this limit is reached, the market is said to be *locked*, and no further trading can take place until the price of the futures contract comes off its limit.[3] Clearly, in such a market the underlying contract cannot always be freely bought or sold.

Additionally, individual traders cannot generally borrow or lend money at the same rate as large financial institutions. If a trader has a debit balance, it will cost him more to carry that debit; if he has a credit balance, he will not earn as much on that credit. There is a spread, and perhaps a fairly large one, between a trader's borrowing and lending rate. Fortunately, as we discussed in Chapter 3, the interest rate component is usually the least important of the inputs into a theoretical pricing model. Even though the applicable interest rate may vary from trader to trader, in general it will only cause small changes in the total profit or loss in relation to the profit or loss resulting from other inputs.

---

3. It is sometimes possible to circumvent the problem of a locked market by either buying or selling the physical commodity rather than the futures contract, or by trading spreads between futures months if one of the months is not locked.

Transaction costs, on the other hand, can be a very real consideration. If such costs are high, the hedge in Figure 5-1 might not be a viable strategy; all the profits could be eaten up by brokerage fees. In theory, the desirability of a strategy will depend not only on the trader's initial transaction costs, but also on the subsequent costs of making adjustments. The adjustment cost is a function of a trader's desire to remain delta neutral. A trader who wants to remain delta neutral at every moment will have to adjust more often, and more adjustments mean more transaction costs.

Suppose a trader initiates a hedge but adjusts less frequently, or does not adjust at all. How will this affect the outcome? Since theoretical evaluation of options is based on the laws of probability, a trader who initiates a theoretically profitable hedge still has the odds on his side. Although he may lose on any one individual hedge, if given a chance to initiate the same hedge repeatedly at a positive theoretical edge, on average he should profit by the amount predicted by the theoretical pricing model, assuming, of course, that his inputs are correct. The adjustment process is simply a way of smoothing out the winning and losing hedges by forcing the trader to make more bets, always at the same favorable odds. A trader's disinclination to adjust simply means that there is greater risk of not realizing a profit on any one hedge. Adjustments do not in themselves alter the expected return; they simply reduce the possibility of short-term bad luck.

Based on the foregoing discussion, a retail customer and a professional trader are likely to approach option trading in a slightly different manner, even though both understand and use the values generated by a theoretical pricing model. A professional trader, particularly if he is an exchange member, has relatively low transaction costs. Since adjustments cost him practically nothing in relation to the expected theoretical profit from a hedge, he is willing to make frequent adjustments. However, a retail customer who establishes the same hedge will probably not adjust, or will adjust less frequently, because any adjustments are likely to significantly reduce the profitability of a hedge. But if he understands the laws of probability, the retail customer will realize that his position has the same favorable odds as the professional trader's position. At the same time he should realize that his position is more sensitive to short-term bad luck. Even though the retail customer may occasionally experience larger losses than the professional trader, he will also occasionally experience larger profits. In the long run, on average, both should end up with approximately the same profit.[4]

Taxes may also be a factor in evaluating an option strategy. When positions are initiated, when they are liquidated, how the positions overlap, and the relationship between different instruments (options, stock, futures, physical commodities, etc.) may have different tax consequences. Such consequences can often have a significant impact on the value of a diversified portfolio, and for this reason portfolio managers must be sensitive to the tax ramifications of a strategy. Since each trader has unique tax considerations, and this book is intended as a general guide to option evaluation and strategies, we will simply assume that each trader wishes to maximize his theoretical pre-tax profits and that he will worry about taxes afterward.

---

4. This of course ignores the very real advantage the professional trader often has from being able to buy at the bid price and sell at the ask price. A retail customer can never hope to match the profit resulting from this advantage, nor should he try to do so.

Returning to our example in Figure 5-1, note that after the hedge was initiated no subsequent trades were made in the option market. The trader's only concern was the volatility, or price fluctuations, in the underlying market. These price fluctuations determined the size and the frequency of the adjustments, and in the final analysis it was the adjustments which determined the profitability of the hedge. We might think of the hedge as a race between the loss in time value of the June 100 calls and the cash flow resulting from the adjustments, with the theoretical pricing model acting as the judge. The model says that if options are purchased at less than theoretical value, the adjustments will win the race; if options are purchased at more than theoretical value, the loss in time value will win the race. The conditions of the race are determined by the inputs into the theoretical pricing model.

While we assumed in our example that the future volatility was known to be 18.3%, we might ask what the outcome would have been had volatility been other than 18.3%? Suppose, for example, it turned out to be higher than 18.3%. Higher volatility means greater price fluctuations, resulting in more and larger adjustments. In our example, more adjustments mean more profit. This is consistent with the principle that options increase in value as volatility increases.

What about the reverse, if volatility had been less than 18.3%? Lower volatility means smaller price fluctuations, resulting in fewer and smaller adjustments. This would have reduced the profit. If the volatility were low enough, the adjustment profit would just be enough to offset the other components, so that the total profit from the hedge would be exactly zero. This break-even volatility is identical to the option's implied volatility at the trade price. Using the Black model, we find that the implied volatility of the June 100 call at a price of 3.25 is 14.6%. At that volatility the race between profits from the adjustments and the loss in the option's time value will end in an exact tie. Above a volatility of 14.6% we expect the hedge, including adjustments, to show a profit; below 14.6% we expect the hedge to show a loss.

Since we needed to make adjustments in order to realize a profit, it may seem that every profitable hedge requires us to maintain the position until expiration. In practice, however, this may not be necessary. Suppose, for example, that immediately after we established the hedge the implied volatility in the option market began to increase. Suppose that it increased from 14.6%, the implied volatility when we bought the June 100 calls, to 18.3%, the future volatility over the life of the option. What would happen to the price of the June 100 call? Its price would rise from 3.25 (an implied volatility of 14.6%) to 3.88 (an implied volatility of 18.3%). We could then sell our calls for an immediate profit of .63 per option. Of course, if we wanted to close out the hedge we would also have to buy back the 57 June futures contracts which we originally sold. What effect would the change in implied volatility have on the price of the futures contracts? Implied volatility is a characteristic associated with options, not with underlying contracts. For this reason we would expect to see the underlying futures contract continue to trade at its original price of 101.35. By purchasing our 57 outstanding futures contracts at 101.35 we would realize an immediate total profit from the hedge of 63.00, exactly the amount predicted by the theoretical pricing model. If we could do all this, there would be no reason to hold the position for the full ten weeks.

How likely is an immediate reevaluation in implied volatility from 14.6% to 18.3%? While violent changes in implied volatility are possible, they are the exception rather than the rule. Changes usually occur gradually over a period of time, and are the result of equally gradual changes in the volatility of the underlying contract. As the volatility of the underlying contract changes, option demand either rises or falls, and this demand is reflected in a corresponding rise or fall in the implied volatility. In our example, if market participants realized that the price of the underlying futures contract were fluctuating at a volatility greater than 14.6%, we would expect implied volatility to begin to rise. If implied volatility ever reached our target of 18.3%, we could sell out our calls and buy in our futures, thereby realizing our expected profit of 63.00 without having to hold the position for the full ten weeks. However, option prices are subject to a wide variety of market forces, not all of them theoretical. There is no guarantee that implied volatility will ever reevaluate up to 18.3%. In that case, we will have to hold the position for the full ten weeks and continue to adjust in order to realize our profit.

Every trader hopes for quick reevaluation of implied volatility towards his volatility forecast. It not only enables him to realize his profits more quickly, but it eliminates the risk of holding a position for an extended period of time. The longer a position is held, the greater the possibility of error from the inputs into the model.

Not only might implied volatility not reevaluate favorably, it might actually move against us, even if the true volatility of the underlying contract moves in our favor. Suppose that after initiating our hedge, implied volatility immediately falls to 13.5% from 14.6%. The price of the June 100 call will fall from 3.25 to 3.06. Now we have a paper loss of $100 \times -.19 = -19.00$. Does this mean we made a bad trade and should close out the position? Not necessarily. If the volatility forecast of 18.3% turns out to be correct, the options will still be worth 3.88 by expiration. If we hold the position and adjust, we can eventually expect a profit of 63.00. Realizing this, we ought to maintain the position as we originally intended. Even though an adverse move in implied volatility is unpleasant, it is something with which all traders must learn to cope. Just as a speculator can rarely hope to pick the exact bottom or top at which to take a long or short position, an option trader can rarely hope to pick the exact bottom or top in implied volatility. He must try to establish positions when market conditions are favorable. But he must also realize that conditions might become even more favorable. If they do, his initial trade may show a temporary loss. This is something a trader learns to accept as a practical aspect of trading.

Let's look at a somewhat more complex hedge, this time in the form of mispriced stock options. Suppose current market conditions are as follows:

Stock price	= 48½
Interest rate	= 8.00%
Time to March expiration	= 10 weeks
Expected dividend	= 50¢ in 40 days

Note that we now have an additional input, the expected dividend. Of course, we still need the volatility over the life of the option. Again looking into our crystal ball, we see that the volatility over the next 10 weeks will be 32.4%. Again, we decide to look at a call which is close to at-the-money, specifically the March 50 call. Feeding all of our inputs into the Black-Scholes model, we find that the March 50 call has a theoretical value of 2.17 and a delta of 46.

Having determined the theoretical value of the call, we still need its price in order to see if there is any profit opportunity available. In this case, it turns out that the call is trading for 3 (an implied volatility of 42.2%). Since the option is overpriced, we want to sell it and establish a delta neutral hedge against the underlying contract. We might, for example, sell 100 March 50 calls and simultaneously buy 46 stock contracts. Assuming this option is trading on a U.S. stock options exchange where each underlying contract consists of 100 shares of stock, it will be necessary to buy 4600 shares of stock.

As in all hedges based on a theoretically mispriced option, it is necessary to maintain a delta neutral position throughout the life of the option. As before, we will make our adjustments at weekly intervals, but now the underlying contract is shares of stock. Figure 5-2 shows the adjustment process for this hedge. Let's go through the hedge step by step and see what the final results are.

Original Hedge: At expiration, with the stock at 52⅜, the 50 calls were worth 2⅜. So on the option we showed a profit of \$300 – \$237.50, or \$62.50. The 4600 shares of stock we purchased at 48½ we were able to sell at 52⅜, for a profit of 3⅞ (\$3.875) per share. The total hedge profit was therefore +(100 × \$62.50) +(4600 × \$3.875) = +\$24,075.

Adjustments: The adjustment process forced us to buy and sell stock to remain delta neutral. At week one we bought 600 shares of stock at 49⅝; at week two we bought 1400 shares at 52⅛; at week three we sold 200 shares at 51¾; and so on. At week ten we sold out our remaining 900 shares of stock at 52⅜. The result of all these

Figure 5-2

Week	Stock Price	Delta of 50 call	Total Delta Position	Adjustment in Shares	Total Share Adjustment	Cash Flow	Interest on Cash Flow
0	48½	0	0	0	0	0	0
1	49⅝	52	–600	buy 600	+600	–29,775	–411.14
2	52⅛	66	–1400	buy 1,400	+2000	–72,975	–895.69
3	51¾	64	+200	sell 200	+1800	+10,350	+111.16
4	50	52	+1200	sell 1,200	+600	+60,000	+552.33
5	47	28	+2400	sell 2,400	–1800	+112,800	+865.32
	ex-dividend 50¢						
6	48⅛	38	–1000	buy 1,000	–800	–48,125	–295.34
7	52	73	–3500	buy 3,500	+2700	–182,000	–837.70
8	52¼	78	–500	buy 500	+3200	–26,125	–80.16
9	50⅛	55	+2300	sell 2,300	+900	+115,288	+176.88
10	52⅜			sell 900		+47,138	

adjustments was a loss of $13,425. (Again, the reader may wish to confirm this by adding up all the numbers in the "cash flow" column.)

Carrying Costs on the Initial Position: Originally we sold 100 options at $300 each, and bought 4600 shares of stock at $48.50 each. This resulted in a total debit of (100 × $300) – (4600 × $48.50) = $193,100. The carrying cost on this debit for ten weeks at an annual rate of 8.00% (our interest rate assumption) was $193,100 × .08 × 70/365 = $2,962.63. Note that this is somewhat different than the futures example, where only the option contracts entailed a carrying cost. Unlike futures trades, the purchase or sale of stock results in an immediate cash flow, and this cash flow becomes part of the carrying cost on the initial hedge.

Interest on the Adjustments: Whenever we bought or sold stock to make an adjustment, the trade resulted in a cash flow, either a debit or a credit. We were able to earn interest on any credit, and we were required to pay interest on any debit, at a rate of 8.00 percent. For example, at week one we bought 600 shares of stock at 49⅝, for a total cash outlay of $29,775. The cost of carrying this debit to expiration (nine weeks hence) was –$29,775 × 63/365 × .08 = –$411.14. The total interest cost from our adjustments is the sum of all the individual interest calculations, or –$814.34.

Dividends: We also assumed that 30 days prior to expiration (between week five and six) the stock paid a dividend of 50¢. What was the dividend earnings or loss to our position? We initially bought 4,600 shares of stock. At the end of week five we were short 1800 shares of stock as part of the adjustment process. This means that on the ex-dividend date we were long a total of 2800 shares of stock. At a dividend of 50¢ per share, we received a dividend payout $1,400.

Interest on Dividends: We were also able to earn interest on the $1,400 dividend payout for the remaining 30 days to expiration at a rate of 8.00%. The proceeds from this were $1,400 × 30/365 × .08 = $9.21.

Summarizing the results, we have:

Original Hedge	Adjustments	Interest on Hedge	Interest on Adjustments	Dividends	Interest on Dividends
+$24,075	–$13,425	–$2,962.63	–$814.34	+$1,400	+$9.21

The total profit on the hedge is therefore:

+$24,075 –$13,425 –$2,962.63 –$814.34 +$1,400 +$9.21 = +$8,282.24

versus a theoretical profit of 100 × ($300 – $217) = 100 × $83 = +$8,300.

As in our last example, our profit depended on our knowing the volatility of the underlying contract over the life of the option. This "known" volatility of 32.4% represents the actual volatility associated with the ten stock price changes in Figure 5-2.

While we continue to assume that markets are frictionless, we noted in our futures option example that this is not necessarily true. In a locked futures market it is not always possible to freely buy and sell the underlying contract. A similar type of restriction can occur in stock option trading. In our example we established the initial hedge by selling calls and purchasing stock. If, however, the calls had been underpriced, we might have chosen to buy calls and sell stock, stock which we might not necessarily own. This type of *short sale*, the sale of stock which is borrowed rather than owned, is prohibited in some markets. This makes it difficult to hedge certain types of option positions. As we shall see later, if we choose to sell puts it is necessary to hedge the position by selling stock. If we are not able to sell stock to hedge the sale of puts, we might hesitate to sell puts, even at a price greater than the theoretical value. Indeed, in markets where short sales are prohibited, puts tend to trade at inflated prices compared to calls.

The short sale of stock is not totally prohibited in U.S. markets, but it is subject to an *up-tick rule*. This rule specifies that a short sale is always prohibited at a price lower than the price at which the previous trade took place (a down-tick). A short sale is always permitted at a price higher than the price at which the previous trade took place (an up-tick). Finally, a short sale may take place at the same price at which the previous trade took place if the previous trade took place on an up-tick (also an up-tick). The up-tick rule was instituted following the market crash of 1929, with the intent of preventing a similar crash by prohibiting the sale, at continuously lower prices, of stock not actually owned. Below are ten consecutive trade prices (reading from left to right) for a stock with the accompanying ticks (a positive sign for an up-tick; a negative sign for a down-tick).

48½ +48⅝ +48⅝ −48½ −48⅜ −48¼ −48¼ +48⅜ +48⅜ +48⅜

Not only might a short sale not be possible because of the up-tick rule, but many brokerage firms which execute short sales of stock for their customers do not pay full interest on the proceeds from a short sale. This can further distort the interest component used in a theoretical pricing model.

Taking one last look at our examples, what enabled us to make a profit approximately equal to that predicted by the theoretical pricing model? A simple way of interpreting the results is to realize that, according to the model, the option's cash flow can be replicated through the adjustment process. If we know the conditions of an option contract and the characteristics of the underlying contract, we can replicate the characteristics of the option, and therefore replicate the cash flow resulting from a position in the option, through an adjustment process in the underlying contract. In our examples, because we knew the exact market conditions which would prevail over the life of the options (primarily, this means knowing volatility), we knew we could replicate the option by continuously calculating the delta and taking an appropriate offsetting position in the underlying contract. According to the model, at expiration the total cash flow from this *dynamic hedge* should exactly equal the value of the option. But in our examples we either bought the option at less than theoretical value (our futures option example) or sold the option at more than theoretical value (our stock option example). Since the cash flow from the adjustment process exactly replicated the option's theoretical value, we were left with a profit equal to the difference between the option's price and its theoretical value.

This type of *option replication*, using the cash flow from continuous hedging in the underlying contract, is the basis for many strategies which make use of option characteristics but do not actually involve options. We will discuss the best known of these strategies, portfolio insurance, in Chapter 13.

❖ 6 ❖

Option Values and Changing Market Conditions

Every trader who enters the marketplace must balance two opposing considerations, reward and risk. A trader hopes that his analysis of market conditions is correct, and that this will lead to profitable trading strategies. But no intelligent trader can afford to ignore the possibility of error. If he is wrong, and market conditions change in a way that adversely affects his position, how badly might the trader get hurt? A trader who fails to consider the risks associated with his position is certain to have a short and unhappy career.

Consider the trader who goes into the marketplace and purchases a futures contract. What is he worried about? Obviously he is worried that the market will fall. Indeed, anyone who takes a position in an underlying contract has only one real concern, that the market will move in the wrong direction. If a trader has a long position, he is at risk from a decline in the market; if he has a short position, he is at risk from a rise in the market.

Unfortunately, the risks with which an option trader must deal are not one-dimensional. A wide variety of forces can affect an option's value. If a trader uses a theoretical pricing model to evaluate options, any of the inputs into the model can represent a risk since there is always a chance that the inputs have been incorrectly estimated. Even if the trader has correctly estimated current market conditions, it's possible that over time conditions will change in a way that will adversely affect the value of his option position. Because of the many forces affecting an option's value, prices can change in ways which may surprise even the most experienced trader. Since decisions must often be made quickly, and sometimes without the aid of a computer, much of an option trader's education consists of learning how changing market conditions are likely to change an option's value and the risks associated with an option position.

First, let's consider the general effects of changing market conditions on an option's value. These changes are summarized in Figure 6-1.

As the price of the underlying rises or falls, options are more or less likely to finish in-the-money, and their values rise and fall accordingly. As volatility rises, extreme outcomes in the underlying contract become more likely, and this increases an option's value. As volatility falls, or as time to expiration grows shorter, extreme outcomes become less likely, and this reduces an option's value.

Figure 6-1: The Effect of Changing Market Conditions on an Option's Theoretical Value

If . . .	Call values will . . .	Put values will . . .
The price of the underlying contract rises	rise	fall
The price of the underlying contract falls	fall	rise
Volatility rises	rise	rise
Volatility falls	fall	fall
Time passes	fall*	fall*

* In some unusual cases it may be possible for an option to rise in value as time passes. The circumstances which can cause this will be discussed later.

Note that we have not considered the effect of changes in interest rates on option values. Since interest rates affect options differently depending on the underlying instrument and the settlement procedure, it is not possible to generalize about the effect of changing interest rates. However, we can logically deduce the effect of changing interest rates on option values by thinking of a call as a substitute for purchasing the underlying contract, and a put as a substitute for selling the underlying contract. For example, suppose we want to purchase a certain stock. The alternative is to purchase a call option. If interest rates are high, we will prefer the call since the outright purchase of stock requires a much larger cash outlay, and therefore a greater carrying cost. On the other hand, if interest rates are low, the carrying cost associated with stock is not as great, and calls become a less attractive alternative to purchasing the stock. Hence, rising interest rates cause stock option calls to rise in value, and falling interest rates cause stock option calls to fall in value.

The effect is just the opposite for stock option puts. If we are considering the sale of stock, the alternative is the purchase of a put. In a high interest rate environment the sale of stock will be more desirable since the cash credit resulting from the sale will earn greater interest. In a low interest rate environment puts become more attractive since the earnings on any cash credit resulting from the sale of stock is reduced. Hence, rising interest rates cause stock option puts to fall in value, and falling interest rates cause stock option puts to rise in value.

The situation is more complex when it comes to options on foreign currencies because a trader must deal with two interest rates, a domestic rate and a foreign rate. The effect of changes in domestic interest rates will be the same as the effect on stock options: a call will avoid the cash outlay required to purchase the currency, and a put will forego the cash credit resulting from the sale of the currency. However, the effect of a change in the foreign interest rate will be just the opposite. If foreign interest rates are high, rather than purchase a call one will always prefer to purchase the currency outright in order to earn the higher interest rate. Hence, higher (lower) foreign interest rates lead to lower (higher) call values. But if foreign rates are high, a put becomes a more desirable alternative to selling the foreign currency since one will want to continue to earn a high rate on the foreign currency. Hence, higher (lower) foreign interest rates lead to higher (lower) put values.

Stock and foreign currency options are always assumed to be subject to stock-type settlement (immediate cash payment for the option). But the settlement procedure for options on futures contracts may vary, depending on the exchange. Sometimes such options are settled like stock and sometimes they are settled like futures. While there is no carrying cost associated with a futures contract, there will be a carrying cost associated with an option if it is subject to stock-type settlement. In such a case, option values will fall when interest rates are high (the option becomes a less desirable alternative to a position in the futures contract) and rise when interest rates are low (the option becomes a more desirable alternative to a futures position). The effect, however, will be small since the value of the option, unless it is very deeply in-the-money, is small relative to the value of the underlying contract. Futures options are therefore much less sensitive to changes in interest rates than options on stocks and foreign currencies. When futures options are subject to futures-type settlement, changes in interest rates have no effect at all on option values since there is no carrying cost associated with either the underlying contract or the option.

The general effects of a change in interest rates are shown in Figure 6-2. In each case, the reader can intuitively arrive at the correct conclusion if he asks himself whether a call (put) is a better or worse substitute for the outright purchase (sale) of the underlying contract.

The dividend which is expected to be paid on stock during the life of a stock option may also affect the value of the option. In a simple sense, we can equate a dividend payment with the foreign interest rate on a currency option. If we own the foreign currency we can earn interest on it. In the same way, if we own the stock we will receive whatever dividend is paid on the stock. If dividends increase, we will prefer to take a long position by purchasing the stock rather than purchasing a call. The call therefore becomes a less desirable alternative to owning the stock. In the case of puts, if dividends increase we will prefer to take a short position by purchasing a put rather than selling the stock, since the sale of the stock will result in the loss of the dividend. Hence, rising dividends will cause stock option calls (puts) to fall (rise) in value, and falling dividends will cause stock option calls (puts) to rise (fall) in value. This is summarized in Figure 6-3.

We can generalize about the effects of changing market conditions on the value of options, but we must still consider the magnitude of the changes. Will the changes be large or small, representing either a major or minor risk, or something in between? Fortunately, along with the theoretical value, pricing models also generate several other numbers which enable a trader to assess not only the direction of the change, but also the relative magnitude of the change. While these numbers will not answer all our questions concerning changing market conditions, they will help us to better assess the risks associated with both individual and complex option positions.

Figure 6-2: The Effect of Changing Interest Rates on Option Values

Interest	If Domestic Interest Rates Rise	If Domestic Interest Rates Fall	If Foreign Interest Rates Rise	If Foreign Interest Rates Fall
Calls on stock will . . .	rise in value	fall in value	(not applicable)	(not applicable)
Puts on stock will . . .	fall in value	rise in value	(not applicable)	(not applicable)
Calls on a foreign currency will . . .	rise in value	fall in value	fall in value	rise in value
Puts on a foreign currency will . . .	fall in value	rise in value	rise in value	fall in value
Calls on a futures contract will . . . (stock type settlement)	fall in value	rise in value	(not applicable)	(not applicable)
Puts on a futures contract will . . . (stock type settlement)	fall in value	rise in value	(not applicable)	(not applicable)
Calls on a futures contract will . . . (futures type settlement)	remain unchanged	remain unchanged	(not applicable)	(not applicable)
Puts on a futures contract will . . . (futures type settlement)	remain unchanged	remain unchanged	(not applicable)	(not applicable)

Figure 6-3: The Effect of Changing Dividends on Stock Options

If . . .	Call values will . . .	Put values will . . .
The dividend is increased	fall	rise
The dividend is decreased	rise	fall

THE DELTA

We touched on the delta (Δ) in the last chapter as needed to determine the number of underlying contracts to option contracts required to establish a neutral hedge. The delta has several other interpretations, any of which may be useful to a trader.

Rate of Change

Figure 6-4[1] shows what happens to the theoretical value of a call as the price of the underlying contract changes. Under some conditions, when the call is very deeply in-the-money, its value changes at a rate almost identical to that of the underlying. If the underlying price moves up or down one point, the call's value will change by an equal amount. Under other conditions, when the call is far out-of-the-money, its value may change only slightly, even with a large change in the price of the underlying. The delta is a measure of how an option's value changes with respect to a change in the price of the underlying contract.

In theory, an option can never gain or lose value more quickly than the underlying, so the delta of a call always has an upper bound of 100. (Again, we will retain the common practice of writing the delta without the decimal point. Hence, a delta of 1.00 will be written as 100. This is sometimes referred to as the percent format.) An option with a delta of 100 will move up or down one full point for each full point move up or down in the price of the underlying. It is moving at 100% of the rate of the underlying. In theory, a call also cannot move in the opposite direction of the underlying market, so the delta of a call has a lower bound of zero. A call with a delta of zero will move negligibly, even if the underlying contract makes a relatively large move.

Most calls, of course, will have deltas somewhere between zero and 100 and will move at a slower rate than the underlying. A call with a delta of 25 can be expected to change its value at 25% of the rate of the underlying. If the underlying rises (falls) 1.00, the option can be expected to rise (fall) .25. A call with a delta of 75 can be expected to change its value at 75% of the rate of the underlying. If the underlying rises (falls) .60, the option can be expected to gain (lose) .45 in value. Call options which are at-the-money have delta values close to 50. They rise or fall in value at just about half the rate of the underlying.

Thus far our discussion of deltas has focused only on calls. Puts have characteristics similar to calls, except that put values move in the opposite direction of the underlying market. In Figure 6-5 we can see that when the underlying rises, puts lose value; when

1. In order to generalize characteristics of the option sensitivities, which in most cases are similar regardless of the type of underlying instrument, we assume an interest rate of zero in Figures 6-4 through 6-21.

Figure 6-4: Call Theoretical Value vs. Underlying Price

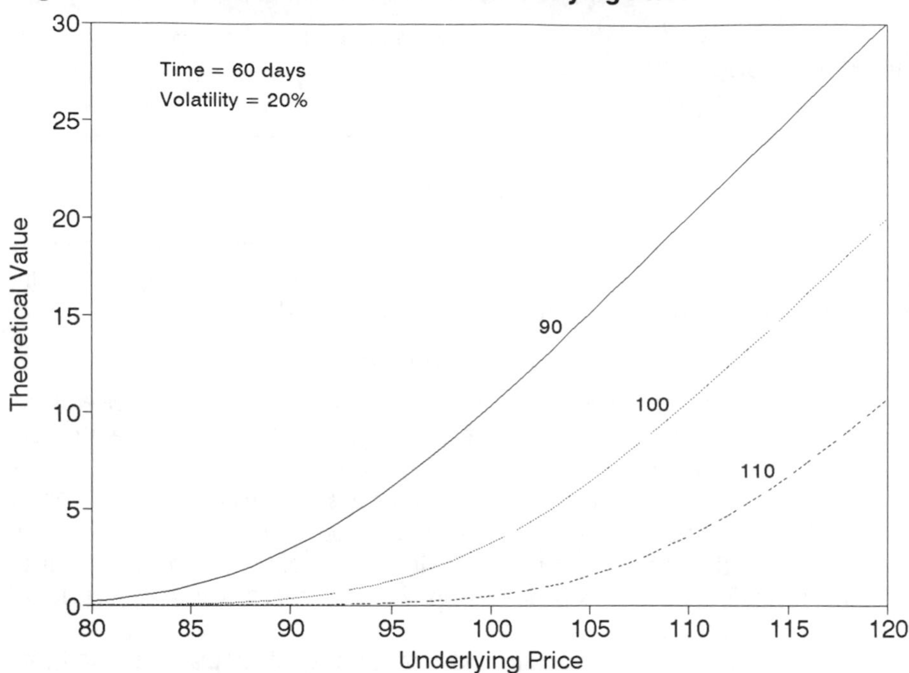

Figure 6-5: Put Theoretical Value vs. Underlying Price

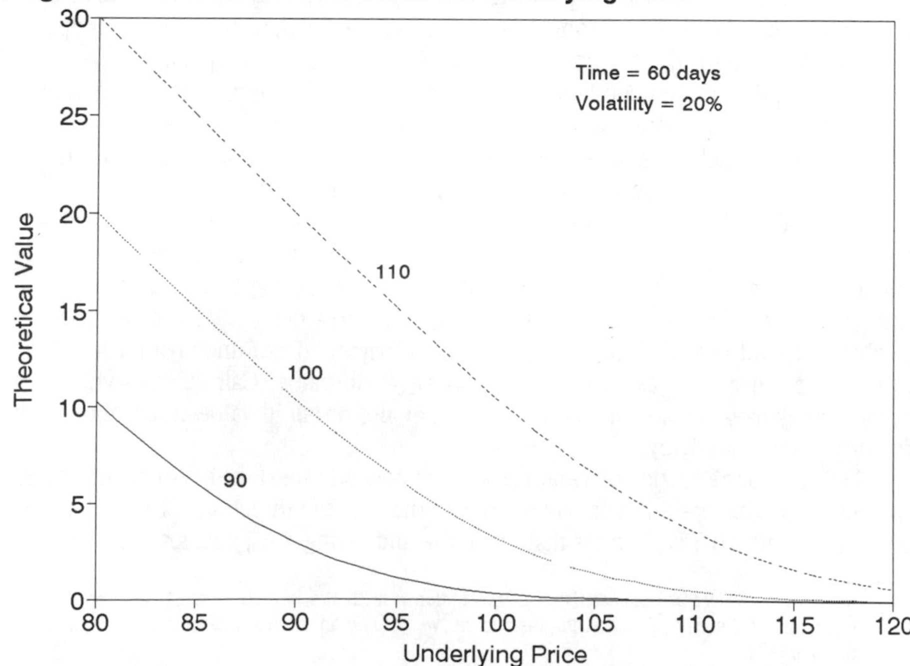

the underlying falls, puts gain value. For this reason, puts always have negative deltas, ranging from zero for far out-of-the-money puts to –100 for deeply in-the-money puts. Just like a call delta, a put's delta is a measure of the rate of change in the put's value with respect to a change in the price of the underlying, but the negative sign indicates that the change will be in the opposite direction of the underlying market. A put with a delta of –10 can be expected to change its value at 10% of the rate of the underlying, but in the opposite direction. If the underlying moves up (down) .50, the put can be expected to lose (gain) .05 in value. At-the-money puts will have deltas of approximately –50, and can be expected to change their value at approximately half the rate of the underlying, but in the opposite direction.

Hedge Ratio

As discussed in Chapter 5, if we wish to hedge an option position against the underlying contract, the delta tells us the proper ratio of underlying contracts to options required to establish a neutral hedge. An underlying contract always has a delta of 100, so the proper hedge ratio can be determined by dividing 100 by the option's delta. An at-the-money option has a delta of 50, so the proper hedge ratio is 100/50, or 2/1. For every two options purchased, we need to sell one underlying contract to establish a neutral hedge. A call with a delta of 40 requires the sale of two underlying contracts for each five options purchased, since 100/40 = 5/2.

Since puts have negative deltas, the purchase of puts will require us to hedge the position by purchasing underlying contracts. A put with a delta of –75 will require the purchase of three underlying contracts for each four puts purchased, since 100/75 = 4/3.

Thus far, all the hedges we have looked at have consisted of options and underlying contracts. But any hedge, whether options versus underlying contracts, or options versus options, is delta neutral as long as all the deltas in the hedge add up to zero. For example, suppose we buy four calls with a delta of 50 each, and ten puts with a delta of –20 each. Our position is delta neutral since $(+4 \times +50) + (+10 \times -20) = 0$. A position can be highly complex, consisting of underlying contracts, calls, and puts, with different exercise prices and expiration dates, but as long as the deltas add up to approximately zero we say that the position is delta neutral.

Theoretical or Equivalent Underlying Position

Many option traders come to the option market after trading in the underlying instruments. Futures option traders often start their careers by trading futures contracts; stock option traders often start by trading stock. If a trader has become accustomed to evaluating his risk in terms of the number of underlying contracts bought or sold (either futures contracts or shares of stock), he can use the delta to equate the directional risk of an option position with a position of similar size in the underlying market.

Since an underlying contract always has a delta of 100, each 100 deltas in an option position represents a theoretical position equivalent to one underlying contract. A trader who owns an option with a delta of 50 is long, or controls, approximately ½ of an underlying contract. If he owns ten such contracts, he is long 500 deltas or, in equivalent terms, five underlying contracts. If the underlying is a futures contract, he is theoretically long five such contracts. If the underlying is a stock contract consisting of 100 shares of stock, he is theoretically long 500 shares of stock. The trader has a similar theoretical position if he sells 20 puts with a delta of –25 each, since $-20 \times -25 = +500$.

It is important to emphasize the theoretical aspect of the delta interpretation as an equivalent to an underlying position. An option is not simply a surrogate for an underlying position. An actual underlying position is almost exclusively sensitive to directional moves in the underlying market. An option position, while also sensitive to directional moves, is also sensitive to other changes in market conditions. An option trader who looks only at his delta position may be ignoring other risks which could have a far greater impact on his option position. He must realize that the delta represents an equivalent underlying position only under very narrowly defined market conditions.

The reader may have already noted that our three interpretations of delta—the hedge ratio, the rate of change in the theoretical value, and the equivalent underlying position—are all essentially the same. How a trader interprets a delta position depends primarily on his trading strategy. For example, suppose a trader has a delta position of +500. If the trader intends to maintain a delta neutral position, he must sell five underlying contracts (the hedge ratio interpretation). However, if he believes the market will rise and wants to maintain his delta position, he knows that in theory he is long five underlying contracts (the equivalent underlying position interpretation). And finally, if he does maintain his delta position of +500, the value of his position will change at five times the rate, or 500%, of the underlying market (the rate of change interpretation). Even though a trader may interpret the delta differently at different times, each interpretation is mathematically the same.

There is one other interpretation of the delta which is perhaps of less practical use but may still be worth mentioning. If we ignore the sign of the delta (positive for calls, negative for puts), the delta is approximately equal to the probability that the option will finish in-the-money. A call with a delta of 25, or a put with a delta of –25, has approximately a 25% chance of finishing in-the-money. A call with a delta of 75, or a put with a delta of –75, has approximately a 75% chance of finishing in-the-money. As an option's delta moves closer to 100, or –100 for puts, the option becomes more and more likely to finish in-the-money. As the delta moves closer to zero, the option becomes less and less likely to finish in-the-money. We can also see why at-the-money options have deltas close to 50. If we assume that price changes are random, there is half a chance that the market will rise (the option goes into-the-money), and half a chance that the market will fall (the option goes out-of-the money).

Of course, the delta is only an approximation of the probability since interest rate considerations and, in the case of stock options, dividends, may distort this interpretation. Moreover, most option strategies depend not only on whether an option finishes in-the-money, but by how much. If a trader sells an option with a delta of 10 in the belief that the option will expire worthless nine times out of ten, he may indeed be correct. But if on the tenth time he loses an amount greater than the total premium he took in the nine times the option expired worthless, the trade will result in a negative expected return. In option trading the primary consideration is not always how often a strategy wins or loses, but also how much it wins or loses. Every experienced trader is willing to accept several small losses if he can occasionally offset these with one big win.

THE GAMMA

In discussing the delta, we noted that under some circumstances, when the option is far out-of-the-money, its delta is close to zero. At other times, when the option is deeply in-the-money, its delta is close to 100 (–100 for puts). We can logically conclude that as the underlying price changes, the delta of an option must also be changing. As the underlying price rises, call deltas move towards 100 and put deltas move towards zero; as the underlying price falls, call deltas move towards zero and put deltas move towards –100. This effect is shown in Figures 6-6 and 6-7.

The *gamma* (Γ), sometimes referred to as the *curvature* of an option, is the rate at which an option's delta changes as the price of the underlying changes. The gamma is usually expressed in deltas gained or lost per one point change in the underlying, with the delta increasing by the amount of the gamma when the underlying rises, and falling by the amount of the gamma when the underlying falls. If an option has a gamma of 5,[2] for each point rise (fall) in the price of the underlying, the option will gain (lose) 5 deltas. If the option originally had a delta of 25, and the underlying moves up (down) one full point, then the new delta of the option will be 30 (20). If the underlying moves up (down) another point, the new delta will be 35 (15).

Note that Figures 6-6 and 6-7 seem to be identical, even though the former represents call gammas and the latter put gammas. This can only mean that both calls and puts with the same exercise price and the same amount of time to expiration have the same curvature.[3] This may at first seem odd, but it becomes logical when we remember that zero is greater than –50 in the same way that –50 is greater than –100. Negative numbers become more positive (or less negative) as one moves towards zero. Therefore, *both calls and puts must have positive gammas.* This often confuses the new trader since, through his use of the delta, he is accustomed to associating positive numbers with calls and negative numbers with puts. But regardless of whether we are working with calls or puts, we always add the gamma to the old delta as the underlying rises, and subtract the gamma from the old delta as the underlying falls. When a trader is long options, whether calls or puts, he has a long gamma position. When he is short options, he has a short gamma position.

For example, suppose an at-the-money call, with a delta of 50, and an at-the-money put, with a delta of –50, both have gammas of 5. If the underlying contract rises one point, we add the gamma of 5 to the call delta of 50, to get the new delta of 55. To get the new put delta if the underlying contract rises one point we also add the gamma of 5 to the put delta of –50 to get the new delta of –45. This corresponds to our intuition

2. When the delta is expressed in the decimal format (0 to 1.00), the gamma is expressed in the same format.

3. If interest rates are zero, as they are assumed to be in Figures 6-6 and 6-7, the gamma of calls and puts with the same exercise price will be identical. If interest rates are not zero, and there is a possibility of early exercise, the gammas may differ slightly.

Figure 6-6: Call Delta vs. Underlying Price

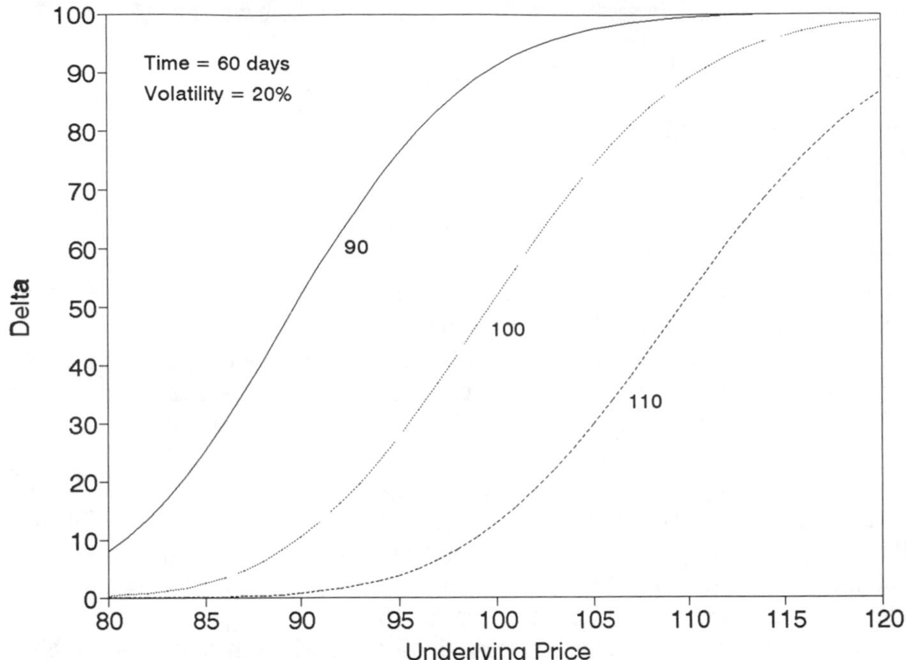

Figure 6-7: Put Delta vs. Underlying Price

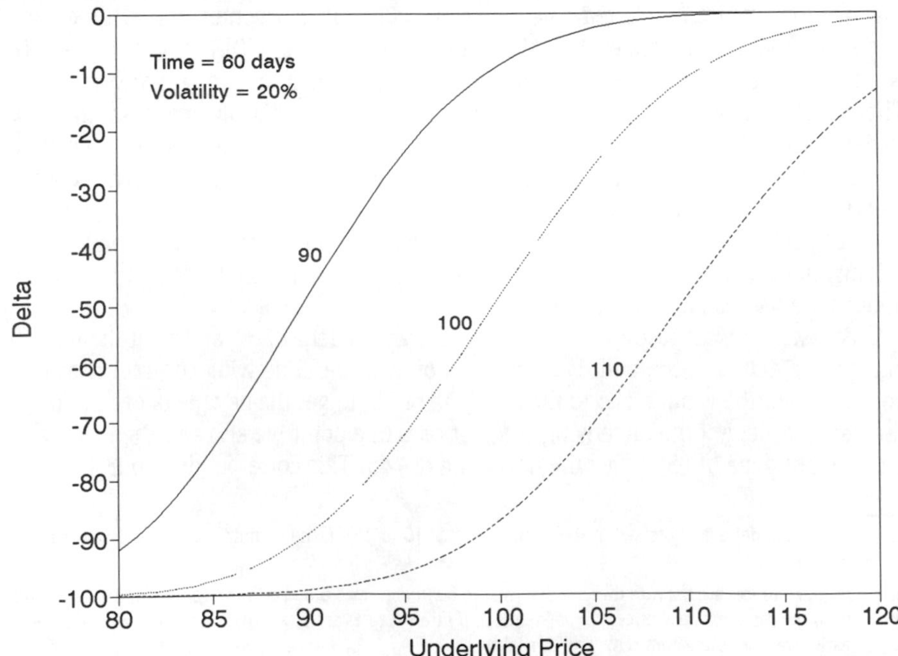

that as the underlying price rises, at-the-money calls move into-the-money and at-the-money puts move out-of-the-money. If the underlying contract falls one full point, in both cases we subtract the gamma, giving the call a delta of 45 (50-5), and the put a delta of –55 (–50–5). Now the call is moving out-of-the-money and the put is moving into-the-money.

We know that an underlying contract has a delta of 100. But what is the gamma associated with an underlying contract? Since the gamma is the rate of change in the delta, and the delta of an underlying contract is always 100, the gamma must be zero.

The gamma is a measure of how fast an option changes its directional characteristics, acting more or less like an actual underlying position. Since directional risk is always important, the gamma is an important risk measurement. Indeed, an option position can change its directional risk dramatically, even if a trader takes no action in the marketplace. A large gamma number, whether positive or negative, indicates a high degree of risk; a low gamma number indicates a low degree of risk. Every option trader learns to look carefully not only at current directional risk (the delta), but also at how that directional risk will change if the underlying market begins to move (the gamma).

Consider a trader who sells ten calls with a delta of 30 each. He is short 300 deltas (–10 × 30), equivalent in theory to being short three underlying contracts. If this trader is accustomed to dealing in lots of five underlying contracts or less, he is, for the moment, within his normal risk limits. If the market rises ten points and he considers only his original delta position of –300, he may assume that he is still, in theory, short the same three underlying contracts. But what if the initial gamma of each call was 6? Then, for each point rise in the underlying contract, each call will gain 6 deltas. When the underlying rises ten points, each call will gain 60 deltas, for a total delta of 90 each. The trader's directional risk has now increased by a factor of three. Instead of the initial delta of –300, the delta position is now –900, well beyond his normal risk limits.

A large gamma can sometimes overwhelm the inexperienced trader. New traders are well advised to avoid large gamma positions, particularly negative ones, because of the speed with which such positions can change. Even experienced traders occasionally take on gamma positions which are too risky. This was dramatically demonstrated in the collapse of the Volume Investors clearing firm on the COMEX in the spring of 1985. Several traders, all clearing their trades through the same firm, built up extremely large negative gamma positions by selling large numbers of out-of-the-money gold options. In the past this had been a very profitable strategy, since the gold market had been relatively quiet with low volatility. But on this occasion the market made a violent upward move, leaving the traders, who had originally been delta neutral, short thousands of deltas in a rapidly rising market. The losses sustained by the traders not only led to the collapse of the clearing firm, but also to a crisis in the COMEX's clearing association. The incident might have been avoided had someone, either the traders themselves, the clearing firm, or the clearing association, realized that the large negative gamma position represented an unacceptable risk. Most firms which trade options or clear option trades for their customers now have risk managers responsible for identifying such dangerous positions.

The gamma can also help a trader maintain a delta neutral position by enabling him to make a quick estimate of how the delta is changing. Suppose a trader has a delta position of +500 prior to the opening of the market. If he wishes to be delta neutral he knows that he will have to sell 500 deltas on the opening. He can accomplish this by selling five underlying contracts. But suppose that his gamma position is +100 and the market is expected to open two points higher. If it does in fact open two points higher his delta position will no longer be +500, but +700 since he will become 100 deltas longer for each point rise in the underlying. He now knows that in order to be delta neutral he must sell 700 deltas, or seven underlying contracts. He can make this calculation without any computer assistance simply by knowing his initial delta and gamma positions.

Since the delta of an option must always remain in the range of zero to 100 (zero to −100 for puts), we can logically conclude that the gamma must also be changing. Otherwise, continuously adding or subtracting a constant gamma would take the delta beyond this range. The effect of changes in market conditions on the value of gammas is shown in Figures 6-8, 6-9, and 6-10. Figure 6-8 demonstrates that the gamma is greatest for an option which is at-the-money, and becomes progressively smaller as an option moves either into- or out-of-the-money. Figures 6-9 and 6-10 show that the gamma of an at-the-money option can increase dramatically as expiration approaches, or as we decrease our volatility assumption. A trader's gamma position, which may have initially been small, can become increasingly large through the passage of time or through changes in volatility. An option position must always be monitored to ensure that its risk characteristics remain within acceptable limits.

While the gamma is perhaps the most common measure of the change in the delta, the delta is also subject to change from market conditions other than movement in the price of the underlying contract. Figures 6-11 and 6-12 show how call and put deltas change as time passes. Figures 6-13 and 6-14 show how deltas change with changes in volatility. Note that all four sets of graphs have the same shape. As we increase the time to expiration or increase volatility, all options tend to become more at-the-money, with call deltas approaching 50 and put deltas approaching –50. Conversely, as we decrease the amount of time to expiration or decrease volatility, all option deltas move away from 50 (–50 for puts). An option which is in-the-money will move further into-the-money, and an option which is out-of-the-money will move further out-of-the-money. Options which are at-the-money and have deltas close to 50 tend to maintain the same delta characteristics regardless of changes in time or volatility.

Perhaps a comment is in order here about what *at-the-money* means. Traders tend to think of an at-the-money option as one whose exercise price is approximately equal to the current price of the underlying contract. By this definition a trader will instinctively assign a delta of 50 to any option whose exercise price is currently at-the-money. However, a theoretical pricing model will interpret the at-the-money option (the one with a delta of 50) as the option whose current exercise price is most likely to be closest to the price of the underlying contract at expiration. Suppose that interest rates are 12% annually and that a certain stock is currently trading at $100. If two five-month calls are available with exercise prices of 100 and 105, which call has a delta closer to 50? We

Figure 6-8: Call or Put Gamma vs. Underlying Price

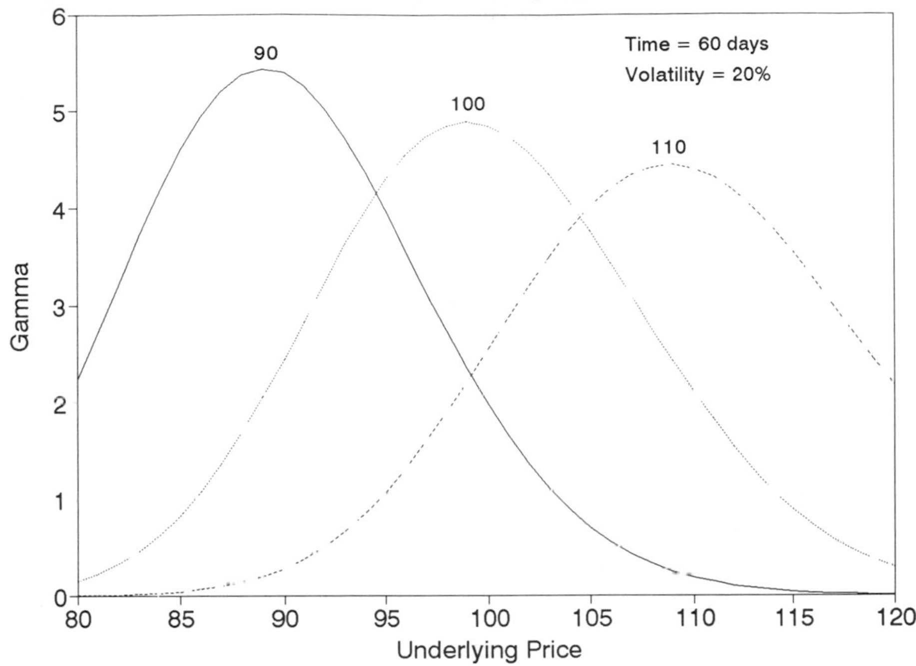

Figure 6-9: Call or Put Gamma vs. Time to Expiration

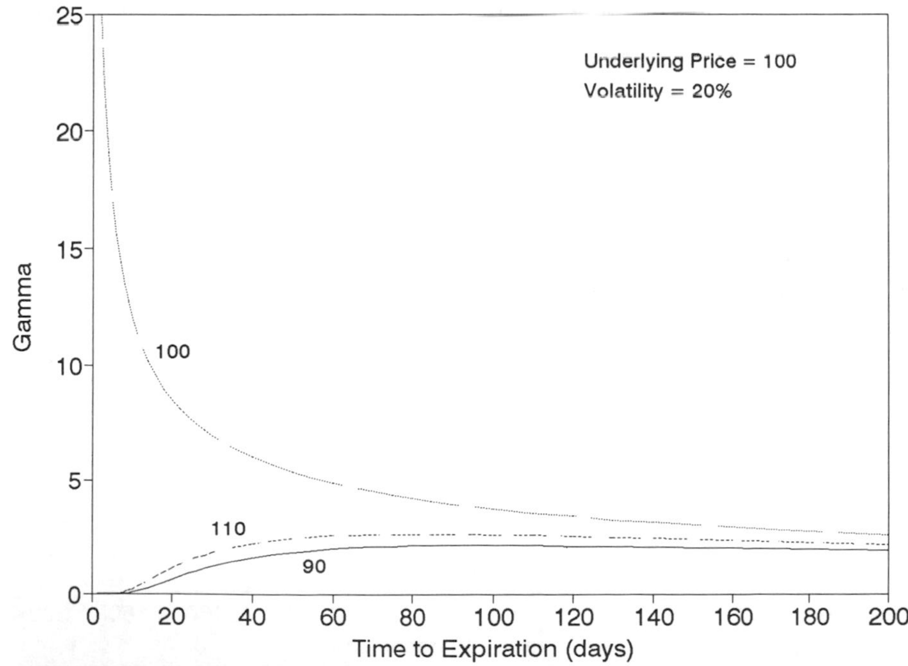

Figure 6-10: Call or Put Gamma vs. Volatility

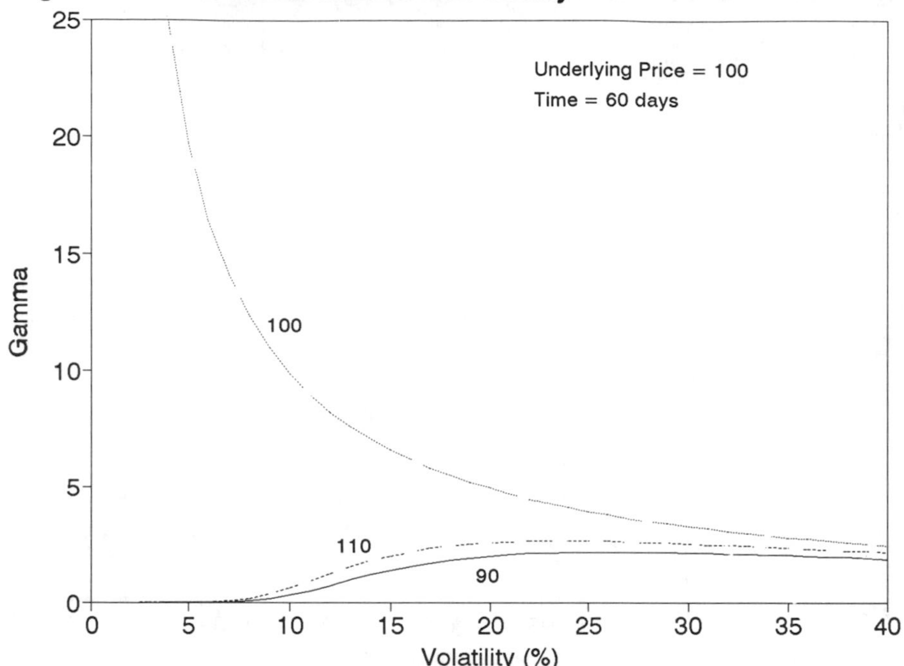

Figure 6-11: Call Delta vs. Time to Expiration

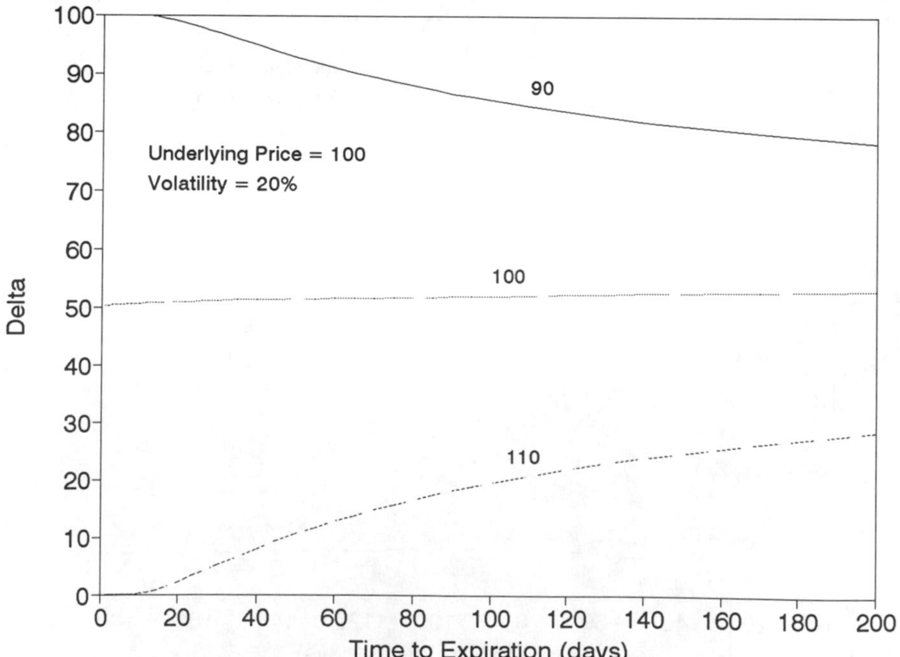

Figure 6-12: Put Delta vs. Time to Expiration

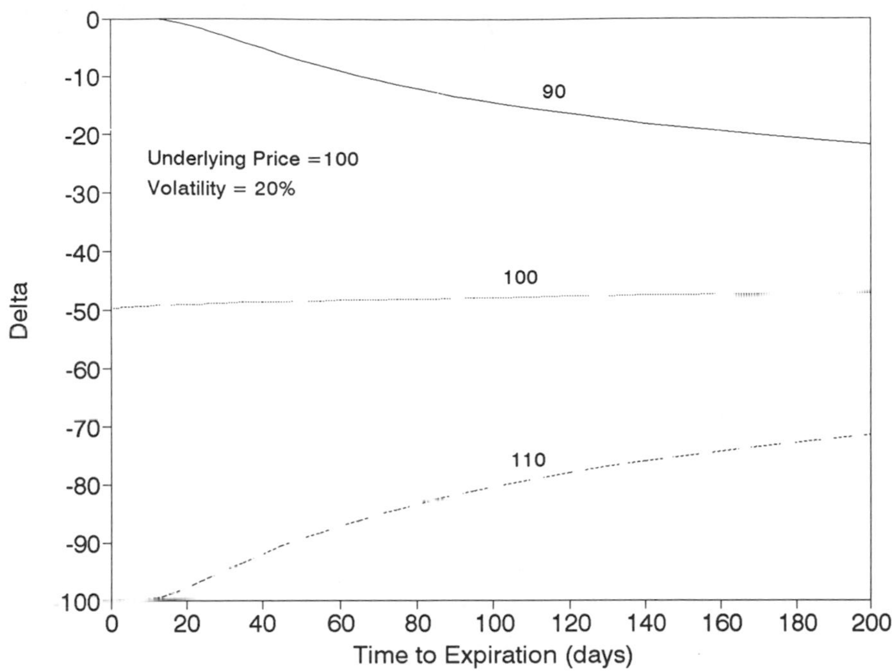

Figure 6-13: Call Delta vs. Volatility

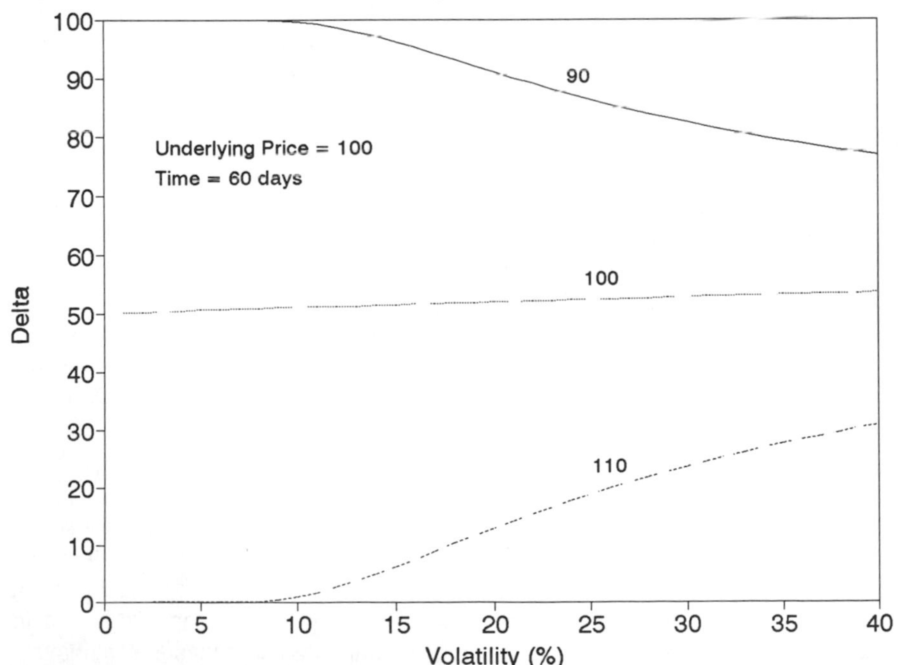

Figure 6-14: Put Delta vs. Volatility

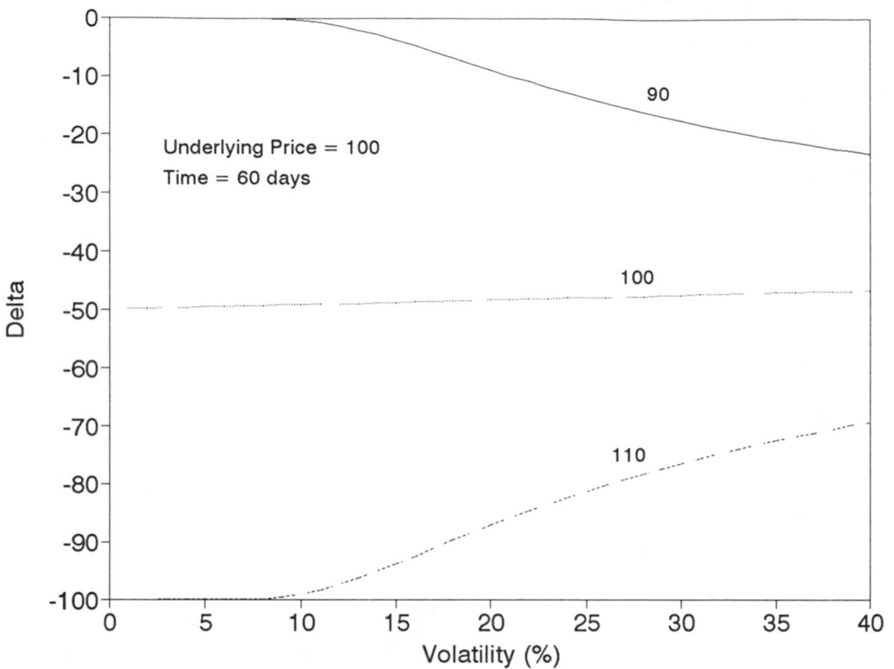

saw in Chapter 4 that the mean of the distribution assumed in most theoretical pricing models is the forward price (the break-even price) for the underlying contract. In our present case, the forward price is the current stock price of $100 plus the $5 carrying costs over the five-month holding period. The 105 call is therefore the one which the model interprets as being at-the-money, and hence will have a delta of 50. Depending on the type of underlying contract, under extreme interest rate conditions or with a great deal of time remaining to expiration, options can have deltas decidedly different from what we might instinctively surmise.

Just as a delta neutral option position can become unbalanced through movement in the underlying contract, it can also become unbalanced through the passage of time or through changes in volatility. No trader knows for certain whether he is delta neutral because he can't be certain about the accuracy of the inputs into the theoretical pricing model. The delta value depends, among other factors, on the volatility assumption. And volatility is just that, an assumption. A trader who sells four calls, each with a delta of 25, and buys one underlying contract, might believe that he is delta neutral. But in order to arrive at a call delta of 25 the trader is required to feed some volatility into a theoretical pricing model. If he subsequently decides that his original volatility assumption was too low, and he now raises it, we can see in Figure 6-13 that the call delta will rise towards 50. Using his new volatility assumption the delta of the call might be 35, and instead of being delta neutral, the trader is now 40 deltas short. All he did to unbalance his delta position was to change his assumptions about market conditions.

Nothing in the foregoing discussion invalidates the concept of delta neutrality, which is still an important one. However, a trader must realize that a delta neutral position depends on an estimate of market conditions, both current and future, and there is no guarantee that this estimate will be correct. As he changes his assumptions about market conditions, he must constantly change his trading strategies to fit these new assumptions. Delta neutral trading is only one aspect of this principle.

THE THETA

The effect of a change in time to expiration on the theoretical values of calls and puts is shown in Figures 6-15 and 6-16. Note that all options, both calls and puts, lose value as expiration approaches. The *theta* (Θ), or time decay factor, is the rate at which an option loses value as time passes. It is usually expressed in points lost per day, when all other conditions remain the same. An option with a theta of .05 will lose .05 in value for each day that passes with no change in other market conditions. If the option is worth 2.75 today, then tomorrow it will be worth 2.70. The day after that, it will be worth 2.65.

Time runs in only one direction and, technically, the theta is a positive number. However, as a convenient notation, and to remind the user that the theta represents a loss in the option's value as time passes, it is sometimes written as a negative number. This is the convention which will be followed in this text. Therefore, the theta of an option which loses .05 per day will be written as –.05. Consequently, a long option position will always have a negative theta, and a short option position will always have a positive theta. Note that this is just the opposite of the gamma, where a long option position has a positive gamma, and a short option position has a negative gamma.

As a general principle, an option position will have a gamma and theta of opposite signs. Moreover, the relative size of the gamma and theta will correlate. A large positive gamma goes hand in hand with a large negative theta, while a large negative gamma goes hand in hand with a large positive theta. We saw that as expiration approaches, the gamma of an at-the-money option becomes increasingly large. The same is also true of the theta. As we get closer to expiration the rate at which an option decays begins to accelerate. If the option is exactly at-the-money, its theta at the moment of expiration becomes infinitely large.

Every option position is a tradeoff between market movement and time decay. If price movement in the underlying contract will help a trader (positive gamma), the passage of time will hurt (negative theta). And vice versa. The trader can't have it both ways. Either he wants the market to move, or he wants it to sit still. This opposing effect can be seen in Figure 6-9 (gamma vs. time to expiration) and Figure 6-17 (theta vs. time to expiration). As the gamma becomes large, so does the theta. Just as a large negative gamma represents a high degree of risk with respect to market movement, a large negative theta represents a high degree of risk with respect to the passage of time.

Is it ever possible for an option to have a positive theta such that if nothing changes the option will be worth more tomorrow than it is today? When futures options are subject to stock-type settlement, as they currently are in the United States, the carrying cost on a deeply in-the-money option, either a call or a put, can, under some circum-

Figure 6-15: Call Theoretical Value vs. Time to Expiration

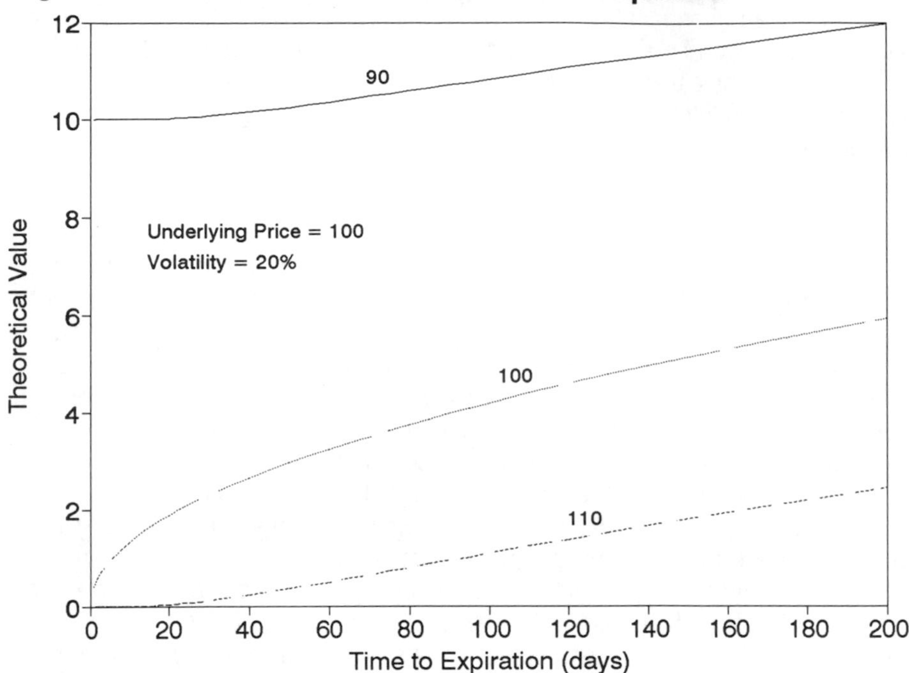

Figure 6-16: Put Theoretical Value vs. Time to Expiration

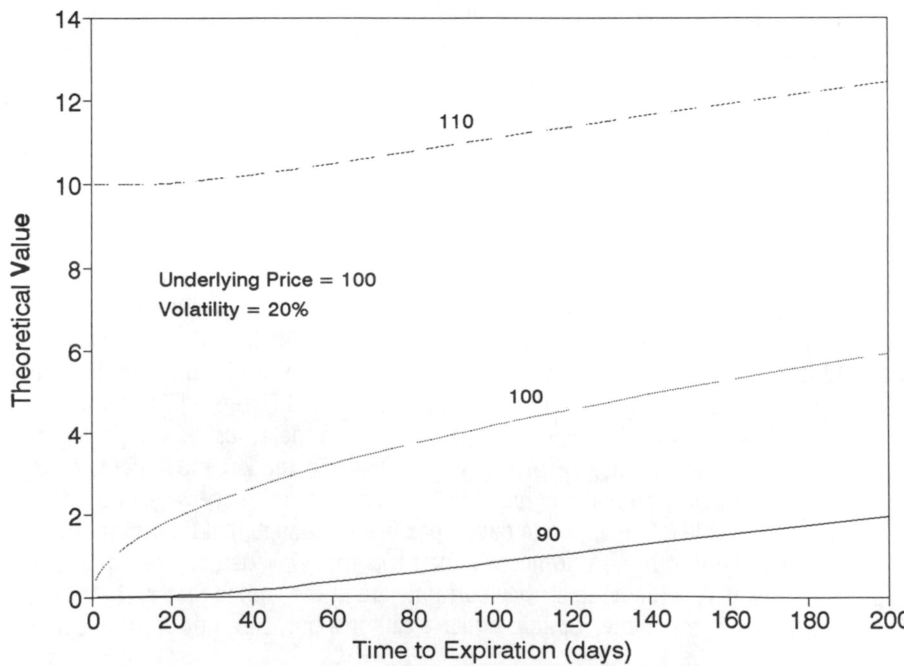

Figure 6-17: Call or Put Theta vs. Time to Expiration

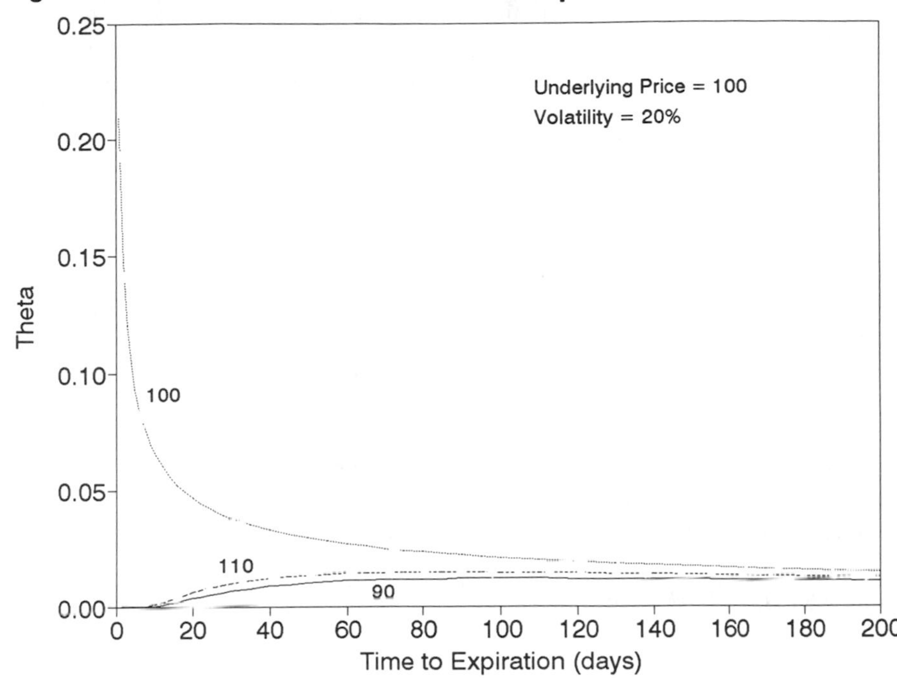

stances, be greater than the volatility component. If this happens, and the option is European (no early exercise permitted), it will have a theoretical value less than parity (less than intrinsic value). As expiration approaches, the value of the option will slowly rise to parity. Hence, the option will have a positive theta. A put option on stock can be similarly affected if the put is deeply in-the-money and, again, no early exercise is permitted. If interest rates are high enough, the put may be worth less than parity, and so will rise to parity as expiration approaches. In both cases, however, the option must be European. American options, where early exercise is a possibility, can never be worth less than parity, and so can never have positive thetas.[4] Since the conditions under which a European option will have a positive theta are rare, in general we can assume that an option will lose value as time passes.

THE VEGA OR KAPPA

Just as we are concerned with the effect on an option's theoretical value by movement in the underlying contract (delta) and the passage of time (theta), we must also be

4. One can argue that a put on a stock which is about to pay a large dividend will also have a positive theta. When the stock gives up the dividend, it will drop by approximately the amount of the dividend, and this drop in price will increase the value of the put. The reader can make his own decision as to whether this reflects a positive theta, or is actually the result of some change in market conditions (the stock going ex-dividend).

concerned with a change in volatility. This effect is shown in Figures 6-18 and 6-19. While the terms delta, gamma, and theta are found in most option texts, there is no generally accepted term for the sensitivity of an option's theoretical value to a change in volatility. The most commonly used term in the trading community is *vega*, and this is the term which will be used in this book. But this is by no means universal. Since vega is not a Greek letter, a common alternative in academic literature, where Greek letters are preferred, is *kappa* (K).

The vega of an option is usually given in point change in theoretical value for each one percentage point change in volatility.[5] Since all options gain value with rising volatility, the vega for both calls and puts is positive. If an option has a vega of .15, for each percentage point increase (decrease) in volatility, the option will gain (lose) .15 in theoretical value. If the option has a theoretical value of 3.25 at a volatility of 20%, then it will have a theoretical value of 3.40 at a volatility of 21%, and a theoretical value of 3.10 at a volatility of 19%.

Note in Figure 6-20 that an at-the-money option always has a greater vega than either an in-the-money or out-of-the-money option when all options are of the same type and have the same amount of time to expiration. This means that an at-the-money option is always the most sensitive in total points to a change in volatility. As a corollary,

Figure 6-18: Call Theoretical Value vs. Volatility

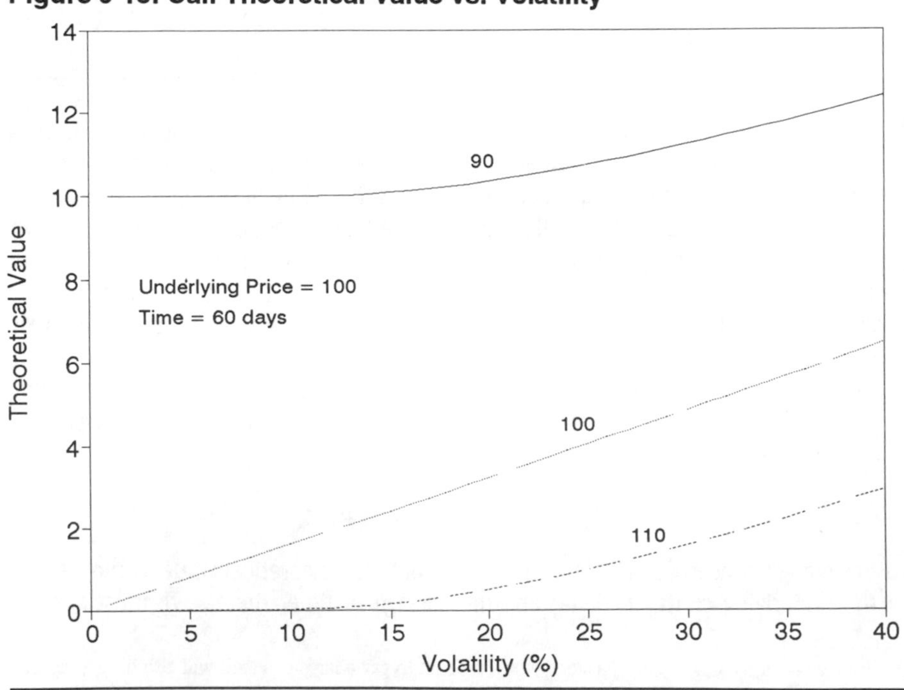

5. The theta and the vega are sometimes expressed in dollar (or other appropriate currency) change in the option's value as time passes or volatility changes.

Figure 6-19: Put Theoretical Value vs. Volatility

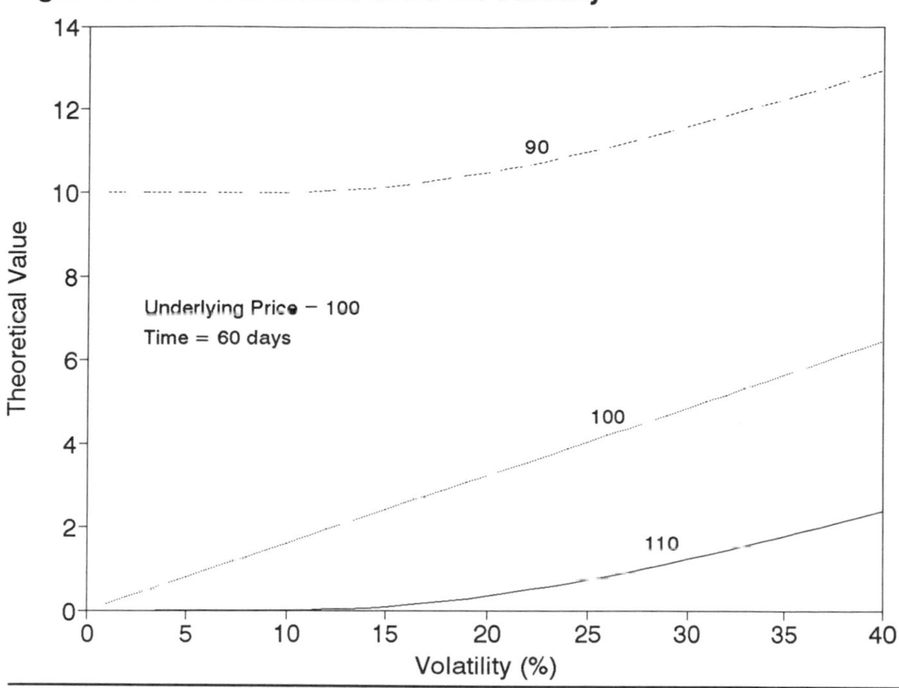

the out-of-the-money option is always the most sensitive in percent terms to a change in volatility. For example, suppose that with a volatility assumption of 15% an at-the-money and an out-of-the-money option have theoretical values of 2.00 and .50, respectively. If we raise our volatility assumption to 20%, the options might now have theoretical values of 3.00 and 1.00. The at-the-money option has shown the greater total point increase (1.00 vs. .50), while the out-of-the-money option has shown the greater percent increase (50% vs. 100%). Since many option strategies involve buying and selling unequal numbers of options, the latter characteristic will be important when we look at trading strategies. (The reader can confirm this by looking again at Figure 4-11.)

Note also in Figure 6-20 that the vega of all options declines as expiration approaches. Therefore, a long-term option will always be more sensitive to a change in volatility than a short-term option with otherwise identical contract specifications. A four-month option will have a greater vega, and therefore be more sensitive to a change in volatility, than a one-month option.

This last point illustrates an important principle of option evaluation, that time and volatility are closely interconnected. More time to expiration means more time for volatility to take effect, while less time to expiration may mean that any change in volatility will have only a minor effect on an option's value. Moreover, changes in the amount of time remaining to expiration and changes in volatility often have similar effects on an option's value. Decreasing volatility is similar to decreasing time to expiration. If a trader cannot remember what effect the passage of time will have on his

Figure 6-20: Call or Put Vega vs. Time to Expiration

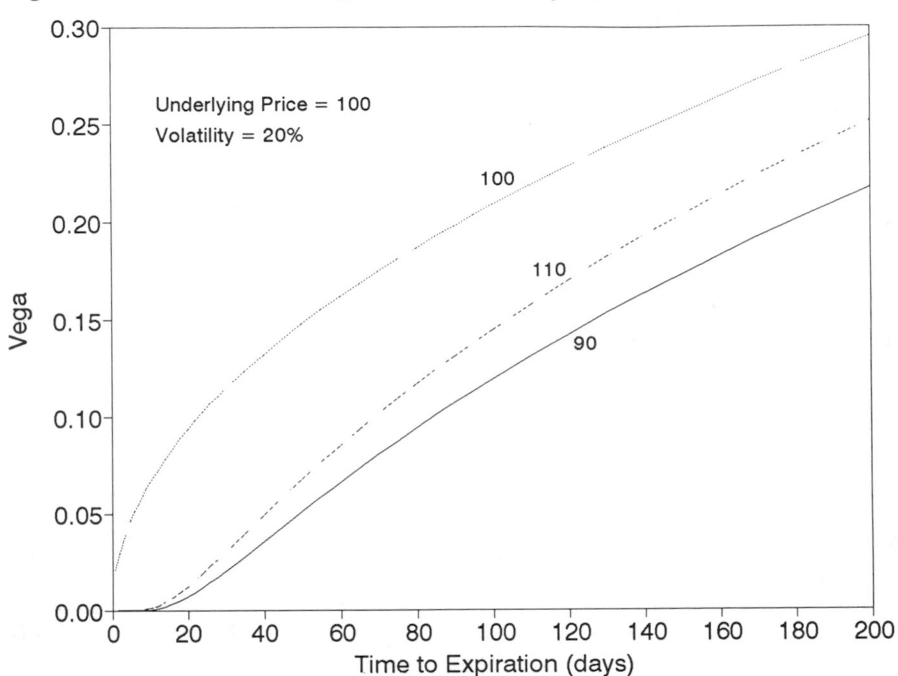

position, he might consider instead what effect a reduction in volatility will have. This can be seen by comparing Figures 6-15 and 6-18 (theoretical values with respect to changes in time and volatility), Figures 6-11 and 6-13 (delta values with respect to changes in time and volatility), and Figures 6-9 and 6-10 (gamma values with respect to changes in time and volatility). In each case the similar shapes of the graphs indicate similar effects of time and volatility.

Finally, we can see in Figure 6-21 that the vega of an at-the-money option is relatively constant, regardless of changes in volatility. This makes it easy to estimate the theoretical value of an at-the-money option under a wide variety of volatility scenarios.

THE RHO

The sensitivity of an option's theoretical value to a change in interest rates is given by its *rho* (P). Unlike the other sensitivities, one cannot generalize about the rho since its characteristics depend on the type of underlying instrument and the settlement procedure for the options. The general effects have already been summarized in Figure 6-2. Note that foreign currency options which require the delivery of the currency, rather than the delivery of a futures contract, are affected by both domestic and foreign interest rates. Hence, such options have two interest rate sensitivities, rho_1 (the domestic interest rate sensitivity) and rho_2 (the foreign interest rate sensitivity). The latter is sometimes denoted with the Greek letter phi (Φ).

Figure 6-21: Call or Put Vega vs. Volatility

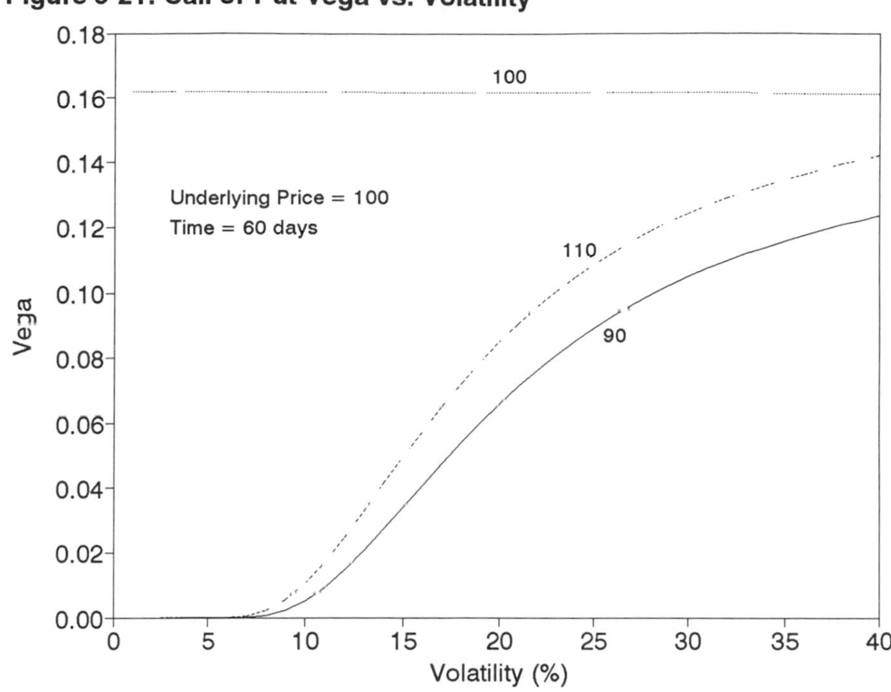

If both the underlying contract and options are subject to futures-type settlement, the rho must be zero, since no cash flow results from either a trade in the underlying contract or a trade in the options. When options on futures are subject to stock-type settlement, the rho associated with both calls and puts is negative. An increase in interest rates will decrease the value of such options since it raises the cost of carrying the options. In the case of stock options, calls will have positive rhos (an increase in interest rates will make calls a more desirable alternative to buying the stock) and puts will have negative rhos (an increase in interest rates will make puts a less desirable alternative to selling the stock).

Although changes in interest rates can affect an option's theoretical value, the interest rate is usually the least important of the inputs into a pricing model. For this reason the rho usually takes a back seat to the other, more critical, sensitivities: the delta, gamma, theta, and vega. Indeed, few traders pay much attention to the rho. However, for completeness, some of the characteristics of the rho are shown in Figures 6-22 (stock options) and 6-23 (futures options). In all cases the options which have the highest rho are those which are deeply in-the-money, because they require the greatest cash outlay. And the greater the amount of time to expiration, the greater the rho. Note also that because an option is a substitute for a position in the underlying instrument, the rho for stock options is much greater in magnitude than the rho for futures options. The purchase or sale of stock results in a much greater cash flow than the purchase or sale of a futures contract. (The vertical scale in Figure 6-23 is approximately ten times greater

Figure 6-22: Futures Option Rho vs. Underlying Price

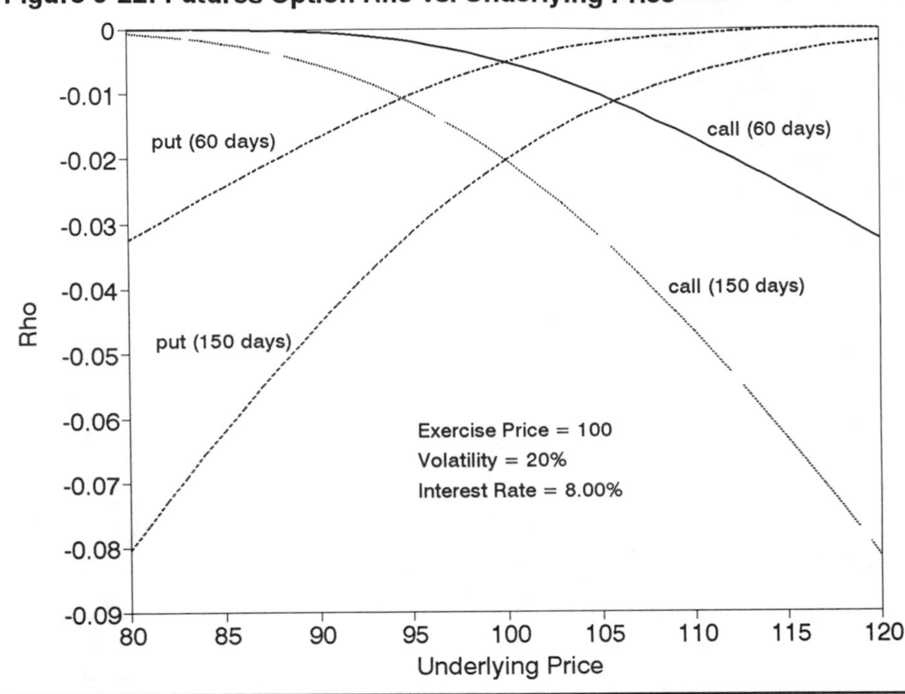

than the vertical scale in Figure 6-22.) Because of its relatively minor importance, we will generally disregard the rho in analyzing option strategies and managing risk.

SUMMARY

It is important for the active option trader to become familiar with delta, gamma, theta, and vega characteristics, since he may need to make quick decisions about trading strategies and risk management, decisions which might well determine his financial fate. The following is a summary of these characteristics:

Delta—Deltas range from zero for far out-of-the-money calls to 100 for deeply in-the-money calls, and from zero for far out-of-the-money puts to –100 for deeply in-the-money puts.

At-the-money calls have deltas of approximately 50, and at-the-money puts approximately –50.

As time passes, or as we decrease our volatility assumption, call deltas move away from 50, and puts deltas away from –50. As we increase our volatility assumption, call deltas move towards 50, and put deltas towards –50.

Gamma—At-the-money options have greater gammas than either in- or out-of-the-money options with otherwise identical contract specifications.

Figure 6-23: Stock Option Rho vs. Underlying Price

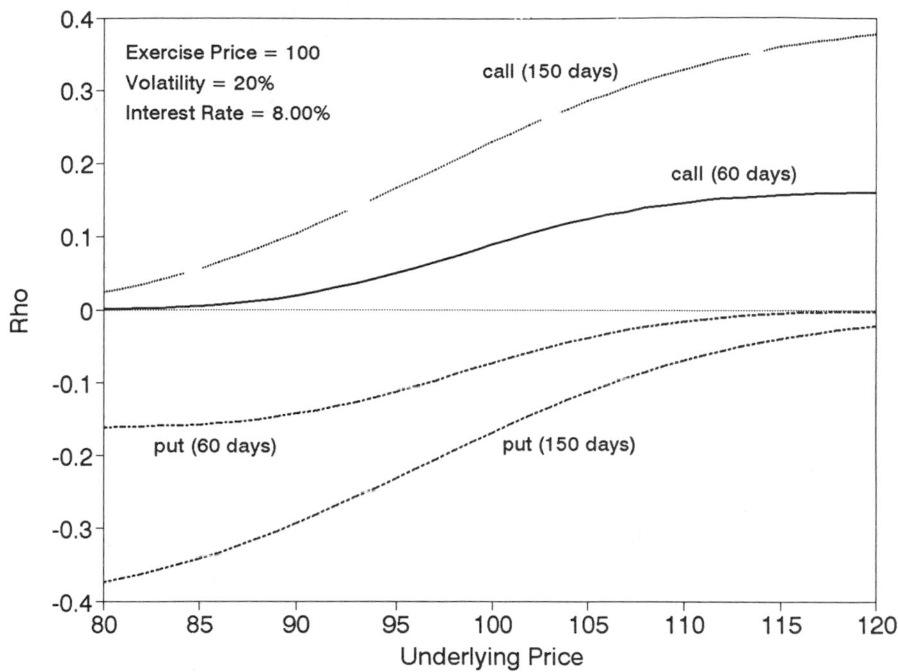

As we increase our volatility assumption, the gamma of an in- or out-of-the-money option rises, while the gamma of an at-the-money option falls. As we decrease our volatility assumption, or as time to expiration grows shorter, the gamma of an in- or out-of-the money option falls, while the gamma of an at-the-money option rises, sometimes dramatically.

Theta—At-the-money options have greater thetas than either in- or out-of-the-money options with otherwise identical contract specifications.

The theta of an at-the-money option increases as expiration approaches. A short-term, at-the-money option will always decay more quickly than a long-term, at-the-money option.

As we increase (decrease) our volatility assumption, the theta of an option will rise (fall). Higher volatility means there is greater time value associated with the option, so that each day's decay will also be greater when no movement occurs.

Vega—At-the-money options have greater vegas than either in- or out-of-the-money options with otherwise identical contract specifications.

Out-of-the-money options have the greatest vega as a percent of theoretical value.

The vegas of all options decrease as time to expiration grows shorter. A long-term option is always more sensitive to a change in volatility than a short-term option with otherwise identical contract specifications.

The vega of an at-the-money option is relatively constant with respect to changes in volatility. If we raise or lower volatility, the option's vega is unlikely to change significantly.

In Figure 6-3 we summarized the general effects on stock option values if the expected dividend payment for the underlying stock changes. But we did not address the question of magnitude. How sensitive is an option's value to a change in dividends? When a stock goes ex-dividend, its price will normally drop by approximately the amount of the dividend. Increasing the dividend is therefore similar to dropping the stock price, and cutting the dividend is similar to increasing the stock price. If a stock had been expected to pay a dividend of $.75 per share, and the dividend is increased to $1.00 per share, this is similar to dropping the stock price by an additional $.25. Since an option's sensitivity to a change in the price of the underlying is given by the delta, the sensitivity to a change in the dividend can also be approximated by the delta. If the dividend is increased by $.25, a call with a delta of 60 will lose about $.15 in value. A put with a delta of –40 will gain about $.10. This approximation applies only when one dividend payment is expected prior to expiration. If multiple dividend payments are expected over the life of the option, the effect on the option's value must be increased accordingly. As we will see, dividend considerations play their greatest role in arbitrage strategies and early exercise.

Two typical evaluation tables with prices, implied volatilities, and all relevant sensitivities are shown in Figures 6-24 and 6-25. Figure 6-24 is for options on September Deutschemark futures on the Chicago Mercantile Exchange as of 22 May 1992. The values are based on a volatility assumption of 10.5% and an interest rate assumption of 4.50%. Figure 6-25 is for options on General Electric stock on the Chicago Board Options Exchange as of the same date. The values are based on a volatility assumption of 22% and an interest rate assumption of 4.50% for all three expiration months (June, September, December).[6] The expected dividends for General Electric stock, and their payment dates, are also included in the assumptions.[7]

We noted previously that the delta, gamma, theta, and vega can be sensitive to changes in volatility. Under some circumstances it may be useful for a trader to ask: if the implied volatility of an option were the correct volatility, what would be its delta, gamma, theta, and vega? The resulting numbers are referred to as the *implied delta, gamma, theta, and vega.* The implied delta and theta, in particular, often appear on computer printouts, the former because many traders prefer to maintain delta neutral

6. This is a simplified example with uniform volatility and interest rates. Under some circumstances it might be more reasonable to vary the volatility and interest rate assumptions for different expiration dates.

7. Due to the greater likelihood of early exercise for stock options, and the fact that the quoted options are American, the calculations in Figure 6-25 were done using a binomial model, which more accurately evaluates the early exercise value of American options. The problem of early exercise will be discussed further in Chapter 12.

Figure 6-24

22 May 1992 (Black Model)

September 1992 Deutschemarks = 60.71; Time to expiration = 105 days; Volatility = 10.5%; Interest rate = 4.50%

	CALLS							PUTS						
Exercise Price	Price	Theoretical Value	Delta	Gamma	Theta	Vega	Implied Volatility	Price	Theoretical Value	Delta	Gamma	Theta	Vega	Implied Volatility
52	—	8.71*	99	.2	0	0	—	.01	0	0	.2	0	.004	12.1
53	—	7.71*	98	.6	0	0	—	.02	.01	–1	.6	–.0003	.009	11.8
54	—	6.71*	97	1.3	0	0	—	.04	.02	–2	1.3	–.0007	.017	11.6
55	—	5.71*	95	2.4	0	0	—	.07	.05	–4	2.4	–.0013	.030	11.2
56	4.78	4.77	92	4.0	–.0016	.044	10.9	.13	.11	–7	4.0	–.0022	.044	10.9
57	3.89	3.88	87	6.0	–.0028	.066	10.7	.23	.22	–12	6.0	–.0033	.066	10.7
58	3.07	3.07	79	8.1	–.0041	.090	10.6	.40	.39	–20	8.1	–.0045	.090	10.6
59	2.32	2.34	70	10.0	–.0053	.111	10.3	.64	.65	–29	10.0	–.0055	.111	10.4
60	1.72	1.72	59	11.2	–.0060	.125	10.5	1.02	1.02	–40	11.2	–.0061	.125	10.5
61	1.20	1.21	47	11.5	–.0063	.128	10.4	1.49	1.50	–52	11.5	–.0062	.128	10.4
62	.83	.82	36	10.9	–.0059	.121	10.6	2.11	2.09	–63	10.9	–.0058	.121	10.7
63	.56	.53	26	9.5	–.0052	.105	10.8	2.82	2.79	–73	9.5	–.0050	.105	10.8
64	.34	.33	18	7.6	–.0042	.085	10.7	3.60	3.57	–81	7.6	–.0039	.085	10.8
65	.21	.19	12	5.7	–.0032	.064	10.8	4.46	4.43	–87	5.7	–.0027	.064	11.0
66	.13	.11	7	4.0	–.0022	.044	11.0	5.37	5.33	–92	4.0	–.0016	.044	11.3
67	.08	.06	4	2.6	–.0015	.029	11.2		6.29*	–95	0	0	0	—
68	.06	.03	2	1.6	–.0009	.018	11.9		7.29*	–97	0	0	0	—

* Using an unadjusted Black model these options would have a theoretical value less than parity. Since they are in fact American options rather than European, their values have been adjusted upward to parity.

Figure 6-25

22 May 1992 (Cox-Ross-Rubenstein Model)

General Electric = 76⅝; Time to expiration: 28 days (June), 119 days (September), 210 days (December); Volatility = 20.5%; Interest rate = 4.50%;

Dividend = .55 on 3 June 92; .55 on 22 September 92; .55 on 3 December 92

	CALLS							PUTS						
Exercise Price	Price	Theoretical Value	Delta	Gamma	Theta	Vega	Implied Volatility	Price	Theoretical Value	Delta	Gamma	Theta	Vega	Implied Volatility
Jun 60	16¾	16.69	100	0	.006	0	—	1/16	0	0	0	0	0	—
Jun 65	11¾	11.70	100	.1	.008	0	—	⅛	0	0	.4	0	.001	34.5
Jun 70	6⅞	6.72	98	3.2	.012	.009	28.3	¼	.10	6	3.6	.008	.023	24.9
Jun 75	2⅜	2.45	67	7.9	.037	.073	19.0	15/16	1.09	37	7.7	.026	.079	18.0
Jun 80	⅜	.47	20	6.3	.023	.060	18.3	4⅛	4.20	81	6.1	.014	.056	18.6
Jun 85	1/16	.04	3	2.2	.005	.014	21.7	8¾	8.84	99	2.0	0	.009	—
Sep 70	8¼	7.75	82	3.1	.017	.112	22.4	1¼	1.04	19	3.2	.008	.114	22.6
Sep 75	4⅝	4.38	62	4.2	.019	.168	20.2	2 7/16	2.73	40	4.5	.011	.169	19.3
Sep 80	2¼	2.15	40	4.2	.017	.166	19.7	5¼	5.54	64	4.7	.019	.157	19.5
Sep 85	⅞	.91	21	3.3	.011	.125	19.0	9	9.34	85	3.5	.003	.091	17.7
Dec 70	8⅞	8.67	77	2.7	.017	.171	21.1	2 3/16	1.80	25	2.8	.006	.179	22.0
Dec 75	6	5.58	61	3.4	.018	.216	21.9	4	3.70	41	3.3	.006	.219	21.4
Dec 80	3⅜	3.33	43	3.4	.015	.221	20.2	6⅜	6.44	58	3.5	.004	.219	19.8
Dec 85	1¾	1.86	28	2.9	.013	.190	19.5	9¾	9.97	74	3.3	.003	.177	19.0

positions using the implied delta, and the latter because the rate at which the price of an option decays is usually more useful than the rate at which the theoretical value decays.

Knowing the total delta, gamma, theta, and vega of an option position can help a trader determine beforehand how the position is likely to react to changing market conditions. Since all these numbers are additive, the total sensitivity of a position can be calculated by adding up the sensitivities of the individual options. For example, a trader who has purchased five options with a gamma of 2.5 each, and sold two options with a gamma of 4.0 each, has a total gamma position of

$$(+5 \times 2.5) + (-2 \times 4.0) = +4.5$$

Similarly, if he has purchased nine options with a theta of –.05 each, and sold four options with a theta of –.08 each, his total theta position is

$$(+9 \times -.05) + (-4 \times -.08) = -.13$$

New traders sometimes find it difficult to remember whether a delta, gamma, theta, or vega position is long or short. The various positions and their respective signs are given in Figure 6-26. The sign of the delta, gamma, theta, or vega, together with the magnitude of the numbers, tell the trader which changes in market conditions will either help or hurt his position, and to what degree. The positive or negative effect of changing market conditions is summarized in Figure 6-27.

Even though a trader can analyze the effect of changing market conditions on his position through its delta, gamma, theta, and vega characteristics, his first and primary concern is that the position be profitable if his assumptions about market conditions are correct. This means that the position ought to have a positive theoretical edge. The theoretical edge can be calculated in the same way as the total delta, gamma, theta, and vega. One need only multiply the theoretical edge of each individual option (the difference between its trade or settlement price and theoretical value) by the number of contracts traded, and add up all the contracts involved. The amount of positive or negative theoretical edge is a reflection of the position's potential profit or loss.

The top portion of Figure 6-28 shows a theoretical evaluation table for individual options on a hypothetical futures contract. Beneath the table are several possible option positions for which the total theoretical edge, delta, gamma, theta, and vega have been calculated. The reader should take a moment to look at the arithmetic of each position, and to consider the risk characteristics associated with each position. Are all the positions likely to be profitable if the assumptions used for theoretical evaluation are correct? What will help or hurt each position?

There is one other option sensitivity that is not generally used by traders, but which the reader may encounter in other option texts. An option's *elasticity*, sometimes denoted with the Greek letter omega (Ω) (or less commonly the Greek letter lambda (λ)), is the relative percent change in an option's value for a given percent change in the price of the underlying contract. For example, suppose a call has a theoretical value of 2.50 with the underlying contract at 50. If the call has a delta of 25, and the underlying contract rises one point to 51, the call should rise to 2.75. In percent terms the call has

Figure 6-26

If you are . . .	Your delta (hedge ratio) position is . . .	Your gamma (curvature) position is . . .	Your theta (time decay) position is . . .	Your vega (volatility) position is . . .
long the underlying	positive	0	0	0
short the underlying	negative	0	0	0
long calls	positive	positive	negative	positive
short calls	negative	negative	positive	negative
long puts	negative	positive	negative	positive
short puts	positive	negative	positive	negative

Figure 6-27

If your delta position is . . .	you want the underlying contract to . . .
positive	rise in price
negative	fall in price
If your gamma position is . . .	**you want the underlying contract to . . .**
positive	move very swiftly, regardless of direction
negative	move slowly, regardless of direction
If your theta position is . . .	**the passage of time will generally . . .**
positive	increase the value of your position
negative	decrease the value of your position
If your vega position is . . .	**you want volatility to . . .**
positive	rise
negative	fall
If your rho position is . . .	**you want interest rates to . . .**
positive	rise
negative	fall

changed its value five times as fast as the underlying: the underlying rose 2% (1/50), while the call rose 10% (.25/2.50). We say that the call has an elasticity of 5. The elasticity is sometimes referred to as the option's *leverage value.* The greater an option's elasticity, the more highly leveraged the option.

An easy method of calculating an option's elasticity is to divide the price of the underlying contract by the option's theoretical value, and multiply this by the option's delta (when calculating the elasticity, we use the decimal format for the delta):

$$\text{elasticity} = \frac{\text{underlying price}}{\text{theoretical value}} \times \text{delta}$$

Figure 6-28

	CALLS						PUTS					
Exercise Price	Price	Theoretical Value	Delta	Gamma	Theta	Vega	Price	Theoretical Value	Delta	Gamma	Theta	Vega
90	10.35	10.22	90	2.0	−.009	.07	.46	.35	−9	2.0	−.011	.07
95	6.26	6.18	74	3.9	−.020	.13	1.34	1.25	−25	3.9	−.021	.13
100	3.13	3.19	51	4.9	−.026	.16	3.12	3.19	−48	4.9	−.026	.16
105	1.38	1.38	28	4.1	−.022	.14	6.29	6.31	−70	4.1	−.021	.14
110	.55	.50	13	2.6	−.014	.08	10.44	10.36	−86	2.6	−.012	.08

Position	Theoretical Edge	Delta Position	Gamma Position	Theta Position	Vega Position
long 20 100 calls	20 × +.06	+20 × +51	+20 × 4.9	+20 × −.026	+20 × .16
short 10 futures	0	−10 ö +100	0	0	0
	+1.20	+20	+98.0	−.520	+3.20
long 10 95 puts	10 × −.09	+10 × −25	+10 × 3.9	+10 × −.021	+10 × .13
short 25 90 puts	25 × +.11	−25 × −9	−25 × 2.0	−25 × −.011	−25 × −.07
	+1.85	−25	−11.0	+.065	−.45
short 10 95 calls	10 × +.08	−10 × +74	−10 × 3.9	−10 × −.020	−10 × .13
short 15 100 puts	15 × −.07	−15 × −48	−15 × 4.9	−15 × −.026	−15 × .16
	−.25	−20	−112.5	+.590	−3.70
long 10 105 calls	10 × 0	+10 × +28	+10 × 4.1	+10 × −.022	+10 × .14
short 10 110 calls	10 × +.05	−10 × +13	−10 × 2.6	−10 × −.014	−10 × .08
	+.50	+150	+15.0	−.080	+.60
short 10 95 calls	10 × +.08	−10 × +74	−10 × 3.9	−10 × −.020	−10 × .13
long 20 100 calls	20 × +.06	+20 × +51	+20 × 4.9	+20 × −.026	+20 × .16
short 10 105 calls	10 × 0	−10 × +28	−10 × 4.1	−10 × −.22	−10 × .14
	+2.00	0	+18.0	−.100	+.50
short 12 90 calls	12 × +.13	−12 × +90	−12 × 2.0	−12 × −.009	−12 × .07
long 12 90 puts	12 × −.11	+12 × −9	+12 × 2.0	+12 × −.011	+12 × .07
short 7 95 calls	7 × +.08	−7 × +74	−7 × 3.9	−7 × −.020	−7 × .13
long 10 100 puts	10 × +.07	+10 × −48	+10 × 4.9	+10 × −.026	+10 × .16
long 15 105 calls	15 × 0	+15 × +28	+15 × 4.1	+15 × −.022	+15 × .14
long 8 110 calls	8 × −.05	+8 × +13	+8 × 2.6	+8 × −.014	+8 × .08
short 3 110 puts	3 × +.08	−3 × −86	−3 × 2.6	−3 × −.012	−3 × .08
long 12 futures	0	+12 × +100	0	0	0
	+1.34	−204	+96.2	−.550	+3.19

In our example we have:

$$\text{elasticity} = \frac{50}{2.50} \times .25 = 5$$

One final observation for the prospective trader. All the numbers we have discussed in this chapter, the theoretical value, delta, gamma, theta, vega, and rho, are constantly changing, so that the profitability and risks associated with different strategies are also changing. The importance of analyzing risk cannot be overemphasized. The great majority of traders who fail at option trading do so because they fail to fully understand risk and how to manage it. But there is another type of trader, one who attempts to analyze every possible risk. When this happens, the trader finds it difficult to make any trading decisions at all; he is stricken with *paralysis through analysis.* A trader who is so concerned with risk that he is afraid to make a trade cannot profit, no matter how well he understands options. When a trader goes into the marketplace he has chosen to take on some risk. The delta gamma, theta, and vega enable him to identify risk; they do not eliminate risk. The intelligent trader uses these numbers to help him decide beforehand which risks are acceptable and which risks are not.

❖ 7 ❖

Introduction to Spreading

In option markets, as in all markets, there are many ways to trade profitably. One type of trading strategy, common among floor traders, is *scalping*. A scalper attempts to buy at the bid price and sell at the offer price as often as possible, without regard to the contract's theoretical value. Although the profit from each trade may be small, if a trader can do this enough times each day he can expect to show a reasonable profit. Scalping, however, requires a highly liquid market, and option markets are rarely sufficiently liquid to support this type of trading.

A different type of trading strategy involves speculating on the direction in which the underlying contract will move. If a speculator correctly anticipates the market direction, and takes an appropriate position, he can also expect to show a profit. But even when the market moves in the expected direction, taking a directional position in an option market will not necessarily be profitable. Many different forces beyond directional considerations can affect an option's price. If a trader's sole consideration is direction, he will usually be better off taking a position in the underlying market. If he does, and he is right, he is assured of making a profit.

The majority of successful option traders engage in *spread* trading. Since option evaluation is based on the laws of probability, and because the laws of probability can be expected to even out only over long periods of time, option traders must often hold positions for extended periods. Unfortunately, over short periods of time, while the trader is waiting for the option price to move towards theoretical value, the trader may be at risk from a wide variety of changes in market conditions which threaten his potential profit. Indeed, over short periods of time there is no guarantee that an option will react in a manner consistent with a theoretical pricing model. Spreading is simply a way of enabling an option trader to take advantage of theoretically mispriced options, while at the same time reducing the effects of short-term changes in market conditions so that he can safely hold an option position to maturity.

WHAT IS A SPREAD?

A spread is a strategy which involves taking simultaneous but opposing positions in different instruments. A spread trader makes the assumption that there is an identifiable price relationship between different instruments and, although he may not know in which direction the market will move, the price relationship between the instruments ought to remain relatively constant. When the relationship appears to be temporarily mispriced, the spread trader will take a long position in the instrument which appears to be underpriced and a short position in the instrument which appears to be overpriced. The trader hopes to profit when the prices of the instruments return to their expected relationship.

Among futures traders the most common type of spread involves taking opposing positions in different delivery months for the same commodity. A trader might purchase October crude oil and sell November crude oil on the New York Mercantile Exchange. Or he might buy December corn and sell July corn on the Chicago Board of Trade. The value of this type of *intra-market spread* depends on a variety of factors, the most important of which is usually the cost of carrying the physical commodity from one delivery month to another.

Suppose that February gold on the COMEX is trading for \$360 per ounce. What should April gold be trading for? A trader who takes delivery of gold in February at \$360 per ounce and holds it until April will incur a debit of \$360 per ounce for a two-month period. If interest rates are 9 percent annually, the two-month financing cost will be:

$$9\% \times 2/12 \times \$360 = \$5.40$$

Given the financing cost of \$5.40 per ounce that can be saved by purchasing an April futures contract rather than purchasing the physical commodity, the April contract ought to be worth \$5.40 more than the February contract, or \$365.40 per ounce. If the February contract is trading at \$360 and the April contract is trading at \$364, the trader knows that the spread is \$1.40 too cheap. He can profit from this mispricing by purchasing the spread for \$4.00 (buy April for \$364, sell February for \$360). If the spread returns to its expected value of \$5.40, the trader can buy back the February contract and sell out the April contract, thereby realizing a profit of \$1.40.

Note that the above spread will be profitable regardless of the general direction of the gold market, as long as the prices of the two delivery months return to their expected \$5.40 spread. If February gold rises to \$370, the trader will lose \$6 on the February side of his spread. If, however, the April contract rises to \$375.40, the gain in the value of the April contract will more than offset the loss on the February contract and result in the expected \$1.40 per ounce profit.

Factors other than financing costs can also affect the price relationship between different futures months for the same commodity. The futures price of some commodities must also include the cost of storing and insuring the commodity for the period between delivery months. In theory, the cost of financing, storing, and insuring a traditional commodity (precious metals, agricultural products, livestock, energy products, etc.) must be some positive number, so that the price of a more distant delivery month ought to be greater than the price of a nearby delivery month. This is known as a *contango* relationship. Any increase in these costs will increase the value of a futures contract.

Supply and demand considerations can also affect the spread relationship of different delivery months. In theory, a November crude oil contract ought to always trade for more than an October crude oil contract. But if crude oil is currently in short supply, refiners may be willing to pay more for an October futures contract in order to ensure an uninterrupted flow of crude oil to their refineries. Markets where the near-by delivery month is trading at a premium to the more distant months are said to be in *backwardation.* Supply and demand for raw materials can often cause traditional commodities markets to go into backwardation. Examples of contango and backwardation markets are shown in Figure 7-1.

The cost of carrying a position in an underlying commodity is only one of many factors which can affect a futures spread relationship. A trader who purchases a stock index futures contract will save the financing costs associated with owning the basket of stocks which make up the index. At the same time, he gives up the rights to any dividends he might receive if he actually owned the stocks. The savings in financing costs add value to the futures contract, but the loss in dividends reduces the contract's value.[1]

Matters can be further complicated if different interest rates play a role in the evaluation of a spread relationship. The value of a treasury bond futures contract depends not only on the carrying costs saved by purchasing a futures contract instead of the actual bond (the short-term rate), but also on the interest lost by not owning the bond (the long-term rate). Depending on the difference between short- and long-term rates, distant delivery months in the treasury bond futures market can be trading at either a premium to the nearby months or at a discount to the nearby months. Similar types of considerations affect relationships in foreign currency futures markets, but here the determining factors are the difference between domestic and foreign interest rates. When foreign rates are low compared to domestic rates, the more distant months trade at a premium; when foreign rates are high, the more distant months trade at a discount.

Calculating the spread relationship between different delivery months can be a complex problem, and is covered more fully in texts focusing specifically on futures trading. The point here is that, in theory, there ought to be a well defined price relationship between different delivery months. When this relationship is violated in the marketplace, a potential profit opportunity exists by selling the overpriced contract and buying the underpriced.

Spreads need not be based solely on the relationship between different delivery months for the same commodity. They can also be based on presumed price relationships between different, though usually related, instruments. The NOB (notes over bonds) spread traded on the Chicago Board of Trade is based on the assumption that there is an identifiable relationship between the price of Treasury Bonds and Treasury Notes. When the spread between the prices of these two futures contracts is more or less than expected, traders will sell one instrument and buy the other. For example, with Treasury Notes at 99-16[2] and Treasury Bonds at 96-00, there is a 3-16 spread between the two instruments. If a trader feels, based on his analysis of interest rates,

---

1. Because of their unique importance in financial markets, we will look at stock index futures and options in detail in Chapter 15.
2. U.S. Treasury Bonds and Notes are traded in points and 32^{nds}. 99-16 represents a price of 99 16/32.

Figure 7-1

Contango Markets

Month	Open	High	Low	Settle	Change	-Lifetime- High	Low
			Friday, October 22, 1993				
COCOA (CSCE); 10 metric tons; $ per gallon (1 = $10.00)							
Dec	1163	1166	1125	1134	-21	1506	919
Mar94	1200	1203	1161	1174	-20	1495	835
May	1215	1215	1172	1183	-24	1518	841
Jul	1226	1226	1190	1200	-23	1530	845
Sep	1237	1237	1220	1220	-20	1536	878
Mar95	1239	1239	1239	1239	-20	1346	980
COTTON (CTN); 50,000 lbs.; ¢ per lb. (.01 = $5.00)							
Dec	57.74	57.94	57.20	57.55	-.19	64.25	54.60
Mar94	59.35	59.45	58.85	59.17	-.20	64.20	55.62
May	60.10	60.30	59.75	59.95	-.30	64.85	57.47
Jul	60.68	60.80	60.30	60.55	-.25	65.00	58.30
Oct	61.80	62.20	61.80	62.00	+.35	64.00	59.81
Dec	61.50	62.20	61.35	62.10	+.35	62.90	59.48
SOYBEAN MEAL (CBT); 100 tons.; $ per ton. (.01 = $10.00)							
Dec	193.30	194.60	192.90	193.10	-.30	235.50	183.40
Jan	193.30	194.70	193.10	193.40	....	231.50	176.90
Mar	194.30	195.90	194.30	194.40	-.10	231.00	175.60
May	196.00	197.00	195.40	195.40	+.40	228.00	177.00
Jul	197.50	198.70	197.20	197.40	+.10	245.00	179.00
Aug	197.50	198.40	197.50	197.50	....	237.50	180.10

Backwardation Markets

Month	Open	High	Low	Settle	Change	-Lifetime- High	Low
			Monday, December 10, 1990				
CATTLE (CME); 44,000 lbs.; ¢ per lb. (.01 = $4.40)							
Dec	79.97	80.75	79.97	80.70	+.78	79.77	71.00
Feb91	76.35	77.00	76.25	76.87	+.70	77.80	72.50
Apr	76.20	76.95	76.20	76.87	+.65	78.05	74.00
Jun	74.10	74.65	74.10	74.55	+.50	75.45	72.15
Aug	72.70	73.12	72.70	72.92	+.35	73.85	70.35
Oct	72.70	73.05	72.70	72.90	+.48	72.85	70.70
COPPER (COMEX); 25,000 lbs.; ¢ per lb. (.01 = $2.50)							
Jan	110.00	110.85	109.60	110.80	+1.30	126.40	91.50
Feb	109.00	109.80	108.90	109.80	+1.60	115.80	99.50
Mar	106.40	108.40	106.30	108.00	+2.00	122.60	92.30
Apr	106.00	108.00	106.00	107.20	+2.00	115.50	99.85
May	105.15	106.70	105.00	106.40	+2.05	117.80	97.00
Jul	103.80	105.30	103.80	104.80	+2.10	110.50	95.50
HEATING OIL (NYMEX); 42,000 gallons; ¢ per gallon (.01 = $4.20)							
Jan	81.60	82.50	80.80	80.97	+1.80	107.25	52.95
Feb	79.00	79.20	77.60	77.76	+1.52	102.00	52.60
Mar	74.00	74.00	72.70	72.82	+.81	96.50	50.70
Apr	69.50	69.50	68.10	68.12	+.46	92.00	49.30
May	66.20	66.25	65.90	66.12	+.11	88.50	48.40
Jun	64.75	64.75	64.00	63.22	-.14	85.75	48.40

that the spread between Notes and Bonds ought to be 3-00, he can sell the spread at 3-16 (sell Notes at 99-16, buy Bonds at 96-00). If the spread returns to its expected value of 3-00, the trader can buy in his Notes and sell out his Bonds, realizing a profit of $^{16}/_{32}$.

Spreads can also be based on more complex relationships. Many traders on the COMEX follow the price relationship between gold and silver. However, with gold at \$300 to \$400 per ounce and silver at \$4 to \$5 per ounce (as of this writing), the relationship is more commonly expressed as a ratio. Suppose a trader decides that the spread between the two metals ought to be 80 ounces of silver to one ounce of gold (an 80:1 ratio). If silver is trading at \$4.50, given the 80:1 price ratio, gold ought to be trading at \$4.50 × 80 = \$360. If, however, gold is at \$375, the spread trader will sell one ounce of gold at \$375, and buy 80 ounces of silver at \$4.50. Regardless of the general trend in prices of precious metals, he expects to make \$15 when the spread returns to its 80:1 ratio. If the precious metals market drops, so that gold is at \$336 and silver is at \$4.20 (the expected 80:1 ratio), the trader's total profit will be:

$$80 \times (\$4.20 - \$4.50) = -\$24 \text{ (silver)}$$

$$\$375 - \$336 = +\$39 \text{ (gold)}$$

As expected, he has shown a profit of \$15.

Spreads can also reflect a trader's opinion that one contract will outperform a different contract. Futures on the New York Stock Exchange Composite Index traded on the New York Futures Exchange represent the value of approximately 1500 actively traded stocks. Futures on the Standard & Poor's 500 Index traded on the Chicago Mercantile Exchange represent the value of 500 such stocks. If a trader believes the relationship between the two index values ought to be 9 to 5 (9 NYSE = 4 S&P 500), and the current prices are 220 and 396, the price relationship is, as expected, 9:5 (9 × 220 = 5 × 396). There does not seem to be any reason to either buy or sell the spread. If, however, a trader believes that in percent terms the 500 stocks in the S&P will outperform the 1500 stocks in the NYSE, he can buy five S&P contracts and sell nine NYSE contracts. If, in percent terms, the S&P rises more quickly, or declines less quickly, the trader will profit from the better performance of the contracts which he owns.

Spread relationships need not be restricted to two instruments. Sometimes three, or even more, different instruments may define a spread relationship. We calculated that if February gold is at \$360, and interest rates are 9%, the spread between February and April gold ought to be \$5.40. If interest rates rise, the carrying costs will also rise, and the February/April spread will widen. If a trader is long February gold and short April gold, and he feels that Eurodollar interest rates correlate closely to his cost of carry, he can sell Eurodollar futures to protect himself against a rise in interest rates. If interest rates do rise, he will lose on his February/April spread, but this will be offset by the profit on his Eurodollar position. He has made the assumption that there is a three-sided spread relationship between the price of February gold, April gold, and Eurodollars.

Much of the most sophisticated trading in derivative markets involves identifying and following spread relationships. When a trader decides that a spread relationship is mispriced in the marketplace, it can be just as profitable to buy or sell the spread as to take an outright long or short position in a single instrument.

In the foregoing examples the price relationship between instruments was defined in point or currency terms. In some cases, however, it may be more practical to define the relationship in other terms. In Chapter 4 we used a theoretical pricing model to determine an option's implied volatility, and we noted that for an option trader the implied volatility might be a more accurate reflection of an option's price than its dollar price. An option trader might therefore express the spread value between two options in terms of the spread between their implied volatilities. An option with an implied volatility of 15% and a different option with an implied volatility of 17% have a two-point volatility spread, regardless of the difference in their dollar prices. If both options have the same underlying instrument, a trader might purchase the option with an implied volatility of 15% and sell the option with an implied volatility of 17%, hoping to profit when the spread between the implied volatilities narrows.

As we shall see, the foregoing example is simplistic. An option trader cannot simply buy options with low implied volatilities and sell options with high implied volatilities. Not only is the spread between implied volatilities important, but also the general level of implied volatility. A two-percentage-point volatility spread may mean one thing if the implied volatilities are 6% and 8%, and something else if the implied volatilities are 26% and 28%. Moreover, there are important considerations of risk arising from difficulties in predicting volatility, as well as the possible inaccuracies in the models themselves. In spite of these factors, volatility spreads form one of the most important classes of option trading strategies. Much of an option trader's education is spent studying volatility relationships, and learning to create spreads based on mispriced volatility.

In the previous examples we assumed that a spreading strategy was static, that once the spread was initiated it was only necessary to wait for the spread to reach its expected value. Spreads can also be dynamic, requiring action over the life of the spread in order to profit from the mispricing. This was the method used in Chapter 5 to take advantage of a mispriced option. The option was spread against the underlying contract, and the position was adjusted over the life of the option. At expiration, the resulting profit was approximately equal to the amount by which the option was originally mispriced.

WHY SPREAD?

We saw in Chapter 3 that most theoretical pricing models depend on the laws of probability to generate option values. Even if we have correctly estimated the probabilities, i.e., volatility, we know that probability theory is only valid over many occurrences or, in the case of options, over long periods of time. A trader will sometimes have to hold an option position for an extended period in order to profit from the option's mispricing. Unfortunately, while he is holding the position, over short periods of time he may have to put up with adverse fluctuations in the position's value. The fluctuations might be severe enough that the trader, because of capital requirements, will not be able to maintain the position. If he is forced to liquidate the position prior to expiration, there is no guarantee that he will profit from the option's mispricing, even if he has accurately estimated all the inputs into the pricing model. By spreading, a trader is attempting to reduce the effect of short-term "bad luck" that goes with any investment based on the laws of probability.

Spreading strategies not only take advantage of the laws of probability by enabling a trader to hold option positions over long periods of time, but such strategies also have the effect of protecting the trader against incorrectly estimated inputs into the theoretical pricing model. Suppose a trader estimates that over the life of an option the volatility of an underlying Deutschemark futures contract will be 13%. Based on this estimate he finds that a certain call trading at the Chicago Mercantile Exchange has a theoretical value of 1.75 but is actually trading for 2.00. If the call has a delta of 25, one strategy is to sell four calls for 2.00 each and buy one futures contract, yielding a theoretical edge of 4 × .25 = 1.00, or $1,250. (Each point in currency contracts at the Chicago Mercantile Exchange is worth $1,250.) Of course, if the trader can make $1,250 with a 4 × 1 spread, it may occur to him that he can make $12,500 if he increases the size of the spread to 40 × 10. Why stop now? He can make $125,000 if he increases the size to 400 × 100.

Even if the market is sufficiently liquid to absorb unlimited size, is this a reasonable approach to trading? Should a trader simply find a theoretically profitable strategy and do it as many times as possible in order to maximize the profit potential? At some point the intelligent trader will have to consider not only the potential profit, but also the risk associated with a strategy. After all, his volatility estimate of 13% is just that, an estimate. What will happen if volatility actually turns out to be some higher number, perhaps 15%, or 17%? If the calls which he sold at 2.00 are worth 2.25 at a volatility of 17%, and volatility actually turns out to be 17%, then his hoped-for profit of $125,000 (assuming a size of 400 × 100) will turn into a loss of $125,000.

A trader must always consider the effects of an incorrect estimate, and then decide how much risk he is willing to take. If the trader in this example decides that he can survive if volatility goes no higher than 15% (a two-percentage-point margin for error), he might only be willing to do the spread 40 × 10. But if there were some way to increase his break-even volatility to 19% (a six-percentage-point margin for error), he might indeed be willing to do the spread 400 × 100. Option spreading strategies enable traders to profit over a wide variety of market conditions by giving them an increased margin for error in estimating the inputs into a theoretical pricing model. No trader will survive very long if his livelihood depends on estimating each input with 100% accuracy. Even when he incorrectly estimates the inputs, the experienced trader can survive if he has constructed intelligent spread strategies which allow for a wide margin of error.

SPREADING AS A RISK MANAGEMENT TOOL

Recall our example in Chapter 3 where a casino is selling a roulette bet with an expected return of 95¢ (American conditions) for $1.00. The casino owner knows that based on the laws of probability he has a 5% theoretical edge. Suppose that one day a bettor comes into the casino and proposes to bet $2,000 on one number at the roulette table. The casino owner knows that the odds are on his side and that he will most likely get to keep the $2,000 bet. But there is always a chance that the player will win, and that the casino will lose $70,000 (the $72,000 payoff less the $2,000 cost of the bet) if the player's number does come up.

Now suppose that two other bettors come into the casino, and each proposes to place a $1,000 bet at the roulette table. They promise, however, to bet on different numbers. Whichever number one bettor chooses, the other bettor will choose some other number. As with the first bettor and his single bet of $2,000, the casino's potential reward in this new scenario is also $2,000, if neither of the two numbers come up. But the risk to the casino is now only $34,000 (the $36,000 payoff if one player wins, less the cost of the two $1,000 bets). Since only one player can win, the two bets are *mutually exclusive*: if one wins, the other must lose.

Given our two scenarios, one bettor wagering $2,000 on one number, or two players wagering $1,000 each on different numbers, what is the theoretical edge to the casino? The edge to the casino in both cases is still the same 5%. Regardless of the amount wagered, or the number of individual bets, the laws of probability say that in the long run the casino gets to keep 5% of everything that is bet at the roulette table. In the short run, however, the risk to the casino is greatly reduced with two $1,000 bets because the bets have been spread around the table.

A casino does not like to see a bettor wager a large amount of money on one outcome, whether at roulette or any other casino game. The odds are still in the casino's favor. But, if the bet is large enough, and the bettor is lucky, short-term bad luck can overwhelm the casino. Indeed, if a bettor knows that the odds are against him, and he wants the greatest chance of showing a profit, his best course is to wager the maximum amount on one outcome, and hope that in the short run he gets lucky. If he continues to make bets over a long period of time, the laws of probability will eventually catch up with him and the casino will end up with the bettor's money. The ideal scenario from the casino's point of view is for 38 players to place 38 bets of $1,000 each on all 38 numbers at the roulette table. Now the casino has a perfect spread position. One player will collect $36,000, but with $38,000 on the table the casino has a sure profit of $2,000.

The option trader prefers to spread for the same reason that the casino prefers the bets to be spread around the table: spreading maintains profit potential but reduces short-term risk. There is no perfect spread position for the option trader, as there is for a casino. But the intelligent option trader learns to spread off his risk in as many different ways as possible in order to minimize the effects of short-term bad luck.

New traders are sometimes astonished at the size of the trades an experienced trader is prepared to make. For example, an independent floor trader in Treasury Bond options at the Chicago Board of Trade who buys 100 calls at 2-00 ($2,000) each has taken a position worth $200,000. How can he afford to do this? His capital resources certainly play a role in the risk he is willing to accept. But equally important is his ability to spread off risk. An experienced trader may know a wide variety of ways to spread off the risk associated with the 100 calls he purchased, either using other options, futures contracts, cash bonds, or some combination of these instruments. He may not be able to completely eliminate his risk. But he may be able to reduce it to such an extent that his risk is actually less than that of a much smaller trader who does not know how to spread, or knows only a limited number of spreading strategies.

❖ 8 ❖

Volatility Spreads

To take advantage of a theoretically mispriced option, it is necessary to hedge the purchase or sale of the option by simultaneously taking an opposing market position. In the examples in Chapter 5, the opposing market position was always taken in the underlying instrument. It is also possible to hedge an option position with other options which are theoretically equivalent to the underlying instrument. For example, suppose we feel a certain call with a delta of 50 is underpriced in the marketplace. If we buy 10 calls, giving us a total delta position of +500, we can hedge our position in any of the following ways:

- Sell five underlying contracts
- Buy puts with a total delta of –500
- Sell calls, different than those which we purchased, with a total delta of +500
- Combine several of these strategies, such that we create a total delta of –500

With many different calls and puts available, as well as the underlying contract, there are many different ways of hedging our ten calls. Regardless of which method we choose, each spread will have certain features in common:

- Each spread will be approximately delta neutral.
- Each spread will be sensitive to changes in the price of the underlying instrument.
- Each spread will be sensitive to changes in implied volatility.
- Each spread will be sensitive to the passage of time.

Spreads with the foregoing characteristics fall under the general heading of volatility spreads. In this chapter we will define the basic types of volatility spreads and look at their characteristics, initially by examining the expiration values of the spread, and then by considering the delta, gamma, theta, vega, and rho associated with each spread.

Before defining the primary types of spreads, it should be noted that spreading terminology is not uniform. Traders sometimes use different terms when referring to the same spread; they sometimes use the same term when referring to different spreads. An attempt has been made to use the most common terminology, but alternative spread definitions are also given where appropriate.

BACKSPREAD
(also referred to as a *ratio backspread* or *long ratio spread)*

A backspread is a delta neutral spread which consists of more long (purchased) options than short (sold) options where all options expire at the same time. In order to achieve this, options with smaller deltas must be purchased and options with larger deltas must be sold. A call backspread consists of long calls at a higher exercise price and short calls at a lower exercise price. A put backspread consists of long puts at a lower exercise price and short puts at a higher exercise price.

Typical backspreads and their values at expiration are shown in Figures 8-1 and 8-2. (These, and the example spreads in the following sections, are taken from the option evaluation table in Figure 8-20.) In each case, a move away from the long option's exercise price will increase the value of the spread. Depending on the type of backspread, movement in one direction may be preferable to movement in the other direction. In a call backspread the upside profit potential is unlimited; in a put backspread the downside profit is unlimited. But the primary consideration is that some movement will occur. If no movement occurs, a backspread is likely to be a losing strategy.

Typically, a backspread is done for a credit. That is, the amount of premium received for the sold options is greater than the premium paid for the purchased options. This ensures that the backspread will be profitable if the market makes a large move in either direction. If the market collapses in the case of a call backspread, or the market

Figure 8-1: Call Backspread

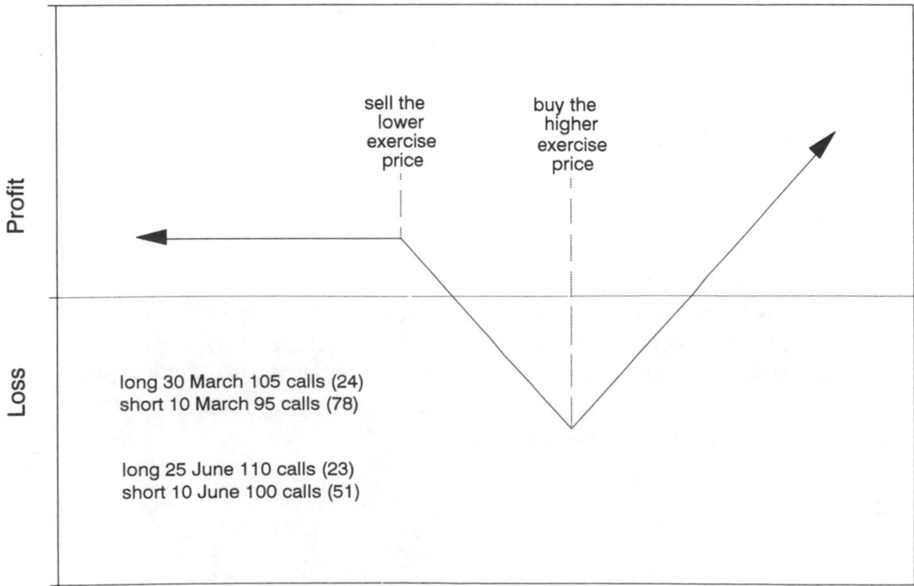

Figure 8-2: Put Backspread

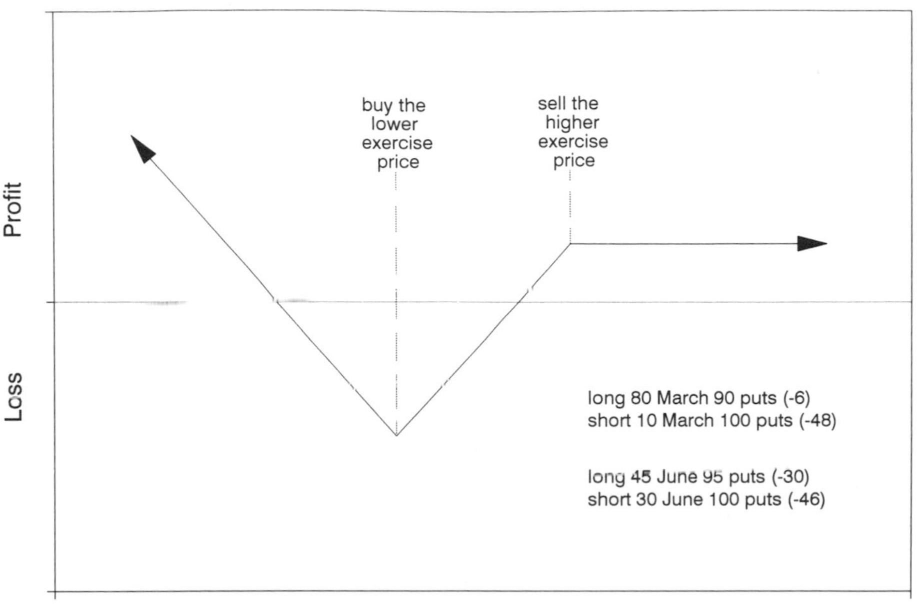

explodes in the case of a put backspread, all options will expire worthless and the trader will keep the credit from the initial transaction.

A trader will tend to choose the type of backspread which reflects his opinion about market direction. If he foresees a market with great upside potential, he will tend to choose a call backspread; if he foresees a market with great downside potential he will tend to choose a put backspread. He will avoid backspreads in quiet markets since the underlying contract is unlikely to move very far in either direction.

RATIO VERTICAL SPREAD
(also referred to as a *ratio spread, short ratio spread, vertical spread,* or *front spread)*

A trader who takes the opposite side of a backspread also has a delta neutral spread, but he is short more contracts than long, with all options expiring at the same time. Such a spread is sometimes referred to as a ratio spread or a vertical spread. However, these terms can also be applied to other types of spreads. In order to avoid later confusion, we will designate the opposite of a backspread as a ratio vertical spread.

Typical ratio vertical spreads, and their expiration values, are shown in Figures 8-3 and 8-4. From these graphs we can see that a ratio vertical spread will realize its maximum profit at expiration when the underlying contract finishes right at the short (sold) option's exercise price. Since a ratio vertical spreader assumes the opposite risks of a backspreader, his risk is unlimited on the upside in a call ratio vertical spread, and

Figure 8-3: Call Ratio Vertical Spread

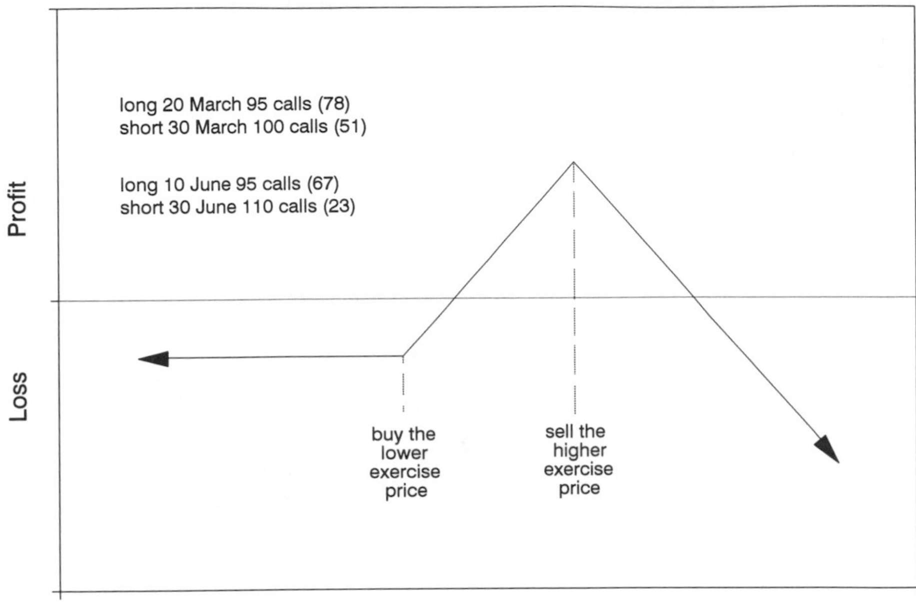

Figure 8-4: Put Ratio Vertical Spread

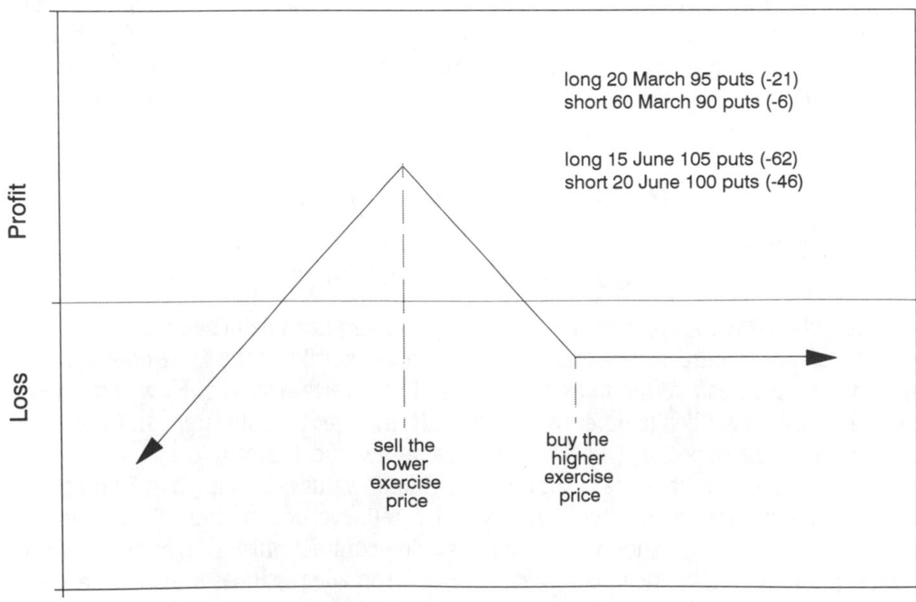

unlimited on the downside in a put ratio vertical spread. While a ratio vertical spreader expects the market to remain relatively stable, he will tend to choose either a call or put ratio vertical spread in order to limit his losses if he is wrong. If he is primarily worried about a swift rise in the market, he will choose a put ratio vertical spread; if he is primarily worried about a swift fall in the market, he will choose a call ratio vertical spread. In both cases, if the market does make a big move, his loss will be limited since the calls can only collapse to zero if the market falls, and the puts can only collapse to zero if the market rises.

STRADDLE

A straddle consists of either a long call and a long put, or a short call and a short put, where both options have the same exercise price and expire at the same time. If both the call and put are purchased, the trader is said to be long the straddle; if both options are sold, the trader is said to be short the straddle. Typical long and short straddles, with their expiration values, are shown in Figures 8-5 and 8-6.

While most straddles are executed with a one-to-one ratio (one call for each put), this is not a requirement. A straddle can also be *ratioed,* so that it consists of unequal numbers of calls and puts. Any spread where the number of long market contracts (long calls or short puts) and short market contracts (short calls or long puts) are unequal is considered a *ratio spread.* The most common types of ratio spreads are backspreads and

Figure 8-5: Long Straddle

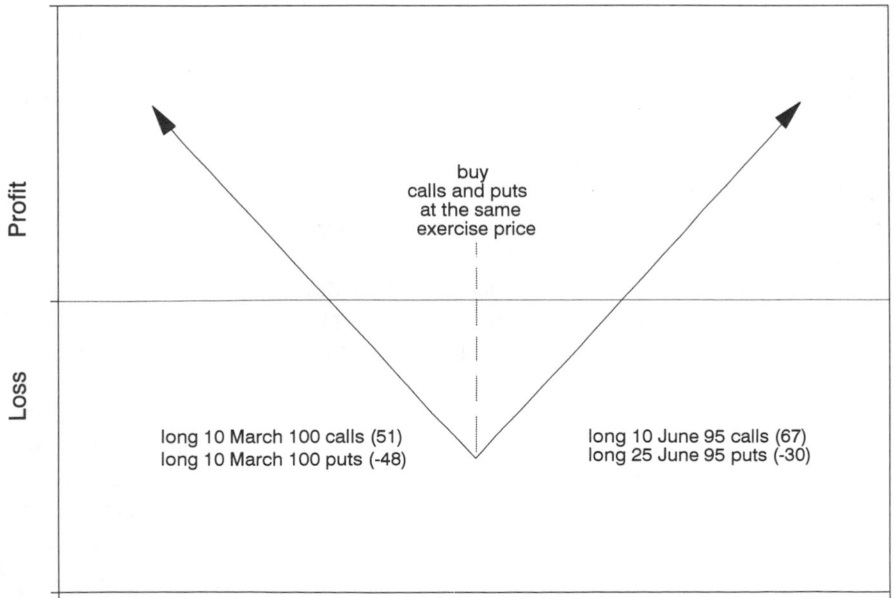

Figure 8-6: Short Straddle

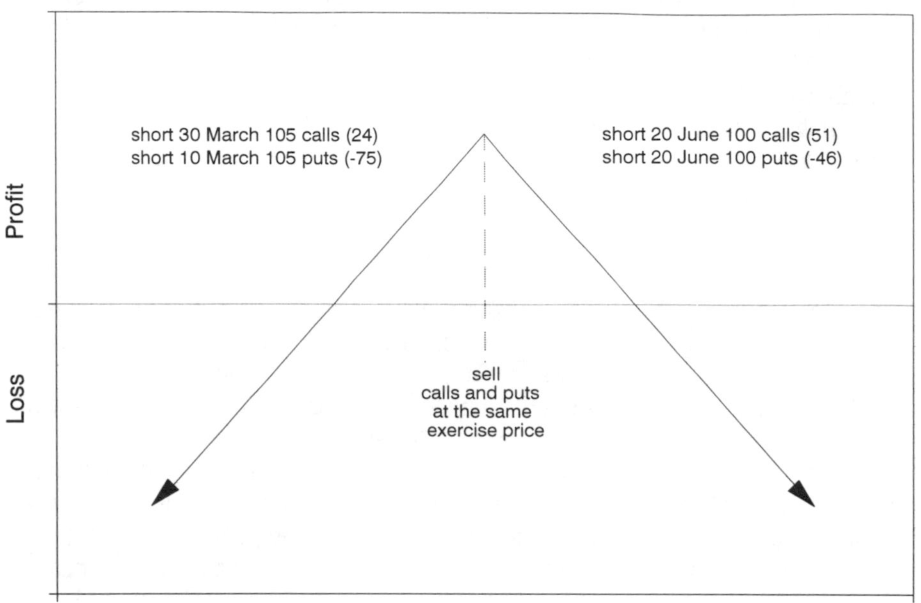

ratio vertical spreads. But other spreads, including straddles, can be ratioed. This is usually done to ensure that the spread is delta neutral.

A long straddle has many of the same characteristics as a backspread. Like a backspread it has limited risk and unlimited profit potential. With a long straddle, however, the trader's potential profit is unlimited in either direction. If the market moves sharply up or down, the straddle will realize ever increasing profits as long as the market continues to move in the same direction.

A short straddle has many of the same characteristics as a ratio vertical spread. The spread will realize its maximum profit if the market stays close to the call and put exercise price. The spread has a limited profit potential, and unlimited risk should the market move violently in either direction.

The new option trader often finds long straddles attractive because strategies with limited risk and unlimited profit potential offer great appeal, especially when the profit is unlimited in both directions. However, if the hoped for movement fails to materialize, he soon finds that losing money little by little, even a limited amount, can also be a painful experience. This is not an endorsement of either long or short straddles. Under the right conditions either strategy may be sensible. But the intelligent trader's primary concern ought to be the total expected return. If the strategy with the greatest expected return also entails unlimited risk, a trader may have to accept that risk as part of doing business.

STRANGLE

Like a straddle, a strangle consists of a long call and a long put, or a short call and a short put, where both options expire at the same time. In a strangle, however, the options have different exercise prices. If both options are purchased, the trader is long the strangle; if both options are sold, the trader is short the strangle. Typical long and short strangles are shown in Figures 8-7 and 8-8.

Strangles have characteristics similar to straddles, and are therefore similar to backspreads and ratio vertical spreads. Like a long straddle, a long strangle needs movement to be profitable, and has unlimited profit potential should such movement occur. Like a short straddle, a short strangle has unlimited risk in either direction, but will show a profit if the underlying market remains in a narrow trading range.

If a strangle is simply identified by its expiration month and exercise prices, there may be some confusion as to the specific options involved. A June 95/105 strangle might consist of a June 95 put and June 105 call. But it might also consist of a June 95 call and a June 105 put. Both these combinations are consistent with the definition of a strangle. To avoid confusion a strangle is commonly assumed to consist of out-of-the-money options. If the underlying market is currently at 100 and a trader wants to purchase the June 95/105 strangle, it is assumed that he wants to purchase a June 95 put and a June 105 call. When both options are in-the-money, the position is sometimes referred to as a *guts*.

Figure 8-7: Long Strangle

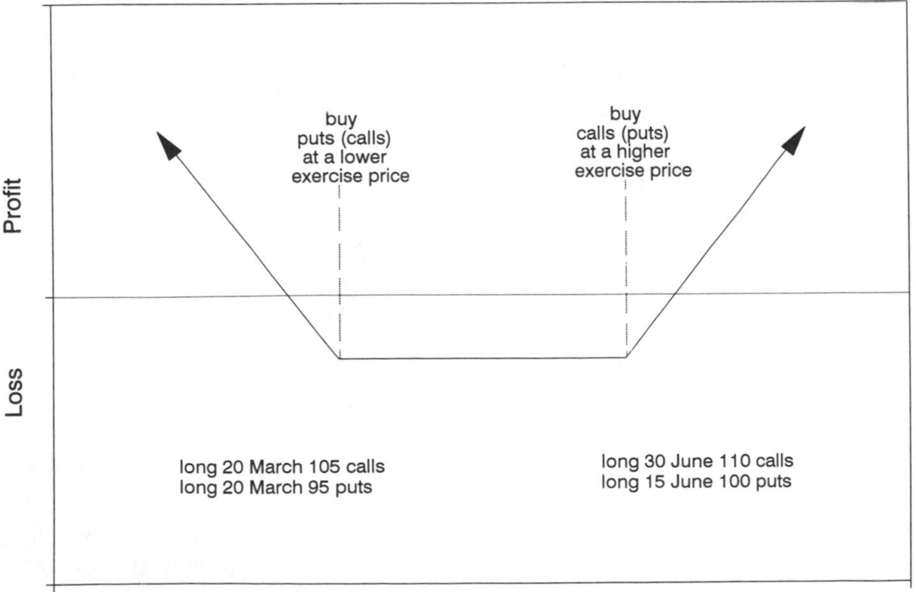

Figure 8-8: Short Strangle

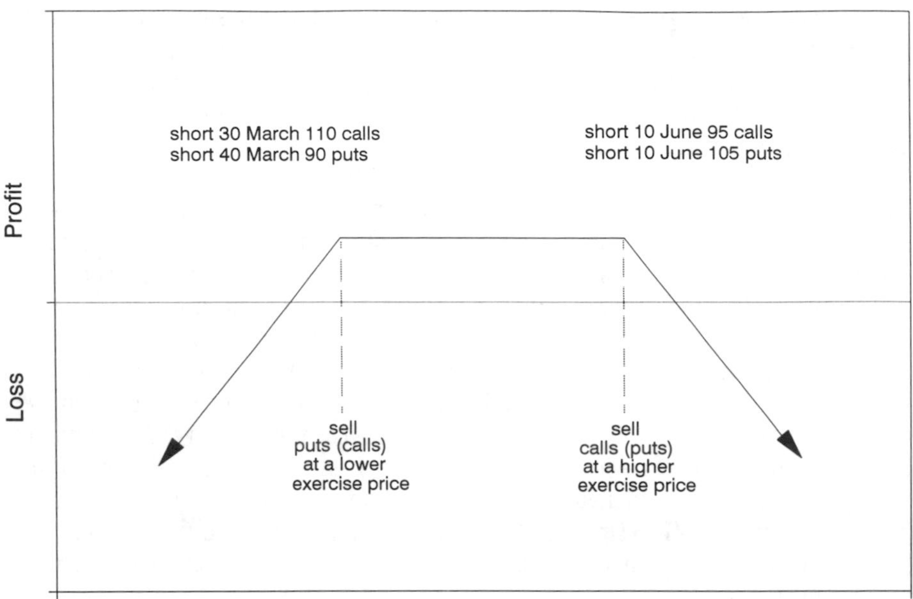

In the absence of other identifying information, strangles, like straddles, are usually executed with a one-to-one ratio (one call for each put). However, there is no law against executing a strangle with some other ratio. If the call has a delta of 15 and the put has a delta of –30, and a trader wants to be delta neutral, it is perfectly acceptable to trade two calls for each put.

If we ignore the limited or unlimited risk/reward characteristics of backspreads, long straddles, and long strangles, these spreads essentially differ in the degree of desired movement. A backspread needs some market movement to show a profit, a long straddle needs more movement, and a long strangle needs even greater movement. Indeed, a strangle is usually considered the most highly leveraged of all option positions because out-of-the-money options are cheap relative to other options. Several strangles can often be purchased for the price of just one straddle. If significant movement occurs with such a position, its value can increase dramatically. But there is a tradeoff. If movement fails to occur, the position will swiftly lose its value through the passage of time.

The same considerations of degree are also true for ratio vertical spreads, short straddles, and short strangles. A ratio vertical spread, a short straddle, and a short strangle all want the market to sit still. But again, the strangle is considered the most highly leveraged of these positions. If a trader sells several strangles and the market does sit still his profits will usually be greater than if he had sold one straddle or done a moderate sized ratio vertical spread. If, however, the market makes an unexpectedly large move, short strangles also entail the greatest risk. All option positions are a tradeoff between risk and reward. If the reward is great, so is the risk; if the risk is small, so is the reward.

Based on their similar characteristics, it is sometimes convenient to classify long straddles and long strangles as special types of backspreads. This follows logically from the definition of a backspread: long more contracts than short, with all options expiring in the same month. A long straddle or strangle consists only of long options (long calls and long puts), with all options expiring at the same time. Hence, these positions are backspreads. (Even though the owner of a put has a short market position, he is said to be long the put because he has purchased it.)

The same reasoning leads us to classify short straddles and strangles as special types of ratio vertical spreads. Short straddles and strangles consist only of short options, with all options expiring at the same time. Hence, the positions conform to our definition of a ratio vertical spread.

BUTTERFLY

Thus far we have looked at spreads which involve buying or selling two different option contracts. However, we need not restrict ourselves to two-sided spreads. We can also construct spreads consisting of three, four, or even more different options. A butterfly consists of options at three equally spaced exercise prices, where all options are of the same type (either all calls or all puts) and expire at the same time. In a long butterfly the outside exercise prices are purchased and the inside exercise price is sold, and vice versa for a short butterfly.[1] Moreover, the ratio of a butterfly never varies. It is always $1 \times 2 \times 1$, with two of each inside exercise price traded for each one of the outside exercise prices. If the ratio is other than $1 \times 2 \times 1$, the spread is no longer a butterfly. Typical examples of long and short butterflies are shown in Figures 8-9 and 8-10.

Since a butterfly consists of equal numbers of long and short options, it does not fit conveniently into the backspread or ratio vertical spread category. However, as commonly traded, a long butterfly tends to act like a ratio vertical spread and a short butterfly tends to act like a backspread. To understand why, consider a trader who buys a 95/100/105 call butterfly (long a 95 call, short two 100 calls, long a 105 call). What will be the value of this position at expiration? If the underlying contract is below 95 at expiration all the calls will expire worthless, and the value of the position will be zero. If the underlying contract is above 105 at expiration, the value of the 95 and 105 calls together will be identical to the value of the two 100 calls. Again, the value of the butterfly will be zero. Now suppose the underlying contract is somewhere between 95 and 105 at expiration, specifically, right at the inside exercise price of 100. The 95 call will be worth 5 points, while the 100 and 105 calls will be worthless. The position will therefore be worth 5 points. If the underlying moves away from 100 the value of the butterfly will decline, but its value can never fall below zero.

---

1. The inside exercise price is sometimes referred to as the *body* of the butterfly, while the outside exercise prices are referred to as the *wings*.

Figure 8-9: Long Butterfly

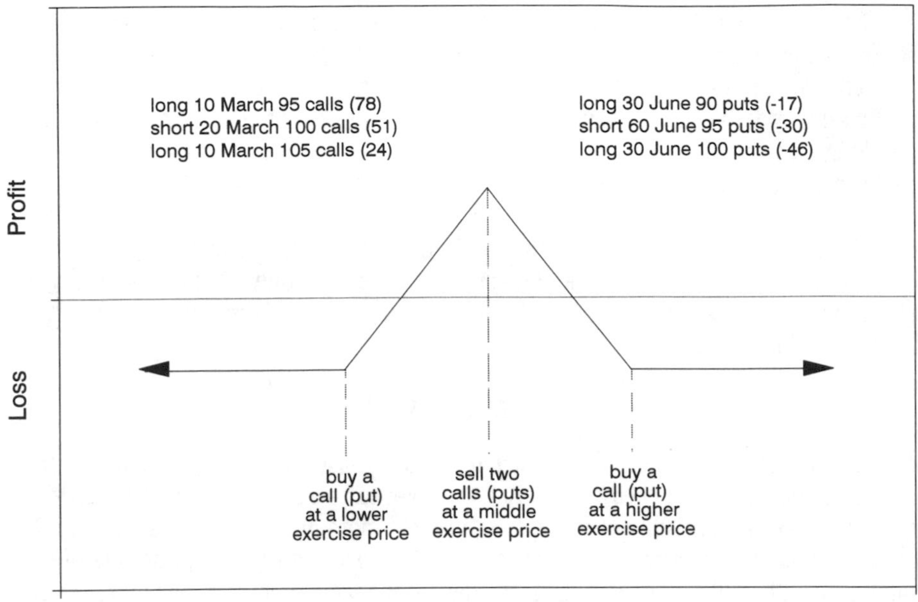
long 10 March 95 calls (78)
short 20 March 100 calls (51)
long 10 March 105 calls (24)
long 30 June 90 puts (-17)
short 60 June 95 puts (-30)
long 30 June 100 puts (-46)
Profit
Loss
buy a call (put) at a lower exercise price
sell two calls (puts) at a middle exercise price
buy a call (put) at a higher exercise price

Figure 8-10: Short Butterfly

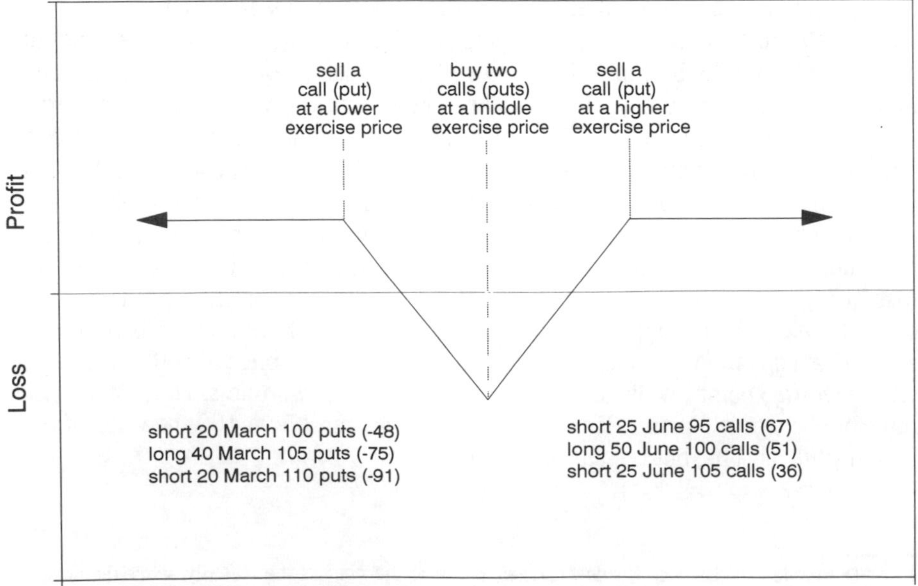
sell a call (put) at a lower exercise price
buy two calls (puts) at a middle exercise price
sell a call (put) at a higher exercise price
Profit
Loss
short 20 March 100 puts (-48)
long 40 March 105 puts (-75)
short 20 March 110 puts (-91)
short 25 June 95 calls (67)
long 50 June 100 calls (51)
short 25 June 105 calls (36)

At expiration a butterfly will always have a value somewhere between zero and the amount between exercise prices. It will be worth zero if the underlying contract is below the lowest exercise price or above the highest exercise price, and it will be worth its maximum if the underlying contract is right at the inside exercise price.

Since a butterfly has a value between zero and the amount between exercise prices (5 points in our example), a trader should be willing to pay some amount between zero and 5 for the position. The exact amount depends on the likelihood of the underlying contract finishing right at or close to the inside price at expiration. If there is high probability of this occurring, a trader might be willing to pay as much as 4¼ or 4½ for the butterfly, since it might very will expand to its full value of 5 points. If, however, there is a low probability of this occurring, and consequently a high probability that the underlying contract will finish outside the extreme exercise prices, a trader may only be willing to pay ½ or ¾, since he may very will lose his entire investment.

Now we can see why a long butterfly tends to act like a ratio vertical spread. If a trader feels that the underlying contract will remain within a narrow range until expiration, he can buy a butterfly where the inside exercise price is at-the-money. If he is right, and the market does stay close to the inside exercise price, the butterfly will expand to its maximum value (Figure 8-9). A long butterfly tends to act like a ratio vertical spread since it increases in value as the underlying market sits still.

In contrast, the trader who sells a butterfly wants the underlying market to move as far away from the inside exercise price as possible so that the position will expire with the underlying contract either below the lowest exercise price or above the highest exercise price. In this case, the butterfly will expire worthless and he will be able to keep the full amount he received when he sold the butterfly (Figure 8-10). A short butterfly tends to act like a backspread since it increases in value with movement in the underlying market.

Why are the strategies in Figure 8-9 referred to as "long" butterflies, and the strategies in Figure 8-10 referred to as "short" butterflies? It is common practice to refer to a spread which requires an outlay of capital as a long, or purchased, spread. If a trader initiates a butterfly by purchasing the outside exercise prices and selling the inside exercise price, he has a position which can never be worth less than zero at expiration. The trader can therefore expect to lay out some amount of capital for the position when he initiates it. When the trader does this, he has purchased, or is "long," the butterfly. (If a trader can initiate a long butterfly for a credit, he should do it as many times as the law will allow; he can't lose.) When the trader sells the outside exercise prices and purchases the inside exercise price, he can expect to receive some amount of capital. He has sold, or is "short," the butterfly.

Since all butterflies are worth their maximum amount when the underlying contract is right at the inside exercise price at expiration, both a call and put butterfly with the same exercise prices and the same expiration date desire exactly the same outcome, and therefore have identical characteristics. Both the March 95/100/105 call butterfly and the March 95/100/105 put butterfly will be worth a maximum of 5 with the underlying contract right at 100 at expiration, and a minimum value of zero with the underlying contract below 95 or above 105. If both butterflies are not trading at the same price, there is a sure profit opportunity available by purchasing the cheaper and selling the more expensive.[2]

If a trader foresees a quiet market, why might he choose a long butterfly over some other type of strategy, for example a short straddle? An important characteristic of a butterfly is its limited risk. If a trader initiates a long butterfly in the belief that the market is unlikely to move very far from the current price, the most he can lose if he is wrong is the amount he laid out to purchase the butterfly. On the other hand, if a trader sells a straddle and the market makes a large move, his potential risk is unlimited. Regardless of theoretical considerations, some traders are not comfortable with the possibility of unlimited risk. If given the choice between purchasing butterflies and selling straddles, they will prefer the former strategy to the latter.

Of course the straddle, while riskier, also has greater profit potential. If a trader intends to purchase butterflies but wants a potential profit commensurate with that of a short straddle, he will have to trade butterflies in much greater size. A trader who is considering the sale of 25 straddles might decide instead to buy 100 butterflies (100 × 200 × 100). While trading 100 spreads may appear riskier than trading 25 spreads, 100 butterflies may in fact be much less risky than 25 straddles because of the risk characteristics associated with a butterfly. A trader should never confuse size and risk. Risk often depends on the characteristics of the strategy, not on the size in which the strategy is executed.

TIME SPREAD
(also referred to as a *calendar spread* or *horizontal spread*)

If all options in a spread expire at the same time, the value of the spread is simply a function of the underlying price at expiration. If, however, the spread consists of options which expire at different times, the value of the spread cannot be determined until both options expire. The spread's value depends not only on where the underlying market is when the short-term option expires, but also on what will happen between that time and the time when the long-term option expires. Time spreads, sometimes referred to as calendar spreads or horizontal spreads,[3] consist of opposing positions which expire in different months.

The most common type of time spread consists of opposing positions in two options of the same type (either both calls or both puts) where both options have the same exercise price. When the long-term option is purchased and the short-term option is sold, a trader is long the time spread; when the short-term option is purchased and the long-term option is sold, the trader is short the time spread. Since a long-term option will have more time value, and therefore a higher price than a short-term option, this is consistent with the practice of referring to any spread which is executed at a debit (credit) as a long (short) spread position.

---

2. This is not necessarily the case if the spreads consist of American options, where there is a possibility of early exercise. A sure profit would exist only if one were certain of carrying the position to expiration.

3. Expiration months were originally listed horizontally on exchange option displays. Hence the term horizontal spread.

Although time spreads are most commonly executed one-to-one (one contract purchased for each contract sold), a trader may ratio a time spread to reflect a bullish, bearish, or neutral market sentiment. For the present we will assume that all time spreads will be ratioed delta neutral. Typical long and short time spreads are shown in Figures 8-11 and 8-12.

A time spread has different characteristics from the other spreads we have discussed, because its value depends not only on movement in the underlying market, but also on other traders' expectations about future market movement as reflected in the implied volatility. If we assume that the options making up a time spread are approximately at-the-money, time spreads have two important characteristics.

A long time spread always wants the underlying market to sit still. An important characteristic of an at-the-money option's theta (time decay) is its tendency to become increasingly large as expiration approaches. As time passes, a short-term at-the-money option, having less time to expiration, will lose its value at a greater rate than a long-term at-the-money option. (Note the value of at-the-money options in Figures 6-13 and 6-14, and the theta values in Figure 6-15.) This principle has an important effect on the value of a time spread.

For example, suppose two at-the-money calls, one with three months to expiration and one with six months to expiration, have values of 6 and 7½, respectively. The value of the spread is therefore 1½. If one month passes and the underlying market is unchanged, both options will lose value. But the short-term option, with its greater theta, will lose a greater amount. If the long-term option loses ¼, the short-term option

Figure 8-11: Long Time Spread (Value at Near Term Expiration)

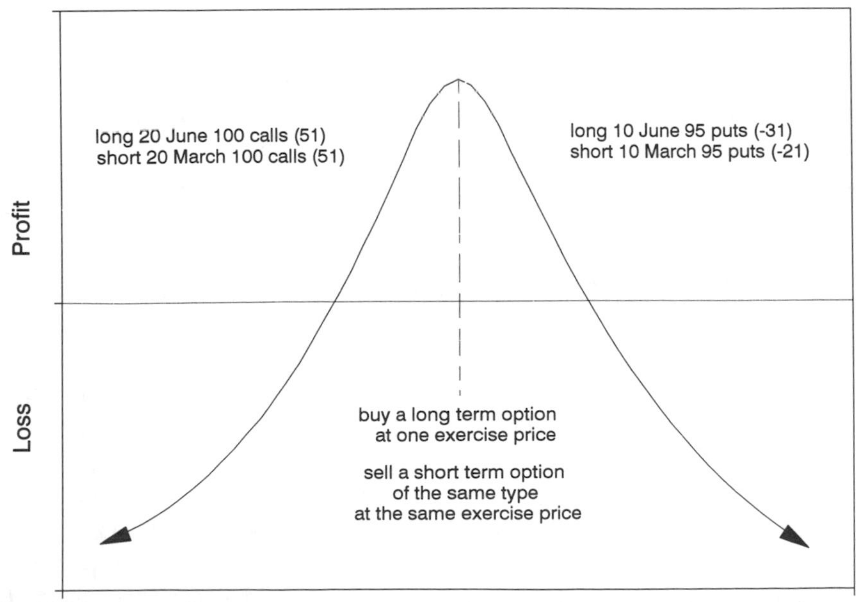

Figure 8-12: Short Time Spread (Value at Near Term Expiration)

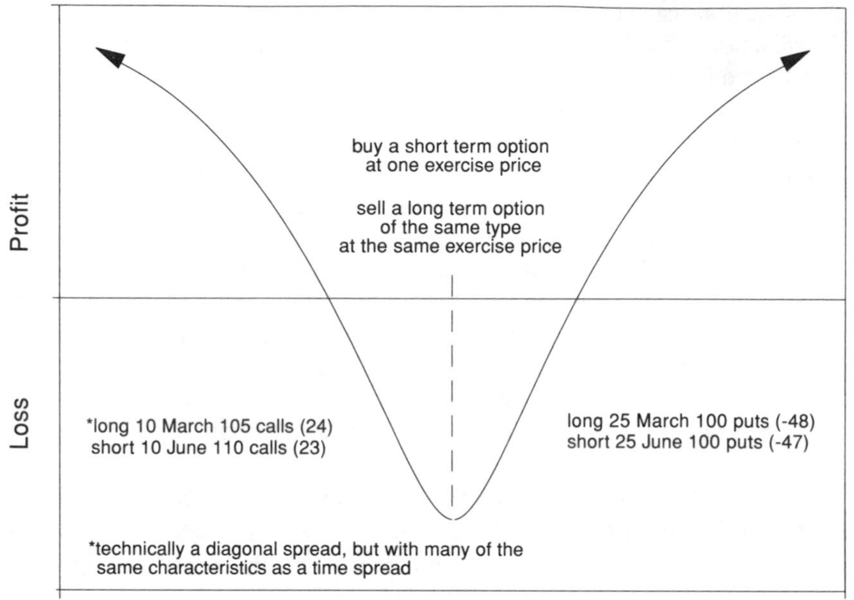

may lose a full point. Now the options are worth 5 and 7¼, and the spread is worth 2¼. If another month passes and the market is still unchanged, both options will continue to decay, But, again, the short-term option, with less time remaining to expiration, will decay at a greater rate. If the long-term option loses ½, the short term option may lose 2 points. Now the options are worth 3 and 6¾, and the spread has increased in value to 3¾. Finally, if at expiration the market is still unchanged, the short-term option, since it is still at-the-money, will lose all of its remaining value of 3 points. The long-term option will continue to decay but will do so at a slower rate. If the long-term option loses ¾, it will be worth 6 points, and the spread will be worth 6 points (Figure 8-13).

What will happen if the underlying market makes a larger move? Assume as before that both options are at-the-money and have values of 7½ and 6. As the underlying market rises and options move more deeply into-the-money, they begin to lose their time value. If the move is large enough, it won't matter that the long-term option has three more months remaining to expiration. Both options will eventually lose all their time value (see Figures 6-15 and 6-16). If the time spread consists of calls, both of which have exercise prices of 100, and the underlying market moves from 100 to 150, both options might trade at parity (intrinsic value), or 50 points. The spread will then go to zero. Even if the long-term option retains as much as ¼ point, the spread will still have collapsed to ¼.

What about a large downward move in the underlying market? The situation is almost identical to an upward move. As an option moves further out-of-the-money its

Figure 8-13: The Effect of Time Passage on Time Spreads

Time to Expiration				
Long-term option	6 months	5 months	4 months	3 months
Short-term option	3 months	2 months	1 month	none
Option Value				
Long-term option	7½	7¼	6¾	6
Short-term option	6	5	3	0
Spread Value	1½	2¼	3¾	6

time value also begins to shrink. Here, however, neither option will have any intrinsic value, so that if the market moves down far enough both options will eventually be worthless. If that happens, the time spread will be worthless. If, as above, the long-term option retains even ¼ point in value, the spread will still collapse to ¼ point.

Since a short-term at-the-money option always decays more quickly than a long-term at-the-money option, regardless of whether the options are calls or puts, both a long call time spread and a long put time spread want the underlying market to sit still. Ideally, both spreads would like the short-term option to expire right at-the-money so that the long-term option will retain as much time value as possible while the short-term option expires worthless.

If a long time spread wants the market to sit still, logically a short time spread wants the market to move. It may therefore seem that, as with backspreads and ratio vertical spreads, the major consideration in deciding whether to initiate a long or short time spread is the likelihood of movement in the underlying market. Certainly time spreads are sensitive to movement in the price of the underlying, but time spreads are also sensitive to changes in implied volatility.

A long time spread always benefits from an increase in implied volatility. Look again at Figure 6-18, the relationship between an option's vega (sensitivity to a change in volatility) and the time remaining to expiration. As time to expiration increases, the vega of an option increases. This means that a long-term option is always more sensitive in total points to a change in volatility than a short-term option with the same exercise price.

For example, assume again that a 100 call time spread is worth 1½ (long- and short-term options with values of 7½ and 6, respectively). Assume also that the value of the spread is based on a volatility of 20%. What will happen to the value of the spread if we raise volatility to 25%? Both options will increase in value since an increase in volatility increases the value of all options. But the long-term option, with more time remaining to expiration and therefore a higher vega, will gain more value as a result of the increase in volatility. If the short-term option gains ½, the long-term option may gain a full point. Now the options will be worth 8½ and 6½, and the spread will have widened from 1½ to 2 (Figure 8-14).

Figure 8-14: The Effect of Volatility on Time Spreads

Volatility	15%	20%	25%
Option Value			
Long term option	6½	7½	8½
Short term option	5½	6	6½
Spread Value	1	1½	2

Conversely, if we lower our volatility estimate to 15%, both options will lose value. But the long-term option, with more time remaining to expiration, will be more sensitive to the change in volatility and will lose a greater amount. The new option values might be 6½ and 5½, causing the spread to narrow to 1 point.

The effects of volatility on a time spread become especially evident when there is a change in implied volatility in the option market. When implied volatility rises, time spreads tend to widen; when implied volatility falls, time spreads tend to narrow. This effect can often be great enough to offset either a favorable or unfavorable move in the underlying market. A trader who is long a time spread expects to lose money if the underlying market makes a swift move in either direction. He knows that time spreads begin to collapse as the options move into- or out-of-the-money. But if this movement is accompanied by a sufficient increase in implied volatility, the increase in the spread's price due to the increase in implied volatility may actually be greater than the loss due to market movement. In that case the trader may find that the spread has actually widened. Conversely, if the market sits still, the trader expects the spread to widen because of the short-term option's greater time decay. But if, at the same time, there is a collapse in implied volatility, the decline in the spread's price due to the decline in implied volatility may more than offset any gain from the passage of time. If this happens, the trader may find that the spread has narrowed.

These two opposing forces, the decay in an option's value due to the passage of time and the change in an option's value due to changes in volatility, give time spreads their unique characteristics. When a trader buys or sells a time spread, he is not only attempting to forecast movement in the underlying market. He is also trying to forecast changes in implied volatility. The trader would like to forecast both inputs accurately, but often an error in one input can be offset by an accurate forecast for the other input.

Ideally, the trader who is long a time spread wants two apparently contradictory conditions in the marketplace. First, he wants the underlying market to sit still so that time decay will have a beneficial effect on the spread. Second, he wants everyone to think the market is going to move so that implied volatility will rise. This may seem an impossible scenario, the market remaining unchanged but everyone thinking it will move. In fact, this happens quite often because events which don't have an immediate effect on the underlying market could be perceived to have a future effect on the market.

Suppose an announcement is made that the finance ministers of the major industrialized countries plan to meet to discuss exchange rates. If no one knows what the outcome of the meeting will be, there is unlikely to be any significant move in the currency markets when the initial announcement is made. On the other hand, all traders will assume that major changes in exchange rates could result from the meeting. This possibility will result in an increase in implied volatility in the currency option market. The lack of movement in the underlying market, together with the increase in implied volatility, will cause time spreads to widen.

Suppose that, as a result of the meeting, the finance ministers decide to maintain the status quo. Now expectations of a major change in exchange rates fade, implied volatility falls, and, as a result, time spreads narrow.

Scenarios with similar consequences also occur in the interest rate options market when a policy statement is expected from the Federal Reserve in the United States, or when a company's earnings are due to be reported in the stock option market. These events are unlikely to have an effect on the underlying market before the fact, but they could have significant repercussions after the fact.

The effect of implied volatility is what distinguishes time spreads from the other types of spreads we have discussed. Backspreads (including long straddles, long strangles, and short butterflies) and ratio vertical spreads (including short straddles, short strangles, and long butterflies) want real volatility (price movement in the underlying market) and implied volatility (a reflection of expectations about future price movement in the underlying market) to either both rise or both fall. A swift move in the underlying market or an increase in implied volatility will help a backspread. A quiet market or a decrease in implied volatility will help a ratio vertical spread. With time spreads, however, real and implied volatility have opposite effects. A big move in the underlying market or a decrease in implied volatility will help a short time spread, while a quiet market or an increase in implied volatility will help a long time spread. This opposite effect is what gives time spreads their unique characteristics.

While the foregoing characteristics of time spreads apply to all option markets, there may be other considerations, depending on the specific underlying market. We previously assumed that the price of the underlying contract for both the short- and long-term option was the same. In the stock option market this will always be true because the underlying for every expiration is the same stock. The underlying contract for all IBM options, regardless of the expiration month, is always IBM stock. And IBM stock can only have a single price at any one time. In contrast, the underlying for a futures option is a specific futures contract. Consider this situation for Eurodollar futures and options traded at the CME:

March Eurodollar Futures = 93.90
June Eurodollar Futures = 93.75

Suppose a trader initiates a long time spread:

long 10 June 94.00 calls
short 10 March 94.00 calls

The underlying for March Eurodollar options is a March Eurodollar futures contract; the underlying for June Eurodollar options is a June Eurodollar futures contract.

While the March and June Eurodollar futures contracts are related, they are not identical. It is not impossible for one futures contract to go up while the other goes down. As a result, in addition to volatility considerations, a trader who buys a June/March Eurodollar option call time spread also has to worry about the risk of the June futures contract falling while the March futures contract is rising. Is there any way to offset this risk?

If, in our example, the spread between the March and June futures contracts, which is currently .15, begins to widen, the option spread will narrow regardless of volatility considerations. If, however, when the trader initiates the option spread, he also executes a futures spread by purchasing March futures and selling June futures, he will have a position which will offset any loss to the option spread resulting from a widening in the futures spread.

How many futures spreads should the trader execute? He ought to trade the number of futures spreads required to be delta neutral. If the delta of both options is 40 and the trader executes the option spread ten times, he will be long 400 deltas in June and short 400 deltas in March. Therefore, he should buy 4 March futures contracts and sell 4 June futures contracts. The entire spread will look like this (deltas are in parentheses):

long 10 June 94.00 calls (40)	short 4 June futures (100)
short 10 March 94.00 calls (40)	long 4 March futures (100)

This type of balancing is not necessary, indeed not possible, in stock options because the underlying for all months is identical. There is no such thing as March IBM stock or June IBM stock.

THE EFFECT OF CHANGING INTEREST RATES AND DIVIDENDS

Thus far we have considered only the effects of changes in the price of the underlying market and changes in volatility on the value of volatility spreads. What about changes in interest rates and, in the case of stocks, dividends?

Because there is no carrying cost associated with the purchase or sale of a futures contract, interest rates have only a minor impact on futures options, and, consequently, a negligible effect on the value of futures option volatility spreads.[4] If, however, we are trading stock options and change the interest rate, we change the forward price of stock (the current stock price plus the carrying cost on the stock to expiration). When all options expire at the same time, as they do in backspreads and ratio vertical spreads, the forward stock price for all options remains the same, so that the effects of the change are practically negligible. If, on the other hand, we are considering stock options with different expiration dates, we must consider two different forward prices. And these two forward prices may not be equally sensitive to a change in interest rates. For example, consider the following situation:

---

4. Interest rates can of course affect the relative value of different futures months. As noted, we can offset this risk by trading a futures spread along with the futures option time spread.

Stock price = 100   Interest rate = 12%   Dividend = 0

Suppose a trader initiates a long time spread:

long 10 June 100 calls
short 10 March 100 calls

If there are three months remaining to March expiration and six months remaining to June expiration, the forward prices for March and June stock are 103 and 106, respectively. If interest rates drop to 8 percent, the forward price for March will be 102 and the forward price for June will be 104. With more time remaining, the June forward price is more sensitive to a change in interest rates. Assuming the deltas of both options are approximately equal, the June option will be more affected in total points by the decline in interest rates than the March option, and the time spread will narrow. In the same way, if interest rates increase, the time spread will widen because the June forward price will rise more quickly than the March forward price. Therefore, a long (short) call time spread in the stock option market must have a positive (negative) rho.

Changes in interest rates have just the opposite effect on stock option puts. In our example, if interest rates fall from 12% to 8% the March forward price will fall from 103 to 102, while the June forward price will fall from 106 to 104. Again, if we assume that the deltas of both options are approximately equal, and recalling that puts have negative deltas, the June put will show a greater increase in value than the March put. The put time spread will therefore widen. In the same way, if interest rates increase, the put time spread will narrow. Therefore, a long (short) put time spread in the stock option market must have a negative (positive) rho.

The degree to which stock option time spreads are affected by changes in interest rates depends primarily on the amount of time between expiration dates. If there are six months between expiration dates (e.g., March/September) the effect will be much greater than if there is only one month between expiration dates (e.g., March/April).

Changes in dividends can also affect the value of stock option time spreads. Dividends, however, have the opposite effect on stock options as changes in interest rates (see Chapter 3). An increase (decrease) in dividends lowers (raises) the forward price of stock. If all options in a volatility spread expire at the same time (backspreads, ratio vertical spreads), the forward stock price will be identical for all options and the effect on the spread will be negligible. But in a time spread, if a dividend payment is expected between expiration of the short-term and long-term option, the long-term option will be affected by the lowered forward price of the stock. Hence, an increase in dividends, if at least one dividend payment is expected between the expiration dates, will cause call time spreads to narrow and put time spreads to widen. A decrease in dividends will have the opposite effect, with call time spreads widening and put time spreads narrowing. The effect of changing interest rates and dividends on stock option time spreads is shown in Figure 8-15.

Even if both options are deeply in-the-money, a call time spread in the stock option market should always have some value greater than zero. If volatility is very low, the spread should still be worth a minimum of the cost of carry on the stock between

Figure 8-15

The Effects of Changing Interest Rates on Stock Option Time Spreads

Stock Price = 100; Volatility = 20%; Dividend = 0
Time to March expiration = 6 weeks
Time to June expiration = 19 weeks

If interest rates are . . .	**0%**	**3%**	**6%**	**9%**	**12%**
June 100 call	4.81	5.35	5.92	6.52	7.15
March 100 call	2.71	2.88	3.05	3.24	3.43
Call Spread Value	2.10	2.47	2.87	3.28	3.72
June 100 put	4.81	4.26	3.76	3.30	2.88
March 100 put	2.71	2.53	2.37	2.21	2.06
Put Spread Value	2.10	1.73	1.39	1.09	.82

The Effect of Changing Dividends on Stock Option Time Spreads

Stock Price = 100; Volatility = 20%; Interest Rate = 6.00%
Time to March expiration = 6 weeks
Time to June expiration = 19 weeks

If the quarterly dividend is . . .	**0**	**1.00**	**2.00**	**3.00**	**4.00**
June 100 call	5.92	4.81	3.82	2.97	2.26
March 100 call	3.05	2.53	2.07	1.66	1.31
Call Spread Value	2.87	2.28	1.75	1.31	.95
June 100 put	3.76	4.62	5.62	6.75	8.01
March 100 put	2.37	2.84	3.37	3.96	4.62
Put Spread Value	1.39	1.78	2.25	2.79	3.39

expiration months. This is only true, however, if a trader can carry a short stock position between expiration months. If a situation arises where no stock can be borrowed, the trader who owns a time spread may be forced to exercise his long-term option, thereby losing the time value associated with the option.

As an example, suppose in February a company's stock is trading at 70, when a tender offer is made to buy a portion of the outstanding stock at a price of 80. If a trader is long a June/March 70 call time spread, he will be assigned on the March 70 call because the holder of that call wants to tender his stock for sale at 80. The trader is now short stock and long a June 70 call. The June call should still carry some time value because of the interest which can be earned on the short stock to June expiration. But in order to carry a short stock position, the trader must deliver the stock to the exerciser of the March 70 call. To deliver the stock, he must borrow it from someone. Unfortunately, no one will lend stock to the trader because everyone wants to tender the stock for sale at the tender price of 80. Unless the trader wants to go into the market and buy the stock at the tender price of 80, he will be forced to exercise his June 70 call. This is the only method by which the trader can obtain stock for delivery to the exerciser of the March 70 call. Even though the June 70 call should in theory have some time value, the trader will be forced to discard the time value in order to fulfill his delivery obligation.

In the foregoing situation, sometimes referred to as a *short squeeze*, a trader is forced to exercise calls with some time value remaining because no stock can be borrowed to carry a short stock position. Anyone who owns the June/March 70 call time spread will be forced to exercise the June 70 call, and the price of the time spread will collapse to zero. Note that this situation is not the same as a buy-out, where all the stock in a company is purchased at one price. Although a tender offer was made at 80, it was for only a portion of the company's outstanding stock. When the tender is completed, the remaining stock will continue to trade, most likely at its pre-tender price of 70.

DIAGONAL SPREADS

A diagonal spread is similar to a time spread, except that the options have different exercise prices. While many diagonal spreads are executed one-to-one (one long-term option for each short-term option), diagonal spreads can also be ratioed, with unequal numbers of long and short market contracts. With the large number of variations in diagonal spreads, it is almost impossible to generalize about their characteristics as we can with backspreads, ratio vertical spreads, and long and short time spreads. Each diagonal spread must be analyzed separately, often using a computer, to determine the risks and rewards associated with the spread.

There is, however, one type of diagonal spread about which we can generalize. If a diagonal spread is done one-to-one, and both options are of the same type and have approximately the same delta, the diagonal spread will act very much like a conventional time spread. An example of a such diagonal spread is shown in Figure 8-12.

OTHER VARIATIONS

The spreads we have thus far defined are the primary types of volatility spreads, and are the ones most commonly executed in the marketplace. There are, however, some variations of which the reader ought to be aware.

A *Christmas tree* (also referred to as a *ladder)* is a term which can be applied to a variety of spreads. The spread usually consists of three different exercise prices where all options are of the same type and expire at the same time. In a long (short) call Christmas tree, one call is purchased (sold) at the lowest exercise price, and one call is sold (purchased) at each of the higher exercise prices. In a long (short) put Christmas tree, one put is purchased (sold) at the highest exercise price, and one put is sold (purchased) at each of the lower exercise prices. Christmas trees are usually delta neutral, but even with this restriction, there are many ways to execute the spread. Some examples of Christmas trees are shown in Figure 8-16.

Long Christmas trees, when done delta neutral, can be thought of as particular types of ratio vertical spreads. Such spreads therefore increase in value if the underlying market either sits still or moves very slowly. Short Christmas trees can be thought of as

Figure 8-16

Long Christmas Trees	**Short Christmas Trees**
long 10 March 95 calls (78)	short 5 June 90 calls (81)
short 10 March 100 calls (51)	long 5 June 100 calls (51)
short 10 March 105 calls (24)	long 5 June 105 calls (36)
long 25 June 110 puts (–75)	short 50 March 110 puts (–91)
short 25 June 100 puts (–47)	long 50 March 105 puts (–75)
short 25 June 95 puts (–31)	long 50 March 95 puts (–21)

particular types of backspreads, and therefore increase in value with big moves in the underlying market.

It is possible to construct a spread which has the same characteristics as a butterfly by purchasing a straddle (strangle) and selling a strangle (straddle) where the straddle is executed at an exercise price midway between the strangle's exercise prices. All options must expire at the same time. Because the position wants the same outcome as a butterfly, it is known as an *iron butterfly*. Like a true butterfly, at expiration an iron butterfly has a minimum value of zero and a maximum value of the amount between exercise prices.

Note that if the straddle is purchased and the strangle is sold, the position will result in a debit (a long iron butterfly). Such a position will show its greatest profit at expiration if the underlying market finishes beyond the outside (strangle's) exercise prices. A long iron butterfly is therefore equivalent to a short butterfly. If the straddle is sold and the strangle is purchased, the position will result in a debit (a short iron butterfly). Such a position will show its greatest profit at expiration if the underlying market finishes right at the inside (straddle's) exercise price. A short iron butterfly is therefore equivalent to a long butterfly. Examples of long and short iron butterflies are shown in Figure 8-17.

Another variation on a butterfly, known as a *condor*, can be constructed by splitting the inside exercise prices. Now the position consists of four options at consecutive exercise prices where the two outside options are purchased and the two inside options sold (a long condor), or the two inside options are purchased and the two outside options sold (a short condor). As with a butterfly, all options must be of the same type (all calls or all puts) and expire at the same time.

At expiration a condor will have its maximum value, equivalent to the amount between consecutive exercise prices, when the underlying contract is at or anywhere between the two inside exercise prices. It will be worthless whenever the underlying contract is outside the extreme exercise prices at expiration. Note that this is very similar to a butterfly, except that a condor has a maximum value over a wider range of underlying prices. A butterfly will achieve its maximum value at expiration at only one underlying price, when the underlying contract is right at the inside exercise price. For this reason a condor will usually have a higher value than a butterfly with approximately the same exercise prices. Examples of long and short condors are shown in Figure 8-18.

Figure 8-17

Long Iron Butterflies	**Short Iron Butterflies**
long 10 March 100 calls (51)	short 15 June 100 calls (51)
long 10 March 100 puts (–48)	short 15 June 100 puts (–47)
short 10 March 105 calls (24)	long 15 June 105 calls (36)
short 10 March 95 puts (–21)	long 15 June 95 puts (–31)
long 50 June 100 calls (51)	short 25 March 105 calls (24)
long 50 June 100 puts (–47)	short 25 March 105 puts (–75)
short 50 June 110 calls (23)	long 25 March 110 calls (8)
short 50 June 90 puts (–17)	long 25 March 100 puts (–48)

SPREAD SENSITIVITIES

Just as every individual option has a unique delta, gamma, theta, vega, and rho associated with it, every spread position has unique sensitivities. These numbers can help a trader determine beforehand how changing market conditions are likely to affect the spread. Before proceeding further the reader may want to review Figure 6-27, which summarizes the significance of the signs associated with the various option sensitivities.

A trader who initiates a volatility spread is concerned primarily with the magnitude of movement in the underlying contract and only secondarily with the direction of movement. Therefore all volatility spreads will be approximately delta neutral (the deltas will add up to approximately zero). It is true that some volatility spreads may prefer movement in one direction rather than the other, but the primary consideration is whether movement of any type will occur. If a trader has a large positive or negative delta, such that directional considerations become more important than volatility considerations, then the position can no longer be considered a volatility spread.

All spreads which are helped by movement in the underlying market have a positive gamma. These include backspreads, long straddles, long strangles, short butterflies, and short time spreads. All spreads which are hurt by movement in the underlying market will have a negative gamma. These include ratio vertical spreads, short straddles, short

Figure 8-18

Long Condors	**Short Condors**
long 10 March 90 calls (93)	short 50 March 95 puts (–21)
short 10 March 95 calls (78)	long 50 March 100 puts (–48)
short 10 March 100 calls (51)	long 50 March 105 puts (–75)
long 10 March 105 calls (24)	short 50 March 110 puts (–91)
long 25 June 95 puts (–31)	short 5 June 90 calls (81)
short 25 June 100 puts (–47)	long 5 June 95 calls (67)
short 25 June 105 puts (–62)	long 5 June 100 calls (51)
long 25 June 110 puts (–75)	short 5 June 105 calls (36)

strangles, long butterflies, and long time spreads. A trader who has a positive gamma is sometimes said to be *long premium* and is hoping for a volatile market with large moves in the underlying contract. A trader who has a negative gamma is sometimes said to be *short premium* and is hoping for a quiet market with only small moves in the underlying market.

Since the effect of market movement and the effect of time decay always work in opposite directions, any spread with a positive gamma will necessarily have a negative theta. Any spread with a negative gamma will necessarily have a positive theta. If market movement helps, the passage of time hurts. If market movement hurts, the passage of time helps. An option trader can't have it both ways.

Spreads which are helped by a rise in volatility have a positive vega. These include backspreads, long straddles, long strangles, short butterflies, and long time spreads. Spreads which are helped by a decline in volatility have a negative vega. These include ratio vertical spreads, short straddles, short strangles, long butterflies, and short time spreads. In theory, the vega refers to the sensitivity of a theoretical value to a change in the volatility of the underlying contract over the life of the option. In practice, however, traders tend to associate the vega with the sensitivity of an option's price to a change in implied volatility. Spreads with a positive vega will be helped (hurt) by any increase (decrease) in implied volatility. Spreads with a negative vega will be helped (hurt) by any decrease (increase) in implied volatility.

The delta, gamma, theta, and vega associated with the primary types of volatility spreads are summarized in Figure 8-19. Since the delta of a volatility spread is assumed to be approximately zero, and since the theta is always of opposite sign to the gamma but of similar magnitude, we can place every volatility spread into one of four categories based on the sign of the gamma and vega associated with the spread:

Category	**Gamma**	**Vega**
Backspread	Positive	Positive
Ratio Vertical Spread	Negative	Negative
Long Time Spread	Negative	Positive
Short Time Spread	Positive	Negative

If a trader is approximately delta neutral—no matter how complex the position, even if it includes options of different types, at many different exercise prices, and with several different expiration dates—he can always place the position in one of these four general categories based on the gamma and vega of the position. The extent to which he is pursuing one of these strategies will depend on the magnitude of the gamma and vega. A trader with a gamma of −100 and vega of +200 would describe his position as a long time spread, but not nearly to the degree of a trader who has a gamma of −1500 and a vega of +3000.

Figure 8-20 is an evaluation table with the theoretical value, delta, gamma, theta, and vega of several different options. Following this table are examples of volatility spreads of the types discussed in this chapter, along with their total delta, gamma, theta, and vega. (Although the examples in Figure 8-20 are based on futures options, the

Figure 8-19: Characteristics of Volatility Spreads

Spread Type	Delta Position	Gamma Position	Theta Position	Vega Position
Backspread	0	+	–	+
Long Straddle	0	+	–	+
Long Strangle	0	+	–	+
Short Butterfly	0	+	–	+
Ratio Vertical Spread	0	–	+	–
Short Straddle	0	–	+	–
Short Strangle	0	–	+	–
Long Butterfly	0	–	+	–
Long Time Spread	0	–	+	+
Short Time Spread	0	+	–	–

spread characteristics are equally valid for stock options.) The reader will see that each spread does indeed have the positive or negative sensitivities summarized in Figure 8-19. Note also that a volatility spread need not be exactly delta neutral. (Indeed, as we saw in Chapter 6, no trader can say with any certainty whether he is delta neutral.) A practical guide is for the delta to be close enough to zero so that the volatility considerations are more important than the directional considerations.

Note that no price is given for any of the option contracts in Figure 8-20, and therefore no theoretical edge can be calculated for any of the spreads. The prices at which a spread is executed may be good or bad, resulting in a positive or negative theoretical edge. But once the spread has been established, the market conditions which will help or hurt the spread are determined by its type, not by the initial prices. Like all traders, option traders must not let their previous trading activity affect their current judgement. A trader's primary concern ought never be what happened yesterday, but what he can do today to make the most of the current situation, whether that means maximizing his potential profit or minimizing his potential loss.

CHOOSING AN APPROPRIATE STRATEGY

With so many spreads available, how do we know which type of spread is best? First and foremost we will want to choose spreads which have a positive theoretical edge to ensure that if we are right about market conditions we can be confident of showing a profit. Ideally, we would like to construct a spread by purchasing options which are underpriced and selling options which are overpriced. If we can do this the resulting spread, whatever its type, will always have a positive theoretical edge.

More often, however, our opinion about volatility will result in all options appearing either underpriced or overpriced. When this happens, it will be impossible to both

Figure 8–20: Examples of Volatility Spreads

5 February 1993
March Futures = 100.00* Time to Expiration = 6 weeks Volatility = 20.0% Interest Rate = 6.00%

Exercise Price	CALLS Theoretical Value	Delta	Gamma	Theta	Vega	PUTS Theoretical Value	Delta	Gamma	Theta	Vega
Mar 90	10.10	93	1.7	–.0069	.040	.17	–6	1.7	–.0090	.040
Mar 95	5.82	78	4.3	–.0221	.100	.85	–21	4.3	–.0232	.100
Mar 100	2.69	51	5.8	–.0313	.134	2.68	–48	5.8	–.0313	.134
Mar 105	.95	24	4.6	–.0250	.107	5.92	–75	4.6	–.0240	.107
Mar 110	.26	8	2.3	–.0124	.055	10.16	–91	2.3	–.0103	.055

June Futures = 100.00* Time to expiration = 19 weeks Volatility = 20.0% Interest Rate = 6.00%

Exercise Price	CALLS Theoretical Value	Delta	Gamma	Theta	Vega	PUTS Theoretical Value	Delta	Gamma	Theta	Vega
Jun 90	10.97	81	2.1	–.0090	.154	1.18	–17	2.1	–.0111	.154
Jun 95	7.45	67	2.9	–.0140	.209	2.55	–31	2.9	–.0151	.209
Jun 100	4.71	51	3.2	–.0166	.234	4.71	–47	3.2	–.0166	.234
Jun 105	2.77	36	3.0	–.0160	.221	7.66	–62	3.0	–.0149	.221
Jun 110	1.52	23	2.5	–.0132	.182	11.30	–75	2.5	–.0111	.182

* For simplicity we assume that both futures contracts are trading at the same price.

Figure 8-20: Examples of Volatility Spreads (continued)

CALL BACKSPREAD: Long more calls than short; all calls expiring at the same time.

	Delta Position	Gamma Position	Theta Position	Vega Position
Long 30 March 105 calls	+30 × 24	+30 × 4.6	+30 × −.0250	+30 × .107
Short 10 March 95 calls	−10 × 78	−10 × 4.3	−10 × −.0221	−10 × .100
	−60	+95.0	−.9710	+2.210
Long 25 Jun 110 calls	+25 × 23	+25 × 2.5	+25 × −.0132	+25 × .182
Short 10 Jun 100 calls	−10 × 51	−10 × 3.2	−10 × −.0166	−10 × .234
	+65	+30.5	−.1640	+2.210

PUT BACKSPREAD: Long more puts than short; all puts expiring at the same time.

	Delta Position	Gamma Position	Theta Position	Vega Position
Long 80 March 90 puts	+80 × −6	+80 × 1.7	+80 × −.0090	+80 × .040
Short 10 March 100 puts	−10 × −48	−10 × 5.8	−10 × −.0313	−10 × .134
	0	+78.0	−.4070	+1.860
Long 45 June 95 puts	+45 × −31	+45 × 2.9	+45 × −.0151	+45 × .209
Short 30 June 100 puts	−30 × −47	−30 × 3.2	−30 × −.0166	−30 × .234
	+15	+34.5	−.1815	+2.385

CALL RATIO VERTICAL SPREAD: Short more calls than long; all calls expiring at the same time.

	Delta Position	Gamma Position	Theta Position	Vega Position
Long 20 March 95 calls	+20 × 78	+20 × 4.3	+20 × −.0221	+20 × .100
Short 30 March 100 calls	−30 × 51	−30 × 5.8	−30 × −.0313	−30 × .134
	+30	−88.0	+.4970	−2.020
Long 10 June 90 calls	+10 × 81	+10 × 2.1	+10 × −.0090	+10 × .154
Short 20 June 105 calls	−20 × 36	−20 × 3.0	−20 × −.0160	−20 × .221
	+90	−39.0	+.2300	−2.880

PUT RATIO VERTICAL SPREAD: Short more puts than long; all puts expiring at the same time.

	Delta Position	Gamma Position	Theta Position	Vega Position
Long 20 March 95 puts	+20 × −21	+20 × 4.3	+20 × −.0232	+20 × .100
Short 60 March 90 puts	−60 × −6	−60 × 1.7	−60 × −.0090	−60 × .040
	−60	−16.0	+.0760	−.400
Long 15 June 105 puts	+15 × −62	+15 × 3.0	+15 × −.0149	+15 × .221
Short 20 June 100 puts	−20 × −47	−20 × 3.2	−20 × −.0166	−20 × .234
	+10	−19.0	+.1085	−1.365

Figure 8-20: Examples of Volatility Spreads (continued)

LONG STRADDLE: Long calls and puts with the same expiration date and exercise price.

	Delta Position	Gamma Position	Theta Position	Vega Position
Long 10 March 100 calls	+10 × +51	+10 × 5.8	+10 × −.0313	+10 × .134
Long 10 March 100 puts	+10 × −48	+10 × 5.8	+10 × −.0313	+10 × .134
	+30	+116.0	−.6260	+2.680
Long 10 June 95 calls	+10 × +67	+10 × 2.9	+10 × −.0140	+10 × .209
Long 25 June 95 puts	+25 × −31	+25 × 2.9	+25 × −.0151	+25 × .209
	−105	+101.5	−.5175	+7.315

SHORT STRADDLE: Short calls and puts with the same expiration date and exercise price.

	Delta Position	Gamma Position	Theta Position	Vega Position
Short 30 March 105 calls	−30 × +24	−30 × 4.6	−30 × −.0250	−30 × .107
Short 10 March 105 puts	−10 × −75	−10 × 4.6	−10 × −.0240	−10 × .107
	+30	−184.0	+.9900	−4.280
Short 20 June 100 calls	−20 × +51	−20 × 3.2	−20 × −.0166	−20 × .234
Short 20 June 100 puts	−20 × −47	−20 × 3.2	−20 × −.0166	−20 × .234
	−80	−128.0	+.6640	+9.36

LONG STRANGLE: Long calls and puts with the same expiration date but different exercise prices.

	Delta Position	Gamma Position	Theta Position	Vega Position
Long 20 March 105 calls	+20 × +24	+20 × 4.6	+20 × −.0250	+20 × .107
Long 20 March 95 puts	+20 × −21	+20 × 4.3	+20 × −.0232	+20 × .100
	+60	+178.0	−.9640	+4.140
Long 30 June 110 calls	+30 × +23	+30 × 2.5	+30 × −.0132	+30 × .182
Long 15 June 100 puts	+15 × −47	+15 × 3.2	+15 × −.0166	+15 × .234
	−15	+123.0	−.6450	+8.970

SHORT STRANGLE: Short calls and puts with the same expiration date but different exercise prices.

	Delta Position	Gamma Position	Theta Position	Vega Position
Short 30 March 110 calls	−30 × +8	−30 × 2.3	−30 × −.0124	−30 × .055
Short 40 March 90 puts	−40 × −6	−40 × 1.7	−40 × −.0090	−40 × .040
	0	−137.0	+.7320	−3.250
Short 10 June 95 calls	−10 × +67	−10 × 2.9	−10 × −.0140	−10 × .209
Short 10 June 105 puts	−10 × −62	−10 × 3.0	−10 × −.0149	−10 × .221
	−50	−59.0	+.2890	−4.300

Figure 8-20: Examples of Volatility Spreads (continued)

LONG BUTTERFLY: Short two options at the same exercise price, and long one option with an immediately higher exercise price and one option with an immediately lower exercise price; all options are of the same type and expire at the same time.

	Delta Position	Gamma Position	Theta Position	Vega Position
Long 10 March 95 calls	+10 × 78	+10 × 4.3	+10 × –.0221	+10 × .100
Short 20 March 100 calls	–20 × 51	–20 × 5.8	–20 × –.0313	–20 × .134
Long 10 March 105 calls	+10 × 24	+10 × 4.6	+10 × –.0250	+10 × .107
	0	–27.0	+.1550	–.610
Long 30 June 90 puts	+30 × –17	+30 × 2.1	+30 × –.0111	+30 × .154
Short 60 June 95 puts	–60 × –31	–60 × 2.9	–60 × –.0151	–60 × .209
Long 30 June 100 puts	+30 × –47	+30 × 3.2	–30 × –.0166	+30 × .234
	–60	–15.0	+.0750	–.900

SHORT BUTTERFLY: Long two options at the same exercise price, and short one option with an immediately higher exercise price and one option with an immediately lower exercise price; all options are of the same type and expire at the same time.

	Delta Position	Gamma Position	Theta Position	Vega Position
Short 20 March 100 puts	–20 × –48	–20 × 5.8	–20 × –.0313	–20 × .134
Long 40 March 105 puts	+40 × –75	+40 × 4.6	+40 × –.0240	+40 × .107
Short 20 March 110 puts	–20 × –91	–20 × 2.3	–20 × –.0103	–20 × .055
	–220*	+22.0	–.1280	+.500
Short 25 June 95 calls	–25 × 67	–25 × 2.9	–25 × –.0140	–25 × .209
Long 50 June 100 calls	+50 × 51	+50 × 3.2	+50 × –.0166	+50 × .234
Short 25 June 105 calls	–25 × 36	–25 × 3.0	–25 × –.0160	–25 × .221
	–25	+12.5	–.0800	+.950

* Note that because the ratio of a butterfly is always 1 × 2 × 1, the butterfly can become unbalanced if the exercise prices are far away from the current underlying price.

LONG TIME SPREAD: Long a long-term option and short a short-term option where all options have the same exercise price and are of the same type.

	Delta Position	Gamma Position	Theta Position	Vega Position
Long 20 June 100 calls	+20 × 51	+20 × 3.2	+20 × –.0166	+20 × .234
Short 20 March 100 calls	–20 × 51	–20 × 5.8	–20 × –.0313	–20 × .134
	0	–52.0	+.2940	+2.000
Long 10 June 95 puts	+10 × –31	+10 × 2.9	+10 × –.0151	+10 × .209
Short 10 March 95 puts	–10 × –21	–10 × 4.3	–10 × –.0232	–10 × .100
	–100	–14.0	+.0810	+1.090

Figure 8-20: Examples of Volatility Spreads (continued)

SHORT TIME SPREAD: Short a long-term option and long a short-term option where all options have the same exercise price and are of the same type.

	Delta Position	Gamma Position	Theta Position	Vega Position
Long 25 March 100 puts	+25 × –48	+25 × 5.8	+25 × –.0313	+25 × .134
Short 25 June 100 puts	–25 × –47	–25 × 3.2	–25 × –.0166	–25 × .234
	–25	+65.0	–.3675	–2.500
*Long 10 March 105 calls	+10 × 24	+10 × 4.6	+10 × –.0250	+10 × .107
Short 10 June 110 calls	–10 × 23	–10 × 2.5	–10 × –.0132	–10 × .182
	+10	+21.0	–.1180	–.750

* Although this is technically a diagonal spread, it will tend to act like a time spread because the options have deltas which are approximately equal.

buy underpriced and sell overpriced options. Such a market can be easily identified by comparing our volatility estimate to the implied volatility in the option marketplace. If implied volatility is generally lower than our volatility estimate, all options will appear underpriced. If implied volatility is generally higher than our estimate, all options will appear overpriced.

If options generally appear underpriced (low implied volatility), look for spreads with a positive vega. This includes strategies in the backspread or long time spread category. *If options generally appear overpriced (high implied volatility), look for spreads with a negative vega.* This includes strategies in the ratio vertical or short time spread category.

It may seem at first glance that if one encounters a market where all options are either underpriced or overpriced, the sensible strategies are either long straddles and strangles, or short straddles and strangles. Such strategies will enable a trader to take a position with a positive theoretical edge on both sides of the spread. Straddles and strangles are certainly possible strategies when all options are too cheap or too expensive. We will see in Chapter 9 that straddles and strangles, while often having a large, positive theoretical edge, can also be among the riskiest of all strategies. For this reason, a trader will often want to consider other spreads in the backspread or ratio vertical spread category, even if such spreads entail buying some overvalued options or selling some underpriced options.

The theoretical values and deltas in Figure 8-20 have been reproduced in Figures 8-21 and 8-22, but now prices have been included which reflect implied volatilities different from the volatility input of 20%. The prices in Figure 8-21 reflect an implied volatility of 17%. In this case the reader will find that only those spreads with a positive vega will have a positive theoretical value:

call and put backspreads
long straddles and strangles

Figure 8-21

IMPLIED VOLATILITY = 17%

March Futures = 100.00 Time to Expiration = 6 weeks Volatility = 20% Interest = 6.00%

	CALLS			PUTS		
Exercise Price	Price	Theoretical Value	Delta	Price	Theoretical Value	Delta
90	10.00	10.10	93	.07	.17	-6
95	5.54	5.82	78	.57	.85	–21
100	2.28	2.69	51	2.28	2.68	–48
105	.65	.95	24	5.62	5.92	–75
110	.12	.26	8	10.05	10.16	–91

June Futures = 100.00 Time to Expiration = 13 weeks Volatility = 20% Interest = 6.00%

	CALLS			PUTS		
Exercise Price	Price	Theoretical Value	Delta	Price	Theoretical Value	Delta
90	10.54	10.97	81	.75	1.18	–17
95	6.83	7.45	67	1.94	2.55	–31
100	4.00	4.71	51	4.00	4.71	–47
105	2.11	2.77	36	7.01	7.66	–62
110	1.00	1.52	23	10.79	11.30	–75

Figure 8-22

IMPLIED VOLATILITY = 23%

March Futures = 100.00 Time to Expiration = 6 weeks Volatility = 20% Interest = 6.00%

	CALLS			PUTS		
Exercise Price	Price	Theoretical Value	Delta	Price	Theoretical Value	Delta
90	10.23	10.10	93	.30	.17	-6
95	6.12	5.82	78	1.16	.85	–21
100	3.09	2.69	51	3.09	2.68	–48
105	1.28	.95	24	6.25	5.92	–75
110	.44	.26	8	10.37	10.16	–91

June Futures = 100.00 Time to Expiration = 13 weeks Volatility = 20% Interest = 6.00%

	CALLS			PUTS		
Exercise Price	Price	Theoretical Value	Delta	Price	Theoretical Value	Delta
90	11.45	10.97	81	1.66	1.18	–17
95	8.08	7.45	67	3.19	2.55	–31
100	5.42	4.71	51	5.42	4.71	–47
105	3.44	2.77	36	8.34	7.66	–62
110	2.08	1.52	23	11.87	11.30	–75

short butterflies
long time spreads

The prices in Figures 8-22 reflect an implied volatility of 23%. Now the reader will find that only those spreads with a negative vega will have a positive theoretical value:

call and put ratio vertical spreads
short straddles and strangles
long butterflies
short time spreads

An important assumption in most theoretical pricing models is that volatility is constant over the life of an option. The volatility input into the model is assumed to be the one volatility which best describes price fluctuations in the underlying instrument over the life of the option. When all options expire at the same time, it is this one volatility which will, in theory, determine the desirability of a spread. In real life, however, a trader may believe that volatility is likely to rise or fall over some period of time. Very often implied volatility will also rise or fall. Since time spreads are particularly sensitive to changes in implied volatility, whether volatility is rising or falling can affect the desirability of time spreads. Consequently, we can add this corollary to our spread guidelines: *Long time spreads are likely to be profitable when implied volatility is low but is expected to rise; short time spreads are likely to be profitable when implied volatility is high but is expected to fall.*

These are only general guidelines, and an experienced trader may decide to violate them if he has reason to believe that the implied volatility will not correlate with the volatility of the underlying contract. A long time spread might still be desirable in a high implied volatility market, but the trader must make a prediction of how implied volatility might change under certain conditions. If the market were to stagnate, with no movement in the underlying contract, but the trader felt that implied volatility would remain high, a long time spread would be a sensible strategy. The short-term option would decay, while the long-term option would retain its value. In the same way, a short time spread might still be desirable in a low implied volatility market if the trader felt that the underlying instrument were likely to make a large move with no commensurate increase in implied volatility.

ADJUSTMENTS

A volatility spread may initially be delta neutral, but the delta of the position is likely to change as the price of the underlying contract rises or falls. Moreover, changes in volatility and time to expiration can also affect the delta of spread. A spread which is delta neutral today may not be delta neutral tomorrow, even if all other conditions remain the same. The optimum use of a theoretical pricing model requires a trader to continuously maintain a delta neutral position throughout the life of the spread. Continuous adjustments are impossible in real life, so a trader ought to give some thought to when he will adjust a position. Essentially, we can consider three possibilities:

1. *Adjust at regular intervals*—In theory, the adjustment process is assumed to be continuous because volatility is assumed to be a continuous measure of the speed of the market. In practice, however, volatility is measured over regular time intervals, so a reasonable approach is to adjust a position at similar regular intervals. If a trader's volatility estimate is based on daily price changes, the trader might adjust daily. If the estimate is based on weekly price changes, he might adjust weekly. This is a trader's best attempt to emulate the assumptions built into the theoretical pricing model.

2. *Adjust when the position becomes a predetermined number of deltas long or short*—Very few traders insist on being delta neutral all the time. Most traders realize that this is not a realistic approach, both because a continuous adjustment process is physically impossible, and because no one can be certain that all the assumptions and inputs in a theoretical pricing model, from which the delta is calculated, are correct. Even if one could be certain that all delta calculations were accurate, a trader might still be willing to take on some directional risk. But a trader ought to know just how much directional risk he is willing to accept. If he wants to pursue delta neutral strategies, but believes that he can comfortably live with a position which is up to 500 deltas long or short, then he can adjust the position any time his delta position reaches this limit. Unlike the trader who adjusts at regular intervals, a trader who adjusts based on a fixed number of deltas cannot be sure how often he will need to adjust his position. In some cases he may have to adjust very frequently; in other cases he may go for long periods of time without adjusting.

The number of deltas long or short a trader chooses for his adjustment points depends on the size of his positions and his capitalization. A small, independent trader may find that he is uncomfortable with a position which is even 200 deltas long or short, while a large trading firm may consider a position which is several thousand deltas long or short as being approximately delta neutral.

3. *Adjust by feel*—This suggestion is not made facetiously. Some traders have good market feel. They can sense when the market is about to move in one direction or another. If a trader has this ability, there is no reason why he shouldn't make use of it. For example, suppose that the underlying market is at 50.00 and a trader is delta neutral with a gamma of –200. If the market falls to 48.00, the trader can estimate that he is approximately 400 deltas long. If 400 deltas is the limit of risk he is willing to accept, he might decide to adjust at this point. If, however, he is also aware that 48.00 represents strong support for the market, he might choose not to adjust under the assumption that the market is likely to rebound from the support level. If he is right, he will have avoided an unprofitable adjustment. Of course, if he is wrong and the market continues downward through the support level, he will regret not having adjusted. If the trader is right more often than not, there is no reason why he shouldn't take advantage of this skill.

ENTERING A SPREAD ORDER

In sophisticated option markets, spreads are traded as if they are one, single contract. This means that a spread is quoted with a single bid price and a single offer price. For example, suppose a trader is interested in buying a certain straddle and receives a quote from a market-maker of 3.45/3.55. If the trader wants to sell the straddle, he will have to do so at a price of 3.45 (the bid price); if he wants to buy the straddle, he will have to pay 3.55 (the ask price). If the trader decides he is willing to pay 3.55, neither he nor the market-maker care whether the trader pays 1.75 for the call and 1.80 for the put, or 1.55 for the call and 2.00 for the put, or some other combination of call and put prices. The only consideration is that the prices of the call and put taken together add up to 3.55.

A market-maker will always endeavor to give one bid price and one ask price for an entire spread. If the spread is a common type, such as a straddle, strangle, butterfly, or time spread, a bid and ask can usually be given very quickly. Of course, market-makers are only human. If a spread is very complex, involving several different options in unusual ratios, it may take a market-maker several minutes to calculate the value of the spread. But regardless of the complexity of a spread, the market-maker will make an effort to give his best two-sided (bid and ask) market.

Spread orders, like individual option orders, can be submitted with qualifying instructions. The most common types are market orders (orders to be filled at the current market price) and limit orders (orders to be filled at a specified price). Other *contingency orders* may also include instructions specifying how the order is to be executed in the marketplace. The following contingency orders, all of which are defined in Appendix A, are often used in option markets:

All Or None
Fill Or Kill
Immediate Or Cancel
Market If Touched
Market On Close
Not Held
One Cancels The Other
Stop Limit Order
Stop Loss Order

Two typical spread orders, submitted with their contingency instructions, are shown in Figures 8-23a and 8-23b.

A broker executing a spread order is responsible for adhering to any special instructions which accompany the order. Unless a trader knows exactly what current market conditions are, or has a great deal of confidence in the broker who will be handling the order, it is always a good practice to submit specific instructions with the order as to how it is to be filled. Additionally, when one considers all the information that must be communicated with a spread order (the expiration months, the exercise prices, the type of options, whether the order is a buy or sell, the ratio), it is easy to see

Figure 8-23a

FUTURES ORDER

Account Number ________ Broker ________ Memo ________

$ A B C D E F G H I J K L M N O P Q R S T U V W X Y Z 2 3 4 5 6 7 8 9 % **S**

BUY	**SELL**
25 Crude Oil Jan. 19 C	25 Crude Oil Feb. 19 C
.24 ← an indication of the prices the broker should look at →	.44
1 x 1 (spread ratio) .20 Credit (spread price)	All or None

how incorrect information might inadvertently be transmitted with the order. For this reason, it is also a good practice to recheck all orders before submitting them for execution. Option trading can be difficult enough without the additional problems of miscommunication.

Figure 8–23b

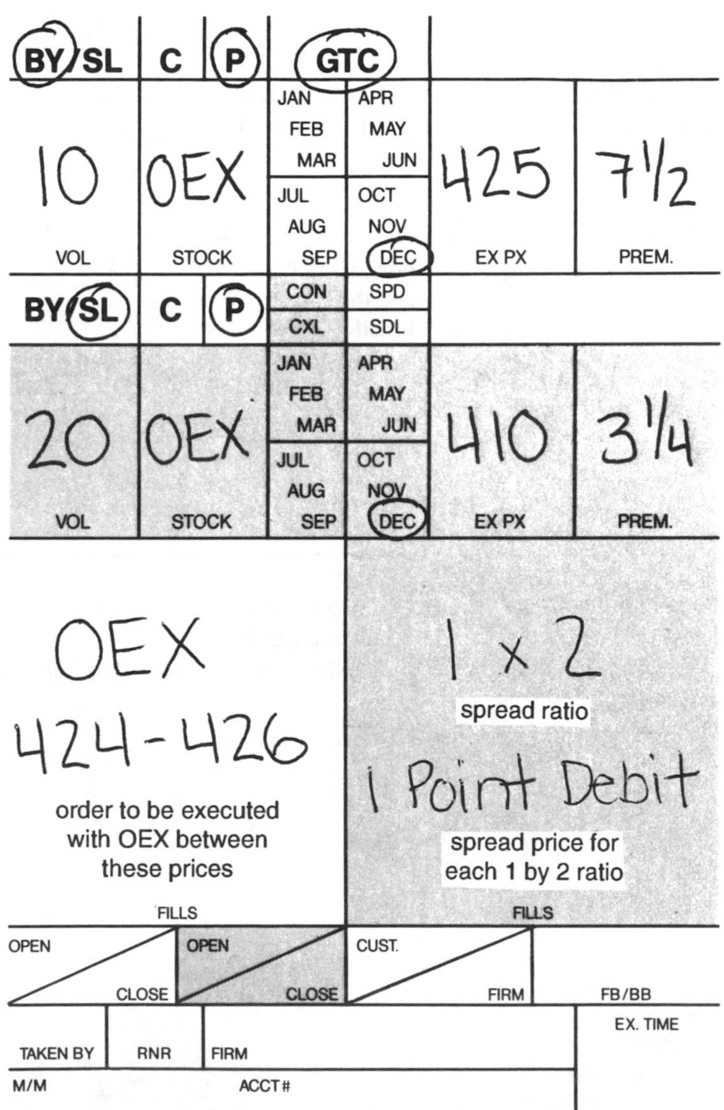
BY/SL
C
P
GTC
JAN
FEB
MAR
APR
MAY
JUN
JUL
AUG
SEP
OCT
NOV
DEC
10
OEX
425
7½
VOL
STOCK
EX PX
PREM.
BY/SL
C
P
CON
CXL
SPD
SDL
JAN
FEB
MAR
APR
MAY
JUN
JUL
AUG
SEP
OCT
NOV
DEC
20
OEX
410
3¼
VOL
STOCK
EX PX
PREM.
OEX
424-426
order to be executed
with OEX between
these prices
1 x 2
spread ratio
1 Point Debit
spread price for
each 1 by 2 ratio
FILLS
FILLS
OPEN
CLOSE
OPEN
CLOSE
CUST.
FIRM
FB/BB
EX. TIME
TAKEN BY
RNR
FIRM
M/M
ACCT#

❖ 9 ❖

Risk Considerations

Consider the prices and theoretical values shown in Figure 9-1. What categories of volatility spreads might be profitable under these conditions? By comparing prices to theoretical values, or by comparing the implied volatilities of the various options to the volatility input of 15%, we can see that all options are overpriced. Recalling the general guidelines in the last chapter, under the given conditions a trader will want to consider spreads with a negative vega:

Call and Put Ratio Vertical Spreads
Short Straddles and Strangles
Long Butterflies
Short Time Spreads

Which of these categories is likely to represent the best spreading opportunity? And within each category, which specific spread might be best?

CHOOSING THE BEST SPREAD

For the moment, let's focus on May options only. Having eliminated the possibility of time spreads, we will have to look for spreads in the ratio vertical category (negative gamma, negative vega). With ten different May options (five calls and five puts), it is possible to construct a wide variety of spreads which fall into this category. How can we make an intelligent decision about which spread might be best?

Suppose we choose three possible strategies and try to analyze them. The three strategies which have been chosen are spreads 1, 2, and 3, shown in Figure 9-2.

These are certainly not the only possible spreads, nor can we be certain that they are the best possible spreads. But in theory each spread ought to be profitable under the given market conditions, since each fits into the ratio vertical spread category: spread 1 is a short straddle, spread 2 is a call ratio vertical spread, and spread 3 is a long put butterfly. How can we evaluate the relative merits of each spread?

Initially it may appear that spread 1 is best since it has the greatest theoretical edge. If the volatility estimate of 15% turns out to be correct, spread 1 will show a profit of 2.86, while spread 2 will show a profit of 1.00, and spread 3 will show a profit of only .40.

But is theoretical edge our only concern? If that were true we could simply do each spread in bigger and bigger size to make the theoretical edge as large as we want. Instead of doing spread 2 at 10 × 15, we might increase the size fivefold to 50 × 75. This will

Figure 9-1

May Futures: 49.50; Time to Expiration: 56 days; Volatility: 15%; Interest Rate: 8.00%

	CALLS							PUTS						
Exercise Price	Price	Theoretical Value	Delta	Gamma	Theta	Vega	Implied Volatility	Price	Theoretical Value	Delta	Gamma	Theta	Vega	Implied Volatility
48	2.19	2.02	70	11.6	–.0083	.066	17.53	.72	.54	–29	11.6	–.0087	.066	17.70
49	1.56	1.40	57	13.3	–.0097	.075	17.08	1.05	.91	–42	13.3	–.0098	.075	16.87
50	1.07	.92	44	13.4	–.0099	.076	16.96	1.59	1.42	–55	13.4	–.0098	.076	17.30
51	.77	.57	31	12.1	–.0090	.068	17.89	2.22	2.06	–68	12.1	–.0087	.068	17.44
52	.53	.33	21	9.8	–.0073	.055	18.39	2.99	2.80	–78	9.8	–.0068	.055	18.24

July Futures: 50.11; Time to Expiration: 112 days; Volatility: 15%; Interest Rate: 8.00%

	CALLS							PUTS						
Exercise Price	Price	Theoretical Value	Delta	Gamma	Theta	Vega	Implied Volatility	Price	Theoretical Value	Delta	Gamma	Theta	Vega	Implied Volatility
48	3.03	2.82	70	8.0	–.0056	.092	17.20	1.00	.76	–28	8.0	–.0060	.092	17.50
49	2.40	2.20	61	8.9	–.0064	.103	16.92	1.34	1.12	–37	8.9	–.0066	.103	17.14
50	1.88	1.67	52	9.3	–.0069	.108	16.92	1.78	1.57	–46	9.3	–.0069	.108	16.98
51	1.46	1.24	42	9.2	–.0069	.106	17.09	2.33	2.11	–56	9.2	–.0067	.106	17.11
52	1.12	.89	34	8.6	–.0065	.100	17.28	2.98	2.73	–64	8.6	–.0061	.100	17.44

Figure 9-2

		Delta Position	Theoretical Edge
Spread 1:	Short 10 May 50 calls @ 1.07	–10 × +44	10 × +.15
	Short 8 May 50 puts @ 1.59	–8 × –55	8 × +.17
		0	+2.86
Spread 2:	Long 10 May 51 calls @ .77	+10 × +44	10 × +.15
	Short 15 May 52 calls @ .53	–15 × +21	15 × .20
		–5	+1.00
Spread 3:	Long 10 May 49 puts @ 1.05	+10 × –42	10 × –.14
	Short 20 May 50 puts @ 1.59	–20 × –55	20 × +.17
	Long 10 May 51 puts @ 2.22	+10 × –68	10 × –.16
		0	+.40

increase the theoretical edge fivefold to 5.00, and ostensibly makes spread 2 a better strategy than spreads 1 and 3. Clearly, theoretical edge can't be the only consideration.

Theoretical edge is only an indication of what we expect to earn if we are right about market conditions. Since there is no guarantee that we will be right, we must give at least as much consideration to the question of risk. If we are wrong about market conditions, how badly might we be hurt?

In order to focus on the risk considerations, let's change the size of spreads 2 and 3 so that their theoretical edge is approximately equal to that of spread 1. We can achieve this by tripling the size of spread 2 to 30 × 45, and increasing the size of spread 3 sevenfold to 70 × 140 × 70. The spreads in their new sizes with their total theoretical edge and risk sensitivities are shown in Figure 9-3.

With all three spreads having approximately the same theoretical edge, we can now focus on the risks associated with each spread.

As with all volatility spreads, one of the risk considerations is the possibility of an incorrect volatility estimate. Since each spread has a negative vega, there will be no problem if volatility turns out to be lower than 15%. In that case, the value of each spread will increase and we will show a greater profit than originally expected. On the other hand, if volatility turns out to be greater than 15%, this could present a problem. What will happen if volatility turns out to be 17%, or 20%, or some higher number? Each spread will be hurt due to the negative vega, but each spread may not be hurt to the same degree.

One way to analyze the volatility risk associated with each spread is to use a theoretical pricing model to simulate the value of each spread at increasingly greater volatilities. From these values we can construct graphs reflecting each spread's theoretical edge versus volatility. Such a graph is shown in Figure 9-4.

With our size adjustments each spread now has approximately the same initial theoretical edge, enabling us to focus on the volatility risk associated with each spread. Looking at Figure 9-4 we can see that each spread, 1, 2, and 3, loses its theoretical edge

Figure 9-3

		Theoretical Edge	Delta Position	Gamma Position	Theta Position	Vega Position
Spread 1:	−10 May 50 calls	10 × +.15	−10 × +44	−10 × 13.4	−10 × −.0099	−10 × .076
	−8 May 50 puts	8 × +.17	−8 × −55	−8 × 13.4	−8 × −.0098	−8 × .076
		+2.86	0	−241.2	+.1774	−1.368
Spread 2:	+30 May 51 calls	30 × −.20	+30 × +31	+30 × 12.1	+30 × −.0090	+30 × .068
	−45 May 52 calls	45 × +.20	−45 × +21	−45 × 9.8	−45 × −.0073	−45 × .055
		+3.00	−15	−78.0	+.0585	−.435
Spread 3:	+70 May 49 puts	70 × −.14	+70 × −42	+70 × 13.3	+70 × −.0098	+70 × .075
	−140 May 50 puts	140 × +.17	−140 × −55	−140 × 13.4	−140 × −.0098	−140 × .076
	+70 May 51 puts	70 × −.16	+70 × −68	+70 × 12.1	+70 × −.0087	+70 × .068
		+2.80	0	−98.0	+.0770	−.630

as volatility increases. But the slope of spread 1 is most severe. It loses its value very quickly as volatility increases, much more quickly than spreads 2 and 3.

For each of our spreads we might logically ask how high volatility can rise before we begin to lose money. That is, we might want to determine the break-even volatility, or *implied volatility*, for each spread. This is simply an extension of the general definition of implied volatility: the volatility which would have to occur over the life of an option, or options, such that a position would show neither a profit nor a loss. It is common among traders to determine the implied volatility of a spread position, just as they determine the implied volatility of individual options. We can see from Figure 9-3 that the implied (break-even) volatilities of spreads 1, 2, and 3 are approximately 17%, 20%, and 22%, respectively.

From a volatility perspective, spread 3 shows the best risk/reward characteristics. With each spread we are, in a sense, selling volatility, and we would like to do so at the highest possible price. Would we rather sell something that's worth 15% (our volatility estimate) at 17% (the implied volatility of spread 1), at 20% (the implied volatility of spread 2), or at 22% (the implied volatility of spread 3)? The higher the implied volatility of the spread, the greater the margin for error in our volatility estimate and, consequently, the greater the likelihood of showing a profit. Spread 1 has only a 2-percentage-point margin for error, while spread 3 has a margin for error more than three times greater, at 7 percentage points. Spread 2 falls somewhere in between.

Why are we so concerned about our volatility estimate being too low? A trader might take the view that he is just as likely to overestimate as underestimate volatility. If this happens, how will it affect the potential outcome of each spread? Suppose we decide to do spread 1 and volatility turns out to be 18%, three percentage points higher than our estimate of 15%. Looking at Figure 9-4 we can see that if this happens we will lose approximately 1.21. Suppose, however, that there is an equal chance that volatility will turn out to be 12%, three percentage points lower than our estimate. In Figure 9-5, where we have extended volatility down to 10%, we can see that in this case we will make approximately 6.95. In a more extreme case, when volatility turns out to be 20% we will lose 3.95. But if volatility turns out to be 10% we will make 9.64. For each time we underestimate volatility and show an unexpected loss, we might assume there will be an equal number of times when we overestimate volatility and show an unexpected profit. The end result of all these outcomes will be an average profit of approximately 2.86, the predicted profit of the spread at a volatility estimate of 15%.

Suppose that the average result of doing any one of our spreads, 1, 2, and 3, is a profit of approximately 2.80. If the outcome in each case is identical, why should it make any difference which spread we choose? While the end result is certainly an important theoretical consideration, how the end result comes about may be an equally important practical consideration.

Every trader knows that there are times when he shows a profit and times when he shows a loss. No one wins all the time. In the long run, however, a good trader's profits will more than offset his losses. For example, suppose a trader chooses a strategy which will show a profit of $7,000 half of the time, and which will show a loss of $5,000 the other half of the time. In the long run he will show an average profit of $1,000. But

Figure 9-4

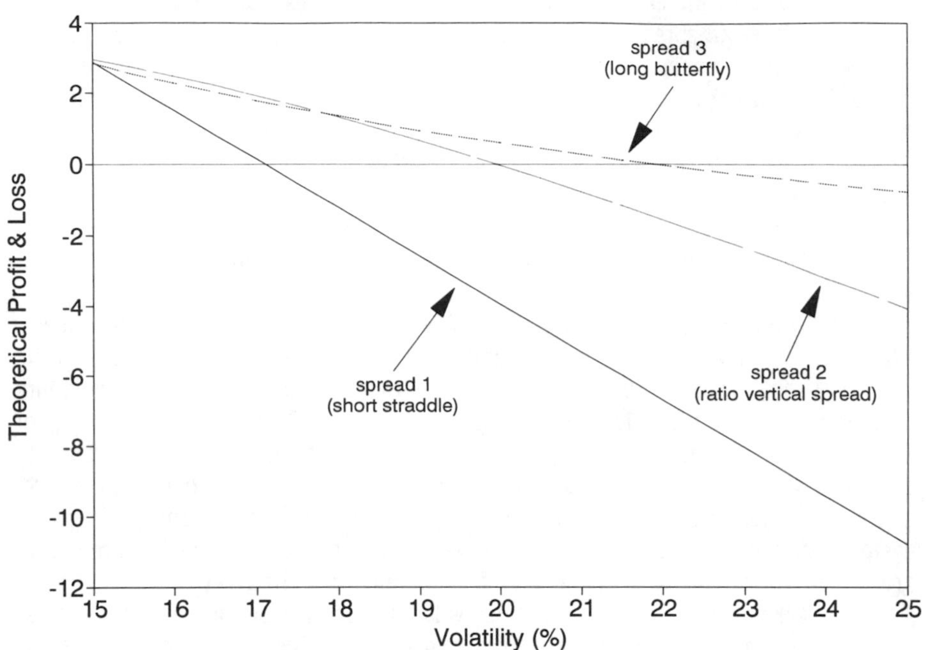

Figure 9-5

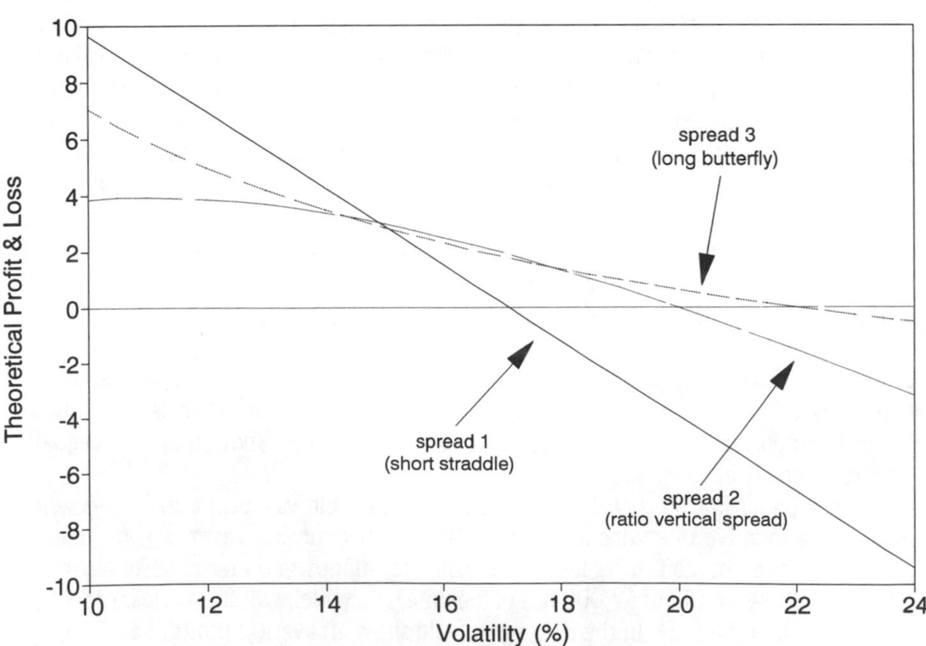

suppose the first time the trader executes the strategy he loses $5,000 and the trader only has $3,000? Now the trader will not be able to stay in business for all those times when he is fortunate enough to show a profit of $7,000. Every trader knows that it is only over long periods of time that good luck and bad luck even out. No experienced trader will initiate a strategy where short-term bad luck might terminate his trading career. This is the reason an experienced option trader will tend to avoid spread 1.

Any financial officer knows that it is much easier to manage a steady cash flow rather than one that swings wildly. This is equally true for an option trader. He must sensibly manage his finances so that he can avoid being ruined by the periods of bad luck which will inevitably occur, no matter how skillfully he trades.

An incorrect volatility estimate may not be the only risk with which an option trader must be concerned. Every input into a theoretical pricing model represents a risk to the trader since an incorrect input may alter an option's theoretical value. These risks are reflected in the delta, gamma, theta, vega, and rho associated with a spread. We can summarize these risks as follows:

Delta (Directional) Risk—The risk that the underlying market will move in one direction rather than another. When we create a position which is delta neutral, we are trying to ensure that initially the position has no particular preference as to the direction in which the underlying instrument will move. A delta neutral position does not necessarily eliminate all directional risk, but it usually leaves us immune to directional risks within a limited range.

Gamma (Curvature) Risk—The risk of a large move in the underlying contract, regardless of direction. The gamma position is a measure of how sensitive a position is to such large moves. A positive gamma position does not really have gamma risk since such a position will, in theory, increase in value with movement in the underlying contract. A negative gamma position, however, can quickly lose its theoretical edge with a large move in the underlying contract. The consequences of such a move must always be a consideration when analyzing the relative merits of different positions.

Theta (Time Decay) Risk—The risk that time will pass with no movement in the underlying contract. This is the opposite side of gamma risk. Positions with positive gamma become more valuable with large moves in the underlying. But if movement helps, the passage of time hurts. A positive gamma always goes hand in hand with a negative theta. A trader with a negative theta will always have to consider the risk in terms of how much time can pass before the spread's theoretical edge disappears. The position wants movement, but if the movement fails to occur within the next day, or next week, or next month, will the spread, in theory, still be profitable?

Vega (Volatility) Risk—The risk that the volatility which we input into the theoretical pricing model will be incorrect. If we input an incorrect volatility, we will be assuming an incorrect distribution of underlying prices over time. Since some positions have a positive vega and are hurt by declining volatility, and some positions have a negative vega and are hurt by rising volatility, the vega represents a risk to every position. A trader must always consider how much the volatility can move against him before the potential profit from a position disappears.

Rho (Interest Rate) Risk—The risk that interest rates will change over the life of the option. A position with a positive rho will be helped (hurt) by an increase (decline) in interest rates, while a position with a negative rho will show just the opposite characteristics.[1] Generally, the interest rate is the least important of the inputs into a theoretical pricing model, and it is unlikely, except for special situations, that a trader will give extensive thought to the rho risk associated with a position.

So far we have compared only the volatility risk associated with spreads 1, 2, and 3. Is there any other risk with which we ought to be concerned? All of our spreads have a negative gamma, so they will all be adversely affected by a large move in the underlying contract. In order to compare the relative gamma risks, we can construct a graph showing the values of the spreads at varying prices of the underlying contract. This has been done in Figure 9-6. Again, we assume that each spread has approximately the same theoretical value under our theoretical assumptions, in this case at the current underlying price of 49.50.

Figure 9-6

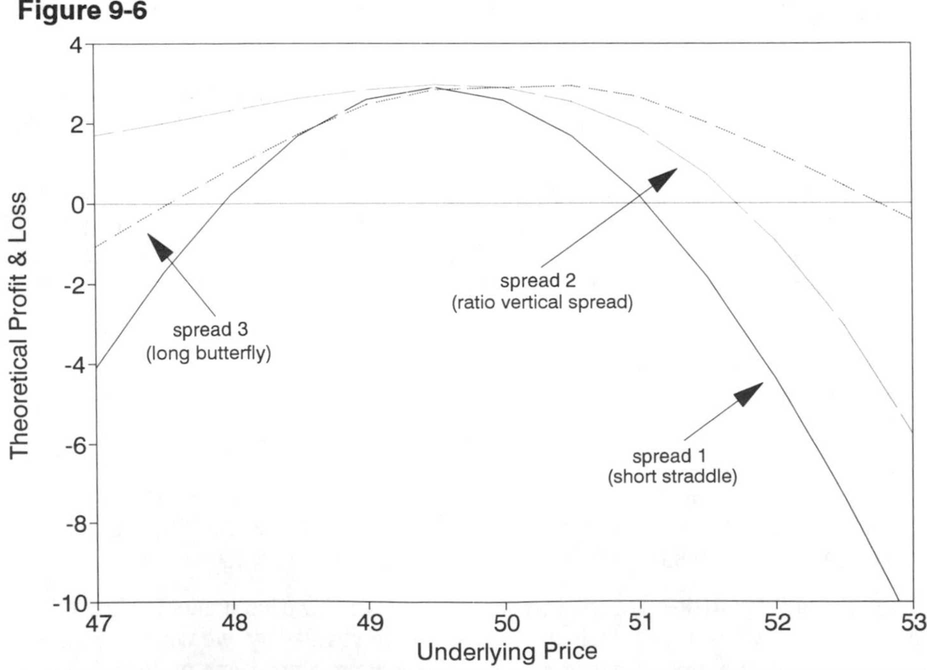

1. Of course, we are only considering the interest rate risk as it applies to the evaluation of options. Changes in interest rates can also affect the evaluation of an underlying contract, such as a bond, or even the shares in a company. But that is a separate matter.

Looking at Figure 9-6 we can see that if the underlying contract makes a large upward move, spread 3 will be the least affected. It can stand a move up to 52.75 without losing its positive theoretical edge. Spreads 1 and 2 can stand upward moves to only 51.05 and 51.75, respectively. On the downside, spread 1 is still the riskiest since it loses all its theoretical edge if the underlying market should make a swift move down to 47.90. Spread 3 is less risky because it can stand a move down to 47.50. But the least risky on the downside is clearly spread 2, since it never loses all its theoretical edge. In the most extreme downward move the theoretical edge of spread 2 will collapse to approximately zero.

PRACTICAL CONSIDERATIONS

Considering the vega and gamma risk, spread 3 seems to have the best risk characteristics. It has a larger margin for error in terms of volatility than either spread 1 or 2. In terms of underlying price movement it can also stand a larger upward move than the other two spreads. Only when we consider the possibility of a large downward move does spread 3 not display the best risk characteristics. In this case spread 2 comes in first. But spread 3 still looks better than spread 1. In theory, a trader ought to be more willing to execute spread 3 than either spread 1 or 2. In the real world, however, practical trading considerations may play a role in the trader's decision.

Even though spread 3, the butterfly, appears to be the best theoretical choice of the three, it has some practical drawbacks which may make it an unrealistic choice. Spread 3 is a three-sided spread, as opposed to spreads 1 and 2, which are two-sided. A three-sided spread will probably be more difficult to execute in the marketplace, and is likely to cost more in terms of the total width of the bid/ask. If a trader wants to execute the complete spread at one time, as is most common, he may not be able to do so at his target prices. If, on the other hand, he tries to execute one leg[2] at a time, he will be at risk from adverse changes in the market until the other legs have been executed.

Additionally, there is the question of market liquidity. In order to obtain a theoretical edge commensurate with spreads 1 and 2, it was necessary to increase the size of the butterfly sevenfold to 70 × 140 × 70. If there is insufficient liquidity in the May 49, 50, and 51 puts to support this size, it may not be possible to execute the butterfly in the size required to meet our profit expectations. Alternatively, we may be able to execute part of the spread at favorable prices, but as we increase the size, the prices may become less satisfactory. Moreover, for a retail customer the increased size may entail significantly greater transaction costs.

If trading considerations make spread 3 impractical, we may have to choose between spreads 1 (the straddle) and 2 (the ratio vertical spread). If that happens, spread 2 is the clear winner. It allows for a much greater margin for error in both volatility (vega risk) and underlying price change (gamma risk). A trader who is given a choice between these two spreads will strongly prefer spread 2.

The choice of spreads may not always be as clear as in this example. The superiority of spread 3, at least from the theoretical standpoint, was relatively obvious. Sometimes,

2. The options which comprise a spread position are sometimes referred to as the *legs* of the spread.

however, one spread may be superior with respect to one type of risk, while a different spread may be superior with respect to a different risk.

Let's consider three new spreads, 4 (a ratio vertical spread), 5 (a short time spread), and 6 (a diagonal spread). The total theoretical edge of each spread, as well as their risk sensitivities (all taken from the theoretical evaluation table in Figure 9-1), are shown in Figure 9-7. In order to again focus on the risks associated with each spread, the size of each spread has been adjusted to yield approximately the same theoretical edge.

Since each spread has a negative vega, we will want to consider the volatility risk if volatility should turn out to be greater than our estimate of 15%. The sensitivity of each spread to increasing volatility is shown in Figure 9-8. We can see that spread 4 has an implied volatility of approximately 18.1%, spread 5 approximately 17.0%, and spread 6 approximately 17.2%. If an increase in volatility is our primary concern, then spread 4 (the ratio vertical spread) seems to offer the best risk characteristics.

In addition to the volatility risk, we can see that spread 4 also has a negative gamma, so that it will be adversely affected by a sudden large move in the underlying contract. If we are concerned about the possibility of such a move we may want to determine exactly how a large move in the price of the underlying contract will affect the value of the spread. Figure 9-9 shows the sensitivity of each of our spreads, 4, 5, and 6, to a change in the price of the underlying contract.[3]

Note that spread 4 has the narrowest profit range of the three spreads, in theory losing all its theoretical value if the market should immediately drop below 46.50 or rise above 52.20. On the other hand, spread 6 has very little downside risk and can still stand an immediate move upward to about 52.30. If a trader were worried about the possibility of a swift fall in the market, he might be willing to give up the extra volatility cushion offered by spread 4 over spread 6 (18.0% vs. 17.2%) for the additional downside protection offered by the latter spread. This is reflected in the smaller negative gamma associated with spread 6 as compared with spread 4.

Finally, we can see that spread 5, while having the least desirable volatility risk, also has a positive gamma. This means that any large move in the underlying contract will increase the value of the position. If a trader were worried about the possibility of a sudden large move in the underlying contract, but were not overly concerned with an increase in volatility, he might be willing to accept the less desirable volatility risk associated with spread 5 for the more desirable positive gamma characteristics.

A trader who executes spread 5 will have a positive gamma, so he has no gamma risk. But he will have a theta risk if the underlying contract fails to move. How great is the risk? Figure 9-10 shows the sensitivity of all three spreads to the passage of time. Since spreads 4 and 6 have negative gammas, they can only gain value with the passage of time. On the other hand, spread 5 loses value as each day passes. Looking at the graph associated with this spread, we can see that if no movement occurs in the underlying contract, the spread loses all its theoretical edge after about 18 days. This is the price one has to pay for the privilege of having a positive gamma.

3. We assume here that the May and July underlying contracts maintain the same approximate relationship. That is, the July contract is always 1.0123 times the May contract since 50.11/49.50 = 1.0123. The x-axis in Figure 9-9 is the price of the May contract.

Figure 9-7

		Theoretical Edge	Delta Position	Gamma Position	Theta Position	Vega Position
Spread 4:	+20 July 50 calls	20 × –.21	+20 × +52	+20 × 9.3	+20 × –.0069	+20 × .108
	–30 July 52 calls	30 × +.23	–30 × +34	–30 × 8.6	–30 × –.0065	–30 × .100
		+2.70	+20	–72.0	+.0570	–.840
Spread 5:	+50 May 48 puts	50 × –.18	+50 × –29	+50 × 11.6	+50 × –.0087	+50 × .066
	–50 July 48 puts	50 × +.24	–50 × –28	–50 × 8.0	–50 × –.0060	–50 × .103
		+3.00	–50	+180.0	–.1350	–1.850
Spread 6:	+10 May 48 calls	10 × –.17	+10 × +70	+10 × 11.6	+10 × –.0083	+10 × .066
	–20 July 52 calls	20 × +.23	–20 × +34	–20 × 8.6	–20 × –.0065	–20 × .100
		+2.90	+20	–56.0	+.0470	–1.340

Figure 9-8

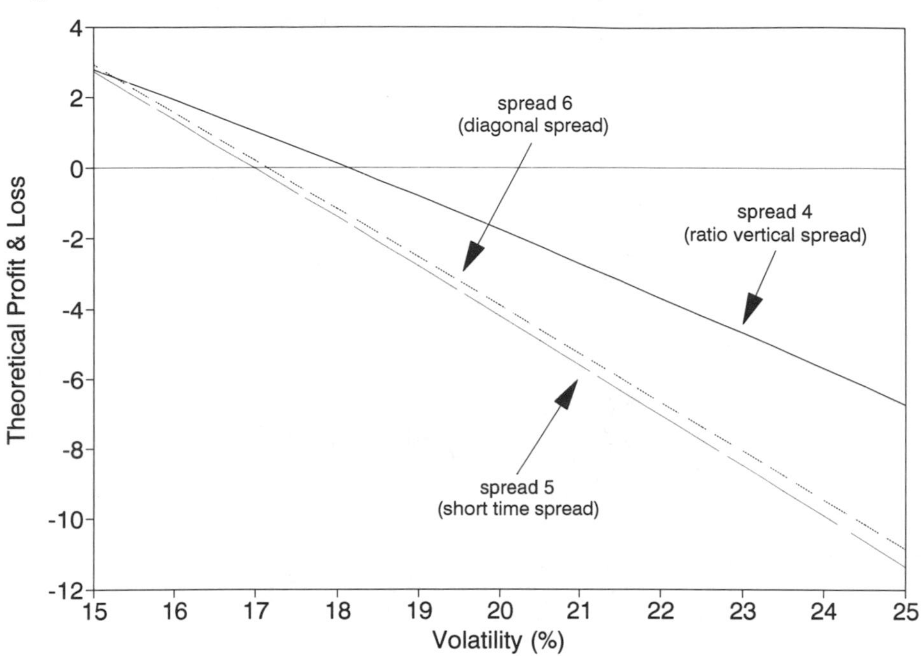

Figure 9-9

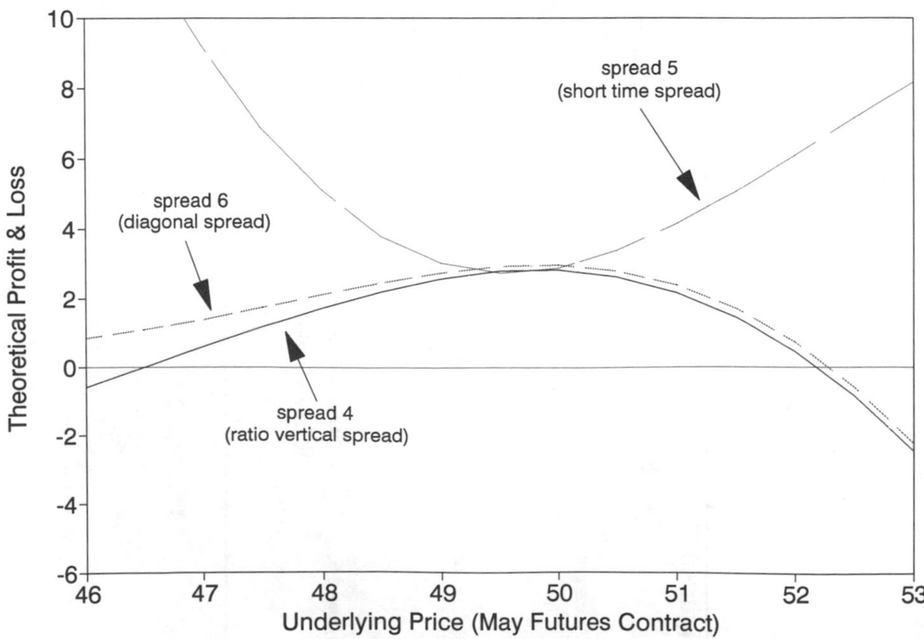

Figure 9-10

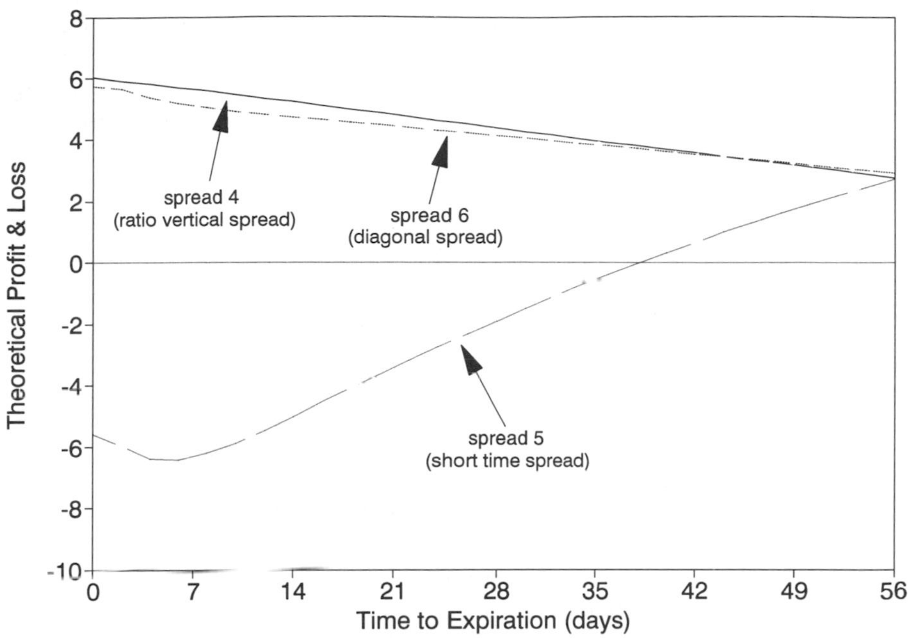

If one has to choose from among spreads 4, 5, or 6, which spread is best? The situation is not clear-cut, and the answer will probably depend on a trader's experience in the market. If he feels that an increase in implied volatility represents the greatest risk, he will probably choose spread 4. If he feels that a large move in the underlying contract represents the greatest risk, he will probably choose spread 5. And if he is willing to settle for partial protection against both volatility and market movement, he will probably choose spread 6.

As must by now be obvious, the choice of spreads is never a simple matter of right and wrong. Like all trading decisions, it is a question of risk and reward. While there are many risks with which an option trader must deal, he will often have to ask himself which risk represents the greatest threat. Sometimes, in order avoid one type of risk, he will be forced to accept a different risk. Even if the trader is willing to accept some risk in a certain area, he may decide that he will only do so to a limited degree. Then he may have to accept increased risks in other areas.

If given the choice between several different spreads a trader can use a computer, as was done in the foregoing examples, to study the risk characteristics of the different spreads. Unfortunately, it may not always be possible to analyze the choices in such detail. A trader may not have the necessary computer support at his disposal, or market conditions may be changing so rapidly that if he fails to make an immediate decision opportunity may quickly pass him by. Is there any way to make a quick comparison of spreads without doing a detailed graphic analysis?

One method that traders sometimes use is to think of every spread as a tradeoff between risk and reward. We might express this tradeoff as a fraction, risk/reward. If a trader goes into the marketplace, he would like to have the greatest possible reward. At the same time he would like to have the least possible risk. Indeed, the ideal risk/reward fraction would be $0 \div \infty$ (zero risk, infinite reward). But $0 \div \infty = 0$, so that if we express the risk/reward characteristics of each spread as a fraction, risk/reward, then in theory the spread whose fraction is closest to zero has the best tradeoff between risk and reward.

What numbers should we use to express the risk and reward for a spread? The reward is what we expect to make when we are right about market conditions. This is simply the theoretical edge, and we can therefore make the theoretical edge the denominator of our fraction. What about the numerator, or risk component? Here we may have to deal with several different numbers since option positions are subject to many different risks. These risks are represented by the various option sensitivities. The practical approach is to express the numerator of our fraction with the sensitivity with which we are most concerned. For example, if a change in volatility is our greatest concern, we can use the vega of the spread as our numerator. If choosing from among several different spreads, the spread whose vega/theoretical edge is closest to zero will have the most desirable risk/reward characteristics. In the same way, if a large price move is our greatest concern, the spread whose gamma/theoretical edge is closest to zero will have the most desirable risk/reward characteristics.

Let's try to analyze spreads 4, 5, and 6 using this method. One risk with which we will certainly have to be concerned is the possibility of a change in volatility. Calculating the vega/theoretical edge, we have:

Spread 4:	–.840/2.70	≈	–.311
Spread 5:	–1.850/3.00	≈	–.617
Spread 6:	–1.340/2.90	≈	–.462

From the above calculations we can see that spread 4 has the best volatility characteristics since its vega/theoretical edge is closest to zero. This is the same conclusion we reached from Figure 9-8, but without the necessity of doing a detailed study of each spread.

Note that when we divide the sensitivity of a spread by its theoretical value, the result is independent of the size of the spread. If we had done spread 4 twice as large (40×60 instead of 20×30) this would have doubled the size of both the vega and the theoretical edge. The resulting fraction would still have been –.311.

What about the risk of a large move in the price of the underlying contract? We do not need to worry about large price moves in spread 5 since its positive gamma means that a large move can only enhance the value of the position. However, we might still want to compare spreads 4 and 6 for gamma risk. Dividing the gamma by the theoretical edge we have:

Spread 4:	–72.0/2.70	≈	–26.7
Spread 6:	–56.0/2.90	≈	–19.3

We can see that spread 6 is at less risk from a large move in the price of the underlying contract because –19.3 is closer to zero than –26.7. This confirms the conclusion from Figure 9-9.

A word of warning about this method of estimating the relative riskiness of a spread. Because an option's sensitivities are only well defined within a narrow range, dividing the risk sensitivity by the theoretical edge offers only an estimate of the relative riskiness of a position. Consider, for example, the relative volatility risks of spreads 1, 2, and 3. Dividing the vega by the theoretical value for each spread we have:

Spread 1:	–1.368/2.86	≈	–.478
Spread 2:	.435/3.00	≈	–.145
Spread 3:	–.630/2.80	≈	–.225

From these numbers it appears that spread 2 is the least risky with respect to volatility since –.145 is closer to zero than –.478 or –.225. But going back to Figure 9-4 we find that spread 3 actually has the highest implied volatility, and therefore the least volatility risk. Even so, this method would have at least warned us away from spread 1, which clearly has the greatest volatility risk.

Sometimes, if a trader is under great pressure to make a quick decision, he may not have the time to make even a cursory analysis of relative riskiness of various spreads. In such cases, he will often have to rely on his instincts in choosing a strategy. While there is no substitute for experience, most traders quickly learn an important rule: *straddles and strangles are the riskiest of all spreads.* This is true whether one buys or sells these strategies. New traders sometimes assume that the purchase of straddles and strangles is not especially risky because such strategies have limited risk. But it can be just as painful to lose money day after day when one buys a straddle or strangle and the market fails to move, as it is to lose the same amount of money all at once when one sells a straddle and the market makes a violent move. Of course, a trader who is right about volatility can reap large rewards from straddles and strangles. But an experienced trader knows that such strategies offer the least margin for error, and he will usually prefer other strategies with more desirable risk characteristics.

HOW MUCH MARGIN FOR ERROR?

New traders sometimes ask what is a reasonable margin for error in assessing the inputs into a theoretical pricing model, particularly when it comes to the volatility input. As is often the case, it will depend on the trader's experience in the market in which he is trading. In some cases, 5 percentage points may be an extremely large margin for error, and the trader will feel very confident with any strategy passing such a test. In other cases, five percentage points may be almost no margin for error at all, and the trader will find that the strategy is a constant source of worry.

Perhaps a better way to approach the question is to ask not what is a reasonable margin for error, but rather to ask what is the correct size in which to do a spread given a known margin for error. Practical trading considerations aside, a trader should always choose the spread with the best risk/reward characteristics. But sometimes even the best spread will have only a small margin for error, and consequently entail significant risk. In such cases a trader, if he wants to make a trade, ought to do so in small size. If, however, a trader can execute a spread with a very large margin for error, he ought to be willing to do the spread in much larger size.

As an example, consider a trader whose best estimate of volatility in a certain market is 15%. If implied volatility is higher than 15% he will look for positions with a negative vega. If the best negative vega strategy the trader can find is a 1 × 2 ratio vertical spread with an implied volatility of 16½% (only a 1½-percentage-point margin for error), he will almost certainly keep the size of his strategy small, perhaps executing the spread only five times (5 × 10). If, however, the same spread has an implied volatility of 25% (a 10-percentage-point margin for error), and the trader has never seen volatility go that high, he may have the confidence to execute the spread in much larger size, perhaps 50 × 100.[4] The size of a trader's positions should depend on the riskiness of the positions, and this in turn depends on how much can go wrong without the strategy turning against the trader.

DIVIDENDS AND INTEREST

In addition to the delta, gamma, theta, and vega risks which all traders must consider, stock option traders might also have to consider the risk of changes in dividends and interest rates.[5] This is especially true of time spreads, since options with different expirations react differently to changes in these inputs.

Consider the evaluation table for stock options shown in Figure 9-11. With implied volatilities well below the forecast of 27%, it makes sense to look for spreads with positive vegas. Suppose we focus on four possible spreads shown in Figure 9-12. Spreads 7 and 8 are long time spreads, while spreads 9 and 10 are diagonal spreads. What are the relative merits of each spread?

As with all option spreads, we have to consider a variety of risks. Note that in the evaluation table in Figure 9-11 we used an interest rate of 8%. Suppose we believe that interest rates are likely to rise sharply in the near future. How might these spreads react to rising interest rates? We can see from Figure 9-13 that spreads 7 and 9 will be hurt by rising interest rates, while spreads 8 and 10 will be helped. If a rise in interest rates is our primary concern, we might focus on spreads 8 and 10, regardless of any desirable vega or gamma characteristics associated with spreads 7 and 9.

If we focus on spreads 8 and 10, we will still want to consider the volatility risk. We can do a cursory comparison of this risk by dividing the vega by the theoretical edge. From this we find:

Spread 8:	1.380/6.45	≈	.214
Spread 10:	2.774/6.14	≈	.452

4. Size, of course, is relative. To a well capitalized, experienced trader even 50 × 100 may be a small trade.
5. Futures options can also be affected by changes in interest rates since a change in interest rates will affect the forward price of the underlying futures contract. Unlike stocks, factors other than interest rates, such as short term supply and demand, can also affect these contracts.

Figure 9-11

Stock Price: 98½; Time: March 56 days, June 147 days; Volatility: March 27%, June 27%; Interest: 8.00%; Expected Dividend: 1.25 in 28 days and 119 days

MARCH	CALLS							PUTS						
Exercise Price	Price	Theoretical Value	Delta	Gamma	Theta	Vega	Implied Volatility	Price	Theoretical Value	Delta	Gamma	Theta	Vega	Implied Volatility
95	5	5.79	64	3.6	–.0436	.142	25.0	2¼	2.66	–36	3.6	–.0281	.142	24.1
100	2⅞	3.29	45	3.8	–.0430	.151	24.3	4¾	5.12	–55	3.8	–.0267	.151	24.6
105	1⅜	1.69	28	3.3	–.0350	.128	24.5	8⅛	8.47	–72	3.3	–.0180	.128	24.3

JUNE	CALLS							PUTS						
Exercise Price	Price	Theoretical Value	Delta	Gamma	Theta	Vega	Implied Volatility	Price	Theoretical Value	Delta	Gamma	Theta	Vega	Implied Volatility
95	7⅝	8.22	61	2.3	–.0298	.233	24.4	4¼	4.93	–39	2.3	–.0145	.233	24.1
100	5	5.85	50	2.4	–.0292	.243	23.5	6½	7.43	–50	2.4	–.0132	.243	23.2
105	3¼	4.03	38	2.3	–.0268	.233	23.6	9¾	10.49	–62	2.3	–.0099	.232	23.8

Figure 9-12

		Theoretical Edge	Delta Position	Gamma Position	Theta Position	Vega Position
Spread 7:	+25 June 95 puts	25 × +.68	+25 × −39	+25 × 2.3	+25 × −.0145	+25 × .233
	−25 March 95 puts	25 × −.41	−25 × −36	−25 × 3.6	−25 × −.0281	−25 × .142
		+6.75	−75	−32.5	+.3400	+2.275
Spread 8:	+15 June 100 calls	15 × +.85	+15 × +50	+15 × 2.4	+15 × −.0292	+15 × .243
	−15 March 100 calls	15 × −.42	−15 × +45	−15 × 3.8	−15 × −.0430	−15 × .151
		+6.45	+75	−21.0	+.2070	+1.380
Spread 9:	+15 June 95 puts	15 × +.68	+15 × −39	+15 × 2.3	+15 × −.0145	+15 × .233
	−10 March 100 puts	10 × −.37	−10 × −55	−10 × 3.8	−10 × −.0267	−10 × .151
		+6.50	−35	−3.5	+.0495	+1.985
Spread 10:	+18 June 105 calls	18 × +.78	+18 × +38	+18 × 2.3	+18 × −.0268	+18 × .233
	−10 March 95 calls	10 × −.79	−10 × +64	−10 × 3.6	−10 × −.0436	−10 × .142
		+6.14	+44	+5.40	−.0464	+2.774

Figure 9-13

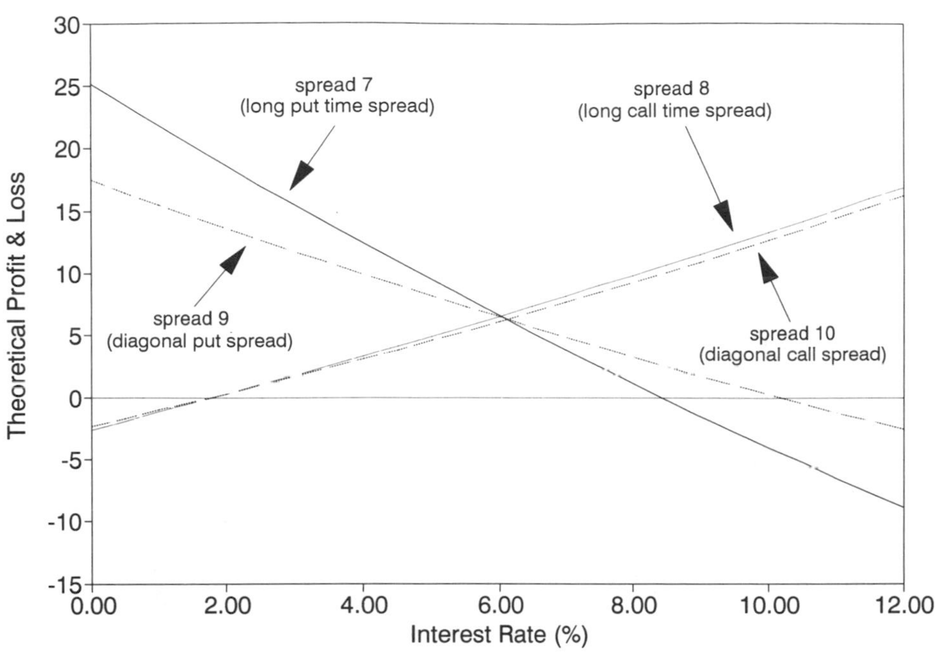

If volatility risk is our second concern, then spread 8 is probably best because its vega divided by theoretical edge is much smaller than that of spread 10. Suppose, however, that we are more concerned with a large move in the underlying stock than with a decline in volatility. Now we can see that spread 10 is best because its positive gamma means that a large move in the price of the underlying stock can only work to our advantage. As always, the choice of strategies will require us to make some judgements as to what risks we are willing to accept, and to what degree.

Finally, let's look at our spreads with respect to a change in dividends. In our evaluation table we assumed a quarterly dividend of 1.25. Suppose we believe that the dividend is likely to be increased. How will this affect our four spreads? From Figure 9-14 we can see that now spreads 7 and 9 look the best since they are helped by an increase in the dividend.

What about volatility and curvature risk? Estimating the relative risks by dividing the sensitivity by theoretical edge, we have:

	Vega Risk	Gamma Risk
Spread 7:	$2.275/6.75 \approx .337$	$-32.5/6.75 \approx -4.8$
Spread 9:	$1.985/6.50 \approx .305$	$-3.5/6.50 \approx -.5$

Since there is not much difference in the spreads in terms of vega risk, we might choose spread 9 since it has much less gamma risk. At the same time, if we believe an

Figure 9-14

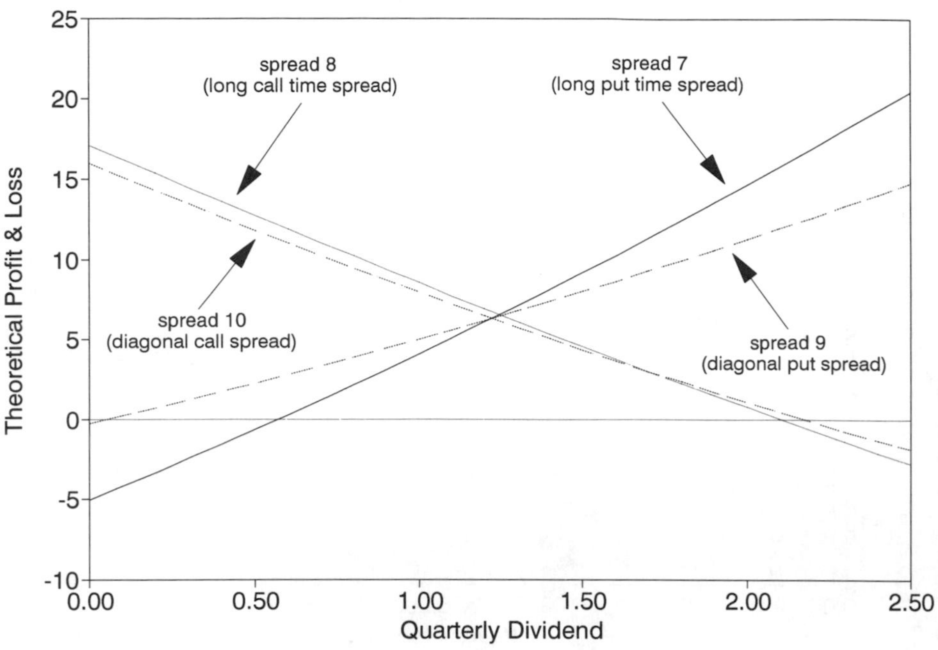

increase in the dividend is very likely, we may prefer spread 7, since we can see from Figure 9-14 that if the dividend is increased, spread 7 shows the greatest increase in value.

WHAT IS A GOOD SPREAD?

Option traders, being human, would rather talk about their successes than their disasters. If one were to eavesdrop on conversations among traders, it would probably seem that no one ever made a losing trade. Disasters, when they do occur, only happen to other traders. The fact is every successful option trader has had his share of disasters. What separates the successful trader from the unsuccessful one is the ability to survive such occurrences.

Consider the trader who initiates a spread with a good theoretical edge and a large margin for error in almost every risk category. If the trader still ends up losing money on the spread, does this mean that the trader has made a poor choice of spreads? Maybe a similar spread, but one with less margin for error, would have resulted in an even greater loss, perhaps a loss from which the trader could not recover.

It is impossible to take into consideration every possible risk. A spread which passed every risk test would probably have so little theoretical edge that it wouldn't be worth doing. But the trader who allows himself a reasonable margin for error will find that even his losses will not lead to financial ruin. A good spread is not necessarily the one that shows the greatest profit when things go well; it may be the one which shows the least loss when things go badly. Winning trades always take care of themselves. Losing trades, which don't give back all the profits from the winning ones, are just as important.

ADJUSTMENTS

In the last chapter we considered the question of when a trader should adjust a position to remain delta neutral. The trader must also consider how best to adjust, for there are many different ways to adjust the total delta position. An adjustment to a trader's delta position may reduce his directional risk, but if he simultaneously increases his gamma, theta, or vega risk, he may inadvertently be exchanging one type of risk for another.

A delta adjustment made with the underlying contract is essentially a risk neutral adjustment. By this we mean that an adjustment made with the underlying contract will not change any of the other risks we have discussed because the gamma, theta, and vega associated with an underlying contract are zero. Therefore, if a trader wants to adjust his delta position, but wants to leave the other characteristics of the position unaffected, he can do so by purchasing or selling an appropriate number of underlying contracts.

An adjustment made with options may reduce the delta risk, but will also change the other risk characteristics associated with the position. Every option, in addition to having a delta, also has a gamma, theta, and vega. When an option is added to or subtracted from a position, it necessarily changes the total delta, gamma, theta, and vega of the position. This is something which new traders sometimes forget.

Consider an option market where the underlying contract is trading at 99.25. If all options appear to be overpriced, a trader might decide to sell the 95/105 strangle (sell the 95 put, sell the 105 call). Suppose the deltas of the put and call are, respectively, −36 and +36, and the trader decides to sell 20 strangles. He is initially delta neutral since

$$(-20 \times -36) + (-20 \times +36) = 0$$

Suppose several days pass and the underlying market has fallen to 97.00, with new delta values for the 95 put and 105 call of −41 and +30. Assuming that no adjustments have been made, the trader's delta position is now

$$(-20 \times -41) + (-20 \times +30) = +220$$

If the trader now decides to make an adjustment he has three basic choices:

1. sell underlying contracts
2. sell calls
3. buy puts

Which method is best?

All other considerations being equal, whenever a trader makes an adjustment he should do so with the intention of improving the risk/reward characteristics of the position. If the trader decides to adjust his delta position by purchasing puts, he also reduces his other risks since the gamma, theta, and vega associated with the put purchase are opposite in sign to the gamma, theta, and vega associated with his existing short strangle position.

Unfortunately, all other considerations may not be equal. Since implied volatility can remain high or low for long periods of time, it is quite likely that if all options were overpriced when the trader initiated his position, they will still be overpriced when he goes back into the market to make his adjustment. Even though the purchase of puts to become delta neutral will reduce his other risks, such an adjustment will also have the effect of reducing the theoretical edge. On the other hand, if all options are overpriced and the trader decides to sell additional calls to reduce the delta, the sale of the overpriced calls will have the effect of increasing the theoretical edge. If the trader decides that adding to his theoretical edge is of primary importance he may decide to sell seven more 105 calls, leaving him approximately delta neutral since

$$(-20 \times -41) + (-27 \times +30) = +10$$

Now suppose several more days pass and the market has rebounded to 101.50, with new delta values for the 95 put and 105 call of –26 and +40. The position delta is now

$$(-20 \times -26) + (-27 \times +40) = -560$$

Again, if the trader wants to adjust he is faced with three choices: buy underlying contracts, buy calls, or sell puts. Assuming that all options are still overpriced and that the trader wants to continue to increase his theoretical edge, he may decide to sell an additional 22 of the 95 puts. The total delta position is

$$(-42 \times -26) + (-27 \times +40) = +12$$

It should be clear what will result from these adjustments. If all options remain overpriced and the trader is always intent on increasing his theoretical edge, he will continue to make whatever adjustments are necessary by continuously selling overpriced options. This method of adjusting may indeed result in the greatest profit to the trader. But notice what is happening. The strangle, which the trader was initially prepared to sell 20 times, has now increased in size to 42 × 27. If the market now makes a violent move in either direction, the negative consequences will be greatly magnified. Unfortunately, the new trader, overly concerned with always increasing his theoretical edge, often finds himself in just such a position. If the market makes a very swift move, the trader may not survive. For this reason, a new trader who is unfamiliar with all the subtleties of an option market should avoid making adjustments which increase the size of his position.

No trader can afford to ignore the effect his adjustments will have on the total risk to his position. If he has a positive (negative) gamma position, buying (selling) any additional options will increase his gamma risk. Likewise, if he has a positive (negative) vega position, buying (selling) any additional options will increase his vega risk. A trader cannot afford to sell overpriced options or buy underpriced options ad infinitum. At some point the size of the spread will simply become too large, and any additional theoretical edge will have to take a back seat to risk considerations. When that happens there are only two choices: decrease the size of the spread or adjust in the underlying market.

A disciplined trader knows that sometimes, because of risk considerations, the best course is to reduce the size of the spread, even if it means giving up some theoretical edge. This may be hard on the trader's ego, particularly if he must personally go back into the market and either buy back options which he originally sold at a lower price, or sell out options which he originally purchased at a higher price. However, if a trader is unwilling to swallow his pride from time to time, and admit that he made a mistake, his trading career is certain to be a short one.

If a trader finds that any delta adjustment in the option market that reduces his risk will also reduce his theoretical edge, and he is unwilling to give up any theoretical edge, his only recourse is to make his adjustments in the underlying market. An underlying contract has no gamma, theta, or vega, so the risks of the position will remain essentially the same.

A QUESTION OF STYLE

Because most option pricing models assume that movement in the underlying contract is random, an option trader who trades purely from the theoretical values generated by a model should not have any prior opinion about the direction in which the underlying market will move. In practice, however, many option traders begin their trading careers by taking positions in the underlying market, where direction is the primary consideration. Many traders therefore develop a style of trading based on presumed directional moves in the underlying market. A trader might, for example, be a trend follower, adhering to the philosophy that "the trend is your friend." Or he might be a contrarian, preferring to "buy weakness, sell strength."

Traders often try to incorporate their personal trading styles into their option strategies. One way to do this is to consider beforehand the adjustments which will be required for a certain strategy if the underlying market begins to move. For example, suppose a trader sells straddles in such a way that he is initially delta neutral. Such spreads have a negative gamma, so that as the market moves higher his delta position is getting shorter, and as the market moves lower his delta position is getting longer. If this trader likes to trade against the trend, he will avoid adjustments as much as possible because his position is automatically trading against the trend. Whichever way the market moves, the position always wants a retracement of this movement.

On the other hand, a trader who sells the same straddles but prefers to trade with the trend will adjust at every opportunity. In order to remain delta neutral, he will be forced to buy underlying contracts as the market rises and sell underlying contracts as the market falls.

The opposite is true for a trader who buys straddles. He has a positive gamma position, so that as the market rises his delta is becoming longer, and as the market falls his delta is becoming shorter. If this trader likes to trade with the trend, he will want to adjust as little is possible in the belief that the market is likely to continue in the same direction. However, if he prefers to trade against the trend, he will want to adjust as often as possible. Every adjustment will represent a profit opportunity if the market does in fact reverse direction.

A trader with a negative gamma is always adjusting with the trend of the underlying market. A trader with a positive gamma is always adjusting against the trend of the underlying market. If a trader prefers to trade with the trend or against the trend, he should choose a strategy and an adjustment process that is appropriate to his preference. A trader who prefers to trade with the trend can choose a strategy with a positive gamma together with less frequent adjustments, or a strategy with a negative gamma with more frequent adjustments. A trader who prefers to trade against the trend can choose a strategy with a negative gamma together with less frequent adjustments, or a strategy with a positive gamma with more frequent adjustments. The purely theoretical trader will not have to worry about this since for him there is no such thing as a trend. However, for most traders old habits, such as trading with or against the trend, die hard.

LIQUIDITY

As long as a trader has an open option position it represents a risk. Even if the risk is limited to the current value of the options, by leaving the position open the trader is risking the loss of that value. If he wants to eliminate the risk, he will have to take some action which will in effect close out the position. Sometimes this can be done through early exercise, or by taking advantage of an opposing position to create an arbitrage. More often, however, in order to close out an open position a trader will be required go into the marketplace and buy in any short options and sell out any long options.

An important consideration in deciding whether to enter into a trade is often the ease with which the trader can reverse the trade. Liquid option markets, where there are many buyers and sellers, are much less risky than illiquid markets, where there are few buyers and sellers. In the same way, a spread which consists of very liquid options is much less risky than a spread which consists of one or more illiquid options. If a trader is considering entering into a spread where the options are illiquid, he ought to ask himself whether he is willing to live with that position until expiration. If the market is very illiquid, that may be the only time he will be able to get out of the position at anything resembling a fair price. If the spread consists of long-term options, say nine months, the trader may find himself married to the position for better or worse, in sickness and in health, for the next nine months. If he is unwilling to commit his capital for that period, perhaps he should avoid the position. Since there is greater risk associated with a long-term investment than with a short-term investment, a trader who does decide to take a position in long-term options ought to expect greater potential profit in the form of larger theoretical edge.

New traders are often advised to begin trading in liquid markets. If a new trader does make an error resulting in a losing trade, in a liquid market he will be able to keep his loss to a minimum because he will be able to exit the trade with relative ease. On the other hand, an experienced trader, especially a market maker, will often prefer to deal in less liquid markets. There may be less trading activity in such markets, but the bid/ask spread is much wider, resulting in greater theoretical edge each time a trade is made. Of course, any mistake can be a problem with which the trader will have to live for a long time. However, an experienced trader is expected to keep his mistakes to a minimum.

The most liquid options in any market are those which are short-term and which are either at- or slightly out-of-the-money. Such options always have the narrowest bid/ask spread, and there are usually traders willing to buy or sell large numbers of these contracts. As a trader moves to longer term options, or to options which are more deeply in-the-money, he finds that the bid/ask spread begins to widen, and there are fewer and fewer traders interested in these contracts. While at-the-money short-term options are constantly traded, deeply in-the-money long-term options may not trade for weeks at a time.

In addition to the liquidity of an option market, a trader should also give some thought to the liquidity of the underlying market. If a trader has an option position and wants to make an adjustment, he may find it difficult to do if the option market is illiquid. If the underlying market is liquid, he will at least he be able to make his adjustment in that market with relative ease. The most dangerous market in which to trade is one where both the options and the underlying contract are inactively traded. Only the most experienced and knowledgeable traders should enter such markets.

End-of-day volume figures and bid/ask spreads in S&P 500 index options traded at the Chicago Board Options Exchange on July 9, 1993 are shown in Figure 9-15. Note the lower volume and wider bid/ask spread for back month and deeply in-the-money options, versus front month and at- and out-of-the-money options.

Figure 9-15

July 9, 1993 S&P 500 Index Options (CBOE)
S&P 500 Index at 448.11

	July Options			August Options			September Options			December Options		
	Bid	Ask	Volume	Bid	Ask	Volume	Bid	Ask	Volume	Bid	Ask	Volume
420 call	27 3/8	28 3/8	0	28 1/4	29 1/4	0	30	31	0	35 1/2	36 1/2	0
425 call	22 1/2	23 1/2	0	24 1/2	25 1/8	0	25 1/2	26 1/2	10	29 5/8	30 5/8	0
430 call	18	18 3/4	0	19 1/2	20 1/4	0	21 1/2	22 1/2	300	no listing		
435 call	13 1/4	14	355	15 5/8	16	0	17 3/8	18 1/8	0	23 1/2	24 1/4	0
440 call	8 5/8	8 7/8	2,532	11 1/8	11 5/8	2,465	13 3/4	14	1	no listing		
445 call	4 5/8	4 3/4	397	7 3/4	8 1/4	50	10 5/8	11	16	no listing		
450 call	1 1/2	1 5/8	1,013	5 1/8	5 3/8	766	7 3/8	7 7/8	27	14 1/8	14 7/8	50
455 call	5/16	7/16	500	2 7/8	3 1/8	755	5	5 3/8	1	no listing		
460 call	1/16	1/8	301	1 5/8	1 3/4	152	3 1/4	3 1/2	585	no listing		
465 call		1/16	469	13/16	7/8	1,190	2	2 1/4	0	no listing		
470 call		1/16	0	5/16	7/16	10	1	1 3/16	10	no listing		
420 put		1/16	372	13/16	1	0	1 11/16	1 13/16	800	5 7/8	6 1/8	100
425 put	1/16	1/8	2	1	1 3/16	50	2 3/8	2 5/8	520	6 3/8	6 3/4	22
430 put	1/16	1/8	932	1 3/8	1 5/8	1,483	3	3 1/4	1	no listing		
435 put	3/16	1/4	1,720	2 1/8	2 3/8	300	3 7/8	4	1,775	9 3/8	9 3/4	0
440 put	3/8	1/2	2,736	3 1/2	3 3/8	935	5 1/4	5 3/4	126	no listing		
445 put	1	1 1/16	1,438	4 1/2	4 5/8	610	6 7/8	7 3/8	8	no listing		
450 put	2 7/8	3 1/8	1,327	6 5/8	7	130	8 1/2	9	7	14 1/4	14 3/4	80
455 put	6 3/4	6 7/8	70	9 5/8	9 7/8	134	11	11 3/4	0	no listing		
460 put	11 3/4	12 1/4	23	13 1/8	13 7/8	6	14 1/4	14 5/8	0	no listing		
465 put	16 3/8	17 1/8	0	17 1/8	17 7/8	0	17 1/2	18 1/4	0	no listing		
470 put	21 1/4	22	0	20 3/4	21 3/4	0	21 1/4	22 1/4	0	no listing		

❖ 10 ❖

Bull and Bear Spreads

While delta neutral strategies are perhaps the most popular among active option traders, many traders prefer to trade with a bullish or bearish perspective in the underlying instrument. The trader who wishes to take a directional position in the underlying instrument has the choice of doing so in either the instrument itself, buying or selling a futures contract or stock, or in the option market. If he chooses the option market, the trader has the opportunity to integrate option pricing theory into a bull or bear strategy in order to take advantage of theoretically mispriced options.

NAKED POSITIONS

Since the purchase of calls or the sale of puts will create a positive delta position, and the sale of calls or purchase of puts will create a negative delta position, we can always take a directional position in a market by taking an appropriate naked position in either calls or puts. If all options are overpriced (high implied volatility), we might sell puts to create a bullish position, or sell calls to create a bearish position. If all options are underpriced (low implied volatility), we might buy calls to create a bullish position, or buy puts to create a bearish position.

The problem with this approach is that, as with all non-hedged positions, there is very little margin for error. If we purchase options, we will lose money not only if the market moves in the wrong direction, but also if the market fails to move enough in our favor to offset the time premium in the option. If we sell options, we face the prospect of unlimited risk if the market moves violently against us. An experienced trader will always look for a way to improve the risk/reward characteristics of his position by looking for positions with the greatest possible margin for error. This philosophy applies no less to directional strategies than to volatility strategies. In directional strategies, as in volatility strategies, this can often be done by finding an appropriate spread.

BULL AND BEAR RATIO SPREADS

If a trader believes that implied volatility is too high, one sensible strategy is a ratio vertical spread. For example, with the underlying market at 100 suppose a June 100 call has a delta of 50 and a June 110 call has a delta of 25. A delta neutral spreader can:

buy 1 June 100 call (50)
sell 2 June 110 calls (25)

Since the spread is delta neutral, it has no particular preference for upward or downward movement in the underlying market.

Now suppose the same trader believes that this ratio vertical spread is a sensible strategy, but at the same time he is also bullish on the market. There is no law that requires him to do this spread in a delta neutral ratio. If he wants this spread to reflect his bullish sentiment, he might change the ratio slightly:

buy 2 June 100 calls (50)
sell 3 June 110 calls (25)

The trader has essentially the same ratio vertical spread, but with a bullish bias. This is reflected in the total delta for the position of +25.

There is, however, an important limitation using this type of ratio strategy to create a bullish or bearish position. In our example the trader is initially bullish, but the position is still a ratio vertical spread. As such, it has a negative gamma. If the trader has underestimated volatility, and the underlying market moves up too quickly, the spread can invert from a positive to a negative delta. If the market rises far enough, to 130 or 140, eventually all options will go deeply into-the-money and the deltas of both the June 100 and June 110 calls will approach 100. Eventually, the trader will be left with a delta position of −100. Even though the trader was correct in his bullish sentiment, the position was primarily a volatility spread, so that the volatility characteristics of the position eventually outweighed any considerations of market direction.

The delta can also invert with a backspread. Unlike a negative gamma position, where the inversion is caused by swift price movement in the underlying contract, a backspread can invert when the market is less volatile than expected. For example, suppose that with the underlying market at 100 a trader believes that implied volatility is too low. He might decide on a delta neutral backspread:

buy 2 June 110 calls (25)
sell 1 June 100 call (50)

If, however, he is bullish on the market, he can, as in the last example, change the ratio to reflect this sentiment:

buy 3 June 110 calls (25)
sell 1 June 100 call (50)

His delta position of +25 reflects this bullish bias.

We know that as time passes, or as volatility declines, all deltas move away from 50. If time begins to pass with no movement in the underlying contract, the delta of the June 100 call will remain at 50, but the delta of the June 110 call will start to decline. If, after a period of time, the delta of the June 100 call declines to 10, the delta of the position will no longer be +25, but will instead be −20. Since this spread is a volatility spread, the primary consideration, as before, is the volatility of the market. Only secondarily are we concerned with the direction of movement. If the trader overestimates volatility, and the market moves more slowly than expected, the spread which was initially delta positive can instead become delta negative.

BULL AND BEAR BUTTERFLIES AND TIME SPREADS

Butterflies and one-to-one (non-ratioed) time spreads can also be chosen in such a way as to reflect a trader's bullish or bearish bias. Like ratio spreads, however, their delta characteristics can also invert as market conditions change.

With the underlying market at 100, a delta neutral trader might buy the June 95/100/105 call butterfly (buy a 95 call, sell two 100 calls, buy a 105 call). The trader hopes that the market will sit still at 100 so that at expiration the butterfly will widen to its maximum value of five points. If, however, a trader wants to buy a butterfly, but is also bullish on the market, he can choose a butterfly where the inside exercise price is above the current price of the underlying contract. If the underlying market is currently at 100, he might choose to buy the June 105/110/115 call butterfly. Since this position wants the underlying market at 110 at expiration, and it is currently at 100, the position is a bull butterfly. This will be reflected in the position having a positive delta.

Unfortunately, if the underlying market moves too swiftly, say to 120, the butterfly can invert from a positive to a negative delta position. Since at expiration the butterfly always has its maximum value with the underlying contract right at the inside exercise price, the trader will now want the market to fall back from 120 to 110. Whenever the underlying market is below 110, the position will be bullish; whenever the underlying market is above 110, the position will be bearish.

Conversely, if the trader is bearish, he can always choose to buy a butterfly where the inside exercise price is below the current price of the underlying market. But again, if the market moves down too quickly and goes through the inside exercise price, the position will invert from a negative to a positive delta.

In a similar manner, a trader can choose time spreads that are either bullish or bearish. A long time spread always wants the near-term contract to expire exactly at-the-money. A long time spread will be initially bullish if the exercise price of the time spread is above the current price of the underlying market.[1] With the underlying market at 100, the June/March 110 call time spread (buy the June 110 call/sell the March 110 call) will be bullish since the trader will want the underlying market to rise to 110 by March expiration. The June/March 90 call time spread (buy the June 90 call/sell the March 90 call) will be bearish, since the trader will want the underlying market to fall to 90 by March expiration. However, like a long butterfly, a long time spread has a negative gamma, so that if the market moves through the exercise price, the delta can invert. If the market moves from 100 to 120, the June/March 110 call time spread, which was initially bullish, will become bearish. If the market moves from 100 to 80, the June/March 90 call time spread, which was initially bearish, will become bullish.

---

1. In the futures market the situation may be complicated by the fact that different futures months may be trading at different prices. Instead of choosing a traditional time spread where both options have the same exercise price, the trader may have to choose a diagonal spread to ensure that the position is either bullish (delta positive) or bearish (delta negative).

VERTICAL SPREADS

It is common for traders to take bull or bear market positions by choosing appropriate ratio spreads, butterflies, or time spreads, but in each of these positions volatility is still the primary concern. A trader can be right about market direction, but if he is wrong about volatility, the spread may not retain the directional characteristics that the trader intended.

If a trader focuses initially on the direction of the underlying market, he might look for a spread where the directional characteristics of the spread are the primary concern, and volatility is of secondary importance. He would like to be certain that if the spread is initially bullish (delta positive) it will remain bullish under all possible market conditions. If it is initially bearish (delta negative) it will remain bearish under all possible market conditions.

The class of spreads which meet the above requirements are known as *vertical spreads*. A vertical spread always consists of one long (purchased) option and one short (sold) option, where both options are of the same type (either both calls or both puts) and expire at the same time. The options are distinguished only by their different exercise prices. Typical vertical spreads might be:

buy 1 June 100 call
sell 1 June 105 call

or

buy 1 March 105 put
sell 1 March 95 put

Vertical spreads are not only initially bullish or bearish, but they remain bullish or bearish no matter how market conditions change. Two options which have different exercise prices but which are identical in every other respect cannot have identical deltas. In the first example, where the trader is long a June 100 call and short a June 105 call, the June 100 call will always have a delta greater than the June 105 call. If both options go deeply into-the-money or very far out-of-the-money, the deltas may be almost identical. Even then, the June 100 call will have a delta fractionally greater than the June 105 call. In the second example, no matter how market conditions change, the March 105 put will always have a delta greater than the March 95 put.

At expiration, a vertical spread will have a minimum value of zero, if both options are out-of-the-money, and a maximum value of the amount between exercise prices, if both options are in-the-money. If the underlying market is below 100 at expiration, the June 100/105 call spread will be worthless because both options will be worthless. If the market is above 105, the same spread will be worth five points because the June 100 call will be worth exactly five points more than the June 105 call. Similarly, the March 95/105 put spread will be worthless if the underlying market is above 105 at expiration, and it will be worth 10 points if the market is below 95. The expiration values of typical bull and bear vertical spreads are shown in Figures 10-1 and 10-2.

Figure 10-1

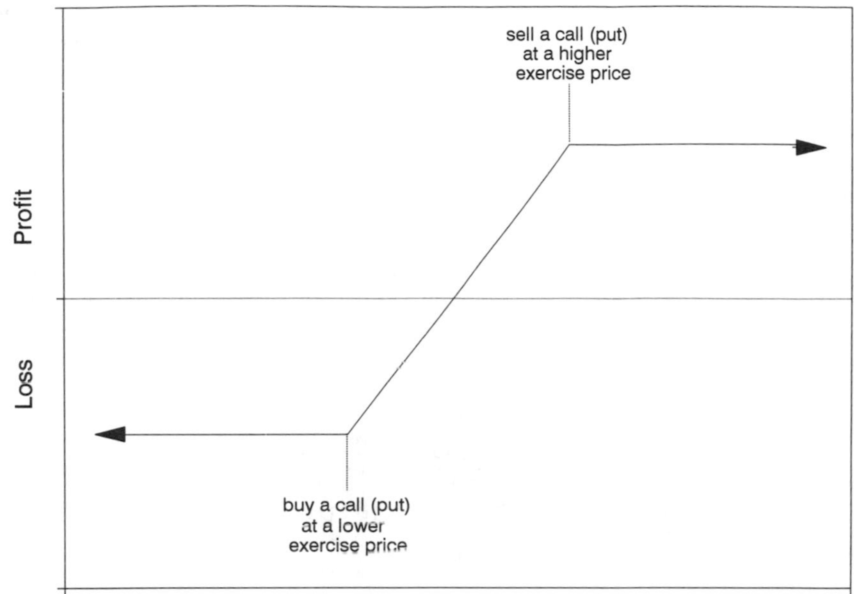

Figure 10-2

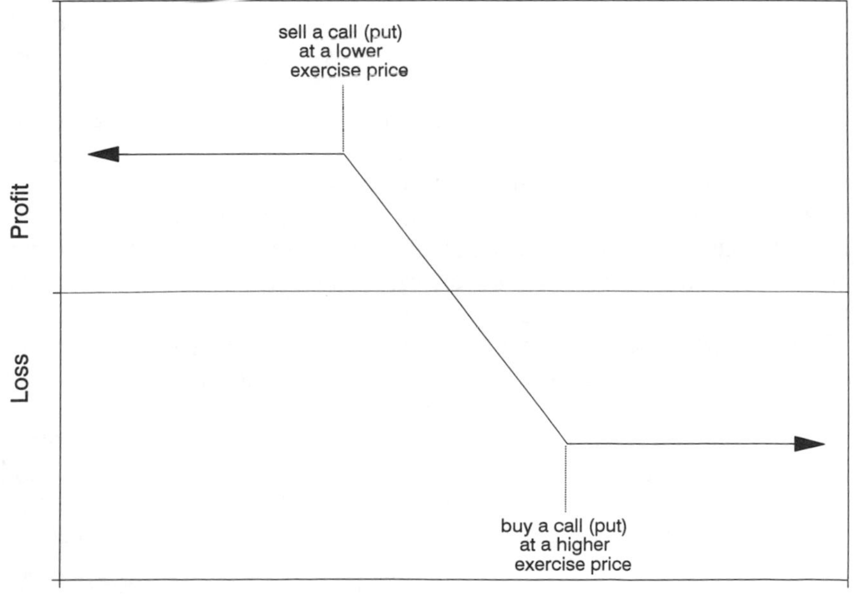

Since a vertical spread at expiration will always have a value between zero and the amount between exercise prices, a trader can expect the price of such a spread to be somewhere within this range. A 100/105 call vertical spread will trade for some amount between zero and five points; a 95/105 put vertical spread will trade for some amount between zero and 10 points. The exact value will depend on the likelihood of the underlying market finishing below the lower exercise price, above the higher exercise price, or somewhere in between. If the market is currently at 80 and gives little indication of rising, the price of the 100/105 call vertical will be close to zero, while the price of the 95/105 puts vertical will be close to 10. If the market is currently at 120 with little likelihood that it will fall, the price of the 100/105 call vertical will be close to five points, while the price of the 95/105 put vertical will be close to zero.

If a trader wants to do a vertical spread, he has essentially four choices. If he is bullish he can choose a bull vertical call spread or a bull vertical put spread; if he is bearish he can choose a bear vertical call spread or a bear vertical put spread. For example:

bull call spread:	buy a June 100 call
	sell a June 105 call
bull put spread:	buy a June 100 put
	sell a June 105 put
bear call spread:	sell a June 100 call
	buy a June 105 call
bear put spread:	sell a June 100 put
	buy a June 105 put

Note that a trader who is bullish can buy a 100 call and sell a 105 call, or buy a 100 put and sell a 105 put. And a trader who is bearish can buy a 105 call and sell a 100 call, or buy a 105 put and sell 100 put. This may seem counter-intuitive, since one expects spreads which consist of puts to have characteristics which are the opposite of those which consist of calls. *Regardless of whether a vertical spread consists of calls or puts, whenever a trader buys the lower exercise price and sells the higher exercise price, the position is bullish; whenever a trader buys the higher exercise price and sells the lower exercise price, the position is bearish.* Call and put vertical spreads which expire at the same time and which consist of the same exercise prices have approximately the same delta, so they have approximately the same bullish or bearish characteristics.[2]

Given the many different exercise prices and expiration months available, how can a trader choose the vertical spread which best reflects his directional expectations and which gives him the best chance to profit from those expectations?

Since options have a limited life with a fixed expiration date, a trader who wants to use options to take advantage of an expected market move must first determine his time horizon. Is the movement likely to occur in the next month, in the next three months, in the next nine months? If it is currently May and the trader foresees upward

2. We are assuming for the moment that all options are European, with no possibility of early exercise.

movement, but believes the movement is unlikely to occur within the next two months, it does not make much sense to take a position in June options. If his expectations are long-term, he may have to take his position in September, or even December, options. Of course, as he moves further and further out in time, market liquidity may become more of a problem. This is a factor that will have to taken into consideration.

Next, a trader will have to decide just how bullish or bearish he is. Is he very confident, and therefore willing to take a very large directional position? Or is he less certain and willing to take only a limited position? Two factors determine the total directional characteristics of a vertical spread:

1. The delta of the specific vertical spread
2. The size in which the spread is executed

For example, a trader who wants to take a position which is 500 deltas long (equivalent to purchasing five underlying contracts) can either choose a vertical spread which is 50 deltas long and execute it 10 times, or choose a vertical spread which is 25 deltas long and execute it 20 times. Both positions will leave him long 500 deltas.

The delta value of a vertical spread is determined by various factors: time to expiration, volatility, and distance between exercise prices. Since a trader will be required to choose an expiration date which covers the period of expected directional movement, and since a trader will always make his best estimate of volatility over a given period, in practice the delta will be a function of the exercise prices which he chooses. The greater the distance between exercise prices, the greater the delta value associated with the spread. A 95/110 bull spread will be more bullish than a 100/110 bull spread, which will, in turn, be more bullish than a 100/105 bull spread. This is shown in Figure 10-3.

Once a trader decides on an expiration month in which to take his directional position, he must decide which specific spread is best. That is, he must decide which exercise prices to use. A common approach is to focus on the at-the-money options. If a trader does this, he will have the following choices:

Bull call spread:	buy an in-the-money call sell an at-the-money call	or	buy an at-the-money call sell an out-of-the-money
Bear call spread:	buy an at-the-money call sell an in-the-money call	or	buy an out-of-the-money call sell an at-the-money call
Bull put spread:	buy an at-the-money put sell an in-the-money put	or	buy an out-of-the-money put sell an at-the-money put
Bear put spread:	buy an in-the-money put sell an at-the-money put	or	buy an at-the-money put sell an out-of-the-money put

With four different bull spreads and four different bear spreads available, how can the trader choose the spread which represents the best value? One way to do this is to use a theoretical pricing model to evaluate several different vertical spreads. This has been done in Figure 10-4 for six different options on an underlying futures contract: an in-the-money, at-the-money, and out-of-the-money call, and an in-the-money, at-the-

Figure 10-3

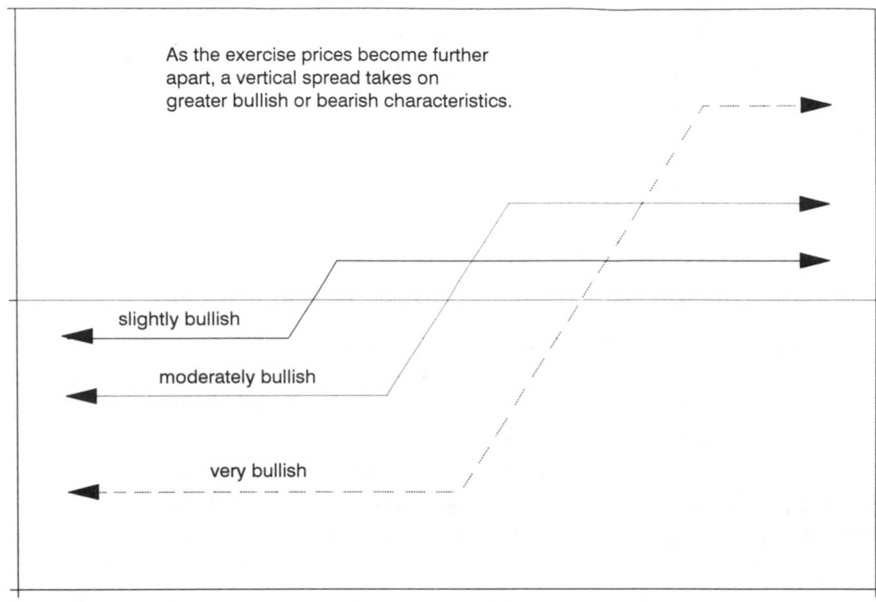
As the exercise prices become further apart, a vertical spread takes on greater bullish or bearish characteristics.
slightly bullish
moderately bullish
very bullish

money, and out-of-the-money put. The assumptions include an underlying price of 100, 12 weeks to expiration, a volatility estimate of 20%, and an interest rate of 8%.

Suppose we are interested in doing a bull call spread. Two possibilities are to buy a 95 call and sell a 100 call, or buy a 100 call and sell a 105 call. The spreads and their theoretical values are:

Spread	Theoretical Value	Delta
95/100 call spread	2.87	+20
100/105 call spread	1.88	+20

Figure 10-4

Futures price = 100; Time = 12 weeks; Volatility = 20%; Interest = 8.00%

Option	Theoretical Value	Delta	Gamma	Theta	Vega
95 call	6.63	71	3.4	–.017	.16
100 call	3.76	51	4.1	–.022	.19
105 call	1.88	31	3.7	–.020	.17
95 put	1.72	–27	3.4	–.019	.16
100 put	3.76	–47	4.1	–.022	.19
105 put	6.79	–67	3.7	–.019	.17

With both spreads having the same delta of +20, it may appear that the 100/105 spread is a better value since it is likely to be less expensive. But should this be the sole determinant in choosing a strategy? As in all spreads, the option trader's goal is to create a position with positive theoretical edge, by either purchasing high value at a low price, or selling low value at a high price. In order to achieve this goal we need to know not only the theoretical values of the spreads, but also the prices of the spreads in the marketplace.

From an option trader's point of view, the relative prices of options in the marketplace is usually represented by the implied volatility. We know the value of the spreads based on our volatility input of 20%. What might be the prices of the spreads if implied volatility in the option market is something other than 20%? We can answer the question by using a theoretical pricing model with the same underlying price, time to expiration, and interest rate, but with volatilities lower and higher than 20%. This has been done in Figure 10-5 using volatilities of 16% and 24%, along with our estimated volatility of 20%.

Going back to our bull call spread, suppose implied volatility is lower than our estimate of 20%, say 16%. We can see that the price of the 95/100 spread will be approximately 3.01, while the price of the 100/105 spread will be approximately 1.78. We have two choices: we can pay 3.01 for a spread that is worth 2.87 (the 95/100 spread), or we can pay 1.78 for a spread that is worth 1.88 (the 100/105 spread). Clearly, we will prefer the 100/105 spread since it will result in a positive theoretical edge of .10. If we were to buy the 95/100 spread we would end up with a negative theoretical edge of .14.

Now suppose implied volatility is higher than our estimate of 20%, say 24%. We can see that the price of the 95/100 spread will be approximately 2.77, while the price of the 100/105 spread will be approximately 1.94. Again, we have two choices: we can pay 2.77 for a spread that is worth 2.87 (the 95/100 spread), or we can pay 1.94 for a spread that is worth 1.88 (the 100/105 spread). Now we will prefer the 95/100 spread since it will result in a positive theoretical edge of .10. The 100/105 spread would result in a negative theoretical edge of .06.

Figure 10-5

Volatility	95 Call	95/100 Spread	100 Call	100/105 Spread	105 Call
16%	6.02	3.01	3.01	1.78	1.23
20%	6.63 (71)	2.87 (20)	3.76 (51)	1.88 (20)	2.57 (31)
24%	7.28	2.77	4.51	1.94	2.57

Volatility	95 Put	95/100 Spread	100 Put	100/105 Spread	105 Put
16%	1.11	1.90	3.01	3.13	6.14
20%	1.72 (–27)	2.04 (20)	3.76 (–47)	3.03 (20)	6.79 (–67)
24%	2.37	2.14	4.51	2.97	7.48

What's happening here? Even though both spreads have the same delta values, under one set of circumstances we seem to prefer the 95/100 spread, while under different circumstances we seem to prefer the 100/105 spread. The reason becomes clear if we recall one of the characteristics of option evaluation introduced in Chapter 6:

> If we consider three options, an in-the-money, at-the-money, and out-of-the-money option which are identical except for their exercise prices, the at-the-money option is always the most sensitive in total points to a change in volatility.

This means that when all options appear overpriced because we believe implied volatility is too high, in total points the at-the-money option will be the most overpriced. When all options appear underpriced because we believe implied volatility is too low, in total points the at-the-money option will be the most underpriced. This characteristic leads to a very simple rule for choosing bull and bear vertical spreads:

> *If implied volatility is too low, vertical spreads should focus on purchasing the at-the-money option. If implied volatility is too high, vertical spreads should focus on selling the at-the-money options.*

Now we can see why the 100/105 call spread is a better value if implied volatility is 16%, while the 95/100 spread is a better value if implied volatility is 24%. If implied volatility is too low (16%), we want to buy the at-the-money (100) call. Having done this, we have only one choice in order to create a bull spread—sell the out-of-the-money (105) call. If implied volatility is too high (24%), we want to sell the at-the-money (100) call. Having done this, we again have only one choice in order to create a bull spread—buy the in-the-money (95) call.

The same principle is equally true for put vertical spreads. We always want to focus on the at-the-money option, buying it when implied volatility is too low, and selling it when implied volatility is too high. For example, suppose we want to do a bear put spread with implied volatility too low. In this case we want to buy the at-the-money (100) put. Having done this, we are forced to sell the out-of-the-money (95) put to create our bear spread. We can see from Figure 10-5 that we will pay approximately 1.90 for this spread, but the spread is worth 2.04. We will end up with a delta position of –20, and a positive theoretical edge of .14.

Of course, a trader is not required to execute any vertical spread by first buying or selling the at-the-money option. Such spreads always involve two options, and a trader can choose to either execute the complete spread in one transaction, or leg into the spread by trading one option at a time. In the latter case, he may decide to first trade the in-the-money or out-of-the-money option, and trade the at-the-money option at a later time. This is a practical trading decision he will have to make based on market conditions and the amount of risk he is willing to accept. Regardless of how the spread is executed, the trader should focus on the at-the-money option, either buying it when implied volatility is too low, or selling it when implied volatility is too high.

In practice it is unlikely that one option will be exactly at-the-money, so that it may be difficult to decide which option to buy and which to sell. In such a case, it is usually best to focus on the option which is closest to at-the-money. If the underlying market is at 103, with 95, 100, 105, and 110 calls available, it is logical to focus on the 105 call since it is closest to at-the-money. If implied volatility is too low, a trader will want to buy the 105 call; if implied volatility is too high, a trader will want to sell the 105 call. He can then trade a different option in order to create a bull or bear vertical spread.

Nor does a trader have to include the option which is closest-to-the-money as part of his spread. A trader who has a strong directional opinion can choose a vertical spread where both options are very far out-of-the-money or very deeply in-the-money. The delta values of such spreads will be very low, but a trader can create a highly leveraged position by executing each spread many times. For example, with the underlying market at 100, a trader who is strongly bullish might buy the 115/120 call spread (assuming such exercise prices are available). The cost of this spread will be very low since there is a high probability that the spread will expire worthless. Hence, the trader will be able to execute the spread many times at a relatively low cost. If he is right and the market does rise above 120, the spread will widen to its maximum value of five points, resulting in very large profits. But regardless of the exercise prices chosen, if implied volatility is low, the trader will attempt to buy the closer-to-the-money option, and if implied volatility is high, the trader will attempt to sell the closer-to-the-money option.

The choice of the at-the-money option is slightly different when we move to stock options. If we define the at-the-money option as the one whose delta is closest to 50, then we may find that the at-the-money option is not always the one whose exercise price is closest to the current price of the underlying contract. This is because the option with a delta closest to 50 will be the one whose exercise price is closest to the forward price of the underlying contract. In stock options, the forward price is the current price of the stock, plus carrying costs on the stock, less expected dividends. Assuming an underlying stock price of 99, six months to expiration, a volatility of 28%, interest rates of 10%, and no dividend, we can see from Figure 10-6 that the 105 call has a delta of 50 and therefore acts like the at-the-money option, even though its exercise price is six points higher than the current underlying price. Therefore, any vertical spread should focus on the 105 call or 105 put.

The approximate prices of vertical spreads with these stock options at implied volatilities of 23% and 33% are shown in Figure 10-7.

Figure 10-6

Stock price = 99; Time = 6 months; Volatility = 28%; Interest = 8.00%

Option	Theoretical Value	Delta	Gamma	Theta	Vega
95 call	11.97	69	1.8	–.031	.24
105 call	6.96	50	2.0	–.030	.27
115 call	3.74	32	1.8	–.025	.25
95 put	4.25	–31	1.8	–.013	.22
105 put	9.20	–50	2.0	–.011	.26
115 put	15.68	–68	1.8	–.004	.24

Figure 10-7

Volatility	95 Call	95/105 Spread	105 Call	105/115 Spread	115 Call
23%	10.77	5.20	5.57	3.05	2.52
28%	11.97 (69)	5.01 (19)	6.96 (50)	3.22 (18)	3.74 (32)
33%	13.21	4.85	8.36	3.34	5.02

Volatility	95 Call	95/105 Spread	105 Call	105/115 Spread	115 Call
23%	3.05	4.41	7.46	6.56	14.02
28%	4.25 (–31)	4.60 (19)	8.85 (–50)	6.39 (19)	15.24 (–68)
33%	5.49	4.76	10.25	6.27	16.52

As always, we can never be certain of the delta values of a spread because we can never be certain that we have the correct inputs into the model, in particular, volatility. If volatility turns out to be lower than our estimate, the deltas will move away from 50. If volatility turns out to be higher than our estimate, the deltas will move towards 50. This will change the delta values of the spreads. However, if we work around the at-the-money option, spreads with approximately the same amount between exercise prices will have approximately the same delta values. Our primary problem will be deciding whether implied volatility is too high or too low.

Notice that in every case, whether with futures options or with stock options, whether using a low volatility or a high volatility, if one leg of our spread always involves an at-the-money option, the vertical spread which includes the in-the-money option always has a higher price than the spread which includes the out-of-the-money option. A new trader might take the view that since both spreads have approximately the same delta values, it must make sense to always purchase the cheaper spread or sell the more expensive. This ignores the purpose of option evaluation: to consider not only the initial cost of a strategy, but to compare that to the strategy's expected return. In our futures option example, a trader will always have to pay more for the 95/100 call spread than the 100/105 call spread. But if implied volatility is too high, the 95/100 spread will also return more to the trader. To see why, suppose a trader is choosing between the 95/100 bull call spread and the 100/105 bull call spread. Consider three possible cases. In case one, the trader is right and the market moves from 100 to 110. If that happens both spreads will be winners since they will both widen to their maximum value of five points. In case two, the trader is wrong and the market drops to 90. In that case both spreads will be losers since they will both collapse to zero. Now consider case three, where the trader is wrong because he expected the underlying market to rise and it didn't. But he wasn't terribly wrong, because it also didn't fall. It simply remained at 100. If that happens the 100/105 spread will collapse to zero, while the 95/100 spread will still widen to its maximum value of five points. The 95/100 spread is always more valuable than the 100/105 spread because it has time on its side. The 100/105 spread needs the market to rise to show a profit. The 95/100 spread doesn't really need the market to rise; it just needs for the market not to fall. The reader can confirm this by calculating the gamma and theta positions of the spreads in Figure 10-5. The 100/105 spread has a positive gamma and a negative theta, whereas the 95/100 spread has negative gamma and a positive theta.

If a trader is considering a bull vertical spread, how likely is it that the market will rise? That depends on his ability to predict market direction. At the same time, he must ask himself how likely it is that the market will move. That depends on his ability to predict volatility. If a trader believes there is a good chance the market will move (high volatility), and at the same time believes the movement will be to the upside (bullish on direction), it makes sense to buy the 100/105 spread. On the other hand, if the trader believes the market is unlikely to move significantly (low volatility), but at the same time believes that whatever movement does occur is likely to come on the upside (also bullish), it makes sense to buy the 95/100 spread. In both cases the trader is trying to maximize the return on his investment when he is right and minimize the loss when he is wrong.

Why might a trader with a directional opinion prefer a vertical spread to an outright long or short position in the underlying instrument? For one thing, a vertical spread is much less risky than an outright position. A trader who wants to take a position which is 500 deltas long can either buy five underlying contracts or buy 25 vertical call spreads with a delta of 20 each. The 25 vertical spreads may sound riskier than five underlying contracts, until we remember that a vertical spread has limited risk while the position in the underlying has open-ended risk. Of course, greater risk also means greater reward. A trader with a long or short position in the underlying market can reap huge rewards if the market makes a large move in his favor. By contrast, the vertical spreader's profits are limited, but he will also be much less bloodied if the market makes an unexpected move in the wrong direction.

Experienced traders accept the fact that they are human, and that their directional forecasts will occasionally be wrong. When that happens the vertical spreader has a distinct advantage over the trader with an outright position in the underlying market. By intelligently estimating volatility, an option trader can decide whether he wants time working for or against him. When he chooses to have time on his side (positive theta), he can sometimes show a profit when the outright trader either breaks even or shows a loss. When he chooses to have time working against him (positive gamma), the option trader's losses when he is wrong about market direction will often be less than the losses from an outright underlying position.

❖ 11 ❖

Option Arbitrage

One important characteristic of options is that they can be combined with other options or underlying contracts to create positions with characteristics which are almost identical to some other contract or combination of contracts. This type of replication leads to a new category of trading strategies which are unique to the option market.

SYNTHETIC POSITIONS

Suppose a trader has the following position where all options are European (no early exercise permitted):

long a June 100 call
short a June 100 put

What will happen to this position at expiration? It may seem that one cannot answer the question without knowing where the underlying contract will be at expiration. Surprisingly, the price of the underlying contract does not affect the outcome. If the underlying contract is above 100, the put will expire worthless, but the trader will exercise the 100 call. This results in his buying the underlying contract at 100. Conversely, if the underlying contract is below 100, the call will expire worthless, but the trader will be assigned on the 100 put. This also results in his buying the underlying contract at 100.

Ignoring for the moment the unique case when the underlying contract is right at 100, at June expiration the above position will always result in the trader going long the underlying instrument at the exercise price of 100. He will go long, either by choice (the underlying contract is above 100 and he exercises the 100 call) or by force (the underlying contract is below 100 and he is assigned on the 100 put). We refer to this position as a *synthetic long underlying*. The position has the same characteristics as the underlying contract, but won't actually become an underlying contract until expiration.

If the trader takes the opposite position, selling a June 100 call and purchasing a June 100 put, he has a *synthetic short underlying*. This position will always result in his selling the underlying contract at the exercise price of 100, either by choice (the underlying contract is below 100 and he exercises the 100 put) or by force (the underlying contract is above 100 and he is assigned on the 100 call).

We can express the foregoing relationships as follows:

synthetic long underlying = long call + short put
synthetic short underlying = short call + long put

where all options expire at the same time and have the same exercise price.

A synthetic position acts very much like its real equivalent. For each point the underlying instrument rises, a synthetic long position will gain approximately one point in value and a synthetic short position will lose approximately one point in value. This leads us to conclude, correctly, that the delta of a synthetic underlying position is approximately 100. If the delta of the June 100 call is 75, the delta of the June 100 put will be approximately –25. If the delta of the June 100 put is –60, the delta of the June 100 call will be approximately 40. Ignoring the positive sign associated with a call and the negative sign associated with a put, the deltas of calls and puts with the same underlying contract, expiration date, and exercise price will always add up to approximately 100. As we will see, interest rates, as well as the possibility of early exercise, can cause the delta of a synthetic underlying position to be slightly more or less than 100. But for most practical calculations, traders tend to look at a synthetic underlying position and mentally assign it a delta of 100.

Rearranging the components of a synthetic underling position, we can create four other synthetic relationships:

synthetic long call = long an underlying contract + long put
synthetic short call = short an underlying contract + short put

synthetic long put = short an underlying contract + long call
synthetic short put = long an underlying contract + short call

Again, all options must expire at the same time and have the same exercise price. Each synthetic position has a delta approximately equal to its real equivalent and will therefore gain or lose value at approximately the same rate as its real equivalent.

If the underlying instrument in our examples is a June futures contract, we can create six synthetic positions:

synthetic long June future = long June 100 call + short June 100 put
synthetic short June future = short June 100 call + long June 100 put

synthetic long June 100 call = long June future + long June 100 put
synthetic short June 100 call = short June future + short June 100 put

synthetic long June 100 put = short June future + long June 100 call
synthetic short June 100 put = long June future + short June 100 call

We need not create a synthetic position using the 100 exercise price. We can choose any available exercise price. A long June 110 call together with a short June 110 put is still a synthetic long June futures contract; however, at June expiration the June futures contract will be purchased at 110. A short June 95 call together with a long June 95 put is a synthetic short June futures contract. But at expiration the June futures contract will be sold at 95.

Suppose an underlying contract is trading at 102.00 and we want to take a long position in the market. We can simply go into the underlying market and buy the contract at 102.00. But we now have an additional choice. We can take a long synthetic position by purchasing a June call and selling a June put at the same exercise price. Which of these strategies is best? As with any option strategy, the decision depends on the prices of the options in the marketplace. Suppose the June 100 call is trading at 5.00 and the June 100 put is trading at 3.00. If we buy the June 100 call for 5.00 and sell the June 100 put for 3.00, we will show an immediate debit of 2.00. If at expiration the underlying contract is at 110.00, we will show a credit of 10.00 when we exercise our June 100 call, for a total profit of 8.00. If we ignore interest considerations, this is identical to the profit we would have realized had we instead bought the underlying contract at 102.00. This is shown in Figure 11-1.

Suppose the underlying contract is still trading at 102.00, but now the June 100 call is trading at 4.90 and the June 100 put is trading at 3.05. If we take a synthetic long underlying position by purchasing the June 100 call and selling the June 100 put, we will show a debit of 1.85. Now if the underlying contract is at 110.00 at expiration we will show a total profit of 8.15 (the debit of 1.85 from the option trades, plus the 10-point credit when we exercise the 100 call). This is .15 better than we would do by taking a long position in the underlying contract at 102.00.

As long as the price of the June 100 call is exactly two points greater than the price of the June 100 put, the profit or loss resulting from a synthetic position will be identical

Figure 11-1

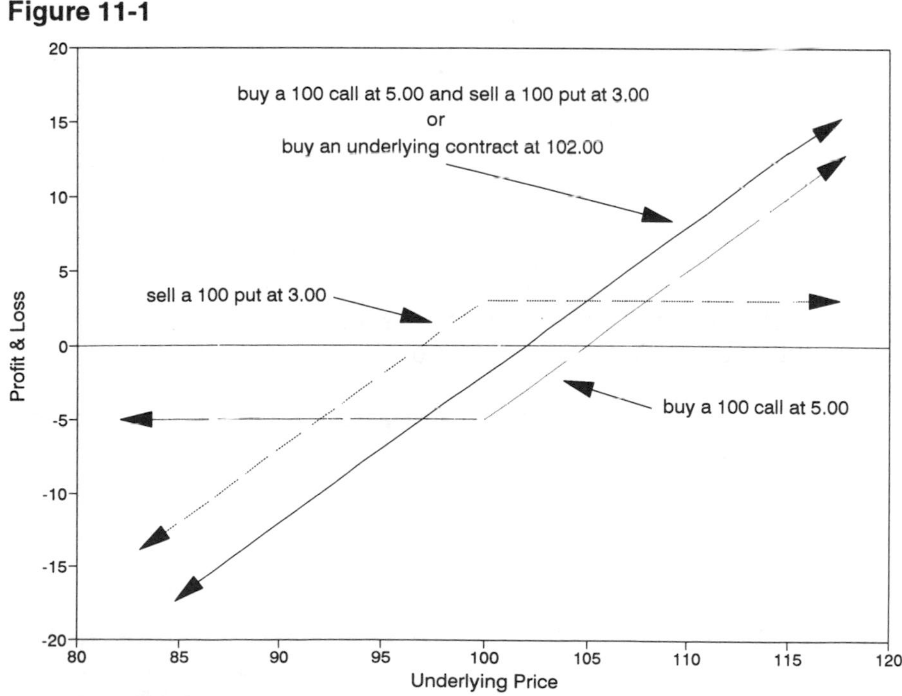

to an actual position taken in the underlying contract at a price of 102.00. The difference between the call and put price is often referred to as the *synthetic market.* In the absence of any interest or dividend considerations, the value of the synthetic market can be expressed as:

$$\text{call price} - \text{put price} = \text{underlying price} - \text{exercise price}$$

If this equality holds, there is no difference between taking a position in the underlying market, or taking an equivalent synthetic position in the option market. With the June 100 call at 5.00 and the June 100 put at 3.00, we can write:

$$5.00 - 3.00 = 102.00 - 100.00$$
$$2.00 = 2.00$$

There is no difference between the synthetic and its real equivalent.

With the June 100 call at 4.90 and the June 100 put at 3.05, we can write:

$$4.95 - 3.05 \neq 102.00 - 100.00$$
$$1.90 \neq 2.00$$

Here the synthetic side is cheaper, and we therefore prefer to take a long underlying position synthetically by purchasing the call and selling the put.

Now suppose the price of the June 100 call is 5.15 and the price of the June 100 put is 2.90, with the underlying contract still trading at 102.00. We have:

$$5.15 - 2.90 \neq 102.00 - 100.00$$
$$2.25 \neq 2.00$$

Now the real side is cheaper, so we prefer to take a long position by purchasing the actual underlying contract. On the other hand, if we want to take a short underlying position, we will prefer to sell the underlying contract synthetically by selling the call and purchasing the put. If we do this, we are selling a contract which is only worth 2.00 for 2.25.

The reader may have noted that the synthetic and real markets will be the same when the time value of the call and the time value of the put are identical. In our example, the synthetic and real markets are identical when the June 100 call and the June 100 put both have the same amount of time value. If this is not true, there is always a synthetic position which is either too cheap or too expensive with respect to its real equivalent.

The three-sided relationship between a call, a put, and its underlying contract means that we can always express the value of any one of these contracts in terms of the other two:

$$\text{underlying price} = \text{call price} - \text{put price} + \text{exercise price}$$
$$\text{call price} = \text{underlying price} + \text{put price} - \text{exercise price}$$
$$\text{put price} = \text{call price} - \text{underlying price} + \text{exercise price}$$

This three-sided relationship is sometimes referred to as *put-call parity.*

CONVERSIONS AND REVERSALS

If we take a synthetic long or short underlying position, our primary concern, as with an actual underlying position, is the direction of the market. If the market moves in our favor, we expect to show a profit; if it moves against us, we expect to show a loss. If we execute the synthetic at favorable prices we may gain more or lose less, but it is still primarily the direction of the market in which we are interested.

Suppose, as before, the underlying contract is trading at 102.00, the June 100 call is trading at 5.10, and the June 100 put is trading at 2.85. The synthetic market should be 2.00 (underlying price less the exercise price), but is actually 2.25. If we wanted to take a short position in the underlying market, we would certainly prefer to do so synthetically (sell the call, buy the put). Suppose we are not interested in taking a directional position. Is there any way we can profit from the difference in price between the real and synthetic markets?

When a trader identifies two contracts which are essentially the same but which are trading at different prices, the natural course is to execute an *arbitrage* by purchasing the cheaper contract and selling the more expensive. Since the synthetic position and its real equivalent are essentially the same, and since they are trading at different prices (2.25 vs. 2.00), an option trader might try to purchase the cheaper contract (the underlying contract) and sell the more expensive (the synthetic equivalent). That is, he might try to purchase the underlying contract for 102.00, and simultaneously sell the call for 5.10 and buy the put for 2.85. The cash flows from these transactions are:

Transaction	**Cash flow**
underlying purchase	–102.00
call sale	+5.10
put purchase	–2.85
exercise or assignment (at 100) at expiration	+100.00
total	+.25

No matter what happens in the underlying market, the underlying position will do exactly .25 better than the synthetic position. The entire position will therefore show a profit of .25, regardless of movement in the underlying market. This is shown in Figure 11-2.

The foregoing position, where the purchase of an underlying contract is offset by the sale of a synthetic position, is known as a *conversion*. The opposite position, where the sale of an underlying contract is offset by the purchase of a synthetic position, is known as a *reverse conversion* or, more commonly, a *reversal*. A reversal would be profitable if the underlying contract were trading at 102.00, and the difference between the prices of the June 100 call and June 100 put were less than 2.00. For example, with the June 100 call at 4.90 and the June 100 put at 3.05, the synthetic price is 1.85. By purchasing the synthetic at 1.85 (buy the call at 4.90, sell the put at 3.05), and selling the underlying contract at 102.00, the reverse conversion would lock in a profit of .15. This is shown in Figure 11-3.

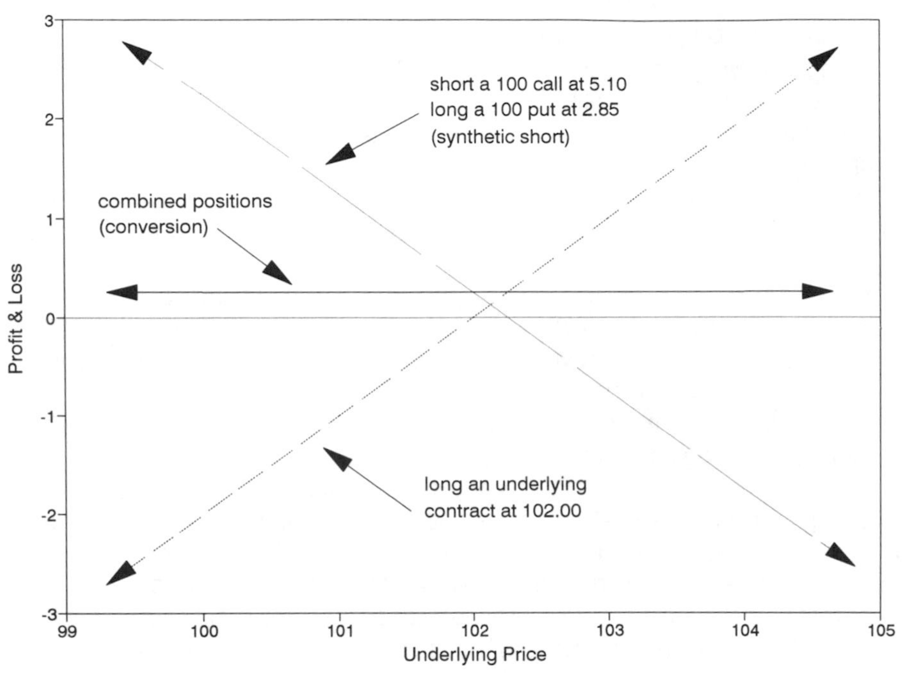

Summarizing:

conversion	=	long underlying + synthetic short underlying
	=	long underlying + short call + long put
reversal	=	short underlying + synthetic long underlying
	=	short underlying + long call + short put

As before, we assume that the call and the put have the same exercise price and expiration date.

Conversions and reversals are classified as arbitrage strategies because of their similarity to traditional arbitrage. Typically, an arbitrageur will attempt to simultaneously buy and sell the same items in different markets to take advantage of price discrepancies between the two markets. He might, for example, buy gold in New York for $389 per ounce, and sell it in London for $392 per ounce. The profit margin of $3, while small, is secure since the risk of a trade in one market is almost immediately offset by an identical but opposing trade in another market. Unlike a speculator, who usually hopes to make a large profit on a small number of trades, an arbitrageur hopes to make a small profit on a large number of trades. An arbitrageur is willing to do much greater size than the speculator because the risk is much smaller.

Like traditional arbitrages, conversions and reversals involve buying and selling the same thing in different markets. A conversion involves buying the underlying instru-

Figure 11-3

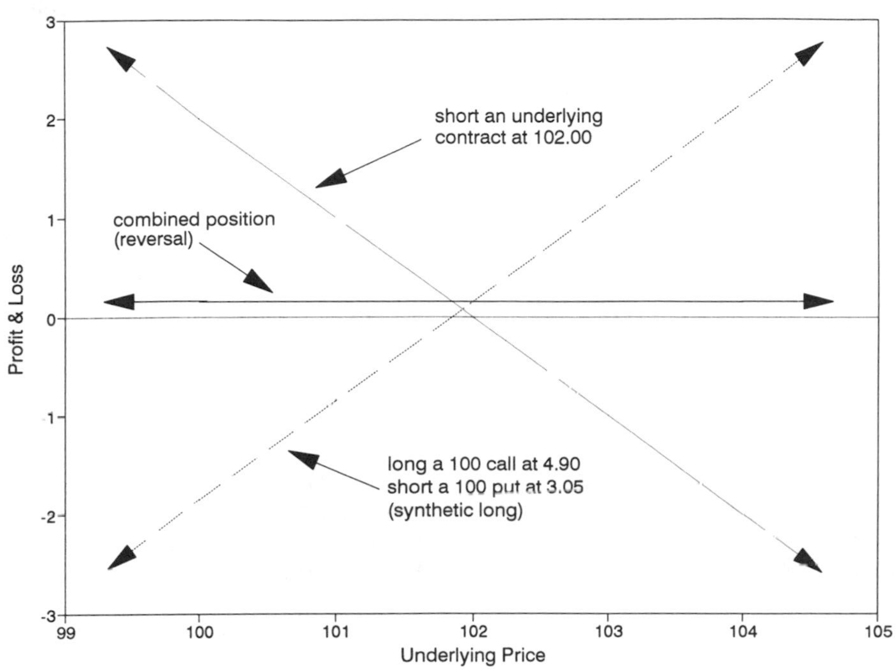

ment, whether a stock or commodity, in the underlying market, and selling the underlying instrument, synthetically, in the option market. A reversal involves selling the underlying instrument in the underlying market, and buying the underlying instrument, synthetically, in the option market. The profitability of these strategies is determined by the relationship between the synthetic price and the actual underlying price. Synthetic positions are often used to execute conversions and reversals, so traders sometimes refer to the synthetic market (the difference between the call price and put price) as the *conversion/reversal market.*

All experienced traders are familiar with the price relationship between a synthetic position and its underlying contract, so that any imbalance in the conversion/reversal market is likely to be short-lived. If the synthetic is overpriced, all traders will want to execute a conversion (buy the underlying, sell the call, buy the put). If the synthetic is underpriced, all traders will want to execute a reversal (sell the underlying, buy the call, sell the put). Such activity, where everyone is attempting to do the same thing, will quickly force the synthetic market back to equilibrium. Indeed, imbalances in the conversion/reversal market are usually small and rarely last for more than a few seconds. When imbalances do exist, an option trader is usually willing to execute conversions and reversals in very large size because of the low risk associated with such strategies.

We initially broke down a synthetic position into its component cash flows, enabling us to identify the basic relationship between a synthetic and its underlying instrument:

call price – put price = underlying price – exercise price

However, when and how the component cash flows occur can alter this relationship. Since there can be different settlement procedures associated with different underlying instruments as well as with options, in order to calculate the exact value of a synthetic position we need to consider how these settlement procedures affect the basic synthetic relationship.

Futures Option Markets

If the cash flow resulting from an option trade and a trade in the underlying instrument is identical, the synthetic relationship is simply:

call price – put price = underlying price – exercise price

This will be true if interest rates are zero, or in futures markets where both the underlying contract and options on that contract are subject to futures-type settlement. In the latter case there is no interest component because no cash changes hands when either the futures contract or the options on that contract are traded. This is currently the procedure on many non-U.S. exchanges.

In futures markets, where options are subject to stock-type (cash) settlement, while no cash will change hands when the futures contract is traded, there will be an exchange of cash when options are traded. The interest considerations on the credit or debit will therefore have to be taken into consideration when calculating the value of a synthetic position.

Using our earlier example, with the June futures contract at 102.00, the June 100 call at 5.00, and the June 100 put at 3.00, we have:

call price – put price = underlying price – exercise price
5.00 – 3.00 = 102.00 – 100.00
2.00 = 2.00

At these prices there does not appear to be any profit opportunity from either a conversion or reversal. If we do either of these strategies, the credit and debits from the two sides of the equation exactly offset each other.

Suppose, however, that we decide to do a reversal by selling the underlying futures contract for two points (underlying price minus exercise price) and buying the synthetic for two points (call price minus put price). Suppose also that the options are subject to stock-type (cash) settlement, as is generally true in U.S. futures markets. We will lay out 2.00 on the option trades, and we will not get this money back until expiration when we will buy the underlying futures contract, which we originally sold at 102, for 100. If interest rates are currently 8% per annum, and there are three months remaining to expiration, there will be a 2% carrying cost on the two-point debit resulting from the option trades. Based on the simple synthetic relationship, we expected to break even on the conversion. In fact we will end up losing 2% × 2.00, or .04, because of the cost of carrying the debit to expiration. If we really want to break even, we will have to find some way to offset this interest cost of .04. We might, for example, purchase the call for .04 less (4.96), or sell the put for .04 more (3.04), or sell the futures contract for .04 more (102.04). Or we might use a combination of these three transactions, for example by purchasing the call for 4.98, selling the put for 3.01, and selling the futures contract for 102.01. The result is a savings of .04, an amount equal to the carrying cost on the debit resulting from the option trades.

Assuming that all options are European (no early exercise permitted), we can now express the synthetic relationship in futures markets where the options are settle in cash as follows:

$$\text{call price} - \text{put price} = \text{futures price} - \text{exercise price} - \text{carrying costs}$$

where the carrying costs are calculated on either the difference between the futures price and the exercise price, or the difference between the call price and put price, both of which will be approximately the same. In our example, if the call is trading for 4.98, the put for 3.01, and the futures contract for 102.01, the synthetic market is exactly balanced since:

$$4.98 - 3.01 = 102.01 - 100.00 - .04$$
$$1.97 = 1.97$$

Using put-call parity, we can always calculate a call, put, or underlying futures price when we know the prices of any two of the other contracts. For example, with a June futures contract at 102.00, and the June 100 put at 2.75, we have:

$$\begin{aligned} \text{call price} &= \text{futures price} - \text{exercise price} + \text{put price} - \text{carrying costs} \\ &= 102.00 - 100.00 + 2.75 - .04 \\ &= 4.71 \end{aligned}$$

With the June 100 call at 5.35 and the June futures contract at 101.90, we have:

$$\begin{aligned} \text{put price} &= \text{call price} + \text{exercise price} - \text{futures price} + \text{carrying costs} \\ &= 5.35 + 100.00 - 101.90 + .04 \\ &= 3.49 \end{aligned}$$

Finally, with the June 100 call at 3.25 and the June 100 put at 1.25, we have:

$$\begin{aligned} \text{futures price} &= \text{call price} - \text{putprice} + \text{exercise price} + \text{carrying costs} \\ &= 3.25 - 1.25 + 100.00 + .04 \\ &= 102.04 \end{aligned}$$

Stock Option Markets

Consider a stock trading at 103, with a June 100 call trading at six and a June 100 put trading at three. If there are no interest or dividend considerations, the synthetic market seems to be balanced since:

$$\text{call price} - \text{put price} = \text{stock price} - \text{exercise price}$$
$$6 - 3 = 103 - 100$$
$$3 = 3$$

Suppose we decide to do a conversion by purchasing the stock for 103 and selling the synthetic for three points (call price minus put price). We will lay out 103 for the stock, take in six for the call, and lay out three for the put. These trades will create a total debit of 100, a debit which we will have to carry to expiration, at which time we will sell the stock for 100, either through exercise of the put or assignment of the call. Since interest rates in the real world are not zero, there will be a cost associated with carrying this debit. If interest rates are currently 8% per annum, and there are three months remaining to expiration, there will be a 2% carrying cost on the 100-point debit resulting from the trades. Based on the simple synthetic relationship, we expected to break even on the conversion. But in fact we will end up losing 2% × 100, or two points, because of the cost of carrying the debit to expiration. If we really want to break even, we will have to find some way to offset this two-point interest cost. We might do this by selling the call for two points more (8), or by purchasing the put for two points less (1), or by purchasing the stock for two points less (101). Or we might use a combination of these three transactions, for example by selling the call for 7, purchasing the put for 2½, and purchasing the stock for 102½. The result is a savings of two points, an amount equal to the carrying cost on the debit resulting from the trades.

Taking into consideration the interest rate component, we can express the synthetic relationship as:

$$\text{call price} - \text{put price} = \text{stock price} - \text{exercise price} + \text{carrying costs}$$

where the carrying costs are calculated on the exercise price.[1] In our example, if the call is trading for 7, the put for 2½, and the stock for 102½, the synthetic market is exactly balanced since:

$$7 - 2\tfrac{1}{2} = 102\tfrac{1}{2} - 100 + 2$$
$$4\tfrac{1}{2} = 4\tfrac{1}{2}$$

Now suppose that prior to expiration the stock will pay a dividend of 1½. When we did our conversion we purchased stock, so we will receive an extra 1½ points when the dividend is paid. Given this, we can afford to pay up to 1½ points more for the conversion and still do no worse than break even. We could, for example, sell the call for 5½, or buy the put for four, or buy the stock for 104. Or, as before, we might combine these three trades by selling the call for six, buying the put for 3½, and buying the stock for 103½.

Assuming that all options are European (no early exercise permitted), and taking into consideration both interest rates and dividends, we can now express the full value of the synthetic relationship in the stock option market as:

1. The exact value depends on the discounted price, or present value, of the exercise price. For a more detailed explanation, see Appendix B.

call price − put price = stock price − exercise price + carrying costs − dividends

where the carrying costs are calculated on the exercise price and the dividends are those expected prior to expiration.

Using put-call parity, we can always calculate a call, put, or underlying stock price when we know the prices of any two of the other contracts. For example, with the stock at 102 and the June 100 put at 3¼, we have:

call price = stock price − exercise price + put price + carrying costs − dividends
= 102 − 100 + 3¼ + 2 − 1½
= 5¾

With the June 100 call at 6½ and the stock at 101¼, we have:

put price = call price + exercise price − stock price − carrying costs + dividends
= 6½ + 100 − 101¼ − 2 + 1½
= 4¾

Finally, with the June 100 call at 7 and the June 100 put at 1¾, we have:

stock price = call price − put price + exercise price − carrying costs + dividends
= 7 − 1¾ + 100 − 2 + 1½
= 104¾

ARBITRAGE RISK

New option traders are often instructed to go into the market and concentrate on executing conversions and reversals because these strategies are riskless. Beware: *There are no riskless strategies.* There are only strategies with greater or lesser risk. The risks of doing conversions or reversals may not be immediately apparent, but they exist nonetheless.

Interest Rate Risk

Whenever there is a cash flow associated with a trade, the value of the trade depends on the interest which can be earned on a credit or which must be paid to carry a debit over the life of the trade. This is a function of interest rates, and since interest rates may not be constant, the interest considerations can change over time. If part of the expected profit from a trade depends on our earning 8% on a credit balance, a reduction in interest rates to 6% will certainly reduce our profit, and might even result in a loss. If part of the expected profit from a trade depends on our paying 7% on a debit balance, an increase in interest rates to 10% will likewise reduce our profit. In practice, large changes in interest rates over the limited life of most options[2] are the exception rather than the

2. We are referring here primarily to exchange traded options with expirations up to approximately nine months. Long-term options with expirations of up to several years will obviously be much more sensitive to changes in interest rates.

rule. For this reason the interest rate risk associated with conversions and reversals is relatively small.

Note also that synthetic strategies in the stock option market are much more sensitive to interest rates than the same strategies in the futures option market. A stock option conversion or reversal includes the cash flow from the underlying stock, while a similar trade in the futures option market includes no such cash flow. The cash flow from a stock trade is always greater than the cash flow from an option trade since the price of stock is always greater than the price of the options.

Execution Risk

Since no market participant wants to give away money, a trader is unlikely to be offered a profitable conversion or reversal all at one time. Consequently, he will have to execute one or two legs of the strategy, and hope to be able to execute the final leg(s) at a later time. He may, for example, initially purchase the underlying contract and puts, and later hope to complete the conversion by selling calls. However, if call prices begin to fall, he may never be able to profitably complete the conversion. Even a professional trader on an exchange, who would seem to be in a good position to know the prices of all three contracts, can be fooled. He may purchase a call and sell a put (synthetic long underlying) at what he thinks are good prices. However, when he tries to sell the underlying contract to complete the reversal, he may find that the price is much lower than what he thought it was. Anytime a strategy is executed one leg at a time, there is always the risk of an adverse change in prices before the strategy can be completed.

Pin Risk

When we introduced the concept of a synthetic position, we assumed that at expiration either the underlying market would be above the exercise price, in which case any call would be exercised, or below the exercise price, in which case any put would be exercised. But what will happen if the underlying market is exactly equal, or *pinned*, to the exercise price at the moment of expiration?

Suppose a trader has executed a June 100 conversion: he is short a June 100 call, long a June 100 put, and long the underlying contract. If the underlying market is above or below 100 at expiration, there is no problem. He will either be assigned on the call or will exercise the put. In either case he will offset his long underlying position so that he will have no market position on the day following expiration.

Now suppose that at the moment of expiration the underlying market is right at 100. The trader would like to be rid of his underlying position. If he doesn't get assigned on the call, he plans to exercise his put; if he does get assigned on the call, he will let the put expire worthless. In order to make a decision, he must know whether the call will be exercised. Unfortunately, he won't know this until the day after expiration, when he either does or does not receive an assignment notice. But then it will be too late because the call will have expired.

It may seem that an option which is exactly at-the-money at expiration will never be exercised since, in theory, it has no value. In fact many at-the-money options do get exercised. Even though such an option has no theoretical value, it does have some practical value. For example, suppose the owner of a call which is exactly at-the-money at expiration wants to take a long position in the underlying contract. He has two choices. He can either exercise the call or buy the underlying contract. Since most exchanges where options are traded include the right of exercise in the original transaction cost, it is almost always cheaper to exercise the call. Even if there is a charge for exercise, it will be less than the cost of trading the underlying contract. Anyone owning an at-the-money option, and choosing to take a long or short position at expiration, will find that it is cheaper to exercise the option than buy or sell the underlying contract.

Clearly, the trader who is short an at-the-money option at expiration has a problem. What can he do?

One course might be to guess whether the trader will be assigned. If the market appears to be strong on the last trading day, the trader might assume that it will continue higher on the day following expiration. If the person who holds the call sees the situation similarly, it is logical to assume that the call will be exercised. Hence, the trader will choose not to exercise the put. Unfortunately, if the trader is wrong, and he does not get assigned on the call, he will find himself with a long underlying position which he would rather not have. Conversely, if the market appears to be weak on the last trading day, the trader might make the assumption that he will not be assigned on the call. He will therefore choose to exercise the put. But again, if he is wrong and does get an assignment notice, he will find himself with an unwanted short underlying position on the day following expiration.

The risk of a wrong guess can be further compounded by the fact that conversions and reversals, because of their low risk, are usually done in large size. If the trader guesses wrong, he may find himself naked long or short not one, but several hundred underlying contracts.

There can be no certain solution to the problem of pin risk. With many, perhaps thousands, of open contracts outstanding, some at-the-money options will be exercised and some won't. If the trader lets the position go to expiration and relies on luck, he is at the mercy of the fates, and that is a position which an intelligent option trader prefers to avoid. The practical solution is to avoid carrying conversions and reversals to expiration when there is a real possibility of expiration right at the exercise price. If the trader has a large number of June 100 conversions or reversals, and expiration is approaching with the underlying market close to 100, the sensible course is to reduce the pin risk by reducing the size of the position. If the trader doesn't reduce the size, he may find that he is under considerable pressure to get out of a large number of risky positions at the last moment.

Sometimes even a careful trader will find that he has some at-the-money conversions or reversals outstanding as expiration approaches. One way to eliminate the pin risk which still exists is to liquidate the position at the prevailing market prices. Unfortunately, this is likely to be a losing proposition since the trader will be forced to trade each contract at an unfavorable price, either buying at the offer or selling at the bid. Fortunately, it is often possible to trade out of such a position all at once at a fair price.

Since conversions and reversals are common strategies in all option markets, a trader who has an at-the-money conversion and is worried about pin risk can be fairly certain that there are also traders in the market who have at-the-money reversals and are also worried about pin risk. If the trader with the conversion could find a trader with a reversal and cross positions with him, both traders would eliminate the pin risk associated with their positions. This is why, on option exchanges, one often finds traders looking for other traders who want to trade conversions or reversals at even money. This simply means that a trader wants to trade out of his position at a price which is fair to everyone involved, so that everyone can avoid the problem of pin risk. Whatever profit a trader expected to make from the conversion or reversal presumably resulted from the initial trade, not from the closing trade.

Certain options, such as stock indices and Eurodollars, are settled at expiration in cash rather than with the delivery of an actual underlying contract. When such an option expires, the amount of cash which flows into or out of a trader's account is simply the amount by which the option is in-the-money, i.e., the difference between the underlying price and the option's exercise price. There is no pin risk associated with options which settle in this manner because no underlying position results from exercise or assignment.

Interest rate risk, execution risk, and pin risk are common to all markets, regardless of the underlying contract. There are, however, certain risks which are unique to a market depending on the characteristics of the underlying market.

Settlement Risk in the Futures Market

Let's go back to our original conversion where a trader is short a June 100 call, long a June 100 put, and long an underlying contract. Suppose the underlying contract is a June futures contract which is trading at 102.00. If there are three months remaining to June expiration, interest rates are 8%, and all options are subject to stock-type (cash) settlement, the value of the June 100 synthetic market (the difference between the June 100 call and the June 100 put) is:

$$\text{futures price} - \text{exercise price} - \text{carry on 2 points for 3 months} =$$
$$102 - 100 - (2 \times 3/12 \times 8\%) = 1.96$$

Suppose a trader is able to sell a June 100 call for 5.00, buy a June 100 put for 3.00, and sell a June futures contract for 102.00. If interest rates do not change, and assuming there will not be a problem with pin risk, at expiration the trader should realize a profit of .04, since he has done the June 100 conversion at .04 better than its value.

Suppose that shortly after the trader initiates this conversion, the underlying June futures contract falls to 98.00. The synthetic (short) side of the position will now show a profit of four points: the short call and long put together will appreciate by four points. But because the options are settled like stock, the profit on the synthetic side will only be a paper profit, and will not be fully realized until expiration. On the other hand, the trader is also long a June futures contract, and this contract, since it is subject to futures-type settlement, will result in an immediate four point debit when the market drops four points. To cover this four point debit, the trader will either have to borrow the money or take the money out of an existing, interest-bearing account. In either case there will be a loss in interest, and this interest loss will not be offset by the paper profit from the option position. If the loss in interest is great enough, it may more than offset the profit of .04 which the trader originally expected from the position. And in the most extreme case, where the trader does not have access to the funds required to feed the futures position, the trader may be forced to liquidate the position. Needless to say, forced liquidations are never profitable.

Of course, this works both ways. A rise in the price of the underlying futures contract to 106.00 will result in a four point loss to the synthetic side: the short call and long put together will decline by four points. But the loss on the synthetic side will only be a paper loss, and will not be fully realized until expiration. On the other hand, the rise in the futures contract will result in an immediate cash credit, a credit on which the trader can earn interest. This interest will increase his potential profit beyond the original expected profit of .04.

Most futures option traders think of conversions and reversals as being delta neutral, but in fact this is not necessarily true. With the underlying futures contract at 102, the deltas in our example might be:

Option Position	**Delta Position**
short June 100 call	−60
long June 100 put	−38
long June futures contact	+100
total	+2

The two extra deltas reflect the fact that the trader would prefer the market to rise rather than fall, so that cash will flow into his account from the futures position. The interest from this cash flow can represent an unexpected profit or loss, in the case of a decline in the futures price.

Two deltas are really no risk, except when we remember that conversions and reversals, because of their low risk, are often done in very large size. A trader who executes 500 conversions has a risk delta equal to $500 \times +2 = +1000$. This is the same as being naked long 10 futures contracts. The risk comes from the interest that can be earned on any cash credit, or which must be paid on any cash debit, resulting from movement in the underlying futures contract.

The amount by which the delta of a synthetic futures position will differ from 100 depends on the interest risk associated with the position. This in turn depends on two factors: the general level of interest rates and the amount of time remaining to expiration. The higher the interest rate and the more time remaining to expiration, the greater the risk. The lower the interest rate and the less time remaining to expiration, the less the risk. A 10% interest rate with nine months to expiration represents a much greater risk than a 4% interest rate with one month remaining to expiration. In the former case, the deltas of a synthetic position may add up to 94, while in the latter case the deltas may add up to 99.

Note that there is no settlement risk when both contracts are subject to the same settlement procedure. If all contracts are subject to stock-type settlement, no cash flow results from fluctuations in the prices of the contracts prior to expiration. If all contracts are subject to futures-type settlement, any credit or debit resulting from changes in the price of the underlying futures contract will be offset by an equal but opposite cash flow from changes in prices of the option contracts.

Dividend Risk in the Stock Market

Consider a stock trading at 102½, with three months to June expiration, interest rates at 8%, and a dividend of 1½ expected prior to expiration. The value of the June 100 synthetic (the difference between the 100 call and the June 100 put) is:

$$\text{stock price} - \text{exercise price} + \text{carry on 100 to expiration} - \text{expected dividends} =$$
$$102\tfrac{1}{2} - 100 + (100 \times 3/12 \times 8\%) - 1\tfrac{1}{2} = 3$$

Suppose a trader is able to sell a June 100 call for 7¾, buy a June 100 put for 4½, and buy stock for 102½. If interest rates do not change, and assuming there will not be a problem with pin risk, at expiration the trader should realize a profit of ¼, since he has done the June 100 conversion at ¼ better than its value.

Since the trader owns the stock, part of his profit comes from the 1½ point dividend which he expects to receive when the stock goes ex-dividend. If the dividend changes unexpectedly, it could affect the trader's eventual profit. If, for example, the company is doing poorly and decides to cut its dividend in half, to ¾, the trader's conversion will be worth ¾ less, and his profit of ¼ will turn into a loss of ½. Of course, if the company is doing well and decides to increase its dividend to two points, the conversion will be worth ½ more, and the trader's profit will increase from ¼ to ¾. Clearly, the possibility of a change in the expected dividend represents a risk to a conversion or reversal. Moreover, if multiple dividends are expected over the life of the strategy, the impact of a change in the company's dividend policy can be greatly magnified.

BOXES

As we have seen, a conversion or reversal entails risk because these strategies combine a synthetic position in options with a position in the underlying contract. The risk arises because a synthetic position in options and an actual position in the underlying contract can have different characteristics, either in terms of settlement procedure, as in the futures option market, or in terms of the dividend payout, as in the stock option market. How might we eliminate this risk?

One way to eliminate this risk is to eliminate the position in the underlying contract. Consider a conversion:

short a call
long a put
long an underlying contract

If we want to maintain this position, but would also like to eliminate the risk that goes with holding an underlying position, we might replace the long underlying position with something that acts like an underlying contract, but which isn't an underlying contract. For example, we might replace the long underlying position with a deeply in-the-money call. Now our position is:

short a call
long a put
long a deeply in-the-money call

If the deeply in-the-money call has a delta of 100, and therefore acts like a long underlying contract, the position will have the same characteristics as the conversion.

In the same way, instead of replacing the underlying position with a deeply in-the-money call, we can sell a deeply in-the-money put:

short a call
long a put
short a deeply in-the-money put

If the deeply in-the-money put has a delta of −100, and therefore acts like an underlying contract, the position will again have the same characteristics as the conversion.

This type of position, where the underlying instrument in a conversion or reversal is replaced with a deeply in-the-money option, is known as a *three-way.* While eliminating some risks, a three-way is not without its own problems. If a trader sells a deeply in-the-money option to complete his three-way, he still has the risk of the market going through the exercise price. Indeed, as the underlying market moves closer and closer to the exercise price of the deeply in-the-money option, the option will act less and less like a position in the underlying contract. The combination of contracts will then act less and less like a true conversion or reversal.

What else acts like an underlying contract but isn't an underlying contract? A synthetic underlying position obviously fills the bill. In addition to a three-way, we might also consider replacing an underlying position in a conversion or reversal with a synthetic equivalent. For example, our original position might be a 100 conversion:

short a June 100 call
long a June 100 put
long an underlying contract

Suppose we also execute a reversal at 90:

long a June 90 call	short a June 100 call
short a June 90 put	long a June 100 put
short an underlying contract	long an underlying contract

The long and short underlying contracts cancel out, leaving:

long a June 90 call	short a June 100 call
short a June 90 put	long a June 100 put

We are left with a synthetic long position at the 90 exercise price, and a synthetic short position at the 100 exercise price. Or we can think of the position as a reversal at one exercise price, and a conversion at a different exercise price.

This position, known as a *box*, is similar to a conversion or reversal, except that any risk associated with holding a position in the underlying contract has been eliminated because the underlying position has been replaced with a synthetic underlying position at a different exercise price. A trader is long (short) the box when he is synthetically long (short) the lower exercise price and synthetically short (long) the higher exercise price. The example position is long a June 90/100 box.

At expiration, regardless of the price of the underlying contract, a trader who has a box will simultaneously buy the underlying contract at one exercise price and sell the underlying contract at the other exercise price. The value of the box at expiration will therefore be exactly the amount between exercise prices. In our example, at expiration the 90/100 box will be worth exactly 10 points because the trader will simultaneously buy the underlying contract at 90 and sell it at 100. If it is worth 10 points at expiration, how much is it worth today? If the options are subject to stock-type settlement, the value of the box today will be the value of the box at expiration less carrying costs. If our 10-point box expires in three months with interest rates at 8%, the value today is:

$$10 - (10 \times 3/12 \times 8\%) = 10 - .20 = 9.80$$

Since a box eliminates the risk associated with carrying a position in the underlying contract, boxes are even less risky than conversions and reversals, which are themselves low-risk strategies. When all options are European (there is no risk of early exercise), and the options are settled in cash rather than through delivery of the underlying contract (there is no pin risk), the purchase or sale of a box is identical to lending or borrowing funds over the life of the options. In our example, a trader who sells a 10-point box for 9.80 has essentially borrowed funds from the buyer of the box for three months at an interest rate of 8%. If a trader were willing to pay a higher rate to borrow funds, he could sell the box at a lower price, for example 9.70. This corresponds to a rate over three months of 12%. When no other method is available, a trading firm might be able to raise needed short-term cash by selling boxes. Since the firm will probably have to sell the boxes at a price lower than the theoretical value, this will increase the firm's borrowing costs. Moreover, if the options can be exercised early, or if there is a danger of pin risk at expiration, this method of borrowing may not be without its own risks.

We originally introduced a box as a conversion at one exercise price and a reversal at a different exercise price. Since the long and short underlying positions cancel out, we are left with two synthetic underlying positions. The June 90/100 box was written:

long a June 90 call	short a June 100 call
short a June 90 put	long a June 100 put

The left side of the box is a synthetic long at 90 and the right side is a synthetic short at 100. Instead of dividing the box into right and left sides, we can also divide it into top and bottom sides. Notice that the top side is a bull vertical call spread (long June 90 call/short June 100 call), while the bottom side is a bear vertical put spread (long June 100 put/short June 90 put). Since a box is a combination of two vertical spreads, the combined prices of the vertical spreads must add up to the value of the box.

For example, with three months remaining to expiration and interest rates at 8%, the value of our June 90/100 box is 9.80. Suppose a trader knows that the June 90/100 vertical call spread is trading for six points. Without any additional information, the trader can estimate the fair market price of for the June 90/100 vertical put spread. He knows 90/100 box is worth 9.80, and that the value of a call and put vertical spread must add up to the value of the box. The price of the put spread must therefore be:

$$9.80 - 6 = 3.80$$

If the trader believes he can either buy or sell the call vertical spread at six points, and he is asked for a market in the put spread, he will probably make his market around an assumed value of 3.80. He might, for example, make a market of 3.50 bid/4.10 ask. If he is able to buy the put vertical for 3.50, he can then try to buy the call vertical for 6.00. If he is successful, he will have paid a total of 9.50 for a box with a theoretical value of 9.80. Conversely, if he is able to sell the put vertical for 4.10, he can then try to sell the call vertical for 6.00. If he is successful, he will have sold a box with a theoretical value of 9.80 at a price of 10.10.

JELLY ROLLS

Another method of eliminating a position in the underlying contract is to take a synthetic position in a different expiration month, rather than at a different exercise price as with a box. For example, suppose we have executed the following reversal:

long a June 100 call
short a June 100 put
short an underlying contract

Suppose we now execute the following conversion:

short a September 100 call
long a September 100 put
long an underlying contract

If the underlying contract for both June and September is identical, they will cancel out, leaving us with:

long a June 100 call	short a September 100 call
short a June 100 put	long a September 100 put

These combined long and short synthetic positions taken at the same exercise prices but in different expiration months is known as a *jelly roll*,[3] or simply a *roll*. The strategy is

3. This very unscientific sounding term seems to have originated among traders on the Chicago Board Options Exchange.

most common in the stock option market where the underlying for both months is the same.

What should be the value of a roll in the stock option market? In our example, the sale of the June/September 100 roll, the trader will buy stock at 100 at June expiration and sell the same stock at 100 at September expiration. The value of the roll is the cost of holding the stock for the three-month period from June to September. If interest rates are 8%, the holding costs are:

$$100 \times 3/12 \times 8\% = 2.00$$

Therefore, the roll should have a value of two points. Expressed another way, the difference between the June 100 synthetic (the June 100 call less the June 100 put) and the September 100 synthetic (the September 100 call less the September 100 put) should be exactly two points.

Now suppose that the stock pays a quarterly dividend of ¾ point. Since the trader will own the stock for the period from June to September, he will receive the ¾ point dividend. The value of the roll is now the two-point carrying cost less the ¾ point dividend, or 1¼. The full value of the roll is:

jelly roll = long term synthetic – short-term synthetic
= cost of carry – expected dividends

where the cost of carry is calculated on the exercise price over the period between expiration months.

In the same way that we evaluated a box as the combination of two vertical spreads, we can also evaluate a jelly roll as the difference between two time spreads:

long a June 100 call	short a September 100 call
short a June 100 put	long a September 100 put

This is simply a short June/September 100 call time spread and a long June/September put time spread. Since the roll is a combination of the sale of a call (put) time spread and the purchase of put (call) time spread, the values of the call and put times spreads should differ by exactly the value of the roll. If the roll is worth 1¼, the difference between the call and put time spreads should also be 1¼. If the call time spread is trading for 3¼, the put time spread should be trading for 2. This is logical when we realize that we can rewrite the jelly roll in a slightly different form:

jelly roll = long-term synthetic – short-term synthetic
= (long-term call – long-term put) – (short-term call – short-term put)
= (long-term call – short-term call) – (long-term put – short-term put)
= carrying costs – expected dividends

The difference between the call and put time spreads should therefore be equal to the cost of carry on the exercise price less the expected dividends.

Since jelly rolls involve holding stock positions for some period of time, they have risks similar to those affecting conversions and reversals. If interest rates rise, or the dividend is cut, a jelly roll will become more valuable. If interest rates fall, or the dividend is increased, a jelly roll will become less valuable.

Finally, we can create a *time box* by taking opposing synthetic positions at different exercise prices and expiration dates:

long a June 90 call	short a September 100 call
short a June 90 put	long a September 100 put

The value of this position is the combined value of purchasing the June 90/100 box and selling the June/September 100 jelly roll. If the June 90/100 box is worth 9¾, and the June/September 100 jelly roll is worth 1¼, the time box should be worth 8½.

USING SYNTHETICS IN VOLATILITY SPREADS

A trader need not restrict himself to using synthetics only in arbitrage strategies. He can also execute a volatility or directional strategy using a synthetic. Consider the following situation. Dealing in a futures option market where the underlying March futures contract is trading very actively at 100.00, a trader wants to execute the following backspread for a one-point credit:

buy 20 March 105 calls
sell 10 March 100 calls

That is, the amount he expects to receive for the sale of one March 100 call less the amount he expects to pay for two March 105 calls should equal one point. Suppose the current market in these options is:

Option	Bid/Ask
March 100 call	2.70/2.90
March 105 call	.85/.95

If the trader were able sell the March 100 calls at the ask price of 2.90, he would be willing to pay the ask price of .95 for the March 105 calls, since 2.90 – (2 × .95) = 1.00. In the same way, if he were able to buy the March 105 calls at the bid price of .85, he would be willing to sell the March 100 calls at the bid price of 2.70, since 2.70 – (2 × .85) = 1.00.

Suppose that an offer comes into the marketplace to sell March 105 calls at .85. The trader immediately buys these calls and is about to offer the March 100 calls at 2.70, when suddenly a bid of 2.80 is made for March 100 puts. Does this affect what the trader might do?

Since the new bid is for the March 100 put, and the trader is interested in selling the March 100 call, it may seem that the put bid will have no affect on his strategy. But recall the synthetic relationship:

synthetic short call = short put + short underlying

In the futures market, the value of the call is:

call price = put price + futures price – exercise price – carrying costs

If the underlying March futures contract is trading at 100, there is no carrying cost associated with a March 100 synthetic because the difference between the futures price and exercise price is zero. Therefore:

March 100 call = March 100 put + 100 – 100 – 0
March 100 call = March 100 put

In other words, if the trader believes he can trade the March futures contract at 100, then the prices of the March 100 call and put ought to be identical. He originally intended to sell the March 100 call at 2.70 to complete his backspread. He is now given the chance to sell the March 100 call, synthetically, at 2.80. If he sells the March 100 put at 2.80, and simultaneously sells the March futures contract at 100.00, he has effectively sold the March 100 call at 2.80, which is .10 better than he originally intended.

Whenever a trader is considering a strategy, he ought to always ask himself whether he can do better by executing some part of his strategy synthetically. Usually he won't be able to because synthetic relationships tend to be very efficient. But every now and then the trader will find that the synthetic position is slightly more favorable. Over a career of trading even small savings can add up.

Using synthetic equivalents, we can also rewrite some volatility spreads in more familiar terms. For example, we said that call and put butterflies with the same exercise prices are identical. Suppose we take a typical call butterfly and rewrite it in terms of its synthetic equivalents:

Contract	**Synthetic Equivalent**
long 1 March 95 call	long 1 March 95 put/long an underlying contract
short 2 March 100 calls	short 2 March 100 puts/short 2 underlying contracts
long 1 March 105 call	long 1 March 105 put/long an underlying contract

Since the long and short underlying contracts in our synthetic equivalent cancel out, we are left with a put butterfly:

long 1 March 95 put
short 2 March 100 puts
long 1 March 105 put

Using synthetic equivalents, we can also express the following strategy in a more familiar form:

long 2 March 100 calls
short an underlying contract

This is simply a long straddle, since we can take one of the March 100 calls and rewrite it synthetically:

long March 100 call = long March 100 put + long underlying contract leaving:

long 1 March 100 call
short an underlying contract
long 1 March 100 put
long an underlying contract

Since the long and short underlying contracts cancel out, we are left with a typical long straddle:

long 1 March 100 call
long 1 March 100 put

TRADING WITHOUT THEORETICAL VALUES

Synthetic relationships can often enable a trader to make logical trading decisions without the aid of values generated by a theoretical pricing model. Usually all that is required is an ability to calculate the carrying cost on a position and, in the case of stocks, to determine the dividend payout.

While a trader can't always be as certain of a profit as he is with arbitrage strategies such as conversions, reversals, boxes, and jelly rolls, there are many logical relationships between options and underlying contracts, or between options and other options, which enable a trader to identify potentially profitable trading strategies without the use of a theoretical pricing model.

Consider the following option prices with the underlying price at 101.50:

95 call	**100 call**	**105 call**
8.00	4.80	1.60

Is there anything wrong with these prices?

If the trader purchases one 95 call for 8.00, sells two 100 calls at 4.80, and purchases one 105 call for 1.60, he has bought the 95/100/105 butterfly for zero since:

$$(2 \times 4.80) - (8.00 + 1.60) = 9.60 - 9.60 = 0$$

Since a butterfly can never be worth less than zero at expiration, and in this case might be worth as much as five points, the purchase of this butterfly represents a riskless trading opportunity.

Another way of reaching the same conclusion is to realize that a butterfly is made up of two consecutive vertical spreads. In our example, the purchase of the 95/100/105 butterfly consists or purchasing the 95/100 vertical call spread and selling the 100/105 vertical call spread. We know that as the market rises, a vertical call spread goes more deeply into-the-money and becomes more valuable. Therefore, as long as there is an equal amount between exercise prices, a vertical call spread with lower exercise prices will always be more valuable than a vertical call spread with higher exercise prices. The opposite is true of vertical put spreads. Those with higher exercise prices are always more valuable than those with lower exercise prices. If two vertical spreads violate this relationship, a trader can take advantage of the situation by purchasing the spread which ought to be more valuable, and selling the spread which ought to be less valuable. In our example, the vertical call spreads are:

95/100 spread	=	8.00 – 4.80	=	3.20
100/105 spread	=	4.80 – 1.60	=	3.20

While both spreads are trading at the same price, the 95/100 spread is intuitively more valuable than the 100/105 spread. Consequently, a trader will try to purchase the 95/100 spread and sell the 100/105 spread. If he succeeds, he will have purchased the butterfly for zero. While there is no guarantee that this will be profitable (the underlying market could finish below 95 or above 105), the strategy still makes sense because there is no risk associated with it.

Consider a different type of relationship:

Underlying price = 99.75 Interest rate = 0

	95	**100**	**105**
calls:	6.85	3.70	1.10
puts:	2.10	3.95	6.35

First, we might check to make sure that all the synthetic relationships balance. Since they do, there is no profit opportunity there. Next, we might check the butterflies. Both the call and put butterflies are trading for .55. This might or might not be a reasonable price; without a theoretical pricing model it would be difficult to say. But at least the butterflies are trading for some positive number, so it is not immediately apparent that they represent a good trading opportunity. Is there any other logical relationship that might be violated?

Look at the prices of the straddles:

	95	**100**	**105**
call + put:	8.95	7.65	7.45

We know that a straddle becomes more valuable as the underlying price moves away from the exercise price, resulting in one side of the straddle, either the call or put, going more deeply into-the-money. With the underlying price at 99.75, the 95 straddle should be more valuable than the 100 straddle, and this is reflected in the respective prices of 8.95 and 7.65. The 105 straddle, being further away from 99.75, should also be more valuable than the 100 straddle. But here the prices do not reflect the additional value. The 105 straddle is .30 cheaper than the 100 straddle. Even though we don't know the theoretical value of either the 100 or 105 straddle, we do know that the 105 straddle is too cheap *with respect to the 100 straddle.* Therefore, if given the opportunity, a trader would attempt to purchase the 105 straddle at 7.45 and sell the 100 straddle at 7.65. There is no guarantee that this strategy will be profitable. The underlying contract could finish above 105, in which case the 100 straddle will be worth five points more than the 105 straddle. But if we assume that movement is random, then the sale of the 100 straddle and the purchase of the 105 straddle puts the laws of probability heavily on the trader's side.

Finally, consider this scenario:

Underlying price = 100.75 Interest rate = 0

	95	100	105
March calls:	7.50	3.85	2.35
June calls:	9.65	5.70	3.30

Is there any apparent mispricing here?

First, we might look at the butterflies. The March butterfly is trading for (7.50 + 2.35) – (2 × 3.85) = 2.15. The June butterfly is trading for (9.65 + 3.30) – (2 × 5.70) = 1.55. Since both butterflies are trading for some positive amount, it isn't immediately clear that we should buy or sell either one? What about the prices of the butterflies with respect to each other? Should the June butterfly, at 1.55, be less expensive than the March butterfly, at 2.15? It may seem that the June butterfly, with more time to expiration, ought to be more expensive. In option evaluation we usually associate more time with greater value. But if the market remains at 100.75, the price of the butterfly will expand towards 4.25 as time passes. Hence, it is logical that the March butterfly is more valuable than the June butterfly.

Is there any other relationship we might consider? When we see options with different expiration dates, time spreads certainly come to mind.

	95	100	105
June call less March call:	2.15	1.85	.95

Is there anything wrong with these prices?

We know that a time spread maintains its greatest value with the underlying contract at the exercise price. The 100 time spread, being more at-the-money, is trading for more than the 105 time spread, as one would expect. The 100 time spread should also be more valuable than the 95 time spread. Here the 95 time spread is trading at a greater price, and, again, if we assume random movement in the underlying contract, this is clearly not logical. Without a theoretical pricing model, we can't be sure what each of these spreads is worth. But we do know that the 95 call time spread is too expensive *with respect to the 100 call time spread.* If we sell the former and buy the latter we can't be certain of a profit, but we do have the laws of probability on our side.

Note that in each of these examples we made an important assumption:

> *Regardless of the exact theoretical value, there ought to be a uniform progression of both individual option prices and spread prices in the marketplace. If this uniform progression is violated, a trader can take advantage of the situation by purchasing the option or spread which is relatively cheap and selling the option or spread which is relatively expensive.*

While the great majority of option traders work with theoretical values, a good habit for the new trader is to quickly check the relationship of option prices and spreads in the market to ensure that there are no obvious mispricings. The trader can start with conversions and reversals, then look at vertical spreads and butterflies, and finally consider straddles and time spreads. Usually there will not be any obvious mispricing. But if there is, the trader can exploit the situation by purchasing the cheap side of the relationship and selling the expensive.

Two evaluation tables, demonstrating typical progressions of option prices and spreads in a stock option and futures option market, are shown in Figures 11-4 and 11-5.

Figure 11-4

Stock price = 100
Time to expiration: March = 13 weeks; June = 26 weeks
Volatility = 25%; Interest rate = 8.00%; Dividend = 0

	80		85		90		95		100		105		110		115		120
March calls	21.68		17.04		12.74		9.00		5.97		3.72		2.17		1.19		.61
March puts	.11		.37		.97		2.13		4.00		6.65		10.00		13.92*		18.24*
March call verticals		4.64		4.30		3.74		3.03		2.25		1.55		.98		.58	
March put verticals		.26		.60		1.16		1.87		2.65		3.35		3.92		4.32	
March butterflies			.34		.56		.71		.78		.70		.57		.40		
March straddles	21.79		17.41		13.71		11.13		9.97		10.37		12.17		15.11		18.85
June calls	23.57		19.30		15.40		11.95		9.02		6.63		4.74		3.30		2.25
June puts	.47		1.00		1.90		3.25		5.12		7.53		10.44		13.80*		17.55*
June call verticals		4.27		3.90		3.45		2.93		2.39		1.89		1.44		1.05	
June put verticals		.53		.90		1.35		1.87		2.41		2.91		3.36		3.75	
June butterflies			.37		.45		.52		54		.50		.45		.39		
June straddles	24.04		20.30		17.30		15.20		14.14		14.16		15.18		17.10		19.80*
Call time spreads	1.89		2.26		2.66		2.95		3.05		2.91		2.57		2.11		1.64
Put time spreads	.36		.63		.93		1.12		1.12		.88		.44		– .12*		– .69*

* Since all options are assumed to be European, with no early exercise permitted, some theoretical values may be less than parity and some spreads may have negative values. The effect of early exercise on spread values will be discussed in Chapter 12.

Figure 11-5

Futures price = .50
Time to expiration: May = 4 weeks; July = 12 weeks
Volatility = 15%; Interest rate = 8.00%

	46		47		48		49		50		51		52		53		54
May calls	3.99*		3.04		2.16		1.41		.82		.43		.20		.08		.04
May puts	.03		.07		.18		.42		.82		1.42		2.18		3.05		4.00
May call verticals		.95		.88		.75		.59		.39		.23		.12		.04	
May put verticals		.04		.11		.24		.40		.60		.76		.87		.95	
May butterflies			.07		.13		.16		.20		.16		.11		.08		
May straddles	4.02		2.11		2.34		1.83		1.64		1.85		2.38		3.13		4.04
July calls	4.13		3.32		2.58		1.94		1.41		.99		.67		.44		.27
July puts	.21		.38		.62		.96		1.41		1.97		2.63		3.38		4.19
July call verticals		.81		.74		.64		.53		.42		.32		.23		.17	
July put verticals		.17		.24		.34		.45		.56		.66		.75		.81	
July butterflies			.07		.10		.11		.11		.10		.09		.06		
July straddles	4.34		3.70		3.20		2.90		2.82		2.96		3.30		3.82		4.46
Call time spreads	.14		.18		.42		.53		.59		.56		.47		.36		.23
Put time spreads	.18		.31		.44		.54		.59		.55		.45		.33		.19

* Since all options are assumed to be European, with no early exercise permitted, some theoretical values may be less than parity. The effect of early exercise on spread values will be discussed in Chapter 12.

❖ 12 ❖

Early Exercise of American Options

Thus far we have assumed that all option strategies involve holding a position to expiration. Since the great majority of exchange traded options are American, carrying with them the right of early exercise, it will be worthwhile to consider some of the characteristics of American options. Specifically, we will want to answer two questions:

1. Given the opportunity, under what circumstances might a trader consider exercising an American option prior to expiration?
2. How much more should a trader be willing to pay for an American option over an equivalent European option?

In order for early exercise to be desirable, there must be some positive cash flow which will result from early exercise, and the value of this cash must be greater than the insurance value of the option. Because the cash flow which results from the exercise of a stock option is significantly different from the cash flow which results from the exercise of a futures option, the conditions under which early exercise will be desirable are different. For this reason, we will look at these two situations separately.

FUTURES OPTIONS

From previous discussions (see Chapter 6) we know that in evaluating an option there are some factors which make the option more valuable and there are some factors which make the option less valuable. Consider a futures option. We might list the factors which affect its value as follows:

$$\text{option value} = \text{intrinsic value} + \text{volatility value} - \text{interest rate value}$$

Since the intrinsic value and volatility components can never be less than zero, these factors always enhance the option's value. As either rises, the option value rises. Only the interest rate component might affect the option's value negatively. As interest considerations rise, the option's value falls. If the negative effects of interest rates are greater than the positive effects of volatility, it might be possible for an option, if it is

European, to be worth less than parity.[1] In such a case, if the option were an American option it would become an early exercise candidate.

For example, suppose a certain futures contract is trading at 100. Suppose also that we own an 80 call which will expire in two months, and that this option is subject to stock-type settlement. When we evaluate the option, we find that it has a theoretical value of 20 and a delta of 100. This means that the option has essentially the same characteristics as the futures contract. If the option is American, and we want to maintain the same delta position, we have three possible choices:

1. Hold the option
2. Exercise the option
3. Sell the option and buy a futures contract

Which of these choices is best?

If we choose the first alternative and hold the position, there is no change to our account. The position we take home is identical to the one with which we begin the next trading day.

If we choose the second alternative and exercise the 80 call, it is as if we had gone into the futures market and purchased a futures contract at 80. Since we now have a futures position, we are subject to futures-type settlement. If the futures contract which we purchased at 80 settles at 100, 20 points will be credited to our account—20 points on which we can earn interest. How much interest will we earn? That depends on the level of interest rates as well as the amount of time remaining to expiration. If interest rates are 6%, with two months remaining to expiration, we will earn:

$$20 \times 2/12 \times 6\% = .20$$

Through early exercise of the option we will earn an additional .20 in interest over the time remaining to expiration. Since no trader wants to throw away an additional profit, exercising the option early makes better sense than simply holding the position.

What about the third choice, selling the option ourselves and buying a futures contract? If the 80 call is trading at exactly its intrinsic value of 20 points, there is no difference between exercising the call, or selling the call and buying a futures contract. Both strategies will result in a 20-point credit, and over the time remaining to expiration we will earn the same interest of .20. But suppose the 80 call is trading at a price other than 20. Suppose it is trading at 19.50. Clearly, this price is not possible in a market where the options are American and can be exercised at any time. Purchasing an 80 call for 19.50 is equivalent to purchasing the futures contract for 99.50. If the futures contract is trading at 100, this means the call is trading at less than parity. If this were indeed true, all traders would buy the call, sell the futures contract, and immediately exercise the call. This would result in a riskless profit of .50, the amount by which the

1. Note that a European option with a theoretical value less than parity will have a positive theta. Its value will gradually rise to parity as expiration approaches.

option was below parity. In a market where options are subject to early exercise, no option ought to be trading at less than parity.

What if the option is trading for more than parity, say 20.50? If we sell the 80 call for 20.50 and buy the futures contract for 100, we will have the same position we would have had through early exercise. But now, instead 20 points, we will have 20.50 points credited to our account. We will realize an additional profit of .50 through the sale of the option, as well as the slight additional interest earnings which go with it.

A trader who exercises a futures option early does so to capture the interest on the option's intrinsic value. This intrinsic value will be credited to his account only if the option is subject to stock-type settlement. When he abandons the option through exercise, he receives the variation resulting from settlement of the futures contract. If, however, futures options are subject to futures-type settlement, as they are on many non-U.S. exchanges, no cash flow results from the early exercise of an option. With an 80 call trading at 20 and the underlying futures contract trading at 100, if the option is subject to futures-type settlement when exercised, 20 points will be credited to the trader's account from the settlement of the futures contract. But 20 points will simultaneously be debited from his account when the 20-point value of the option disappears. Since the cash credits and debits exactly offset each other, no additional interest earnings can accrue.

In futures markets where the options are subject to futures-type settlement there is never any economic justification for early exercise, and early exercise can never be an optimal choice. A trader will always be better off either holding the option or selling it, rather than exercising it early.

STOCK OPTIONS

Early Exercise of Calls for the Dividends

We can separate a stock option call into its components, as we did with a futures option. Now we have the additional consideration of dividends:

call value = intrinsic value + interest rate value + volatility value – dividend value

Since the intrinsic value, interest rate, and volatility components can never be less than zero, these factors always enhance the call's value. As any one of them rises, the call value rises. Only the dividend component might affect the option's value negatively. As the dividend rises, the call option's value falls. If the underlying stock pays no dividend, or no dividend is expected prior to expiration of the option, a call option can never have a value less than parity (intrinsic value). If, however, the negative effects of the dividend are greater than the positive effects of interest rates and volatility, it might be possible for a call, if it is European, to be worth less than parity.

For example, suppose a certain stock is trading at 100 and that the stock will go ex-dividend two points tomorrow. Suppose also that there is a 90 call available which will expire in two weeks. When we evaluate the option, we find that it has a theoretical value of 10 and a delta of 100. This means that the option has essentially the same characteristics as the stock. If the option is American, and we want to maintain the same delta position, we have three possible choices:

1. Hold the option
2. Exercise the option
3. Sell the option and buy stock

Which of these choices is best?

Suppose we simply hold the option. Certainly we will maintain our delta position. But what will happen tomorrow when the stock gives up its dividend? If the stock opens unchanged, it will open ex-dividend at 98,[2] since the two-point dividend will be deducted from its price. Since the option has a value of parity, it will open not at 10, the previous day's parity price, but at 8, today's parity price. In other words, if we hold the option we can be certain of losing two points on our position.

Can we do any better with the second choice, exercising the option? If we exercise the option, we will pay the exercise price of 90 for the stock, and we will discard the 10-point value of the option, effectively purchasing the stock at 100. When the stock goes ex-dividend we will lose two points when it opens two points lower the next day, but we will also receive the dividend since we now own the stock. We will break even because the two-point loss on the stock price will be offset by the two-point dividend we receive. Clearly, we are better off exercising the option than holding it, not because we will show some additional profit, but because we will avoid a two-point loss. We must exercise the option to ensure that we break even.

What about the third choice, selling the option and buying stock ourselves? This seems to be very similar to early exercise. In both cases we are replacing the option with the stock. If the option is trading at parity, in this case 10, there is no difference between exercising the option, or selling the option and buying the stock. In each case the cash flow will be identical and we will own the stock when it goes ex-dividend. But suppose the 90 call is trading at a price other than 10. Suppose, for example, it is trading at 9½. Clearly, this price is not possible in a market where the options are American and can be exercised at any time. Purchasing a 90 call for 9½ is equivalent to purchasing the stock for 99½. If the stock is trading at 100, this means the call is trading at less than parity. If this were indeed true, all traders would buy the call, sell the stock, and immediately exercise the call. This would result in a riskless profit of ½ point, the amount by which the option was below parity. In a market where options are subject to early exercise, no option ought to be trading at less than parity.

What if the 90 call is trading for more than parity, say 10½? Now if we sell the option and purchase the stock we will still receive the dividend, since we will own the stock. But we will end up with an additional ½ point which we would not have

2. On the day a stock gives up its dividend, prices are typically disseminated with the dividend already deducted from the stock's price. Hence, a 100-point stock which gives up a 2-point dividend overnight and opens the next day at 98 would be deemed to have opened unchanged since the 2-point drop in its price results from the dividend payout, not from any change in investor demand.

collected through exercise of the call. Therefore, our third choice, selling the call and buying the stock, is the optimum choice.

Since the only reason a trader would ever consider exercising astock option call early is to receive the dividend, if a stock pays no dividend there is no reason to exercise a call early. If the stock does pay a dividend, the only time a trader ought to consider early exercise is the day before the stock goes ex-dividend. At no other time in its life is a stock option call an early exercise candidate.

We noted that in an American (exercise) market an option should never trade at less than parity. Is the same true in a European (exercise) market? In our example of the 90 call and stock at 100, with an expected two-point dividend, the call price will clearly drop when the stock goes ex-dividend. If the option cannot be turned into stock through exercise prior to the ex-dividend date, the option is clearly going to lose value. If it has very little time value, the amount it will lose when the dividend is given up may make the option worth less than parity. In our example, if the option expires in two weeks with interest rates at 8% and a volatility of 20%, the European value of the 90 call is approximately 8¼. This is 1¾ under parity, due to the fact that a call option, no matter how deeply in the-money, does not carry with it the right to the dividend. Only ownership of the stock carries that right.

Early Exercise of Puts for Interest

As we did with a stock option call, we can express a stock option put's value in terms of its components:

put value = intrinsic value – interest rate value + volatility value + dividend value

In the case of a put, the only component that affects its value negatively is the interest rate component. If the negative effects of interest rates are greater than the positive effects of volatility and dividends, it might be possible for a put, if it is European, to be worth less than parity. Consider this situation:

Stock price = 100, Time to expiration = 8 weeks, Volatility = 20%
Interest rate = 8.00%, Dividend = 0

With these assumptions, the value of a 110 call is approximately .70. Using the put/call parity relationship, we can calculate the value of the 110 put:

put value = call value + exercise price – stock price – carrying costs

The carrying costs on the exercise price of 110 are:

$$110 \times 56/365 \times 8\% = 1.35$$

The European put value is therefore:

$$.70 + 110 - 100 - 1.35 = 9.35$$

Since the 110 put is only worth 9.35 if we hold it to expiration, but is worth 10 points if we exercise it today, the option is apparently worth more dead (exercised) than alive (unexercised). When we exercise the 100 put we get to sell stock at 110, and we can earn interest on this 110-point credit to expiration.

Whereas a stock option call can only be an early exercise candidate on the day prior to the stock's ex-dividend date, a stock option put can become an early exercise candidate anytime the interest which can be earned through the sale of the stock at the exercise price is sufficiently large. Determining exactly when this happens is a difficult problem, but if the stock pays a dividend it is most likely to occur on the day after the stock goes ex-dividend. Since a put is a substitute for a short stock position, one of the advantages of holding a put is to avoid paying the dividend. Hence, a trader will almost always want to hold the put through the ex-dividend date. Then, if the interest considerations are sufficient, the trader will exercise his put.

In an American (early exercise) market no put option can be trading at less than parity. Otherwise there is an immediate arbitrage opportunity available by purchasing the stock, purchasing the put, and immediately exercising the put. The profit will be equal to the amount by which the put is trading at less than parity. This is not necessarily true in a European (no early exercise) market, where the option must be carried to expiration. In our example of the 110 put where the theoretical value derived from the call price was 9.35 (.65 less than parity), the market in the European 110 put might be 9¼-9½. A market maker is willing to sell the option at 9½ (½ less than parity) because he can hedge himself by selling stock, and he will be confident in the knowledge that he will not be required to buy back the stock until expiration. The interest he earns on the stock to expiration will more than offset the amount he will lose by selling the put below parity.

Conditions for Early Exercise

If given the chance, there are clearly reasons why a trader might want to exercise an American option early. In the case of futures options, when the option is subject to stock-type settlement, the trader is trying to capture the interest on the option's intrinsic value. In the case of stock option calls, he is trying to capture the dividend which the stock pays. In the case of stock option puts, he is trying to capture the interest on the proceeds from the sale of the stock at the exercise price. From the foregoing discussion we can infer two conditions which are necessary before a trader considers exercising an option early to capture this additional profit:

1. The option must be trading at parity.

2. The option must have a delta close to 100.

If the option is trading at more than parity, the trader will always do better selling the option and taking a position in the underlying market himself. Determining whether an option is trading at parity is simply a matter of finding out what the market in that option is. In the great majority of cases, if an option is deeply enough in-the-money to be an early exercise candidate, the bid/ask spread is probably so wide that for practical purposes the option is trading at parity.

Why should the delta be close to 100? If we exercise an option early, we are trading in the option for a position in the underlying contract. We therefore want to be reasonably certain that the option and the underlying contract have the same characteristics. In other words, we want to be certain that the option has no additional insurance value left, so that when we exercise the option we are not throwing away this insurance value.

For example, suppose there is an 80 call available with the underlying contract trading at 100. If we want to take a long position we can purchase either the 80 call or the underlying contract. If we feel there is no chance that the market can fall below 80 prior to expiration, there is no difference between holding the 80 call or holding the underlying contract. But suppose we feel that there is some chance that the market could fall below 80. In that case we will prefer to hold the 80 call. If the market were to fall below 80, holding the call would limit our potential loss to the option's premium. If, however, we hold a long underlying position and the market drops below 80, our potential loss is unlimited.

Recall that one interpretation of the delta is the probability that the option will finish in-the-money. A delta close to 100 means that the underlying market has almost no chance of going through the exercise price, and the option therefore has almost no chance of going out-of-the-money.

What degree of certainty justifies early exercise? With a delta of 100 one certainly would consider early exercise. What about 99? 96? 90? With a delta above 95, many traders will at least consider early exercise. How much interest will be earned, or what dividend will be collected, through early exercise? With a delta of 95 or lower, the risk is probably too great to consider early exercise. There is at least a 5% chance that the underlying market will go through the exercise price. If that happens, a trader will regret having exercised an option early, regardless of the additional benefits to be gained through early exercise.

By ensuring that the delta is close to 100, we are also ensuring that we do not throw away any insurance value that the option might still retain. As an option goes more deeply into-the-money, its time value (insurance value) begins to disappear. With a delta of 100, in theory the option has no time value left. However, as the delta declines, the time value increases. If the delta were significantly less than 100, the option would still retain a significant amount of time value. If we were to exercise such an option, we would be throwing away this insurance value.

Since the desirability of early exercise is dependent, at least in part, on the option's delta, the accuracy of the delta is important. But there are many factors which affect the delta, and we might incorrectly assess any one of these factors. If we feel that the correct volatility is 15%, an option might have a delta of 98. But if we decide to raise our volatility to 17%, the delta of the option will decline. Under the new conditions its delta might only be 93. At a 15% volatility a trader might consider early exercise, while at a 17% volatility he might not. For this reason, options in low-volatility markets are exercised early much more often than options in high-volatility markets.

In the same way, an option with three months remaining to expiration might have a delta of 92, and would therefore not be an early exercise candidate. But if two months pass, and the price of the underlying contract is unchanged, the delta will rise, and the new delta might be 99. With three months remaining the option was not an early exercise candidate, but with one month remaining the option might be early exercise candidate.

Of course, we ought to ask why we were considering early exercise in the first place. In many cases, we exercise to earn interest over the life of the option. We can earn more interest over three months than over one month, so from this point of view a three-month option is more likely to be an early exercise candidate than a one-month option. We can see that many factors affect the desirability of early exercise, and these factors can pull in different directions, with some factors dictating for early exercise and some dictating against.

Thus far we have only addressed the question of when a trader might find it desirable to exercise an option early. There should be an additional value associated with an American option over an identical European option because the American option carries with it additional rights. Even an out-of-the-money option, which no one would consider exercising today, might someday go deeply enough into-the-money so that it could become an early exercise candidate. This possibility should always make an American option more valuable than a European option.

How much more should a trader be willing to pay for an American option over an identical European option? The Black-Scholes model makes no attempt to answer this question since it is a European pricing model. In spite of the fact that Black-Scholes generated values are likely to show some inaccuracies in an American market, for many years traders continued to use the model because no model with equal ease of use existed to evaluate American options. The problem of early exercise was dealt with through intuition, or through slight adjustments to Black-Scholes generated values. For example, when a stock is expected to pay a dividend, an American call value can be approximated by comparing the Black-Scholes value of the call option under two circumstances:

1. The call expires the day before the stock goes ex-dividend.
2. The call expires on its customary date, but the underlying stock price used to evaluate the call is the current price less the expected dividend.

Whichever value is greater is the *pseudo-American* call value.

In the case of options on futures, or of put options on stock, traders used Black-Scholes generated values, but raised any option with a theoretical value less than parity to exactly parity.

Models eventually were developed to more accurately evaluate American options. The most widely used of these are the Cox-Ross-Rubenstein model, developed by John Cox, Stephen Ross, and Mark Rubenstein; and the Whaley model, developed by Giovanni Barone-Adesi and Robert Whaley. Unlike the Black-Scholes model, neither of these models is closed form. One can't simply sit down and add up all the numbers to get the correct value. Rather, both models are algorithms, or loops, and each time the user makes a pass through the loop, the closer he comes to the true American value of the option. While the Cox-Ross-Rubenstein model is quite easy to understand, both intuitively and mathematically, it may require numerous passes through the loop to generate an acceptable value. On the other hand, the Whaley model is more complex mathematically, but converges to an acceptable value much more quickly. The Cox-Ross-Rubenstein model may require 40 or 50 passes through the loop to reach the same degree of accuracy as the Whaley model achieves with four or five passes through the loop. In addition to evaluating American options, both models also determine when an option should be exercised early. We were somewhat vague on this point in our earlier discussion, stating that the delta of an option should be close to 100 to justify early exercise. When using a true American model, an option is optimally exercised early when its theoretical value is exactly parity and its delta is exactly 100.

While the Cox-Ross-Rubenstein and Whaley models in most cases generate similar values, more and more computer services are using the Whaley model to evaluate American options because of the speed with which it can achieve results. However, the Cox-Ross-Rubenstein model, while slower, is still very widely used because it offers some advantages which are not available in the Whaley model. For example, the Whaley model handles the dividend payout of a stock as if it were a continuous interest payment over the life of the option. In reality dividends are paid all at once, and the Cox-Ross-Rubenstein model more accurately reflects the impact of this one-time payment on a call option on the stock. Unlike the Whaley model, the Cox-Ross-Rubenstein model can also be used to evaluate some of the recently introduced, exotic options. Such options are *path dependent* since their value depends not only on the likely price distribution of the underlying contract at expiration, but also on the various paths which the underlying price might take to achieve that distribution. Both these models are discussed further in Appendix B.

Regardless of the model a trader chooses, the accuracy of model-generated values will depend at least as much on the inputs into the model as the theoretical accuracy of the model itself. If a trader evaluates an American option using an incorrect volatility, or an incorrect interest rate, or an incorrect underlying price, the fact that he derives his values from an American rather than a European model is likely to make little difference. Both models will generate incorrect values because the inputs are incorrect. The American model may produce less error, but that will be small consolation if the incorrect inputs lead to a large trading loss.

American option values are most important when there is a significant difference between the carrying cost associated with the option and the carrying cost associated with the underlying contract. The greater the difference between the two carrying costs, the greater the value of early exercise. When the underlying contract is a futures contract and the option on the contract is subject to futures-type settlement, the cost of carrying either position is, in theory, zero. This is the same as assuming an effective interest rate of zero. If we use a zero interest rate, there is no difference between European and American option values.

When the options on a futures contract are subject to stock-type settlement, there is a small difference between the carrying cost on the option and the carrying cost on the underlying contract. Although the option is subject to stock-type settlement, the price of the option is only a small fraction of the price of the underlying contract. The additional value for early exercise is therefore small, and is only likely to show up in deeply in-the-money options. Even in this case, the difference between European and American values is often less than the minimum price increment. In such a market, a trader is unlikely to profit significantly because he is using an American pricing model while other traders are using a European pricing model. Practical considerations, such as the accuracy of the trader's volatility estimate, his ability to anticipate directional trends in the underlying market, and his ability to control risk through effective spreading strategies, will far outweigh any small advantage gained by using an American rather than a European model.

The importance of early exercise is greatest when the underlying contract is a stock or physical commodity.[3] In such a case there is a significant difference between the carrying cost on an option and the carrying cost on an underlying position. This difference will especially affect the difference between European and American put values, since early exercise will allow the trader to earn interest on the proceeds from the sale at the exercise price. An option trader in either the stock or physical commodity market will find that the additional accuracy offered by an American model, such as the Cox-Ross-Rubenstein or Whaley models, will indeed be worthwhile. The significance of this difference is shown in Figure 12-1.

THE EFFECT OF EARLY EXERCISE ON TRADING STRATEGIES

The delta of an American option will always be greater than the delta of an equivalent European option. The extent to which it is greater will depend on how deeply in-the-money the option is, as well as the interest considerations resulting from early exercise. In most cases the delta of an American option will differ only slightly from a European option, and the possibility of early exercise is therefore unlikely to have a significant impact on volatility or directional strategies. In the former case, a trader may have to adjust the ratio of a strategy slightly if he wants to remain close to delta neutral. In the latter case, a trader may find that he is a few deltas longer or shorter than he would be if employing the same strategy with European options.

Because early exercise of an option is not automatic, there are strategies which depend on someone making an error and not exercising an option early when he ought to do so. For example, a stock option trader might try to execute a *dividend play*. This strategy consists of buying stock and selling deeply in-the-money calls as the ex-dividend

3. Early exercise can also be an important consideration in the foreign exchange market if the interest rates associated with the domestic currency (the currency in which the option is settled) and foreign currency (the currency to be delivered in the event of exercise) are significantly different.

Figure 12-1

European vs. American Put Values

Stock price = 100.00 Volatility = 25%; Interest rate = 8.00%; Dividend = 0

4 weeks to expiration:

	Black-Scholes Value	Black-Scholes Delta	Cox-Ross Value	Cox-Ross Delta
80 put	.00	0	.00	0
90 put	.15	–5.0	.15	–5.1
100 put	2.46	–45.1	2.51	–46.4
110 put	9.67	–89.5	10.03	–95.3
120 put	19.28	–99.4	20.00	–100.0

13 weeks to expiration:

	Black-Scholes Value	Black-Scholes Delta	Cox-Ross Value	Cox-Ross Delta
80 put	.11	–2.2	.11	–2.3
90 put	.97	–14.3	1.00	–14.9
100 put	4.00	–41.2	4.20	44.0
110 put	10.00	–70.6	10.71	–78.2
120 put	18.25	–89.2	20.00	–100.0

26 weeks to expiration:

	Black-Scholes Value	Black-Scholes Delta	Cox-Ross Value	Cox-Ross Delta
80 put	.46	–5.7	.50	–6.1
90 put	1.89	–18.1	2.02	–19.6
100 put	5.11	–37.7	5.55	–42.1
110 put	10.43	–58.9	11.58	–68.8
120 put	17.56	–76.4	20.04	–94.8

date for the stock approaches. If the trader is not assigned on the calls, he will break even on the stock (the stock price will fall, but he will collect the dividend). At the same time he will profit when the deeply in-the-money calls which he has sold fall by the amount of the dividend. Of course, if he is assigned on the calls, as he ought to be, he will only break even. But for each call which goes unexercised the trader will profit by the amount of the dividend. Dividend plays were much more common in the early days of option trading when the market was less sophisticated and many options which should have been exercised were not. As markets have become more efficient, only a professional trader, with very low transaction costs, can afford to take advantage of such a possibility. Even then, he may find that he is assigned on the great majority of the calls he has sold.

A trader can execute a similar type of *interest play* by selling stock and simultaneously selling deeply in-the-money puts. Now, instead of profiting by the amount of the dividend, the trader will profit by the amount of the interest he can earn on the exercise price (the proceeds of the stock sale and the put sale combined). This profit will continue to accrue as long as the puts remain unexercised. If the puts are exercised, the trader does no worse than break even. Again, only a professional trader, with his low transaction costs, is likely to employ such a strategy.

If options are subject to stock-type settlement, an interest play can also be done in the futures option market by either purchasing a futures contract and simultaneously selling a deeply in-the-money call, or selling a futures contract and simultaneously selling a deeply in-the-money put. If the option is deeply enough in-the-money, it ought to be exercised early. If, however, the option remains unexercised, the trader will continue to earn interest on the proceeds from the option sale. Since the amount on which the trader will earn interest is the difference between the exercise price and futures price, this will not be as profitable as a similar strategy in the stock option market, where the trader will earn interest on the exercise price. Still, if the transaction costs are low enough, it may be worth doing.

A variation on dividend and interest plays can also be executed using deeply in-the-money vertical spreads. For example, suppose a stock is trading at 100 with the ex-dividend date approaching If both the 80 and 85 calls are deeply enough in-the-money to be early exercise candidates, a trader might try to purchase the 80/85 call vertical spread for five points. If he does so, he will exercise his 80 call in order to collect the dividend, and at the same time hope not to be assigned on the 85 call. Oddly, if both the 80 and 85 calls are early exercise candidates, the trader should also be willing to sell the 80/85 call vertical for five points. If he does so, he will exercise his 85 call in order to collect the dividend, and at the same time hope not to be assigned on the 80 call. In other words, a professional trader might logically make a market under these circumstances of 5 bid/5 ask. He is willing to buy or sell the 80/85 call vertical at five points. He intends to immediately exercise whichever call he buys, while hoping not be assigned on the call which he sells.

The possibility of early exercise can also have an impact on arbitrage strategies. For example, suppose a stock option trader executes a reverse conversion:

buy a call
sell a put
sell stock

If he executes this strategy at what he believes to be profitable prices, part of his profit will come from the interest he expects to earn on the sale of the stock. But what will happen if the stock price begins to fall, and in fact falls so far that the trader is assigned on the put? This will eliminate the interest earnings, since he will be required to buy back the stock. Of course, he can still sell the call and take in some cash. But if the value of the call is insufficient to offset the interest loss, the trader may find that his profitable reversal has in fact become unprofitable.

The trader in our example is worried about being assigned on his put. If the market drops there will be a greater likelihood of assignment; if the market rises there will be a lesser likelihood of assignment. Since the trader prefers the market to rise, he must be delta long. This is confirmed by the following delta values:

Stock price = 100; Time to expiration = 3 months; Volatility = 25%
Interest rate = 8.00%; Dividend = 0

Option	European Value	European Delta	American Value	American Delta
100 call	5.97	58.8	5.97	58.8
100 put	4.00	–41.2	4.20	–44.0

If these are European options, the total delta of the reversal is:

$$+58.8 + 41.2 - 100 = 0$$

If, however, the options are American, the total delta is:

$$+58.8 + 44.0 - 100 = +2.8$$

The positive delta of 2.8 reflects a slight preference for the market to rise so that the trader will avoid being assigned on the put.

For a similar reason, if the trader executes a conversion (sell call, buy put, buy stock), he is 2.8 deltas short. He wants the stock to fall so that he can exercise his put early and thereby avoid the interest costs of carrying a long stock position.

Because the desirability of early exercise, and therefore the likelihood of early exercise, can increase or decrease as the underlying market rises or falls, conversions and reversals using American options are not delta neutral. While these strategies may be unbalanced by only two or three deltas, the fact that they are often done in large size can result in an additional risk that the trader cannot afford to ignore. This also applies to boxes and jelly rolls, which are simply combinations of conversions and reversals. Consider these option values:

Stock price = 100; Volatility = 25%; Interest rate = 8.00%; Dividend = 0
Time to expiration: March = 3 months, June = 6 months

Option	European Value	European Delta	American Value	American Delta
March 95 call	9.00	73.7	9.00	73.7
March 95 put	2.13	–26.3	2.24	–27.8
March 100 call	5.97	58.8	5.97	58.8
March 100 put	4.00	–41.2	4.20	–44.0
June 95 call	11.96	72.7	11.96	72.7
June 95 put	3.24	–27.3	3.49	–29.9
June 100 call	9.03	62.3	9.03	62.3
June 100 put	5.11	–37.7	5.55	–42.1

We can see how the possibility of early exercise affects the values and deltas of various arbitrages:

Strategy	European Value	European Delta	American Value	American Delta
March 95/100 box	4.90	0	4.99	−1.3
June 95/100 box	4.80	0	4.99	−1.8
March/June 95 jelly roll	1.85	0	1.71	+1.1
March/June 100 jelly roll	1.95	0	1.71	+1.6

Boxes become more valuable using American options because a trader who is long the box owns a put with a higher exercise price. If a trader buys the 95/100 box, he is long a 95 call and a 100 put, and short a 95 put and 100 call. The 100 put will become an early exercise candidate before the 95 put, making the American box more valuable than the same European box. The delta of the box is negative with American options because a trader who owns the box would like the market to decline so that he will be able to exercise the 100 put as quickly as possible.

Jelly rolls become less valuable using American options because a trader who owns the jelly roll has sold a long-term put. If a trader buys the March/June 100 jelly roll, he is long a March 100 put and June 100 call, and is short a March 100 call and June 100 put. The June 100 put, being a longer term option, has more potential for early exercise than the March 100 put. The delta of the jelly roll is therefore positive because there is a greater danger of being assigned on the June 100 put. Hence, the trader who owns the jelly roll would like the market to rise so that he is less likely to be assigned on the June 100 put.

A unique, early exercise situation affecting the value of boxes can also arise in a stock option market if there is a tender offer to buy a portion of the stock in a company. For example, with a stock trading at 100, one would expect to see the 100/105 box trading at close to five points. But suppose that a tender offer is made to buy half the outstanding shares at a price of 110. A trader who owns the 100/105 box will exercise his 100 calls in order to be able to tender stock. If he tenders 1000 shares, he might expect half, or 500 shares, to be accepted at the tender price of 110. But after the tender is completed, because it was for only half the outstanding shares, the stock price will return to its pre-tender price of 100. The trader's remaining 500 shares will still be trading at 100. In other words, prior to the tender offer the 100 calls are worth 10, but after the tender the 105 puts are worth a minimum of five. Of course, one cannot say that the box is worth 15, because only half the outstanding shares are worth 110. The other half are worth 100. Still, the 100/105 box is likely to trade for significantly more than its usual price of five.

The possibility of early exercise can also affect arbitrage strategies in the futures option market, but the difference between American versus European values is much less than in the stock option market because there is less interest consideration associated with futures options. For practical purposes, unless the options are very deeply in-the-money or are very long-term, the difference between American and

European values for futures options is negligible. Some sample option and arbitrage values are shown below (we assume that all options are subject to stock-type settlement):

Futures price = 100; Volatility = 25%; Interest rate = 8.00%;
Time to expiration: March = 3 months, June = 6 months

Option	European Value	European Delta	American Value	American Delta
March 95 call	7.60	66.9	7.67	67.5
March 95 put	2.70	−31.2	2.73	−31.3
March 100 call	4.88	51.5	4.88	51.8
March 100 put	4.88	−46.6	4.88	−46.9
June 95 call	9.27	62.2	9.34	63.5
June 95 put	4.46	−33.9	4.48	−34.2
June 100 call	6.76	51.4	6.80	52.2
June 100 put	6.76	−44.7	6.80	−45.4

Strategy	European Value	European Delta	American Value	American Delta
March 95 conversion	4.90	+1.9	4.94	+1.2
June 95 conversion	4.81	+3.9	4.86	+2.3
March 100 conversion	0	+1.9	0	+1.3
June 100 conversion	0	+3.9	0	+2.4
March 95/100 box	4.90	0	4.94	+.1
June 95/100 box	4.81	0	4.86	+.1
March/June 95 jelly roll	1.85	0	1.71	+1.1
March/June 100 jelly roll	1.95	0	1.71	+1.6

Many new traders seem to worry unduly about the possibility of early exercise: "If I sell an option, what happens if I am suddenly assigned?" It is true that sometimes early assignment can cause a loss. But there are many factors which can cause a trader to lose money; early exercise is only one such factor. A trader should be prepared to deal with the possibility of early exercise just as he should be prepared to deal with the possibility of movement in the price of the underlying contract, or the possibility of changes in volatility. Margin requirements established by the clearing houses usually require a trader to keep sufficient funds in his account to cover the possibility of early assignment. But this is not always true. If he is short deeply in-the-money options, an early assignment notice may cause a cash squeeze. If this happens, he will need sufficient capital to cover the situation. Otherwise, he may be forced to liquidate some or all of the remaining position. And forced liquidations are invariably losing propositions.

An experienced trader should be able to foresee the likelihood of early exercise. He need only ask himself: "If I owned this option, would I logically exercise it now?" If the answer is "yes," then the trader ought to be prepared for assignment. Early exercise rarely comes as a surprise. If it does, it is probably good for the trader who was assigned. If an option is exercised too early, someone has erroneously abandoned the time value or protective characteristics associated with the option. When that happens, the trader who is assigned will find that he has just received an unexpected gift.

❖ 13 ❖

Hedging with Options

The original justification for introducing options and futures was to enable market participants to transfer part or all of the risk associated with holding a position in the underlying instrument from one party to another. Options and futures act as insurance contracts. Unlike a futures contract, an option transfers only part of the risk from one party to another. In this respect an option acts much more like a traditional insurance policy than a futures contract.

Even though options were originally intended to function as insurance policies, option markets have evolved to the point where, in most markets, hedgers (those wanting to protect an existing position), make up only a small portion of market participants. Other traders, including arbitrageurs, speculators, and spreaders, typically outnumber true hedgers. Nevertheless, hedgers still represent an important force in the marketplace, and any sophisticated market participant must be aware of the strategies hedgers use to protect their positions.

Many hedgers come to the marketplace as either natural longs or natural shorts. Through the course of normal business activities they will profit from either a rise or fall in the price of some underlying instrument. The producer of a commodity (grain, oil, precious metals) is a natural long; if the price of the commodity rises, he will receive more when he goes to sell it in the marketplace. The user of a commodity is a natural short; if the price of the commodity falls, he will have to pay less for it when he goes to buy it in the marketplace. In the same way, lenders and borrowers in the financial markets are natural longs and shorts in terms of interest rates. A rise in interest rates will help lenders and hurt borrowers. A decline in interest rates will have the opposite effect.

Other potential hedgers come to the marketplace because they have voluntarily chosen to take long or short positions, and now wish to lay off part or all of the risk of that position. A speculator may have taken a long or short position in a certain contract, but wishes to temporarily reduce the risk associated with an outright long or short position. For example, a portfolio manager is usually paid to choose which stocks to buy for a portfolio. He is a voluntary long. If he wants to continue to hold certain stocks, but believes that the stocks might decline in the short term, he may find it cheaper to temporarily hedge the stocks with options or futures than to sell the stocks and buy them back at a later date.

As with insurance, there is a cost to hedging. The cost may be immediately apparent because it requires an immediate cash outlay. But the cost may also be more subtle, either in terms of lost profit opportunity, or in terms of additional risk under some circumstances. Every hedging decision is a tradeoff: what is the hedger willing to give up under one set of market conditions in order to protect himself under another set? A hedger with a long position who wants to protect his downside will almost certainly have to give up something on the upside; a hedger with a short position trying to protect his upside will have to give up something on the downside.

PROTECTIVE CALLS AND PUTS

The simplest way to hedge an underlying position using options is to purchase either a call to protect a short position, or a put to protect a long position. In each case, if the market moves adversely, the hedger is insulated from any loss beyond the exercise price. The difference between the exercise price and the current price of the underlying is analogous to the deductible portion of an insurance policy. And the price of the option is analogous to the premium which one has to pay for the insurance policy.

For example, suppose an American firm expects to take delivery of DM 1,000,000 worth of German goods in six months. If the contract requires payment in Deutschemarks at the time of delivery, the American firm has automatically acquired a short position in Deutschemarks against U.S. dollars. If the Deutschemark rises against the dollar, the goods will cost more in dollars; if the Deutschemark falls against the dollar, the goods will cost less. If the Deutschemark is currently trading at .60 (60¢ per DM) and remains there for the next six months, the cost to the American firm will be $600,000. If, however, at delivery the Deutschemark has risen to .70 (70¢ per dollar), the cost to the American firm will be $700,000.

The American firm can offset the risk it has acquired by purchasing a call option on Deutschemarks, for example a .64 call. If the firm wants an exact hedge, the underlying contract will be DM 1,000,000, and the option will have an expiration date corresponding to the date of delivery of the goods. If the value of the Deutschemark begins to rise against the U.S. dollar, the firm will have to pay a higher price than expected when it takes delivery of the goods in six months. But the price it will have to pay for Deutschemarks can never be greater than .64. If the price of Deutschemarks is greater than .64 at expiration, the firm will simply exercise its call, effectively purchasing Deutschemarks at .64. If the price of Deutschemarks is less than .64 at expiration, the firm will let the option expire worthless since it will be cheaper to purchase Deutschemarks in the open market.

A hedger who chooses to purchase a call to protect a short position, or a put to protect a long position, has risk limited by the exercise price of the option. At the same time, the hedger still maintains open-ended profit potential. If the underlying market moves in the hedger's favor, he can let the option expire and take advantage of the enhanced value of his position in the open market. If, in our example, the Deutschemark were to fall to .55 at the time of delivery, the firm would simply let the .64 call expire unexercised. At the same time, the firm would purchase DM 1,000,000 for $550,000, resulting in an unexpected windfall of $150,000.

There is a cost involved in buying insurance in the form of a protective call or put, namely the price of the option. The cost of the insurance is commensurate with the amount of protection afforded by the option. If the price of a six-month .64 call is .0075 (3⁄4¢), the firm will pay an extra $7,500 (.0075 × 1,000,000) no matter what happens. A call option with a higher exercise price will cost less, but it also offers less protection in the form of an additional deductible amount. If the firm chooses to purchase a .66 call trading at .0025 (1⁄4¢), the cost for this insurance will only be $2,500 (.0025 × 1,000,000). But the firm will have to bear any loss up to a Deutschemark price of .66. Only above .66 is the firm fully protected. In the same way, a lower exercise price call will offer additional protection, but at a higher price. A .62 call will protect the firm against any rise above .62, but if the price of the call is .015 (1 1⁄2¢), the purchase of this protection will add an additional $15,000 (.015 × 1,000,000) to the final costs.

The cost of purchasing a protective option and the insurance afforded by the strategy is shown in Figures 13-1 (protective call) and 13-2 (protective put). Since each strategy combines an underlying position with an option position, it follows from Chapter 11 that the resulting protected position is a synthetic option:

short underlying + long call = long put
long underlying + long put = long call

A hedger who buys a call to protect a short underlying position has effectively purchased a put at the same exercise price. A hedger who buys a put to protect a long underlying position has effectively purchased a call. In our example, if the firm purchases a .64 call to protect a short Deutschemark position, the result is identical to owning a .64 put.

Figure 13-1: A Protective Call

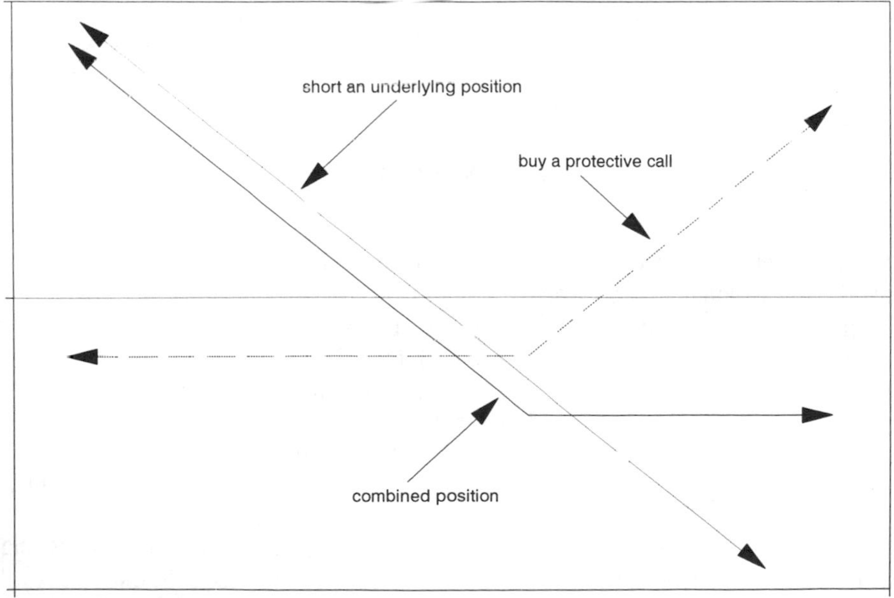

Figure 13-2: A Protective Put

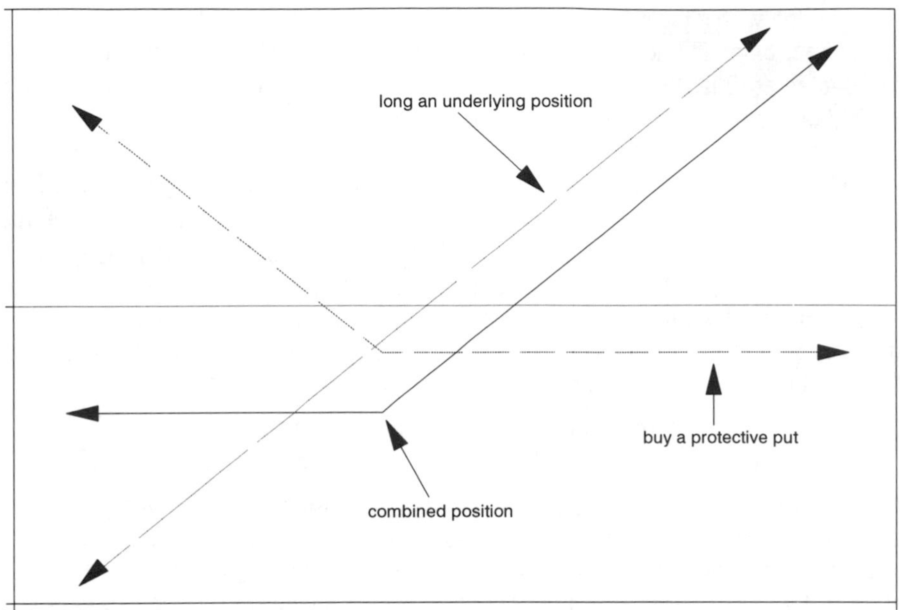

Which protective option should a hedger buy? That depends on the amount of risk the hedger is willing to bear, something which each market participant must determine individually. One thing is certain. There will always be a cost associated with the purchase of a protective option. If the insurance afforded by the option enables the hedger to protect his financial position, the cost may be worthwhile.

COVERED WRITES

While the purchase of a protective option offers a limited and known risk, a hedger might be willing to accept more risk in return for some other advantage. Instead of purchasing an option to protect an existing position, a hedger might consider selling, or writing, an option against the position. This strategy does not offer the limited risk afforded by the purchase of a protective option but, in its favor, the strategy results in a cash credit rather than a debit. This credit offers some, though not unlimited, protection against an adverse move in the underlying market.

Consider a fund manager whose portfolio consists of a long position in a certain stock. If the manager is worried about a decline in the price of the stock, he might choose to sell a call option against the stock. The amount of protection the manager is seeking, as well as the potential upside appreciation, will determine which call is sold, whether in-the-money, at-the-money, or out-of-the-money. Selling an in-the-money call offers a high degree of protection, but will eliminate most upside profit potential. Selling an out-of-the-money call offers less protection but leaves room for large upside profit potential.

For example, if the stock is currently trading at 100, the fund manager might sell a 95 call. If the 95 call is trading at 6½, the sale of the call will offer a high degree of protection against a decline in the price of the stock. As long as the stock declines by no more than 6½, to 93½, the manager will do no worse than break even. Unfortunately, if the stock begins to rise, the fund manager will not participate in the rise since the stock will be called away when the manager is assigned on the 95 call. Still, even if the stock rises, the manager will get to keep the 1½-point time premium he received from the sale of the 95 call.

If the manager wants to participate in upside movement in the stock, and is also willing to accept less protection on the downside, he might sell a 105 call. If the 105 call is trading at two, the sale of this option will only protect him against a two-point fall, to 98, in the price of the stock. If, however, the stock begins to rise, he will participate point for point in this advance up to a price of 105. Above 105, he can expect the stock to be called away.

Which option should the manager sell? Again, that is a subjective decision based on how much risk the manager is willing to take as well as the amount of upside appreciation in which he wants to participate. Many covered write programs involve selling at-the-money options. Such options offer less protection than in-the-money calls, and less profit potential than out-of-the-money options. An at-the-money option is pure time premium. If the market sits still, a portfolio of at-the-money options have been sold against an existing position in the underlying instrument will show the greatest appreciation in value.

The value of typical covered writes, also known as *overwrites*, are shown in Figures 13-3 (covered call) and 13-4 (covered put). When the underlying is purchased and calls are simultaneously sold against the position, a covered write is also referred to as a *buy/write*. As with the purchase of a protective option, a covered write consists of a position in the underlying and an option. It can therefore be expressed as a synthetic position:

long underlying + short call = short put
short underlying + short put = short call

A hedger who sells a call to protect a long underlying position has effectively sold a put at the same exercise price. A hedger who sells a put to protect a short underlying position has effectively sold a call. In our example, if the portfolio manager sells a 100 call to protect a long stock position, the result is identical to selling a 100 put.

The purchase of a protective option and the sale of a covered option are the two most common hedging strategies involving options. If given a choice between these strategies, which one should a hedger choose? In theory, the hedger ought to base his decision on the same criteria as the pure trader: price versus value. In general, if the price of an option is lower than its value, then the purchase of a protective call or put makes the most sense. If the price of an option is higher than its value, then the sale of a covered call or put makes the most sense. By comparing implied volatility to a forecast

Figure 13-3: A Covered Call

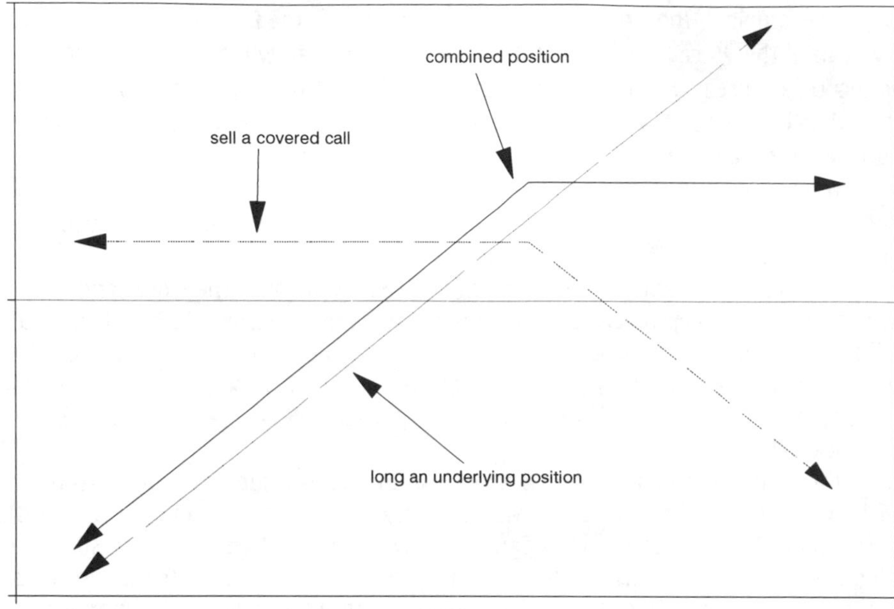

Figure 13-4: A Covered Put

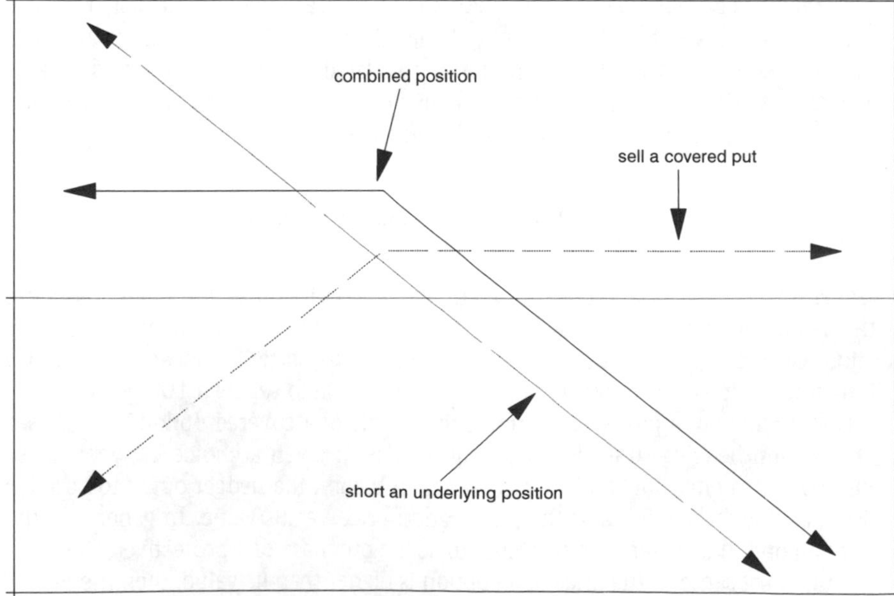

volatility, a hedger ought to be able to make a sensible determination as to whether he wants to buy or sell options. Of course, he is still left with the choice of exercise prices. This will depend on the amount of adverse or favorable movement the hedger foresees, as well as the risk he is willing to accept if he is wrong.

While theoretical considerations will often play a role in a hedger's decision, practical considerations may also be important. If a hedger knows that he will be forced out of business if the underlying contract moves beyond a certain price, then the purchase of a protective option at that exercise price may be the most sensible strategy, regardless of whether the option is theoretically overpriced.[1]

Most hedgers find, however, that there is a psychological barrier to buying options. "Why should I lay out money for an option when I will probably lose the premium?" The hedger is right. Most of the time he will lose the premium because most of the time the option will expire worthless. But the same hedger who refuses to purchase an option to protect his business dealings would never consider leaving his home or family uninsured. Like options, the great majority of insurance policies expire without claims ever being made against them. Houses do not burn down; people live on; cars are not stolen. That is the reason insurance companies make a profit. But the purchaser of an insurance policy is willing to accept the fact that insurance companies make profits. Unlike the insurance company, which is selling the insurance contract with the clear intent of making a profit, the purchaser of an insurance contract is not purchasing the contract to make money. He is purchasing it for the peace of mind which it affords. The same philosophy should apply to the purchase of options. If a hedger needs the protection afforded by the option, the purchase makes sense in spite of the fact that it is likely to be a losing proposition in the long run.

FENCES

Suppose a hedger desires the limited risk afforded by the purchase of a protective option, but also wants to avoid the cash outlay associated with such a strategy. What can he do? A popular strategy, known as a *fence,* is to simultaneously combine the purchase of a protective option with the sale of a covered option. For example, with an underlying contract at 50, a hedger with a long position might choose to simultaneously sell a 55 call and purchase a 45 put. The hedger is insulated from any fall in price below 45, since he can then exercise his put. At the same time, he can participate in any upward move to 55, at which point his underlying position will be called away. The cost of the complete hedge depends on the prices of the 45 put and 55 call. If they are the same, the cost of the hedge is zero. If the price of the 55 call is greater than the price of the 45 put, the hedge can be established for a credit which the hedger gets to keep no matter where the underlying finishes. With prices of 1.25 and 1.75 for the 45 put and 55 call, the hedger will receive a credit of .50. This will reduce his break-even price on the underlying position to 49.50.

1. Of course, if the options are wildly overpriced, a hedger might be reluctant to buy a protective option. But this is unlikely to happen. If option prices are high, there is usually a valid reason.

Recalling the basic synthetic relationships, we find that a long fence (long the underlying, short a covered call, long a protective put) is simply a bull vertical spread done synthetically. Suppose in our example fence consisting of a long 45 put and short 55 call, we replace the 45 put with its synthetic equivalent:

long 45 put = short underlying + long 45 call
45/55 fence = long underlying + long 45 put + short 55 call
= long underlying + (short underlying + long 45 call) + short 55 call
= long 45 call + short 55 call

A short fence consists of a short underlying position together with the purchase of a protective call and sale of a covered put. Since we can always rewrite one of the options with its synthetic equivalent, this is simply a bear vertical spread. Long and short fences are shown in Figures 13-5 and 13-6.

Fences are popular hedging tools because they offer known protection at a low cost, or even a credit. At the same time, they still allow a hedger to participate, at least partially, in favorable market movement. Fences go by a variety of names: *range forwards*, *tunnels*, *cylinders;* among floor traders they are sometimes known as *split-price conversions* and *reversals.*

As the borrowing and lending of funds has become more widespread, and since such activity is often based on a floating interest rate, the use of options to hedge long or short interest rate positions has become especially popular. A firm which borrows

Figure 13-5: A Long Fence

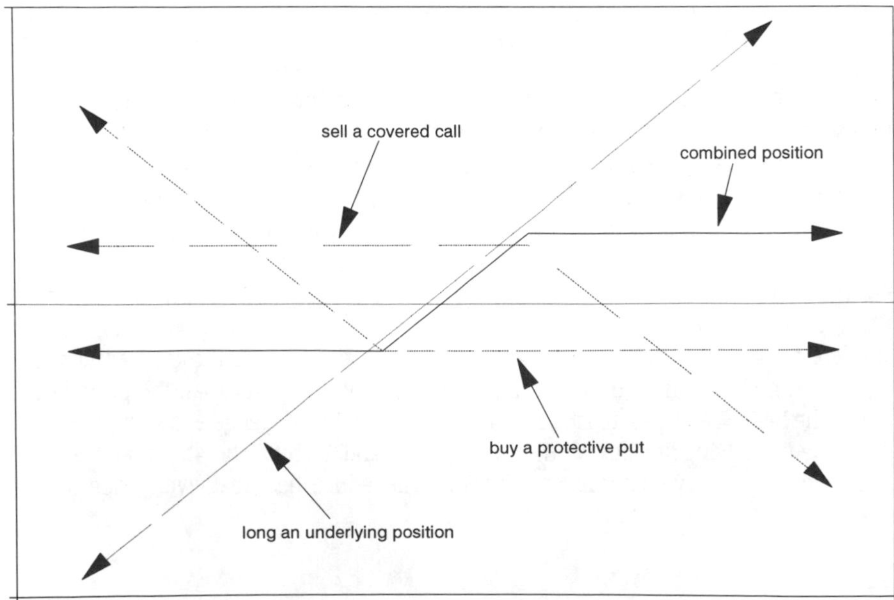

Figure 13-6: A Short Fence

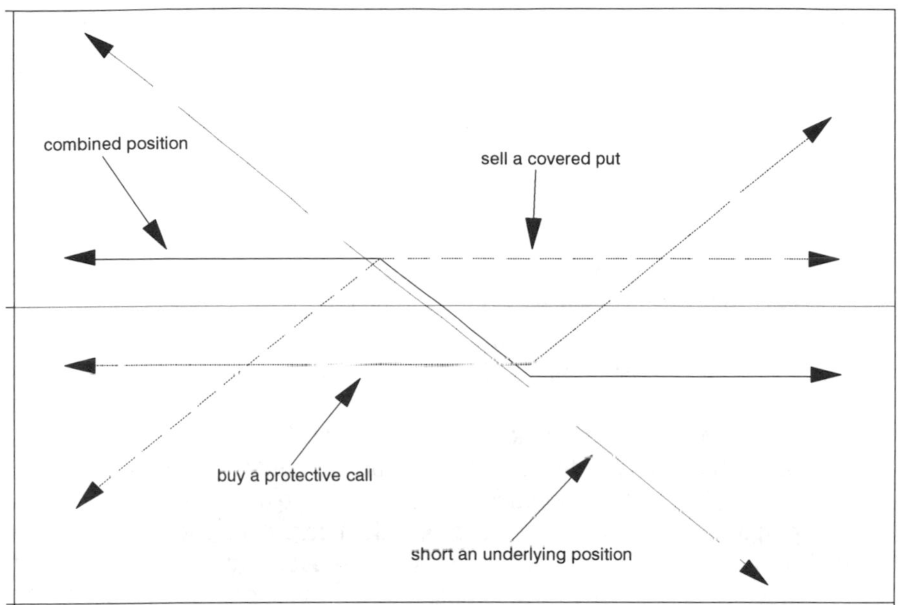

funds at a variable interest rate has a short interest rate position. A fall in interest rates will reduce its cost of borrowing, while a rise in interest rates will increase its costs. To *cap* the upside risk, the firm can purchase an interest rate call, thereby establishing a maximum amount it will have to pay for borrowed funds. No matter how high interest rates rise, the borrower will never have to pay more than the cap's exercise price.

An institution which lends funds at a variable interest rate has a long interest rate position. A rise in interest rates will increase its returns, while a fall in interest rates will reduce its returns. To set a *floor* on its downside risk, the institution can purchase an interest rate put, thereby establishing a minimum amount it will receive for loaned funds, no matter how low interest rates fall. No matter how low interest rates fall, the lender will never receive less than the floor's exercise price.

If a borrower (lender) simultaneously buys a cap (floor) and sells a floor (cap), he has established a *collar* to his position. This is simply a fence done in the interest rate market.

COMPLEX HEDGING STRATEGIES

Since most hedgers are not professional option traders, and have neither the time nor desire to carefully analyze option prices, simple hedging strategies involving the purchase or sale of single options are the most widely used. However, if one is willing to do a more detailed analysis of options, it is possible to construct a wide variety of hedging strategies which involve both volatility and directional considerations. In order to do this, a hedger must be familiar with both volatility and its impact on option values, and the delta as a measure of directional risk. The hedger can then combine his knowledge of options with the practical considerations of hedging.

As a first step in choosing a strategy, a hedger might consider the following:

1. Does the hedge need to offer protection against a "worst case" scenario?
2. How much of the current directional risk should the hedge eliminate?
3. What additional risks is the hedger willing to accept?

A hedger who needs disaster insurance in order to protect against a "worst case" scenario only has a choice of which option(s) to buy. Even so, he still needs to decide which exercise price to purchase and how many options. For example, suppose a hedger has a long position in a certain underlying contract currently trading at 100. Suppose also that the hedger decides to buy a put because he needs to limit the downside risk to some known and fixed amount. Which put should he buy?

Suppose the hedger has determined that options are generally overpriced (implied volatility is too high). Clearly, any option purchase will be to the hedgers' disadvantage. If his sole purpose is to hedge his downside risk without regard to upside profit potential, he ought to avoid options and hedge himself in the futures or forward market. If, however, he still wants upside profit potential, he must ask himself how much of a long position he wants to retain. For example, he might be willing to retain 50% of his current long position. This simply means that he has to purchase puts with a total delta of –50. He can do this by purchasing one at-the-money put with a delta of –50, or several out-of-the-money puts whose deltas add up to –50. But in a high implied volatility market one usually tries to buy as few options as possible and sell as many options as possible. (This is analogous to constructing a ratio vertical spread.) Hence, purchasing one put with a delta of –50 will be less costly, theoretically, than purchasing several options with a total delta of –50. If the hedger wants to eliminate even more of the directional risk, say 75%, under these circumstances he would be better off purchasing one put with a delta of –75.

All other factors being equal, in a high implied volatility market a hedger should buy as few options as possible and sell as many options as possible. Conversely, in a low implied volatility market a hedger should buy as many options as possible and sell as few options as possible.

This means that if all options are overpriced (implied volatility is too high), and the hedger decides he is willing to accept the unlimited downside risk that goes with the sale of a covered call, in theory he ought to sell as many calls as possible to reach his hedging objectives. If he is trying to hedge 50% of his long underlying position, he can do a *ratio write* by selling several out-of-the-money calls with a total delta of 50, rather than selling a single at-the-money call with a delta of 50.

There is an additional problem if one sells several calls against a single long underlying position. Now the hedger not only has the unlimited downside risk which goes with a covered call position, but he also has unlimited upside risk because he has sold more calls than he can cover with the underlying. If the market moves up far enough, he will be assigned on all the calls. Most hedgers want to restrict their unlimited risk to one direction, usually the direction of their natural position. A hedger with a long underlying position may be willing to accept unlimited downside risk, but he is probably unwilling to accept unlimited upside risk. A hedger with a short underlying position may be willing to accept unlimited upside risk, but he is probably unwilling to accept unlimited downside risk. A hedger who constructs a position with unlimited risk in either direction is presumably taking a volatility position. There is nothing wrong with this, since volatility trading can be highly profitable. But a true hedger ought not lose sight of what his ultimate goal is: to protect an existing position, and to keep the cost of this protection as low as possible.

A hedger can also protect a position by constructing one-to-one volatility spreads with deltas which yield the desired amount of protection. For example, a hedger who wants to protect 50% of a short underlying position can buy or sell time spreads or butterflies with a total delta of +50. Such spreads offer partial protection within a range. The position still has unlimited upside risk, while it also retains unlimited downside profit potential. Such volatility spreads also give the hedger the choice of buying or selling volatility. If implied volatility is generally low, with the underlying market currently at 100, the hedger might protect a short position by purchasing a 110 call time spread (purchase a long-term 110 call, sell a short-term 110 call). This spread has a positive delta and, at the same time, is theoretically attractive since the low implied volatility makes a long time spread relatively inexpensive. If the 110 call time spread has a delta of +25, to hedge 50% of his directional risk the hedger can buy two time spreads for each short underlying position. Conversely, if implied volatility is high, the hedger can consider selling time spreads. Now he will have to choose a lower exercise price to achieve a positive delta. If he sells the 90 call time spread (purchase a short-term 90 call, sell a long-term 90 call), he will have a position with a positive delta and a positive theoretical edge. If he wants to protect 75% of his position, and the spread has a delta of +25, he can sell the spread three times for each underlying position.

In the same way, a hedger can also buy or sell vertical spreads to achieve a desired amount of protection. Depending on whether options are generally underpriced or overpriced (implied volatility is too low or too high), the hedger will work around the at-the-money option. With the underlying market currently at 100, the hedger who wants to protect a long position can sell a vertical call spread with a negative delta (sell the lower exercise price call, buy the higher exercise price call). If implied volatility is high, he will prefer to sell an at-the-money option and buy an out-of-the-money option. If implied volatility is low, he will prefer to sell an in-the-money option and buy an at-the-money option. Each spread will have a negative delta, but will also have a positive theoretical edge since the at-the-money option is the most sensitive to changes in volatility.

As is obvious, using options to hedge a position can be just as complex as using options to construct trading strategies. Many factors go into the decision-making process. When a potential hedger is confronted for the first time with the multitude of possible strategies, he can understandably feel overwhelmed, to the point where he decides to abandon options completely. When this happens the hedger, or someone advising the hedger, should lay out a limited number of strategies (perhaps four or five) which make sense, and compare the various risk/reward characteristics of the strategies. Given the hedger's general market outlook, and his willingness or unwillingness to accept certain risks, it should then be possible to make an intelligent decision. A summary of common hedging strategies, with some of their advantages and disadvantages, is given in Figure 13-7.

PORTFOLIO INSURANCE

Suppose a hedger holds a long position in a certain asset, and he wants to protect his holding against downward movement by purchasing a put option. Unfortunately, the hedger finds that no option market for this asset exists. Nor is any other source, such as an option dealer, available. Is there any way the hedger can create the put option himself?

If the hedger were really able to purchase a put, his position would be:

long underlying + long put

But we know from the synthetic relationships in Chapter 11 that a long underlying position together with a long put is equivalent to a long call. Therefore, the hedger really wants to own a call with the same exercise price as the put.

What would be the characteristics of this call? We could analyze the call using a theoretical pricing model. In order to do that, we need to know what the underlying asset is, and then we need to determine the inputs into the model. Suppose the underlying asset is a futures contract, and that we plan to use the following inputs:

exercise price = 100
time to expiration = 10 weeks
underlying price = 101.35
interest rate = 8%
volatility = 18.3%

Feeding these inputs into a theoretical pricing model, we find that the call option which the hedger would like to own has a delta of 57. This means that if the hedger actually owned the call (instead of owning the underlying asset together with a 100 put) in theory he would have a position equivalent to owning 57% of his asset. Therefore, if he wants to replicate the combination of the underlying asset and the 100 put, he must sell off 43% of his holdings in the asset. When he does that, he will have a position theoretically equivalent to owning a 100 call.

Now suppose a week passes and the value of his asset has risen to 102.26. What would be the delta of the 100 call which the hedger desires to own? Again, feeding all the inputs into a theoretical pricing model, we find that the call now has a delta of 62. If the hedger wants a position which is equivalent to a long call, he now needs to own

Figure 13-7: Summary of Hedging Strategies

Position	Hedging Strategy	Advantages	Disadvantage
long underlying	buy a protective put	limited downside risk/unlimited upside profit potential positive theoretical edge	potential negative theoretical edge
	sell a covered call	potential positive theoretical edge	unlimited downside risk potential negative theoretical edge
	long fence (buy a put, sell a call)	limited downside risk potential credit if call price exceeds put price	limited upside profit potential debit if put price exceeds call price
	ratio put purchase	unlimited upside profit/unlimited downside profit potential positive theoretical edge	potential negative theoretical edge
	ratio call write	potential positive theoretical edge	unlimited downside risk/unlimited upside risk potential negative theoretical edge
	bear vertical spread	unlimited upside profit potential positive theoretical edge	unlimited downside risk potential negative theoretical edge
	bear time spread	unlimited upside profit potential positive theoretical edge	unlimited downside risk potential negative theoretical edge
short underlying	buy a protective call	limited upside risk/unlimited downside profit potential positive theoretical edge	potential negative theoretical edge
	sell a covered put	potential positive theoretical edge	unlimited upside risk potential negative theoretical edge
	short fence (buy a call, sell a put)	limited upside risk potential credit if put price exceeds call price	limited downside profit potential debit if call price exceeds put price
	ratio call purchase	unlimited downside profit/unlimited upside profit potential positive theoretical edge	potential negative theoretical edge
	ratio put write	potential positive theoretical edge	unlimited upside risk/unlimited downside risk potential negative theoretical edge
	bull vertical spread	unlimited downside profit potential positive theoretical edge	unlimited upside risk potential negative theoretical edge
	bull time spread	unlimited downside profit potential, positive theoretical edge	unlimited upside risk potential negative theoretical edge

62% of his original holding in the underlying asset. He must therefore buy back 5% of his original holding in the asset.

Suppose another week passes and the value of the asset has fallen to 99.07. Using the new market conditions, the 100 call would now have a delta of 46. In order to replicate the call position, the hedger must now sell off 16% of the asset, so that he owns only 46% of his original holding.

Notice what the hedger is doing. He is periodically rehedging his original holding to create a position with the same delta characteristics as the call. If he continues to do this over the ten-week period, he has, in effect, created a ten-week call at an exercise price of 100.

The reader may have already realized that we are simply repeating the example in Figure 5-1, but in a slightly different form. In that example, we purchased an underpriced call and replicated the sale of the same call through a continuous rehedging process. In our current example we are also replicating the call through a continuous rehedging process. But here we want to purchase the call rather than sell it. All our adjustments are therefore the opposite of those in Figure 5-1. Note also that at week ten (expiration), instead of liquidating the position, as we did in Figure 5-1, we plan to buy in the remainder of the asset. It was always our intention to retain our entire holding of the asset at expiration. The replicated position in our current example is shown in Figure 13-8.

In order to replicate the call, the hedger will have to buy back some of the asset when the market rises and sell some of the asset when the market falls. The unfavorable adjustments (buying high, selling low) suggests that there will be a cost associated with this rehedging process. What will the cost be? If the replication process offers the same protection as owning a 100 put, then one might expect the cost of the replication process to be the same as the theoretical value of the ten week 100 put. This is indeed the case. Using the previously listed inputs, the Black-Scholes model yields a theoretical value for the 100 put of 2.55. This is identical to the cost of the replication process described in Figure 13-8.

The rehedging process is an attempt to replicate the automatic rehedging characteristics of the option. As a hedge against an underlying position, an option has the very desirable characteristic of offering greater protection as the market moves adversely, and less protection as the market moves favorably. In effect, the option automatically rehedges itself to fit the required amount of protection. This is the influence of the gamma on the option's delta. When a hedger attempts to replicate the characteristics of an option by continuously rehedging the underlying position himself, he is simply trying to replicate the automatic rehedging (gamma) characteristics of the option. The cost of the option, or the cost of the rehedging process, is the price the hedger pays for the option's gamma characteristics.

Since we need to continuously compute the delta to replicate an option through a rehedging process, this method of replication requires us to use a theoretical pricing model. We are therefore likely to encounter many of the same problems which we encounter anytime we use a theoretical pricing model to evaluate an option. Is the model itself correct? Do we have the right inputs? Leaving aside the question of the

Figure 13-8

Week	Asset Value	Delta of 100 call	% of Asset Needed for Replication	Required Adjustment
0	101.35	57	57%	sell 43%
1	102.26	62	62%	buy 5%
2	99.07	46	46%	sell 16%
3	100.39	53	53%	buy 7%
4	100.76	56	56%	buy 3%
5	103.59	74	74%	buy 18%
6	99.26	45	45%	sell 29%
7	98.28	35	35%	sell 10%
8	99.98	50	50%	buy 15%
9	103.78	93	93%	buy 43%
10	102.54	100	100%	buy 7%

model's correctness, anyone wishing to use this method will have to come up with a reasonable volatility estimate. If the volatility estimate turns out to be too high or too low, the cost of replicating the option will be more or less than originally expected. But notice that the cost of replication will always be the right cost. If the market is more volatile than expected, the cost will be greater in terms of required adjustments. But the value of the option would also have been greater. Higher volatility means a higher theoretical value. In the same way, if the market is less volatile than expected, the cost will be less in terms of required adjustments. The value of the option would also have been less. Lower volatility means a lower theoretical value.

This process of continuously rehedging an underlying position to replicate an option position is often referred to as *portfolio insurance*. The method can be used to protect any long or short position against adverse movement, but it is most commonly used by fund managers who wish to insure the value of the securities in a portfolio against a drop in value. For example, suppose a manager has a portfolio of securities currently valued at $100 million. If he wants to insure the value of the portfolio against a drop in value below $90 million, he can either buy a $90 million put, or he can replicate the characteristics of a $90 million call. If he is unable to find someone willing to sell him a $90 million put, he can evaluate the characteristics of the $90 million call and continuously buy or sell the portion of his portfolio required to replicate the call position. In effect, he has created his own put.

Unfortunately, the costs of buying and selling a large number of securities in odd amounts may be quite high. While the concept of portfolio insurance may be attractive from a theoretical perspective, the transaction costs may make the process too expensive to be of practical value. Is there any way a fund manager can use portfolio insurance while keeping transaction costs within acceptable bounds? One common method involves using futures contracts as a substitute for the portfolio holding. If the mix of securities in a portfolio approximates an index, and futures contracts are available on that index, the manager can approximate the results of portfolio insurance by purchasing or selling futures contracts to increase or decrease the holdings in his portfolio. In the United States several index futures are available, the most popular being the futures contract on the S&P 500 index traded at the Chicago Mercantile Exchange. Many fund managers use S&P 500 futures to insure their portfolios against adverse movement in the stock market. This method is not without risk, since the S&P 500 index is unlikely to exactly duplicate the holdings of any one portfolio. Still, the risk may be acceptable given the reduced transaction costs.

Even if options are available on an underlying asset, a hedger may still choose to effect a portfolio insurance strategy himself rather then purchasing the option in the marketplace. For one thing, he may consider the option too expensive. If he believes the option is theoretically overpriced, in the long run it will be cheaper to continuously rehedge the portfolio. Or he may find insufficient liquidity in the option market to absorb the number of option contracts he needs to hedge his position. Finally, the expiration of options which are available may not exactly correspond to the period over which he wants to protect his position. If an option is available, but expires earlier than desired, the hedger might still choose to purchase options in the marketplace, and then pursue a portfolio insurance strategy over the period following the option's expiration. For all these reasons, portfolio insurance has become an increasingly popular method of protecting a position in an underlying asset.

❖ 14 ❖

Volatility Revisited

While there are many ways in which traders interpret volatility, in theory the value of an option depends on only one volatility, the volatility of the underlying contract which will occur over the life of the option. Of course, this volatility is unknown to a trader since it will occur in the future. Nevertheless, if a trader wants to use a theoretical pricing model, he will be required to make some prediction about the volatility of the underlying contract over the life of the option.

Making an intelligent volatility forecast can be a difficult and frustrating exercise, especially for a new option trader. The forecasting of directional price movements through technical analysis is a commonly studied area in trading, and there are many sources to which a trader can turn for information on this subject. Unfortunately, volatility is a much newer concept, and there is relatively little to guide a trader. In spite of this difficulty, an option trader must make some effort to come up with a reasonable volatility input if he is going to rely on a theoretical pricing model to make intelligent trading decisions.

SOME VOLATILITY CHARACTERISTICS

The first step in making a sensible volatility forecast is to understand some of the basic characteristics of volatility. First, let's compare two graphs. Figure 14-1 shows Deutschemark prices from 1982 to 1991. Figure 14-2 shows the 50-day volatility of Deutschemarks over the same period. Are there any generalizations one can make from these graphs? Obviously both prices and volatility sometimes rise and sometimes fall. But unlike the prices of an underlying instrument, which appear to move freely in either direction, there seems to be an equilibrium number to which the volatility always returns. Over a period of three years, from early 1985 to late 1987, the price of Deutschemarks rose from a low of 29 to a high of 63. While prices fluctuated after 1987, they never reached the lows of the early 1980s. Someday, economic forces may cause Deutschemarks to rise or fall dramatically, never again returning to prices in the 50s or 60s. In other words, prices of an underlying contract are open-ended. There is no reason why they have to return to some previous level.

Such does not appear to be the case with volatility. The 50-day volatility of Deutschemarks over the 10-year period in question fluctuated from a low of 5% to a high of 20%. Yet no matter how much it fluctuated, at some point volatility always reversed itself and retraced almost all of its previous rise or fall. Indeed, we might try to find an equilibrium volatility such that there are equal fluctuations above and below this

Figure 14-1: Deutschemark Prices 1982–1991

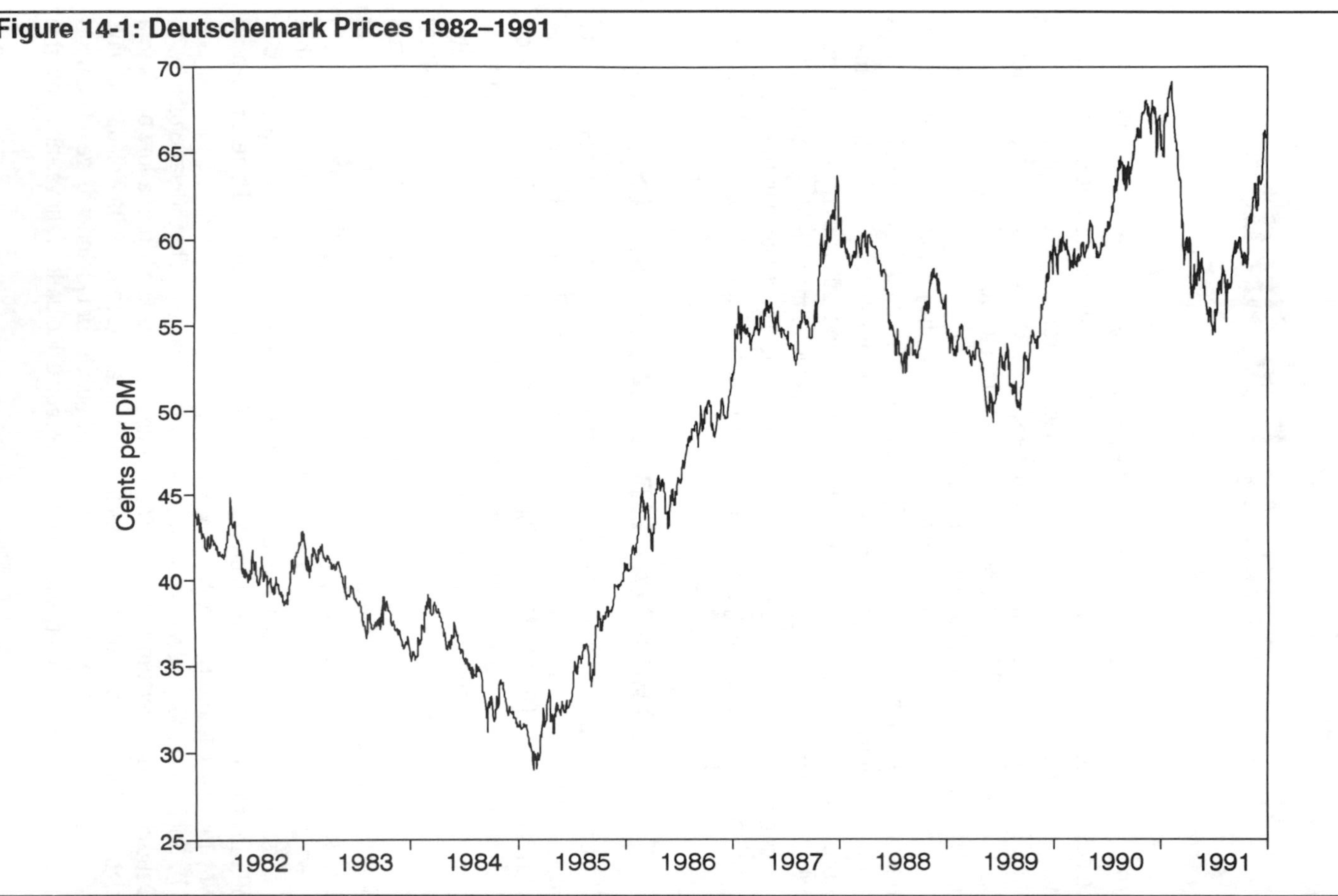

number. In the case of Deutschemarks, this equilibrium volatility seems to be about 11% to 12%. Volatility may rise well above 12%, or fall well below 11%, but eventually it always seems to return to this area.

If we were to generalize about volatility characteristics from the Deutschemark volatility in Figure 14-2, we might surmise that an underlying contract is likely to have a typical long-term average, or *mean volatility*. Moreover, the volatility of the underlying contract appears to be *mean reverting*. When volatility rises above the mean, one can be fairly certain that it will eventually fall back to its mean; when volatility falls below the mean, one can be fairly certain that it will eventually rise to its mean. There is a constant gyration back and forth through this mean.

This mean reverting characteristic of volatility can also be seen in Figure 14-3, which shows the distribution of Deutschemark volatility from 1982 to 1991. Beginning at the extreme left on the x-axis (the amount of time remaining to expiration), we can see that over any two-week period during the 10 years in question, there was a 20% chance that volatility would be either less than 6.0% or greater than 17.3% (the 10th and 90th percentiles). There was a 50% chance that volatility would be either less than 7.6% or greater than 13.0% (the 25th and 75th percentiles). The mean volatility for any two week period was 9.7%. Moving to the extreme right on the x-axis, we can see that over any 50 week period there was a 20% chance that volatility would be either less than 9.8% or greater than 14%. There was a 50% chance that volatility would be either less than 10.6% and greater than 12.7%. The mean volatility for any 50-week period was about 11.5%.

Figure 14-3 has an easily identifiable structure. As one moves further out in time the percentile lines tend to converge towards the mean, and the mean becomes stable. This reinforces the assumption that volatility is indeed mean reverting. This type of volatility graph, sometimes referred to as a *volatility cone*, is an effective method of presenting the volatility characteristics of an underlying instrument.[1]

What else can we say about volatility? Looking at the more detailed Deutschemark volatility chart in Figure 14-4, we might surmise that volatility has some trending characteristics. From July 1989 through June 1990 there was a downward trend in volatility. From July 1990 to April 1991 there was an upward trend. And from April 1991 to October 1991 there was again a downward trend. Moreover, within these major trends there were minor trends as volatility rose and fell for short periods of time. In this respect volatility charts seem to display some of the same characteristics as price charts, and it would not be unreasonable to apply some of the same principles used in technical analysis to volatility analysis. It is important to remember, however, that while price changes and volatility are related, they are not the same thing. If a trader tries to apply exactly the same rules of technical analysis to volatility analysis, he is likely to find that in some cases the rules have no relevance, and that in other cases the rules must be modified to take into account the unique characteristics of volatility. Since the author

---

1. For a more detailed discussion of volatility cones, see:
Burghardt, Galen and Lane, Morton; "How to Tell if Options are Cheap"; *The Journal of Portfolio Management*, Winter 1990, pages 72–78.

Figure 14-2: 50-Day Deutschemark Volatility 1982–1991

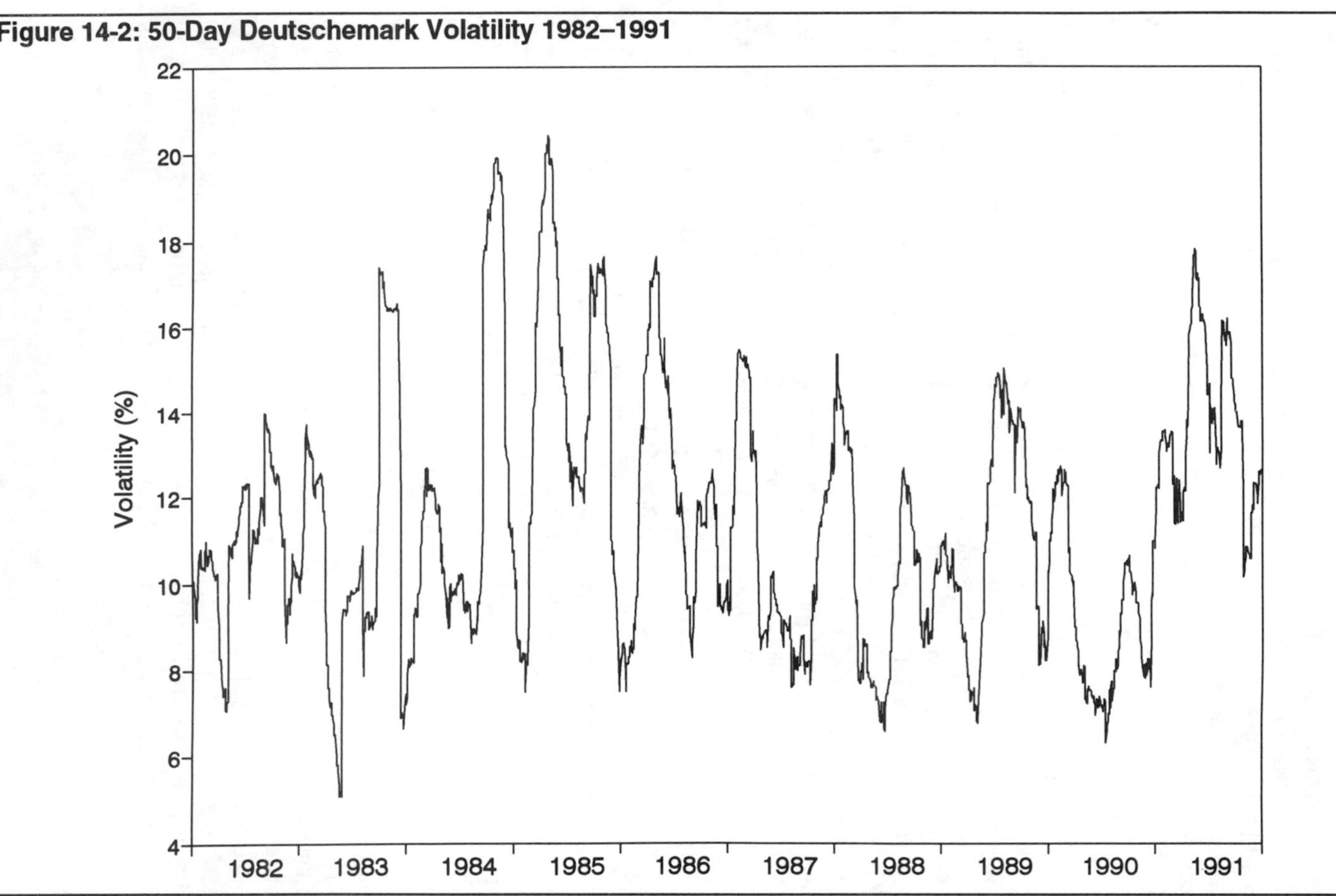

Figure 14-3: Deutschemark Volatility Distribution 1982–1991

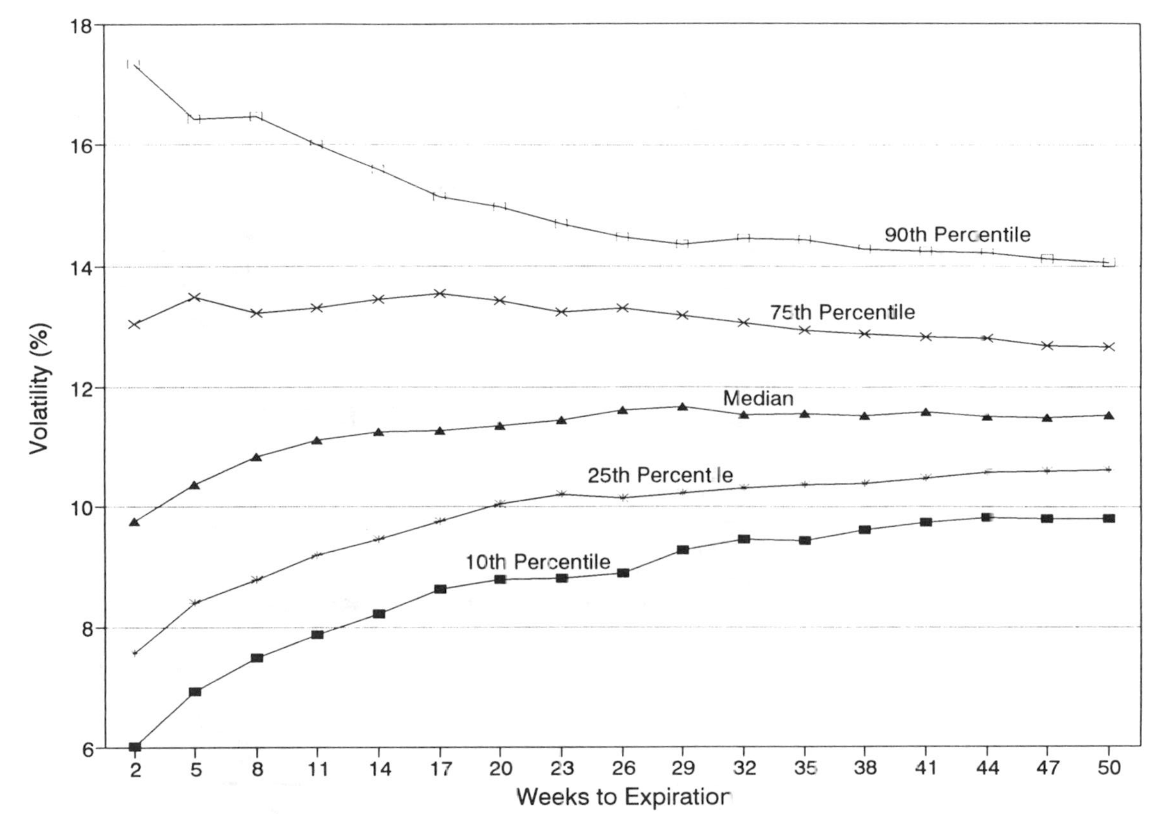

Figure 14-4: 50-Day Deutschemark Volatility 1989–1991

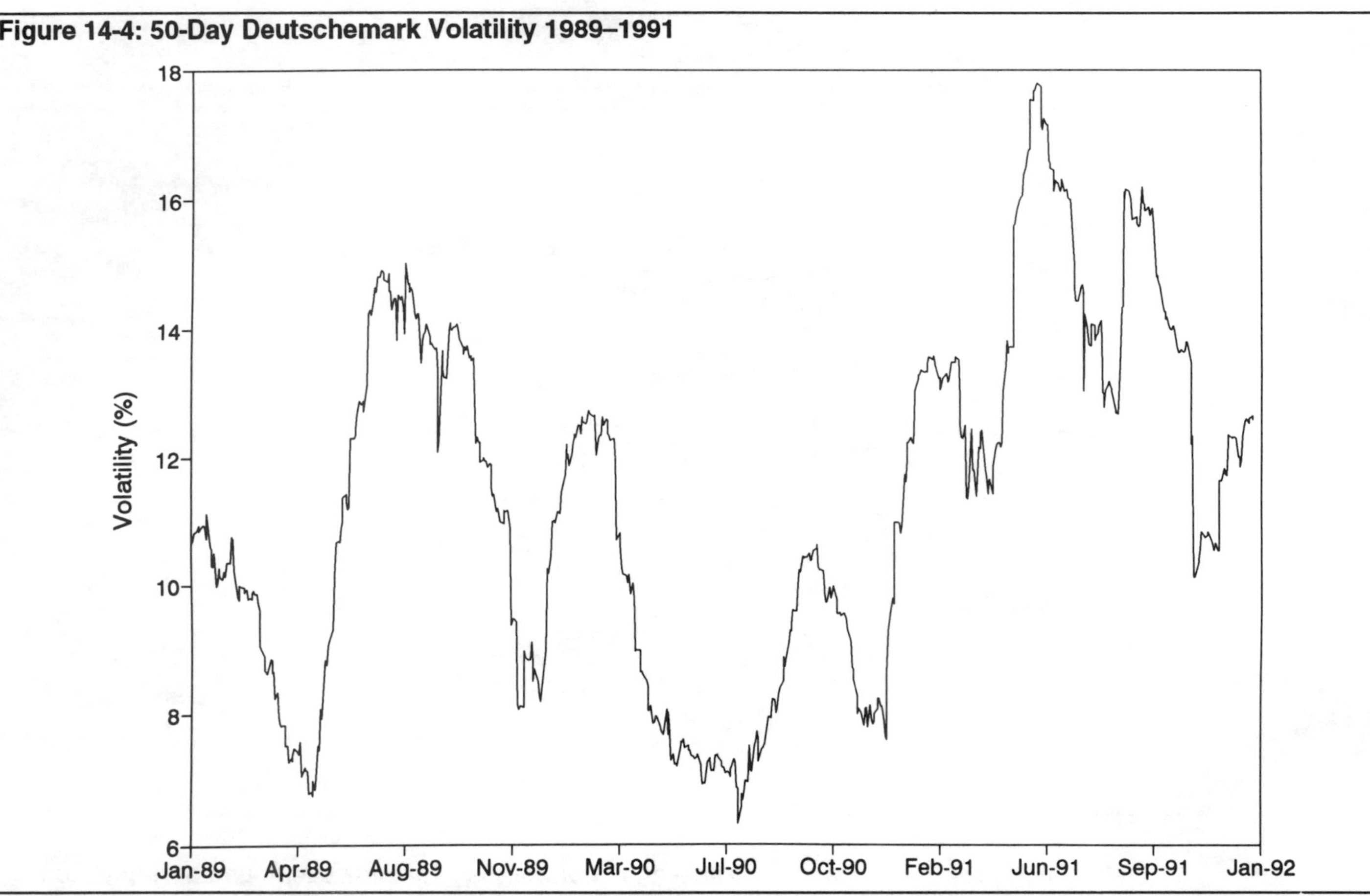

claims no particular expertise in the area of technical analysis, the reader is left to his own devices in this regard.

VOLATILITY FORECASTING

Given the volatility characteristics that we have identified, how might we go about making a volatility forecast? First we need some volatility data. Suppose we have the following historical volatility data on a certain underlying instrument:

last 30 days	24%
last 60 days	20%
last 120 days	18%
last 250 days	18%

Certainly, we would like as much volatility data as possible. But if this is the only data available, how might we use it to make a forecast? One method might be to simply take the average volatility over the periods which we have:

$$(24\% + 20\% + 18\% + 18\%) / 4 = 20\%$$

Using this method, each piece of data is given identical weight. Might it not be reasonable to assume that some data is more important than other data? A trader might assume, for example, that the more current the data, the greater its importance. Since the 24% volatility over the last 30 days is clearly more current than the other volatility data, perhaps 24% should play a greater role in our volatility forecast. We might, for example, give twice as much weight to the 30-day data as to the other data:

$$(40\% \times 24\%) + (20\% \times 20\%) + (20\% \times 18\%) + (20\% \times 18\%) = 20.8\%$$

Our forecast has gone up slightly because of the extra weight given to the more recent data.

Of course, if it is true that the more recent volatility over the last 30 days is more important than the other data, it follows that the volatility over the last 60 days ought to be more important than the volatility over the last 120 days and 250 days. It also follows that the volatility over the last 120 days must be more important than the volatility over the last 250 days. We can factor this into our forecast by using a regressive weighting, giving more distant volatility data progressively less weight in our forecast. For example, we might calculate:

$$(40\% \times 24\%) + (30\% \times 20\%) + (20\% \times 18\%) + (10\% \times 18\%) = 21.0\%$$

Here we have given the 30-day volatility 40% of the weight, the 60-day volatility 30% of the weight, the 120-day volatility 20% of the weight, and the 250-day volatility 10% of the weight.

We have made the assumption that the more recent the data, the greater its importance. Is this always true? If we are interested in evaluating short-term options, it may be true that data which covers short periods of time is the most important. But suppose we are interested in evaluating very long-term options. Over long periods of time the mean reverting characteristic of volatility is likely to reduce the importance of any short-term fluctuations in volatility. In fact, over very long periods of time the most reasonable volatility forecast is simply the long-term mean volatility of the instrument. Therefore the relative weight we give to the different volatility data will depend on the amount of time remaining to expiration for the options in which we are interested.

In a sense, all the historical volatility data we have at our disposal are current data; they simply cover different periods of time. How do we know which data is the most important? In addition to the mean reverting characteristic, volatility also tends to exhibit *serial correlation.* The volatility over any given period is likely to depend on, or correlate with, the volatility over the previous period, assuming that both periods cover the same amount of time. If the volatility of a contract over the last four weeks was 15%, the volatility over the next four weeks is more likely to be close to 15% than far away from 15%. We can again use the weather analogy from Chapter 4. If the high temperature yesterday was 25°, and we had to guess what the high temperature today would be, a guess of 30° would make more sense than a guess of 50°. Once we realize this, we might logically choose to give the greatest weight to the volatility data covering a time period closest to the life of the options in which we are interested. That is, if we are trading very long-term options, the long-term data should get the most weight. If we are trading very short-term options, the short-term data should get the most weight. And if we are trading intermediate-term options, the intermediate-term data should get the most weight.

Suppose we are interested in evaluating six-month options. How should we weight our data? Since 120 (trading) days is closest to six months, we can give the 120-day data the greatest weight, and give other data correspondingly lesser weight:

$$(15\% \times 24\%) + (25\% \times 20\%) + (35\% \times 18\%) + (25\% \times 18\%) = 19.4\%$$

Alternatively, if we are interested in 10-week options, we can give the greatest weight to the 60-day volatility data:

$$(25\% \times 24\%) + (35\% \times 20\%) + (25\% \times 18\%) + (15\% \times 18\%) = 20.2\%$$

In the foregoing examples we used only four historical volatilities, but the more volatility data which is available, the more accurate any volatility forecast is likely to be. Not only will more data, covering different periods of time, give a better overview of the volatility characteristics of an underlying instrument, but it will enable a trader to more closely match historical volatilities to options with different amounts of time to expiration. In our example we used historical volatilities over the last 60 days and 120 days as approximations to forecast volatilities for six-month and 10-week options. Ideally, we would like historical data covering exactly a six-month period and exactly a 10-week period.

The method we have described is one which many traders intuitively use to forecast volatility. It depends on identifying the typical characteristics of volatility, and then projecting a volatility over the forecasting period. Theoreticians have recently tried to take essentially the same approach to volatility forecasting, and this has led to the development of autoregressive conditional heteroskedasticity (ARCH) and generalized autoregressive conditional heteroskedasticity (GARCH) volatility models. A detailed discussion of such models is beyond the scope of this text, since they can be mathematically complex and are not widely used among traders. Nevertheless, an option trader should be aware that these models do exist, and that they are simply an attempt to apply the mean reverting and serial correlation characteristics of volatility to volatility forecasting.[2]

Thus far we have focused only on the historical volatility characteristics of the underlying instrument in trying to forecast a volatility. Is there any other information which might be useful? No individual trader can hope to know everything affecting price changes in an underlying contract. Perhaps there are factors which could affect the future volatility, but about which the trader is unaware. If one believes that such information is likely to be reflected in the prices of the contracts being traded, one way to ferret out additional volatility information is to look at the prices of options. In other words, a trader will want to look at the implied volatility in the marketplace to find the consensus volatility. Once he has done this, he will want to use this information in any volatility forecast he intends to make.

How much weight should a trader give the implied volatility? Some traders subscribe to the efficient market principle, and believe that the implied volatility is always the best volatility forecast since it reflects all available information. Most traders believe, however, that while the implied volatility is important, it isn't the whole story. Typically, a trader might give the implied volatility a weighting somewhere between 25% and 75% in making a volatility forecast. How much depends on the trader's confidence in forecasting a volatility based on historical volatility data? If a trader feels very confident about his forecast, he might give the implied volatility as little as a 25% weight; if he feels uncertain about his forecast, he might give the implied volatility as much as a 75% weight. Of course, his confidence level will depend on his experience, as well as how conclusive the historical data is.

For example, suppose a trader has made a volatility forecast of 20% based on historical data, and that the implied volatility is currently 24%. If the trader decides to give the implied volatility 75% of the weight, his final forecast will be:

$$(75\% \times 24\%) + (25\% \times 20\%) = 23\%$$

On the other hand, if the trader decides to give the implied volatility 25% of the weight, his final forecast will be:

2. For further information on ARCH and GARCH models see:

Engle, R.F., "Autoregressive Conditional Heteroskedaticity with Estimates of the Variance of United Kingdom Inflation," *Econometrica,* Vol. 50, No. 4, 1982, pages 987–1000.

Bollerslev, T., "Generalized Autoregressive Conditional Heteroskedasticity," *Journal of Economics,* No. 31, April 1986, pages 307–327.

Bollerslev, T., "A Conditional Heteroskedastic Time Series Model for Speculative Prices and Rates of Return," *Review of Economics and Statistics,* No. 69, August 1987, pages 542–547.

Nelson, David B., "Conditional Heteroskedasticity in Asset Returns: A New Approach," *Econometrica,* No. 59, 1991, pages 347–370

Kuberek, Robert C., "Predicting Interest Rate Volatility: A Conditional Heteroskedastic Model of Interest Rate Movements," *Journal of Fixed Income,* Vol. 1, No. 4, March 1992, pages 21–27.

$$(25\% \times 24\%) + (75\% \times 20\%) = 21\%$$

Finally, if the trader decides to give the implied volatility half the weight, his final forecast will be:

$$(50\% \times 24) + (50\% \times 20) = 22\%$$

A PRACTICAL APPROACH

No matter how painstaking a trader's method, he is likely to find that his volatility forecasts are often incorrect, and sometimes to a large degree. Given this difficulty, many traders find it easier to take a more general approach. Rather than asking what the correct volatility is, a trader might instead ask, given the current volatility climate, what's the right strategy? Rather than trying to forecast an exact volatility, a trader will try to pick a strategy that best fits the volatility conditions in the marketplace. To do this, a trader will want to consider several factors:

1. What is the long-term mean volatility of the underlying contract?
2. What has been the recent historical volatility in relation to the mean volatility?
3. What is the trend in the recent historical volatility?
4. Where is implied volatility and what is its trend?
5. Are we dealing with options of shorter or longer duration?
6. How stable does the volatility tend to be?

For example, suppose there are ten weeks (approximately 50 trading days) to expiration and we are trying to decide on an appropriate volatility strategy. To make a decision, we might look at the 50-day historical volatility (the historical volatility which corresponds to the amount of time remaining to expiration), its relationship to the long-term mean volatility, and of course the implied volatility. Having done this, suppose we find the conditions shown in Figure 14-5A. What are our conclusions?

Clearly we are coming off a period of high volatility and seem to be moving downward. The recent 50-day historical volatility (approx. 20.6%) is still above the long-term historical mean (approx. 18.7%), so there is reason to believe that the volatility will continue to decline. The implied volatility is also declining, but still appears to be about 1½ percentage points higher (22.1%) than the 50-day historical volatility. All volatility conditions seem to be pointing in the same direction. The historical volatility is above the mean but declining, and the implied volatility is above the historical volatility and also declining. A short volatility position (negative gamma/negative vega) is strongly indicated.

There are of course a variety of short volatility strategies available, and the best strategy will still depend on a trader's experience in the market and the amount of risk he is willing to take. Suppose we have additional volatility data (perhaps a volatility cone of the type in Figure 14-3) showing that the 50-day volatility can easily vary by as much as 10 percentage points. We still want to sell volatility, but given this instability and the

Figure 14-5a

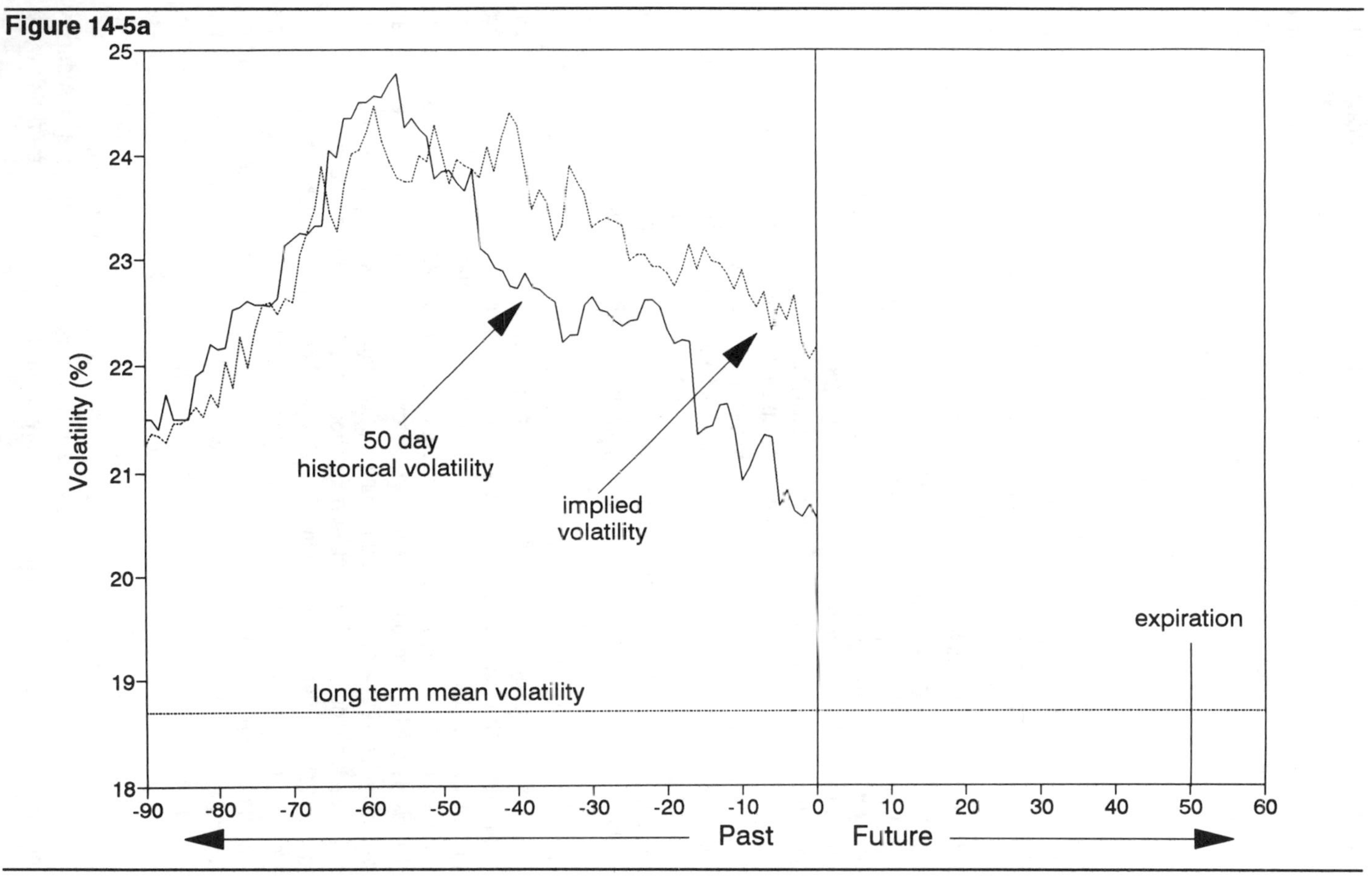
Volatility (%)
25
24
23
22
21
20
19
18
-90
-80
-70
-60
-50
-40
-30
-20
-10
0
10
20
30
40
50
60
Past
Future
50 day
historical volatility
implied
volatility
expiration
long term mean volatility

fact that implied volatility at 22.2% is only slightly above the 50-day historical volatility, perhaps the wisest choice is a less risky strategy such as the purchase of butterflies. If a riskier strategy is chosen, perhaps it should be done only in small size. On the other hand, if implied volatility is currently 25% and we find that the volatility tends to be quite stable, varying only five or six percentage points for any 50-day period, a trader may be willing to take on a much riskier position, perhaps selling a straddles or strangles.

In real life the situation is rarely as simple as in Figure 14-5A. For example, consider Figure 14-5B. Now the historical volatility is above the historical mean and declining, but the implied volatility has already moved ahead of the historical volatility. A trader may still choose a short volatility position, but he is unlikely to have the same degree of confidence. Indeed, the situation may be even more confused. Suppose the historical volatility is above the long-term mean but seems to be increasing (Figure 14-5C). Or suppose implied volatility is moving in the opposite direction of the historical volatility (Figure 14-5D). In each of these situations some factors dictate one type of position, while other factors dictate a different position.

Consider the situation in Figure 14-6A where we are thinking of taking a position in six-week options (approximately 30 trading days). The 30-day historical volatility, currently at 15.8%, is well above the long-term mean of 11.2%. However, the trend in volatility seems to be up, and there is no telling how long it will take for the volatility to revert to its mean of 11.2%. The current implied volatility of 14.6% is also well above the long term mean volatility, but is lower than the 30-day historical volatility. Corresponding to the upward trend in historical volatility, there also seems to be an upward trend in the implied volatility. With so many contradictory signals, a trader is unlikely to have a strong opinion about whether he should buy or sell volatility. He may choose to take no position at all, preferring to wait for clearer indications.

Suppose, in addition to six-week options, we also have available 19-week options (approximately 95 trading days). Volatility data for this contract is shown in Figure 14-6B. While a trader may be hesitant to take a position in six-week options alone, when combined with 19-week options, he may be able to construct a strategy with much more acceptable risk characteristics. Here the 95-day historical volatility of 12.6% is above the 11.2% mean volatility. Moreover the current implied volatility of 19-week options, at 14.5%, is well above both the 95-day historical volatility and the long-term mean volatility. There is a much better chance that the volatility will revert to its mean over a 19-week period than over a six-week period, so there are much stronger reasons for taking a short volatility position in 19-week options than in six-week options. Still, the upward trend in both the historical and implied volatilities will cause some worry if we do take a short volatility position. However, if we were to simultaneously take a long volatility position in six-week options, we would at least be protected against a continuing increase in the volatility of the underlying contract over the next six weeks. By creating a short time spread (buy six-week options/sell 19-week options) we can take a position which should be profitable based on our knowledge of volatility characteristics, but which also has acceptable risk characteristics if we are wrong.

A short time spread will not eliminate every risk. The market might suddenly become very quiet, with historical volatility quickly dropping to, or even below, its

Figure 14-5b

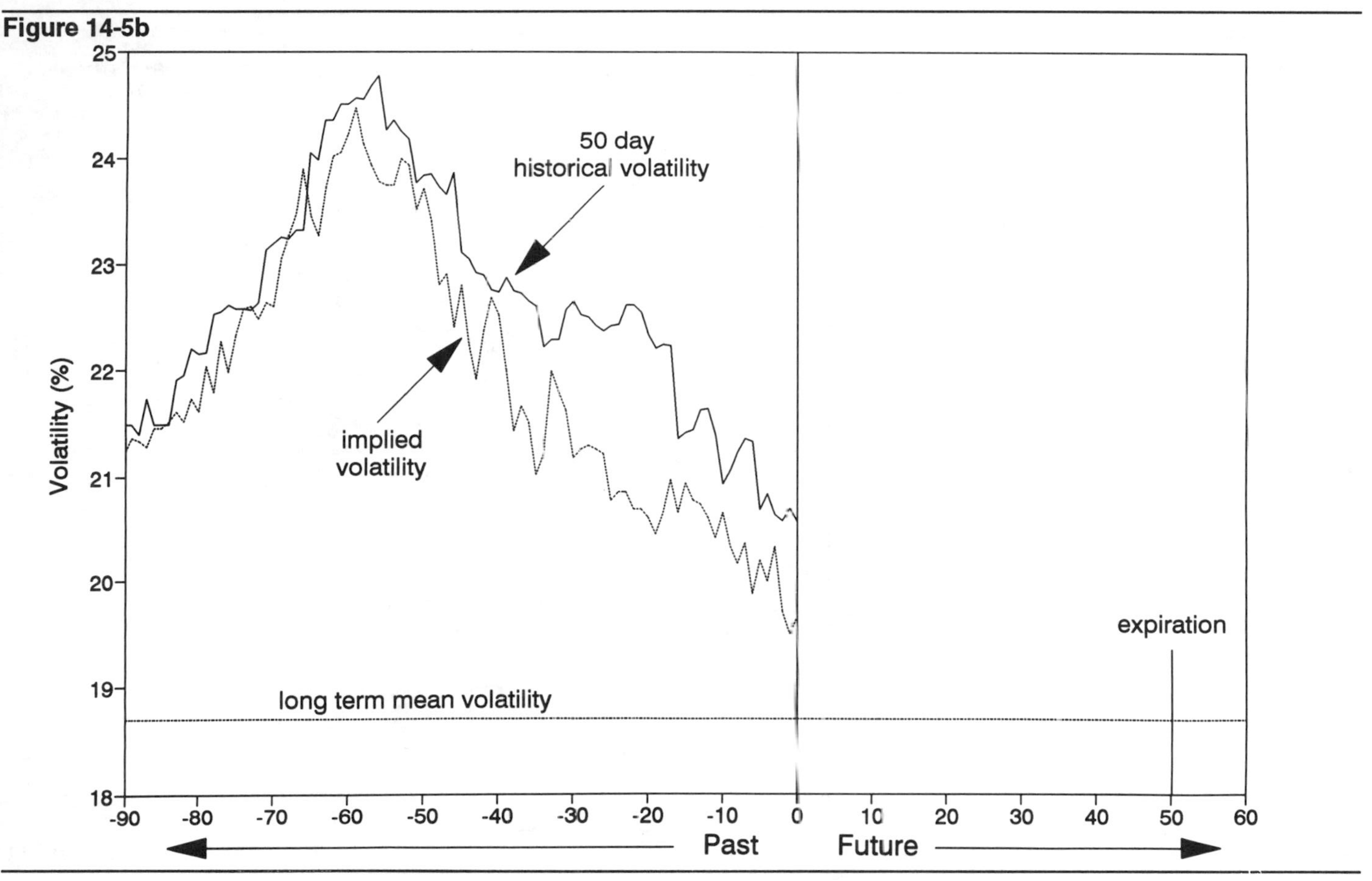
Volatility (%)
25
24
23
22
21
20
19
18
-90
-80
-70
-60
-50
-40
-30
-20
-10
0
10
20
30
40
50
60
Past
Future
50 day
historical volatility
implied
volatility
long term mean volatility
expiration

Figure 14-5c

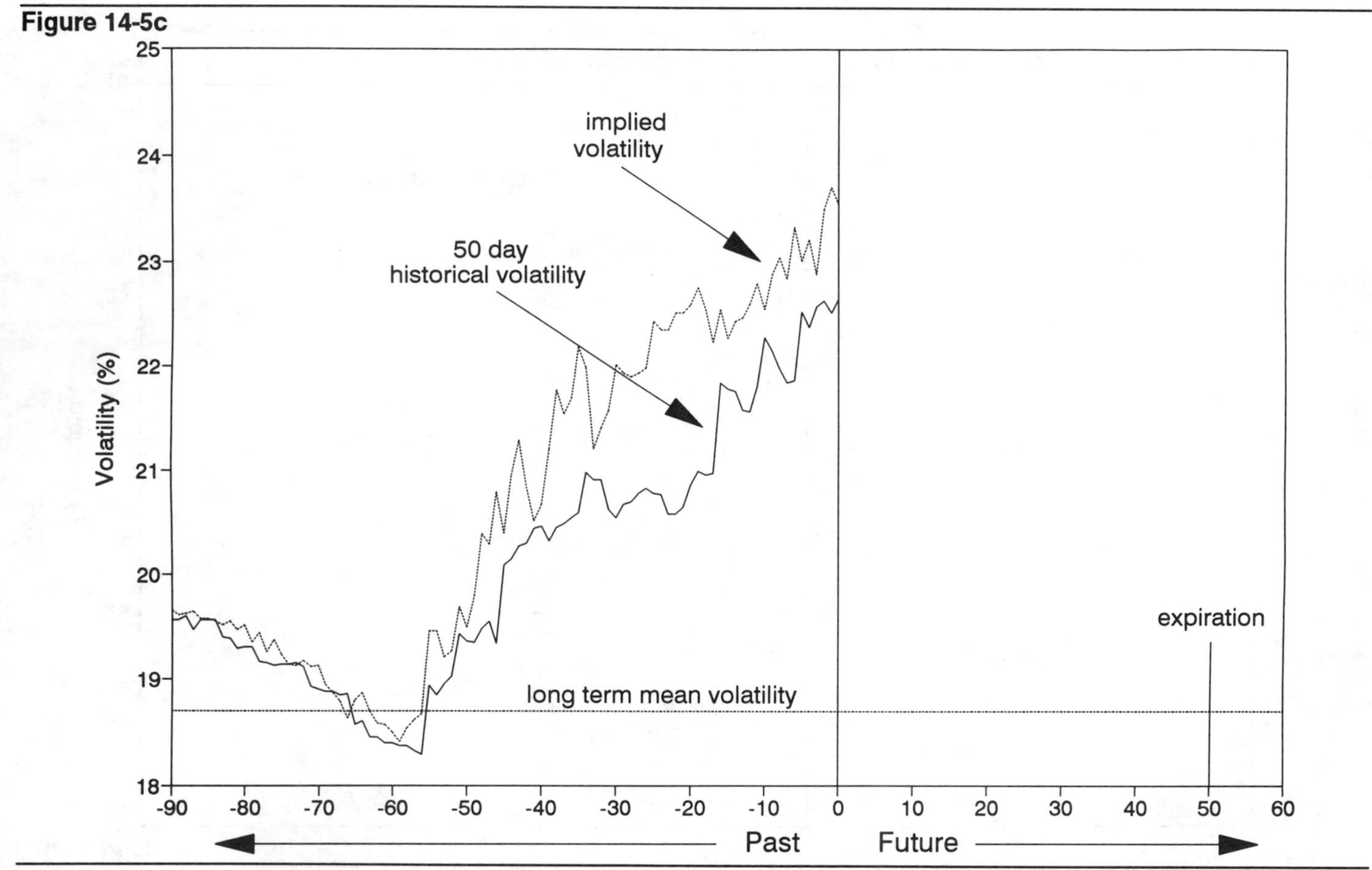
Volatility (%)
25
24
23
22
21
20
19
18
-90
-80
-70
-60
-50
-40
-30
-20
-10
0
10
20
30
40
50
60
Past
Future
implied volatility
50 day historical volatility
long term mean volatility
expiration

Figure 14-5d

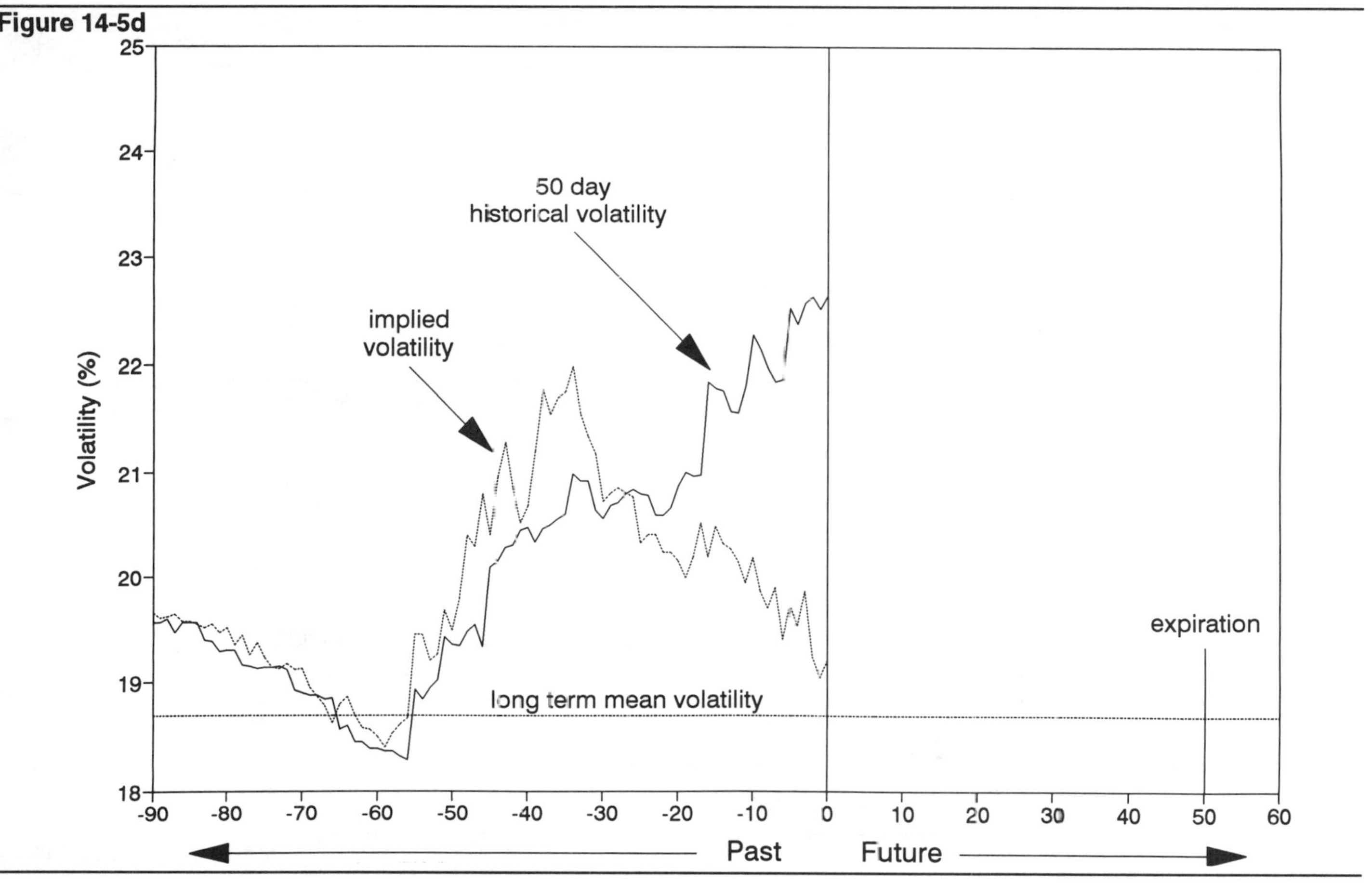
Volatility (%)
25
24
23
22
21
20
19
18
-90
-80
-70
-60
-50
-40
-30
-20
-10
0
10
20
30
40
50
60
50 day
historical volatility
implied
volatility
long term mean volatility
expiration
Past
Future

Figure 14-6a

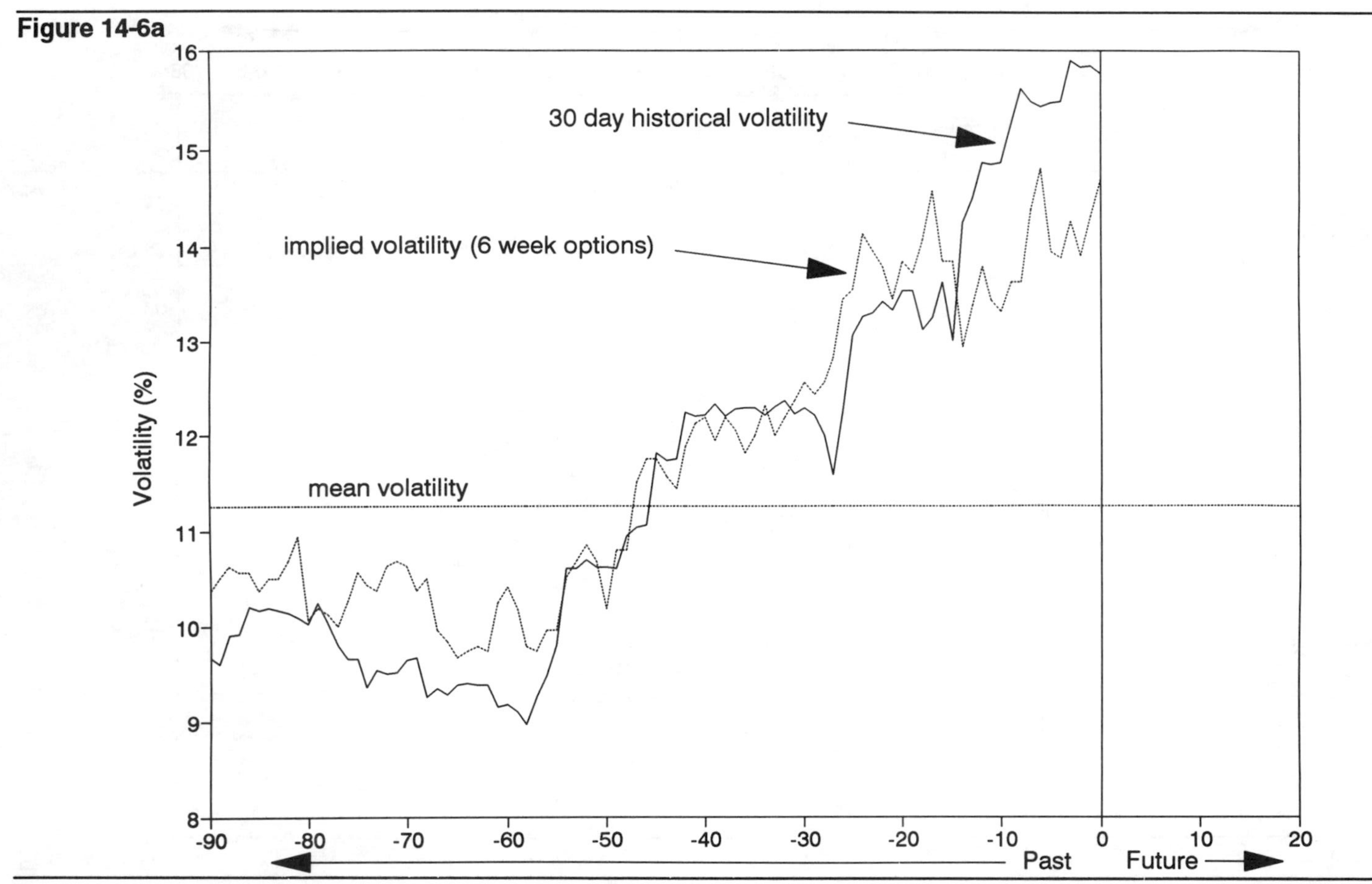
30 day historical volatility
implied volatility (6 week options)
mean volatility
Volatility (%)
16
15
14
13
12
11
10
9
8
-90
-80
-70
-60
-50
-40
-30
-20
-10
0
10
20
Past
Future

Figure 14-6b

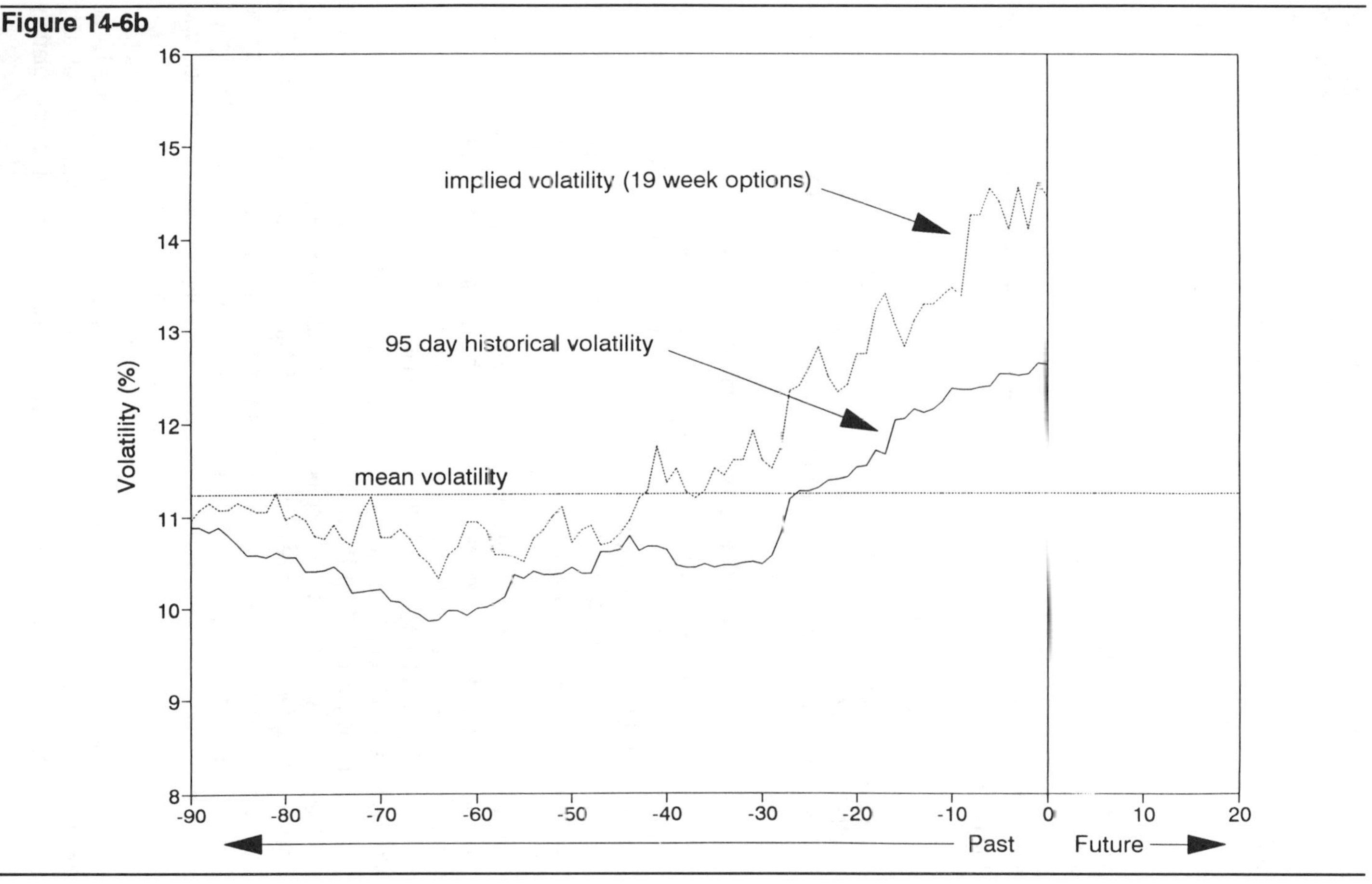
implied volatility (19 week options)
95 day historical volatility
mean volatility
Volatility (%)
16
15
14
13
12
11
10
9
8
-90
-80
-70
-60
-50
-40
-30
-20
-10
0
10
20
Past
Future

long-term mean. At the same time, implied volatility may remain relatively high. Such conditions will do the most damage to a short time spread. Still, if we believe that the implied volatility tends to follow the historical volatility, we may conclude that it is unlikely that the implied volatility will stay high if the historical volatility drops.

A trader will always attempt to pick the strategy which best fits his opinion of market conditions, whether a directional opinion or a volatility opinion. Given the fact that there is such a wide variety of market conditions, a trader who is familiar with the greatest number of strategies will have the best chance of surviving and prospering. He will be in a position to pick strategies with the best risk/reward characteristics, strategies which will be profitable when things go right, but which won't give back all the profits when things go wrong. This skill comes not only from a technical knowledge of option evaluation and theory, but also from a practical knowledge of what really happens in the marketplace.

SOME THOUGHTS ON IMPLIED VOLATILITY

Since many option strategies are sensitive to changes in implied volatility, and since implied volatility will often play a role in forecasting the volatility of the underlying contract, it may be worthwhile to consider some of the characteristics of implied volatility.

Implied versus Historical Volatility

Implied volatility can be thought of as a consensus volatility among all market participants with respect to the expected amount of underlying price fluctuation over the remaining life of an option. In the same way that an individual trader is likely to change his volatility forecast in response to changing historical volatility, it is logical to assume that the marketplace as a whole will also change its consensus volatility in response to changing historical volatility. As the market becomes more volatile, implied volatility can be expected to rise; as the market becomes less volatile, implied volatility can be expected to fall. Market participants are making the logical assumption that what has happened in the past is a good indicator of what will happen in the future.

The influence of historical volatility on implied volatility can be seen in Figure 14-7, the historical and implied volatility of U.S. Treasury Bond futures traded on the Chicago Board of Trade from 1989 to 1991. In late 1989, and again in mid-1991, there were declines in the volatility of Treasury Bond futures, and these were accompanied by corresponding declines in implied volatility. From August 1990 through January 1991 (the period of the Iraqi invasion of Kuwait), there were several sharp increases in the volatility of the futures, and these were accompanied by similar increases in implied volatility. Clearly, the marketplace, in the form of changing implied volatility, was responding to the changing historical volatility of the underlying contract.

Notice, however, that the fluctuations in implied volatility were usually less than the fluctuations in historical volatility. When the historical volatility declined, the implied volatility rarely declined by an equal amount. And when historical volatility increased, the implied volatility rarely increased by an equal amount. Because volatility

Figure 14-7: Treasury Bond Futures Volatility

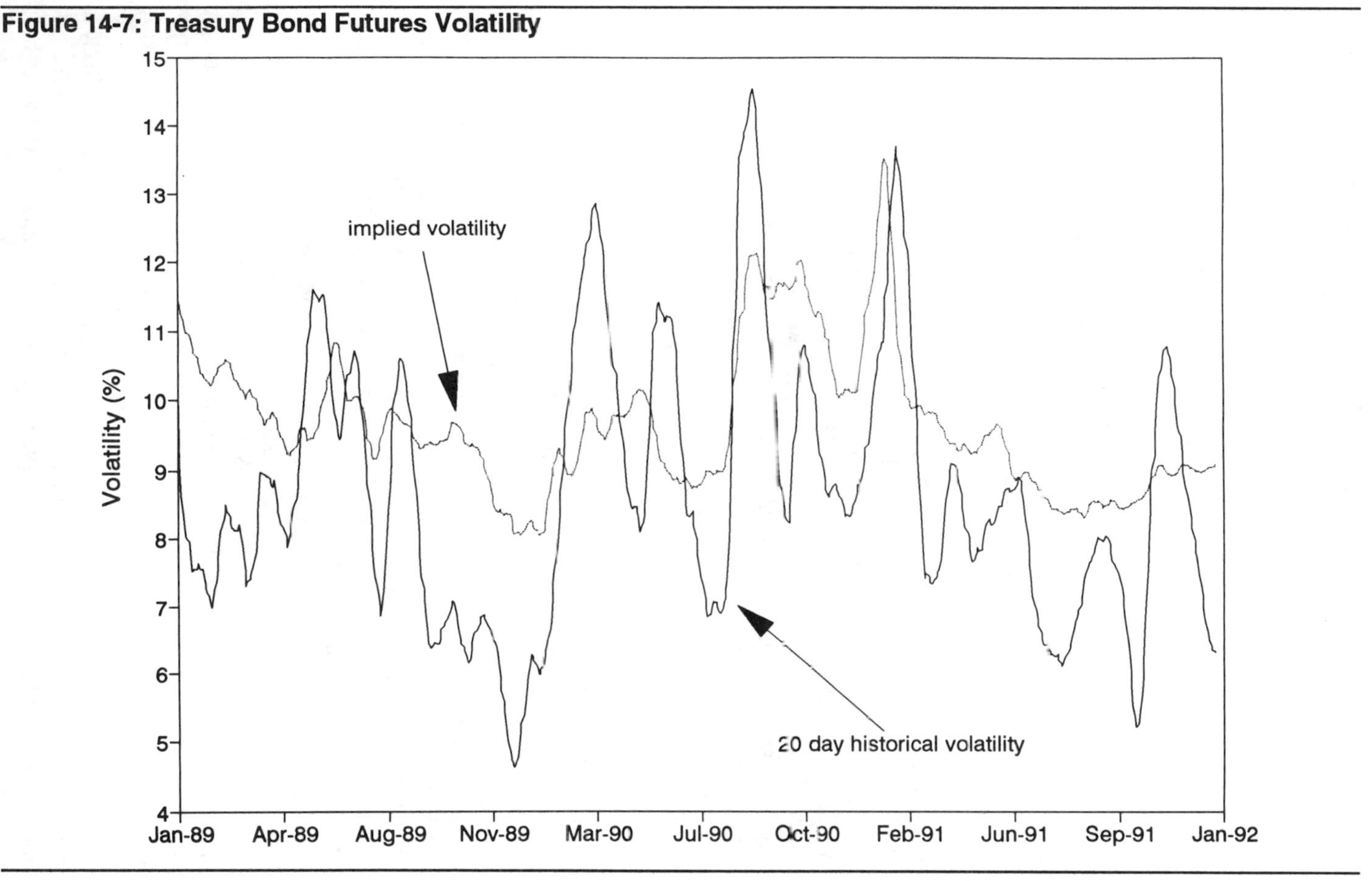

tends to be mean reverting, when historical volatility is above its mean there is a greater likelihood that it will decline, and when historical volatility is below its mean there is a greater likelihood that it will increase.

Moreover, the further out in time we go, the greater the likelihood that the volatility of the underlying contract will return to its mean. (Look again at Figure 14-3.) Consequently, the implied volatility of long-term options tends to remain closer to the mean volatility of an underlying contract than the implied volatility of short-term options. As historical volatility rises, the implied volatility of all options is likely to rise. But given the stronger mean reverting characteristics of volatility over long periods of time, the implied volatility of long-term options will tend to rise less than the implied volatility of short-term options. As historical volatility falls, the implied volatility of all options is likely to fall. But the implied volatility of long-term options will tend to fall less than the implied volatility of short-term options. This is born out by Figure 14-8, the implied volatility of Treasury Bond options for various expiration months from September 1990 to May 1991. Note the increase in implied volatilities during January 1991. But the increase in the implied volatility of the short-term contract (March) was much greater than the increase in the implied volatility of the mid-term (June) contract, which was in turn greater than the increase in the implied volatility of the long-term (September) contract. When implied volatility began to decline in late January 1991 the roles were reversed. The March contract declined the most rapidly, followed by the June contract, and the September contract. This is typical of the way in which implied volatility tends to change in response to changing volatility environments.

Over long periods of time the historical volatility of the underlying contract will be the dominant factor affecting implied volatility. Over short periods of time, however, other factors can also play a significant, perhaps even a dominant, role. If the marketplace foresees events which could cause the underlying contract to become more volatile, anticipation of these events might cause implied volatility to change in ways that are not necessarily consistent with historical volatility. For example, government reports on economic conditions are issued periodically, and these reports have been known to contain surprises for the interest rate and foreign exchange market. This potential for surprise can cause uncertainty in the marketplace, and this uncertainty is often reflected in an increase in implied volatility. Going into government reports, there is a strong tendency for implied volatility to rise, even in the face of low historical volatility in the underlying instrument.

Government reports are not the only factors which add uncertainty to the market. Any future events which could have unexpected consequences can have an effect on implied volatility. In the currency markets, upcoming meetings of finance ministers—or in the energy markets upcoming OPEC meetings—often cause implied volatility to rise. In the stock option market, earnings news, the potential success or failure of new products, or (most dramatically) the possibility of a takeover, can all cause increases in implied volatility, regardless of the historical volatility of the stock.

In a similar way, if the marketplace believes that no significant events are likely to occur in the foreseeable future, uncertainty is removed from the market. In such a case the implied volatility may start to fall, even if the actual historical volatility has been

Figure 14-8: Treasury Bond Futures Implied Volatility

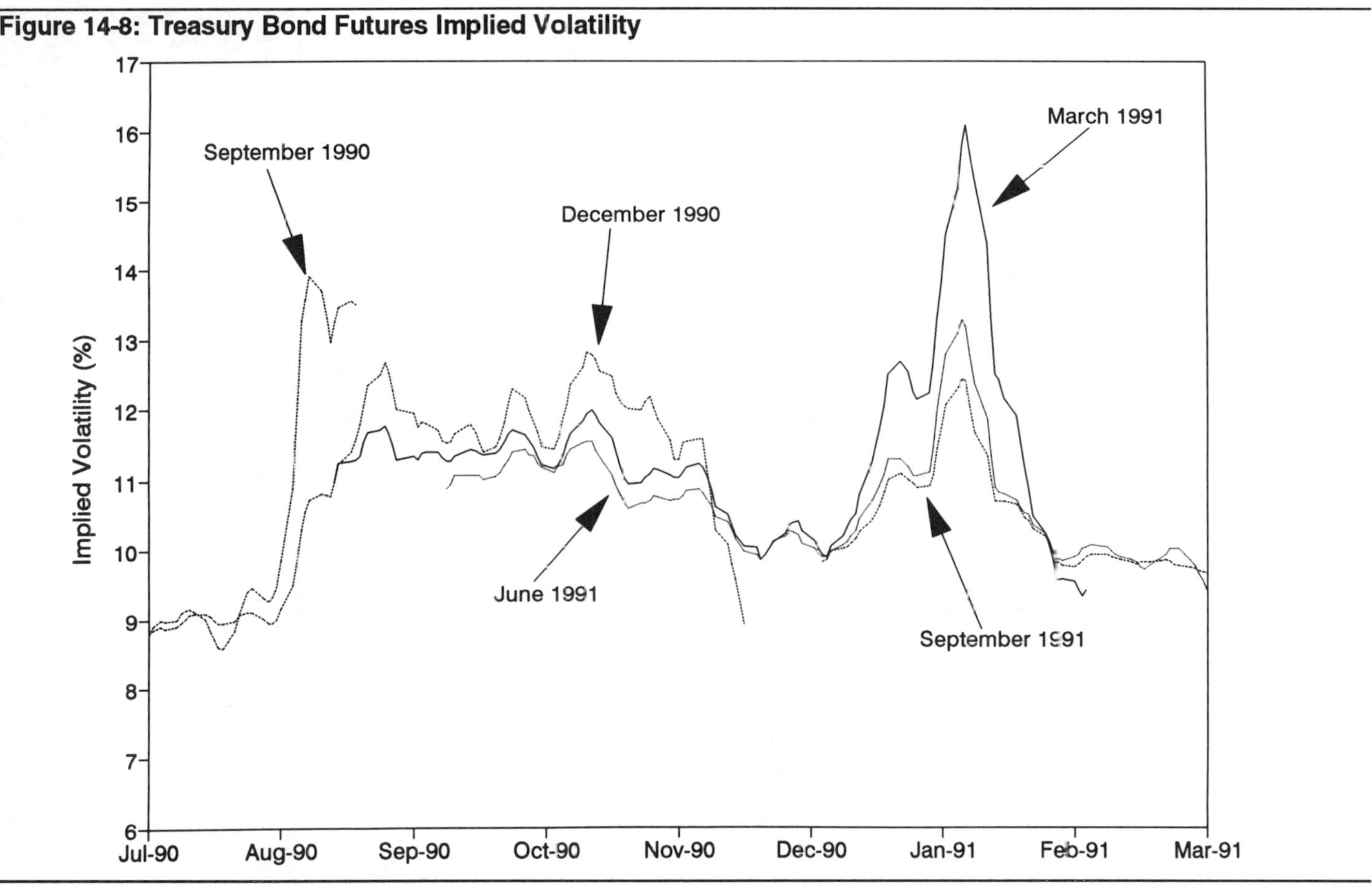

relatively high. This is why implied volatility sometimes drops right after large moves in the underlying contract. Once the big event has occurred, there may be a perception that all the uncertainty has been removed from the market.

Regardless of short-term changes in implied volatility, it is still important for a trader to remember that the volatility of the underlying contract will eventually overwhelm any considerations of implied volatility. As an example, consider the following situation:

futures price = 97.73
time to expiration = 60 days
interest rate = 6%
implied volatility = 20%

Given these conditions, the 100 call would be trading for 2.17, with an implied delta of 40. Suppose we create a delta neutral position by purchasing ten 100 calls for 2.17 each, and selling four futures contracts at 97.73. What will happen to our position if implied volatility rises to 22%?

If implied volatility immediately goes to 22%, the new price of the 100 call will be 2.47, and we will show a profit of

$$10 \times (2.47 - 2.17) = +3.00$$

Suppose, however, that the increase in implied volatility occurs very slowly, over a period of 20 days, and during this period the price of the underlying futures contract remains at 97.73. Under these conditions, even if implied volatility rises from 20% to 22%, the 100 call will now be worth only 1.87. Our position will then show a loss of

$$10 \times (1.87 - 2.17) = -3.00$$

Even though the implied volatility increased, the fact that the underlying futures contract failed to make any significant move resulted in the option's price declining.

Now suppose we have the same position (long ten 100 calls, short four futures contracts) but this time instead of rising to 22%, the implied volatility drops to 18%. What will be the effect on our position?

If implied volatility immediately drops to 18%, the new price of the 100 call will be 1.86, and we will show a loss of

$$10 \times (1.86 - 2.17) = -3.10$$

Suppose, however, that the decline in implied volatility is accompanied by a swift move in the underlying contract. If the underlying futures contract falls to 93.00, and implied volatility falls to 18%, the price of the 100 call will be .59, and we will show a profit of

$$4 \times (97.73 - 93.00) - 10 \times (2.17 - .59) = +3.12$$

On the other hand, if the underlying futures contract rises to 102.50 while implied volatility falls to 18%, the price of the 100 call will be 4.32, and we will again show a profit

$$4 \times (97.73 - 102.50) + 10 \times (4.32 - 2.17) = +2.42$$

In both cases the movement in the underlying contract has more than offset any decline in the option's price due to a decline in implied volatility.

The foregoing examples are of course simplified. As market conditions change-an active trader may very well make adjustments to his position in order to remain delta neutral. If so, the actual profit or loss will be affected by the cash flow from this adjustment process. The important point is that the volatility of the underlying contract, whether the contract moves or sits still over time, will eventually overwhelm any changes in implied volatility. This is not to say that implied volatility is unimportant. The price of a contract is always an important consideration in making trading decisions. But in order to trade intelligently, we need to know value as well as price. The value of an option is determined by the volatility of the underlying contract over the life of the option.

Implied versus Future Volatility

If, as many traders believe, prices in the marketplace reflect all available information affecting the value of a contract, the best predictor of the future volatility ought to be the implied volatility. Just how good a predictor of future volatility is implied volatility? While it would be impossible to answer this question definitively, since that would require a detailed study of many markets over long periods of time, we might still gain some insight by looking at a limited number of examples.

Clearly, no one knows the future volatility. We can, however, record the implied volatility at any moment in time and then, when expiration arrives, look back and calculate the actual volatility of the underlying contract between the time we recorded the implied volatility and expiration. We can do this every day during an option's life, recording the implied volatility and then at expiration calculating the actual volatility that occurred over this period. This has been done in Figures 14-9A, 9B, and 9C for the June 1992, March 1993, and December 1993 options on Treasury Bond futures. It is admittedly dangerous to generalize from such limited data, but are there any conclusions we might draw from these graphs?

We can see that with a great deal of time remaining to expiration, the future volatility of the underlying contract (the solid line) is relatively stable. But as we get closer to expiration the future volatility can become much less stable. This is logical if we again recall that the mean reverting characteristics of volatility are much less certain over short periods of time than over long periods. One large move in the underlying contract with only several days remaining to expiration will result in a sharp increase in the volatility to expiration (see Figure 14-9C). On the other hand, if the underlying contract is relatively quiet over the last several days in an option's life, the volatility to expiration will collapse (see Figure 14-9B).

How does the marketplace react to these volatility characteristics? With long periods of time remaining to expiration, the volatility to expiration is relatively stable. One would therefore expect the implied volatility to also be relatively stable. Conversely, with short periods of time remaining to expiration, the volatility to expiration can be very unstable, and one would therefore expect the implied volatility to be unstable. These conclusions are born out by the implied volatility (the broken line) in

Figure 14-9a

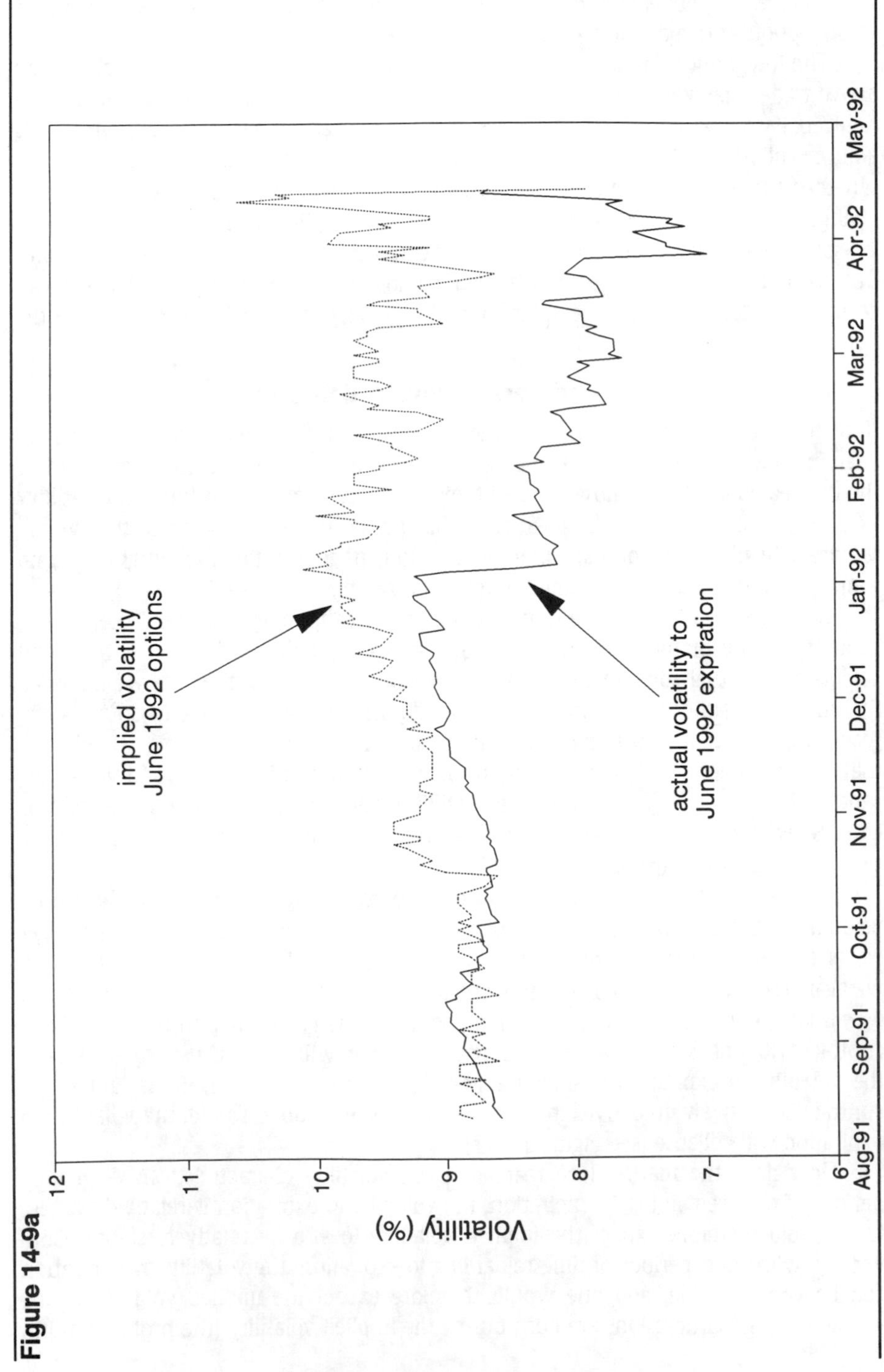

Volatility (%)
12
11
10
9
8
7
6
Aug-91
Sep-91
Oct-91
Nov-91
Dec-91
Jan-92
Feb-92
Mar-92
Apr-92
May-92
implied volatility
June 1992 options
actual volatility to
June 1992 expiration

Figure 14-9b

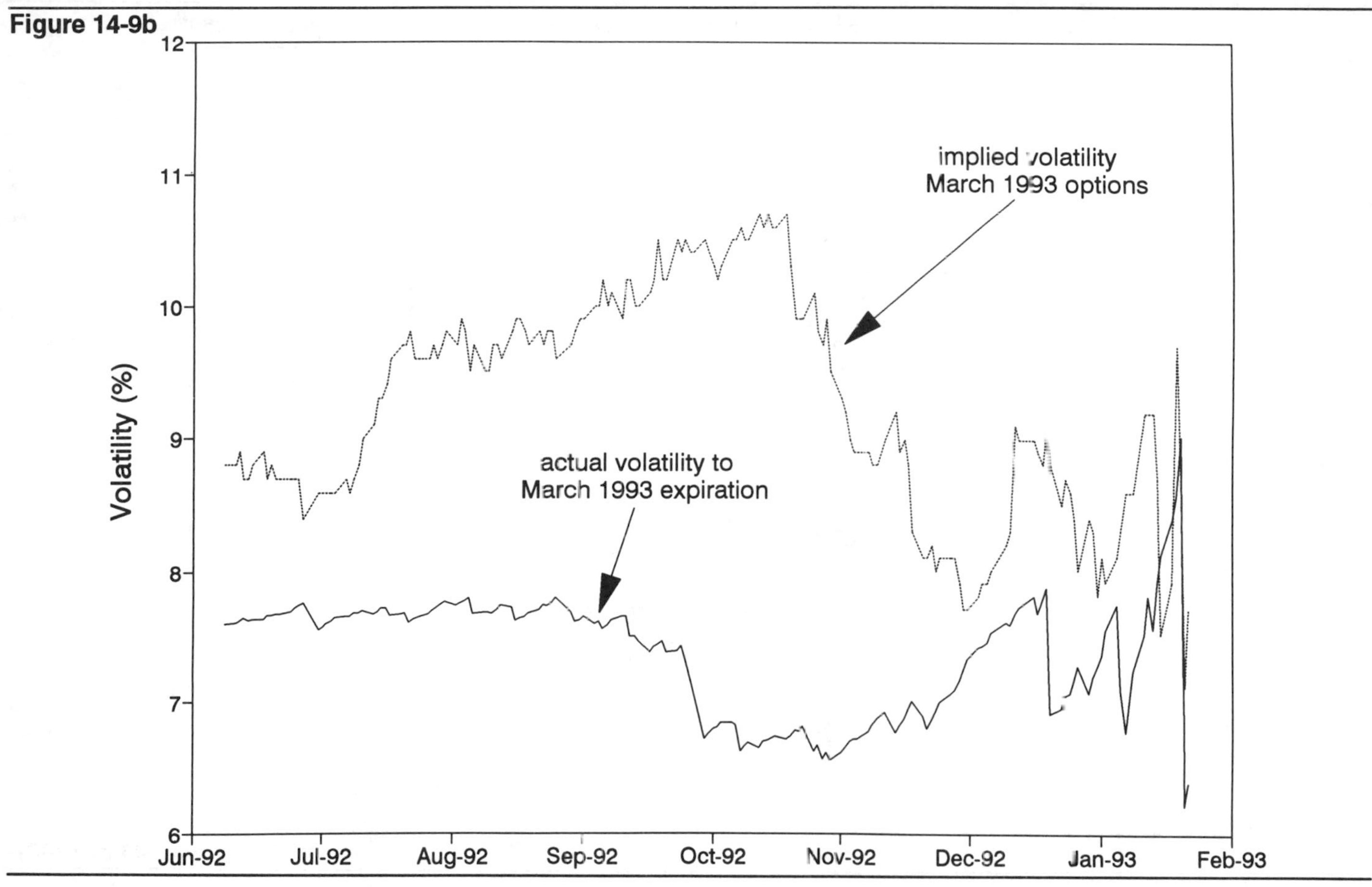
implied volatility
March 1993 options
actual volatility to
March 1993 expiration
Volatility (%)
12
11
10
9
8
7
6
Jun-92
Jul-92
Aug-92
Sep-92
Oct-92
Nov-92
Dec-92
Jan-93
Feb-93

Figure 14-9c

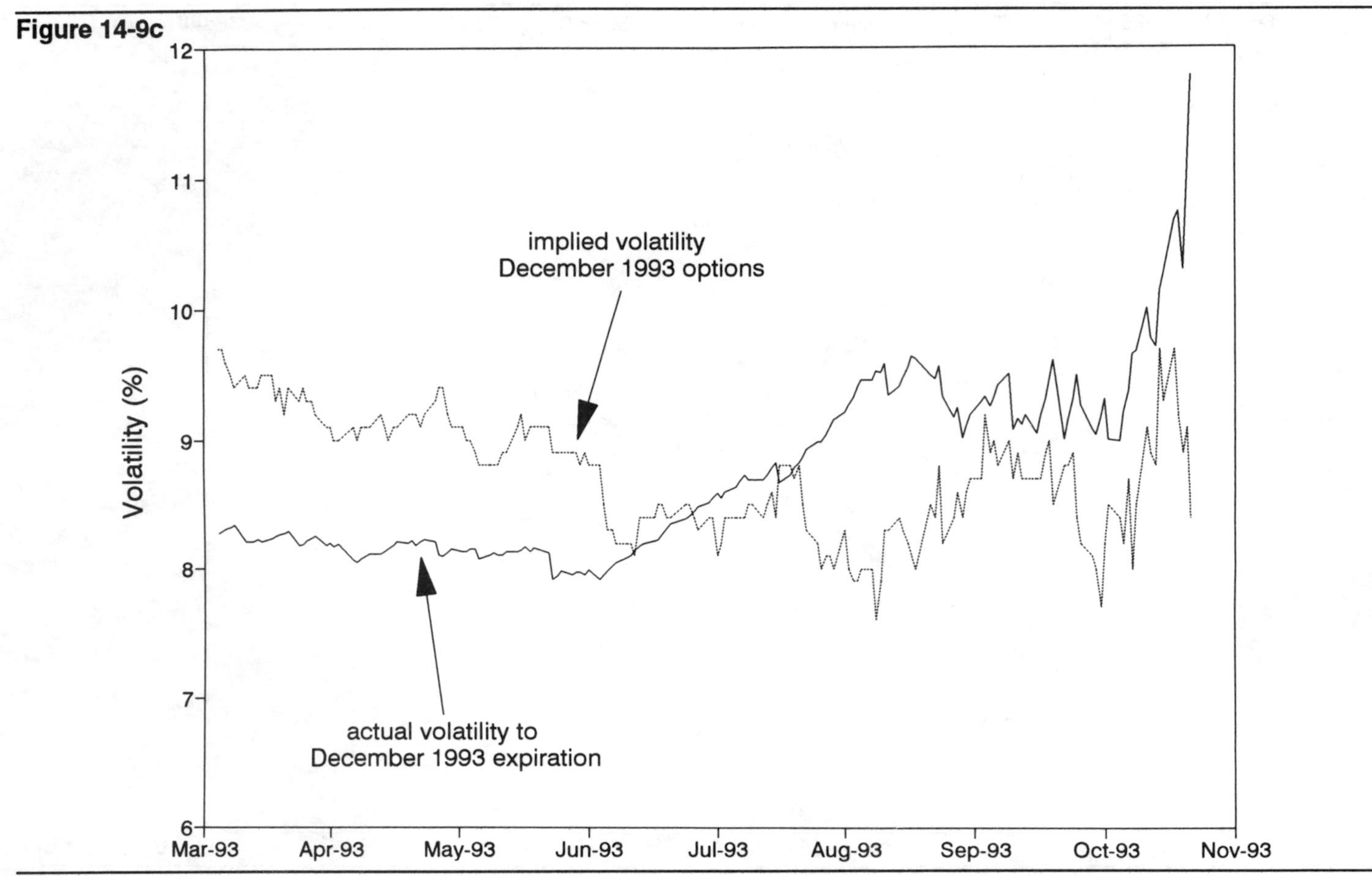
Volatility (%)
12
11
10
9
8
7
6
Mar-93
Apr-93
May-93
Jun-93
Jul-93
Aug-93
Sep-93
Oct-93
Nov-93
implied volatility
December 1993 options
actual volatility to
December 1993 expiration

Figures 14-9A, 9B, and 9C. Over long periods of time, the marketplace is reacting to many events. This is easier than reacting to a limited number of events, which is what the marketplace is faced with over a short period of time. The marketplace knows that the laws of probability are more likely to balance out over many occurrences than over only a few occurrences.

Note also that there is no guarantee that the marketplace will have the correct implied volatility. The implied volatility is a guess, and guesses carry with them the possibility of error, sometimes very large error. In Figure 14-9B the implied volatility turned out to be much too high over almost all of the option's life. Had a trader sold premium at any time, he would have shown a profit. At its most extreme, during October 1992, there was almost a four-percentage point difference between the implied volatility of the March 1993 options and the future volatility of the March 1993 futures contract. In Figure 14-9C the implied volatility was too high during the early part of the option's life, but too low during the latter part. During the few weeks prior to expiration, the implied volatility was too low by as much as three percentage points. Finally, in Figure 14-9A the implied volatility was relatively accurate over the early part of the option's life, but too high during the latter part.

It should be clear by now that dealing with volatility is a difficult task. To facilitate the decision-making process we have attempted to make some generalizations about volatility characteristics. Even then, if one decides to become involved in a market it may not be at all clear what the right strategy is. Moreover, we have looked at a limited number of examples, making the generalizations even less reliable. Every market has its own characteristics, and knowing the volatility characteristics of a particular market, whether interest rates, foreign currencies, stocks, or a physical commodity, is at least as important as knowing the technical characteristics of volatility. And this knowledge can only come from careful study of a market combined with actual trading experience.

❖ 15 ❖

Stock Index Futures and Options

Since their introduction on U.S. exchanges in the early 1980s, stock index futures and options have experienced phenomenal growth, with increasing participation by all segments of the trading community. Both retail and institutional investors use these instruments to invest in the market as a whole, thereby eliminating the laborious job of trying to pick individual stocks. Portfolio managers can use index instruments to create a wide variety of risk/reward scenarios for large, diversified stock portfolios. Finally, professional arbitrageurs find that in spite of the highly liquid and usually efficient index markets, pricing disparities occur often enough to warrant close monitoring of these markets. When a disparity does exist, a trader can execute an arbitrage by hedging the mispriced index against either other stock indices or against a basket of stocks. Such arbitrage strategies are commonly referred to as *index arbitrage.*

For all of the foregoing reasons, no book on options would be complete without at least some discussion of index options. However, index futures and options are so closely related, and so many strategies involve both instruments, that it is almost impossible to discuss one without discussing the other. We will therefore include both instruments in our discussion.

WHAT IS AN INDEX?

An index is a number which represents the composite value of a group of items. In the case of stock indices, the value of the index is determined by the value of a group of specified stocks, with the value of the stocks usually being determined by their prices in the marketplace. As the stocks which make up the index rise in price, the value of the index also rises, reflecting the increased value of the stocks; as the stocks fall in price, the value of the index also falls, reflecting the declining value of the stocks. If some stocks in the index rise while others fall, the offsetting changes in stock prices may result in the index itself remaining unchanged, even though it's possible that every stock in the index changed price. The value of the index always reflects the total value of the stocks which make up the index.

CALCULATING AN INDEX

There are several different methods of calculating stock index values, but the most common methods entail weighting the stocks either by price or by capitalization. To see how these methods work, consider an index composed of the following four stocks:

Stock	Price	Total Shares Outstanding	Total Capitalization
1	125	10,000	1,250,000
2	80	5,000	400,000
3	52	25,000	1,300,000
4	17	40,000	680,000

If an index is *price weighted,* each stock's value in the index is directly proportional to its price. Using this method, the total value of the index is simply the sum of the prices of all the stocks in the index:

$$125 + 80 + 52 + 17 = 274$$

The price weighting of each stock is therefore:

stock 1:	125/274 =	45.6%
stock 2:	80/274 =	29.2%
stock 3:	52/274 =	19.0%
stock 4:	17/274 =	6.2%
		100.0%

Since the importance of each stock is directly proportional to its price, when measured in percent terms movement in higher priced stocks will have a greater impact on the value of the index than equal movement in lower priced stocks. If a trader were monitoring a price weighted index for possible changes, he would do well to look for movement in the higher priced stocks in the index.

If an index is *capitalization weighted,* the index value is the total value of all the outstanding stock of the firms in the index. The total value, or capitalization, of a firm is the price of a share multiplied by the number of shares issued by the firm. The total capitalization of the four stocks making up our index is:

$$(125 \times 10{,}000) + (80 \times 5{,}000) + (52 \times 25{,}000) + (17 \times 40{,}000) =$$
$$1{,}250{,}000 + 400{,}000 + 1{,}300{,}000 + 680{,}000 = 3{,}630{,}000$$

The capitalization weighting of each stock is therefore:

stock 1:	1,250,000/3,630,000 =	34.5%
stock 2:	400,000/3,630,000 =	11.0%
stock 3:	1,300,000/3,630,000 =	35.8%
stock 4:	680,000/3,630,000 =	18.7%
		100.0%

If an index is capitalization weighted, in percent terms the stocks which will have the greatest effect on the index are those with the greatest market value. These are often stocks which are very widely held, even though they may not be the highest priced stocks.

For convenience, when an index is first introduced it is common to set the index value equal to some round number, most often 100. In order to achieve this number, the actual value of the index must be either multiplied or divided by some number. For example, when we calculated the price weighted value of our four-stock index, the value was 274. To transform the index value to 100, we solve:

$$274/x = 100$$
$$x = 2.74$$

This number, 2.74, is referred to as the *index divisor*, and is used in all subsequent index calculations. Whenever a new value of the index is calculated, that value will always be divided by 2.74 to yield the published index value. If we wanted to set the value of our capitalization weighted index to 100, we solve:

$$3{,}630{,}000/x = 100$$
$$x = 36{,}300$$

In this case, the index divisor is 36,300.

An index divisor is not constant, but can change as the capitalization of the index changes. If stocks in the index split or declare special stock dividends, or if stocks are replaced by other stocks due to buyouts, liquidations, or bankruptcies, the index value might go up or down, even though the market prices of the stocks making up the index remain unchanged. To offset this effect, when any capitalization change occurs in the stocks making up the index, the divisor is changed to reflect the relative value of index, and to ensure that the index value represents a true picture of price changes in the marketplace.

Regardless of the method used to calculate an index, prices for each of the component stocks must be determined. If a stock is traded on only one exchange, there is never any doubt as to the stock's price. It is simply the last trade price. But what if a stock is traded on more than one exchange? If the last trade for a stock on one exchange is \$52, while the last trade on a different exchange is \$52½, what price should be used in calculating the index? The answer is usually specified in the index prospectus, and is most commonly the primary marketplace for that stock. In the United States the primary marketplace for many stocks is the New York Stock Exchange, although this is not always the case. Some stocks may be primarily traded on the American, Chicago, Pacific, or Philadelphia Stock Exchanges, or in the over-the-counter market. A trader who follows a stock index should always know the source of the stock prices used to calculate that index.

REPLICATING AN INDEX

Suppose a trader wanted to create a holding of stocks that exactly replicated the value of the index. What would he have to do?

If each point in our four-stock price weighted index is worth exactly $1, then the total value of the index is $274. A trader could simply purchase one share of each stock in the index to exactly replicate the index. Very often, however, for trading purposes the value of each point is assigned a value other than $1. If, for example, each point in the index is assigned a value of $100, the total dollar value of the index is:

$$274 \times \$100 = \$27{,}400$$

Now in order to exactly replicate the index, a trader would have to purchase 100 shares of each stock. The value of his holding would then be:

$$(125 + 80 + 52 + 17) \times 100 = \$27{,}400$$

Not only must a trader consider the value of each point in an index, he must also consider the effect the divisor will have on the index. Suppose that instead of 274, the index in our example has been set to 100 by using a divisor of 2.74. If the point value of the index is still $100, then the total value of the index is:

$$100.00 \text{ (index value)} \times \$100 \text{ (point value)} = \$10{,}000$$

Now if we purchase 100 shares of each stock, the dollar value of our stock holding ($27,400) greatly exceeds the dollar value of the index ($10,000). Clearly, our stock holding does not replicate the index. Notice, however, that the index value of $10,000 is simply our stock value of $27,400 divided by the divisor of 2.74. In other words, if we divide each purchase of 100 shares of stock by 2.74, we will have a stock holding equal to the value of the index. To achieve this, we need to purchase 100/2.74, or approximately 36½ shares of each stock.[1] If we do, the value of our stock holding will replicate the value of the index since:

$$(125 + 80 + 52 + 17) \times 36.5 = \$10{,}000$$

The procedure is slightly more complex if we are attempting to replicate a capitalization weighted index. Consider our four-stock capitalization weighted example with a divisor of 36,300. Suppose each point in the index has a value of $500, so that the dollar value of the index is:

$$100.00 \text{ (index value)} \times \$500 \text{ (point value)} = \$50{,}000$$

How can we create a capitalization weighted stock holding with a value of $50,000?

In our price weighted example, we purchased shares of stock equal to the point value divided by the divisor. We can take the same approach with a capitalization weighted index, with one important change: we must multiply the resulting number by

1. Obviously, one cannot trade fractional shares of stock. In the real world, a trader attempting to replicate the sample index would have to buy either 36 or 37 shares of each stock.

the total number of outstanding shares of the stock. The proper number of shares of each stock required to replicate our capitalization index is:

	Outstanding Shares		Point Value		Divisor		Required Shares
stock 1:	10,000	×	500	÷	36,300	=	137.7
stock 2:	5,000	×	500	÷	36,300	=	68.9
stock 3:	25,000	×	500	÷	36,300	=	344.4
stock 4:	40,000	×	500	÷	36,300	=	551.0

We can see that this replicates the $50,000 value of the index since:

$$(137.7 \times 125) + (68.9 \times 80) + (344.4 \times 52) + (551.0 \times 17) = 50{,}000$$

Summarizing, the number of shares of each stock required to replicate an index

for a price weighted index: point value / index divisor
for a capitalization weighted index: outstanding shares × point value / index divisor

STOCK INDEX FUTURES

In theory one can create a futures contract on a stock index in exactly the same way that futures contracts have been created on traditional commodities. At expiration, the holder of a long stock index futures position would be required to take delivery of all the stocks, in their correct proportions, which make up the index. The holder of a short position would be required to make delivery of the stocks.

In fact, very few stock index futures contracts are settled through the physical delivery of the stocks making up the index. Such a process, requiring the delivery of the correct number of shares of many different stocks, would be unmanageable for most clearing organizations. To be perfectly fair, such a settlement procedure might require the delivery of fractional shares of stock, which is impossible.

For all these reasons, exchanges have chosen to settle stock index futures at expiration in cash. Since futures contracts are settled daily in cash, the final cash transfer between the buyer and seller of a stock index futures contract is equal to the difference between the expiration value of the index and the previous day's settlement price. For example, suppose an index is at 462.50 at the moment of expiration and the previous day's settlement price for the futures contract was 461.00. If each point in the index is worth $100, the holder of a long position will be credited with a final payment of $150, since (462.50 – 461.00) × $100 = $150. The holder of a short position will be debited by the same amount.

What should be the fair value of a stock index futures contract?

Recall from Chapter 1 that an important difference between a futures contract and stock is the settlement procedure. Whereas the purchase of stock requires the buyer to actually pay cash, the purchase of a futures contract requires only an initial margin deposit. The cash paid for the stock will result in an interest cost, while the margin deposit results in no such interest loss. Moreover, any profits or losses resulting from stock trading are only paper profits or losses until the stock position is liquidated. In futures markets, however, profits and losses accrue whenever the price of the futures contract fluctuates, regardless of whether the position is closed out. These profits or losses are typically calculated daily from the settlement price of the futures contract. Such profits and losses result in variation, the amount of cash which is credited to or debited from a trader's account based on the daily price fluctuation. Variation and margin requirements are separate and distinct. Margin in theory entails no carrying costs, while credits or debits resulting from daily variation do indeed earn (in the case of a credit) or lose (in the case of a debit) interest.

Clearly, the purchase of a futures contract offers one important advantage over the purchase of the component stocks: no cash outlay is required to purchase a futures contract. Consequently, there is an interest rate savings equal to the cost of borrowing sufficient cash to purchase all the stocks in the index.

The amount of interest saved by purchasing a stock index futures contract rather than the actual stocks in the index can be calculated by multiplying the current index value by the risk-free interest rate, and then multiplying this number by the amount of time remaining to expiration of the futures contract. By adding the resulting number to the index value, we have the fair value of the futures contract based on carrying costs.

For example, suppose there are three months remaining to expiration with our four-stock index at 274.00. If the risk-free interest rate over this period is 8%, what are the carrying costs on the index?

$$8\% \times 3/12 \times 274.00 = 2\% \times 274.00 = 5.48$$ [2]

If carrying costs are the only consideration, the fair value for the futures contract will be the 274.00 value of the index plus the 5.48-point carrying cost to expiration, or 279.48.

What other advantages or disadvantages are associated with holding a futures contract?

If we buy a futures contract, we may have a very good substitute for the stocks in the index, but we don't actually own the stocks. Since ownership of a stock is necessary for the receipt of a stock dividend, if we buy a futures contract we will have to give up any dividends which the stocks in the index might pay. If the stocks in the index are non-dividend paying, or will not pay any dividends prior to expiration of the futures contract, no further calculations are necessary. The fair value will simply be the current index value plus carrying costs to expiration. More often, however, some, and perhaps all of the stocks in the index will pay dividends prior to futures expiration. In this case we must deduct the amount of dividends lost by holding a futures position rather than the actual stocks.

Suppose that the stocks in our four-stock index are expected to pay the following dividends prior to expiration of the futures contract:

---

2. For simplicity we assume simple interest payments. We can be slightly more accurate by assuming compound interest (see Appendix B).

Stock	Price	Expected Dividend
1	125	$1.80
2	80	0
3	52	$.90
4	17	$.35

If we buy one share of each of the four stocks which make up the index, we will receive by futures expiration a total dividend payout of:

$$\$1.80 + \$.90 + \$.35 = \$3.05$$

If we buy the futures contract instead of the stocks we will have to forego this 3.05. Therefore, we will want to pay 3.05 less for the futures contract. Taking into consideration carrying costs, we showed that with the index at 274.00, the fair value of the futures contract was 279.48. Deducting the dividends, the fair value of the futures contract is:

274.00 (index value) + 5.48 (carrying costs) – 3.05 (expected dividends) = 276.43

If we own the stocks in the index we not only receive the dividends paid by the stocks, we also have use of the dividend funds. If we own stock 1, we will receive a dividend of $1.80 on the ex-dividend date and, in theory, we can also earn interest on this amount to expiration of the futures contract. If the dividend will be paid two months prior to expiration and interest rates are 8%, the interest earnings are:

$$1.80 \times 2/12 \times 8\% \approx .02$$

To calculate an exact futures price, in addition to deducting the dividends themselves, we must also deduct the interest earnings from each dividend payment. This could become a rather complicated exercise, but in practice the interest earnings on dividends are so small in relation to the actual index that most traders simply deduct the dividend payments themselves from the index value, and ignore the accompanying interest earnings.

If the index is price weighted, replication of the index requires an equal number of shares of each stock. So the total dividend payout is simply the sum of all the dividends. If the index is capitalization weighted, replication of the index requires a different number of shares for each stock. In that case, the total dividend payout will be the dividend payout for each stock multiplied by the number of shares required for replication.

Given the apparently complex dividend calculations, as well as the interest considerations on the index and dividends, determining the exact fair value of a futures contract might seem a daunting task. In practice, however, active trading firms have computers which can quickly, and continuously, calculate the fair value for futures contracts on most commonly traded stock indices.

Even when it is not possible to calculate the exact fair value, many traders find it almost as effective to estimate the fair value by adding the carrying cost to the index and subtracting the average dividend payout. For example, suppose there are nine weeks

(63 days) to expiration on a stock index futures contract with the underlying index currently at 425.00. If interest rates are 8% annually, and the average annual dividend payout on the stocks making up the index is 6%, we have:

$$(8\% - 6\%) \times 63/365 \times 425.00 = 1.47$$

Therefore, the approximate fair value of the futures contract is 425.00 + 1.47 = 426.47. The reader should be aware that this is only an estimate. If it turns out that a large number of stocks do not pay their regular dividends during this nine-week period, or if the dividend payout is unusually large, this estimate could prove to be far from accurate.

The daily dividend payout for the S&P 500 index for one quarterly cycle, from March 1993 to June 1993 expiration, is shown in Figure 15-1. Note the large amounts which were paid at the beginning of May, compared to the relatively small amounts paid during April. The cumulative effect of this dividend payout, in terms of the total of dividends expected to June expiration, is shown in Figure 15-2. The line drops only slightly during April, but declines sharply during the first two weeks in May. A trader who intended to initiate some type of arbitrage strategy either just prior to, or just after, a large dividend payout, would need more than a rough estimate of the fair value of an S&P 500 futures contract. If he were not aware of the exact dividend payout, a strategy which he expected to be profitable might turn out to be just the opposite.

It is also possible to reverse the calculations and ask, given an observed futures price, where would the index have to be for the futures to be fairly valued? For example,

Figure 15-1: S&P 500 Index Dividend Payout
(March 1993 to June 1993 Expiration)

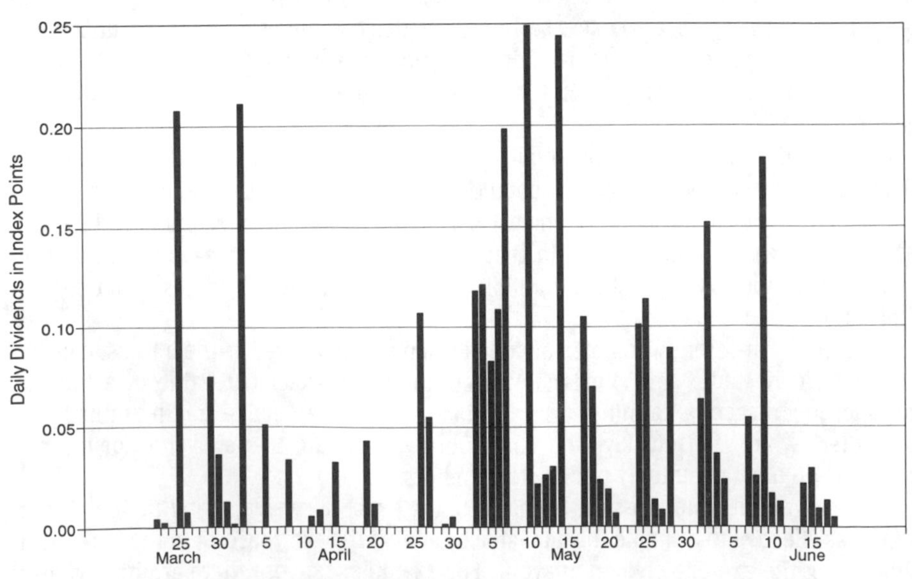

Figure 15-2: S&P 500 Dividends to Expiration
(March 1993 to June 1993 Expiration)

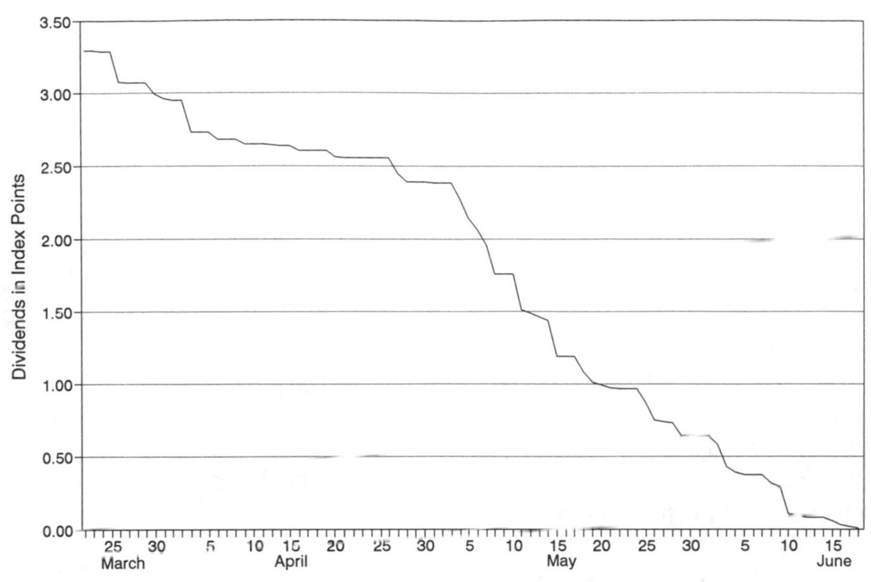

if the futures price is 432.70, and we assume that it is trading at fair value, what should the index price be if there are 6 weeks (42 days) to expiration, interest rates are 6%, and the expected dividend payout is 2.23? First we can add the dividend payout of 2.23 to the futures price of 432.70, giving a value of 434.93. Then we can deduct the carrying costs on this amount over the next six-weeks:

$$434.93 \times 42/365 \times 6\% = 3.00$$

The *implied index value* is therefore 434.93 – 3.00 = 431.93.

INDEX ARBITRAGE

In theory, the price of a futures contract should always reflect the fair value of holding the futures contract rather than holding the stocks making up the index. But markets are not always one hundred percent efficient. If the futures price doesn't reflect the fair value, a trader can execute a profitable arbitrage by purchasing the undervalued asset, either the basket of stocks or the futures contract, and selling the overvalued asset. If a trader believes that the fair value of a stock index futures contract is 386.75, and finds that the futures contract is trading at 387.40, he will attempt to buy all the stocks in their correct proportion and simultaneously sell the futures contract. If the trader succeeds, and if the point value of the futures contract is $500, for each futures contract he executes he will show a theoretical profit of:

$$(387.40 - 386.75) \times \$500 = .65 \times \$500 = \$325$$

Of course, this profit will only be fully realized at expiration, when the futures contract is automatically settled at the index value. At the same time, the trader will also have to liquidate his stock holdings to ensure that at the moment of expiration both his futures position and stock position zero out. This can be done by placing a *market on close* order, guaranteeing that the last trade price for each stock which determines the final index value will be the liquidation price for the trader's stock holdings.

What would happen if the fair value for the stock index futures contract were 386.75, but the futures contract were actually trading at 385.95? Now the trader would take just the opposite position, buying the undervalued futures contract and selling the basket of stocks. The theoretical profit would be:

$$(386.75 - 385.95) \times \$500 = .80 \times \$500 = \$400$$

Unfortunately, some practical problems might affect the workability of this strategy. If the trader wants to sell stock which he doesn't own, he will have to borrow it. If no stock is available, or if the market in which he is dealing does not freely permit the short sale of stock, he may not be able to execute the arbitrage, no matter how mispriced the futures contract. Finally, a trader might not earn full interest on the short sale of stock. If the actual interest earned is less than the interest rate used to calculate the fair value of the futures contract, the fair value of the futures contract, for trading purposes, may be less than the presumed fair value of 386.75.

This type of trading strategy, where one buys or sells a mispriced stock index futures contract and takes an opposing position in the underlying stocks, is one type of index arbitrage. Since computers can often be programmed to calculate the fair value of a futures contract, and to execute the arbitrage when the futures contract is mispriced, such a strategy is also commonly referred to as *program trading.* A buy program consists of buying the stocks and selling the futures contract, and a sell program consists of selling the stocks and buying the futures contract.

How great a mispricing of a futures contract relative to the price of the underlying stocks justifies futures arbitrage? If markets are totally frictionless, a trader would attempt to execute an arbitrage if there were any mispricing, no matter how small. Unfortunately, markets are not totally frictionless. An arbitrage which in theory is profitable because of a mispriced futures contract may be unprofitable when transaction costs are factored in. If a trader believes that it will cost approximately ½ index point to execute all the trades required for an arbitrage, he will not attempt to enter into a program trade unless the futures contract is at least .50 too expensive or too cheap. If he also considers the problems associated with the short sale of stock, he may decide that the futures contract must be .75 too cheap before he will initiate a sell program. With the fair value of the futures contract at 386.75, the trader will initiate a program trade only if the price of the futures contract is outside the range

$$386.75 - .75 \text{ and } 386.75 + .50$$

or less than 386.00 and more than 387.25.

Even if the quoted index price is 386.75, and the futures contract is higher than 387.25 or lower than 386.00, the trader cannot be certain that a profit opportunity exists. In order to execute an arbitrage, it is necessary to trade all the stocks at a price consistent with the index value of 386.75. But there is a bid price and an offer price for each individual stock, and it is likely that the last trade price for some of the stocks in the index took place at the bid price, some at the ask price, and some at prices in between. If a trader wants to immediately execute a buy program, he will have to purchase every stock in the index at the ask price, and this may be at a price well above the quoted index value.

Moreover, the quoted index price can sometimes present a distorted picture of actual market conditions. The index itself may be quoted at 386.75, but does that represent the price at which all the stocks in the index are trading? Perhaps trading in some of the stocks has been halted due to pending news. Or perhaps the last sale for one or more of the stocks took place at a price outside the current market for the stock. The last sale in a stock may have been at 38¼, but if the market in the stock is falling very quickly, the offered price for the stock may be 37¾. The index value is based on the last sale price of 38¼, but the actual price is at least as low as 37¾, and possibly even lower. If a trader hopes to profit from a mispriced futures contract he must know the true market for all the stocks which underlie that contract.

Assuming the trader can execute all purchases and sales at theoretically profitable prices, is there anything which could go wrong with a program trade consisting of stocks against stock index futures? Suppose a trader buys an underpriced futures contract and simultaneously sells the underlying stocks. If the index starts to fall, and the futures contract follows, the trader will show a profit on his stock trades and a loss on his futures trade, and presumably these two components will offset each other. Unfortunately, the stock trades, being subject to stock-type settlement, only result in a paper profit, while the futures trade, being subject to futures-type settlement, results in a cash loss. If the index drops far enough, and the trader must borrow cash to meet the variation requirements for the futures contract, the interest cost may be so great that the arbitrage which initially appeared profitable actually turns into a loss. This is similar to the settlement risk for a conversion or reversal in the futures option market described in Chapter 11.

From this, we can see that a program trade always wants the market to move in the direction of the futures contract so that cash will flow into the trader's account. This will increase the trader's potential profit, since he will be able to earn interest on this cash over the life of the futures contract. In this respect, we can apply the concept of the delta to futures contracts in much the same way we do to an option contract. The delta is the rate at which a contract will change its theoretical value with respect to movement in the underlying contract. For example, assume that a stock index is quoted at 300.00. If there are three months to expiration, with interest rates at 8%, and an expected dividend payout of 4.50, the fair value of a futures contract is approximately:

$$300.00 + (300.00 \times 3/12 \times .08) - 4.50 = 301.50$$

Suppose the index immediately rises 10% to 330.00. The new fair value of the futures contract is:

$$330.00 + (330.00 \times 3/12 \times .08) - 4.50 = 332.10$$

The index rose 30.00 while the futures contract rose 30.60. The delta of the futures contract is therefore 102, since 30.60/30.00 = 1.02. The futures contract is changing its value at 102% the rate of the underlying index.

If we assume that the dividend payout remains constant, the delta of a futures contract is simply a function of interest rates. The extra two deltas associated with the futures contract results from an interest rate of 8% and a time to expiration of three months, since $3/12 \times .08 = .02$. As the amount of time to expiration changes, or as interest rates change, the delta of the futures contract will also change.

We can now express in delta terms the amount by which a program trade is unbalanced. If a trader buys 50 futures contracts, each with a delta of 102, and sells an appropriate amount of the underlying stocks, his delta total position is

$$(50 \times 102) - (50 \times 100) = +100$$

He is long as if he had purchased stock outright corresponding to one index contract. If he wants to be exactly delta neutral, he must sell a basket of stocks corresponding to one index contract.

A change in interest rates will not only affect the delta of the futures contract, but can also affect the profitability of a program trade. If a trader institutes a buy program (buy the stocks, sell the futures), he is effectively borrowing cash in order to purchase the stocks. If the cost of funds is tied to a floating interest rate, any increase in rates will hurt his position and any decrease will help. If he institutes a sell program (sell the stocks, buy the futures) he is effectively lending cash. Now any increase in rates will help his position and any decrease will hurt. If the change in interest rates is sufficiently large, an initially profitable program trade might become unprofitable. This can be especially true if the program trade consists of very long-term futures contracts. In such a case, the interest considerations are magnified because of the increased costs of borrowing or lending over extended periods. In the same way, because of reduced interest considerations, changes in interest rates are unlikely to affect program trades consisting of short-term futures.

We have thus far assumed that the dividend payout of all the stocks in an index remains constant, but this is not necessarily true. Companies can have good years and bad years, and their dividend policies can change accordingly. In a buy program (buy the stocks, sell the futures), any increase in dividends will help the position, and any decrease will hurt. In a sell program (sell the stocks, buy the futures), the effect is just the opposite. In a broadly based index consisting of hundreds of stocks it is unlikely that a change in the dividend policy of any one company, or even several companies, will have a significant impact on the profitability of a program trade. But in a narrowly based index consisting of only a few stocks, a change in the expected dividend payout of even one firm can alter the potential profitability of the trade. In such a case, the trader must carefully consider beforehand the possibility of a dividend change in the companies making up the index.

INDEX OPTIONS

There are really two types of stock index options, those where the underlying is a stock index futures contract, and those where the underlying is the index itself. Although they are alike in many respects, they also have unique characteristics which set them apart from each other. For this reason, we will look at each market separately.

Options on Stock Index Futures

Since an option on a stock index futures contract is often evaluated in the same way as a traditional futures option, a trader in such a market has all the usual problems which go with futures option evaluation. He must pick a suitable pricing model, determine the correct inputs into the model, choose appropriate strategies, and consider the risks that go with these strategies. Since exercise or assignment of a futures option contract will result in the trader taking a long or short position in the stock index futures contract, the trader might logically use the current futures price as the underlying price input into his theoretical pricing model. But a futures option trader is often faced with a new problem. Should he also use the current price of the futures contract as his price input if the futures contract is clearly mispriced and trading at other than fair value?

For example, if a stock index futures contract is trading at 424.00 but an option trader believes that the fair value is 425.00, which value should the trader feed into his theoretical pricing model? If the trader really believes that the futures contract ought to be trading at 425.00, and also believes that all the assumptions upon which the theoretical pricing model is based are valid, then he might very well choose to use 425.00 as the underlying price in his model. He can then take option positions, whether outright or spread positions, by purchasing options which he believes are underpriced and selling those which he believes are overpriced.

Notice, however, that with the futures contract trading at 424.00, he cannot use 425.00 as his price input and still use the futures contract to hedge his option position. If he were to do so, whatever positive theoretical edge he achieved because of his option trades would automatically be offset by the negative theoretical edge resulting from his futures trades. This becomes obvious when we recall the basic synthetic relationship for futures options from Chapter 11:

$$\text{call price} - \text{put price} = \text{futures price} - \text{exercise price}$$

If the trader believes the underlying futures contract ought to be trading at 425.00, then he also believes that the 425 call and the 425 put ought to be trading at an identical price. The difference between the presumed futures price and the exercise price is zero, so the difference between the call price and put price ought to also be zero. But with the underlying futures market actually trading at 424.00, the call price will be approximately 1.00 less than the put price. If the 425 call is trading for 8.50 and the 425 put is trading for 9.50, the call will appear too cheap to the trader and the put will appear too expensive. Unfortunately, if the trader buys the call for 8.50 and sells the put for 9.50, he has no way to lock in his presumed profit of 1.00. If he attempts to complete the reverse conversion (buy the call, sell the put, sell the underlying), he will have to do so by selling the futures contract at 424.00. What he makes on the options he will give back on the futures contract.

If a trader simply wants to execute volatility or directional spreads based on a presumed underlying price of 425.00, then it might very well make sense to use that price as the input into the theoretical pricing model. But professional option traders rely heavily on arbitrage relationships for many of their trading strategies. If a price other than the actual underlying price is used, these arbitrage relationships will no longer be valid. Because the choice of underlying price may vary from trader to trader, many on-line option evaluation services give traders the choice of using either the actual futures price or the theoretical futures price as the basis for theoretical evaluation.

Although the ultimate decision about the underlying price is the trader's, in a stock index futures option market a trader should be very careful about using an underlying futures price different from the quoted price. As we have already seen, the theoretical value of a stock index futures contract depends on information which may not be readily available to the trader. If he is wrong about the price at which the index is actually trading because the individual stock prices do not reflect the true market, his theoretical evaluation of the futures contract will be incorrect. Most traders have learned through experience that the apparent mispricing of a stock index futures contract is often illusory, or at least smaller than it appears.

Options on a Cash Index

The exercise or assignment of a stock option requires the buyer or seller to take delivery or make delivery of the underlying stock. In theory there is no reason why the exercise or assignment of a stock index option could not be treated the same way. If a trader were to exercise such an option, he would take delivery or make delivery of all the stocks in the index, in their correct proportion, at a price equivalent to the value of the index. The trader who was assigned would take an opposing position at the same price.

While this sounds reasonable, in practice it presents the same problems that would arise if we were to settle a stock index futures contract through the physical delivery of all the stocks. The delivery of many different stocks, in their appropriate amounts (which might include fractional shares), would overwhelm the clearing organization. As with futures, the popular solution is to settle the contract in cash rather than through physical delivery. If a trader holds a 440 call and exercises it with the index at 450, he is credited with a cash amount equivalent to 10 index points. If each index point has a value of $100, his account is credited with $1,000. The account of the trader who is assigned on the same call is debited $1,000. In the same way, if a trader exercises a 475 put with the index at 450, his account will be credited with $2,500. The account of the trader who is assigned will be debited $2,500.

In theory, if the index option is American, carrying with it the right of early exercise, the cash settlement should be based on the index value at the time the trader exercises his option. But this is impractical since exercise is not an instantaneous transaction. An exercise notice must be filled out by the trader, submitted to the clearing firm, and then submitted to the clearing house. Even if one could pinpoint the precise time at which an option was exercised, it might be difficult to ascertain the exact value of the index. For all these reasons, the exercise or assignment value for an index option is calculated from the index value at the end of the trading day.[3] Whether an exercise notice is submitted at 10:00 AM or 3:00 PM, both traders will be credited with cash equal to the difference between the exercise price and the index value at the close of trading on that day.[4]

Evaluating a Cash Index Option

The most common method for evaluating cash options on a stock index is based on the assumption that the underlying contract for a cash index option is a basket of stocks which, taken together, have the characteristics of one individual stock. Therefore, a trader might logically choose to evaluate options on an index using a traditional stock option model, the Black-Scholes model for European options or the Cox-Ross-Rubenstein model for American options. In either case, it will be necessary to feed into the model the usual information: time to expiration, exercise price, underlying price, interest rates, volatility, and dividend payout. Unfortunately, the dividend payout presents a problem which we have already touched upon in the discussion of stock index futures. If the options are European, with no possibility of early exercise, the total amount of dividend payout expected to expiration is sufficient for theoretical evaluation. But if the options are American, where early exercise is a possibility, we need to know the exact date of the dividend payout. There is, however, no one exact date since dividends on different stocks are paid at different times. In order to accurately evaluate American options, we need to create a matrix of dividend payouts with the dates and amounts, and then feed this into our theoretical pricing model. If a trader wants an exact evaluation of a stock index option, he will need software which is capable of exact dividend calculations.

A less accurate method, but one which might be practical for many traders, is to assume a constant dividend payout. A trader can attempt to determine the average percent dividend paid by each stock, deduct this from the interest rate component, and use the result as the interest rate input. For example, if the average dividend payout is 4%, and interest rates are 6%, the trader can ignore the dividend input and simply use an interest rate of 2%. Some models allow the user to enter the interest rate and the dividend payout (as a percent) individually, and from these inputs the model calculates the value of an American option. In both cases, however, the value of early exercise will be distorted since stock option calls are often exercised just prior to a dividend payout, and puts are often exercised just after a dividend payout. When no exact dividend date has been entered into the model, optimum early exercise cannot be calculated. The distortion can sometimes be quite large if many stocks in the index happen to pay a large

3. Because of the order imbalances which can occur in individual stocks when a large number of stock index arbitrages are liquidated at the same time, some exchanges have chosen to settle stock index options and futures on expiration day based on the opening index price. This opening price is determined by the opening prices of each stock in the index on that day. Since stocks can open at different times, the index value may not represent simultaneous stock trades.

4. There is usually a cut-off time after which an index option may not be exercised on a given day. In the United States this is usually within an hour after the index has been fixed at the end of the trading day.

dividend on the same date, or pay no dividend for an extended period. Figure 15-1 shows that this is often the case for the S&P 500.

A Phantom Variable

In some markets, stocks or their derivative products continue to trade after the closing index price has been fixed for the day. In the United States, most stock indices are fixed at 4:00 PM Eastern Time when trading ceases on the New York Stock Exchange. However, many of the stocks in the index continue to trade on regional stock exchanges, and futures and options on the indices may also continue to trade for some period after the close. The fact that the underlying index may be fixed while options and futures on the index continue to trade results in an anomaly concerning early exercise.

Suppose a trader owns a stock which settles at a price of $50 when trading ceases at 4:00 PM on the primary stock exchange. Suppose also that the trader has the right to sell that stock to someone at the settlement price of $50 until 12:00 midnight the same day. If the trader's intention is to hold onto the stock, their is no reason for him to exercise this right. But suppose some negative news on the stock comes out at 4:30 PM, and he finds that the stock is now trading on other exchanges at $48. What will he do? If he decided that he wanted to sell the stock because of the bad news, the trader would certainly exercise his right to sell at $50 rather than selling it at $48 on some other exchange. Even if he wanted to retain ownership of the stock, he would immediately realize that he could show an extra $2 profit by exercising his right to sell at $50, and buying the stock back at $48. Indeed, he would be foolish not to do so since if he did not, he would be throwing away $2.

A similar situation occurs in stock index options where early exercise is a possibility, and where alternative instruments are available on the index after the index has been fixed at the close of the trading day. To see what can happen, consider an option market on a very simple, non-dividend paying index which has been fixed at 400.00 when the stock exchange ceases trading at 4:00 PM. If there are 30 days remaining to expiration, with implied volatility at 14%, interest rates at 6%, and no dividend expected, option prices and implied deltas might be the following:

Index = 400.00
Time to June expiration = 30 days   Implied volatility = 14%
Interest rates = 6%   Dividend = 0

Exercise Price	Call Price	Call Delta	Put Price	Put Delta
380	22.44	92	.59	–8
390	13.98	78	2.12	–23
400	7.42	56	5.62	–46
410	3.24	32	11.71	–72
420	1.14	14	20.12	–94

Suppose that at 4:05 PM some very negative economic news comes out. Stocks start to fall on other exchanges which are still open, and traders in the index futures and option markets, which continue to trade after 4:00 PM, react as if the index will open 10 points lower the next morning. If the option market does open the next day at 390.00, option prices and deltas might then look like the following:

Index = 390.00
Time to June expiration = 29 days   Implied volatility = 14%
Interest rates = 6%   Dividend = 0

Exercise Price	Call Price	Call Delta	Put Price	Put Delta
380	13.70	79	1.95	–22
390	7.10	55	5.40	–46
400	2.98	31	11.55	–73
410	.98	13	20.08	–95
420	.25	4	30.00	–100

Suppose a trader originally owned ten 380 calls. What should he do when the negative news hits the market? If he holds his calls, and the market does open at 390.00 the next morning, his calls will be trading at 13.70. He will show a loss of 22.44 – 13.70, or 8.74 per call. But if he exercises his calls today, he will receive 20.00 points, the difference between the exercise price of 380 and that day's index settlement price of 400.00. If he exercises, his loss will only be 22.44 – 20.00, or 2.44 per option. If he fails to exercise, he will automatically show an additional loss of 6.30.

Anytime after the index value has been fixed for the day, a trader who finds that the next day's presumed theoretical value is less than parity will be better off exercising an index option early rather than holding it. In this scenario the 390 calls will also become early exercise candidates, although the savings will not be as great as with the 380 calls. Prior to the news, the 390 calls might be trading for 13.98. But if the market drops to 390.00 the next morning, the 390 calls will only be trading for 7.10. If the trader owns 390 calls and doesn't exercise, he will lose 13.98 – 7.10, or 6.88 per call. If he does exercise, he will lose only 13.98 – 10.00, or 3.98. He will save 2.90 per call through early exercise.

Of course, implied volatility might increase following such a violent drop in the market. But even if implied volatility jumps to 18%, the prices of the 380 and 390 calls the next morning will only be 15.06 and 8.84, respectively. This is still less than parity, so a trader holding these calls would still want to exercise them early.

Although it does seem that stock index markets are more susceptible to bad news than good, puts might also become early exercise candidates if the market were to jump following unusually bullish news. If, in our example, there was a perception that the market would open the next morning 10 points higher, at 410.00, the option prices might look like this:

Index = 410.00
Time to June expiration = 29 days   Implied volatility = 14%
Interest rates = 6%   Dividend = 0

Exercise Price	Call Price	Call Delta	Put Price	Put Delta
380	31.92	98	.12	–2
390	22.45	92	.61	–8
400	14.01	78	2.16	–23
410	7.46	55	5.67	–46
420	3.28	32	11.75	–72

Now the 410 and 420 puts have become early exercise candidates. Based on the closing index price of 400.00, their parity values are 10.00 and 20.00. But with the index perceived to be at 410.00 their prices are only 5.67 and 11.75. Even if implied volatility were to rise to 18%, their prices would only be 7.49 and 13.37, respectively. This is still well below parity, so a trader would want to exercise the puts rather than hold them.

In a market where early exercise is a possibility, options should never trade for less than parity. If a stock index option market remains open after the index has been fixed for the day (as it does for 15 minutes in the United States), even if traders begin to trade the options as if the market will open the next morning at a price significantly different than that day's closing index price, all options must trade at a price of at least parity. If this were not true, there would be an immediate arbitrage opportunity. If the 390 call were really trading at 7.04 as a result of the negative news, a trader would buy as many calls as possible and immediately submit exercise notices, in the process collecting 10 points per option. He would realize an immediate profit of 2.96 per option.

What would happen if the marketplace were wrong about where the index would open the next morning? Suppose that traders believe the market will open the next morning 10 points lower, but in fact the market opens unchanged, or even several points higher. Wouldn't a trader who exercised the 380 or 390 calls regret his actions? Regardless of what happens the following morning, a trader will always be better off exercising as long as he takes action to offset the effects of the exercise.

For example, suppose the trader initiated the following delta neutral ratio spread before the negative news reached the market:

long 10 June 390 calls at 13.98   delta = 78
short 25 June 410 calls at 3.24   delta = 32

If the trader holds the position, including his 390 calls, and the market opens the next morning at 390, he will show a loss of 12.75, since:

$$-10 \times (13.98 - 7.10) + 25 \times (3.24 - .98) = -12.30$$

But suppose the trader decides to exercise his 390 calls. He still needs to balance his delta position by taking in the 780 deltas which disappeared when he exercised his calls.

One way to do this is to simply close out the spread by buying back the 410 calls at their new price of .98. If he does this, he will show a profit of 16.85, since:

$$-10 \times (13.98 - 10.00) + 25 \times (3.24 - .98) = +16.70$$

If the trader does not want to liquidate his short position in the 410 calls, he can look for another way of taking in 780 deltas. If other stock exchanges are still open and the trader can purchase the stocks making up the index at the new, lower prices and in the correct proportion, he might consider buying stock equivalent to eight index contracts (800 deltas) to make up his loss of 780 deltas. Or, if a futures contract is available on the index, and the futures market, in reaction to the negative news, is now trading 10 points lower, he might buy eight futures contracts since each contract will have approximately 100 index deltas.[5]

It may seem odd, but in fact it doesn't matter whether the index opens the next morning at a higher price, lower price, or unchanged. What matters is that the marketplace believes that the market will change, and that all contracts are priced accordingly. In such a case, the trader must exercise those options which, given the perceived change in the underlying price, now have a value less than parity, and replace them with other contracts which are not limited by parity constraints.

There is clearly an additional early exercise value associated with cash index options, a value which does not result from the usual early exercise considerations of dividends or interest. This value arises because under some circumstances a trader can exercise index options and replace them with other instruments at more favorable prices. How much is this replacement value worth? The answer depends on the probability of some significant event occurring between the time the index is fixed and the close of trading in other instruments linked to the index: stocks, futures, and options. It is doubtful that anyone really knows how to quantify that probability, and traders tend to regard the possibility of a significant event occurring as a phantom variable. No one knows how to evaluate it, but everyone agrees that it exists.

The extra early exercise value resulting from this phantom variable is most evident in the trading of boxes in an index option market. Suppose we are interested in buying a 420/430 box (buy the 420 call and 430 put, sell the 420 put and 430 call). If the box is made up of European options where early exercise is not a possibility, the value of the box is simply the 10-point difference between exercise prices less the carrying cost on 10 points to expiration. If there are four weeks to expiration and interest rates are 6%, the value of the box is approximately:

$$10.00 - (28/365 \times 6\% \times 10.00) = 9.95$$

If these are American options there will be some early exercise value attached to them because of dividend and interest considerations. The extra value will be greatest for the 420 call and 430 put, so the value of the box will be slightly greater than 9.95. Using a binomial model, and given a normal dividend payout, we might find that a 10-point box in the S&P 100 (OEX) market has a value of approximately 10.05. Yet such boxes in the

5. For simplicity, we ignore the likelihood that the trader who continues to hold a spread position will make adjustments to his delta position as a result of the movement in the underlying index.

S&P 100 market often trade for as much as 10¼ to 10⅜. The additional amount over expected theoretical value is the value the marketplace places on the possibility of early exercise after the index has been fixed at the end of the day.

If the right of early exercise can represent an additional reward to the holder of a stock index option, then the possibility of early assignment must represent an additional risk to the seller of such an option. Indeed, the risk to the seller of an index option may seem even greater than the reward to the buyer. The seller is not only at the mercy of the buyer in terms of when the option will be exercised; he may not even find out that he has been assigned until it is too late to take protective action.

The problem for the seller is that index options are settled in cash, and cash does not carry a delta value. When a trader is assigned in a normal stock option market, the assignment may result in a loss to the trader in terms of dividends or interest costs, but at least it does not upset his delta position. If the stock option is deeply enough in-the-money to be exercised, it probably has a delta very close to 100. When the option is exercised, the 100 deltas associated with the option disappear, but they are immediately replaced with the 100 deltas associated with the stock contract. But when a trader is assigned on an in-the-money stock index option, not only does assignment cause a negative cash flow, but the deltas associated with the assigned options completely disappear. If the trader knows immediately that he has been assigned, he might be able to do something to rebalance his delta position. Unfortunately, exercise notices are processed overnight, so the trader will not find out that he has been assigned until the next trading day. If he is short deeply in-the-money index options and is assigned, the following day he may find himself with a big positive or negative delta position, perhaps much bigger than he would like. If the market moves substantially on the opening, the trader could find himself with severe losses before he ever has a chance to take any defensive action.

Synthetic Relationships

Suppose a stock is trading at 100. With two months to expiration, interest rates at 6%, and no dividend expected prior to expiration, what should be the relationship between the 100 call and the 100 put? If we ignore the possibility of early exercise, we know from the synthetic relationship in Chapter 11 that the call price should exceed the put price by approximately the carrying costs on the exercise price of 100:

$$\text{call price} - \text{put price} = \text{exercise price} - \text{stock price} + \text{carrying costs}$$

Since the carrying costs on the exercise price are

$$100 \times 6\% \times 2/12 = 1.00$$

we know that the call should be 1.00 more expensive than the put. If the put is trading for 4.00, the call should be trading for 5.00.

Suppose that the stock is trading for 100 and the put 4.00, but the call is actually trading for 4.25. What should a trader do? Regardless of the trader's opinion about volatility, it's clear that the call is .75 too cheap with respect to the put. A trader familiar with synthetic relationships will attempt to take advantage of this relative mispricing by executing a reverse conversion: buy the call for 4.25, sell the put for 4.00, sell the stock for 100. The result will be a profit at expiration of .75 when the trader closes out the position by either exercising the put or being assigned on the call.

True arbitrage relationships are unlikely to be violated in an option market where there is a well defined and freely traded underlying contract. If such a relationship is violated, a trader can always trade the underlying instrument against the mispriced arbitrage relationship and essentially lock in a profit equal to the mispricing. The cumulative effect of all traders attempting to profit from a mispriced relationship is that the mispricing quickly disappears.

Now consider a trader who encounters a similar mispricing in a stock index option market where the options are settled in cash. Suppose that the index is at 400 and that, according to the synthetic relationship, the 400 call should be 3.00 greater than the 400 put. With the 400 put trading at 6.00, the trader would expect to see the 400 call trading at 9.00. What should he do if he finds that the 400 call is actually trading at 7.50?

The trader would like to take the same action in the index that he would take if he were dealing with options in an individual stock: buy the call for 7.50, sell the put for 6.00, and sell the index for 400.00. This ought to result in a profit of 1.50, the amount by which the call and put are mispriced relative to each other. Is this a practical strategy in the index option market?

Certainly the trader can buy the 400 call and sell the 400 put. But when the trader goes to sell the index he may find that it is not as easy as he originally thought. Depending on how broadly based the index is, the trader may have to sell several hundred stocks in various proportions. It might be possible to do so, but it will certainly not be as easy as selling one stock.

Even if he is able to sell all the stocks in the index in the right proportion, has he executed a true reverse conversion? A true reverse conversion consists of being long a call and short a put, and short the underlying instrument, where the underlying instrument is the instrument to be delivered when an option is exercised. If the basket of stocks were the true underlying instrument, the trader would make delivery of, or take delivery of, the basket if the 400 call or 400 put were exercised. But this is not what happens in an index market. If the trader exercises the call, or is assigned on the put, there is a cash transfer. But the trader is still left holding the basket of stocks.

The fact that the index is settled in cash can make a conversion or reverse conversion a much riskier strategy in an index option market than in an individual stock option market, especially if the options are American. Moreover, arbitrage strategies are typically done in large size because of their narrow profit margin. If a trader executes such a strategy and finds himself assigned overnight, his position might become horribly unbalanced. The next day even a small adverse move in the index could prove disastrous.

If a trader could execute all the stocks in the index, and could be certain of holding the position to expiration, he would still have to physically liquidate his stock position. Since the option values at expiration are determined by the closing index value, and since the index value is determined by the closing trades in each individual stock, the trader must ensure that he closes each of his individual stock positions at the closing price on the exchange from which the index is calculated. In many cases, he can accomplish this by placing market-on-close (MOC) orders for each individual stock. But he must be very careful. If he fails to close out each stock position at the appropriate price, his arbitrage may not produce the profit originally expected.

Because it can be difficult to trade a complete and correctly proportioned basket of stocks, and because there is the additional risk of early exercise after an index arbitrage has been executed, mispriced synthetic relationships are not as easy to exploit in index option markets as in other option markets. Not only do such mispricings occur more frequently in index option markets, they can persist for long periods of time.

Finding a Substitute for the Index

Regardless of the difficulty in executing arbitrage strategies, if a synthetic relationship appears to be sufficiently mispriced a trader will look for some way to exploit the situation, even with the additional risks that go with such a strategy. This means either trying to execute the basket of stocks underlying the index, or looking for an acceptable substitute for the basket.

If the index is narrowly based, with only 20 or 30 stocks, it may not be unreasonable to try and execute a complete basket of stocks. If the index is more broadly based, with several hundred stocks, the difficulties of executing every stock in the right quantity may make it impractical to execute a complete basket. In such a case, a trader may question whether a complete basket is really necessary for his purposes. In most indices not every stock has the same weighting. If an index is very broadly based, price changes in the smallest companies may have very little impact on the index. It may be possible to eliminate these companies and still have a basket which is almost identical to the index.

In the search for an acceptable tradeoff between ease of execution and correlation with the index, traders are always experimenting with different *pseudo-baskets*, a selection of stocks in the index which can be easily bought or sold, and which will react to changing market conditions in a way which is almost identical to the actual index. The primary question for most traders is one of correlation. What degree of correlation is sufficient for the trader's purposes? 100 percent? 99%? 95%? A correlation of 99% between a pseudo-basket and the index may sound good. But if the index is at 400.00 and a trader executes a conversion with the synthetic market mispriced by 1.00, the 99% correlation means he could be wrong by as much as 1% of 400.00, or 4.00. Under some conditions, his presumed profit of 1.00 might turn into a loss of 3.00. Of course, the laws of probability are still in the trader's favor. The pseudo-basket's deviation from the true index could also work in the trader's favor, occasionally giving him a profit greater than 1.00. Arbitrages tend to be done in large size because they are supposed to be very low-risk strategies. If the trader executes a large number of conversions or reverse conversions using a pseudo-basket in place of the actual index, he may find that the correlation risk has a greater impact than he expected.

Another possible substitute for the index is a futures contract on the index which underlies the cash options. If such a contract is available, a trader can use the futures contract in place of the underlying basket in his arbitrage strategies. The futures contract is not only easier to execute than a basket, with lower transaction costs, but there will be a 100% correlation between the futures contract and the actual index. If the futures contract and the index expire at the same time, the futures contract and the option values will converge to the same price at expiration. Moreover, the trader will not have to worry about liquidating either his option or futures position. The clearing house will automatically settle all contracts in cash at expiration.

Providing that the futures contract and the options expire at the same time, a futures contract on the same index which underlies the cash option market is a perfect substitute for the basket. Indeed, if the options are European with no chance of early exercise, an arbitrage between the futures contract and options is virtually riskless. Once the trader has completed his arbitrage, he knows that the futures contract and index will correlate perfectly and will converge at expiration. In the United States, traders in the S&P 500 options market at the Chicago Board Options Exchange often treat the S&P 500 futures contract traded at the Chicago Mercantile Exchange as the underlying contract in their strategies.[6] Traders take a similar approach on many European and Asian exchanges which trade index options on cash and where a futures contract with the same underlying index is also available.

If the futures contract offers an acceptable substitute for the index basket, the problem then becomes one of the prices at which an arbitrage can be executed. While it may be easy to buy and sell a futures contract, can it be done at prices which make a conversion or reverse conversion profitable? If the synthetic market is mispriced by 1.00 in the index option market, and we can trade the futures contract at exactly its fair value, there is no problem. But is that likely to be the case? If it were, everyone in the marketplace would line up to buy or sell a synthetic in the option market, and take an opposing position in the futures market. This activity would force the markets back to fair value, and any arbitrage opportunity would quickly disappear. Traders find that if contracts are mispriced in one index market, they are often mispriced by an equal amount in other index markets. If a synthetic underlying position (long call, short put) is 1.00 too cheap in the option market, a trader usually finds that the futures contract is also 1.00 too cheap. If this were not the case, everyone would take advantage of the situation by purchasing the cheaper contract, either the synthetic or futures contract, and selling the more expensive. In this respect, markets are typically very efficient. A mispricing in one market usually means a similar mispricing in all related markets.

If it can be traded at the right price, a futures contract on an index is perhaps the best substitute an option trader can find. If such a contract is not available, a trader might instead consider a futures contract on a different, but similar, index. For example, the largest index option market in the United States is the S&P 100 (OEX) market at the Chicago Board Options Exchange. Traders in this market are always searching for an acceptable substitute for the underlying basket of 100 stocks. A futures contract on this

---

6. Options on S&P 500 futures are also traded at the CME. Because there is so little early exercise premium in futures options, and because the S&P 500 cash options traded at the CBOE are European, it turns out that the markets for both the futures options and cash options are almost identical.

index would be an ideal substitute but, unfortunately, one does not exist.[7] However, there is a strong correlation between the S&P 100 and S&P 500 indices and, as noted earlier, a futures contract on the latter index is actively traded at the Chicago Mercantile Exchange.

Using an alternative index futures contract as a substitute for the actual underlying index presents several problems. The first is correlation. Just as a pseudo-basket may not correlate exactly, not all indices correlate exactly, even those with many of the same stocks. Figure 15-3 shows the spread between two highly correlated indices, the S&P 500 and the S&P 100, during 1992 and 1993. Note that the spread had a range of almost 20 index points over this period. Moreover, it was not uncommon for the spread to change by as much as five points over a period of several weeks. This highlights the trading risk that can arise when one index is used as a substitute for another.

In addition, not all indices expire at the same time. S&P 100 options are settled from the closing stock prices on the last trading day, while the S&P 500 futures are settled from the opening stock prices on the same day. Because of this, holding an S&P 100 option versus an S&P 500 futures position to expiration represents a substantial and, for most traders, unacceptable risk. If a trader uses S&P 500 futures as a hedge against S&P 100 options, he will almost certainly close one side of the position prior to expiration. Traders have found that using S&P 500 futures contracts as a hedge against S&P 100 options is a short-term solution at best.

The best solution for most index option traders is to avoid using substitute index contracts whenever possible, and to attempt to execute all strategies within the same index market. For arbitrage traders, this means focusing on boxes and jelly rolls, and the time spreads, vertical spreads, and butterflies from which these strategies are constructed. For example, a trader might buy a call time spread, and then try to sell the companion put time spread, thereby creating a jelly roll. Or he might buy a bull vertical call spread, and then try to buy the companion bear vertical put spread, thereby creating a box. Or he might look for butterflies which he believes are mispriced, and try to combine them later with other butterflies to create relatively low risk strategies which act much like an arbitrage.

But even boxes and jelly rolls can present problems. Both carry the risk of early exercise. And a trader who executes a jelly roll still has to decide what to do with his near-term synthetic position as near-term expiration approaches. For example, suppose a trader is long the March/June 410 jelly roll:

short March 410 call	long June 410 call
long March 410 put	short June 410 put

At March expiration the March synthetic will be settled in cash, and the trader will be left with the June synthetic position. If he wants to hold the position and convert it into a reverse conversion, he will have to sell the underlying basket or a suitable substitute. When he tries to do this he will encounter the same problems we have already

7. In the early 1980s the Chicago Mercantile Exchange did trade an S&P 100 futures contract. But the contract was delisted due to insufficient activity.

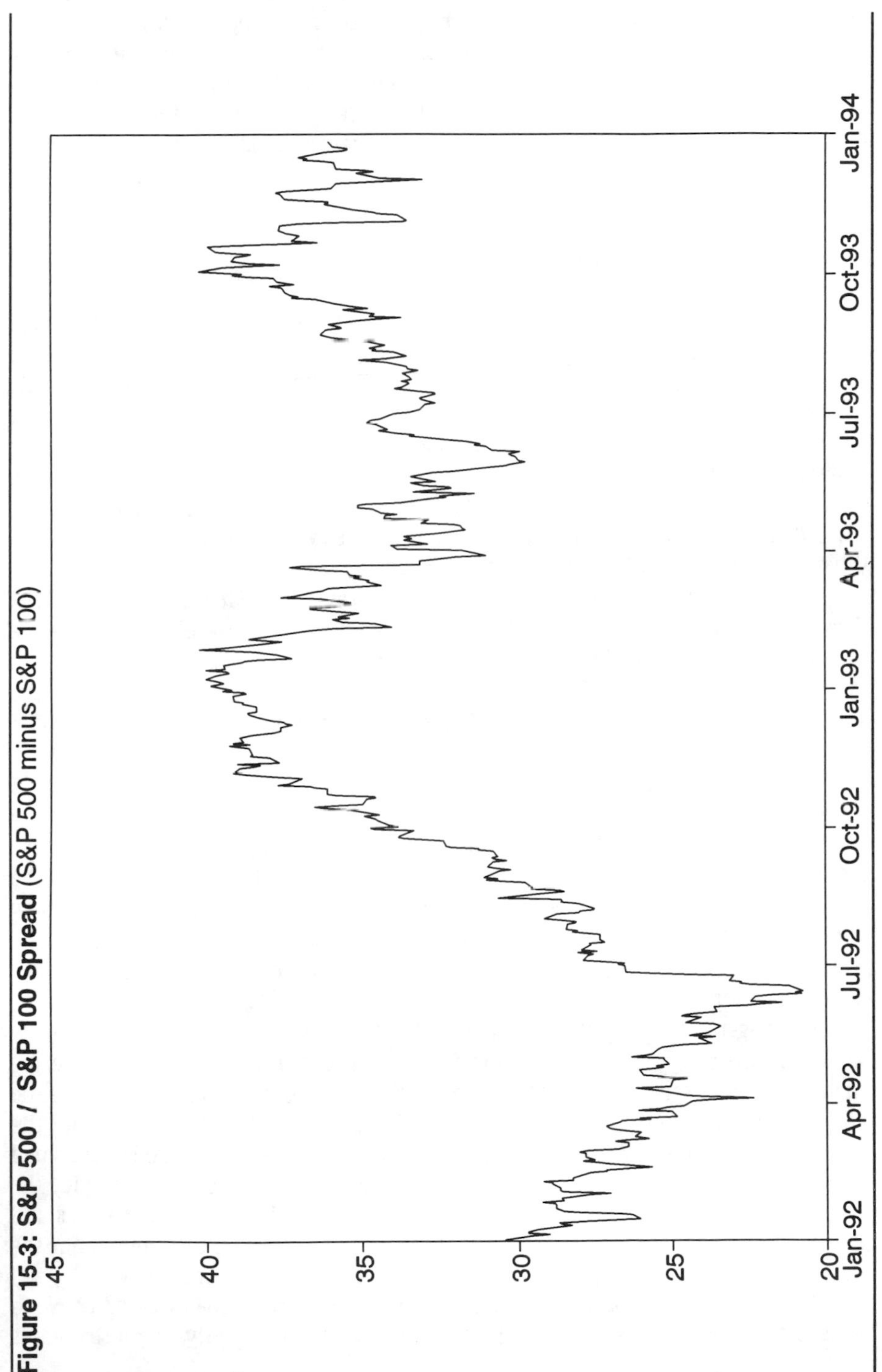

Figure 15-3: S&P 500 / S&P 100 Spread (S&P 500 minus S&P 100)

discussed. This means that jelly rolls, involving two expiration months, can be mispriced in the same way a simple synthetic relationship can be mispriced within one expiration month. If the March 410 synthetic is 1.00 too cheap, while the June 410 synthetic is 1.50 too cheap, the March/June 410 jelly roll will be .50 too cheap. But this is only in theory, since to take advantage of the mispricing, a trader would have to be able to carry the underlying index from March to June expiration. But there is usually no true underlying available, only reasonable substitutes.

BIASES IN THE INDEX MARKET

Although there can be widespread mispricing of synthetic relationships in an index option market, especially where early exercise is a possibility and options are subject to cash settlement, we might assume that this mispricing is random. Sometimes synthetic markets will be too expensive and sometimes they will be too cheap compared to their theoretical values. In the real world, however, synthetic markets always seem to be under pressure. That is, the synthetic market tends to trade at less than theoretical value. If the synthetic market (the difference between a call price and its companion put price) is worth 1.00, the actual market price usually seems to be something less than 1.00. What causes this systematic, downward bias?

Index markets, with their great liquidity, are the most popular of all option markets. They offer all types of traders—directional, volatility, arbitrage—a chance to make decisions based on general market conditions rather than on the unique factors which can affect individual stocks. True or not, most traders believe that the general market is less subject to manipulation than individual stocks, so that index options markets offer a more level playing field.

One especially active participant in index markets is the portfolio manager. A portfolio manager is responsible for going into the market and generating a maximum return on capital with a minimum amount of risk. Historically, portfolio managers have achieved this goal in the equity markets by maintaining a portfolio of stocks which the manager believed would outperform the general market. As the manager identified new stocks which met this criteria he added them to the portfolio, while at the same time selling off other stocks in the portfolio which had either met his performance goals or ceased to perform as expected.

A manager with an equity portfolio might naturally want to protect his holding by taking advantage of the hedging opportunities in an option market. For example, he might want to buy puts to protect the stocks in the portfolio, or sell calls to enhance the stocks' performance. Until the introduction of index options he had to execute the hedging strategy for each individual stock within that stock's option market. If he owned 40 stocks and wanted to execute a uniform hedging strategy for the portfolio, the manager had to go into the individual option markets for the 40 different stocks and execute each hedging strategy separately. This was not only time consuming, but the transaction costs tended to reduce the expected benefits of the hedge.

With the introduction of index options, a manager with a broadly based portfolio realized that his holdings often mimicked an index on which derivative instruments were available. If the manager believed that the characteristics of his portfolio were sufficiently similar to the index, index options now offered a way of hedging the stocks in the portfolio without the time consuming and costly process of executing a hedging strategy in each individual stock.

However, the effect of portfolio hedging strategies on stock index derivatives has been one-sided. Whereas a professional trader will take either a long or short position in the underlying instrument, as market conditions dictate, the vast majority of equity portfolio managers take only long positions in equities. Even if a manager believes a stock will underperform the market, one rarely hears of a manager selling stock short (selling stock which he doesn't own) as part of his investment program. Therefore, a portfolio manager is almost always trying to hedge a long position in the market. This means that the manager is either buying protective puts, selling covered calls, or pursuing some combination of these strategies. The result is that there is constant selling pressure on calls and constant buying pressure on puts.

This downward bias is also evident in stock index futures markets, where a portfolio manager can pursue a dynamic hedging strategy, such as portfolio insurance, by selling futures contracts to protect his equity holdings against adverse market movement. The effect is the same as in option markets—there is always downward pressure on the markets.

If there were a sure way to profit from this downward bias in the market, arbitrageurs would take the opposite position in the underlying index. But we have seen that executing an exact basket is not always possible. Moreover, when the portfolio manager protects his long equity position by selling calls, buying puts, or selling futures, a market maker or arbitrageur ends up taking the opposite position. He is long calls, short puts, or long futures. If he wants to hedge his position with an underlying basket of stocks, he must sell stocks short. And selling stocks short is never as easy as buying stocks. While not totally prohibited in the United States, as it is in many markets, traders who want to sell short are subject to an uptick rule (see Chapter 5). And there is no guarantee that an uptick will occur in even one stock, let alone several hundred.[8] Moreover, most traders are subject to different borrowing and lending rates. Even if a trader can sell short all the stocks in the basket, the interest earnings from the short stock sale may not be the same as the interest cost when stock is purchased.

Given all these factors, the stock index market is not a symmetrical one. Many more factors seem to result in downward pressure on synthetics and futures than upward pressure. This does not mean that such markets can never become inflated, with calls trading for more than expected with respect to puts, or with futures contracts trading at greater than fair value. But this is by far the exception. In stock index markets around the world, there tends to be constant downward pressure on derivative products.

---

8. The Chicago Stock Exchange has tried to facilitate the trading of index products by introducing the Chicago Basket (CMX), a basket of 20 major U.S. stocks which can be traded at one time, and which is not subject to the uptick rule. Hence, a trader who wants to be short all 20 stocks can sell the basket without worrying about finding an uptick in each individual stock.

Figure 15-4: OEX 30-Day Historical Volatility versus OEX Implied Volatility Index (VIX)

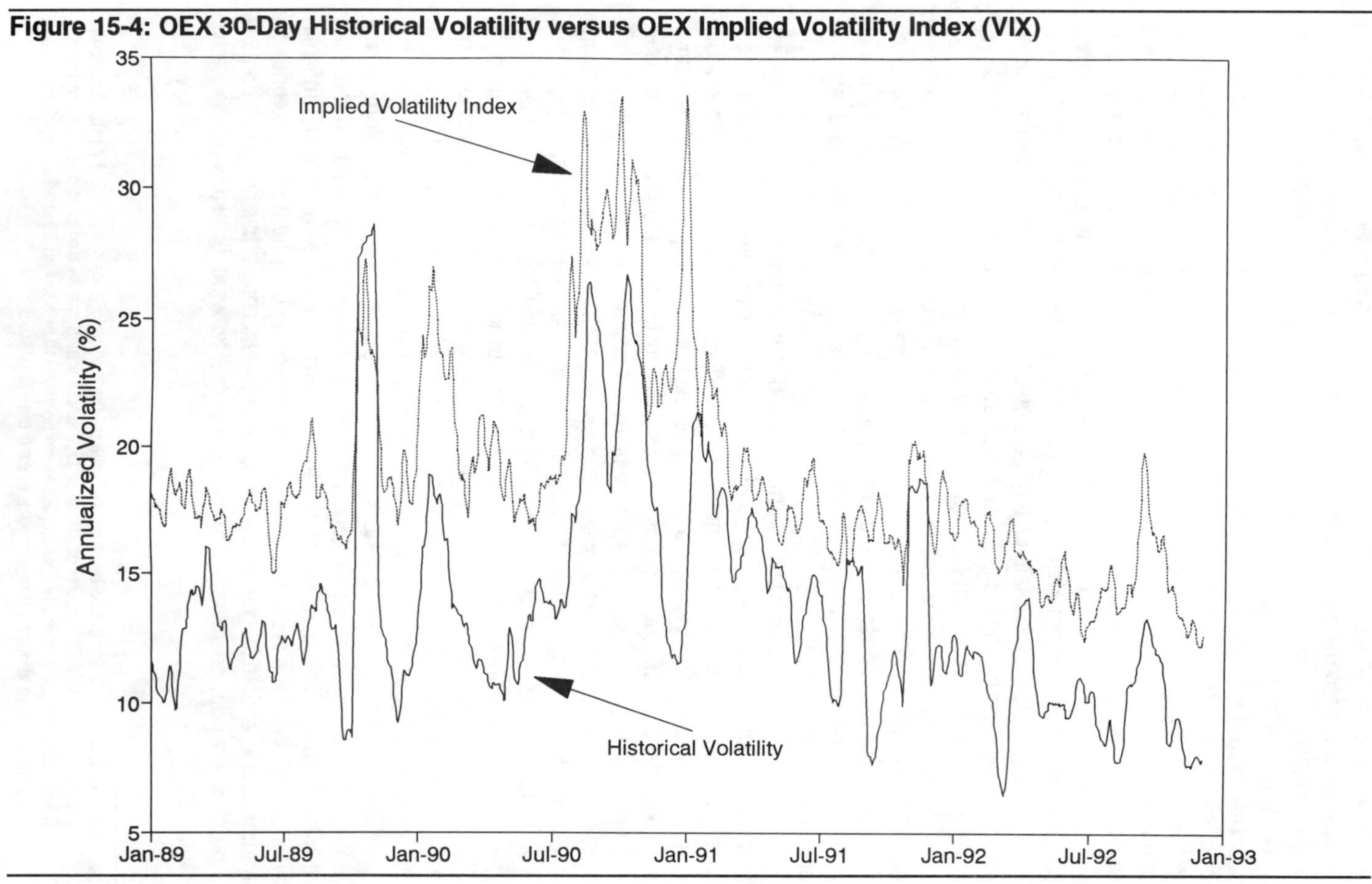

Finally, there also tends to be a consistent bias in premium levels in index option markets. This can be seen in Figure 15-4, a comparison of the 30-day historical volatility of the OEX with the OEX implied volatility index from 1989 to 1992.[9] Note that the implied volatility is almost always greater than the historical volatility. If one believes that the traditional theoretical pricing models are reasonably accurate, it is clear that those who purchase index options are consistently overpaying for them.

While a professional trader would not expect to be very successful if he consistently paid more for options than their theoretical values, such an approach is not necessarily unreasonable for a hedger. If one thinks of options as insurance protection, there are definite benefits that go with owning options. In particular the owner of an option has limited risk with unlimited profit potential. Regardless of theoretical value, these are benefits for which hedgers are very often willing to pay an extra amount. To see why, consider a homeowner who buys insurance to protect his family. Since the insurance company is in business to make a profit, the homeowner knows that the premiums being charged are more than the policy's theoretical value. Nonetheless, the homeowner is willing to pay the extra premium for the privilege of knowing his family is protected against calamity. In the same way, a portfolio manager who believes that his selection of stocks will outperform the market may be willing to pay something more than theoretical value to protect the value of the portfolio when the market moves against him. If he believes that his portfolio will consistently appreciate by more than the cost of the options, he may be willing to overpay since the options will protect him, while at the same time leaving him ahead in the long run.

9. The OEX volatility index (VIX), disseminated by the Chicago Board Options Exchange, represents the implied volatility of a theoretical at-the-money OEX option with 30 days remaining to expiration.

❖ 16 ❖

Intermarket Spreading

While most spreading takes place within one underlying stock, commodity, or index (*intramarket spreading*), a trader need not limit himself to such a narrow playing field. If a trader can identify a relationship between contracts in two different markets, and finds that the instruments are mispriced relative to each other, it is possible to spread one instrument or its derivative products against another instrument or its derivative markets (*intermarket spreading*).

For example, suppose a trader follows two instruments, ABC and XYZ, and decides that ABC will be stronger than XYZ over the next several months. Based on this assessment, the trader might create a spread by purchasing ABC and selling XYZ.

Let's assume the trader purchases ABC at its current price of 50, and sells XYZ at its current price of 100. If ABC rises to 53 and XYZ falls to 98, the trader will show a five-point profit since he can buy back the spread, which he originally sold for 50, at 45. Note that it is not necessary for ABC to rise and XYZ to fall. If ABC rises to 60 and XYZ rises to 105, the trader will still realize a five-point profit. Or if ABC falls to 47 and XYZ falls to 92, the trader will realize the same five-point profit. All that is necessary is that in total points ABC is stronger, or less weak, than XYZ.

Suppose that after initiating the spread, the trader finds that ABC has risen to 60, while XYZ has risen to 115. The spread seems to have gone against the trader as it has widened from the original price of 50 to 55. In point terms the trader was wrong since XYZ was five points stronger than ABC. But many traders would still contend that ABC was stronger than XYZ since ABC rose 20% (10/50) while XYZ only rose 15% (15/100) over the same period. If a trader chooses to measure movement in percent terms, he cannot simply buy ABC and sell XYZ. In order to equalize the percent price changes, his spread must be long and short an equal number of points. In order to accomplish this, for each 100-point XYZ contract the trader sells, he must purchase two 50-point ABC contracts. Now he is long and short an equal number of points. If ABC rises to 60 (a 20% gain) and XYZ rises to 115 (a 15% gain), he will show a profit of:

$$2 \times (60 - 50) - 1 \times (115 - 100) = 5$$

If ABC falls 6% to 47 and XYZ falls 10% to 90, the trader will likewise realize a profit since:

$$-2 \times (50 - 47) + 1 \times (100 - 90) = 4$$

Now in order to make a profit, ABC need only be stronger (or less weak) than XYZ in percent terms.

In our example we tried to ensure that we were long and short the same number of points on each side of our spread. However, the situation can be further complicated if the point values of the instruments are unequal. Suppose that each point in ABC is worth \$400, while each point in XYZ is worth \$100. Now if we buy two ABC contracts and sell one XYZ contract to equalize the point values, we find that the dollar value of our ABC position is $\$400 \times 2 \times 50 = \$40{,}000$, while the dollar value of our XYZ position is $\$100 \times 1 \times 100 = \$10{,}000$. If ABC falls 6% to 47 and XYZ falls 10% to 90, the result will be:

$$[-2 \times (50 - 47) \times \$400] + [1 \times (100 - 90) \times \$100] = -\$2{,}400$$

Even though ABC outperformed XYZ in percent terms, we still ended up losing because the dollar values of each point were different.

The trader's ultimate goal is to equalize the dollar value of each side of his spread. If he wants to achieve this, he must ensure that:

$$\begin{gathered}(\text{ABC contracts}) \times (\text{price of ABC}) \times (\text{point value of ABC}) = \\ (\text{XYZ contracts}) \times (\text{price of XYZ}) \times (\text{point value of XYZ})\end{gathered}$$

He must therefore sell two contracts of XYZ for each one contract of ABC which he buys, since:

$$1 \times 50 \times \$400 = 2 \times 100 \times \$100$$

Putting things in slightly different form, we can express the proper ratio of XYZ contracts to ABC contracts required for a balanced spread as:

$$\begin{aligned}&(\text{price ABC} / \text{price XYZ}) \times (\text{point value of ABC} / \text{point value of XYZ}) \\ &\qquad = (50 / 100) \times (40/10) \\ &\qquad = 2 \ (2{:}1 \text{ ratio})\end{aligned}$$

Now suppose that instead of creating his spread using the underlying instruments ABC and XYZ, the trader decides to create his spread using options on one or both instruments. That is, the trader wants to get long ABC and/or short XYZ by either buying or selling an appropriate number of options. A logical starting point might be to consider the delta positions of each spread. In traditional terms each underlying contract has a delta of 100, and if we buy one ABC contract and sell one XYZ contract we seem to have a neutral spread. But we already know that the price and the point value of the instruments are different. For purposes of intermarket spreading it might be useful to consider the *dollar delta* (\$delta) of each instrument, the total dollar value of the contract divided by 100:

$$\$\text{delta} = (\text{contract price} \times \text{point value}) / 100$$

We can interpret the \$delta as the dollar value change for a one-percent change in the price of the underlying contract. This is slightly different than the traditional interpretation of the delta, the change in a contract's value for a one-point change in the price of the underlying contract. However, the \$delta makes it easier to create and evaluate delta positions between instruments trading at different prices and with different point values.

Using the \$delta calculations, for ABC we have a \$delta of 50 × \$400 / 100 = \$200. For XYZ we have 100 × \$100 / 100 = \$100. For purposes of delta calculations we can see that each delta of ABC is worth two deltas of XYZ. A balanced spread therefore requires us to sell (buy) two deltas of XYZ for each one delta of ABC which we buy (sell). This is simply another way of expressing the proper ratio of underlying instruments required for a balanced spread.

We can also assign a \$delta to an option by multiplying the \$delta of the underlying contract by the option's delta, keeping in mind that, even though deltas are often expressed in whole numbers for convenience, they really represent a percent or decimal fraction:

$$\text{option \$delta} = \text{underlying \$delta} \times \text{option's delta}$$

An option's \$delta represents the dollar change in its theoretical value for a one percent change in the price of the underlying contract. An ABC call with a delta of 80 has a \$delta of:

$$\$200 \times .80 = \$160$$

An XYZ put with a delta of –30 has a \$delta of:

$$\$100 \times -.30 = -\$30$$

Given the \$delta relationship, if we want to get long ABC and short XYZ, and we want to have the same number of dollars at risk on each side of the spread, we need to be long and short an equal number of \$deltas. In other words, in a \$delta neutral position:

number of ABC contracts × contract delta × \$delta of ABC
must equal
number of XYZ contracts × contract delta × \$delta of XYZ

Suppose ABC and XYZ are futures contracts with the following options available:

ABC			XYZ		
Exercise price	**Call delta**	**Put delta**	**Exercise price**	**Call delta**	**Put delta**
45	80	–20	95	70	–30
50	50	–50	100	50	–50
55	20	–80	105	30	–70

Some typical \$delta neutral spreads might be:

long 10 ABC futures / short 40 XYZ 100 calls
long 10 ABC 45 calls / short 16 XYZ futures
long 10 ABC 50 calls / long 20 XYZ 100 puts
short 30 ABC 45 puts / long 40 XYZ 95 puts
long 35 ABC 55 calls / short 20 XYZ 95 calls

Each of these spreads is essentially balanced, because our $delta position in ABC options is exactly offset by an opposing $delta position in XYZ. Since we are always long ABC deltas and short XYZ deltas, for small movements in the underlying contracts, each spread will be profitable as long as ABC is stronger than XYZ.

Why would a trader consider taking a position in options rather than the underlying instrument? When a trader considers an option's theoretical value, in a sense he is comparing the option's value to the value of the underlying instrument. That is why the correct use of an option's theoretical value requires us to establish a hedge against the underlying instrument. If options are underpriced compared to theoretical value, a trader will want to buy options rather than take an equivalent position in the underlying instrument; if options are overpriced compared to theoretical value, a trader will want to sell options rather than take an equivalent position in the underlying instrument. From an option trader's point of view, the determination of whether options are overpriced or underpriced depends on one's opinion of volatility. If implied volatility is low compared to a trader's forecast, options are underpriced; if implied volatility is high, options are overpriced. An option trader will prefer to take a position in the option market rather than in the underlying instrument if he believes that implied volatility is too low or too high.

In our example, if a trader is in agreement with the implied volatility in both ABC and XYZ options, there is nothing to be gained by taking an option position rather than a position in the underlying instrument. Suppose, however, that implied volatility in ABC options is 22% but the trader believes that 24% is a more reasonable volatility. Now options are underpriced. If the trader wants to take a long position in ABC as part of his spread, he will be better off doing so by purchasing ABC calls. He will not only have his intermarket spread, but will, at the same time, be creating a position with a positive theoretical edge. On the other hand, if the trader believes that 20% is a reasonable volatility for ABC options, but implied volatility is 22%, the trader will be better off selling ABC puts. The sale of overpriced puts will create a long position in the ABC market while also creating a positive theoretical edge.

A trader can take the same approach in the XYZ market. If he wants to take a short position in XYZ as part of his intermarket spread, and believes implied volatility in XYZ options is fairly priced, he can simply sell the underlying XYZ contract. Alternatively, if he believes implied volatility is too low, he can buy puts; if he believes implied volatility is too high, he can sell calls.

What types of markets lend themselves to intermarket spreading? Since a trader who enters into an intermarket spread makes the assumption that there is a relationship between the markets involved, the important question for most traders is the closeness of that relationship. A trader is much more likely to construct an intermarket spread in markets which have similar characteristics, or where the markets are driven by the same forces, than in those where no apparent similarity exists. While a trader might find it difficult to identify a relationship between corn and Deutschemarks, he might very well find a relationship between corn and soybeans, or between Deutschemarks and Swiss Francs. In the same way, he might not find a relationship between gold and the stock of General Motors Corp., but he might find a relationship between gold and silver, or between General Motors Corp. stock and Ford Motor Co. stock. Clearly, some instruments are more closely related than others. The closer the relationship, the more such instruments lend themselves to intermarket spreading.

AN INTERMARKET HEDGE

Because intermarket spreading is most common in markets with close relationships, it is not surprising that among the most common markets for intermarket spreading are those where one or more products are derived from some other product. For example, since both heating oil and gasoline are derived from crude oil one would expect price movements in these three markets to be closely correlated. If demand rises for heating oil or gasoline, forcing up the price of these products, then the price of crude oil is also likely to rise. Similarly, if the supply of crude oil is disrupted and prices consequently rise, then the price of gasoline and heating oil is also likely to rise.

Refiners who purchase crude oil and refine it into gasoline and heating oil are often sensitive to the value of *crack spreads*, the spread between the price of crude oil and its derivative products. For example, a refiner who purchases crude oil and refines it into gasoline is concerned that the price of crude oil will rise and that the price of gasoline will fall. If crude oil is at $19.00 per barrel and gasoline at $.5400 per gallon, the price of a simple crude oil/gasoline crack spread is:[1]

$$(\$.54 \times 42) - \$19.00 = \$3.68 \text{ per barrel}$$

If the refiner is satisfied with the $3.68 profit margin, he might protect his position by purchasing crude oil futures at $19.00 and selling an equal number of gasoline futures at $.5400.[2] If, however, he has an opinion on the volatility of either crude oil or gasoline, and this opinion differs from the implied volatility in the option market, he can take either position in options. If he feels that implied volatility in crude oil is unusually low (high), he can take his long position by purchasing calls (selling puts). If he feels that implied volatility in gasoline is unusually low (high), he can take his short position by purchasing puts (selling calls).

While most intermarket spreads consist of opposing positions in two different markets, there is no reason why an intermarket spread cannot be extended to multiple instruments. For example, some refining operations produce a combination of both gasoline and heating oil. In a typical combination 3:2:1 crack spread, from each three barrels of crude oil which the refiner purchases he expects to produce two barrels of gasoline and one barrel of heating oil. With crude oil at $19.00 per barrel, gasoline at $.5400 per gallon, and heating oil at $.5800 per gallon, the value of a 3:2:1 crack spread is:

$$[(2 \times 42 \times \$.5400) + (1 \times 42 \times \$.5800) - (3 \times \$19.00)] / 3 = \$4.24 \text{ per barrel}$$

1. Since gasoline and heating oil are quoted in cents per gallon, and a barrel contains 42 gallons, the gasoline or heating oil price must be multiplied by 42 in order to calculate its price per barrel.

2. Although this is not a $delta neutral position, since the dollars at risk in crude oil are not equal to the dollars at risk in gasoline, it is still an intermarket spread since one market is being spread off against another market.

Again, if the refiner is satisfied with the $4.24 profit margin, he can simply buy crude oil futures and sell gasoline and heating oil futures in a 3:2:1 ratio. For each three crude oil futures which he purchases, he can sell two gasoline futures and one heating oil future. If, however, the refiner has an opinion on the volatility of any of these products, he may find it advantageous to take his long or short position in the option market rather than in the futures market.

VOLATILITY RELATIONSHIPS

A close price relationship between markets may also mean that the markets have similar volatility characteristics. This may enable the trader to identify mispriced options without the necessity of picking the right volatility for either market. Returning to our ABC and XYZ contracts, suppose that a trader thinks ABC will be stronger than XYZ, and wants to take a long position in ABC and a short position in XYZ. If the implied volatility of ABC is 20% and the implied volatility of XYZ is 24%, the trader might now have reason to take his position in options rather than in the underlying instruments. If the market were to rise, the trader expects ABC to go up faster than XYZ since ABC is expected to be stronger than XYZ. In the trader's estimation, ABC ought to have a greater volatility. But the implied volatilities reflect the opposite view. The marketplace seems to believe that if both ABC and XYZ rise in price, XYZ (with its implied volatility of 24%) will rise more quickly than ABC (with its implied volatility of 20%). Clearly, the prices in the marketplace do not reflect the trader's opinion of market conditions. The trader can take advantage of this situation by purchasing ABC calls and selling XYZ calls.

Note that the trader has not made any attempt to predict the right volatility for either ABC or XYZ. He has simply made the assumption that the implied volatilities do not reflect his view of market conditions.

If the trader wants to construct a $delta neutral spread he must still determine the delta of the options involved. Since the $delta, like all deltas, is sensitive to changes in volatility, it may seem that the trader will need a specific volatility to calculate the $delta. He can avoid this problem if he decides to use at-the-money options. No matter what the volatility, he knows that an at-the-money option will have a delta of approximately 50. If ABC is trading at 50 and XYZ is trading at 100, he can buy ABC 50 calls with an implied volatility of 20%, and sell XYZ 100 calls with an implied volatility of 24%. If there are 70 days remaining to expiration, with interest rates at 6%, the price of the ABC 50 call would be 1.73 (a dollar price of $692) and the price of the XYZ 100 call would be 4.14 (a dollar price of $414). Since the $delta of ABC is $200 and the $delta of XYZ is $100, a typical $delta neutral spread might consist of purchasing 10 ABC 50 calls and selling 20 XYZ 50 calls. The value of such a spread at expiration is shown in Figure 16-1.

In Figure 16-1 we can see that if ABC is stronger than XYZ, as the trader believes, the spread will show an ever increasing profit as ABC continues to outperform XYZ. Note that the trader will also show a profit if the market falls in both ABC and XYZ, or if ABC and XYZ move up at the same rate. This is because the trader received more for the XYZ options which he sold than he paid for the ABC options which he bought. If

Figure 16-1: Long 10 ABC 50 Calls/Short 20 XYZ 100 Calls

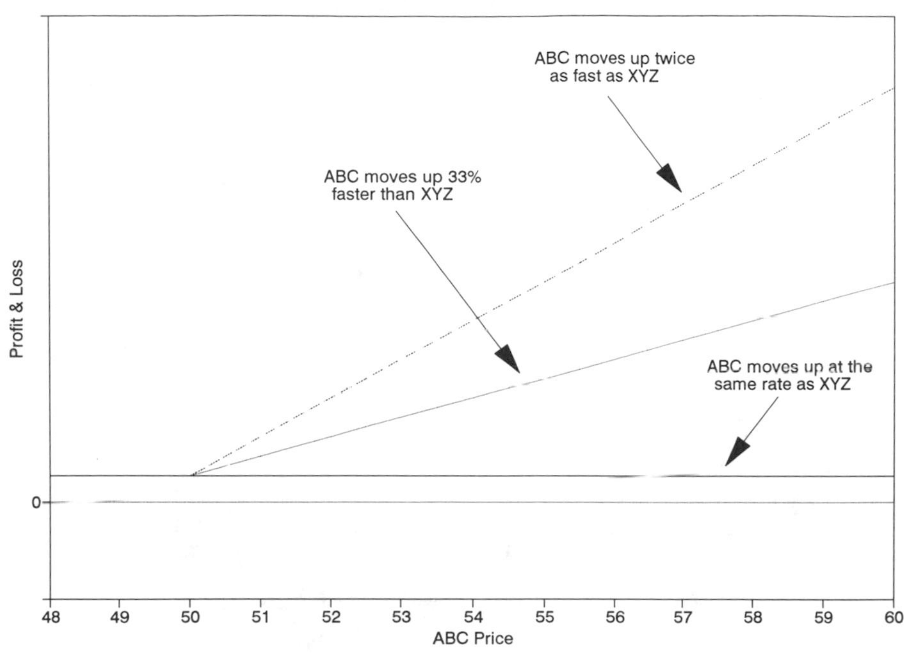

the market falls and the entire position ends up worthless, or if ABC and XYZ move up at the same rate, the trader is left with a profit equal to the excess price of XYZ options. The only market conditions which would hurt this spread would be an upward move in both ABC and XYZ, with XYZ outperforming ABC.

What action could the trader take if the implied volatilities were reversed, with ABC having an implied volatility of 24% and XYZ having an implied volatility of 20%? Now if ABC and XYZ both rise, the marketplace expects ABC to outperform XYZ. Since this is also what the trader believes, there does not seem to be any opportunity. But suppose, instead of buying calls in ABC and selling calls in XYZ, the trader decides to take his long position in ABC by selling puts, and his short position in XYZ by purchasing puts. Assuming, again, that he uses at-the-money puts which he knows to have a delta of approximately –50, he might create a $delta neutral position by selling 10 ABC 50 puts and buying 20 XYZ 100 puts. If the market moves up, and ABC is stronger than XYZ, all the options will collapse to zero. He will be left with a profit equal to the excess credit when he sold ABC 50 puts at an implied volatility of 24% and bought XYZ 100 puts at an implied volatility of 20%. And if the market moves down, based on his assumption that ABC will be stronger than XYZ, the trader expects XYZ to move down more quickly than ABC. Hence, the XYZ puts will appreciate more rapidly than the ABC puts, leaving the trader with an ever-increasing profit. The results of this strategy is shown in Figure 16-2.

Figure 16-2: Short 10 ABC 50 Puts/Long 20 XYZ 100 Puts

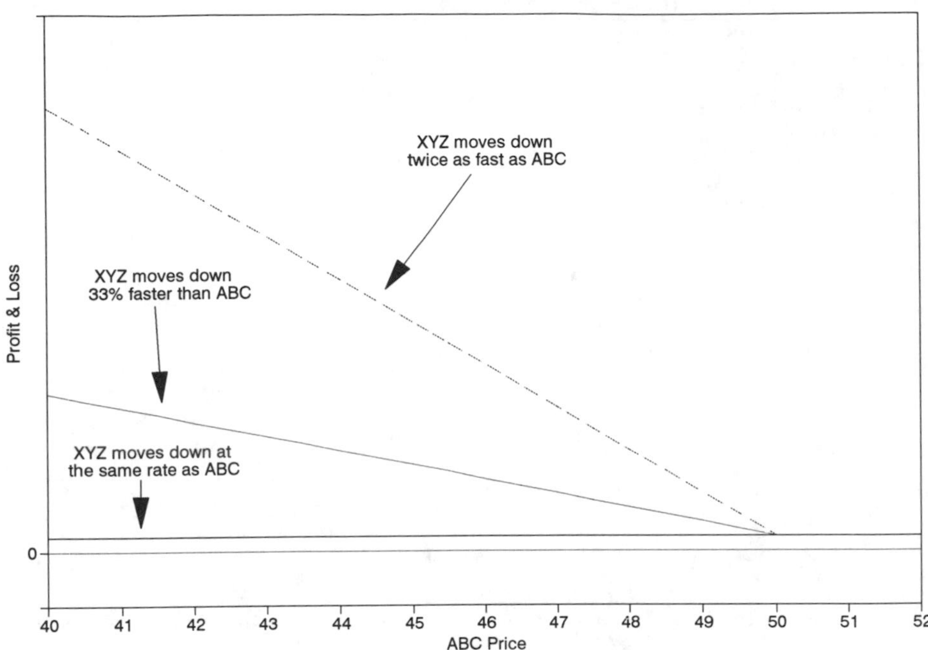

In the foregoing examples we used at-the-money options which we knew to have a delta of 50. What about using either in-the-money or out-of-the-money options? Now the situation becomes more complex. If we use at-the-money options we are only required to determine that ABC and XYZ implied volatilities are mispriced with respect to each other. If, however, we start to vary the options' exercise prices, we need to determine not only whether ABC and XYZ options are mispriced with respect to each other, but also whether the individual implied volatilities are too high or too low. Whenever options appear cheap because implied volatility is lower than a trader's volatility forecast, the trader will try to buy out-of-the-money options (options with lower deltas). Whenever options appear expensive because implied volatility is higher than a trader's volatility forecast, the trader will try to sell out-of-the-money options.

For example, if ABC options not only appear too cheap with respect to XYZ options, but also appear too cheap compared to a trader's volatility forecast for ABC, the trader will try to buy ABC options with smaller deltas and sell XYZ options with larger deltas. Assuming the trader wants to be long ABC and short XYZ, he might buy ABC 55 calls and sell XYZ 100 calls. Or he might buy ABC 50 calls and sell XYZ 95 calls. He is trying to create an *intermarket call backspread,* by purchasing options with smaller deltas, and selling options with larger deltas. In the same way, if ABC options appear too expensive with respect to XYZ, and also appear too expensive compared to a trader's volatility forecast, he might take his long position in ABC by selling puts with lower deltas, and take his short position in XYZ options by purchasing puts with higher deltas. This will create an *intermarket put ratio vertical spread.* Examples of an intermarket call backspread and an intermarket put ratio vertical spread are shown in Figures 16-3 and 16-4. Note that such spreads are sensitive not only to the volatility relationship between ABC and XYZ, but also to the general level of volatility. A backspread wants the market to become more volatile; a ratio vertical spread wants the market to become less volatile.

INTERMARKET VOLATILITY SPREADS

Suppose a trader has decided that ABC and XYZ ought to have very similar volatilities, but he finds that the implied volatility of ABC options, at 20%, is markedly different than the implied volatility of XYZ options, at 25%. If the trader also believes that one market will outperform the other, he might take a position by purchasing calls (puts) in one market and selling calls (puts) in the other market. But suppose the trader has no opinion on the relative strengths of the two markets. His only opinion is that options in one market are too cheap or expensive in relation to options in the other market. He simply wants to be long volatility in one market and short volatility in the other. What can he do?

Suppose the trader purchases ABC calls and sells XYZ calls. If he is right about volatility and both markets move in the same direction, he will always show some profit (Figure 16-1). But his profit will be greatest when ABC and XYZ rise in price. In the same way, if the trader purchases ABC puts and sells XYZ puts, he will always show

Figure 16-3: Long 21 ABC 55 Calls/Short 12 XYZ 95 Calls

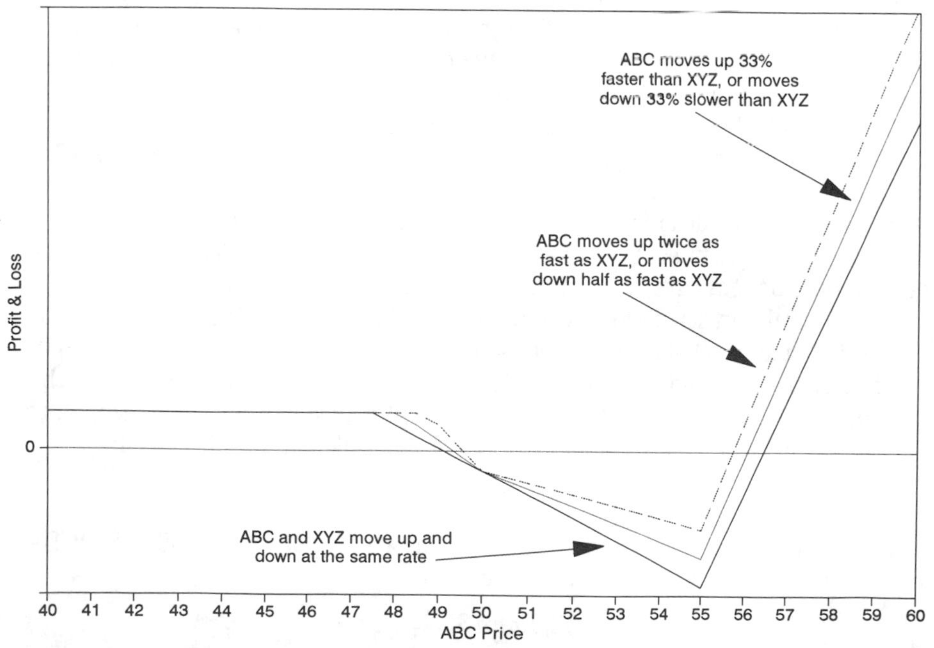

Figure 16-4: Short 21 ABC 45 Puts/Long 12 XYZ 105 Puts

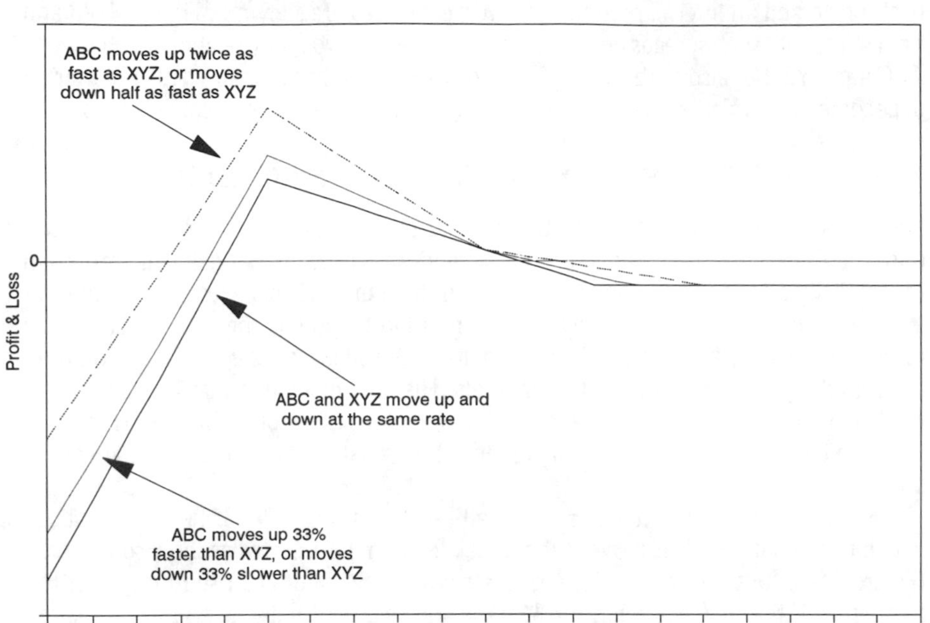

some profit (Figure 16-2). But now his profit will be greatest when ABC and XYZ fall in price. A trader who has only a volatility opinion can combine these strategies to create an intermarket spread which is based solely on the assumption of a mispriced volatility relationship between the two markets. That is, the trader can buy straddles or strangles in one market and sell straddles or strangles in the other market.

Since the trader is not taking a position on what the correct volatility is for ABC or for XYZ, but rather on the relative volatility between the two markets, he can't determine the exact delta for the options. The easiest way to solve this problem is to focus on at-the-money straddles. Regardless of the correct volatility, he knows that at-the-money options have deltas of approximately 50.

Suppose the trader decides to buy 20 ABC 50 straddles. How many XYZ 100 straddles should he sell if he wants the value of the total position to be dependent only on the volatility relationship between the two markets? The trader can think of his position as an ABC/XYZ call spread, combined with an ABC/XYZ put spread. Since ABC has a $delta of $200, the trader's total $delta position in ABC 50 calls is:

$$20 \times \$200 \times .50 = \$2000$$

The $delta of XYZ is $100, so each XYZ call has a $delta of $100 × .50 = $50. The correct number of XYZ calls to sell is therefore:

$$\$2{,}000 \ / \ \$50 = 40$$

The arithmetic is essentially the same for ABC and XYZ puts, each having a delta of −50. If the trader buys 10 ABC 50 puts, his $delta position is:

$$10 \times \$200 \times -.50 = -\$2000$$

With the $delta for the XYZ 100 put of −$50 we need to sell 40 XYZ 100 puts to balance the 20 ABC 50 puts which we purchased. The complete position is:

long 20 ABC 50 calls	short 40 XYZ 100 calls
long 20 ABC 50 puts	short 40 XYZ 100 puts

The value of this position at expiration is shown in Figure 16-5.

Note in Figure 16-5 that if ABC and XYZ move at the same rate, the position will always show a profit equal to the excess premium received for XYZ options (implied volatility = 25%) over the premium paid for ABC options (implied volatility = 20%). Suppose the implied volatilities of 20% for ABC and 25% for XYZ turn out to be correct. This means that XYZ will move 25% faster than ABC since 25/20 = 1.25. If this happens we can see from Figure 16-5 that the spread will now act like a short straddle, showing its maximum value if the market sits still and showing a loss if the market makes a big move.

If the trader believes that XYZ will move faster than ABC, as indicated by the implied volatilities, he might alter the ratio. If XYZ does have a volatility 25% greater than ABC, the trader can rebalance the spread by purchasing 25% more ABC straddles than he originally intended. Instead of purchasing 20 ABC straddles he can purchase 25 ABC straddles. The effect of doing the spread in this new ratio is shown in Figure 16-6.

We can see from Figure 16-6 that in the new size of 25 × 40 the spread breaks even if XYZ does move 25% faster than ABC. But the position acts like a long straddle if ABC and XYZ move at the same rate. In the new size of 25 × 40 the volatility difference between the two contracts has become a factor in determining the correct ratio. Originally, the trader balanced his spread based on the following relationship:

ABC contracts × $delta of ABC × ABC option delta
must equal
XYZ contracts × $delta of XYZ × XYZ option delta

But taking into consideration the different volatilities of the two contracts, the spread is now balanced if:

ABC contracts × $delta of ABC × ABC option delta × ABC volatility
equals
XYZ contracts × $delta of XYZ × XYZ option delta × XYZ volatility

Our XYZ call position is:

$$40 \times \$100 \times .50 \times .25 = \$500$$

Taking into consideration the volatility, each ABC call has a $delta of

$$\$200 \times .50 \times .20 = \$20$$

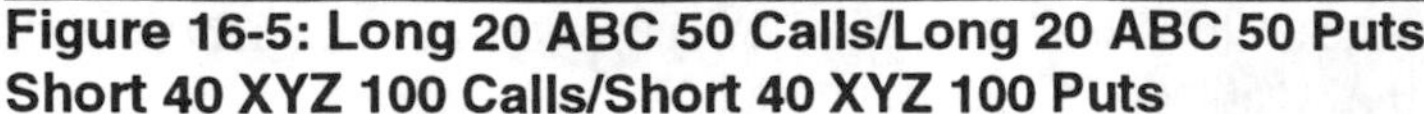

Figure 16-5: Long 20 ABC 50 Calls/Long 20 ABC 50 Puts Short 40 XYZ 100 Calls/Short 40 XYZ 100 Puts

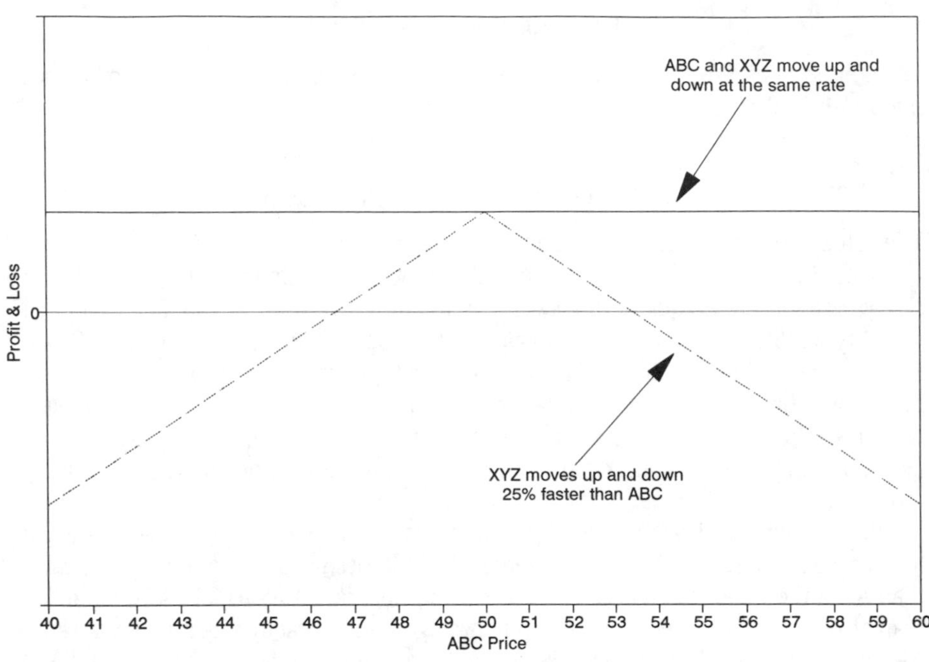

Therefore, the proper number of ABC contracts required to balance the spread is 500/20, or 25 contracts. The spread is now completely balanced since:

$$25 \times \$200 \times .50 \times .20 = 40 \times \$100 \times .50 \times .25$$

We can see that the volatility relationship between the two contracts can be an important factor in determining the proper ratio in an intermarket volatility spread. Since predicting the correct volatility of even one underlying contract can be such a difficult task, what chance does the trader have of being correct about the volatility of two different contracts? The important consideration in an intermarket spread is not necessarily the volatility of each individual contract, but the volatility relationship between the contracts. If a trader can determine the relationship, the actual volatility might not affect the spread value. For example, if we determine that XYZ is always 25% more volatile than ABC, the actual volitilities of ABC and XYZ don't really matter. The ratio is the same whether the volatility of ABC is 20% and XYZ is 25%, or ABC is 12% and XYZ is 15%, or ABC is 28% and XYZ is 35%. In each case XYZ is 25% more volatile than ABC, so the ratio of XYZ to ABC is the same.

Is it possible to identify markets with well defined volatility relationships? While there can be no absolute answer, some markets do seem to be so closely related that their volatilities take on a well defined relationship.

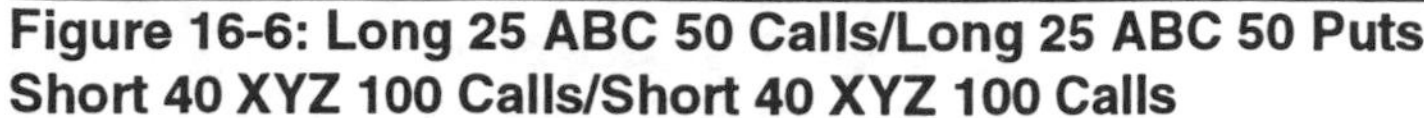

Figure 16-6: Long 25 ABC 50 Calls/Long 25 ABC 50 Puts Short 40 XYZ 100 Calls/Short 40 XYZ 100 Calls

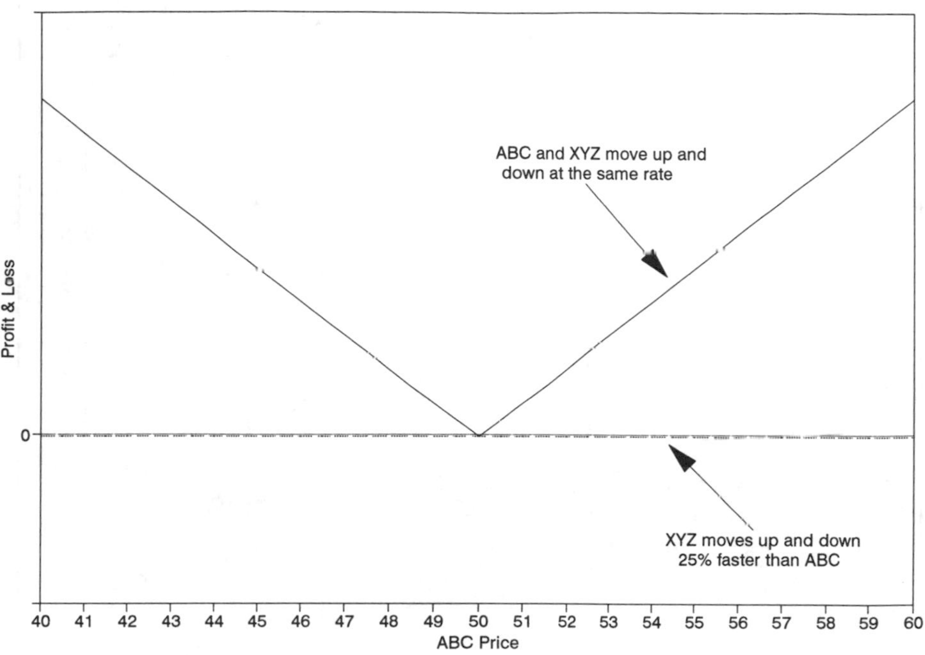

For example, several indexes exist which track the performance of the U.S. stock market. Not only might we expect these indexes to move up or down together, at least over longer periods of time, but we might also expect them to have similar volatility characteristics. As an example, the 50-day historical volatilities of two of these indexes, the S&P 100 (OEX) and the New York Stock Exchange Composite Index (NYA), are shown in Figure 16-7. There is clearly some relationship between the volatility of these two indexes, but how close is the relationship? To help answer the question, NYA volatility has been plotted as a percent of OEX volatility in Figure 16-8. We can see that NYA volatility is typically somewhere between 80% and 95% of OEX volatility. As a rough estimate we might decide that on average NYA volatility is approximately 87% of OEX volatility.

Suppose we find that OEX options, traded on the Chicago Board Options Exchange, and NYA options, traded on the New York Stock Exchange, are trading at approximately the same implied volatility. Since we expect the NYA to be approximately 13% less volatile than the OEX, how can we construct a strategy which exploits this apparent mispricing between OEX and NYA options? If we decide to buy at-the-money OEX straddles and sell at-the-money NYA straddles, and also take into consideration the relative volatilities of the two markets, we know that in a balanced spread:

Figure 16-7: OEX versus NYA Historical Volatility

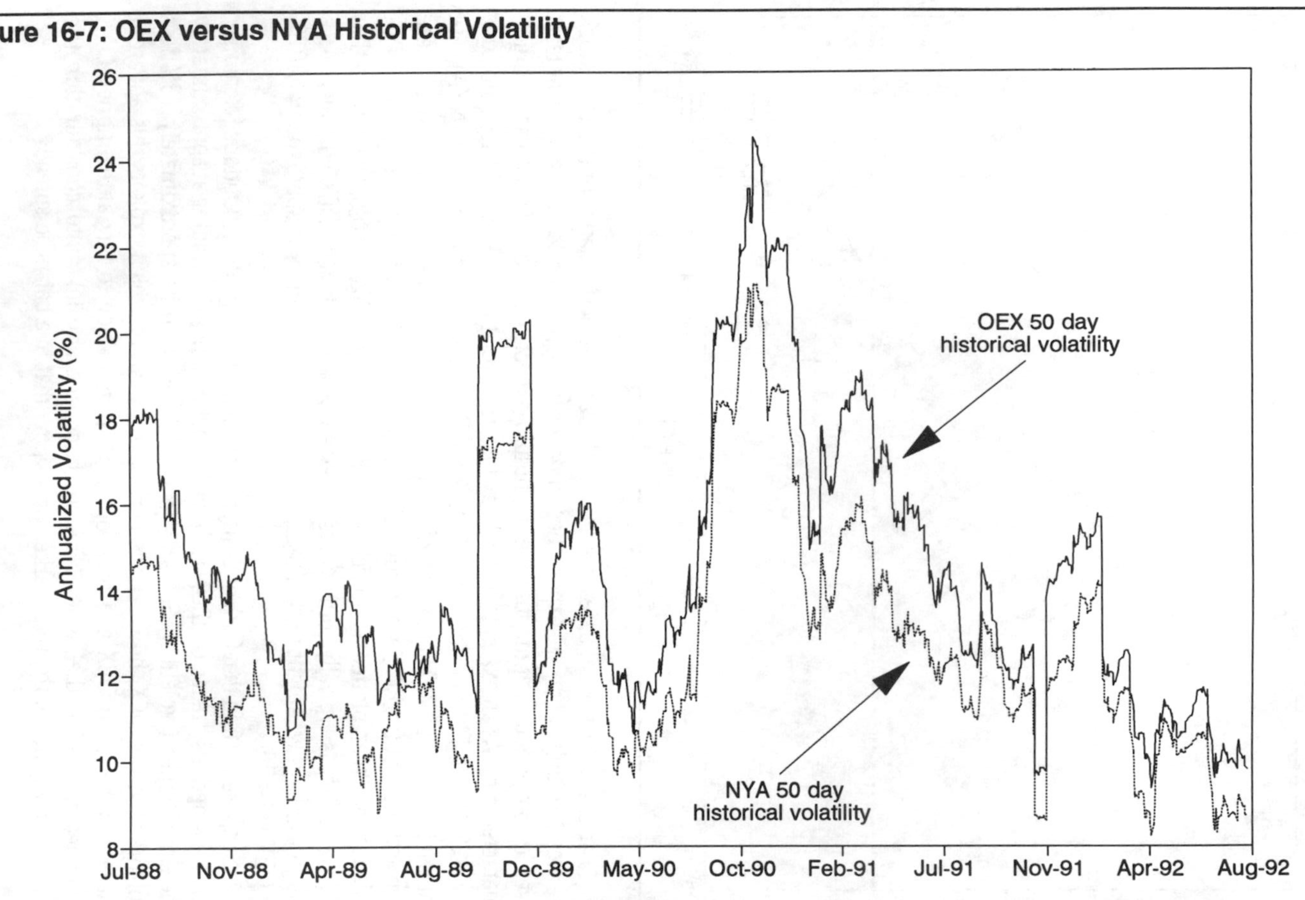

Figure 16-8: NYA Volatility as a Percent of OEX Volatility

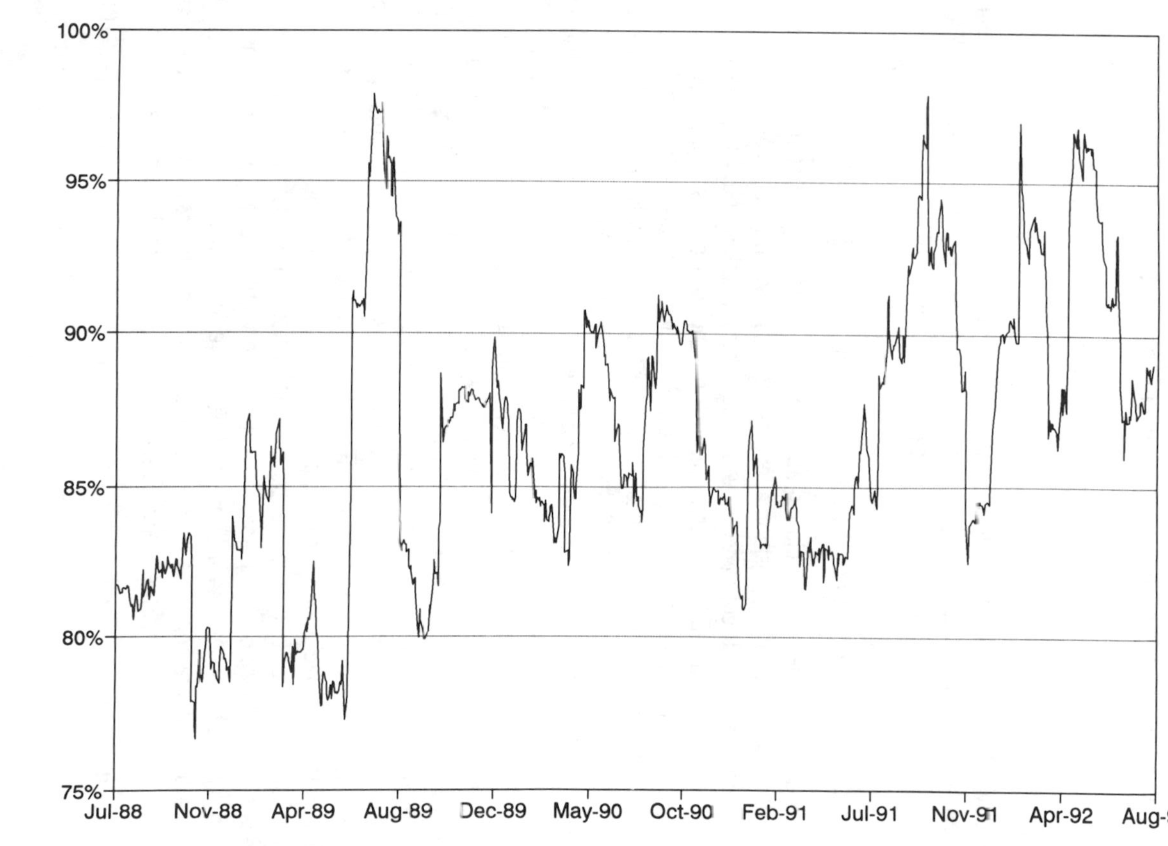

number of OEX straddles × OEX $delta × .87
must equal
number of NYA straddles × NYA $delta

Suppose the OEX is at 440 and the NYA is at 260. Since both contracts have the same point value of $100, the $deltas for the two indexes are:

OEX $delta = 440 × $100 / 100 = $440
NYA $delta = 260 × $100 / 100 = $260

For each NYA straddle which we sell, we must purchase .87 × 260/440, or approximately .51 OEX straddles. If we were to purchase 20 OEX 440 straddles, a balanced intermarket volatility spread would require us to sell approximately 39 NYA 260 straddles, since 39 × .51 = 20. Our spread might consist of:

long 20 OEX 440 calls / long 20 OEX 440 puts
short 39 NYA 260 calls / short 39 NYA 260 calls

If the OEX straddles are purchased and the NYA straddles sold at the same implied volatility, the value of the position at expiration is shown in Figure 16-9.

Note that if both contracts move in the same direction and, as we expect, NYA volatility is 87% of OEX volatility, the position shows a constant profit equal to the expected 13% difference in the volatilities. Even if we double or triple volatility, the profit to the position will be identical, as long as NYA volatility is 87% of OEX volatility.

We can see from Figure 16-8 that NYA volatility need not be exactly 87% of OEX volatility. What will our position look like if NYA volatility turns out to be near the upper range of OEX volatility, perhaps 95%, or near the lower range of OEX volatility, perhaps 80%. These two possibilities have also been plotted in Figure 16-9. In the former case our position will begin to act like a short straddle, and any increase in volatility will reduce the value of the position. In the latter case our position will begin to act like a long straddle, and any increase in volatility will increase the value of the position. Obviously, if we were to focus on a risk to our position, the risk would be that NYA volatility would increase relative to OEX volatility. Even with this risk the spread still looks very attractive since we have considerable margin for error.

In a typical volatility spread a trader often focuses on the delta, gamma, theta, and vega characteristics of the spread. We might also want to consider these sensitivities with respect to an intermarket spread. Just as we found it convenient to calculate a $delta to compare contracts in different markets, we will also find it convenient to calculate the $gamma, $theta, and $vega. The definitions and interpretations are:

$gamma = underlying $delta × option's gamma × underlying point value / 100

(the change in an option's $delta for a one-percent change in the price of the underlying contract)

$theta = underlying point value × option's theta

(the dollar change in an option's theoretical value with the passage of one day)

Figure 16-9: Long 20 OEX 440 Calls/Long 20 OEX 440 Puts Short 39 NYA 260 Calls/Short 39 NYA 260 Puts

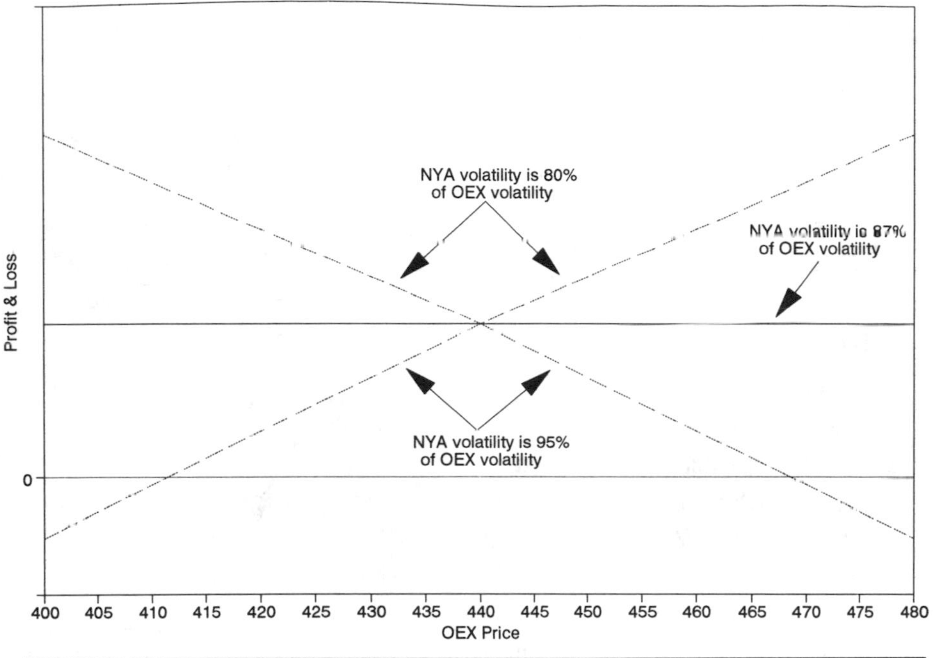

$vega = underlying point value × option's vega

(the dollar change in an option's theoretical value for a one-percentage-point change in volatility)

If we use implied volatilities of 11%, an interest rate of 5%, and assume 70 days remaining to expiration, the dollar sensitivities for several OEX and NYA options might be approximately the following:[3]

OEX = 440.00; time to expiration = 70 days;
volatility = 11%; interest rate = 5%

NYA = 260.00; time to expiration = 70 days;
volatility = 11%; interest rate = 5%

Option	$delta	$gamma	$theta	$vega
OEX 425 call	364	23	–8.57	49
OEX 440 call	259	36	–9.29	75
OEX 455 call	140	33	–6.87	69

3. These figures are approximations only. While early exercise was taken into consideration through the use of the Cox-Ross-Rubenstein model, no dividends were used. In addition, the numbers have been rounded for convenience.

Option	**$delta**	**$gamma**	**$theta**	**$vega**
OEX 425 put	-81	25	–3.09	51
OEX 440 put	–196	42	–4.00	74
OEX 455 put	–339	43	–2.36	54
NYA 250 call	221	13	–4.93	27
NYA 260 call	152	21	–5.49	44
NYA 270 call	75	18	–4.05	39
NYA 250 put	-41	13	–1.85	28
NYA 260 put	–117	24	–2.36	44
NYA 270 put	–211	26	–1.26	28

The total dollar sensitivities of our OEX/NYA position is:

Position	**$delta**	**$gamma**	**$theta**	**$vega**
long 20 OEX 440 calls	5180	720	–185.80	1500
long 20 OEX 440 puts	–3920	840	–80.00	1480
short 39 NYA 260 calls	–5928	–819	214.11	–1716
short 39 NYA 260 puts	4563	–936	92.04	–1716
Totals	–105	–195	+40.35	–452

How can we interpret these sensitivities? Although the $delta of –105 indicates a preference for the market to fall rather than rise, in practice most traders would consider the position essentially $delta neutral since the preference is only very slight. In relative terms the $delta of –105 represents a position which is short only about 24% of an OEX contract (with a $delta of 440), or about 40 percent of an NYA contract (with a $delta of 260).[4]

But why does the position have a negative $gamma, positive $theta, and negative vega?

The total negative $gamma of –195 seems to suggest that movement in the underlying contracts will hurt our position. If both the OEX and NYA were to move at the same rate, we can see from Figure 16-9 that this would indeed be true. But we don't expect the OEX and the NYA to move at the same rate; we expect the NYA to move at only 87 percent the rate of the OEX. If we multiply our NYA $gamma position by .87, and then add it to our OEX $gamma position, it turns out that the total $gamma is very close to zero:[5]

$$(720 + 840) - .87 \times (819 + 936) \approx 33$$

This reflects the fact that we are relatively insensitive to movement in the two indexes as long as the NYA moves at 87% the rate of the OEX.

---

4. In a perfectly balanced intermarket spread the total $delta, $gamma, $theta, and $vega would in fact add up to exactly zero.

5. Ibid.

The same reasoning applies to our $vega position. The total negative $vega of –452 suggests that an increase in volatility will hurt our position. If the volatility of the OEX and NYA were to increase by the same amount this would be true. But if volatility rises, we expect NYA volatility to rise by only 87% of OEX volatility. If we multiply our NYA $vega position by .87, and then add it to our OEX $vega position, the total the total $vega is approximately zero:[6]

$$(1500 + 1480) - .87 \times (1716 + 1716) \approx -6$$

This reflects the fact that we are insensitive to changes in volatility as long as NYA volatility is 87% of OEX volatility.

From these examples, we can see that the actual $gamma, $theta, and $vega positions should reflect the relative volatilities of the underlying contracts. In our example we have:

total $gamma = OEX $gamma + (NYA $gamma × [NYA volatility/OEX volatility])
total $theta = OEX $theta + (NYA $theta × [NYA volatility/OEX volatility])
total $vega = OEX $vega + (NYA $vega × [NYA volatility/OEX volatility])

When we do this, we find that our intermarket spread is insensitive to price movement, to the passage of time, and to changes in volatility, *as long as the NYA moves at 87% the rate of the OEX.*

Suppose that instead of selling at-the-money NYA straddles to offset our purchased at-the-money OEX straddles, we decided to sell NYA strangles. For example, we might establish the following $delta neutral position:

buy 20 OEX 440 calls	sell 69 NYA 270 calls
buy 20 OEX 440 puts	sell 96 NYA 250 puts

Since the OEX 440 call has a $delta of 259 and the NYA 270 call has a $delta of 75, for each OEX 440 call we buy, we must sell 259/75, or approximately 3.45 NYA 270 calls. In the same way, since each OEX 440 put has a $delta of –196 and each NYA 250 put has a delta of –41, for each OEX 440 put which we buy, we must sell 196/41, or approximately 4.78 NYA 250 puts. Having purchased 20 OEX 440 straddles, to establish a $delta neutral intermarket spread we must sell 69 NYA 270 calls and 96 NYA 250 puts.

The sensitivities of this position are:

Position	**$delta**	**$gamma**	**$theta**	**$vega**
long 20 OEX 440 calls	5180	720	–185.80	1500
long 20 OEX 440 puts	–3920	840	–80.00	1480
short 69 NYA 270 calls	–5175	–1242	279.45	–2691
short 96 NYA 250 puts	3936	–1248	177.60	–2688

Taking into consideration the multiplication factor of .87 for the NYA $gamma, $theta, and $vega, the total sensitivities for our spread are:

6. Ibid.

\$delta = 5180 – 3920 – 5175 + 3936 = +21
\$gamma = 720 + 840 – .87 × (1242 + 1248) = –606
\$theta = –185.80 – 80.00 + .87 × (279.45 + 177.60) = +131.83
\$vega = 1500 + 1480 – .87 × (2691 + 2688) = –1700

Even though the \$delta position is approximately neutral, the negative \$gamma, positive \$theta, and negative \$vega suggest that the spread will act like a short straddle: any large move in the underlying market or increase in volatility will hurt the position, and the passage of time or a decline in volatility will help the position. If we do such a spread, we are not only taking a position on the relative volatilities of the two underlying markets, we are also taking a position that the implied volatilities in the two markets are too high.

What type of position would we initiate if the relative volatilities were incorrect, and at the same time the trader felt that implied volatilities were too low? In this case we would try to create a position with a positive \$gamma, negative \$theta, and positive \$vega. For example, we might buy the OEX 425/455 strangle and sell the NYA 260 straddle:

buy 20 OEX 425 calls	sell 18 NYA 260 calls
buy 20 OEX 455 puts	sell 14 NYA 260 puts

Since the OEX 455 call has a \$delta of 140 and the NYA 260 call has a \$delta of 152, for each OEX 455 call we buy, we must sell 140/152, or approximately .92 NYA 260 calls. In the same way, since each OEX 425 put has a \$delta of –81 and each NYA 260 put has a delta of –117, for each OEX 455 put which we buy, we must sell 81/117, or approximately .69 NYA 260 puts. Having purchased 20 OEX 425/455 strangles, to establish a \$delta neutral intermarket spread we must sell approximately 18 NYA 260 calls and 14 NYA 260 puts.

The sensitivities of this position are:

Position	\$delta	\$gamma	\$theta	\$vega
long 20 OEX 455 calls	2800	660	–137.40	1380
long 20 OEX 425 puts	–2736	500	–61.80	1020
short 18 NYA 260 calls	–1620	–378	98.82	–792
short 16 NYA 260 puts	1638	–336	33.04	–616

Taking into consideration the multiplication factor of .87 for the NYA \$gamma, \$theta, and \$vega, the total sensitivities for our spread are:

\$delta = 2800 – 2736 – 1620 + 1638 = +82
\$gamma = 660 + 500 – .87 × (378 + 336) = -1781
\$theta = –137.40 – 61.80 + .87 × (98.82 + 33.04) = +84.48
\$vega = 1380 + 1020 – .87 × (792 + 616) = -1175

The positive \$gamma, negative \$theta, and positive \$vega suggest that the spread will act like a long straddle: any large move in the underlying market or increase in volatility will help the position, and the passage of time or a decline in volatility will hurt the position. If we do such a spread, we are not only taking a position on the relative volatilities of the two underlying markets, we are also taking a position that the implied volatilities in the two markets are too low.

While intermarket volatility spreads begin with a trader's opinion about the relative volatilities in two different markets, such spreads can be carried one step further. When the implied volatilities appear to be incorrect with respect to each other, the trader can simply buy straddles in the market which is relatively cheap and sell straddles in the market which is relatively expensive. However, if the trader also has an opinion that implied volatilities in the two markets are generally too high or too low, by taking an appropriate $gamma and $vega position the trader can create volatility spreads which also exploit this mispricing. Depending on his opinion, he will want to create one of the four basic types of volatility spreads:

positive $gamma / positive $vega (backspread)
negative $gamma / negative $vega (ratio vertical spread)
negative $gamma / positive $vega (long time spread)
positive $gamma / negative $vega (short time spread)

For a more detailed discussion of volatility spreads and their characteristics, the reader should refer to Chapter 8.

OPTIONS ON SPREADS

There is one last type of intermarket spread worth mentioning. Even though such spreads are not currently traded on exchanges, it is possible to create an option where the value of the option at expiration depends on a spread between two different underlying markets. For example, suppose two underlying markets, ABC and XYZ, are trading at 175 and 150, respectively. The ABC over XYZ spread is therefore trading at 25. If a trader believes this spread might widen to as much as 60 points, he might like to buy an option on the spread with an exercise price below the projected spread of 60. If he buys a spread with an exercise price of 25, and the spread does widen to 60 at expiration, he will receive a payoff of 35, the difference between the 60-point spread and the 25-point exercise price.

Such a spread is not as exotic as it sounds, since there are many situations where a trader might believe that a spread will expand or contract over time. A portfolio manager might believe that the stock market of one country will outperform the stock market of another country. If such an option were available, the manager might want to buy a call option on the spread between the stock indexes of the two countries. If the spread widened to the point where it was greater than the chosen exercise price, the call would go into-the-money and would have unlimited profit potential. If the spread either failed to widen or narrowed, the call would finish out-of-the-money and the manager's loss would be limited to the amount he paid for the call.[7]

---

7. Of course, such an option would be complicated by the relative values of the currencies involved. The buyer of the option would have to devise a method of offsetting the currency risk.

Note that the underlying value of an option on a spread might take on a negative value. The ABC over XYZ spread, with ABC at 175 and XYZ at 150, has a value of 25. But if ABC rises to 185 while XYZ rises to 200, the spread will have a value of −15. Most traditional theoretical pricing models, with their assumption of a lognormal distribution, do not allow for negative prices for the underlying contract. If one were to create a pricing model to evaluate options on spreads, a more realistic assumption might be a normal distribution, which does allow for negative prices. Such a variation on the Black-Scholes model has been suggested in a paper prepared by Darrell Wilcox. This variation is reproduced in Appendix B.

❖ 17 ❖

Position Analysis

When a trader first enters an option market, his initial concern is usually finding strategies with sufficient profit potential to justify making a trade. As a trader becomes more actively involved in options, he finds that an increasingly greater portion of his time is spent analyzing the positions he has already taken. What are the risks to the position? What are the rewards? And what action should be taken if market conditions change either in the trader's favor or against him? Simple volatility spreads, directional spreads, or arbitrage strategies are relatively easy to analyze. As positions become more complex, the risks associated with the position may not be as easy to identify.

The first step in analyzing a position is to determine how the position will react to changing market conditions. One way to accomplish this is by looking at the total risk sensitivities of the position (delta, gamma, theta, vega, rho). Unfortunately, the risk sensitivities are only reliable under narrowly defined market conditions. Since it is often dramatic changes in market conditions about which a trader must be concerned, simply looking at the risk sensitivities rarely enables a trader to grasp fully the risks associated with a position. Moreover, most traders find it easier to interpret graphic information than a series of numbers. For all of these reasons, it is oftenuseful to graph a position's value under a variety of market conditions.

SOME SIMPLE EXAMPLES

Let's start with a simple position:[1]

Stock price = 99.00; Time to June expiration = 7 weeks
Volatility = 20%; Interest rate = 6%; Dividend = 0

Position	Option Price	Option Th. Val.	Option Delta	Option Imp. Vol.
long 10 June 95 calls	6.25	5.82	76	23.7
short 30 June 105 calls	1.63	1.08	26	24.5

The position is a typical ratio vertical call spread which we might take if we feel that implied volatility is too high, as it appears to be here. The total theoretical edge is:

$$-10 \times (6.25-5.82) + 30 \times (1.63-1.08) = +12.20$$

1. The analyses in this chapter were done using either the Black-Scholes model for stock options or the Black model for futures options.

While the position is currently delta neutral, we know that a ratio vertical spread has a negative gamma, positive theta, and negative vega. The gamma, theta, and vega sensitivities of the spread confirm this:

Option	Gamma	Theta	Vega
June 95 call	4.3	–.0344	.113
June 105 call	4.4	–.0278	.117
position totals	–89.0	+.4900	–2.380

The negative gamma is an indication that any large move in the underlying stock will hurt the position. This is shown in Figure 17-1a. Under current conditions, if the stock price begins to fall and we want to remain delta neutral, for each point decline in the stock price we will need to sell approximately 89 shares of stock (or take some similar negative delta action). If the stock begins to rise, for each point rise in the stock price, we will need to buy approximately 89 shares of stock.

A ratio vertical spread also has a positive theta, so the passage of time will help the position. This is confirmed in Figure 17-1b where the value of the position is shown as the time remaining to expiration grows shorter. Note that not only does the position's potential profit change as time passes, the risks associated with the position also change. As time passes the deltas of options tend to move away from 50, with the delta of in-the-money options moving towards 100 and the delta of out-of-the-money options

Figure 17-1a: Long 10 June 95 Calls @ 6.25
Short 30 June 105 Calls @ 1.63

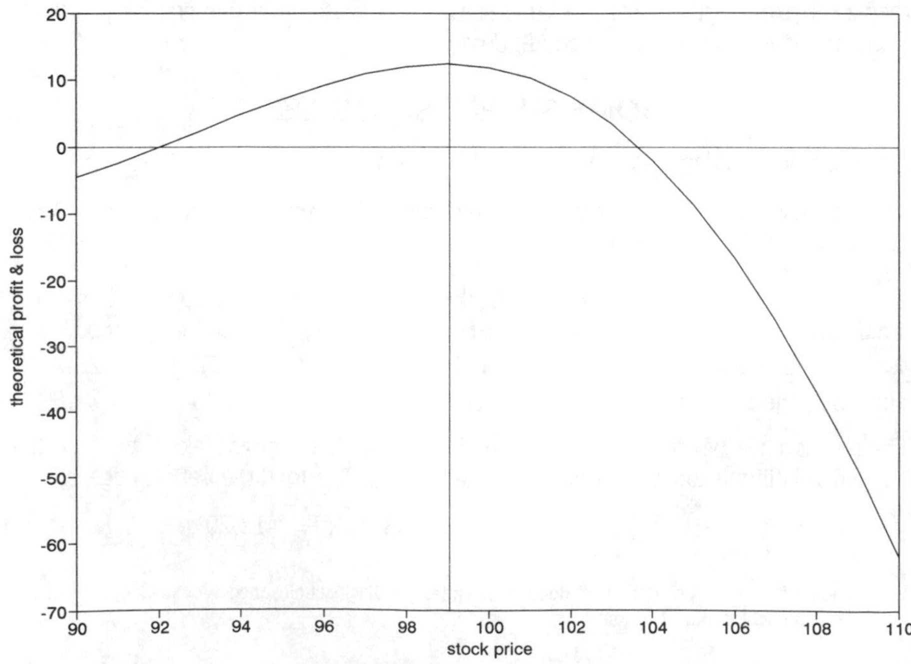

Figure 17-1b: Long 10 June 95 Calls @ 6.25
Short 30 June 105 Calls @ 1.63

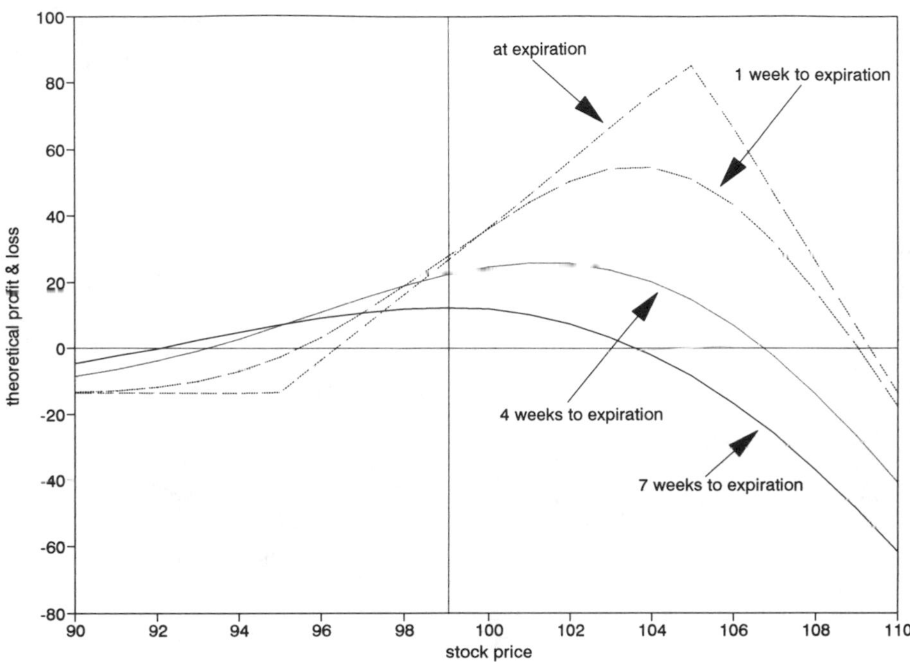

moving towards zero. The net effect is that with the stock price anywhere below 105 our delta position will be getting longer as time passes. If, however, the stock price rises above 105, the 95 call and the 105 call will be in-the-money, and the deltas of both options will move towards 100. This will cause our delta position to become shorter with the passage of time. This is shown in Figure 17-1b where the downward slope of the graph above 105 becomes more pronounced as time passes.

Gamma can also change as time passes. At-the-money options always have the highest gamma, and the gamma of an at-the-money option can increase rapidly as expiration approaches. As time passes note how the curvature of the position becomes more severe around the stock price of 105. If the stock should rise to 105 and remain there as expiration approaches, the position will take on increasingly greater gamma risk.

Since a ratio vertical spread has a negative vega, any rise in volatility will hurt the position, and any decline will help. The theoretical value of the position at various volatilities is shown in Figure 17-1c. Under current conditions the position has an implied volatility of approximately 25%, the volatility at which the position approximately breaks even, showing neither profit nor loss. (We can also approximate the implied volatility of the position by dividing the total theoretical edge of 12.20 by the vega of 2.38, and adding the result to the 20% volatility we are currently using.) If the stock price should change, the implied volatility of the position will also change. At a

Figure 17-1c: Long 10 June 95 Calls @ 6.25
Short 30 June 105 Calls @ 1.63

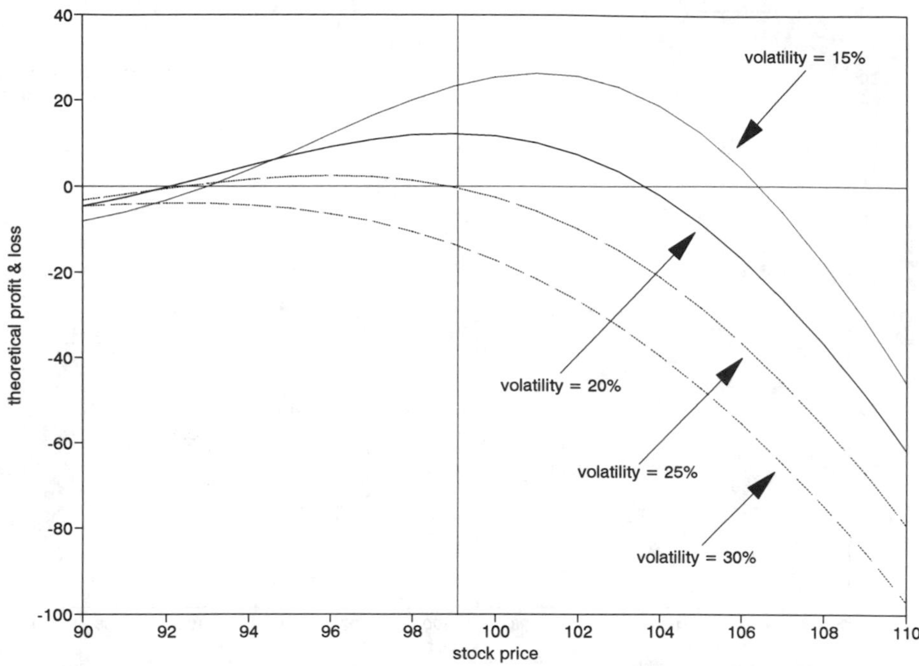

stock price of 104, the position has an implied volatility of approximately 20%. At a stock price of 106, the position has an implied volatility of approximately 15%. As the stock price rises, we hope for a lower and lower volatility.

The delta risk will also change as volatility changes since deltas move away from 50 as volatility falls and towards 50 as volatility rises. If volatility falls, the position will become delta positive; if volatility rises, the position will become delta negative. We can see this by looking at the slope of the graph at the current stock price of 99. With a volatility below 20%, the graph has a positive slope; with a volatility above 20%, the graph has a negative slope.

Let's look at another position:

Stock price = 100.00
Time to expiration: June = 7 weeks, September = 20 weeks
Volatility = 20%; Interest rate = 6%; Dividend = 0

Position	Option Price	Option Th. Val.	Option Delta	Option Imp. Vol.
long 20 June 105 calls	1.88	1.35	30	24.0
short 20 September 110 calls	3.13	2.22	30	24.1

This position is a diagonal spread, but with both options having equal deltas the position will tend to act like a short time spread. The total theoretical edge is:

$$-20 \times (1.88-1.35) + 20 \times (3.13-2.22) = +7.60$$

We know that a short time spread has a positive gamma, negative theta, and negative vega. The gamma, theta, and vega sensitivities of the spread are:

Option	Gamma	Theta	Vega
June 105 call	4.3	−.0308	.128
September 110 call	2.8	−.0200	.216
position totals	+30.0	−.2160	−.760

The positive gamma means that movement in the underlying stock price is working in our favor, as shown in Figure 17-2a. As the stock price rises, our delta position is becoming longer, and as the stock price falls, it is becoming shorter. If we want to stay delta neutral we will need to sell stock as the price rises, and buy stock as the price falls.

Since a positive gamma is always accompanied by a negative theta, the passage of time will work against us, as shown in Figure 17-2b. Under current conditions, for each day that passes with no movement in the underlying stock price, our position will deteriorate by approximately .216. We can also see that with the stock below 105 the slope of the graph becomes negative as time passes, reflecting the fact that our delta

Figure 17-2a: Long 20 June 105 Calls @ 1.88
Short 20 September 110 Calls @ 3.13

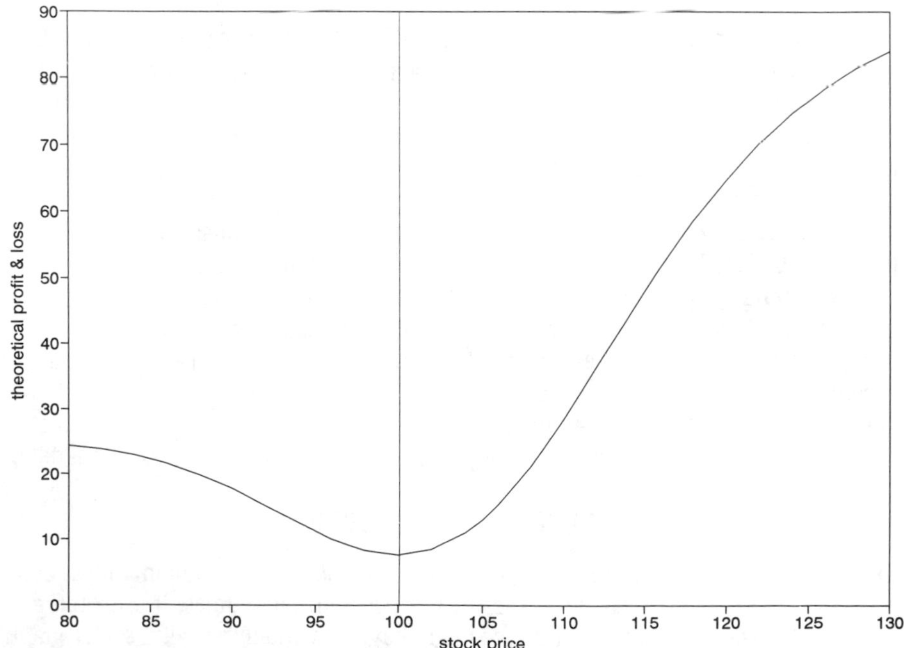

Figure 17-2b: Long 20 June 105 Calls @ 1.88
Short 20 September 110 Calls @ 3.13

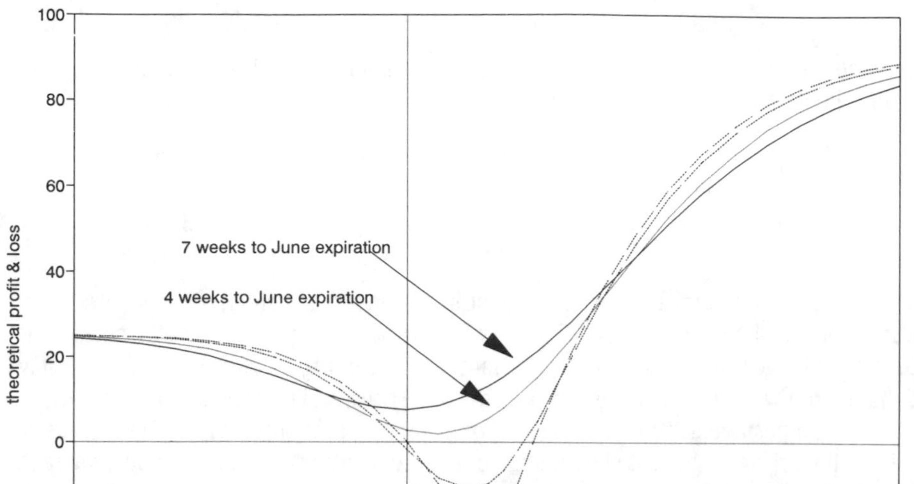

position is becoming shorter with the passage of time. If the stock price should rise above 105, our delta position becomes longer with the passage of time. At June expiration we want the stock to be as far away from 105 as possible.

As the stock price moves toward 105, the curvature of the position also becomes more severe, reflecting the fact that the gamma of an at-the-money option increases with the passage of time.

In Figure 17-2c we can see how the position's value declines (rises) with rising (falling) volatility. The implied volatility of the position is just under 25%.

While changing volatility can affect the delta and gamma of a position, we can see in Figure 17-2c that in this spread the delta and gamma are generally unaffected by changes in volatility. Regardless of volatility, the delta position remains neutral at the current stock price of 100, becomes shorter anywhere below 100, and becomes longer anywhere above 100. Moreover, the graphs all have the same general shape, reflecting the fact that the position's gamma is not particularly sensitive to changes in volatility.

GRAPHING A POSITION

Every trader should know what a graph of his position looks like, if not in minute detail at least the approximate characteristics of the position. Sometimes, if a computer is unavailable to do the graphing for us, we might have to mentally visualize such a graph.

Figure 17-2c: Long 20 June 105 Calls @ 1.88
Short 20 September 110 Calls @ 3.13

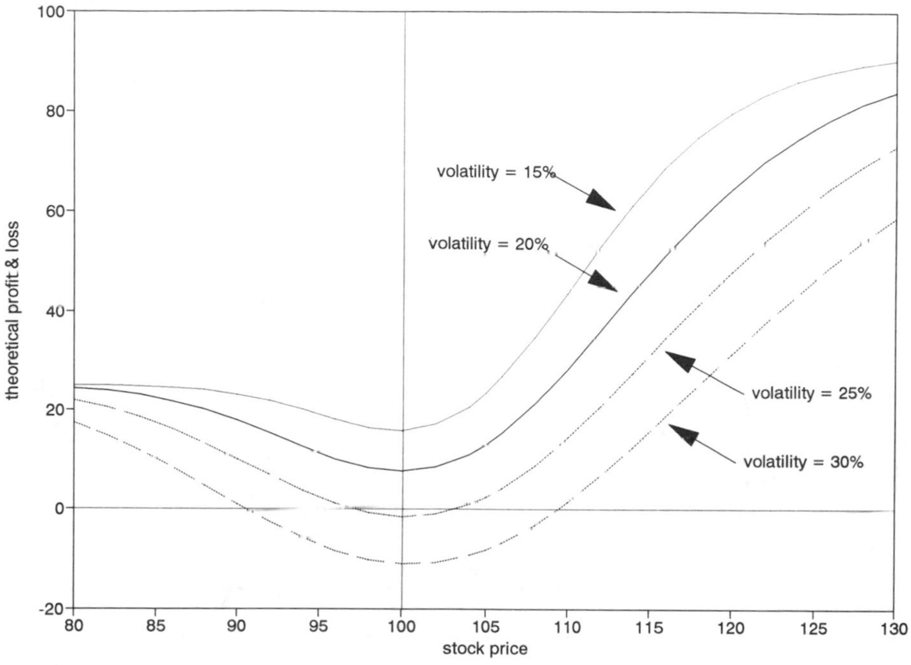

From the foregoing examples, perhaps we can formulate some rules which will enable us to do this.

Using, as before, a grid where the horizontal axis (x-axis) represents movement in the underlying contract and the vertical axis (y-axis) represents profit or loss, we can interpret the theoretical edge, delta, and gamma as follows:

1. *Theoretical Edge*—The graph of a position with a positive theoretical edge will cross the current underlying price at a point above the zero profit & loss line. This is the first thing a trader should look for. When a trader is right about market conditions, he wants to know that his position will be profitable.

2. *Delta* (Figure 17-3a)—A positive delta is theoretically equivalent to a long position in the underlying contract. The graph of such a position will cross the current underlying price at an angle extending from the lower left to the upper right. A negative delta is theoretically equivalent to a short position in the underlying contract. The graph of this position will cross the current underlying price at an angle extending from the upper left to the lower right. The exact slope of the graph as it crosses the current underlying price is determined by the magnitude of the delta. As the delta position becomes larger, the slope becomes more severe; as the delta position becomes smaller, the slope becomes less severe. The graph of a

Figure 17-3a: Positive and Negative Delta (Slope)

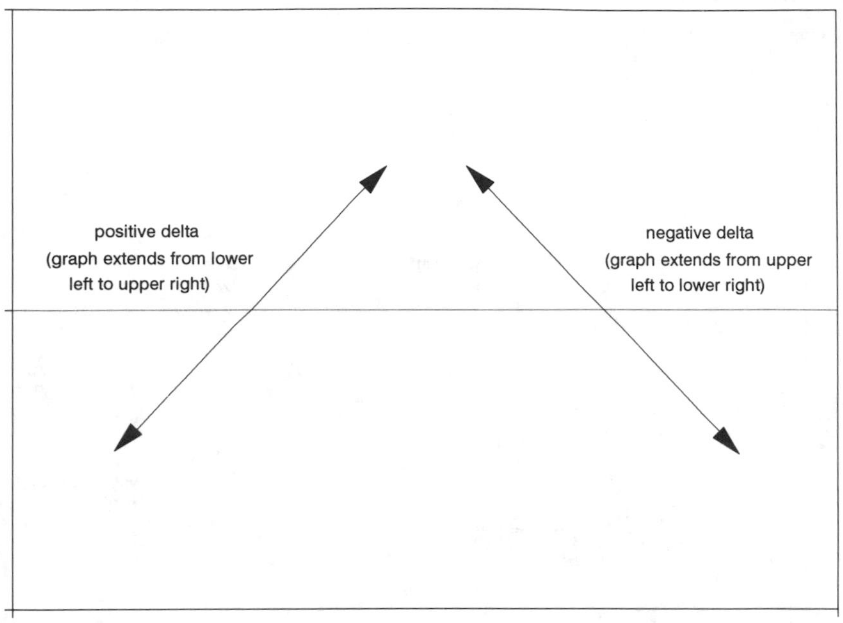

position which is delta neutral will be exactly horizontal as it crosses the current price of the underlying contract.

3. *Gamma* (Figure 17-3b)—A positive gamma position will begin to bend upward as the underlying price moves away from the current price in either direction. This reflects the fact that a positive gamma position likes movement. The graph of such a position will take on a generally convex shape (a smile). A negative gamma position will begin to bend downward as the underlying price moves away from the current price in either direction. This reflects the fact that a negative gamma position prefers for the market to sit still. The graph of such a position will take on a generally concave shape (a frown).

In order to complete a graph there is one other piece of information we need. Suppose the underlying contract makes such a large upward move that all calls go into-the-money and all puts go out-of-the-money, or such a large downward move that all puts go into-the-money and all calls go out-of-the-money. In other words, what will the graph of a position look like at the extreme right or left tail? We can determine this by adding up our *contract* or *lot position.* This is a measure of how many contracts a position will be naked long or short if the underlying market makes such a large move that either all calls or all puts act like underlying contracts.

On the upside (extreme right tail) all puts will collapse to zero while all calls will eventually act like long underlying contracts. The graph of a position which is long more

Figure 17-3b: Positive and Negative Gamma (Curvature)

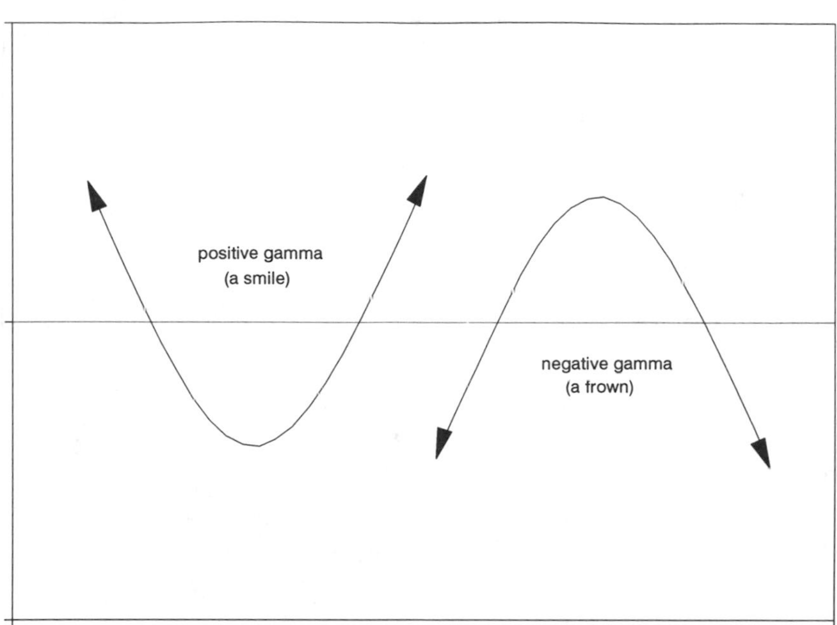

calls than short will angle up and to the right infinitely far (unlimited upside profit). The graph of a position which is short more calls than long will angle down and to the right infinitely far (unlimited upside risk). If the number of long and short calls are equal, or if the position consists only of puts, the position will eventually flatten out (limited upside risk/reward).

On the downside (extreme left tail) all calls will collapse to zero while all puts will eventually act like short underlying contracts. The graph of a position which is long more puts than short will angle up and to the left infinitely far (unlimited downside profit). The graph of a position which is short more puts than long will angle down and to the left infinitely far (unlimited downside risk). If the number of long and short puts are equal, or if the position consists only of calls, the position will eventually flatten out (limited downside risk/reward).

The value of a position may also change over time or as volatility conditions change. The changes will be determined by the theta and vega associated with the position:

4. *Theta* (Figure 17-3c)—As time passes a positive theta position will become more valuable, and the graph of such a position will shift upward. As time passes a negative theta position will become less valuable, and the graph will shift downward.

5. *Vega* (Figure 17-3d)—A positive vega position will be helped by increasing volatility and hurt by declining volatility. The graph of such a position will shift

Figure 17-3c: Positive and Negative Theta (Time Decay)

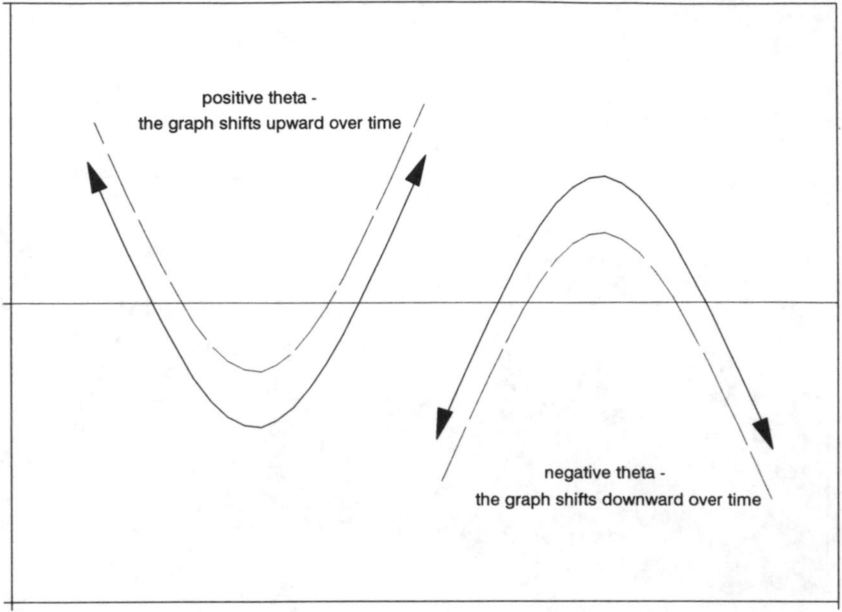

Figure 17-3d: Positive and Negative Vega (Volatility)

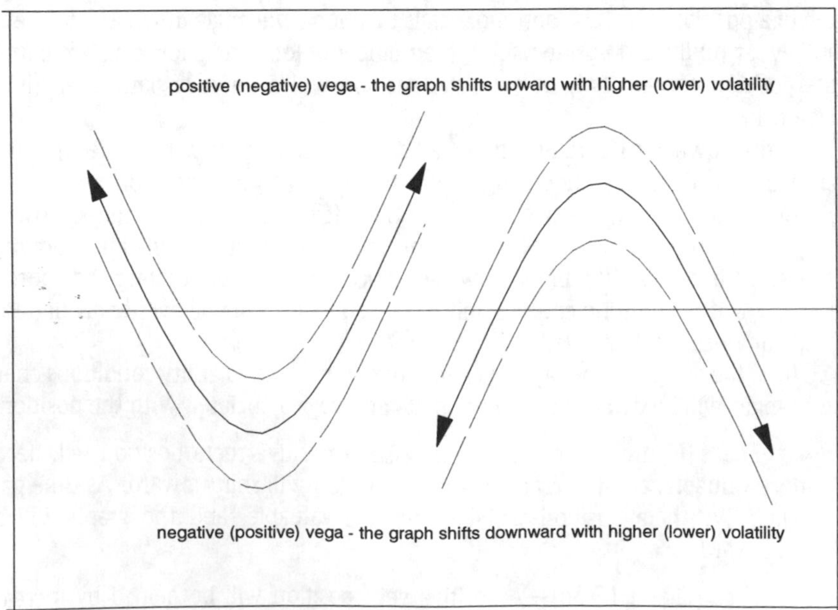

upward when volatility increases and downward when volatility decreases. A negative vega position will be hurt by increasing volatility and helped by declining volatility. The graph of this position will shift downward when volatility increases and upward when volatility decreases.

Note that time and volatility have similar effects on an option position. But unlike time, which can only move in one direction, volatility can either rise or fall. If a trader has a positive (negative) gamma position, he will necessarily have a negative (positive) theta position. He need only worry about one or the other, either gamma or theta. But a trader can have a positive or negative gamma position and still be concerned with volatility. A positive gamma position can still be hurt by a rise in volatility (e.g., a short time spread), while a negative gamma position can still be hurt by a decline in volatility (e.g., a long time spread).

Let's try to put these graphing principles together to analyze a position.

Stock price = 98.75; Time to June expiration = 7 weeks
Volatility = 20%; Interest rate = 6%; Dividend = 0

Position	Option Price	Option Th. Val.	Option Delta	Option Imp. Vol.
long 20 June 105 calls	.75	1.02	25	17.6
short 20 June 95 puts	1.38	1.12	–25	22.1
short 10 stock contracts[2]				

Even though the position is delta neutral, it does not appear to fall into any easily recognized category. The calls appear to be underpriced and the puts appear to be overpriced, and the position combines trades in both these options. The total theoretical edge is:

$$20 \times (1.02-.75) + 20 \times (1.38-1.12) = +10.60$$

The sensitivities of the position are:

Option	Gamma	Theta	Vega
June 105 call	4.3	–.0270	.114
June 95 puts	4.4	–.0192	.115
position totals	–2.0	–.1560	–.020

First we ought to try to visualize what the graph of this position looks like. Since the position has a positive theoretical edge of 10.60, it will cross the current stock price of 98.75 at a point 10.60 above the zero P&L line. The position is delta neutral, so the graph will be exactly horizontal at this point. The position is also very close to gamma neutral at this point, so the graph will have no curvature. This means that it is bending neither upward (concave) nor downward (convex).

2. Since the number of shares in an underlying stock contract varies from market to market, we simply express the underlying in terms of contracts. In U.S. markets where one option contract typically controls 100 shares of stock, this position would be short 1,000 shares.

To complete the graph we need the upside and downside contract position. If the market makes a large upward move, all the puts will eventually collapse to zero while the calls will act like long underlying contracts. In our example the 20 long calls will act like 20 long stock contracts. These will be partially offset by the actual 10 short underlying contracts, but the total will still be an upside contract position which is long 10. If the market moves up far enough the position will take on a slope of +10. For each point the stock price rises, the position will gain ten points in value.

If the market makes a large downward move, all the calls will eventually collapse to zero while the puts will act like short underlying contracts. Since a short put is a long market position, our short 20 puts will act like 20 long stock contracts. These will be partially offset by the actual 10 short underlying contracts, but the total will still be a downside contract position which is long 10 contracts. If the market moves down far enough the position will take on a slope of +10. For each point the stock price falls, the position will lose ten points in value.

The initial characteristics of our spread are shown in Figure 17-4a.

We know that the characteristics of a position are likely to change as market conditions change. How might our position change as time passes? Since deltas move away from 50 with the passage of time, if no movement takes place in the underlying stock, the deltas of both the 95 put and 105 call (currently at –25 and +25) will move

Figure 17-4a: Long 20 June 105 Calls @ .75
Short 20 June 95 Puts @1.38
Short 10 Stock Contracts @98.75

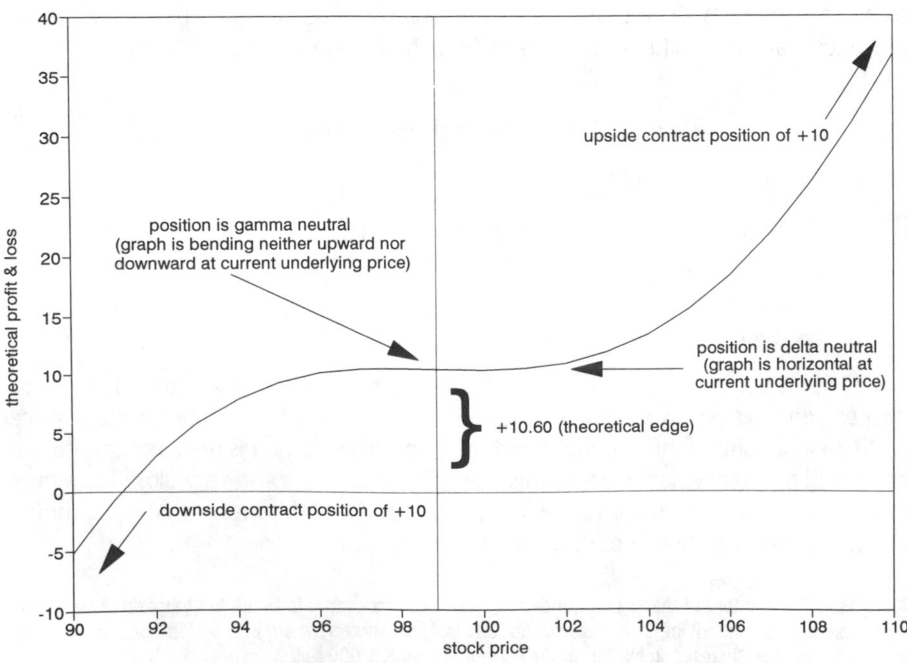

towards zero. This means our position will act more and more like a position which is naked short 10 stock contracts. Therefore, as time passes the slope of the graph is becoming more and more negative between the exercise prices of 95 and 105 (Figure 17-4b).

What about changes in the gamma with respect to stock price movement? If the stock price remains near the current price of 98.75, the gamma (curvature) of the position remains near zero. As the price moves toward either the 95 or 105 exercise price, the position takes on greater gamma characteristics as time passes. As the stock approaches 95 the position begins to act like a short straddle (negative gamma), and as it approaches 105 the position begins to act like a long straddle (positive gamma).

Since the gamma of our position at the current price of 98.75 is very close to zero, we might expect the theta to also be close to zero. In this case the theta is actually –.1560. This means the position is becoming less valuable each day. The reason is that the sale of stock has resulted in a cash credit, a credit on which we can earn interest. As time passes the amount of interest which we expect to earn declines, so the expected profit also declines. This would not be the case if the underlying instrument were a futures contract, since the sale of a futures contract does not result in a cash inflow, and consequently no interest can be earned. The theta of such a position would therefore be close to zero.

Figure 17-4b: Long 20 June 105 Calls @ .75
Short 20 June 95 Puts @1.38
Short 10 Stock Contracts @98.75

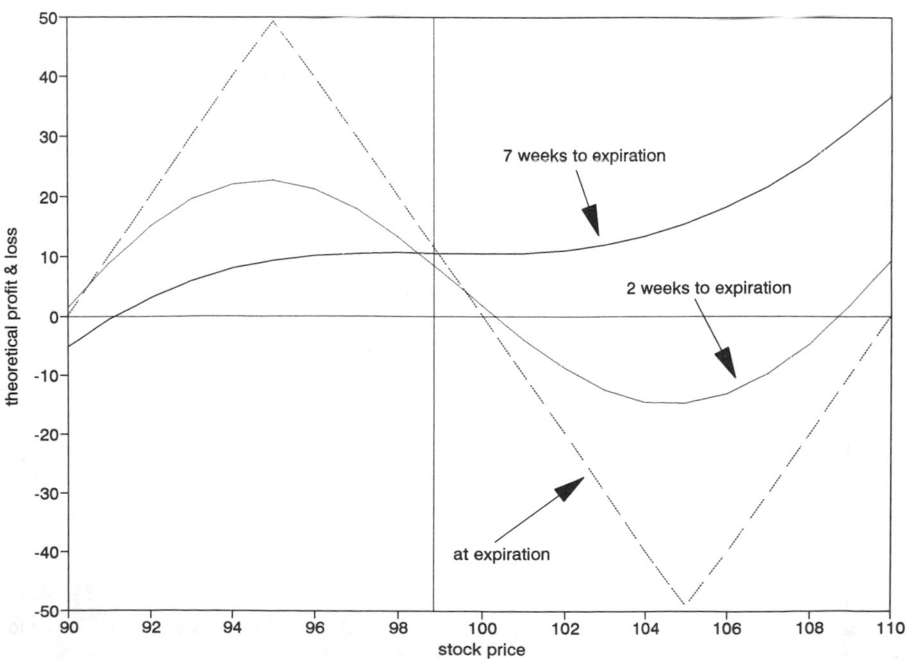

Changes in volatility will also affect the characteristics of the position. Falling volatility is similar to the passage of time. All deltas will move away from 50, and the total delta position will become shorter around the current price of 98.75. If volatility rises all deltas will move towards 50, and the total delta position will become longer. As volatility rises (falls), the position looks more and more like a position which is naked long (short) 10 stock contracts (Figure 17-4c).

Regardless of changes in volatility, the gamma will stay close to zero near the midpoint price of 100. But as we move towards 95 or 105 the gamma begins to increase as either the 95 put or 105 call becomes more and more at-the-money. At the same time the gamma of an at-the-money option falls as volatility rises and rises as volatility falls. The result is that in a low-volatility market any move away from 100 can cause the gamma risk to increase very quickly, becoming negative as the stock price moves toward 95 and positive as the stock price moves toward 105.

Finally, the contract position remains the same, regardless of the passage of time or changes in volatility. If the market makes a big move, rising far above 105 or falling far below 95, we still have the same contract position of +10 (long 10 underlying contracts).

This last example illustrates an important aspect of spreading. Many traders, in addition to focusing on delta neutral strategies, will try to construct positions which are

Figure 17-4c: Long 20 June 105 Calls @ .75
Short 20 June 95 Puts @1.38
Short 10 Stock Contracts @98.75

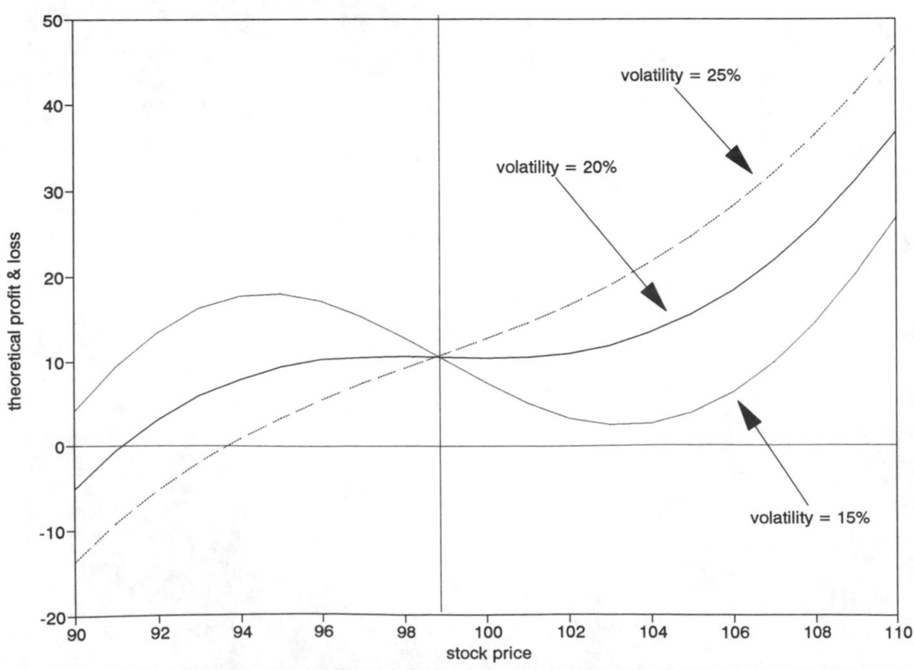

also gamma neutral or vega neutral. Such strategies may be sensible if a trader is concerned with a move in the underlying contract, or with a change in volatility. But a trader should not make the assumption that if he is delta neutral, gamma neutral, and vega neutral, there is nothing that can go wrong. Even if a position has a positive theoretical edge and all the risk sensitivities are small, a profit is not necessarily certain. A position is only delta neutral, or gamma neutral, or vega neutral if the theoretical pricing model is itself correct, and if all the information which the trader has fed into the model is also correct. If any of these assumptions are wrong, the values generated by the theoretical pricing model are also likely to be wrong. As a result, the trader might find that a position which initially appears to be neutral in terms of a risk sensitivity is in fact not neutral at all.

A COMPLEX POSITION

Each of our previous examples consisted of only two different options. A more complex position may consist of options at several different exercise prices. Consider the position shown in Figure 17-5.

We can determine many of the characteristics of this position simply by looking at the total sensitivities. Since the position has a positive gamma, negative theta, and positive vega, it will initially act like a backspread. In addition, we can see that the

Figure 17-5

Stock price = 202.50; Time to June expiration = 6 weeks; Volatility = 24.0%
Interest rate = 6.00%; Dividend = 0

June Contract	Position	Price	Th. Value	Delta	Gamma	Theta	Vega	Imp. Vol.
190 call		15.50	15.50	82	1.6	–.077	.18	24.0
195 call	–23	11.63	11.80	72	2.0	–.088	.23	23.3
200 call	+55	8.25	8.63	61	2.3	–.094	.26	22.6
205 call	–35	5.75	6.06	49	2.4	–.094	.27	22.9
210 call	–20	4.00	4.08	37	2.3	–.086	.26	23.7
215 call	+41	2.63	2.63	27	2.0	–.074	.23	24.0
190 put	–42	1.63	1.70	–18	1.6	–.046	.18	23.6
195 put	+85	2.75	2.95	–28	2.0	–.056	.23	23.1
200 put	+8	4.5	4.76	–39	2.3	–.062	.26	23.0
205 put	–18	6.88	7.15	–51	2.4	–.060	.27	23.0
210 put		10.00	10.13	–63	2.3	–.052	.26	23.5
215 put	–30	13.75	13.65	–73	2.0	–.039	.23	24.5
stock	–18			100				

	Stock	Calls	Puts	Delta	Gamma	Theta	Vega	P&L
totals:	–18	+18	+3	–277	+50.5	–2.244	+6.10	+18.82

downside contract position is net short 21 (short 18 stock contracts, long 3 puts) while the upside contract position is flat (short 18 stock contracts, long 18 calls). The position has unlimited downside reward and limited upside risk/reward. Based on these characteristics, the position can essentially be described as a put backspread. The theoretical graph of the position under current conditions is shown by the solid line in Figure 17-5a.

In Figure 17-5a we also see how the position will change as time passes. Because the trader is long a large number of June 195 puts and June 200 calls, as expiration approaches the position will act more and more like a long June 195/200 strangle. Although the position is now slightly delta short, with the stock at its current price of 202.50, the June 200 calls will tend to dominate, causing the delta position to become increasingly long as time passes. Should the stock drop below 195, the June 195 puts will tend to dominate, and the delta will become increasingly short with the passage of time. Consequently, as time passes the gamma of the position will become very large with the stock price between 195 and 200. The total delta and gamma of the position as time passes is shown in Figures 17-5b and 17-5c.

Figure 17-5d shows the sensitivity of the position to a change in volatility. As we would expect, any increase in volatility will help the position and any decline in volatility will hurt. Even if we increase or decrease volatility by 20%, to 30% or 18%, the shape of the position remains essentially the same. While the delta and gamma will change with changes in volatility, these numbers are not as sensitive to a change in

Figure 17-5a

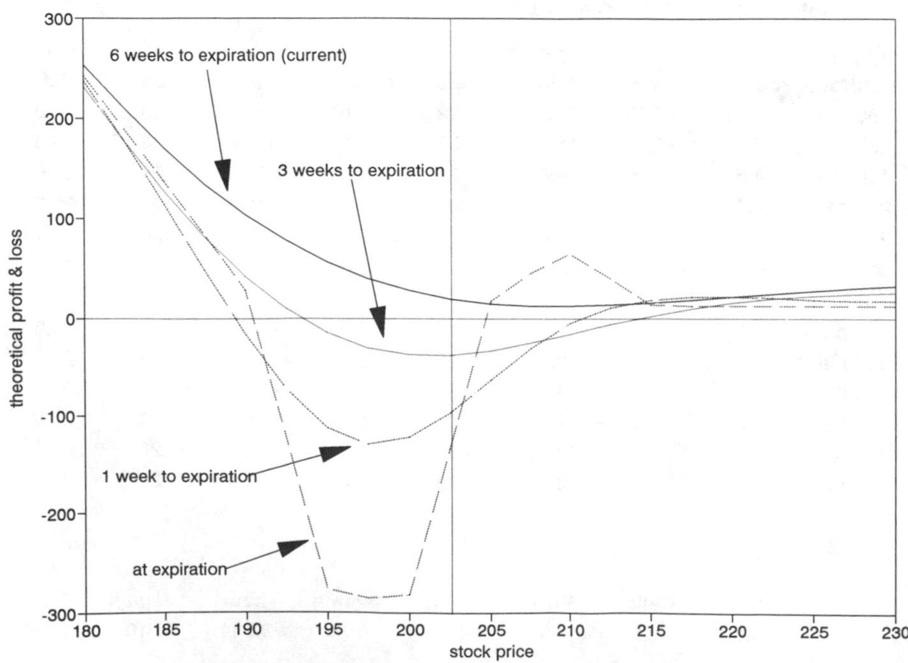

Figure 17-5b

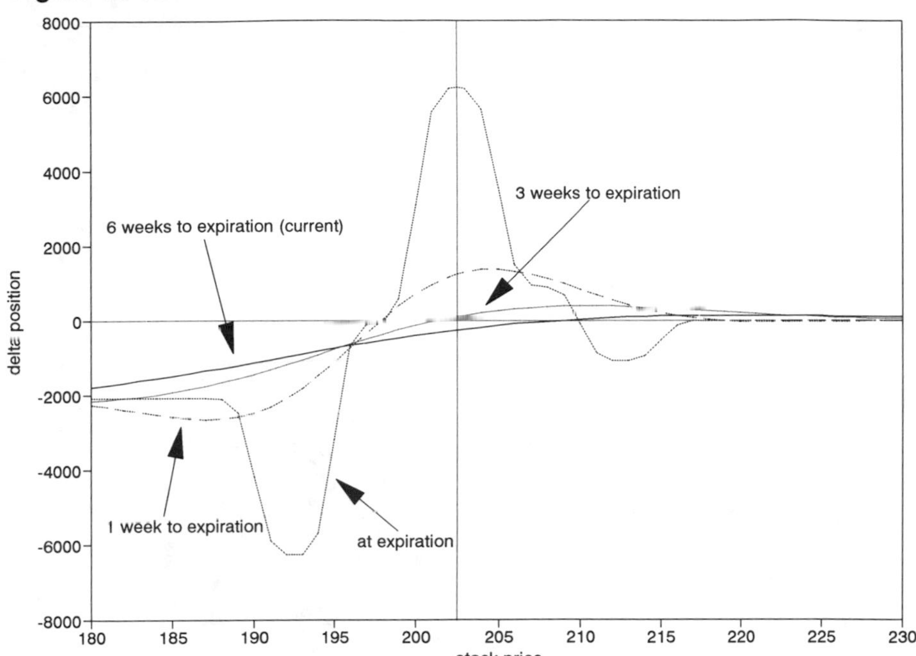

Figure 17-5c

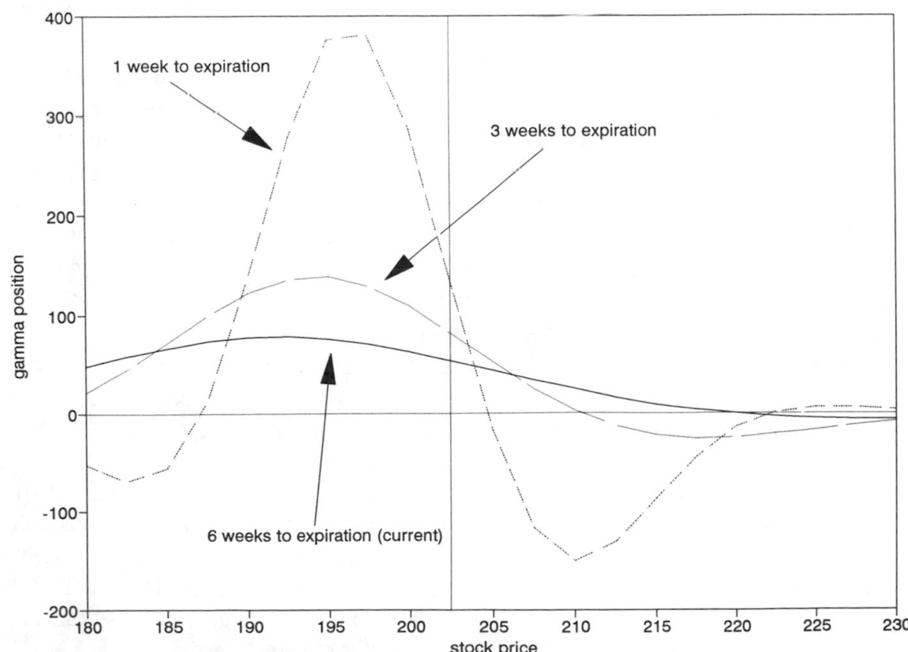

Figure 17-5d

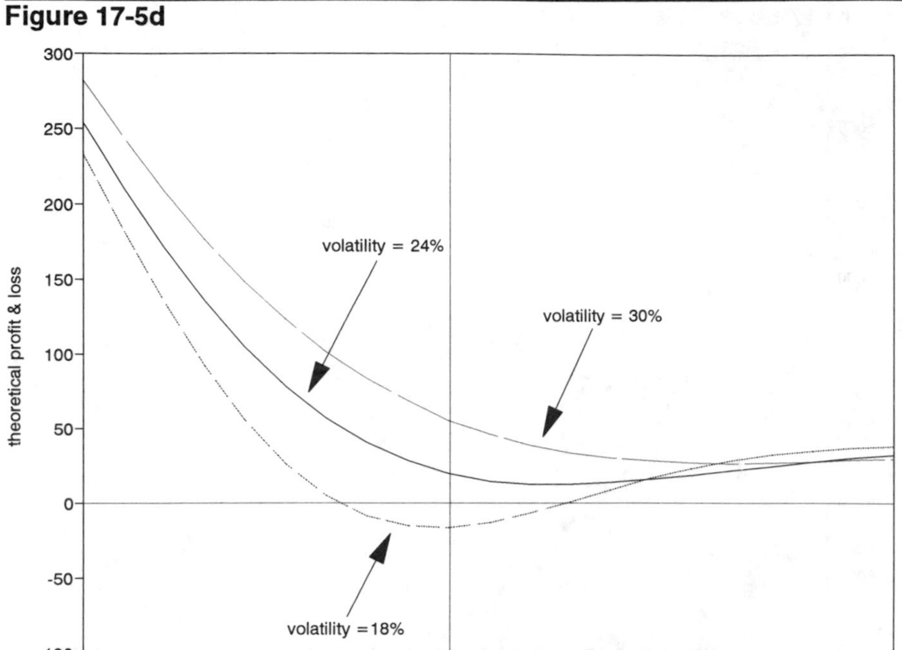

volatility as they are to the passage of time. The total delta and gamma of the position as volatility changes is shown in Figures 17-5e and 17-5f.

A trader with this position must be concerned with a significant decline in volatility. He will be especially worried about a slow decline in the market over time. Each day that passes is costing him 2.244 (the theta) in potential profit, and this number will accelerate as time passes. If several weeks should pass with little movement in the stock price, he will come under increasing pressure to reduce his theta risk. If he decides to take some protective action, he will have to sell some options, either calls or puts. If he considers a large move in the underlying stock a possibility, he may not want to sell calls since this will leave him net short contracts on the upside. This will probably lead him to sell off some of the puts which he is long, either the 195 or 200 puts.

Up to now we have not considered the risk associated with a change in interest rates or, in the case of stock options, dividends. While these risks are usually small with respect to the other risks, if the position is large enough we might want to consider how a change in interest rates or dividends will impact the position.

The sale of 18 stock contracts has created a cash credit for this trader, and the interest earned on this credit will be a part of his profit. Assuming that he is subject to a floating interest rate, any increase in rates will help, since he will earn more on his cash credit, and any decline in interest rates will hurt, since he will earn less on his cash credit. We can estimate the impact on the position of a 1% change in interest rates by calculating the interest earned to expiration at the current stock price:

Figure 17-5e

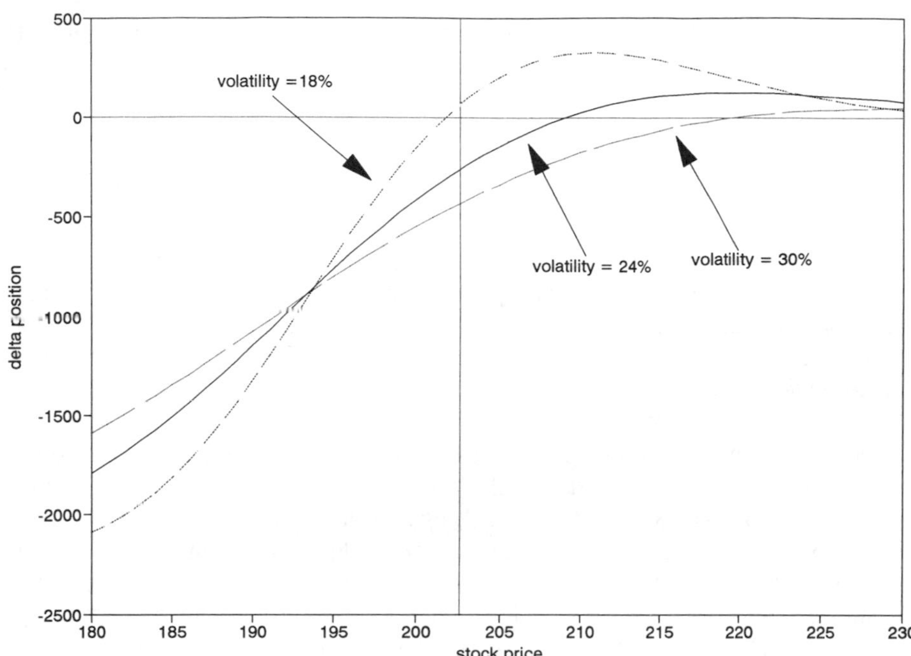

Figure 17-5f

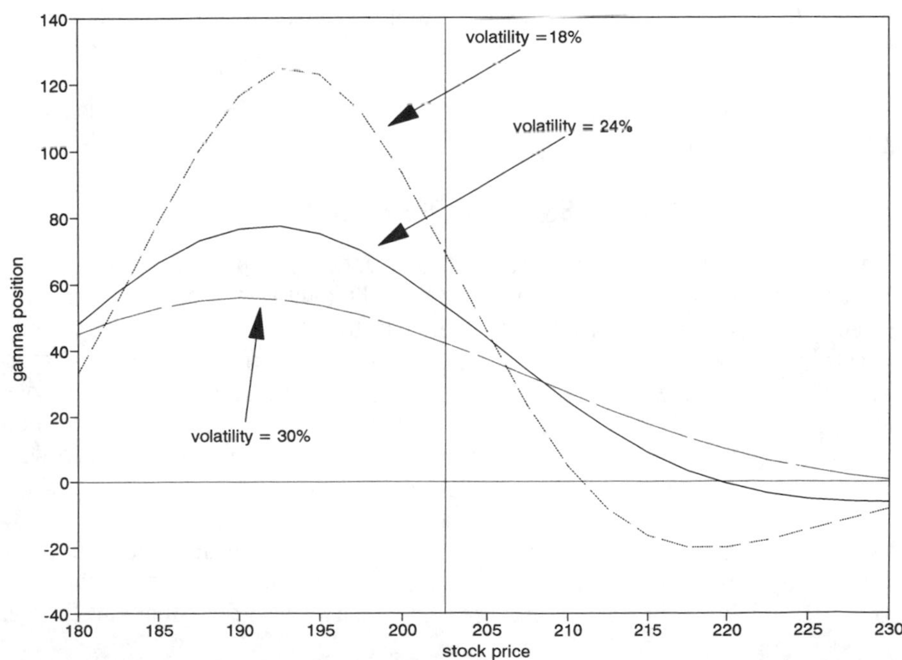

$$1\% \times 42/365 \times 202.50 = .233$$

Since the trader is short 18 stock contracts, the total impact of a 1% change in interest rates is:

$$.233 \times 18 = 4.19$$

For each percentage point increase in interest rates, his position will increase in value by approximately 4.19; for each percentage point decline in interest rates, his position will decline in value by approximately 4.19. If interest rates were to immediately drop from 6% to 4%, the position's potential profit would drop by approximately 8.38.

The underlying stock for this position currently pays no dividend, but the trader may want to consider the possibility that the company will decide to start paying a dividend. If the company decides to pay a dividend prior to June expiration, the trader, as a borrower of stock, will be required to pay this dividend amount to the stock lender. Since he is short 18 stock contracts, for each point increase in the dividend, the trader will lose 18 times the dividend in potential profit. If the company decides to pay a dividend of 2.00, the trader's position will be reduced in value by approximately 36.00.

If the trader believes that the company might in fact decide to pay a dividend prior to June expiration, or if he feels that interest rates could fall significantly, he will want to take some action to reduce his risk. Since the risk results from the short stock position, he can eliminate most of his risk by eliminating the 18 short stock contracts. Assuming that the trader wants to maintain the same delta position, he can accomplish this by buying back the short stock and replacing it with either deeply in-the-money options (buy deeply in-the-money puts or sell deeply in-the-money calls), or by selling synthetic stock contracts (sell calls and buy puts at the same exercise price). The former strategy would be the same as executing a three-way; the latter strategy would be the same as executing a conversion.

The sensitivity of the position to a change in interest rates and dividends is shown in Figures 17-5g and 17-5h.

FUTURES OPTION POSITIONS

The foregoing positions have all consisted of stock options, but delta, gamma, and vega characteristics are similar whether a trader is dealing with stock or futures options. Except for the effect of interest rates and dividends, the analyses of the positions would be essentially the same for futures options. While futures options are not subject to dividend considerations, nor are they as sensitive to changes in interest rates as stock options, there is an additional dimension to the analysis of a futures option position because the relationship between futures months is often less well defined than with stock options. For example, consider the position in Figure 17-6.

This is typical of the type of position an active trader often ends up with: a seemingly disjointed collection of options and underlying contracts which cannot be easily categorized. Nonetheless, it is important that the trader recognize the risks which the position currently presents, as well as those risks which might arise if conditions change.

Figure 17-5g

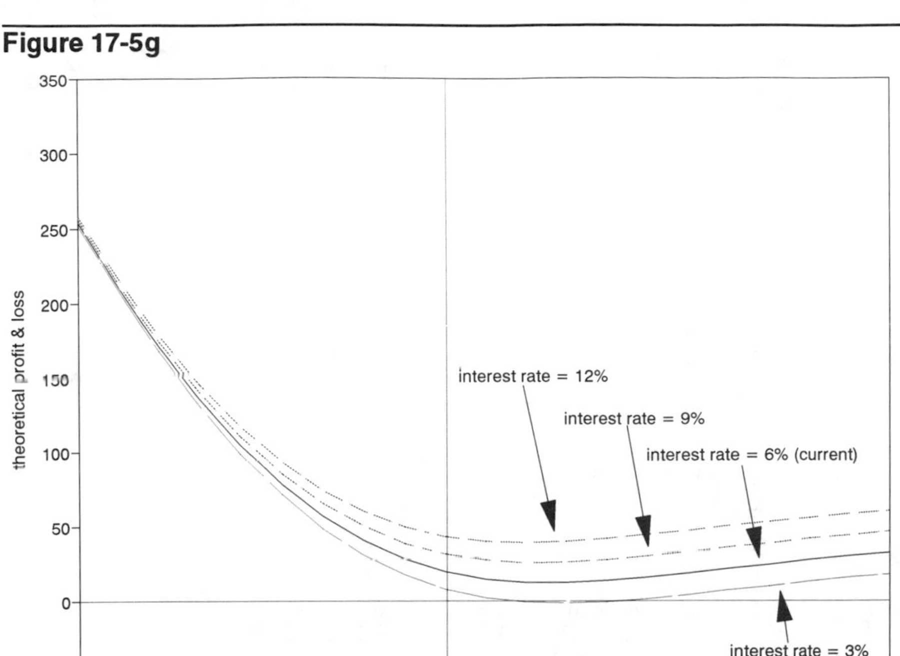

Figure 17-5h

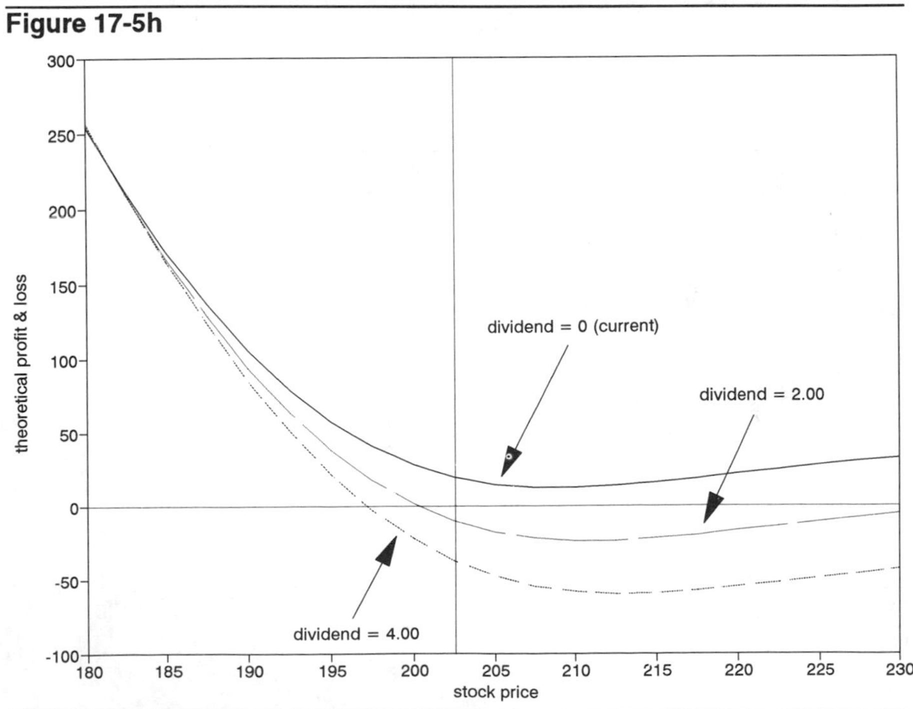

Figure 17-6

May futures = 49.40; Time to expiration = 5 weeks; Volatility = 15.0%: Interest = 6.00%

Contract	Position	Price	Theoretical Value	Delta	Gamma	Theta	Vega	Implied Volatility	Implied Delta
46 call	–28	3.46	3.44	93.5	5.1	–.0033	.018	16.03	92.3
47 call		2.56	2.55	85.8	9.5	–.0067	.033	15.37	85.3
48 call	–39	1.76	1.76	73.5	14.1	–.0103	.049	15.01	73.5
49 call	+36	1.10	1.12	57.5	17.0	–.0126	.059	14.68	57.7
50 call	+156	.62	.65	40.4	16.8	–.0125	.059	14.53	40.1
51 call	–135	.32	.34	25.2	13.9	–.0104	.049	14.61	24.6
52 call	–15	.15	.16	13.9	9.6	–.0072	.034	14.72	13.4
53 call	–60	.07	.07	6.8	5.7	–.0043	.020	15.15	7.0
54 call		.03	.03	2.9	2.88	–.0022	.010	15.46	3.3
46 put		.08	.06	–5.9	5.1	–.0039	.018	16.05	–7.2
47 put	–114	.17	.16	–13.6	9.5	–.0071	.033	15.26	–14.0
48 put	+41	.36	.37	–25.9	14.1	–.0105	.049	14.84	–25.7
49 put	–93	.70	.72	–41.9	17.0	–.0126	.059	14.64	–41.8
50 put	+36	1.21	1.24	–59.0	16.8	–.0124	.059	14.42	–59.5
51 put		1.91	1.93	–74.2	13.9	–.0101	.049	14.59	–74.8
52 put	–24	2.74	2.74	–85.5	9.6	–.0068	.034	14.87	–85.7
53 put		3.65	3.65	–92.7	5.7	–.0037	.020	15.18	–92.4
54 put		4.61	4.60	–96.5	2.8	–.0014	.010	15.99	–95.6
futures	–28			100.0					

July futures = 49.85; Time to expiration = 13 weeks; Volatility = 16.0%; Interest = 6.00%

Contract	Position	Price	Theoretical Value	Delta	Gamma	Theta	Vega	Implied Volatility	Implied Delta
46 call		4.10	4.10	84.0	5.7	–.0043	.057	15.94	84.0
47 call		3.29	3.32	77.0	7.3	–.0058	.072	15.60	77.5
48 call	+15	2.56	2.62	68.6	8.7	–.0071	.086	15.35	69.2
49 call		1.93	2.01	59.2	9.6	–.0080	.095	15.20	59.5
50 call		1.40	1.49	49.3	9.9	–.0084	.098	15.03	49.2
51 call	–35	.99	1.08	39.7	9.6	–.0082	.095	15.05	38.9
52 call	90	.67	.76	30.8	8.8	–.0075	.087	14.98	29.5
53 call	–45	.45	.52	23.0	7.6	–.0065	.075	15.12	21.6
54 call	+111	.30	.34	16.6	6.2	–.0054	.062	15.34	15.5
46 put		.31	.31	–14.6	5.7	–.0049	.057	15.99	–14.5
47 put		.48	.51	–21.5	7.3	–.0063	.072	15.57	–21.0
48 put	–66	.74	.79	–29.9	8.7	–.0074	.086	15.38	–29.3
49 put	+174	1.09	1.17	–39.3	9.6	–.0081	.095	15.17	–39.0
50 put	+8	1.55	1.64	–49.2	9.9	–.0083	.098	15.05	–49.4
51 put	+28	2.12	2.21	–58.8	9.6	–.0080	.095	15.02	–59.6
52 put	–21	2.79	2.88	–67.7	8.8	–.0072	.087	15.00	–69.0
53 put	–30	3.55	3.62	–75.5	7.6	–.0060	.075	15.07	–77.0
54 put	+15	4.38	4.43	–81.9	6.2	–.0047	.062	15.20	83.3
futures	+6			100.0					

Totals	Futures	Calls	Puts	Delta	Gamma	Theta	Vega	Theoretical P & L	Implied Delta
May	–28	–85	–154	+382.5	–1526.2	+1.1205	–5.357	+3.54	+484.4
July	+6	+136	+108	–635.5	+2052.5	–1.7545	+20.346	+17.34	–726.7
All Months*	–22	+51	–46	–253.0	+526.3	–.6341	+14.989	+20.89	+242.3

* Totals may not sum exactly due to rounding.

Since we are analyzing a position which includes two different futures months, we will have to make some assumptions about the relationship between the two futures contracts. The simplest relationship is based on a constant cost of carry. The current spread of .45 (49.85 – 49.40) between the May and July futures months is based on this relationship, since:

$$56/365 \times 6\% \times 49.40 \approx .45$$

If the spread were based only on cost of carry, and interest rates remained constant at 6%, July futures would always be .92% (56/365 × 6%) greater than May futures. Unfortunately, many markets, particularly in energy and agricultural products, are subject to supply and demand forces which often distort the cost of carry relationship between futures months. For this reason, traders often choose to assume a fixed spread relationship when analyzing option positions in several different futures months. In our example, we will make the assumption that the spread between May and July futures is always .45.

We have also added the assumption that July futures will be slightly more volatile (16%) than May futures (15%). Even though these volatility assumptions seem to be slightly higher than the implied volatilities in the marketplace, the trader's volatility relationship between May and July is consistent with the marketplace's opinion where the July implied volatility seems to be slightly higher than the May implied volatility.

Figures 17-6a through 17-6f show the current characteristics of the position, as well as the characteristics under different time and volatility assumptions. At the current underlying price (May futures = 49.40, July futures = 49.85), the passage of time or any decline in volatility will hurt the position (negative theta, positive vega). But if the underlying market should either decline or rise several points, the passage of time will begin to help the position (Figure 17-6a). Even though the theta may become positive with a move of several points, the vega of this position always remains positive (Figure 17-6b). Regardless of underlying price, any increase (decline) in volatility will help (hurt) the position. The position acts like a long straddle with the underlying close to 50, but it acts like a long time spread with the underlying close to 46 or 53. This is typical of how difficult it can sometimes be to classify complex positions. If the position is large enough, even small changes in market conditions can cause the position to change its characteristics radically.

Note that if one were to look only at the delta and gamma, it might seem that the best thing which could happen to this trader would be a swift decline in the underlying market (negative delta, positive gamma). If, however, the decline is too violent, with the market falling five or six points, the trader will have to consider his net contract position. All calls will collapse to zero, but the net total of 46 puts which he is short will begin to act like long futures. These will be partially offset by the 22 futures which he is actually short. But the result will be a position which is net long 24 contracts, leaving the trader with unlimited downside risk. Of course, a violent upside move will never be a problem since the trader has an upside contract position which is net long 29 contracts (long 51 calls, short 22 futures).

Figure 17-6a

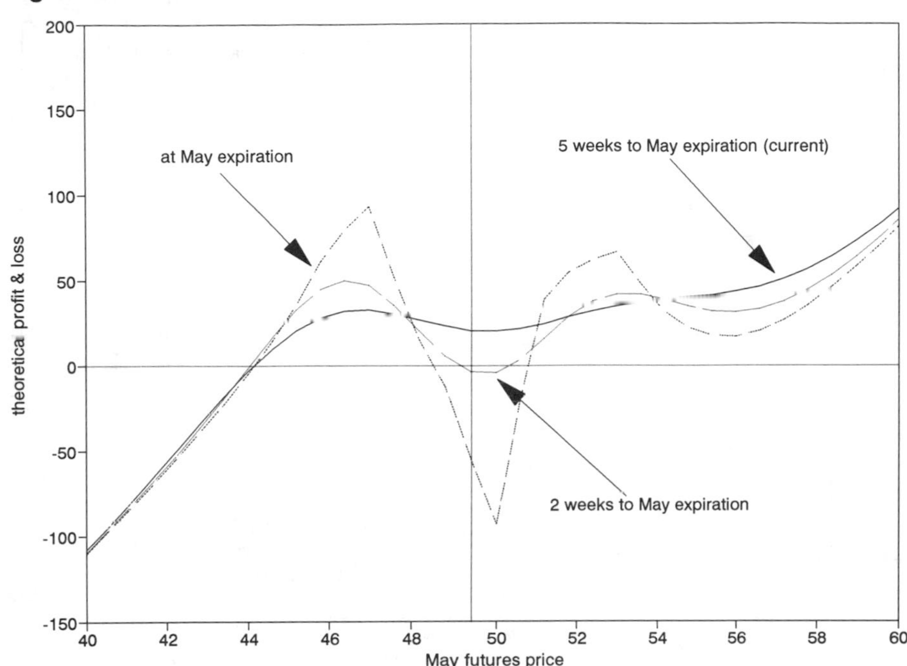

Figure 17-6b

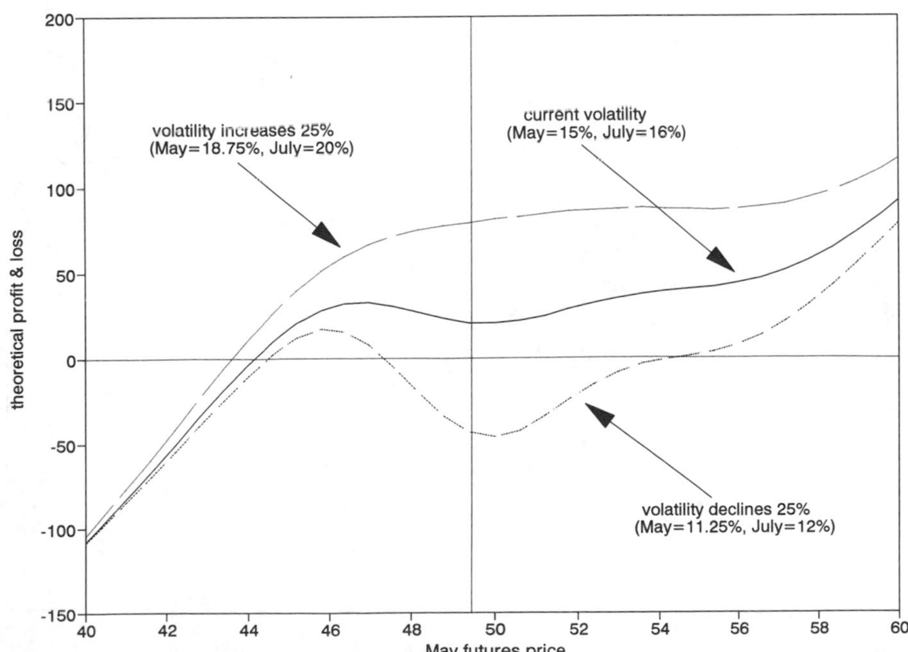

Figure 17-6c

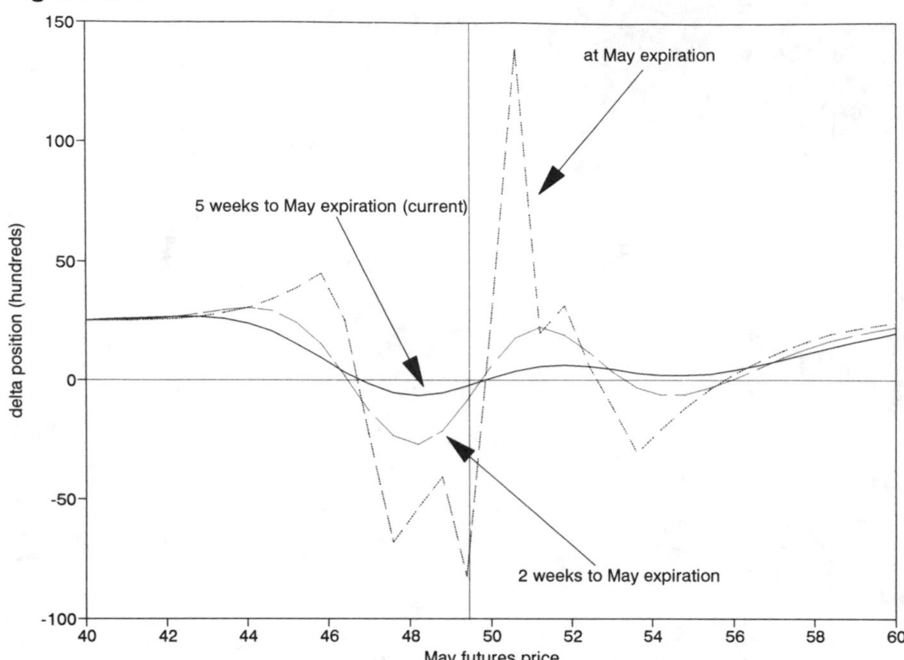

Figure 17-6d

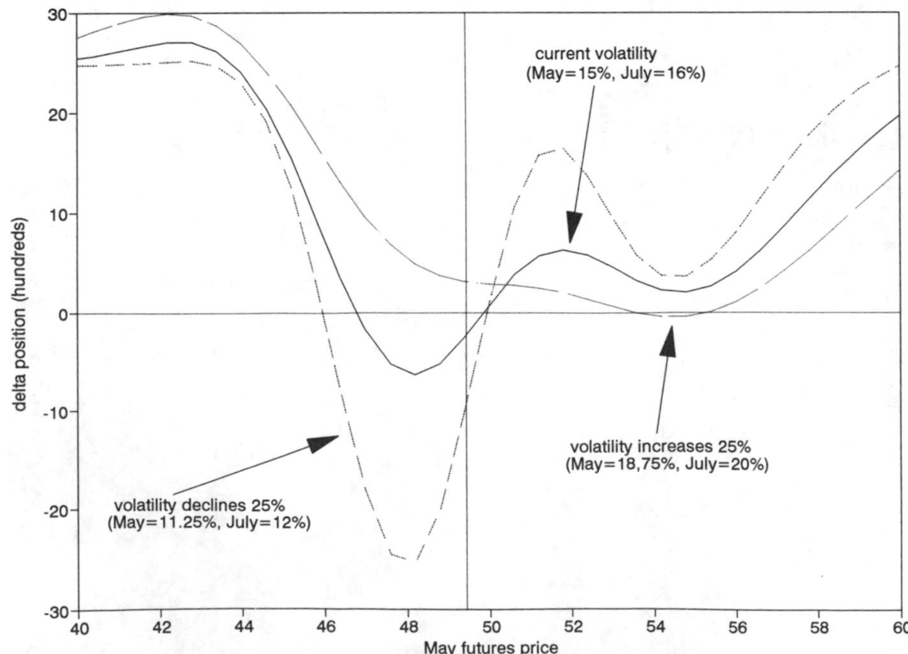

Figure 17-6e

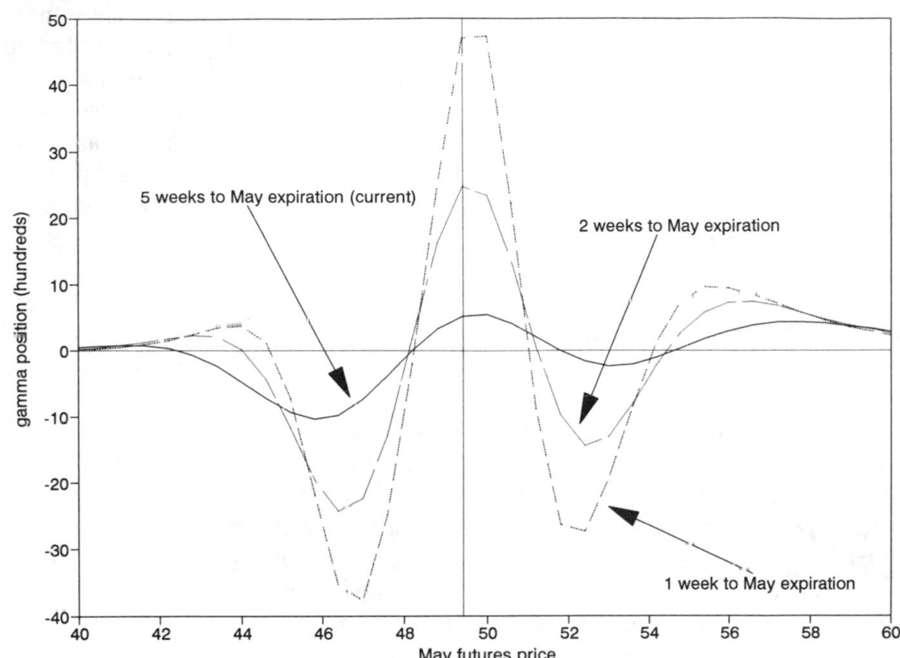

Figure 17-6f

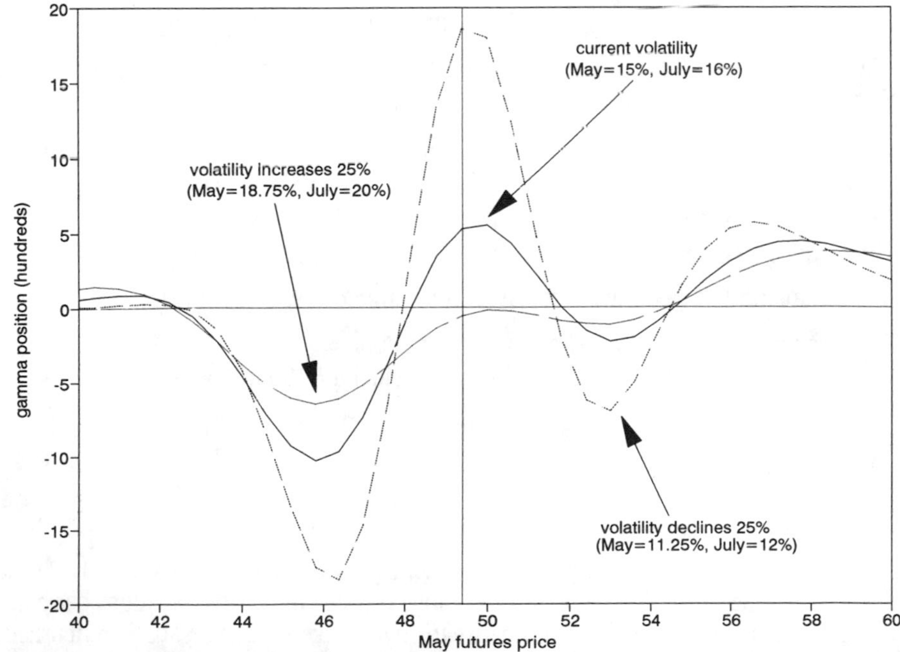

Figure 17-6 also gives the implied delta for the individual options as well as for the total position. This can sometimes be a useful number because a trader may want to take into consideration current market conditions when deciding how to hedge his position. In this example there is little difference between the trader's presumed delta position (-253) and his implied delta position (-242). But this is not always the case. If the trader's volatility assumption is dramatically different than the implied volatility in the marketplace, the presumed delta position might be significantly different than the implied delta position. Since no one can be sure what the right volatility is, no trader can be sure that his delta calculations are correct. Given this uncertainty, it is not uncommon among traders to hedge a position somewhere between the trader's own delta and the implied delta. If, for example, a trader calculated his delta position as +600, but found that the implied delta was +200, he might treat the position as if it had a delta of +400. If he wanted to get delta neutral, the trader might sell four underlying contracts.

We made the assumption that the spread between the July and May futures contracts will remain constant at .45. What will happen if the spread begins to widen or narrow? The total delta of –252 indicates that the trader would like a decline in the market. With a July delta of –635 and a May delta of +382, the trader would prefer July to go down faster than May. The ideal would be for July futures to decline and at the same time for May futures to rise, but any narrowing of the July/May spread should help the position. In futures equivalents, we might describe the position as being roughly short three July/May futures spreads, and short an additional 2½ July futures.

Finally, we might want to analyze a total position which consists of contracts which are not directly related, but which have somewhat similar characteristics. For example, suppose we have the ratio vertical call spread presented at the beginning of this chapter:

ABC stock price = 99.00; Time to June expiration = 7 weeks
Volatility = 20%; Interest rate = 6%; Dividend = 0

Position	**Option Price**	**Option Th. Val.**	**Option Delta**	**Option Imp. Vol.**
long 10 June 95 calls	6.25	5.82	76	23.7
short 30 June 105 calls	1.63	1.08	26	24.5

At the same time, suppose we also have a long strangle in a different stock:

XYZ stock price = 62.00; Time to July expiration = 11 weeks
Volatility = 23%; Interest rate = 6%; Dividend = .50 in 8 weeks

Position	**Option Price**	**Option Th. Val.**	**Option Delta**	**Option Imp. Vol.**
long 20 July 65 calls	1.38	1.52	36	21.6
long 20 July 60 puts	1.50	1.57	–34	22.3

If we combine these two positions, how might we analyze the overall risk? One possible method might be to look at the change in value of the two positions per point move in the underlying stocks. But because the two stocks are trading at different prices, and because they are expected to have different volatilities, a one-point move in ABC is unlikely to be matched by a one-point move in XYZ. To equate movement in ABC with movement in XYZ, it may be more useful to look at price changes in terms of standard deviations. For example, we can approximate a weekly standard deviation for each stock by dividing the annual volatility by $\sqrt{52}$, and multiplying this by the stock price:

$$\text{ABC:}\quad 20\%/7.2 \times 99 = 2.75$$
$$\text{XYZ:}\quad 23\%/7.2 \times 62 = 1.98$$

From these numbers we can generate graphs showing the position value given various standard deviation price changes in each underlying stock. This has been done in Figure 17-7a. Since we have a ratio vertical spread in ABC stock options and a long strangle in XYZ stock options, it should come as no surprise that the position will show its maximum theoretical profit when ABC sits still and XYZ makes a big move.

In order to complete our analysis we might want to look at the delta, gamma, theta, and vega of the position. But, again, with the stocks at different prices it may be difficult to equate the sensitivities of the ABC options with the sensitivities of the XYZ options. Since our total position is an intermarket spread, rather than looking at the delta, gamma, theta, and vega of the position, we might instead look at the $delta, $gamma, $theta, and $vega sensitivities introduced in Chapter 16. These sensitivities are shown in Figures 17-7b through 17-7e.[3]

Figure 17-7a

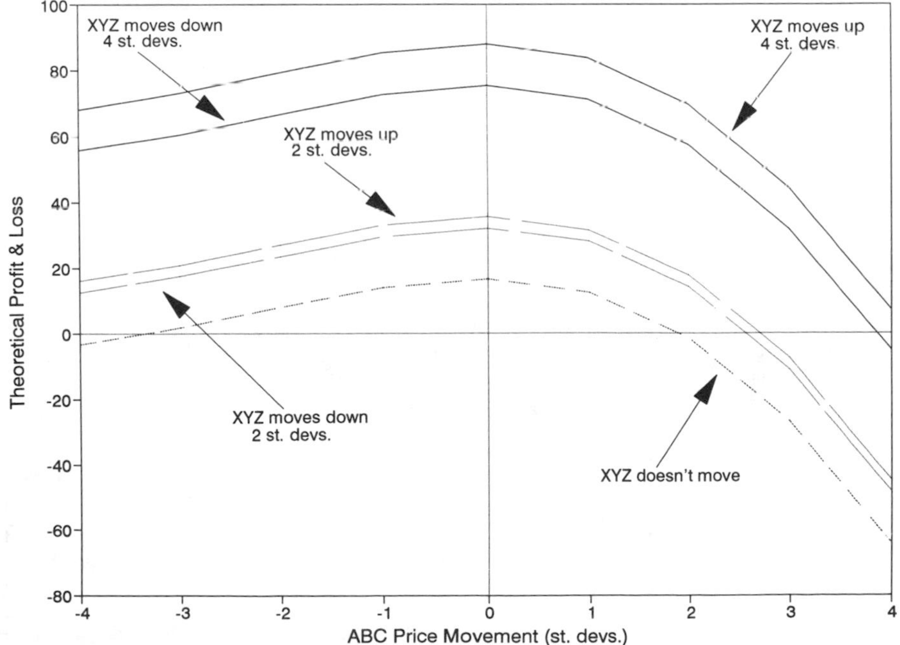

3. In Figures 17-7b through 17-7e we make the assumption that each point is worth $100.

Figure 17-7b

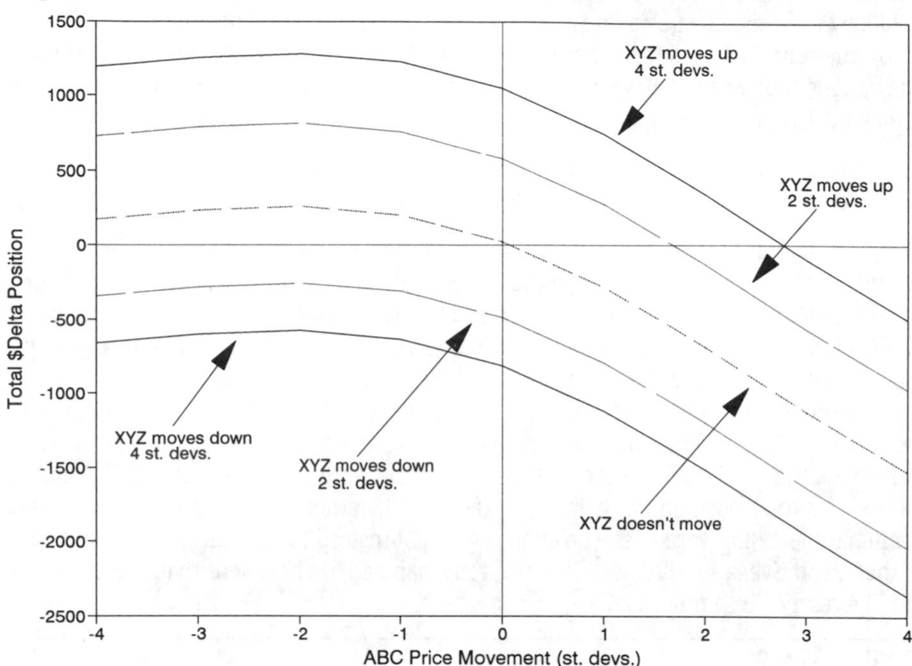

Figure 17-7c

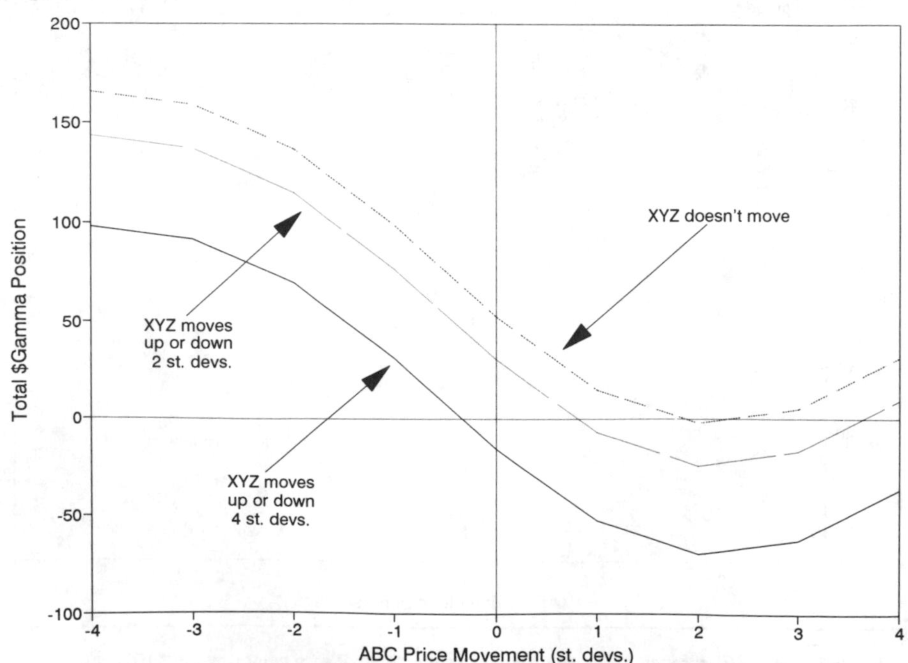

Figure 17-7d

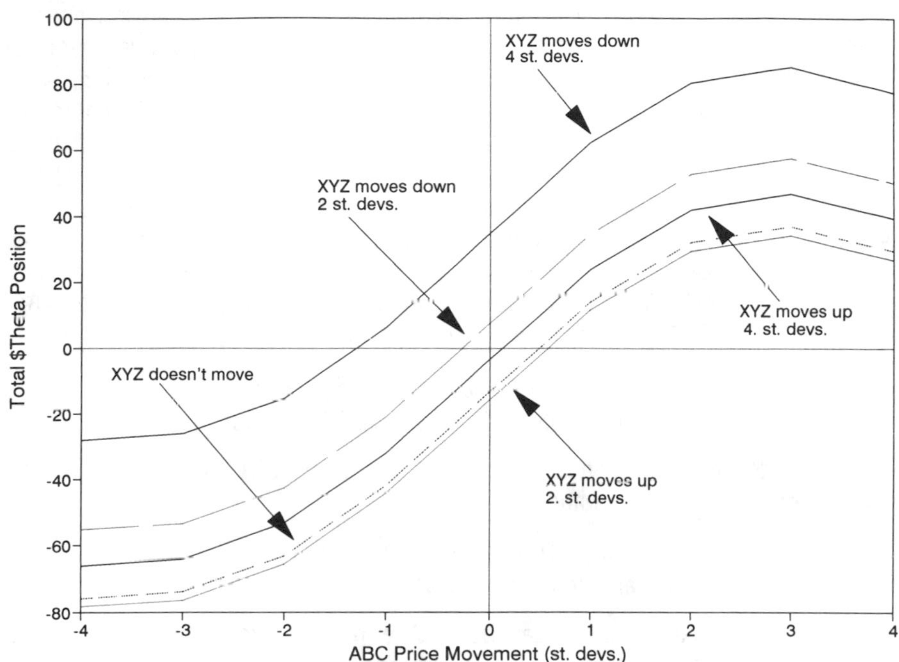

Figure 17-7e

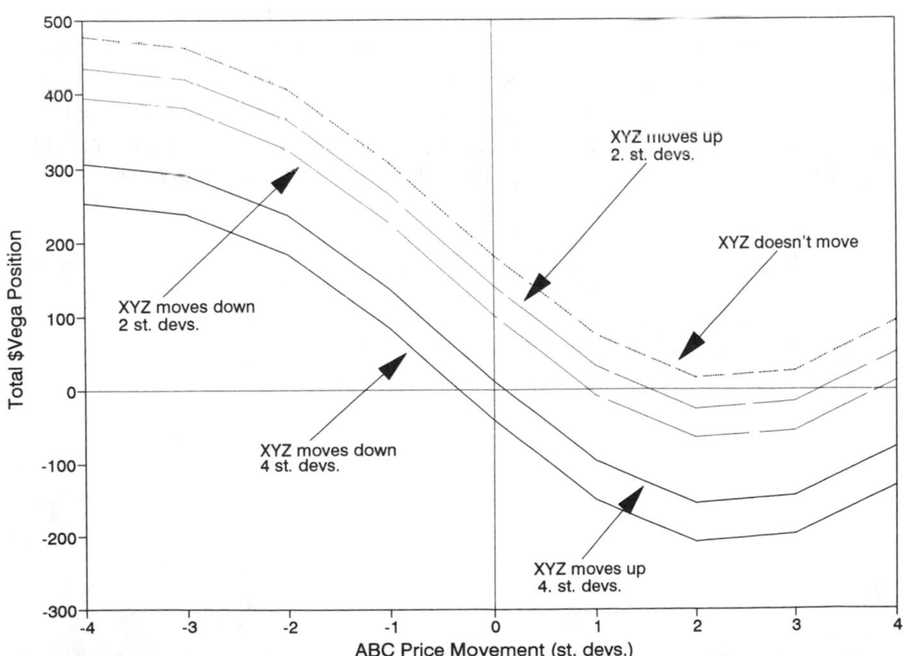

It may initially be difficult to grasp why the $gamma, $vega, and $theta are changing as they are. If one recalls that the gamma, theta, and vega are always greatest for an at-the-money option, the position should show its greatest positive $gamma, negative $theta, and positive $vega when ABC is close to 95 (the position is long ABC 95 calls) and when XYZ is close to either 60 or 65 (the position is long XYZ 60 puts and XYZ 65 calls). The position should show its greatest negative $gamma, positive $theta, and negative $vega when ABC is close to 105 (the position is short ABC 105 calls) and the when XYZ is as far away from 60 and 65 as possible. Since price movement in Figures 17-7a through 17-7e is expressed in standard deviations, in order to interpret the graphs we need to know where the exercise prices are in terms of standard deviations. With ABC at 99 and a one standard deviation price change of 2.75, the ABC exercise prices in terms of standard deviations are:

$$\text{95 call:} \quad (95 - 99) / 2.75 \approx -1.5 \text{ st. devs.}$$
$$\text{105 call:} \quad (105 - 99) / 2.75 \approx +2.2 \text{ st. devs.}$$

With XYZ at 62 and a one standard deviation price change of 1.98, the XYZ exercise prices in terms of standard deviations are:

$$\text{60 put:} \quad (60 - 62) / 1.98 \approx -1 \text{ st. dev.}$$
$$\text{65 call:} \quad (65 - 62) / 1.98 \approx +1.5 \text{ st. devs.}$$

With these values in mind, the reader should take some time to study the graphs and confirm that the $delta, $gamma, $theta, and $vega of the position are in fact consistent with the principles of option evaluation.

The foregoing example consisted of positions in only two different underlying markets. If a trader had option positions in several different underlying markets, a detailed analysis of the total position would require multidimensional graphs. Even if they could be constructed, such graphs would be too complex for most traders to interpret. Under such circumstances the only practical solution is to separate positions by the underlying instrument and do an individual analysis of each market.

❖ 18 ❖

Models and the Real World

The accuracy of values generated by a theoretical pricing model rests on two points: the accuracy of the assumptions upon which the model is based, and the accuracy of the inputs into the model. Thus far, we have tended to focus on the second area, the accuracy of the inputs. Through attention to the sensitivities of an option position (delta, gamma, theta, vega, and rho), a trader can identify those inputs which represent the greatest risk to his position, and thereby prepare to take protective action if things go wrong. While all the inputs into the model represent a risk to the trader, we have placed special emphasis on volatility, since it is the one input which cannot be directly observed in the marketplace.

However, the active option trader cannot afford to ignore the first area, the possibility that the assumptions which form the foundation of the model are themselves inaccurate or unrealistic. Some of these assumptions pertain to the way business is transacted in the marketplace, while others pertain to the mathematics of option pricing.

To begin, we might list the most important assumptions built into a traditional pricing model:[1]

1. Markets are frictionless
    a. The underlying contract can be freely bought or sold, without restriction
    b. There are no tax consequences associated with trading
    c. Everyone can borrow and lend money freely, and one interest rate applies to all transactions
    d. There are no transaction costs
2. Interest rates are constant over the life of an option
3. Volatility is constant over the life of an option
4. Trading is continuous with no gaps in the price changes of an underlying instrument
5. Volatility is independent of the price of the underlying contract
6. Over short periods of time the percent price changes in an underlying contract are normally distributed, resulting in a lognormal distribution of underlying prices at expiration

1. By "traditional pricing model" we mean those that are most commonly used: the Black-Scholes model and its variations, the Cox-Ross-Rubenstein model, or the Whaley model.

The reader may already have an opinion about the accuracy of these assumptions, but let's consider them one by one.

MARKETS ARE FRICTIONLESS

In Chapter 5 we came to the obvious conclusion that markets are not frictionless. The underlying contract cannot always be freely bought or sold; there are sometimes tax consequences; a trader cannot always borrow and lend money freely, nor at the same rate; there are always transaction costs.

In the futures markets the underlying cannot always be freely bought or sold because exchanges sometimes set daily price limits beyond which a futures contract may not trade. When that limit is reached, trading is halted until the market comes off its limit. If it doesn't come off limit, trading does not resume until the next business day.

The consequences of a locked futures market are usually not severe, and there are several ways for a trader to circumvent the problem. Instead of trading in the futures market, a trader might be able to trade in the cash market. Or the trader might be able to trade the underlying market by trading a futures spread where one side of the spread is not locked. For example, suppose a trader wants to buy a June futures contract which is up limit. If a March futures contract is still trading because it is not up its limit, the trader can buy a June/March spread (buy June, sell March), and then go back into the market and buy the March futures contract. This leaves him long a June futures contract, which is what he wanted. Finally, if the underlying futures market is locked, but the option market is not locked, a trader can trade synthetic long or short futures contracts.

In the stock market, there may be prohibitions against the sale of stock not actually owned. Or if short sales are allowed, there may be restrictions on when such sales can be made. If a trader cannot freely sell stock, put prices become inflated compared to call prices, and all the conversions and reversals appear to be mispriced with respect to their theoretical values. If short sales are not freely permitted, many stock option traders try to carry some long stock so they will always be in a position to sell stock if the need arises. Also, we saw in Chapter 5 in the discussion of time spreads, and in Chapter 12 in the discussion of boxes, that tender offers for a stock can distort the value of these positions. In the case of time spreads, traders may be forced to exercise call options with some time value remaining because no stock can be borrowed to carry a short position. A box may be trading at greater than its theoretical value if a partial tender offer is made and early exercise is a possibility.

While there are occasionally tax considerations, for most market participants these are usually minor. When considering a strategy, a trader is unlikely to ask himself, "If this trade makes or loses money, what will be the tax consequences?" Nor should most traders ask such a question. Differences in tax consequences, or changing tax consequences, rarely make one strategy better than another.[2]

---

2. This is not to say that tax consequences are always insignificant. Tax considerations can sometimes play a role in portfolio management. They can also play a role in stock option strategies involving dividends, when the dividends are subject to different tax rules than the gains or losses from stock or options.

The assumption that a trader can always borrow or lend money freely is a more serious weakness in pricing models. Even if a trader has sufficient funds to initiate a trade, he may find at some later date that he is required to come up with additional funds in the form of increased margin requirements.[3] If money were freely available margin would never be a problem. A trader could always borrow margin money and deposit the money with the clearing house. Since the borrowing and lending rate are assumed to be the same, and since the clearing house in theory pays interest on the margin deposit, there would never be a problem obtaining margin money, nor would there ever be a cost associated it.

In the real world traders do not have unlimited borrowing capacity. If a trader cannot meet a margin requirement he may be forced to liquidate a position prior to expiration. Since all models, even those which allow for early exercise, assume that a trader will always have the choice of holding a position to expiration, the inability to meet margin requirements, and therefore maintain the position, can make the values generated by the theoretical pricing model less reliable. Experienced traders learn to consider the risk of a position not only from the standpoint of how much the position might lose if things go wrong, but how much margin might be required to maintain the position over the life of the options. A trader should always have sufficient margin money available to meet this latter requirement.

Even if a trader had unlimited borrowing capacity, the fact that for most traders borrowing and lending rates are not the same can also cause problems with strategies based on model generated values. A trader who borrows margin money at one rate will almost certainly receive a lower rate when he deposits this money with the clearing house. The difference between these rates, which will result in a loss to the trader, is something of which the model is unaware. And the greater the difference between borrowing and lending rates, the less reliable will be the values generated by the model.

The most serious flaw in the frictionless markets hypothesis is the assumption that there are no transaction costs. While a strategy might or might not be affected by tax or interest rate considerations, there are always transaction costs. These costs can come in the form of brokerage fees, clearing fees, or an exchange membership. For many market participants, transaction costs may be so great that a strategy which looks sensible based on model-generated values may not be worth doing when transaction costs are also taken into consideration. Moreover, transaction costs can accrue not only when the strategy is initiated or liquidated, but also every time an adjustment is made. If a strategy will require many adjustments because it has a high gamma and the trader intends to stay delta neutral, the transaction costs can have an especially great impact on model-generated values.

---

3. The possibility that a trader in a futures option market may also have to come up with additional variation money, as opposed to margin money, subsequent to establishing an option position is incorporated into most models. This is why a conversion or reversal in a futures option market may not be delta neutral.

INTEREST RATES ARE CONSTANT OVER THE LIFE OF AN OPTION

The interest rate component assumed in a theoretical pricing model is the riskless rate over the life of an option. Any credits or debits associated with an option strategy will be subject to an interest rate identical to the least risky rate corresponding to the term of the option. In most markets the least risky rate is the rate associated with government issued securities. A trader in a U.S. option market who sells straddles consisting of three-month calls and puts is assumed by the model to have invested the resulting credit in three-month government treasury bills. If both the option position and the treasury bills are held to expiration, this effectively locks in one interest rate (that associated with three-month treasury bills) over the life of the options.

In reality few traders actually take the proceeds from an option trade and invest it in government securities. More often, a trader will put the proceeds in a trading account, where it is subject to a variable interest rate. Moreover, while a trader can lend money to the government by purchasing government securities, he cannot do the reverse and borrow money from the government at the same rate. If he wants to borrow, he may have to go to a bank where the cost of borrowing could be subject to a variable interest rate. Given the realities of the marketplace, most traders' transactions are not subject to a fixed and riskless rate, as the model assumes, but to a constantly changing interest rate. Is this a cause for worry?

While a changing interest rate will cause the value of a trader's option position to change, interest rates usually do not change in a way which will have a significant impact on an option's value, at least in the short run. Since the effect of changing interest rates is a function of time to expiration, and since most listed options have terms of less than nine months, interest rates would have to change violently to have an impact on any but the most deeply in-the-money options. Changing interest rates become even less of a concern when one considers how much more sensitive option values are to changes in the price of the underlying instrument or to changes in volatility.

This is not to say that a trader should completely ignore the possibility of changing interest rates. As we saw in Chapter 8, changing interest rates can have an impact on time spreads in the stock option market. But even then, interest rates would have to change several percentage points over a short period of time to have a significant impact (see Figure 8-15).

With the introduction of long-term equity options, known as LEAPS, the consequences of changing interest rates may well become more of a concern. Using the Black-Scholes model, we can see in Figure 18-1 that the values of two-year stock options changes significantly with only small changes in interest rates (delta values are in parentheses). Note particularly how quickly the 120 put drops below its parity value of 20.00. In a high interest rate environment, a long-term in-the-money American put will quickly become an early exercise candidate. Everyone will prefer to exercise the put in order to earn a high rate of interest on the proceeds from the sale of the stock.

Figure 18-1

Stock price = 100; Time to expiration = 2 years; Volatility = 20%; Dividend = 0

Interest Rate:	**2%**	**4%**	**6%**	**8%**	**10%**	**12%**	**14%**
80 call	25.48 (86)	27.90 (89)	30.34 (91)	32.77 (93)	35.17 (95)	37.54 (96)	39.87 (97)
80 put	2.34 (–14)	1.75 (–11)	1.29 (–9)	.94 (–7)	.67 (–5)	.47 (–4)	.33 (–3)
100 call	13.10 (61)	15.08 (66)	17.20 (71)	19.42 (76)	21.72 (80)	24.09 (84)	26.50 (87)
100 put	9.17 (–39)	7.39 (–34)	5.89 (–29)	4.63 (–24)	3.59 (–20)	2.75 (–16)	2.08 (–13)
120 call	5.95 (36)	7.22 (41)	9.00 (47)	10.28 (52)	12.05 (58)	13.96 (64)	16.00 (69)
120 put	21.24 (–64)	18.00 (–59)	15.10 (–53)	12.54 (–48)	10.29 (–42)	8.35 (–36)	6.70 (–31)

VOLATILITY IS CONSTANT OVER THE LIFE OF THE OPTION

When a trader feeds a volatility into a theoretical pricing model, he is telling the model the magnitude of price changes which will occur over the life of the option. Given the characteristics of a normal distribution, the model uses the volatility to extrapolate a certain number of one, two, three, or more standard deviation price changes. Moreover, the model assumes that occurrences of each particular magnitude will be evenly distributed over the life of the option. Two standard deviation price changes will be evenly distributed among the one standard deviation price changes; three standard deviation price changes will be evenly distributed among the one and two standard deviation price changes; and so on.

Look at Figures 18-2a and 18-2b, daily bar charts of an underlying contract over the life of a certain option. Both bar charts exhibit exactly the same volatility over the period in question, 16.7%. Yet it is obvious that the order in which the volatility occurs is completely different. In Figure 18-2a all the large price changes occur during the early part of the option's life, while in Figure 18-2b all the large price changes occur during the latter part of the option's life. This is often how price changes actually occur in the real world, rather than the even distribution which the model assumes. A trader typically encounters periods of high volatility where all the two and three standard deviation price changes seem to be bunched together. Or he encounters periods of low volatility where all the one standard deviation price changes seem to be bunched together. A graph of historical volatility is never a straight line. (For a good example of this, the reader should look again at Figure 14-2.) But the theoretical pricing model cannot differentiate between our two volatility scenarios. The model simply sees a volatility of 16.7% and assumes that all price changes are evenly distributed, and consistent with this volatility, over the life of the option.

Suppose a trader were to buy a 105 straddle and assumed, correctly, a volatility of 16.7%. If he bought and sold underlying contracts in order to remain delta neutral over the life of the option, the model tells him, because it assumes a constant volatility of 16.7%, that the profit or loss to the trader will be identical in either of our scenarios. Is this likely to be the case?

Notice that the underlying market is moving through 105 both at the beginning and at the end of the options' life. We can therefore consider the 105 call and put as being at-the-money during these periods. Since at-the-money options have the highest gamma, the 105 straddle will be a relatively high gamma position both early and late in the spread's life. Short-term at-the-money options always have greater gammas than long-term at-the-money options, so any increase in volatility which occurs during the latter part of the option's life, as it does in Figure 18-2b, will have a much greater impact on the position than volatility which occurs during the early part of the option's life, as it does in Figure 18-2a.

Because the gamma of a position determines both the magnitude and frequency of the adjustment process, the 105 straddle will be much more valuable under the movement represented in Figure 18-2b. The movement back and forth through the

Figure 18-2a

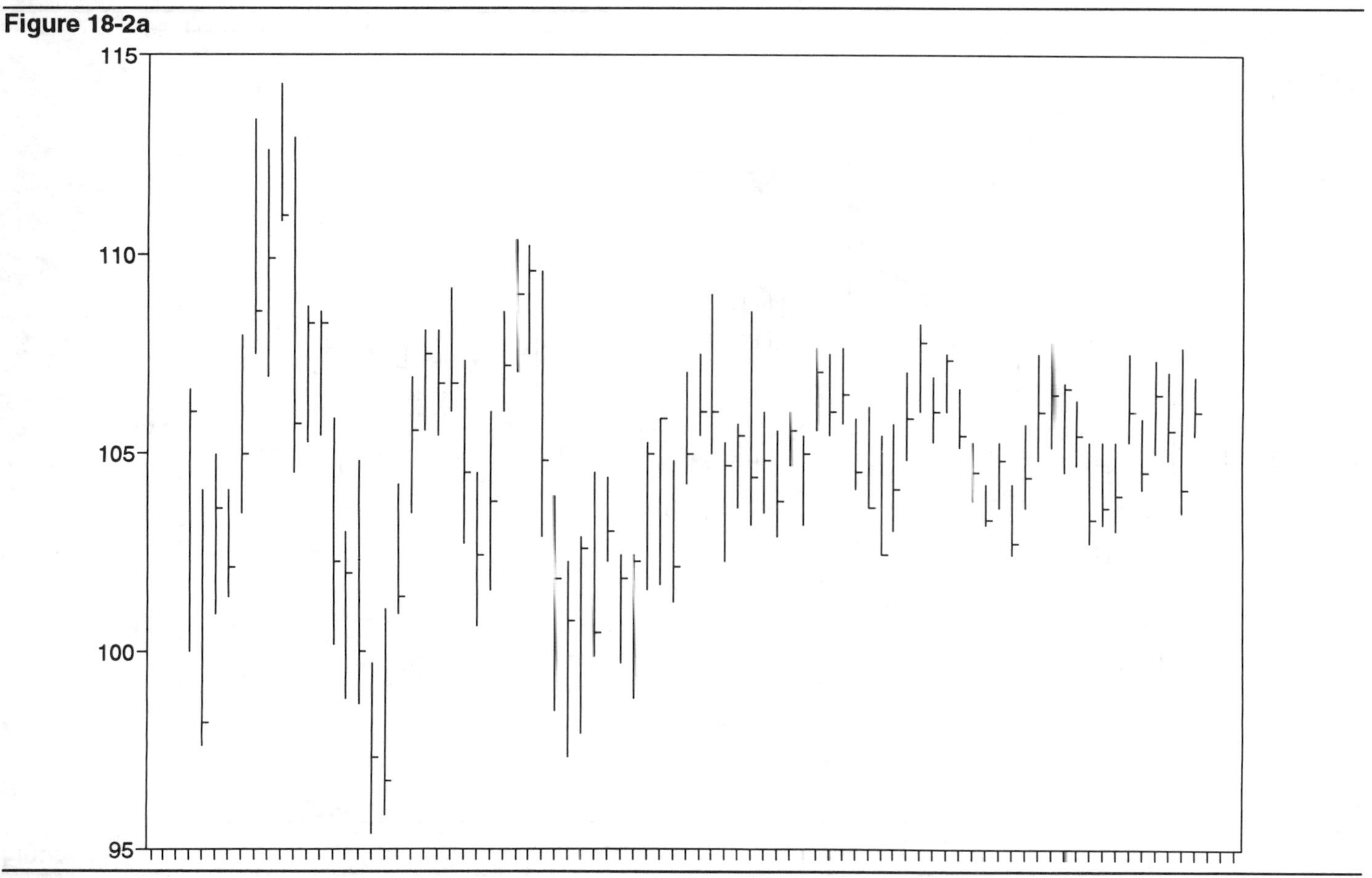

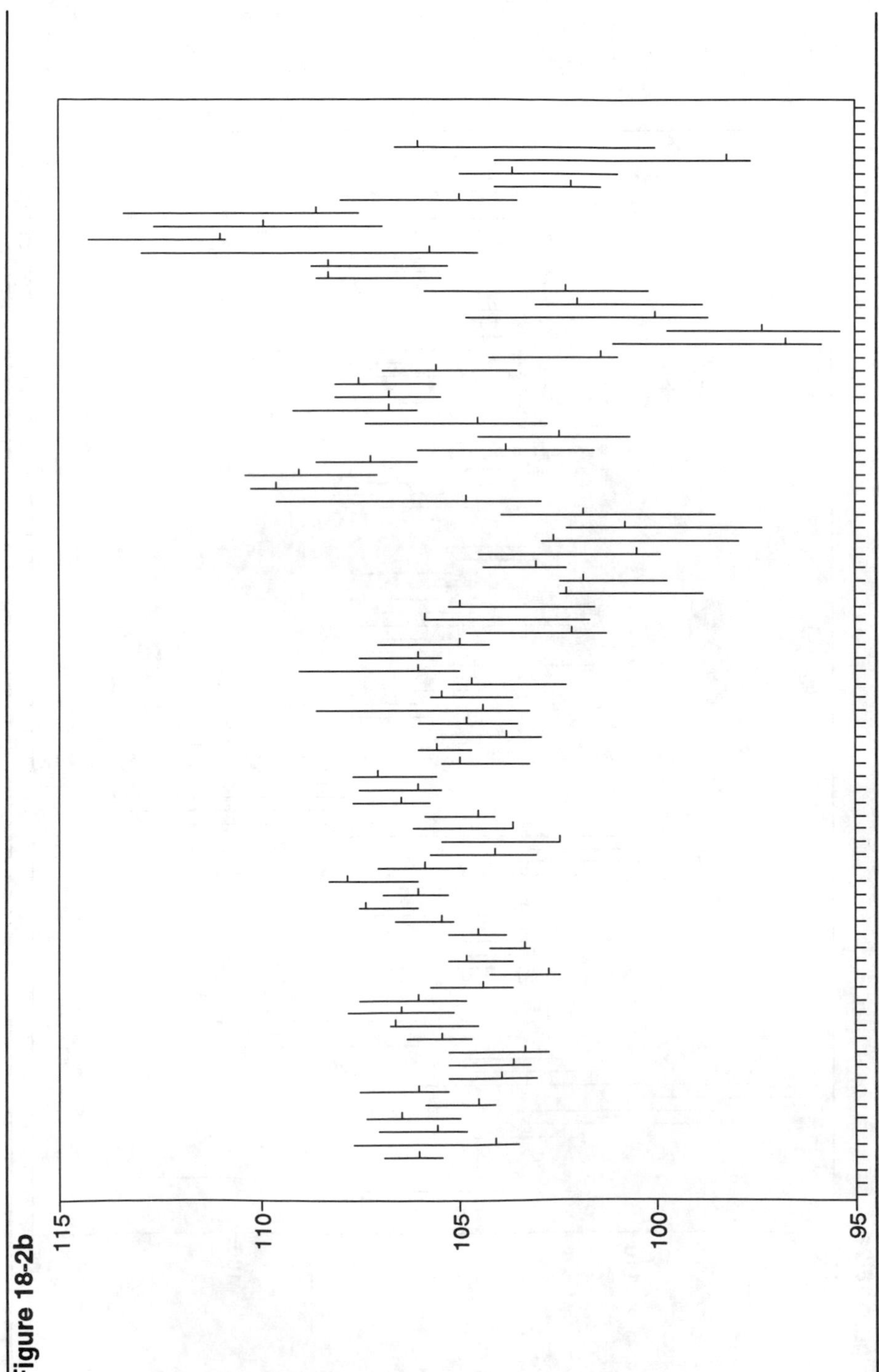

Figure 18-2b

exercise price late in the option's life will require larger and larger adjustments, each of which is favorable to the holder of the 105 straddle. The scenario in Figure 18-2a will also require adjustments. But the adjustments now will be relatively small because the movement in the underlying contract is much less dramatic.

Through experience most traders have come to the conclusion that the order in which volatility occurs does matter. It matters especially for at-the-money options, because they have the greatest gammas. Any period of high volatility which occurs near expiration will have a greater impact on an at-the-money option than the same high volatility which occurs when the option has a great deal of time remaining to expiration. Consequently, even if one knows the actual volatility over the life of an option, a model will tend to undervalue at-the-money options in a rising volatility market, and overvalue at-the-money options in a falling volatility market.

We have only considered one alternative volatility scenario, where volatility is either increasing or decreasing. But there are an infinite number of paths which volatility might follow over the life of an option. A trader might even assume that volatility is itself random, and that predicting volatility with any degree of accuracy is not possible. Models which assume *stochastic volatility* do exist and might, under some conditions, be more suitable than a traditional pricing model. At the same time, such models add another dimension of complexity to a trader's life, and for this reason are not widely used.[4]

Some contracts, by their very nature, are known to change their volatility characteristics over time. Interest rate products, in particular, fall into this category. As a bond approaches maturity, the price of the bond moves inexorably towards par. At maturity, regardless of interest rates, the bond will have a fixed and known value. Clearly, one cannot assume that the price of the bond follows a random walk through time. Even if one assumes that interest rates move randomly, and that the volatility of interest rates is constant, interest rate instruments will change their volatility over time because instruments of different maturities have different sensitivities to changes in interest rates. If we take into consideration the fact that interest rates also vary for different maturities, a traditional Black-Scholes type model is obviously inadequate for the evaluation of such products. This has led to the development of special models to evaluate interest rate instruments.[5]

---

4. For a more detailed discussion see:
   Hull, John and White, Alan, "The Pricing of Options with Stochastic Volatilities," *Journal of Finance,* Vol. 42, No. 2, June 1987, pages 281–300.
   Scott, Louis D., "Option Pricing when Variance Changes Randomly: Theory, Estimation, and Application," *Journal of Finance and Quantitative Analysis,* No. 22, December 1987, pages 419–438.
   Wiggins, J.B., "Option Values under Stochastic Volatility: Theory and Empirical Results," *Journal of Financial Economics,* No. 19, December 1987, pages 351–372.

5. See for example:
   Ho, Thomas, T.S.Y. and Lee, Sang-Bin, "Term Structure Movements and the Pricing of Interest Rate Contingent Claims," *Journal of Finance,* Vol. 41, No. 5, December 1986, pages 1011–1029.
   Heath, David; Jarrow, Robert; and Morton, Andrew, "Bond Pricing and the Term Structure of Interest Rates: A New Methodology," *Econometrica,* Vol. 60, 1992, pages 77–105.

TRADING IS CONTINUOUS

A theoretician trying to develop a realistic price distribution for use in a theoretical pricing model might first ask how the prices of an underlying contract change over time. Perhaps not all contracts change prices in the same way. Price changes might, for example, follow a *diffusion process* (see Figure 18-3). In a diffusion process there are smooth and continuous changes from one price to the next, with no gaps between consecutive prices. Moreover, the longer the period of time between price readings, the greater the dispersion in prices. An example of a typical diffusion process might be the temperature readings in a specific location. While the temperature can change very quickly, there will never be any gaps. If the temperature at one moment is 15° but at a later time is 18°, then at some intermediate time, even if only very briefly, the temperature must have also been 16° and 17°. And there is likely to be a greater temperature change over six weeks than over six days.

Prices might also follow a *jump process.* In a strict jump process, the price of a contract remains constant for a period of time, then instantaneously jumps to a new price, where it again remains constant for some period of time. The way in which central banks set interest rates is typical of a jump process. In the United States, when the Federal Reserve sets the discount rate, it remains there until it is fixed at a new rate. It remains at this new rate until the Federal Reserve again announces a change in the discount rate. A jump process is a combination of fixed prices and instantaneous jumps.

Most theoretical pricing models assume that trading in the underlying contract follows a diffusion process. Trading is assumed to be continuous, proceeding 24 hours per day, seven days per week, without interruption. There can be no gaps in the price of the underlying contract. If a contract trades at 46.05, and at some later time trades at 46.08, then at some intermediate time it must have also traded, even if only briefly, at 46.06 and 46.07. If one were to draw a graph of price changes under a diffusion process, one would never lift the pencil from the paper.

A diffusion process is a convenient, but clearly inexact, approximation of how prices change in the real world. Exchange-traded contracts cannot follow a pure diffusion process because exchanges are not open 24 hours per day. At the end of the trading day a contract often closes at one price, and then opens the next day at a different price. This causes a price gap, something which a diffusion process does not permit. Even during normal trading hours prices may not follow a diffusion process. If major news hits the market, the impact can be almost instantaneous, causing prices to gap up or down.

If a theoretical pricing model makes the assumption that prices follow a diffusion process, when in fact they don't, how is this likely to affect values generated by the model? Consider a situation where an underlying futures contract is trading at 100 and a trader feels that implied volatility in the option market is much too high. Because all options are overpriced, the trader decides to sell the 100 straddle. Unfortunately, immediately after he sells the straddle the market gaps up to 105. How will the gap affect the trader's position?

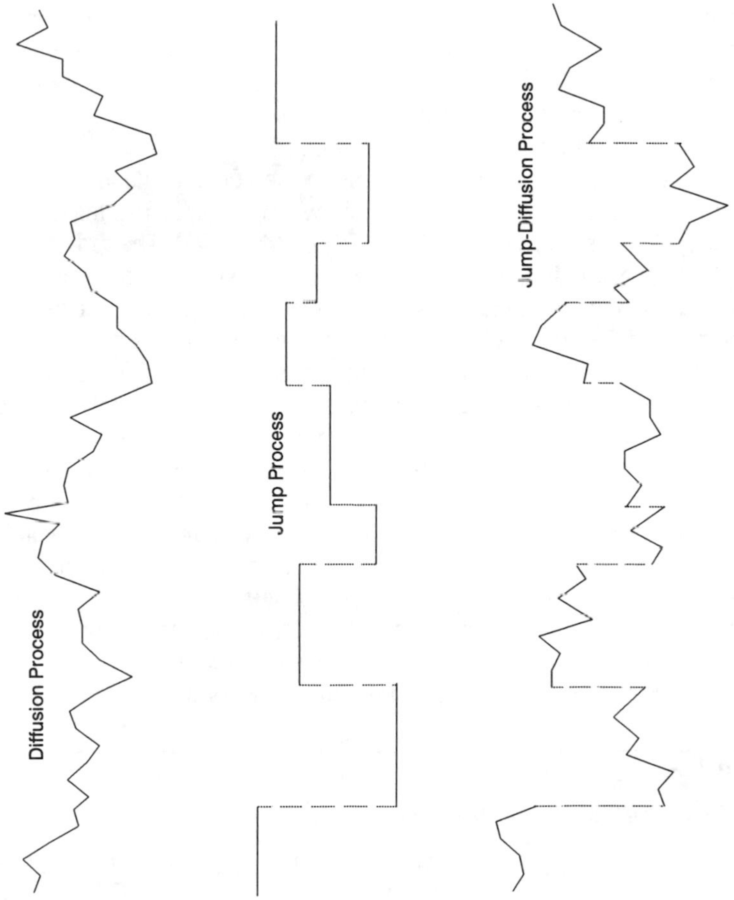

Figure 18-3

A trader who is short straddles does not want to see a gap in the market. The fact that a gap has occurred will hurt the trader, but will it cause him only minor pain, or will it destroy him? If the options are relatively long-term, say nine months, the gap in the underlying price is unlikely to be the end of the world. After all, with nine months remaining to expiration the underlying market could easily fall back to 100. And while the gap has clearly hurt the trader, it is probably not disastrous.[8] But if the gap occurs with only a very short time remaining to expiration, say one day, the trader is now in a situation where he might very well be ruined. With only one day to expiration, there is simply not enough time for the market to retrace its movement. The 100 calls which the trader sold as part of his short straddle will act like short futures contracts. While the spread began approximately delta neutral, after the gap the trader will find himself naked short deeply in-the-money calls, each with a delta of 100, in a market which has just made a giant leap upward. Figure 18-4 shows how prices might change with nine months versus one day remaining to expiration.

With nine months remaining to expiration the 100 straddle increased in value by approximately 7% (14.04/13.18 = 1.07). But with one day remaining to expiration the 100 straddle increased in value by 495% (5.00/.84 = 5.95). The gap was painful with nine months to expiration, but it was devastating with one day to expiration.

The reason that the gap caused such a dramatic change in the one-day straddle was that the delta of the 100 straddle was much more sensitive to a change in the price of the underlying contract. With nine months to expiration the 100 call and put have a gamma of only 2.2. But with one day to expiration they have a gamma of 38.1. In the latter situation, with such a high negative gamma, any movement will undoubtedly be very painful. The trader could reduce some of the damage if he were able to adjust the position by purchasing futures as the market moved upward. But a gap is an instantaneous move; there is no opportunity to adjust. The very high gamma, combined with an inability to make any adjustment, is what makes the gap so devastating.

Options have the unique characteristic of automatically, and continuously, rehedging themselves by changing their deltas as the price of the underlying contract changes. It is this characteristic which buyers of options are paying for. A trader who uses a theoretical pricing model attempts to take advantage of a mispriced option by estab-

Figure 18-4

Implied Volatility = 20%; Interest Rate = 6%

	9 months to expiration		1 day to expiration	
	Futures at 100	Futures at 105	Futures at 100	Futures at 105
100 call price	6.59	9.41	.42	5.00
100 put price	6.59	4.63	.42	0
100 straddle price	13.18	14.04	.84	5.00

8. For simplicity, we assume that there is no change in implied volatility after the gap. Admittedly, this is unlikely to be the case.

lishing a delta neutral hedge against the underlying, and then manually performing the rehedging process himself over the life of the option. This was the basis for the examples in Chapter 5. If a model assumes, as most do, that prices follow a diffusion process, the model assumes that one can continuously maintain a delta neutral hedge. But when the market gaps, the assumptions on which the model is based are violated. Consequently, the values generated by the model are rendered invalid. This problem extends to any application which attempts to replicate option characteristics through a continuous rehedging in the underlying market. The proponents of portfolio insurance suffered their greatest setbacks on October 19 and 20, 1987, when the market made several large gap moves. Because of the gaps, the portfolio insurers were unable to make continuous delta adjustments to their positions. As a consequence, they found that the cost of protection offered by portfolio insurance was much greater than they had ever expected.

Since traditional pricing models make an unrealistic assumption about how prices change, perhaps a model which makes a more realistic assumption would yield more accurate theoretical values. Theoreticians tend to agree that underlying contracts in most markets follow a combination of both a diffusion process and a jump process. Most of the time prices change smoothly and continuously, with no gaps. Every now and then, however, a gap will occur, instantaneously sending the price to a new level. From there prices will again follow a smooth diffusion process until another gap occurs. If one could generate a underlying price distribution which resulted from this *jump-diffusion process*, and feed this distribution into a theoretical pricing model, the model should give more accurate values.

A variation of the Black-Scholes model which assumes that the underlying contract follows a jump-diffusion process has in fact been developed. If used correctly, this *jump-diffusion model* does give values which are probably more accurate than traditional Black-Scholes values.[7] Unfortunately, the model is considerably more complex mathematically than the traditional Black-Scholes model. Moreover, in addition to the five customary inputs, the model also requires two new inputs: the average size of a jump in the underlying market, and the frequency with which such jumps are likely to occur. Unless the user can accurately estimate these new inputs, the values generated by a jump-diffusion model may be no better, and might be worse, than those generated by a traditional model. Most traders take the view that whatever weaknesses are encountered in a traditional model can be best offset through intelligent decision making based on actual trading experience, rather than through the use of a more complex jump-diffusion model.

Since a gap in the market will have its greatest effect on a high gamma option, and since at-the-money options close to expiration have the highest gamma, it is these options which are likely to be mispriced by a traditional theoretical pricing model with its continuous diffusion process. The closer one gets to expiration, the more suspect

7. Information on the jump-diffusion model can be found in most advanced texts on option theory. For additional information see:
Merton, Robert, "Option Pricing when Underlying Stock Returns are Discontinous," *Journal of Financial Economics*, Volume 3, March 1976, pages 125–144.
Beckers, Stan, "A Note on Estimating the Parameters in the Jump-Diffusion Model of Stock Returns," *Journal of Financial and Quantitative Analysis*, March 1981, pages 127–140.

model-generated values become. Consequently, traders pay less and less attention to model-generated values as expiration approaches. It is common practice among floor traders on option exchanges to take with them to the trading floor sheets with theoretical values to enable them to make markets which are consistent with a theoretical pricing model. But as expiration approaches traders are more likely to discard their sheets because the values on the sheets become less reliable. With only one or two days to expiration, most traders simply make decisions based on experience and intuition. While this is perhaps unscientific, it sometimes makes better sense than trading from model-generated values when the model is known to be incorrect.

As a result of the gaps which occur in the real world, both a trader's experience and empirical evidence seem to indicate that a traditional model, with its built-in diffusion assumption, tends to undervalue at-the-money options as expiration approaches. From a risk standpoint, this means that it can be very dangerous to sell a large number of at-the-money options close to expiration, since any gap in the underlying market can have devastating results. New traders, in particular, are advised to avoid such positions. No risk manager will appreciate even experienced traders being short large numbers of at-the-money options as expiration approaches.

Expiration Straddles

If it is dangerous to sell at-the-money options going into expiration, perhaps there is some sense in taking the opposite position by purchasing at-the-money options as expiration approaches. This may seem to contradict conventional option wisdom, which contends that a trader should sell at-the-money options in order to take advantage of the rapid time decay associated with such options. What traders tend to forget is that there is always a tradeoff between risk and reward. If one sells at-the-money options, the reward may be an accelerated profit if the market doesn't move (high positive theta). But the risk is an increased loss if the market does move (high negative gamma). Because the model does not know about the possibility of a gap in the underlying market, the risk is often greater than the reward. If one sells at-the-money options, the losses from an occasional gap will more than offset the profits resulting from increased time decay. An experienced trader will therefore tend to do the opposite of conventional wisdom. If conditions are right, he will tend to buy at-the-money options close to expiration.

This is not to suggest that every time expiration approaches, a trader should run out and buy at-the-money options. As with any strategy, conditions must make the strategy attractive. But because so many traders are intent on selling time premium as expiration approaches, it is often possible to find cheap at-the-money options. For example, suppose that with three days remaining to expiration the Black-Scholes model generates a value for an at-the-money call of .50, but that it is priced at .45. What can we say about this call? While we may not know the exact value, we can certainly say that the call is likely to be worth more than .50, since there is always the possibility of a gap in the market. Clearly, if the call is trading at .45, but has a value in excess of .50, it must be a good buy.

As with any strategy based on volatility, the trader who buys these calls will try to establish a delta neutral position. Because of the synthetic relationship, if the calls are underpriced the puts at the same exercise price will also be underpriced. A logical strategy might be the purchase of at-the-money straddles. This enables a trader to buy both underpriced calls and underpriced puts, and to profit if the underlying market gaps either up or down.

In theory all volatility strategies, including an expiration straddle, ought to be periodically adjusted in order to remain delta neutral. However, with little time remaining to expiration the model is not only unreliable with respect to theoretical values, it is also unreliable with respect to deltas. Because it is impossible to say what the right delta is, it is also impossible to say what the correct adjustment is. For this reason, traders who initiate expiration straddles often forget about trying to adjust, and simply sit on the position to expiration. This may not be the theoretically correct way to handle a volatility position. But it may be the practical choice given all the uncertainties associated with theoretical evaluation as expiration approaches.

Even if a trader carefully chooses his expiration straddles, the great majority of time no gap will occur in the market. In any single case he is more likely to show a loss than a profit. A trader needs to remember that the primary concern is not the profit or loss from any single trade, but what happens in the long run. Going back to the roulette example in Chapter 3, a player who buys a number at a roulette table can expect to win only once in 38 plays. But if the theoretical value of the bet is 95¢, and the player can buy the bet for less than 95¢, he expects to be a winner in the long run. If he pays a very low price for the bet, say 50¢, he still expects to lose 37 times out of 38. But now the bet is very attractive because even if he only wins once in 38 plays, this will still be often enough to more than offset the small losses he takes each time he loses. The same logic is true of expiration straddles. A trader may lose several times before winning. When he does win, he can expect a return great enough to more than offset all the previous losses.

Because a trader knows that he will lose much more often than he will win, a trader should only invest an amount in expiration straddles which he is prepared to lose. But when conditions are right, a trader ought to be willing to make the investment. Even if he loses several times in succession, in the long run he will encounter gaps in the market, or sudden increases in volatility, often enough to make such strategies profitable.

VOLATILITY IS INDEPENDENT OF THE PRICE OF THE UNDERLYING CONTRACT

When a trader feeds a volatility into a theoretical pricing model, the volatility defines a one standard deviation price change at any time during the life of the option, regardless of whether the underlying contract happens to be rising or falling in price. If a contract is currently at 100, and we assume a volatility of 20%, a one standard deviation price change is always based on this volatility of 20%. If at some later time during the life of the option the contract should move up to 150 or down to 50, 20% is still assumed to be the operative volatility.

Unfortunately, this assumption seems to fly in the face of most traders' experience. If one were to ask a stock index or bond trader whether his market were more volatile when rising or falling, he would probably say that it was more volatile when falling. On the other hand, if one were to ask an agricultural or precious metal trader the same question about his market, he would almost certainly give the opposite answer. Those markets tend to be more volatile when rising. In other words, the volatility of a market is not independent of the price of the underlying contract. On the contrary, the volatility over time seems to be dependent on the direction of movement in the underlying contract. In some cases a trader expects the market to become more volatile if the movement is downward and less volatile if the movement is upward; in other cases a trader expects the market to become more volatile if the movement is upward and less volatile if the movement is downward.

Because volatility in some markets does seem to be dependent on the price of the underlying contract, a further variation of the Black-Scholes model has been proposed. The *constant-elasticity of variance*, or *CEV*, model[8] is based on an assumed relationship between volatility and the price level of the underlying contract. This relationship determines the probability of price moves of various magnitudes at each moment in time. Price changes are still random under a CEV assumption, but the randomness varies with the price of the underlying contract.

Like the jump-diffusion model, the CEV model is mathematically complex, and therefore difficult for most traders to compute. And like the jump-diffusion model it requires additional input in the form of a mathematical relationship between the volatility and price movement in the underlying contract. Given these difficulties, the CEV model has not found wide acceptance among option traders.

Over small periods of time the percent price changes in an underlying contract are normally distributed, resulting in a lognormal distribution of underlying prices at expiration

Does the real world look like a lognormal distribution? One way to answer the question is to ask how percent price changes over small periods of time are distributed. If this distribution is normal, then the prices at expiration are likely to be lognormally distributed.

Figure 18-5a is a frequency distribution of daily price changes in the S&P 500 stock index from 1989 through 1993. Each bar represents the number of occurrences of a given price change to the nearest ¼ percent. As one would expect, most of the changes are relatively small and close to zero. As we move away from the zero in either direction,

---

8. For information on the CEV model see:
   Cox, John C.; and Ross, Stephen A.; "The Valuation of Options for Alternative Stochastic Processes"; *The Journal of Financial Economics*; Volume 3, March 1976; pages 145–166.
   Beckers, Stan; "The Constant Elasticity of Variance Model and Its Implications for Option Pricing"; *Journal of Finance;* June 1980; pages 661–673.
   Schroder, Mark; "Computing the Constant Elasticity of Variance Option Pricing Model"; *Journal of Finance*; Vol. 44, No. 1; March 1989; pages 211–219.

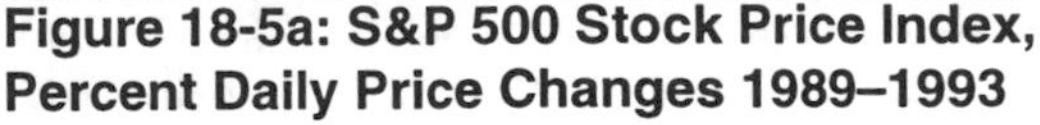

Figure 18-5a: S&P 500 Stock Price Index, Percent Daily Price Changes 1989–1993

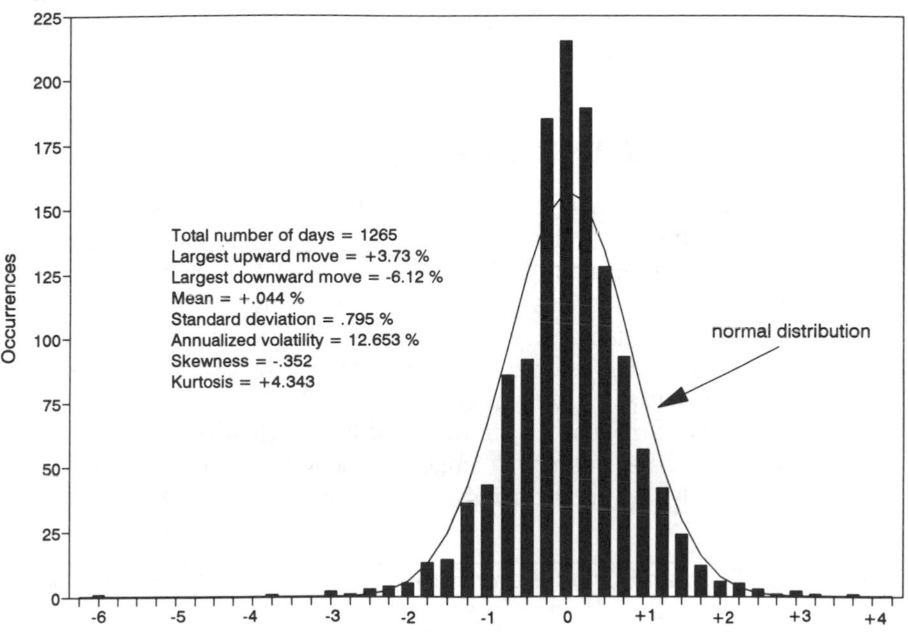

we encounter fewer and fewer occurrences. The distribution certainly seems to have many of the characteristics of a normal distribution. But is it really a normal distribution, and if it isn't, how does it differ from such a distribution?

If the frequency distribution conforms exactly to a normal distribution, the tops of the bars should coincide exactly with a true normal distribution. To find out if this is the case, the mean (+.044%) and standard deviation (.795%) have been calculated for all 1,265 daily price changes over the five-year period. From these numbers, a theoretically exact normal distribution has been overlaid on our frequency chart. Note that the actual frequency distribution is similar to the normal distribution, but there are some clear differences. Because the bars representing the small price changes rise above the normal distribution curve, there seem to be more small price changes than one would expect from a true normal distribution. There are also several large price changes, or *outliers*, which rise above the extreme tails of the normal distribution. These outliers seem to indicate that there are more large moves in our frequency distribution than one would expect from a true normal distribution. Finally, in the midsections, between the peak of the distribution and the extreme tails, there seem to be fewer occurrences than one would expect.

One might at first surmise that differences in Figure 18-5a between the S&P 500 frequency distribution and the true normal distribution are either unique to the S&P 500, or an aberration of the five-year period in question. It turns out, however, that price change distributions for almost all underlying markets exhibit characteristics which are very similar to our S&P 500 distribution. There are usually more days with small moves, more days with large moves, and fewer days with intermediate moves than are predicted by a true normal distribution. These differences between the real world and a theoretical distribution can also be seen in Figures 18-5b and 18-5c, the distribution of price changes for German Bonds and soybeans over the same five-year period.

SKEWNESS AND KURTOSIS

Distributions such as those in Figures 18-5a, 18-5b, and 18-5c are approximately normal, but still differ from a true normal distribution. If one is trying to make decisions based on the characteristics of a distribution, it might be useful to know how the actual distribution differs from the normal. A perfectly normal distribution can be fully described by its mean and standard deviation. But two other numbers, the *skewness* and *kurtosis*, are often used to describe the extent of the difference between an actual frequency distribution and a true normal distribution.

The skewness of a distribution (Figure 18-6a) can be thought of as the lopsidedness of the distribution, or the extent to which one tail is longer than the other tail.[9] If a distribution is positively skewed, the right-hand tail is longer than the left-hand tail. If

Figure 18-5b: German Bonds, Percent Daily Price Changes 1989–1993

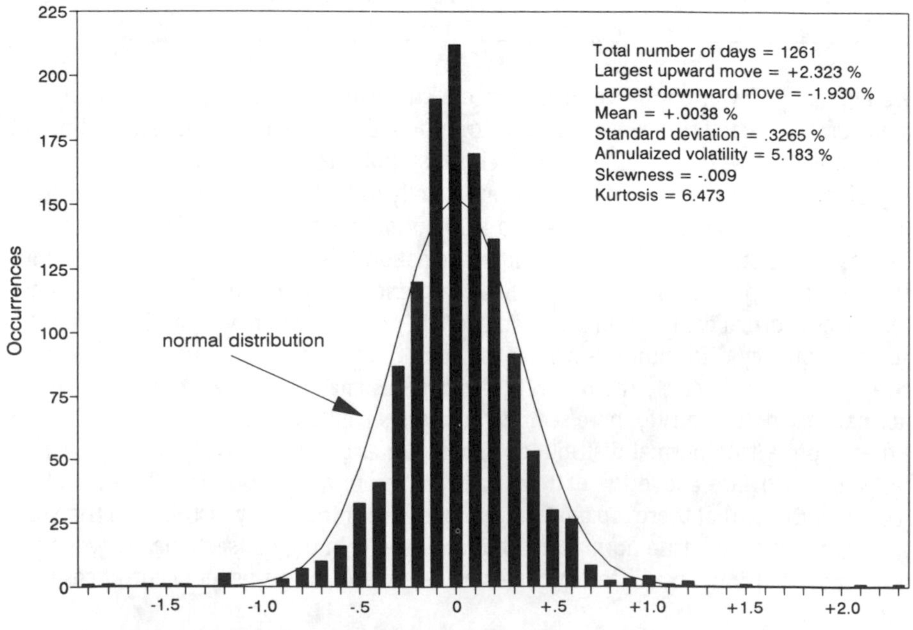

9. The calculation of skewness and kurtosis can be found in Appendix B.

Figure 18-5c: Soybeans, Percent Daily Changes 1989–1993

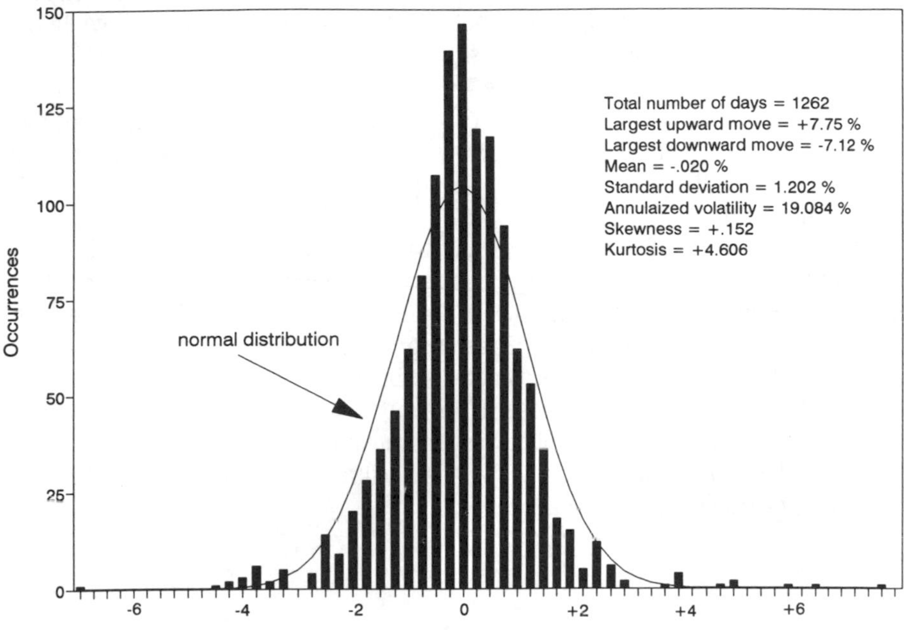

Figure 18-6a: Skewness

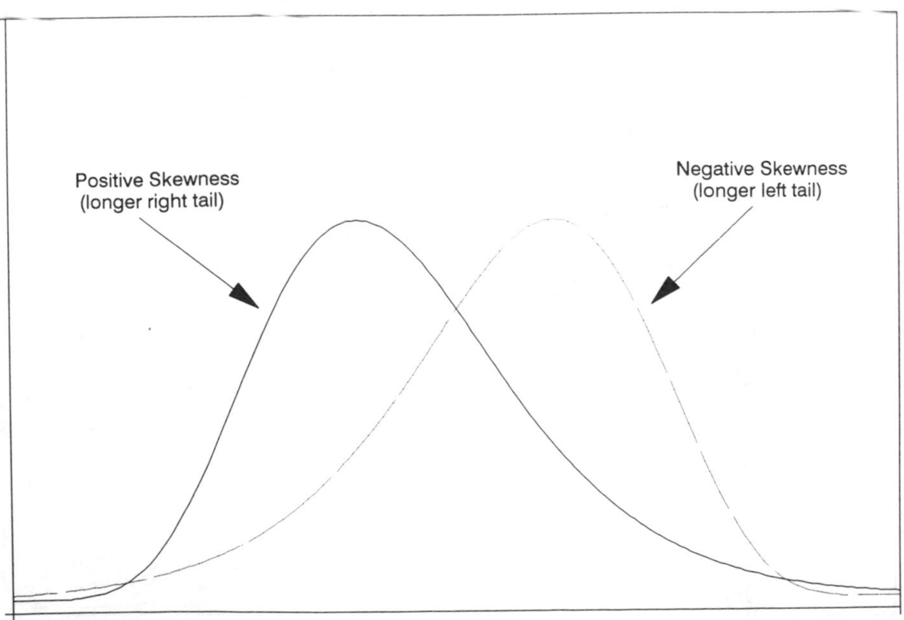

the distribution is negatively skewed, the left-hand tail is longer than the right-hand tail. A true normal distribution has a skewness of zero. The frequency distributions in Figures 18-5a (S&P 500) and 18-5b (German Bonds) are slightly negatively skewed, while the distribution in Figure 18-5c (soybeans) is slightly positively skewed.

The kurtosis of a distribution (Figure 18-6b) is the extent to which the peak of the distribution is unusually tall and pointed, or low and flat. A distribution with a positive kurtosis has a tall, pointed peak (*leptokurtic*), while a distribution with a negative kurtosis has a low, flat peak (*platykurtic*). A perfectly normal distribution has a kurtosis of zero (*mesokurtic*).

Note that a distribution with a low standard deviation also has a pointed peak, just as a distribution with positive kurtosis. But a distribution with a low standard deviation also has narrow tails, while a distribution with a positive kurtosis has long tails. A positive kurtosis distribution is also narrower, or squeezed inward, in the midsection between its peak and tails. The frequency distributions in Figures 18-5a, 18-5b, and 18-5c exhibit the same positive kurtosis, as do almost all underlying markets. They have higher peaks (more days with small moves), more elongated tails (more days with big moves), and narrower midsections (fewer days with intermediate moves) than are predicted by a true normal distribution.

Figure 18-6b: Kurtosis

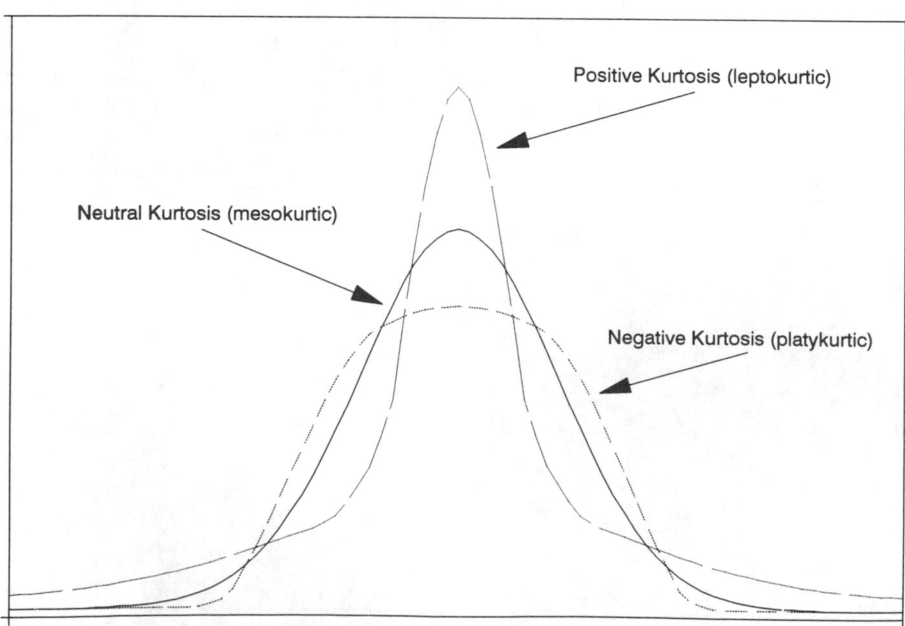

VOLATILITY SKEWS

There are clearly real problems associated with the use of a traditional theoretical pricing model. Markets are not frictionless; prices do not always follow a diffusion process; volatility may vary over the life of an option; the real world may not look like a lognormal distribution. With all these weaknesses, one might wonder whether theoretical pricing models have any practical value at all. In fact, most traders have found that pricing models, while clearly not perfect, are an invaluable tool for making decisions in the option market. While models don't always work perfectly, they have proven to be far better than any other method of evaluating options.

Still, a trader who wants to make the best possible decisions cannot afford to ignore the problems associated with a theoretical pricing model. Consequently, a trader who uses a pricing model might look for a way to reduce the potential errors resulting from these weaknesses. Initially, one might simply look for a better theoretical pricing model. If such a model exists, then it will certainly be worth replacing the old model with the new one. But "better" is a relative term. A model might be better in the sense that it gives slightly more accurate theoretical values. But if the model is extremely complex and difficult to use, or if it requires additional inputs of which a trader cannot always be certain, then the model may merely substitute one set of problems for another. Given the fact that most traders are not theoreticians, a more realistic solution might be to use a less complex model and somehow fine-tune it so that it is consistent with the realities of the marketplace.

A trader trying to offset weaknesses in a pricing model might make the assumption that the marketplace is using the same model as the trader, and then ask how the marketplace is dealing with the weaknesses in the model. This is somewhat analogous to calculating implied volatility where we assumed that everyone was using the same model, that the price of the option was known, and that everyone agreed on all the inputs except volatility. From these assumptions we were able to determine the volatility that the marketplace was implying to the underlying contract. Now we want to take the same general approach, but ask what weaknesses the marketplace is implying to the model. This is a more difficult question to answer.

Figure 18-7 shows the settlement prices and implied volatilities for December options on German Government Bond (Bund) futures traded on the London International Financial Futures and Options Exchange (LIFFE) on July 17, 1992. Since options on LIFFE are settled like futures contracts, the effective interest rate for theoretical calculations is zero. As a result, there is no economic value to early exercise, and one can calculate all implied volatilities using the Black-Scholes model.

By most standards German Government Bonds are a very low-volatility contract. Even so, the numbers do reflect many of the characteristics of option markets with which traders have become familiar. Note that the implied volatilities for calls and puts at the same exercise price are always the same. If this were not true, the prices would reflect an arbitrage opportunity. A trader could profitably execute a conversion if the calls were overpriced with respect to the puts; a trader could profitably execute a reverse conversion if the puts were overpriced with respect to the calls. The fact that call and

Figure 18-7

July 27, 1992; German Government Bond (Bund) Futures
December Futures Contract = 87.86; Days to Expiration = 119; Interest Rate = 0%

Exercise Price	Call Price	Call Implied Volatility	Put Price	Put ImpliedVolatility
84.50	3.40	3.98	.04	3.98
85.00	2.92	3.82	.06	3.82
85.50	2.46	3.76	.10	3.76
86.00	2.02	3.68	.16	3.68
86.50	1.61	3.62	.25	3.62
87.00	1.25	3.62	.39	3.62
87.50	.93	3.58	.57	3.58
88.00	.67	3.58	.81	3.58
88.50	.46	3.56	1.10	3.56
89.00	.31	3.60	1.45	3.60
89.50	.20	3.62	1.84	3.62
90.00	.13	3.69	2.27	3.69
90.50	.08	3.73	2.72	3.73
91.00	.05	3.81	3.19	3.81
91.50	.03	3.87	3.67	3.87

put implied volatilities all line up indicates an efficient market with respect to arbitrage relationships.[12]

Unfortunately, the implied volatilities at different exercise prices do not line up, and this presents a problem to someone who believes that the Black-Scholes model is one hundred percent efficient. Can those traders trading the 89 call or put really believe that the December futures contract will have a volatility of 3.60, while those trading the 85 call or put believe the December contract will have a volatility of 3.82?

If we assume that the exercise price, time to expiration, underlying price, and interest rate are known, the theoretical value of an option in a Black-Scholes world will depend solely on the volatility of the underlying contract over the life of the option. There can be only one volatility over this period. It's true we won't know what that volatility is until expiration arrives, at which point we can look back in time to see what the volatility was. But the December Bund future can have only one volatility over its life. Since all the December Bund options have the same underlying contract, it doesn't make sense for every exercise price to have a different implied volatility. A true adherent of the Black-Scholes model would plug in his best guess about volatility and begin selling those options which appeared to be overpriced and buying those options which appeared to be underpriced. We might think of the marketplace as one big trader. If the activity in the marketplace were a result of everyone believing in the efficiency of the

12. Settlement prices, such as those in Figure 18-7, are intended to reflect an efficient market with respect to arbitrage relationships. During the trading day, because there is a bid/ask spread for each option, and because all trades do not take place simultaneously, markets may appear less efficient.

Black-Scholes model, the selling of overpriced options and the buying of underpriced options would eventually cause the implied volatility of every option to line up exactly. Yet this almost never happens in any market.

The marketplace, like every individual trader, is trying to evaluate options as efficiently as possible, given all the information available. Whether one believes that markets are efficient or not, one can certainly argue that the marketplace is at least trying to be efficient. From the wide range of implied volatilities found in almost every option market, we can reasonably infer that the marketplace does not think the Black-Scholes model is one hundred percent efficient. Unfortunately, trying to identify the source of the inefficiency may not be possible. It might have to do with the fact that markets are not frictionless; or the fact that prices do not always follow a diffusion process; or that volatility may vary over the life of an option; or that the real world may not look like a lognormal distribution. Whatever the reason, the marketplace believes that options at any moment are priced efficiently, even if those prices happen to differ from model-generated values.

For traders using a theoretical pricing model, prices are often expressed in terms of their implied volatilities. A trader who wants to continue using a theoretical pricing model, but wants to use it in a way which is consistent with the way the marketplace is apparently using the model, might look to the distribution of implied volatilities for additional information. He might begin by plotting the implied volatilities across different exercise prices, and then draw a graph that fits the data points. This has been done in Figure 18-8a for December Bund options.

The resulting graph, usually referred to as the *volatility skew*, has a well defined shape. The low point of the graph is close to the price of the underlying contract (87.86), and the tails of the graph rise as we move to exercise prices further away from the underlying price. One inference which most traders draw from this shape is that the marketplace appears to believe there is a better chance for a large price move in the real world than is predicted by the Black-Scholes model. This is not unreasonable if we look again at Figures 18-5a, 18-5b, and 18-5c. The outliers seem to indicate that large moves occur more frequently in the real world than is predicted by a normal distribution. It is the possibility of these large moves which apparently causes the marketplace to inflate the prices of options which are far out-of-the-money or deeply in-the-money.

We can also see that some options are clearly too expensive or too cheap with respect to their neighbors. We may not know exactly what the 88.50 call is worth, but we can see that it is clearly too cheap with respect to the 88 and 89 calls. In the same way, we may not know what the 87 put is worth. But it is clearly too expensive with respect to the 86.50 and 87.50 puts. In the former case, a trader might try to sell the 88.50/89.00/89.50 butterfly. In the latter case, a trader might try to buy the 86.50/87.00/87.50 butterfly. Whatever we think of the skew, there ought to be a smooth progression of implied volatilities from one exercise price to the next.

A trader using the Black-Scholes model might take the view that the volatility skew contains useful information which can be incorporated into the decision-making process. While he might believe that options are generally either overpriced or underpriced, he might also believe that the volatility skew reflects the relative value of options. He

Figure 18-8a

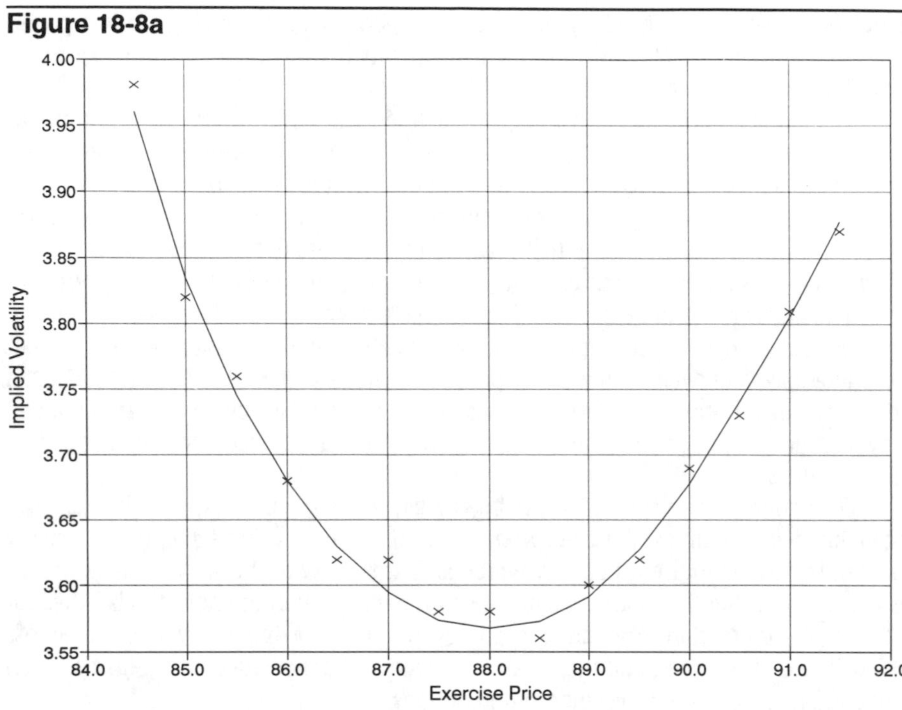

might therefore look for a method of using the skew as part of his method of evaluating options. Unfortunately, dealing with a volatility skew can be a problem because there is no exact formula to use as a guide. Moreover, each trader tends to use the skew in a way that best serves his ultimate goal. A market maker might treat the skew one way, while a speculator or hedger treats the skew in a different way. Additionally, each trader must determine the relative accuracy of the information reflected in the skew. A trader who disagrees with a skew will find that some strategies will be more attractive than others.

For example, consider a trader who is active in the Bund option market, and who is trying to find a simple way to integrate a volatility skew into his theoretical pricing model. He wants his theoretical values to be consistent with the skew, but he also has an opinion on volatility. What might the trader do? Going back to Figure 18-7, we can see that the at-the-money implied volatility in the Bund option market is approximately 3.58. Suppose a trader felt that implied volatility was too low, and that a more reasonable volatility was .25 percentage points higher, at 3.83. If the trader still believed that the skew represented the relative value of options, he might raise the whole skew .25 volatility points and use these new volatilities to evaluate options at different exercise prices. This would reflect his opinion that implied volatility was too low, but would also take into consideration the relative value of options reflected by the skew.

In a similar manner, the trader could also shift the skew right or left as the price of the underlying contract changed. If the underlying contract several weeks later were to move up 2.00, a trader could keep the shape of the skew constant but shift the whole skew up 2 points. At the same time, he could raise or lower the skew, using the at-the-money options as a reference point, to reflect his opinion that the implied volatility was either too high or too low. He could again use the resulting skew to evaluate options at different exercise prices, and from this information to decide on a strategy. The result of shifting a skew either up or down, or from side to side, is shown in Figure 18-8b.

Shifting the whole skew might be a reasonable approach if a trader believes that the skew will remain constant in the face of changing market conditions. But is this likely? The implied volatilities at different exercise prices are likely to depend on how the marketplace views the likelihood of large moves in the underlying market. But all moves are relative, both with respect to the underlying price and to time. In relative terms a 4 point move in the underlying contract is larger with the underlying contract at 80 (a 5% move) than with the underlying contract at 100 (a 4% move). In relative terms a four-point move over a two-week period is larger than a four-point move over a two-month period.

The fact that the volatility skew is likely to change with changing market conditions is born out in Figure 18-8c. The skew changed its shape, generally becoming more severe, as time passed. It also changed its position as both the price of the underlying contract and implied volatility changed. This poses a problem for a trader trying to incorporate a volatility skew into a theoretical pricing model. Pricing models are not

Figure 18-8b

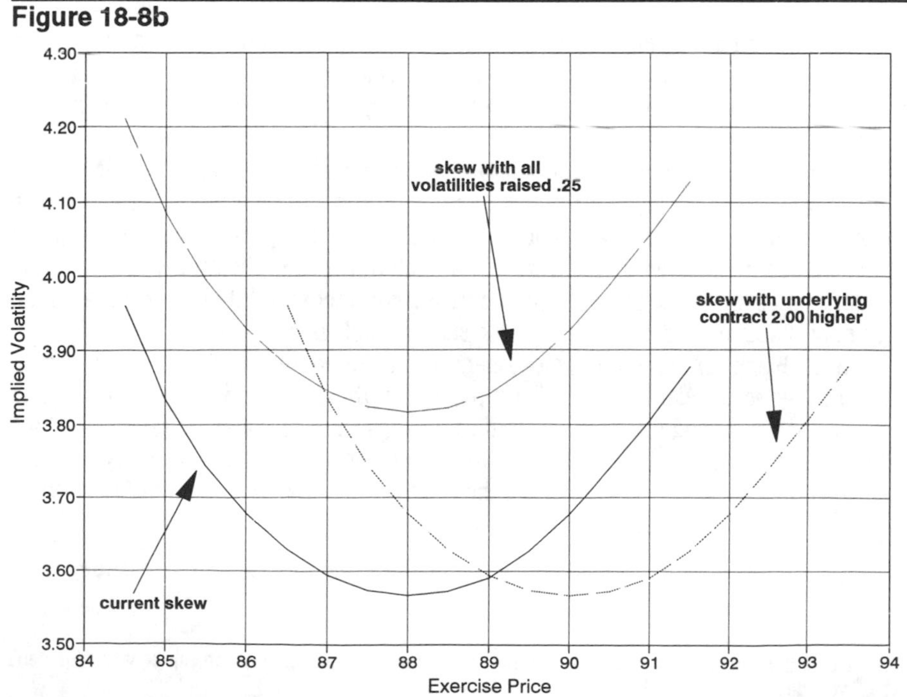

Figure 18-8c

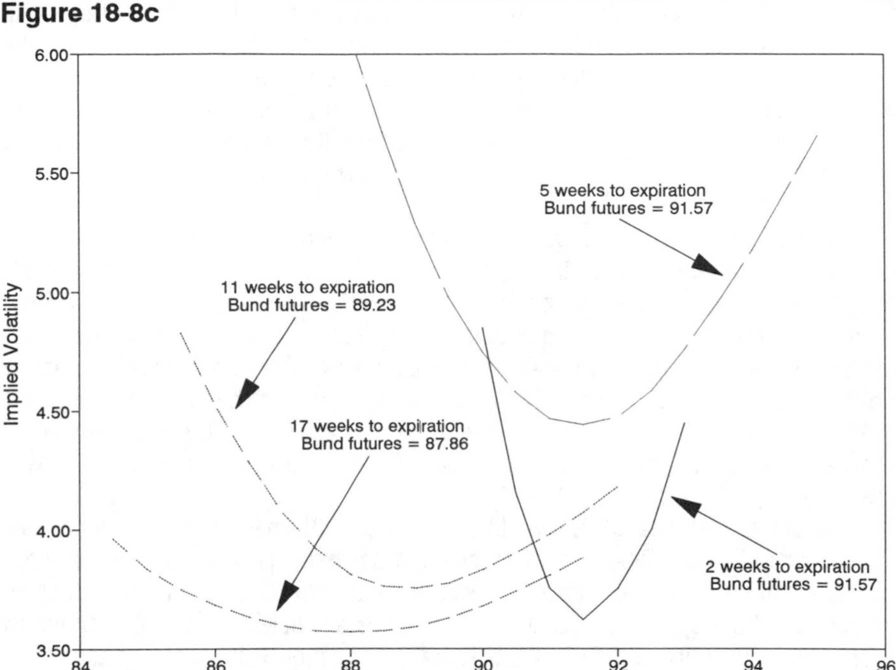

only used to evaluate options under current conditions. They are also used to evaluate risk under changing market conditions. If a trader wants to fully incorporate a skew into his model, he needs to know how the skew is likely to change with changing market conditions.

We noted that movement in the underlying contract is relative, both with respect to the current price of the underlying contract and time to expiration. If we are using a theoretical pricing model, we might ask how the model expresses movement in the underlying contract. If we know this, we can determine how the model expresses the relationship between the price of the underlying contract and different exercise prices. This may enable us to determine how the skew will change.

In the Black-Scholes model, movement in the underlying contract is measured on a logarithmic scale,[13] and the relationship between the exercise price of an option and the current underlying price is expressed as the logarithm of the exercise price divided by underlying price. At the same time, movement over time is governed by a square root relationship, so that in the Black-Scholes model the relative amount of movement required to reach an exercise price is fully expressed as

[natural logarithm (exercise price / underlying price)] / square root (time)

13. For a more detailed discussion of the logarithmic function, and the relationship between time and volatility, see Appendix B.

where time is expressed in terms of years. Since we are using the Black-Scholes model to calculate the implied volatilities of the various options, and since the Black-Scholes model expresses exercise prices in the way we have just described, perhaps it makes sense to express the skew exercise prices in the same way. This has been done in Figure 18-8d.

With our new x-axis measurements the skews start to look very much alike. We still need to take into consideration the fact that the skews occupy different positions because they represent different volatilities. In order to generalize the volatility scale (the y-axis), we might consider expressing all volatilities for a given skew in terms of the volatility of a theoretical at-the-money option. For example, going back to Figure 18-8a, we can see from the graph that with the underlying contract at 87.86, the implied volatility of an option with an exercise price of 87.86 (a theoretically at-the-money option) would be approximately 3.57%. We can therefore express the volatility at each exercise price as the difference between that exercise price's volatility and 3.57. Using this approach, the 91 exercise price, with an implied volatility of 3.81 (the point where the graph crosses the 90 exercise price), would be assigned a value of

$$3.81 - 3.57 = .24$$

The 86 exercise price, with an implied volatility of 3.68, would be assigned a value of

$$3.68 - 3.57 = .11$$

Figure 18-8d

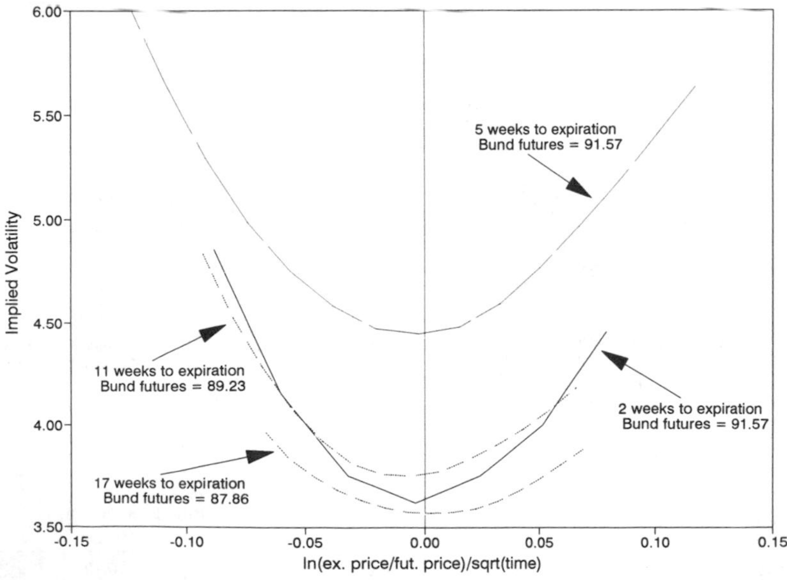

This method is satisfactory when implied volatilities remain relatively constant. But suppose the implied volatility in the Bund option market were to double to 7.00%. Under these circumstances, the implied volatilities at each exercise price can also be expected to double. The 90 exercise price, instead of having an implied volatility of 3.81, will have an implied volatility of 7.62. And the 86 exercise price, instead of having an implied volatility of 3.68, will have an implied volatility of 7.36. Since implied volatility can change in the marketplace, we need a method of relating the overall change in implied volatility to the change in each exercise price's implied volatility. The easiest way to do this is to express the implied volatility at each exercise price as a percent of the at-the-money implied volatility.

For example, with an at-the-money implied volatility of 3.57, the 90 exercise price, with an implied volatility of 3.81, would be assigned a value of

$$3.81 / 3.57 = 106.7\%$$

The 86 exercise price, with an implied volatility of 3.68, would be assigned a value of

$$3.68 / 3.57 = 103.1\%$$

Combining this method of expressing the implied volatility in terms of a percent of at-the-money volatility, together with the logarithmic/time method of expressing the exercise price, yields the transformations shown in Figure 18-8e.

Figure 18-8e

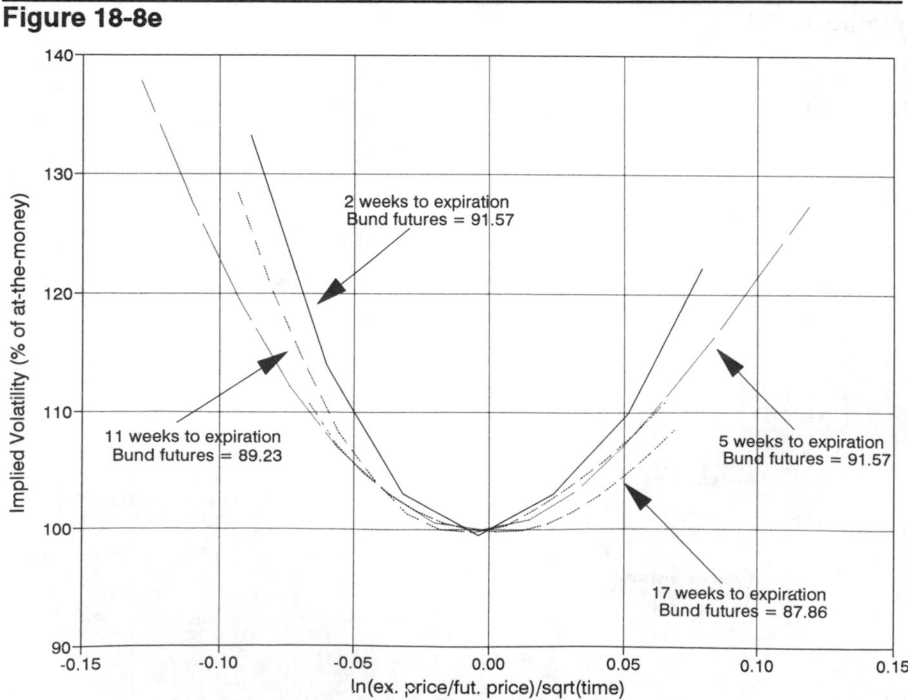

With our new x-axis and y-axis the skews, while not identical, tend to look much alike. If we were to make the assumption that the skew would look similar to those in Figure 18-8e under all conditions, we might think of the skew as an additional variable in a theoretical pricing model. Instead of the five usual variables (time to expiration, exercise price, underlying price, interest rates, volatility), we now have six (Figure 18-9).

If we are going to feed the skew into the model as a variable, we need to do it in a way which the model understands. This means we need to find a formula by which to express the skew. While this may sound difficult, many skews can be expressed as simple equations. In Figure 18-10 a function has been graphed out which approximates the shape of the volatility skews in Figure 18-8. If we make the assumption that this function gives a good approximation of the skew, we can use the function as the volatility skew variable in our theoretical pricing model. To analyze the value of an option position under changing assumptions about underlying price, time to expiration, and volatility, we need only express the volatility at each exercise price using this function:

volatility at an exercise price =
the at-the-money volatility times f(x)

where the exercise price, E, is always expressed in relation to its underlying price, U, and the amount of time to expiration, t:

$$\ln(E/U) / \sqrt{t}$$

There is no law that says a trader must agree with the skew implied in the option market. A trader might believe that there is little chance of an unexpectedly large move in the underlying market. In this case, he can lower the wings of the skew. On the other

Figure 18-9

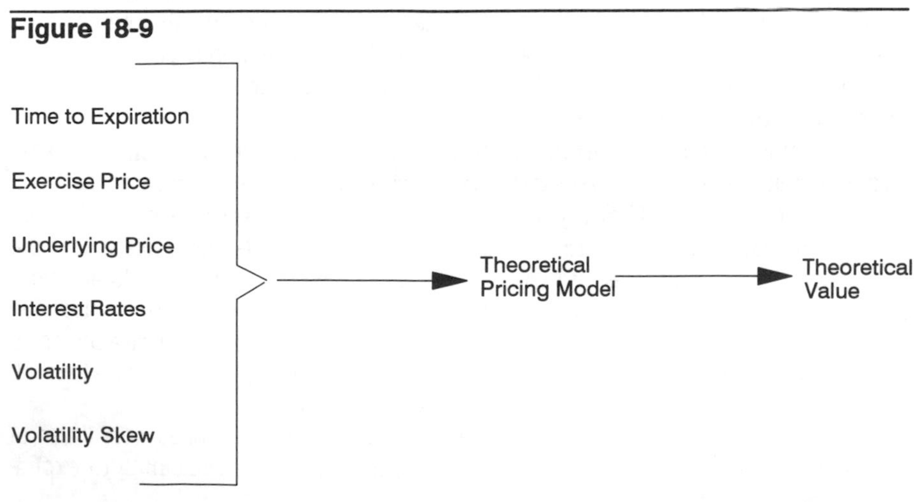

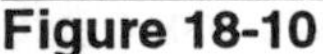
Figure 18-10

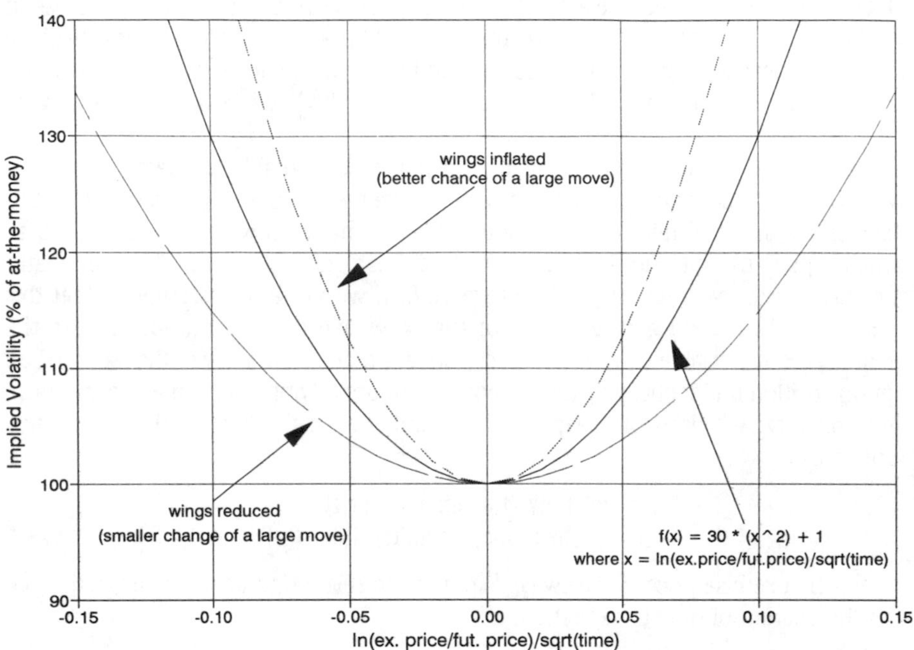

hand, if he believes that a there is a high probability of an unusually large move, he can raise the wings of the skew. This type of modification is also shown in Figure 18-10.

A market maker can also use the skew to adjust his bids and offers. If the market maker finds himself with a large positive gamma position and wants to sell options to cut back on the risk associated with the position, he can shift the skew slightly downward. This will have the effect of lowering his bids and offers on all options. If the market maker finds himself short a large number of out-of-the-money calls or puts, he can adjust his skew by raising the wings. This will have the effect of raising his bids and offers on out-of-the-money options.

The Bund options in our example form what is probably the most common skew shape, a smile which is approximately symmetrical. But this is not always the case. Skews can be symmetrical or asymmetrical, and they can reflect inflated or deflated implied volatilities across exercise prices, depending on how the marketplace sees the possibility, and consequences, of various moves in the underlying market. In addition, in stock index markets, because it is not always possible to take advantage of a mispriced arbitrage relationship (see Chapter 15), calls and puts with the same exercise prices do not necessarily trade at the same implied volatility. For this reason, many traders in stock index markets prefer to evaluate call and put skews separately.

As an example, Figures 18-11a and 18-11b represent the implied volatilities of March 1993 OEX calls and puts with different amounts of time remaining to expira-

Figure 18-11a: OEX March 1993 Calls

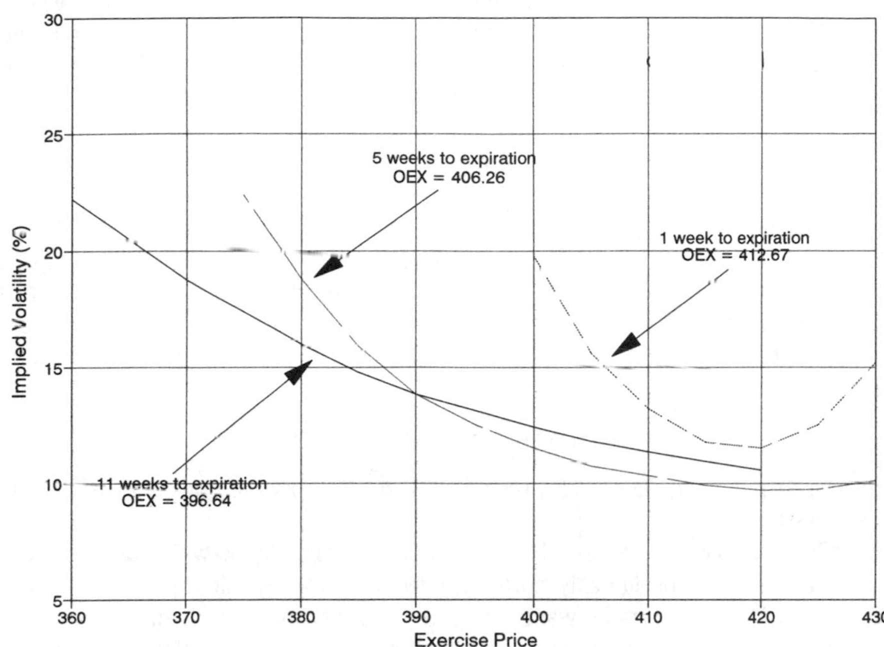

Figure 18-11b: OEX March 1993 Puts

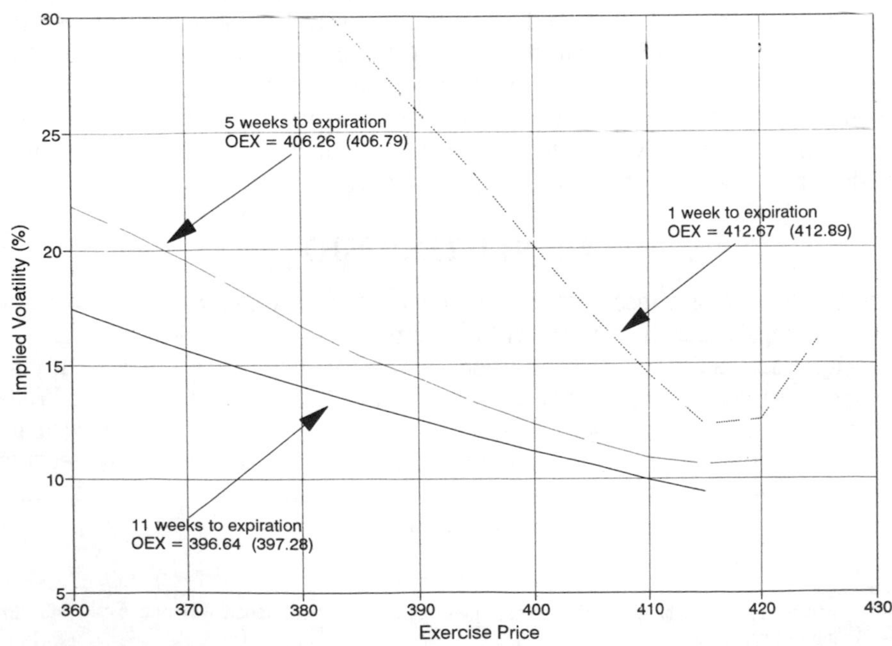

tion.[12] Note the extreme inflation of downside exercise prices, both for calls and puts. While it may not be possible to determine exactly what is causing the skew to have this particular shape (it may indicate that the marketplace believes stock markets go down faster than they go up—as witness October 1987—or it may reflect the fact that stock index options are often used to hedge long stock portfolios), the marketplace seems to be giving greater relative value to lower exercise prices. A trader who wanted to use the marketplace's relative evaluation might try to integrate the skew into his theoretical pricing model.

As before, we might try to generalize the skew by expressing each exercise price in terms of a logarithmic relationship to the underlying index price. Stock index prices, like stock prices, are assumed to be lognormally distributed around the forward price of the index, i.e., the current index price plus carrying costs less dividends. It therefore makes sense to express the exercise price in relation to the forward price rather than to the index price:

$$\ln(\text{exercise price}/\text{forward price}) \,/\, \sqrt{\text{time}}$$

This has been done in Figures 18-11c and 18-11d. (The forward price of the OEX is in parenthesis.)

While there are clearly some differences between volatility skews in Figures 18-11c and 18-11d, there is considerably more consistency than one would expect from Figures 18-11a and 18-11b. If a trader wanted to find functions, one for calls and one for puts, by which the skews could be expressed, he could use these functions to analyze a position under a wide variety of market conditions.

It is only in the last several years that traders have begun to appreciate the importance of volatility skews, both as an evaluation tool and as a risk management consideration. This section is intended not as a solution to all the problems that traders encounter in analyzing and using volatility skews, but as an introduction to how traders approach the problem. Each trader as he gains more experience must decide how best to deal with the volatility skew, given the characteristics of the market in which he is dealing, as well as his ultimate goal in that market.

A FINAL THOUGHT

Because the use of a theoretical pricing model requires a trader to make so many different decisions, both with respect to the inputs into the model and the degree to which the assumptions on which the model is based are likely to be accurate, the new option trader may feel that making the right decisions is simply a matter of luck. While luck undoubtedly plays a role in the short run, in the long run those traders who are willing to put in the effort required to understand how models work always seem to come out ahead. Experienced traders know that using a model, with all its problems, is still the best way to evaluate options and manage risk.

12. Because of the possibility of early exercise, the Cox-Ross-Rubenstein model was used to calculate OEX implied volatilities.

Figure 18-11c: OEX March 1993 Calls

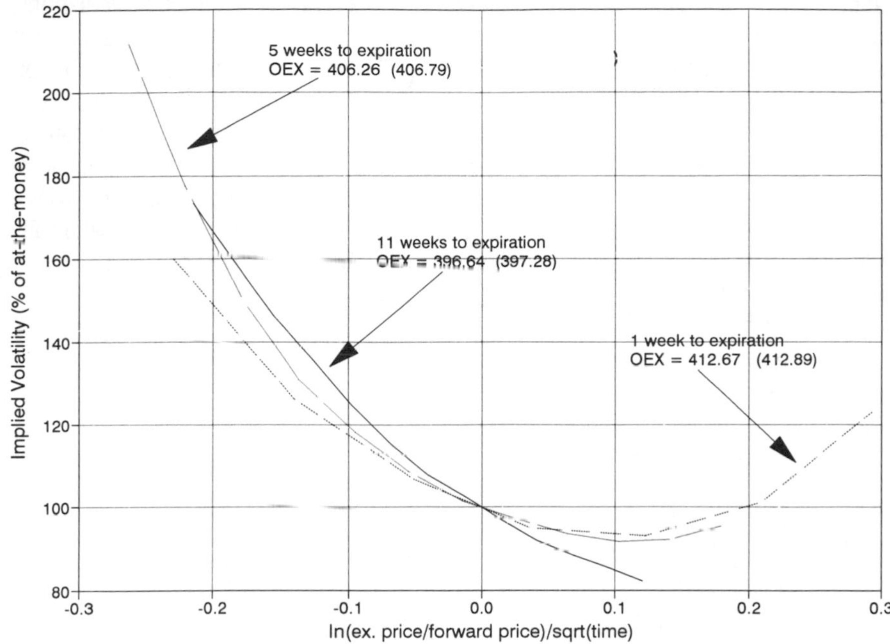

Figure 18-11d: OEX March 1993 Puts

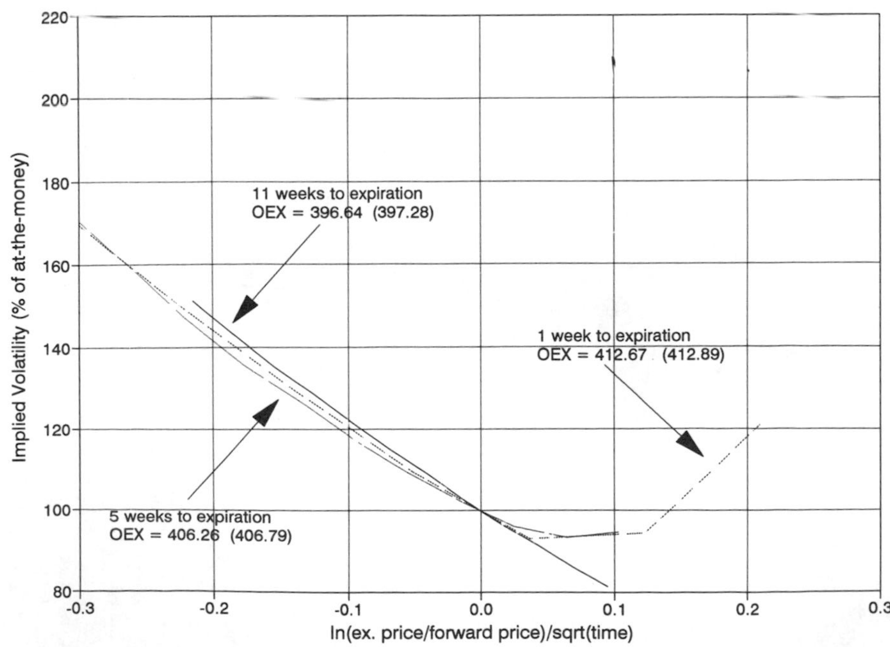

This text, like many others on options, may have left the reader with the impression that option evaluation and trading can be reduced to a series of arithmetic calculations. The science of option evaluation is an important part of any trader's education, but mathematical models are only a tool to help the trader make decisions. Successful option trading is at least as much an art as a science, and a trader must know where science leaves off, and other intangible assets, whether intuition or market feel or experience, begin. This brings us to one final point, and perhaps the most important principle of option trading: *there is no substitute for common sense.* A trader who slavishly uses a model to make every trading decision is heading for disaster. Only a trader who fully understands what a model can and cannot do will be able to make the model his servant rather than his master.

❖ Appendix A ❖

A Glossary of Option and Related Terminology

All or None (AON)—An order which must be filled in its entirety or not at all.

American Option—An option which can be exercised at any time prior to expiration.

Arbitrage—The purchase and sale of the same product in different markets to take advantage of a price disparity between the two markets.

Asian Option—Average price option.

Assignment—The process by which the seller of an option is notified of the buyer's intention to exercise.

At-the-Money—An option whose exercise price is equal to the current price of the underlying contract. On listed option exchanges the term is more commonly used to refer to the option whose exercise price is closest to the current price of the underlying contract.

Automatic Exercise—The exercise by the clearing house of an in-the-money option at expiration, unless the holder of the option submits specific instructions to the contrary.

Average Price Option—An option whose value at expiration is determined by the average price of the underlying instrument over some period of time.

Backspread—A spread, usually delta neutral, where more options are purchased than sold, and where all options have the same underlying contract and expire at the same time.

Backwardation—A futures market where the more distant delivery months trade at a discount to the nearterm delivery months.

Barrier Option—An option which will either become effective or cease to exist if the underlying instrument trades at some predetermined price prior to expiration.

Bear Spread—Any spread which will theoretically increase in value with a decline in the price of the underlying contract.

Box—A long call and short put at one exercise price, together with a short call and long put at a different exercise price. All options must have the same underlying contract and expire at the same time.

Bull Spread—Any spread which will theoretically increase in value with a rise in the price of the underlying contract.

Butterfly—The sale (purchase) of two options with the same exercise price, together with the purchase (sale) of one option with a lower exercise price and one option with a higher exercise price. All options must be of the same type, have the same underlying contract, and expire at the same time, and there must be an equal increment between exercise prices.

Buy/Write—The purchase of an underlying contract together with the sale of a call option on that contract.

Cabinet Bid—On some exchanges, a bid smaller than the minimum increment, permissible between traders desiring to close out positions in very far out-of-the money options.

Calendar Spread—A time spread.

Call Option—A contract between a buyer and a seller whereby the buyer acquires the right, but not the obligation, to purchase a specified underlying contract at a fixed price on or before a specified date. The seller of the call option assumes the obligation of delivering the underlying contract should the buyer wish to exercise his option.

Cap—A contract between a borrower and a lender of floating rate funds, whereby the borrower is assured of paying no more than some maximum interest rate for borrowed funds. This is analogous to a call option where the underlying instrument is an interest rate on borrowed funds.

Chooser Option—A straddle where the owner must decide by some predetermined date whether to keep either the call or the put.

Christmas Tree—A spread involving three exercise prices. One or more calls (puts) are purchased at the lowest (highest) exercise price and one or more calls (puts) are sold at each of the higher (lower) exercise prices. All options must expire at the same time, be of the same type, and have the same underlying contract.

Class—All options of the same type with the same expiration date and same underlying instrument.

Clearing House—The organization which guarantees the integrity of all trades made on an exchange.

Clearing Member—A member firm of an exchange which is authorized by the clearing house to process trades for its customers, and which guarantees, through the collection of margin and variation monies, the integrity of its customers' trades.

Collar—A contract between a borrower and a lender of floating rate funds, whereby the borrower is assured of paying no more than some maximum interest rate for borrowed funds, and whereby the lender is assured of receiving no less than some minimum interest rate on loaned funds. This is analogous to an option fence where the underlying instrument is an interest rate on borrowed funds.

Combination—A two-sided option spread which does not fall into any well defined category of spreads. Most commonly it is used to refer to a long call and short put, or short call and long put, which together make up a synthetic position in the underlying contract.

Compound Option—An option to purchase an option.

Condor—The sale (purchase) of two options with different exercise prices, together with the purchase (sale) of one option with a lower exercise price and one option with a higher exercise price. All options must be of the same type, have the same underlying contract, and expire at the same time, and there must be an equal increment between exercise prices.

Contango—A futures market where the more distant delivery months trade at a premium to the nearterm delivery months.

Contingency Order—An order which becomes effective only upon the fulfillment of some predetermined condition(s) in the marketplace.

Conversion—A long underlying position together with a short call and long put, where both options have the same exercise price and expire at the same time.

Covered Write—The sale of a call (put) option against an existing long (short) position in the underlying contract.

Cylinder—A fence or collar.

Deferred Start Option—A forward start option.

Delta (Δ)—The sensitivity of an option's theoretical value to a change in the price of the underlying contract.

Delta Neutral—A position where the sum total of all the positive and negative deltas adds up to approximately zero.

Diagonal Spread—A long call (put) at one exercise price and expiration date, together with a short call (put) at a different exercise price and expiration date. All options must have the same underlying stock or commodity. This is simply a time spread using different exercise prices.

Elasticity—The percent change in an option's value for a given percent change in the value of the underlying instrument. Sometimes referred to as the leverage value.

Exchange Option—An option to exchange one asset for another asset.

Ex-dividend—The day on which a dividend paying stock is trading without the right to receive the dividend.

Exercise—The process by which the holder of an option notifies the seller of his intention to take delivery of the underlying contract, in the case of a call, or to make delivery of the underlying contract, in the case of a put, at the specified exercise price.

Exercise Price—The price at which the underlying contract will be delivered in the event an option is exercised.

Expiration (Expiry)—The date and time after which an option may no longer be exercised.

European Option—An option which may only be exercised at expiration.

Extrinsic Value—Time value.

Fair Value—Theoretical value.

Fence—A long (short) underlying position, together with a long (short) out-of-the-money put and a short (long) out-of-the-money call. All options must expire at the same time.

Fill or Kill (FOK)—An order which will automatically be cancelled unless it can be executed immediately and in its entirety.

Flex Option—An exchange-traded option where the buyer and seller are permitted to negotiate the exact terms of the option contract. Typically, this includes the exercise price, the expiration date, and the terms of exercise (either European or American).

Floor—A contract between a borrower and a lender of floating rate funds, whereby the lender is assured of receiving no less than some minimum interest rate for loaned funds. This is analogous to a put option where the underlying instrument is an interest rate on loaned funds.

Forward Contract—A contract between a buyer and a seller whereby the buyer is obligated to take delivery and the seller is obligated to make delivery of a fixed amount of a commodity at a predetermined price on a specified future date. Payment in full is due at the time of delivery.

Forward Price—Taking into consideration all carrying costs on a contract, the price at which a contract would have to be trading on some future date such that a trade made at today's price would just break even.

Forward Start Option—An option whose exercise price will be equal to the price of the underlying instrument on some predetermined date.

Front Spread—A ratio vertical spread.

Fugit—The expected amount of time remaining to optimum early exercise of an American option.

Futures Contract—A contract, usually exchange-traded, between a buyer and a seller whereby the buyer is obligated to take delivery and the seller is obligated to make delivery of a fixed amount of a commodity at a predetermined price on some future date. All profits and losses are realized immediately, and result in a cash credit or debit based on daily changes in the settlement price of the contract.

Futures-Type Settlement—A settlement procedure used by commodity exchanges whereby an initial margin deposit is made, but under which no immediate cash payment is made by the buyer to the seller. Cash settlement takes place at the end of each trading day based on the difference between the current day's settlement price and the previous day's settlement price or the original trade price.

Gamma (Γ)—The sensitivity of an option's delta to a change in the price of the underlying contract.

Good 'til Cancelled (GTC)—An order to be held by a broker until it can either be executed or is cancelled by the customer.

Guts—A strangle where both the call and the put are in-the-money.

Haircut—On equity option exchanges, money deposited by a trader with the clearing house to ensure the integrity of his trades. This is similar to a margin requirement on a commodity exchange.

Hedge Ratio—Delta

Hedger—A trader who enters the market with the specific intent of protecting an existing position in an underlying contract.

Horizontal Spread—A time spread.

Immediate or Cancel (IOC)—An order which will automatically be cancelled if it is not filled immediately. An IOC order need not be filled in its entirety.

Implied Volatility—Assuming all other inputs are known, the volatility which would have to be input into a theoretical pricing model in order to yield a theoretical value identical to the price of the option in the marketplace.

In-Option—A type of barrier option which becomes effective only if the underlying instrument trades at some predetermined price prior to expiration.

In-Price—The price at which the underlying instrument must trade before an in-option becomes effective.

In-the-Money—A call (put) option whose exercise price is lower (higher) than the current price of the underlying contract.

Index Arbitrage—One of several strategies attempting to take advantage of the relative mispricing of options, futures contracts, or the physical stocks underlying a stock index.

Intermarket Spread—A spread consisting of opposing market positions in two different underlying securities or commodities, or their derivative products.

Intrinsic Value—The amount by which an option is in-the-money. Out-of-the-money options have no intrinsic value.

Iron Butterfly—A long (short) straddle, together with a short (long) strangle. All options must expire at the same time and have the same underlying contract.

Jelly Roll (Roll)—A long call and short put with one expiration date, together with a short call and long put with a different expiration date. All four options must have the same exercise price and same underlying stock or commodity.

Kappa (K)—Vega.

Knock Out Option—An out-option

Ladder—A Christmas tree.

Long-Term Equity Anticipation Security (LEAPS)—A long-term (usually more than one year) exchange traded equity option.

Leg—One side of a spread position.

Limit—The maximum allowable price movement over some time period for an exchange traded contract.

Limit Order—An order to be executed at a specified price or better.

Local—An independent trader on a commodity exchange. Locals perform functions similar to market makers on stock and stock option exchanges.

Locked Market—A market where trading has been halted because prices have reached their limit.

Long—A position resulting from the purchase of a contract. The term is also used to describe a position which will theoretically increase (decrease) in value should the price of the underlying contract rise (fall). Note that a long (short) put position is a short (long) market position.

Long Premium—A position which will theoretically increase in value should the underlying contract make a large move in either direction. The position will theoretically decrease in value should the underlying market sit still.

Long Ratio Spread—A backspread.

Look Back Option—An option whose exercise price will be equal to either the lowest price of the underlying instrument, in the case of a call, or the highest price of the underlying instrument, in the case of a put, over the life of the option.

Margin—Money deposited by a trader with the clearing house to ensure the integrity of his trades.

Market Maker—An independent trader or trading firm which stands ready to buy or sell contracts in a designated market. Market makers perform duties similar to locals on commodity exchanges, the primary difference being that a market maker is obligated to make a two-sided (bid and ask) market in his designated contract.

Market If Touched (MIT)—A contingency order which becomes a market order if the contract trades at or beyond a specified price.

Market On Close (MOC)—An order to be executed at the current market price as near as possible to the close of that day's trading.

Market Order—An order to be executed immediately at the current market price.

Naked—A long (short) market position with no offsetting short (long) market position.

Neutral Spread—A spread which is delta neutral. A spread may also be lot neutral, where the total number of long contracts and short contracts of the same type are equal.

Not Held—An order submitted to a broker, but over which the broker has discretion as to when and how the order is executed.

Omega (Ω)—The Greek letter sometimes used to denote an option's elasticity.

One Cancels the Other (OCO)—Two orders submitted simultaneously, either of which may be executed. If one order is executed, the other is automatically cancelled.

Order Book Official (OBO)—An exchange official responsible for executing market or limit orders for public customers.

Out-of-the-Money—An option which currently has no intrinsic value. A call (put) is out-of-the-money if its exercise price is more (less) than the current price of the underlying contract.

Out-Option—A type of barrier option which is deemed to have expired if the underlying instrument trades at some predetermined price prior to expiration.

Out-Price—The price at which the underlying instrument must trade before an out option is deemed to have expired.

Out-trade—A trade which cannot be processed by the clearing house due to conflicting information reported by the two parties to the trade.

Overwrite—The sale of an option against an existing position in the underlying contract.

Parity—Intrinsic value.

Pin Risk—The risk to the seller of an option that at expiration the option will be exactly at-the-money. The seller will not know whether the option will be exercised.

Portfolio Insurance—A process whereby the quantity of holdings in an underlying instrument is continuously adjusted to replicate the characteristics of an option on the underlying instrument.

Position—The sum total of a trader's open contracts in a particular underlying market.

Position Limit—For an individual trader or firm, the maximum number of open contracts in the same underlying market permitted by an exchange or clearing house.

Premium—The price of an option.

Program Trading—An arbitrage strategy involving the purchase or sale of a mispriced stock index futures contract against an opposing position in the stocks underlying the index.

Put Option—A contract between a buyer and a seller whereby the buyer acquires the right, but not the obligation, to sell a specified underlying contract at a fixed price on or before a specified date. The seller of the put option assumes the obligation of taking delivery of the underlying contract should the buyer wish to exercise his option.

Range Forward—A fence.

Ratio Backspread—A backspread.

Ratio Spread—Any spread where the number of long market contracts (long underlying, long call, or short put) and short market contracts (short underlying, short call, or long put) are unequal.

Ratio Vertical Spread—A spread, usually delta neutral, where more options are sold than are purchased, and where all options have the same underlying contract and expire at the same time.

Ratio Write—The sale of multiple options against an existing position in an underlying contract. This is simply a covered write using more than one option.

Reverse Conversion (Reversal)—A short underlying position together with a long call and short put, where both options have the same exercise price and expire at the same time.

Rho (ρ)—The sensitivity of an option's theoretical value to a change in interest rates.

Risk Conversion (Risk Reversal)—A fence which includes a long (short) underlying position.

Roll—A jelly roll.

Scalper—A floor trader on an exchange who hopes to profit by continually buying at the bid price and selling at the offer price in a specific market. Scalpers usually try to close out all positions at the end of each trading day.

Serial Expiration—On commodity exchanges, options on the same futures contract which expire in more than one month.

Series—All options with the same underlying contract, same exercise price, and same expiration date.

Short—A position resulting from the sale of a contract. The term is also used to describe a position which will theoretically increase (decrease) in value should the price of the underlying contract fall (rise). Note that a short (long) put position is a long (short) market position.

Short Premium—A position which will theoretically increase in value should the underlying contract sit still. The position will theoretically decrease in value should the underlying contract make a large move in either direction.

Short Ratio Spread—A ratio vertical spread.

Short Squeeze—A situation in the stock option market, usually resulting from a partial tender offer, where no stock can be borrowed to maintain a short stock position. If assigned on a short call position, a trader may be forced to exercise a call early in order to fulfill his delivery obligations, even though the call still has some time value remaining.

Sigma (σ)—The commonly used notation for standard deviation. Since volatility is usually expressed as a standard deviation, the same notation is often used to denote volatility.

Specialist—A market maker given exclusive rights by an exchange to make a market in either a specified contract or group of contracts. A specialist may buy or sell for his own account, or act as a broker for others. In return, a specialist is required to maintain a fair and orderly market.

Speculator—A trader who hopes to profit from a specific directional move in an underlying contract.

Spread—A long market position and an offsetting short market position usually, but not always, in the same underlying market.

Stock-Type Settlement—A settlement procedure in which the purchase of a contract requires full and immediate payment by the buyer to the seller. All profits or losses from the trade are unrealized until the position is liquidated.

Stop Limit Order—A contingency order which becomes a limit order if the contract trades at a specified price.

Stop (Loss) Order—A contingency order which becomes a market order if the contract trades at a specified price.

Straddle—A long (short) call and a long (short) put, where both options have the same underlying contract, the same expiration date, and the same exercise price.

Strangle—A long (short) call and a long (short) put, where both options have the same underlying contract, the same expiration date, but different exercise prices.

Strap—An archaic term for a position consisting of two long (short) calls and one long (short) put where all options have the same underlying contract, the same expiration date, and the same exercise price.

Strike Price (Strike)—Exercise price.

Strip—An archaic term for a position consisting of one long (short) call and two long (short) puts where all options have the same underlying contract, the same expiration date, and the same exercise price. *Also:* A series of futures or futures options designed to replicate the characteristics of a long-term contract or option.

Swap—An agreement to exchange different cash flows. Most commonly a swap involves exchanging variable rate interest payments for payments calculated from a fixed interest rate.

Swaption—An option to enter into a swap agreement.

Synthetic—A combination of contracts having approximately the same characteristics as a different contract.

Synthetic Call—A long (short) underlying position together with a long (short) put.

Synthetic Put—A short (long) underlying position together with a long (short) call.

Synthetic Underlying—A long (short) call and short (long) put, where both options have the same underlying contract, the same expiration date, and the same exercise price.

Tau (τ)—The commonly used notation for the amount of time remaining to expiration.

Theoretical Value—An option value generated by a mathematical model given certain prior assumptions about the terms of the option, the characteristics of the underlying contract, and prevailing interest rates.

Theta (θ)—The sensitivity of an option's theoretical value to a change in the amount of time remaining to expiration.

Three-Way—A position similar to a conversion or reversal, but where the long or short position in the underlying instrument has been replaced with a very deeply-in-the-money call or put.

Time Box—A long call and short put with the same exercise price and expiration date, together with a short call and long put at a different exercise price and expiration date. This is simply a jelly roll using different exercise prices.

Time Premium—Time value.

Time Spread—The purchase (sale) of one option expiring on one date and the sale (purchase) of another option expiring on a different date. Typically, both options are of the same type, have the same exercise price, and have the same underlying stock or commodity.

Time Value—The price of an option less its intrinsic value. The price of an out-of-the-money option consists solely of time value.

Type—The designation of an option as either a call or a put.

Underlying —The instrument to be delivered in the event an option is exercised.

Variation—The cash flow resulting each day from changes in the settlement price of a futures contract.

Vega—The sensitivity of an option's theoretical value to a change in volatility.

Vertical Spread—The purchase of one option and sale of one option, where both options are of the same type, have the same underlying contract, and expire at the same time, but have different exercise prices.

Volatility—The degree to which the price of an underlying instrument tends to fluctuate over time.

Volatility Skew—The tendency of options at different exercise prices to trade at different implied volatilities.

Warrant—A long-term call option. The expiration date of a warrant may under some circumstances be extended by the issuer.

Write—Sell an option.

❖ Appendix B ❖
The Mathematics of Option Pricing

OPTION PRICING MODELS

I. The Black-Scholes Model and Its Variations

Abbreviations used in the following mathematical formulae:

C	=	theoretical value of a call
P	=	theoretical value of a put
U	=	price of the underlying contract
E	=	exercise price
t	=	time to expiration in years
v	=	annual volatility expressed as a decimal fraction
r	=	risk-free interest rate expressed as a decimal fraction
e	=	base of the natural logarithm
ln	=	natural logarithm
N′(x)	=	the normal distribution curve
	=	$\frac{1}{\sqrt{2\pi}} e^{(-x^2/2)}$
N(x)	=	the cumulative normal density function (the area under N′(x))

A. *The Black-Scholes Model* for evaluating European options on non-dividend paying stocks (U = price of the underlying stock):[1]

$$C = UN(h) - Ee^{-rt} N(h - v\sqrt{t})$$

$$P = -UN(-h) + Ee^{-rt} N(v\sqrt{t} - h)$$

where

$$h = \frac{\ln\left(\frac{U}{E}\right) + \left(r + \frac{v^2}{2}\right)t}{v\sqrt{t}}$$

1. Black, Fischer and Scholes, Myron, "The Pricing of Options and Corporate Liabilities," *Journal of Political Economy*, Vol. 81, No. 3, May/June 1973, pages 637–654.

For stocks which pay dividends, the stock price (U) can be replaced by the current stock price less the present value of the expected dividends:

$$U = \sum_{j=1}^{n} d_i e^{-rt(i)}$$

where d_i = each expected dividend payout over the life of the option

t_i = the time in years to each dividend payout

The sensitivities of the Black-Scholes Model are:

$$\text{call delta} = N(h)$$
$$\text{put delta} = -N(-h)$$
$$\text{call gamma} = \text{put gamma} = \frac{N'(h)}{Uv\sqrt{t}}$$
$$\text{call theta} = \frac{Uv\,N'(h)}{2\sqrt{t}} + rEe^{-rt}N(h - v\sqrt{t})$$
$$\text{put theta} = \frac{Uv\,N'(h)}{2\sqrt{T}} - rEe^{-rt}N(v\sqrt{t} - h)$$
$$\text{call vega} = \text{put vega} = U\sqrt{t}\,N'(h)$$
$$\text{call rho} = tEe^{-rt}N(h-v\sqrt{t})$$
$$\text{put rho} = -tEe^{-rt}N(v\sqrt{t}-h)$$

B. *The Black Model* for evaluating European options on futures contracts (U = price of the futures contract):[2]

$$C = Ue^{-rt}N(h) - Ee^{-rt}N(h - v\sqrt{t})$$
$$P = -Ue^{-rt}N(-h) + Ee^{-rt}N(v\sqrt{t} - h)$$

$$\text{where } h = \frac{\ln\left(\frac{U}{E}\right) + \frac{v^2}{2}t}{v\sqrt{t}}$$

The sensitivities of the Black Model are:

$$\text{call delta} = e^{-rt}N(h)$$
$$\text{put delta} = -e^{-rt}N(-h)$$
$$\text{call gamma} = \text{put gamma} = \frac{e^{-rt}N'(h)}{Uv\sqrt{t}}$$
$$\text{call theta} = -rUe^{-rt}N(h) + rEe^{-rt}N(h - v\sqrt{t}) + Ue^{-rt}vN'(h)/2\sqrt{t}$$
$$\text{put theta} = rUe^{-rt}N(-h) - rEe^{-rt}N(v\sqrt{t}-h) + Ue^{-rt}vN'(h)/2\sqrt{t}$$

2. Black, Fischer, "The Pricing of Commodity Contracts", *Journal of Financial Economics*, No. 3, 1976, pages 167–179.

call vega = put vega = $Ue^{-rt}N'(h)\sqrt{t}$
call rho = $-tC$
put rho = $-tP$

C. *The Garman Kohlhagen Model* for evaluating European options on foreign currencies (U = price of the foreign currency in domestic currency units):[3]

$$C = Ue^{-r_f t}N(h) - Ee^{-r_d t}N(h - v\sqrt{t})$$

$$P = -U^{-r_f t}N(-h) + Ee^{-r_d t}N(v\sqrt{t} - h)$$

$$\text{where} \quad h = \frac{\ln\left(\frac{U}{E}\right) + \left(r_d - r_f + \frac{v^2}{2}\right)t}{v\sqrt{t}}$$

r_d = the risk-free rate in the domestic currency
r_f = the risk-free rate in the foreign currency

The sensitivities of the Garman-Kohlhagen Model are:

call delta	=	$e^{-r_f t}N(h)$
put delta	=	$-e^{-r_f t}N(-h)$
call gamma	=	put gamma = $\dfrac{e^{-r_f t}N^1(h)}{Uv\sqrt{t}}$
call theta	=	$r_f Ue^{-r_f t}N(h) - r_d Ee^{-r_d t}N(h - v\sqrt{t}) - Ue^{-r_f t}vN'(h)/2\sqrt{t}$
put theta	=	$-r_f Ue^{-r_f t}N(-h) + r_d Ee^{-r_d t}N(v\sqrt{t} - h) - Ue^{-r_f t}vN'(h)/2\sqrt{t}$
call vega = put vega	=	$Ue^{-r_f t}N'(h)\sqrt{t}$
call domestic rho	=	$te^{-r_d t}EN(h - \sqrt{t})$
put domestic rho	=	$-te^{-r_d t}EN(\sqrt{t} - h)$
call foreign rho	=	$-te^{-r_f t}EN(h)$
put foreign rho	=	$te^{-r_f t}EN(-h)$

Notes: The theta in the foregoing formulae is expressed in terms of decay over one full year. To express the theta in the more common form of daily decay, the resulting number must be divided by 365.

The vega is expressed in terms of the sensitivity to a one-full-point (100-percentage-point) change in volatility. To express the vega in the more common form of the sensitivity to a one-percentage-point change in volatility, the resulting number must be divided by 100.

3. Garman, Mark B. and Kohlhagen, Steven W., "Foreign Currency Option Values", *Journal of International Money and Finance*, Vol. 2, No. 3, December 1983, pages 231–237.
Grabbe, J. Orlin, "The Pricing of Call and Put Options on Foreign Exchange", *Journal of International Money and Finance*, Vol. 2, No. 3, December 1983, pages 239–253.

D. Darren Wilcox has suggested a variation on the Black Model where the underlying contract (U) is assumed to be normally distributed and may therefore take on negative values.[4]

$$C = e^{-rt}(U-E)N(h) + e^{-rt}N'(h)v\sqrt{t}$$

$$P = e^{-rt}(U-E)N(h) + e^{-rt}N(h)v\sqrt{t} - e^{-rt}(U-E)$$

where $h = \dfrac{U-E}{v\sqrt{t}}$

Note: Since this variation assumes a normal, rather than lognormal, distribution, the volatility, v, is the standard deviation of absolute price changes, rather than the standard deviation of logarithmic price changes.

The only difficulty in using the Black-Scholes Model or its variations is the calculation of N(x), the cumulative normal density function. Values for N(x) can be found in most statistical tables. Alternatively, the following approximation is suitable for most practical applications:

If $x \geq 0$, then
$N(x) = 1 - N'(x)(.4361836k - .1201676k^2 + .9372980k^3)$
where $k = 1/(1 + .33267\,|\,x\,|\,)$
and N′(x) is the normal distribution curve previously described.
If $x < 0$, then $N(x) = 1 - N(x)$

II. The Cox-Ross-Rubenstein (Binomial) Model[5]

The Cox-Ross-Rubenstein Model makes the assumption that over any period of time the underlying contract can move up (u) or down (d) by a given amount. The probability of an up move is given by p, and the probability of a down move is given by 1 – p. For example, suppose a certain contract is trading at 100, and over the next time period the contract will move up to 105 (u=5) or down to 95 (d=–5), and that there is a 50 percent chance (p=.5) of either outcome. If this is the only time period remaining to expiration, and there are no interest considerations, we can calculate the value of a 100 call as its expected return at the end the period. The call is worth intrinsic value if the underlying contract is above the exercise price, and zero if the underlying contract is below the exercise price. Its expected return is:

$$.5 \times (105 - 100) + 0 = 2.50$$

4. Wilcox, Darren, "Spread Options in Energy Markets", Research Paper, Goldman, Sachs & Co., March 1990.

5. Cox, John C.; Ross, Stephen A.; and Rubenstein, Mark; "Option Pricing: A Simplified Approach"; *Journal of Financial Economics*; No. 7, 1979; pages 229–263
For a good discussion of the computation required, see: Meisner, James E. and Labuszewski, John W.; "The Cox-Ross-Rubenstein Model for Alternative Underlying Instruments"; *Advances in Futures and Options Research*; Vol. 2, 1987; pages 263–278

In the same way we can calculate the value of a 90 call as:

$$.5 \times (105 - 90) + .5 \times (95 - 90) = 10$$

We can extend this approach by dividing the time to expiration into many small periods, and assume that over each period the underlying contract will always move up (u) or down (d). The result at expiration will be a *binomial tree*, with many possible prices at expiration for the underlying contract. An example of a three-period binomial tree is shown in Figure B-1.

If we assume that the probability, p, of an up move and the probability, 1-p, of a down move, is the same at each node of the binomial tree, it is a simple matter to calculate the probability of each price outcome at expiration. The expected return for the option is the sum, for each outcome where the option is in-the-money, of the difference between the option's exercise price and the underlying price, multiplied by the probability of that outcome. All outcomes where the option is out-of-the-money are set to zero.

In order to create a binomial tree which will approximate a lognormal distribution we can define the following:

$$u = e^{v\sqrt{t/n}}$$

$$d = 1/u$$

where n = the number of periods to expiration (the number of branches on the binomial tree)

Figure B-1

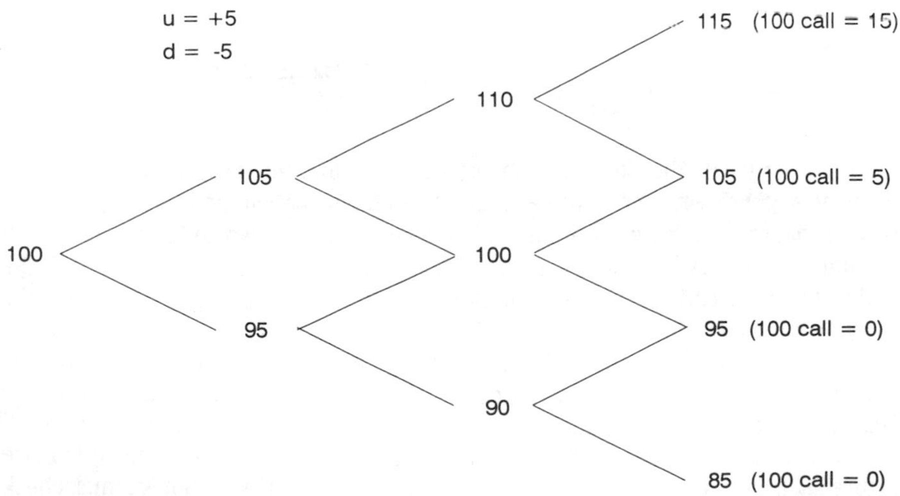

v = the annual volatility of the underlying contract
t = the time to expiration in years

As n becomes very large, the resulting terminal prices of the binomial tree converge to a lognormal distribution.

The probability, p, of an up move is determined by the requirement that the underlying market be arbitrage-free, i.e., that no profit can be made trading the underlying contract. If there are no interest considerations, which is the case with a futures contract, we can ensure that the underlying futures market is arbitrage-free by defining the probability, p, of an up move as:

$$p = (1-d)/(u-d)$$

In an arbitrage-free stock market, the stock price must increase by the amount of carrying costs over each period. If r is the risk-free rate, the rate, rr, by which the stock price must increase over each period is:

$$rr = 1 + (rt/n)$$

We can ensure that the underlying stock market is arbitrage-free by defining the probability, p, as:

$$p = (rr-d)/(u-d)$$

Finally, we must discount the expected return for the option by the carrying costs over the life of the option by multiplying the expected return by $1/(rr)^n$.

The basic form of the Cox-Ross-Rubenstein Model is:

$$C = \frac{1}{(rr)^n}\left[\sum_{k=0}^{n} \frac{n!}{k!(n-k)!}\, p^k(1-p)^{n-k}\max(0, u^k d^{n-k}U - E)\right]$$

$$P = \frac{1}{(rr)^n}\left[\sum_{k=0}^{n} \frac{n!}{k!(n-k)!}\, p^k(1-p)^{n-k}\max(0, E - u^k d^{n-k}U)\right]$$

In order to use the Cox-Ross-Rubenstein Model to evaluate an American option, we need to check whether at the beginning of each time period the value of the option is such that early exercise is warranted. For example, in our two-period example with the underlying at 100, we saw that the expected return for the 90 call was 10. If the option were settled in cash, the theoretical value of the option would be 10 less the carrying costs over the holding period. If the carrying costs were .25, the theoretical value of the option would be 9.75. If, however, the option were American, everyone would exercise the option in order to obtain 10 points right now. In other words, the fact that the option is American would require us to set the theoretical value at 10.

If we define U(i,j) as the jth underlying price at the end of the ith time period (see Figure B-2), and C(i,j) or P(i,j) as the call or put value at each U(i,j), then we must check to see whether each $C(i,j) < U(i,j) - E$, if we are evaluating an American call, or whether

Figure B-2

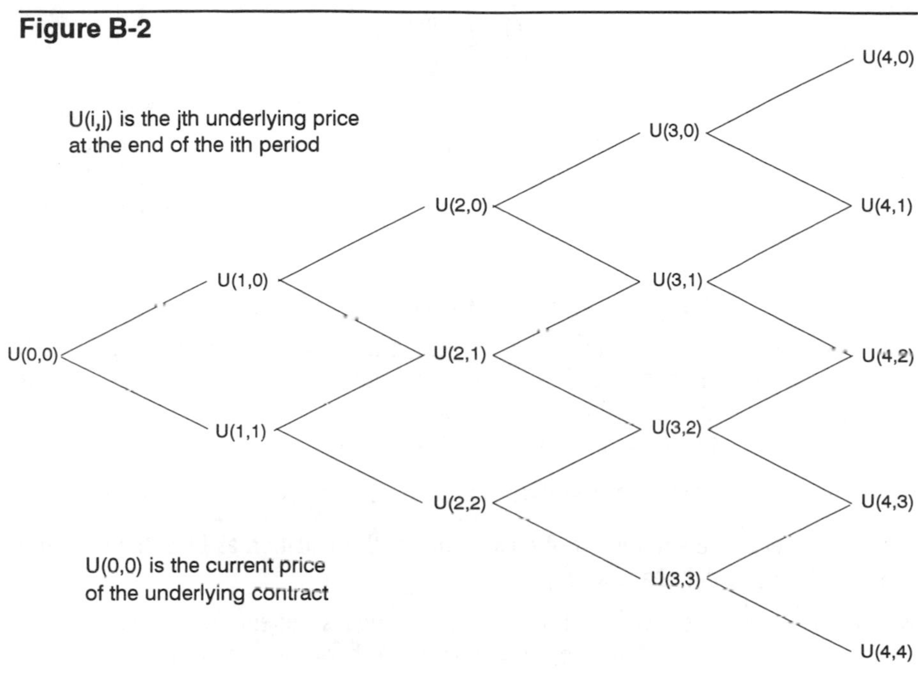

each P(i,j) < E–U(i,j), if we are evaluating an American put. If either condition is true the option becomes an early exercise canditate, and we set the value of C(i,j) equal to U(i,j)–E, or the value of P(i,j) equal to E–U(i,j).

We begin by calculating each terminal value U(n,j) for j=0,...,n. From these values we can calculate the value of the option at each previous node, C(n–1,j) or P(n–1,j) for j=0,...,n–1. If C(n-1,j) turns out to be less than U(n-1,j)–E, or if P(n-1,j) turns out to be less than E-U(n-1,j), the option value is set to parity, and the iterative procedure continues. We continue to work backwards to C(0,0) or P(0,0) (the current value of the call or put), always setting the value at each node, U(i,j), to max[C(i,j), U(i,j)-E] for a call, or max[P(i,j), E-U(i,j)] for a put:

$$C(i, j) = \max\left[\frac{pC(i+1, j) + (1-p)\,C(i+1, j+1)}{rr},\; U(i, j) - E\right]$$

$$P(i, j) = \max\left[\frac{pP(i+1, j) + (1-p)\,P(i+1, j+1)}{rr},\; E - U(i, j)\right]$$

Since the delta of an option is its change in value for a given change in the price of the underlying contract, we can also calculate call and put deltas from a binomial model:

$$\text{call } \Delta = \frac{C(1,1) - C(1,0)}{U(1,1) - U(1,0)}$$

$$\text{put } \Delta = \frac{P(1,1) - P(1,0)}{U(1,1) - U(1,0)}$$

The larger n is chosen, the more accurate the option value generated by the model will be. Unfortunately, as n increases, the number of calculations required to evaluate an American option increases geometrically. Most traders who use the Cox-Ross-Rubenstein model choose n somewhere between 25 and 50. This represents a reasonable trade-off between computer time and accuracy.

III. The Whaley (Quadratic) Model[6]

The Whaley Model uses an approximation technique to estimate the critical price, U^*, at which an American option should optimally be exercised early. This critical price is then used to determine the value of the option.

In order to find U^* for a call, we must solve the equation:

$$E - U^* = e^{(b-r)t}[U^*N(h) - EN(h - v\sqrt{t})] + [(1 - e^{(b-r)t}N(h - v\sqrt{t}))(U^*/q_2)]$$

(For convenience we will refer to the two sides of this equation as LHS [the left-hand side] and RHS [the right-hand side].)

where b = carrying costs on the underlying instrument (for futures $b = 0$; for stock $b = r$) and all other abbreviations are those used in the Black-Scholes Model

$$h = \frac{\ln\left(\frac{U^*}{E}\right) + \left(b + \frac{v^2}{2}\right)t}{v\sqrt{t}}$$

$$q_2 = [-(N-1) + \sqrt{((N-1)^2 + 4M/k)}]/2$$

$$M = 2r/v^2$$

$$N = 2b/v^2$$

$$k = 1\text{-}e^{-rt}$$

To solve for U^* we pick a desired degree of accuracy, ε, satisfying:

$$(\text{LHS} - \text{RHS}) / E < \varepsilon$$

We then perform progressive iterations, each time replacing U^*_i with:

$$U^*_{i+1} = [E + \text{RHS} - b_i U^*_1] / (1 - b_i)$$

where $b_i = e^{(b-r)t} N(hU^*_i)(1 - 1/q_2) + [1 - e^{(b-r)t} N'(hU^*_i/(v\sqrt{t})]/q_2$

Once U^* has been calculated to the desired degree of accuracy, the value of an American call, C, and its delta, Δ, can be found by solving:

$$C = c + A_2(U/U^*)^{q_2}$$

6. Barone-Adesi, Giovanni and Whaley, Robert E., "Efficient Analytic Approximation of American Option Values," *Journal of Finance*, Vol. 42, No. 2, June 1987, pages 301–320.

$$\Delta = \delta + A_2 q_2 (U/U^*)^{q_2}/U$$

where c = the value of a European call
δ = the delta of a European call
A_2 = $(U^*/q_2)[1\text{-}e^{(b-r)t}N(hU^*)]$

In order to find U^* for a put, we must solve the equation

$$E - U^* = e^{(b-r)t}[EN(h - v\sqrt{t}) - U^*N(h)] - [(1 - e^{(b-r)t}N(h))(U^*/q_1)]$$

(We again refer to the two sides of this equation as LHS [the left-hand side] and RHS [the right-hand side].)

where b = carrying costs on the underlying instrument (for futures $b = 0$; for stock $b = r$) and all other abbreviations are those used in the Black-Scholes Model

$$h = \frac{-\ln\left(\frac{U^*}{E}\right) + \left(b + \frac{v^2}{2}\right)t}{v\sqrt{t}}$$

q_1 = $[-(N-1) - \sqrt{((N-1)^2 + 4M/k)}]/2$
M = $2r/v^2$
N = $2b/v^2$
k = $1\text{-}e^{-rt}$

To solve for U^* we pick a desired degree of accuracy, ε, satisfying:

$$(LHS - RHS) / E < \varepsilon$$

We then perform progressive iterations, each time replacing U^*_i with:

$$U^*_{i+1} = [E - RHS - b_i U^*_i] / (1\text{-}b_i)$$

where $b_i = e^{(b-r)t}N(hU^*_i)(1 - 1/q_1) + [1 - e^{(b-r)t}N'(hU^*_i)/(v\sqrt{t})]/q_1$

Once U^* has been calculated to the desired degree of accuracy, the value of an American put, P, and its delta, Δ, can be found by solving:

$$P = p + A_1(U/U^*)^{q_1}$$
$$\Delta = \delta + A_1 q_1 (U/U^*)^{q_1}/U$$

where p = the value of a European put
δ = the delta of a European put
A_1 = $-(U^*/q_1)[1 - e^{(b-r)t}N(hU^*)]$

NORMAL DISTRIBUTIONS

Since the assumption that price changes are normally distributed plays such an important role in many theoretical pricing models, it may be useful to know how to compute some of the numbers associated with a normal distribution.

The Mean (m)

The mean (m) of a distribution of n occurrences is the average outcome of all the occurrences (x_i):

$$m = \frac{1}{n}\sum_{i=1}^{n} x_i$$

The Standard Deviation (σ)

The standard deviation (σ) of a distribution of n occurrences is defined as:[7]

$$\sigma = \sqrt{\frac{1}{n-1}\sum_{i=1}^{n} (x_i - m)^2}$$

If a distribution is normal, approximately 68.3 percent of the occurrences fall within one standard deviation of the mean, approximately 95.5 percent of the occurrences fall within two standard deviations of the mean, and approximately 99.7 percent of the occurrences fall within three standard deviations of the mean.

Skewness (Sk) and Kurtosis (Ku)

If a distribution is approximately normal, it may be useful to know how the distribution deviates from a true normal distribution. We can determine this by computing the skewness and kurtosis of the distribution.

Many of the measures associated with a distribution are derived from a group of numbers called *moments*. In general, the jth moment of a distribution about the mean is:

$$m_j = \frac{1}{n}\sum_{i=1}^{n} (x_i - m)^j$$

To determine the skewness and kurtosis of a distribution, we need the second, third, and fourth moments:

$$m_2 = \frac{1}{n}\sum_{i=1}^{n} (x_i - m)^2$$

---

7. Because we are dividing by (n-1) this is technically the *sample standard deviation*. This is the form which is most commonly used for volatility calculations.

$$m_3 = \frac{1}{n}\sum_{i=1}^{n}(x_i - m)^3$$

$$m_4 = \frac{1}{n}\sum_{i=1}^{n}(x_i - m)^4$$

The skewness of a distribution is defined as:

$$\text{skewness} = \frac{m_3}{m_2\sqrt{m_2}}$$

A perfectly normal distribution has a skewness of zero. If the distribution is positively skewed (Sk > 0), the right tail is longer than the left. If the distribution is negatively skewed (Sk < 0), the left tail is longer than the right.

The kurtosis of a distribution is defined as:

$$\text{kurtosis} = \frac{m_4}{{m_2}^2} - 3$$

A perfectly normal distribution has kurtosis of zero (mesokurtic). If a distribution has a positive kurtosis (Ku > 0), more occurrences fall in the middle and at the extreme tails of the distribution (leptokurtic). If a distribution has a negative kurtosis (Ku < 0), fewer occurrences fall in the middle and at the extreme tails of the distribution (platykurtic).

While almost all spreadsheets include the mean and standard deviation functions, and many also include skewness and kurtosis, it may be worthwhile to do a sample calculation.

Consider, for example, the pinball distribution in Figure 4-2 (reproduced in Figure B-3). In order to compute the mean, we must multiply the number of balls in each trough by the number of the trough, add up the total (563), and divide by the total number of balls (75):

$$\text{mean} = 563/75 = 7.507$$

To compute the standard deviation, for each ball we square the difference between its trough and the mean, add up all 75 results, divide by the number of occurrences less one (74), and take the square root of this number.

$$\text{standard deviation} = \sqrt{\frac{1}{n-1}\sum_{i=1}^{n}(x_i - m)^2}$$

$$= \sqrt{\frac{1}{74}\sum_{i=1}^{75}(x_i - 7.507)^2}$$

Figure B-3

Trough Number	Number of Occurrences	Value	Deviation from the Mean	Deviation Squared	Number of Occurrences × Deviation^2
0	0	0	–7.507	56.350	0
1	2	2	–6.507	42.337	84.673
2	2	4	–5.507	30.323	60.647
3	3	9	–4.507	20.310	60.930
4	5	20	–3.507	12.297	61.484
5	7	35	–2.507	6.283	43.984
6	8	48	–1.507	2.270	18.160
7	10	70	–.507	.0257	2.567
8	10	80	.493	.243	2.434
9	9	81	1.493	2.230	20.070
10	7	70	2.493	6.217	43.517
11	6	66	3.493	12.203	73.220
12	3	36	4.493	20.190	60.570
13	1	13	5.493	30.177	30.177
14	1	14	6.493	42.163	42.163
15	1	15	7.493	56.150	56.150
	75	563			660.747

$$= \sqrt{\frac{660.747}{74}}$$

$$= \sqrt{8.929}$$

$$= 2.988$$

While a detailed calculation of the skewness and kurtosis would require an inordinate amount of space, the relevant values are:

$$m_2 = 8.810$$
$$m_3 = .185$$
$$m_4 = 213.455$$

$$\text{skewness} = \frac{m_3}{m_2\sqrt{m_2}}$$
$$= \frac{.185}{8.810\sqrt{8.810}}$$
$$= \frac{.185}{26.149}$$

$= +.007$ (the right tail is slightly longer than the left)

$$\text{kurtosis} = \frac{m_4}{m_2{}^2} - 3$$
$$= \frac{213.455}{8.810^2} - 3$$
$$= 2.750 - 3$$

$= -.250$ (the distribution has a slightly flatter peak than one would expect)

VOLATILITY CALCULATIONS

Historical Volatility

The historical volatility is defined as the standard deviation of the logarithmic price changes measured at regular intervals of time. Since settlement prices are usually considered the most reliable, the most common method of computing volatility involves using settlement-to-settlement price changes. We define each price change (x_i) as:

$$x_i = \ln\left(\frac{P_i}{P_{i-1}}\right)$$

where P_i is the price of the underlying contract at the end of the ith time interval

P_i/P_{i-1} is sometimes referred to as the *price relative.*

As an example, consider the volatility of the price changes in Figure 5-1.

Week	Underlying Price	ln(P_i/P_i-1)	Mean	Deviation from Mean	Deviation Squared
0	101.35				
1	102.26	+.008939		.007771	.000060
2	99.07	−.031692		−.032859	.001080
3	100.39	+.013236		.012069	.000146
4	100.76	+.003679		.002512	.000006
5	103.59	+.027699	+.001167	.026532	.000704
6	99.26	−.042698		−.043865	.001924
7	98.28	−.009922		−.011089	.000123
8	99.98	+.017150		.015982	.000255
9	103.78	+.037303		.036136	.001306
10	102.54	−.012020		−.013188	.000174
		+.011674			.005778

We first calulate the standard deviation of the logarithmic price changes:

$$\begin{aligned}\text{standard deviation} &= \sqrt{(.005778/9)}\\ &= \sqrt{.000642}\\ &= .025338\end{aligned}$$

We then calculate the annual volatility by multiplying the standard deviation by the square root of the time interval between price changes. Since we looked at price changes every week, the time interval is 365/7:

$$\begin{aligned}\text{annualized volatility} &= .025338 \times \sqrt{(365/7)}\\ &= .025338 \times \sqrt{52.14}\\ &= .025338 \times 7.22\\ &= .1829\ (18.29\%)\end{aligned}$$

We can calculate the volatility of a stock, such as in Figure 5-2, in the same way except that we must remember that the volatility is based on the forward price. This requires two modifications. Over any interval of time, in order to maintain a theoretically arbitrage-free market, the stock price is expected to increase by the carrying costs on the stock over that period. If we record stock price changes at weekly intervals, the stock price is expected to rise by r/52, where r is the annualized, risk-free interest rate. The price changes are therefore expressed as:

$$x_i = \ln\left(\frac{P_i}{(1+r/52)P_{i-1}}\right)$$

When the stock gives up its dividend, this does not really cause a change in the stock price. We therefore include the dividend, D, in the price of the stock when calculating price change over the period when the stock goes ex-dividend:

$$x_i = \ln\left(\frac{P_i+D}{(1+r/52)(P_{i-1})}\right)$$

Over short periods of time, or in a low-interest-rate environment, the impact of interest rates on the forward price is small, and can usually be ignored when calculating historical stock price volatility.

The Extreme Value Method[8]

When reliable settlement prices are unavailable, the extreme value method is an acceptable alternative method of calculating historical volatility. The method uses high and low prices during a period, and each data point, x_i, is equal to:

$$x_i = .601 \cdot \ln(H_t/L_t)$$

where H_t = the highest price over time period t
L_t = the lowest price over time period t

The volatility is the standard deviation of all x_i, annualized by multiplying by the square root of the number of time periods, t, in a year. If t is a daily interval, we must

Figure B-4: Using a Newton-Raphson Search to Find the Implied Volatility

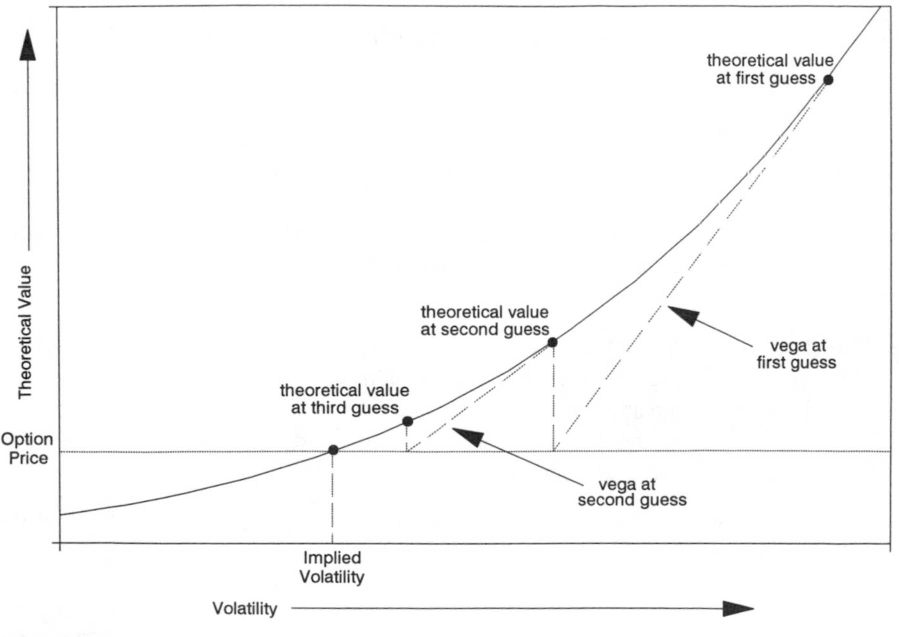

8. Parkinson, Michael, "The Extreme Value Method for Estimating the Variance of the Rate of Return", *Journal of Business*, Vol. 53, No.1, 1980, pages 61–65.

multiply by the square root of the number of trading days in a year (approximately 253); if t is a weekly interval, we must multiply by the square root of the number of trading weeks in a year (approximately 52).

Calculation of Implied Volatility

While it is not possible to invert the Black-Scholes Model to arrive at an implied volatility from a known option price, a Newton-Raphson search can be used to converge on the implied volatility quite quickly. We first make a guess as to the option's implied volatility, and then use the option's vega (sensitivity to a change in volatility) to come progressively closer to the true implied volatility. This method is illustrated in Figure B-4.

Because an option's vega is relatively linear, the method converges very quickly, usually with no more than four iterations, even with a poor first guess. The iterative process is:

$$x_{i+1} = x_i - \frac{y_i - p}{v_i}$$

where p = the option's price
x_i = the volatility
y_i = the option's theoretical value at volatility x_i
v_i = the option's vega at volatility x_i

We choose a desired degree of accuracy, ε, and continue with the process until $|y_i - p| < \varepsilon$, at which point x_i is the desired implied volatility.

THE EXPONENTIAL AND NATURAL LOGARITHM FUNCTIONS

Since the natural logarithm ($\ln(x)$) and exponential function (e^x) play such an important role in most theoretical pricing models, a brief discussion of their use may be worthwhile.

Suppose r = an annual interest rate, expressed as a decimal fraction
I = the amount of an investment
t = the time period over which the investment is made, expressed in years

When r is continuously compounded, the value, V, of I at the end of the time period, t, is given by:

$$V = e^{rt} \cdot I$$

When r is continuously compounded, the initial investment, I, required to yield V at the end of the time period is given by:

$$I = e^{-rt} \cdot V$$

I is referred to as the *present value* of V, i.e., V discounted by its carrying costs.

The yield, y, resulting from the continuous compounding of the interest rate, r, over the time period is given by:

$$y = e^{rt} - 1$$

The annualized yield is y/t.

Example: If r=10% (.10), the value of a $2,000 investment in three months (t–.25) if interest is compounded continuously will be:

$$\begin{aligned} V &= e^{rt} \cdot \$2{,}000 = e^{.10 \cdot .25} \cdot \$2{,}000 \\ &= e^{.025} \cdot \$2{,}000 = 1.0253 \cdot \$2{,}000 = \$2{,}050.63 \end{aligned}$$

Example: If r=6% (.06) and is compounded continuously, the amount of money one would need to invest to have $5,000 after eight months (t=.667) would be:

$$\begin{aligned} I &= e^{-rt} \cdot \$5{,}000 = e^{.06 \cdot .667} \cdot \$5{,}000 \\ &= e^{-.04} \cdot \$5{,}000 = .9608 \cdot \$5{,}000 = \$4{,}803.95 \end{aligned}$$

Example: If r=15% (.15) and is compounded continuously, the total yield on a six-month (t=.5) investment will be:

$$y = e^{rt} - 1 = e^{.15 \cdot .5} - 1 = e^{.075} - 1 = .0779\ (7.79\%)$$

The total annualized yield is:

$$y/t = .0779/.5 = .1558\ (15.58\%)$$

If I is the amount initially invested, the continuously compounded rate of return, r_t, needed to yield V over some period of time, t, is given by:

$$r_t = \ln(V/I)$$

If V is greater than I, the resulting rate of return will be a positive number. If V is less than I, the resulting rate of return will be a negative number. The annualized rate of return is:

$$r = r_t/t = \ln(V/I)/t$$

Example: Assuming continuous compounding, the annual rate of return required for an initial investment of $3,000 to yield $3,200 in nine months (t=.75) is:

$$\begin{aligned} r &= \ln(3{,}200/3{,}000)/.75 = \ln(1.0667)/.75 \\ &= .0645/.75 = .0861(8.61\%) \end{aligned}$$

Note that the exponential and logarithmic functions are inverses:

$$\ln(e^{x}) = e^{\ln(x)} = x$$

Because volatility is also a rate of return, and is assumed to be continuously compounded, the exponential and logarithmic functions can be used to calculate expected price changes of an underlying contract.

Example: Suppose a certain futures contract is trading at a price, P, of 50 and has an annual volatility, v, of 12%. A one standard deviation upward price change is

$$e^{v} \cdot P = e^{.12} \cdot 50 = 1.1275 \cdot 50 = 56.37$$

A one standard deviation downward price change is

$$e^{-v} \cdot P = e^{-.12} \cdot 50 = .8869 \cdot 50 = 44.35$$

Since we know that one standard deviation takes in about 68 percent of all outcomes, we know that if the volatility figure of 12% is correct, there is a 68 percent chance that one year from now the same futures contract will be trading between 44.35 and 56.37.

What about a two standard deviation price change? If the move is upward, we calculate:

$$e^{.12 \cdot 2} \cdot 50 = e^{.24} \cdot 50 = 1.2712 \cdot 50 = 63.56$$

If the move is downward, we calculate:

$$e^{-.12 \cdot 2} \cdot 50 = e^{-.24} \cdot 50 = .7866 \cdot 50 = 39.33$$

Since we know that two standard deviations takes in about 95% of all outcomes, we know that if the volatility figure of 12% is correct, there is a 95% chance that one year from now the same futures contract will be trading between 63.56 and 39.33.

For time periods other than one year we must also take into consideration the square root relationship between time and volatility. If a one standard deviation price change over a period is given by v, then a one standard deviation price change over a period which is twice as long is $v\sqrt{2}$. Similarly, a one standard deviation price change over a period only half as long is $v\sqrt{.5}$. The generalized rule is:

$$\text{volatility (standard deviation) over the period } t = v \cdot \sqrt{t}$$

where v is the annualized volatility and t is the time period in years. This enables us to express a move of n standard deviations over t as either:

$$e^{n \cdot v \cdot \sqrt{t}} \cdot P \text{ (an upward move)}$$

or

$$e^{-n \cdot v \cdot \sqrt{t}} \cdot P \text{ (a downward move)}$$

where P is the current price of the contract.

Example: With an underlying contract at 84.00 and an annual volatility of 16%, a one and two standard deviation price change over a three-month period (t = .25) is:

$$\begin{aligned} e^{.16\sqrt{.25}} \cdot 84.00 &= e^{.16 \cdot .5} \cdot 84.00 = e^{.08} \cdot 84.00 \\ &= 1.0833 \cdot 84.00 = 91.00 \text{ (up 1 standard deviation)} \end{aligned}$$

$$e^{2\cdot.16\sqrt{.25}} \cdot 84.00 = e^{2\cdot.16\cdot.5} \cdot 84.00 = e^{.16} \cdot 84.00$$
$$= 1.1735 \cdot 84.00 = 98.57 \text{ (up 2 standard deviations)}$$

$$e^{-.16\sqrt{.25}} \cdot 84.00 = e^{-.16\cdot.5} \cdot 84.00 = e^{-.08} \cdot 84.00$$
$$= .9231 \cdot 84.00 = 77.54 \text{ (down 1 standard deviation)}$$

$$e^{-2\cdot.16\sqrt{.25}} \cdot 84.00 = e^{-2\cdot.16\cdot.5} \cdot 84.00 = e^{-.16} \cdot 84.00$$
$$= .8521 \cdot 84.00 = 71.58 \text{ (down 2 standard deviations)}$$

Given a volatility and time period we can always calculate the number of standard deviations required to reach an outcome. If we have a table of standard deviations and their associated probabilities, we can then find the probability associated with that outcome.

In the case of options, we might often be interested in the probability of an option with a certain exercise price being in-the-money at expiration. The movement, in standard deviations, required for an underlying contract with price, P, to go through an exercise price, E, at expiration is given by:

$$\text{number of standard deviations} = \frac{\ln(E/P)}{v\sqrt{t}}$$

Example: If conditions are the same as in the last example (v=.16, P=84.00), the movement, in standard deviations, required for a 95 call to finish in-the-money three months from now is:

$$\ln(95/84)/(.16\cdot\sqrt{.25}) = \ln(1.1310)/.08 = .1231/.08 = +1.5383 \text{ st. devs.}$$

Checking a table of standard deviations, we find that there is approximately a 6.2% chance, or about one chance in 16, of an upward move of 1.5383 standard deviations.

In the case of a stock, a slight modification is necessary because the volatility represents price movement away from the forward price. If P is the current stock price, t is the time period, r is the risk-free interest rate, and D is the amount of dividends expected over the period, the forward price of the stock, P_f, is:

$$P_f = P \cdot e^{rt} - D$$

Example: Suppose interest rates are at 8%. If a certain non-dividend paying stock is trading at 38 and has an annual volatility of 27%, the movement, in standard deviations, needed for a 35 put to finish in-the-money six months (t=.5) from now is:

$$\ln[35/(38\cdot e^{.08\cdot.5})/(.27\cdot\sqrt{.5}) = \ln(35/39.55)/.191$$
$$= -.122/.191 = -.64 \text{ standard deviations}$$

Checking a table of standard deviations, we find that there is approximately a 26% chance, or about one chance in four, of a downward move of .64 standard deviations.

❖ Appendix C ❖

Characteristics of Volatility Spreads

Figure C-1: Characteristics of Volatility Spreads

(all spreads are assumed to be approximately delta neutral)

Spread Type	Initial Delta	Initial Gamma	Initial Theta	Initial Vega	A large move in the underlying generally	An increase(decrease) in implied volatility generally	The passage of time generally	Upside contract position	Downside contract position
Call backspread	0	+	–	+	helps	helps (hurts)	hurts	long	0
Put backspread	0	+	–	+	helps	helps (hurts)	hurts	0	short
Call ratio vertical spread	0	–	+	–	hurts	hurts (helps)	helps	short	0
Put ratio vertical spread	0	–	+	–	hurts	hurts (helps)	helps	0	long
Long straddle	0	+	–	+	helps	helps (hurts)	hurts	long	short
Short straddle	0	–	+	–	hurts	hurts (helps)	helps	short	long
Long strangle	0	+	–	+	helps	helps (hurts)	hurts	long	short
Short strangle	0	–	+	–	hurts	hurts (helps)	helps	short	long
Long butterfly	0	–	+	–	hurts	hurts (helps)	helps	0	0
Short butterfly	0	+	–	+	helps	helps (hurts)	hurts	0	0
Long time spread (1:1 ratio)	0	–	+	+	hurts	helps (hurts)	helps	0	0
Short time spread (1:1 ratio)	0	+	–	–	helps	hurts (helps)	hurts	0	0

❖ Appendix D ❖

What's the Right Strategy?

The following chart is designed to help the reader choose the types of strategies which are most likely to be profitable given a trader's opinion on market direction and volatility. Even though several strategies may be appropriate under the same market conditions, each strategy will have its own unique risk/reward characteristics. The reader should refer to the text for a more detailed analysis of each strategy.

The implied volatility component, whether low, moderate, or high, is in comparison to a trader's own volatility forecast. If the trader believes that 15% is a reasonable forecast, but implied volatility is 13%, then implied volatility is low. If the trader believes that 20% is a reasonable forecast, but implied volatility is 24%, then implied volatility is high. If the trader's volatility forecast is approximately the same as the implied volatility, then implied volatility is moderate.

Any of the listed strategies can be done synthetically. Instead of buying (selling) a call, a trader can buy (sell) a put with the same exercise price and buy (sell) an underlying contract (synthetic long (short) call). Instead of buying (selling) a put, a trader can buy (sell) a call with the same exercise price and sell (buy) an underlying contract (synthetic long (short) put).

The only scenario for which there is no appropriate strategy is one in which a trader has no opinion on either implied volatility or market direction. In such a case a disciplined trader will choose to sit on the sidelines until trading conditions become more opportune.

In-the-money call butterflies and time spreads, and out-of-the-money put butterflies and time spreads, are those in which all exercise prices are lower than the current price of the underlying contract. Out-of-the-money call butterflies and time spreads, and in-the-money put butterflies and time spreads, are those in which all exercise prices are higher than the current price of the underlying contract.

Figure D-1: What's the Right Strategy?

ITM = in-the-money ATM = at-the-money OTM = out-of-the-money

MARKET DIRECTION	IMPLIED VOLATILITY: Low	Moderate	High
Bearish	buy naked puts bear vertical spreads buy ATM call/sell ITM call buy ATM put/sell OTM put sell OTM (ITM) call (put) butterflies buy ITM (OTM) call (put) time spreads	sell the underlying	sell naked calls bear vertical spreads: buy OTM call/sell ATM call buy ITM put/sell ATM put buy ITM (OTM) call (put) butterflies sell OTM (ITM) call (put) time spreads
Neutral	backspreads buy straddles/strangles sell ATM call or put butterflies buy ATM call or put time spreads	go on vacation	ratio vertical spreads sell straddles/strangles buy ATM call or put butterflies sell ATM call or put time spreads
Bullish	buy naked calls bull vertical spreads: buy ATM call/sell OTM call buy ATM put/sell ITM put sell ITM (OTM) call (put) butterflies buy OTM (ITM) call (put) time spreads	buy the underlying	sell naked puts bull vertical spreads: buy ITM call/sell ATM call buy OTM put/sell ATM put buy OTM (ITM) call (put) butterflies sell ITM (OTM) call (put) time spreads

❖ Appendix E ❖

Synthetic and Arbitrage Relationships

SYNTHETIC EQUIVALENTS AND ARBITRAGE STRATEGIES

(Unless otherwise noted, options are assumed to have the same exercise price and expiration date.)

Synthetic Equivalents:

synthetic long underlying = long call + short put
synthetic short underlying = short call + long put

synthetic long call = long underlying + long put
synthetic short call = short underlying + short put

synthetic long put = short underlying + long call
synthetic short put = long underlying + short call

Arbitrage Strategies:

conversion = long underlying + synthetic short underlying
= long underlying + short call + long put

reverse conversion = short underlying + synthetic long underlying
= short underlying + long call + short put

box = synthetic long underlying at one exercise price + synthetic short underlying at a different exercise price

jelly roll = synthetic long underlying in one expiration month + synthetic short underlying in a different expiration month

ARBITRAGE VALUES FOR EUROPEAN OPTIONS
(no early exercise permitted)

(In the following relationships "carrying cost" is meant to be the cost of carry to expiration. "Present value" is the value at expiration discounted by the carrying costs. For a more detailed discussion of "present value", see the description of the exponential function in Appendix B.)

For Futures Markets

synthetic underlying market = call – put price
= underlying price – exercise price – carrying cost (futures price – exercise price)

box market = present value (amount between exercise prices)

(When options in a futures market are subject to futures-types settlement, all carrying costs are zero, and the present value is identical to the expiration value.)

For Stocks

synthetic underlying market = call price – put price
= underlying price price – exercise price + carrying price (exercise price) – expected dividends

box market = present value (amount between excise prices)

jelly roll market = carrying costs on the exercise price from one expiration to the next – expected dividends
= present value (long–term exercise price) – present value (short–term exercise price) – expected dividends

OTHER USEFUL RELATIONSHIPS

box = conversion at one exercise price + reverse conversion at a different exercise price
= bull (bear) vertical call spread + bear (bull) vertical put spread

call butterfly = put butterfly with the same exercise prices and expiration dates

long (short) call butterfly + short (long) put butterfly with the same exercise prices
= long (short) box at the lower exercise prices + short (long) box at the higher exercise prices

long (short) butterfly = short (long) iron butterfly
= short (long) straddle + long (short) strangle

jelly roll = conversion in one month + reverse conversion in a different month
= long (short) call time spread + short (long) put time spread

❖ Appendix F ❖
Recommended Reading

This book represents only one of many possible approaches to option evaluation and trading. The reader who desires a complete proficiency in options is strongly advised to seek out as many different sources of information as possible.

The following list includes those books which are likely to be of interest to the serious option trader. An attempt has been made to categorize books according to their level of difficulty (usually in terms of the mathematics involved), although categorizations are subjective and in some cases may overlap. Where possible, the primary focus of the book (stock options, futures options, interest rates, currencies, etc.) has also been noted.

(References to academic articles, including the original presentation of the more commonly used pricing models, appear as footnotes in the text.)

ELEMENTARY BOOKS

Barenblat, Scot G.; and Mesler, Donald T.
Stock Index Options (stock indexes)
Probus Publishing Co.; Chicago, IL
1992; 206 p.

Caplan, David
The Options Advantage (futures)
Probus Publishing Co.; Chicago, IL
1991; 222 p.

Colburn, James T.
Trading in Options on Futures (futures)
The New York Institute of Finance; New York, NY
1990; 310 p.

Frost, Ronald J.
Options on Futures, Revised Edition (futures)
Probus Publishing Co.; Chicago, IL
1994; 254 p.

Fullman, Scott H.
Options: A Personal Seminar (stocks)
New York Institute of Finance; New York, NY
1992; 373 p.

Hexton, Richard
Dealing in Traded Options (stocks)
Prentice-Hall International Ltd.; Hertfordshire, UK
1989; 192 p.

Luft, Carl F.; and Sheiner, Richard K.
Understanding and Trading Listed Stock Options, Rev. Ed. (stocks)
Probus Publishing Co.; Chicago, IL
1994, 231 p.

Mayer, Terry S.
Commodity Options (futures)
New York Institute of Finance; New York, NY
1983; 300 p.

McMillan, Lawrence G.
Options as a Strategic Investment (stocks)
The New York Institute of Finance; New York, NY
Third Edition, 1993; 882 p.

The Options Institute (editor)
Options: Essential Concepts and Trading Strategies (stocks)
Business One Irwin; Homewood, IL
1990; 403 p.

Smith, Courtney
Option Strategies (stocks)
John Wiley & Sons, Inc.; New York, NY
1987; 256 p.

Thomsett, Michael C.
Getting Started in Options (stocks)
John Wiley & Sons, Inc.; New York, NY
1989; 229 p.

Walker, Joseph A.
How the Options Markets Work (stocks)
New York Institute of Finance; New York, NY
1991; 229 p.

Wasendorf, Russell R.; and McCafferty, Thomas A.
All About Options
Probus Publishing Co.; Chicago, IL
1993; 213 p.

INTERMEDIATE BOOKS

Baird, Allen Jan
Option Market Making (futures)
John Wiley & Sons, Inc.; New York, NY
1993; 201 p.

Bookstaber, Richard M.
Option Pricing and Investment Strategies (stocks)
Third Edition
Probus Publishing Co.; Chicago, IL
1991; 300 p.

Bookstaber, Richard M.; and Clarke, Roger G.
Option Strategies for Institutional Investment Management (stocks)
Addison-Wesley Publishing Co., Inc.; Menlo Park, CA
1983; 168 p.

Clasing, Henry K, Jr.; Lombard, Odile; and Marteau, Didier
Currency Options (currencies)
Business One Irwin; Homewood, IL
1992; 270 p.

Denning, Hugh
Equity Options: Valuation, Trading & Practical Strategies (stocks)
Longman Professional; Melbourne, Australia
1991; 183 p.

DeRosa, David F.
Options on Foreign Exchange (currencies)
Probus Publishing Co.; Chicago, IL
1992; 272 p.

Fabozzi, Frank J.
Winning the Interest Rate Game: A Guide to Debt Options (interest rates)
Probus Publishing Co.; Chicago, IL
1985; 300 p.

Fabozzi, Frank J.
The Handbook of Fixed-Income Options (interest rates)
Probus Publishing Co.; Chicago, IL
1989; 657 p.

Figlewski, Stephen; Silber, William L.;
and Subrahmanyam, Marti G. (editors)
Financial Options: From Theory to Practice
Business One Irwin; Homewood, IL
1992; 579 p.

Fitzgerald, Desmond M.
Financial Options (stocks)
Euromoney Publications; London, England
1987; 262 p.

Gastineau, Gary
The Options Manual (stocks)
McGraw Hill; New York, NY
Third Edition, 1988; 440 p.

Gemmill, Gordon
Option Pricing: An International Perspective
McGraw-Hill; London
1993; 267 p.

Kolb, Robert W.
Options: The Investor's Complete Toolkit (stocks)
New York Institute of Finance; New York, NY
1991; 216 p.

Labuszewski, John W.; and Nyhoff, John E.
Trading Options on Futures (futures)
John Wiley & Sons, Inc.; New York, NY
1988; 264 p.

Labuszewski, John; and Sinquefield, Jeanne
Inside the Commodity Option Markets (futures)
John Wiley & Sons, Inc.; New York, NY
1985; 384 p.

Smith, A.L.H.
Trading Financial Options
Butterworths; London, England
1986; 200 p.

Sutton, W. H.
Trading Currency Options (currencies)
The New York Institute of Finance; New York, NY
1988; 208 p.

Tompkins, Robert
Options Explained (futures/interest rates)
MacMillan Publishers Ltd.; Basingstoke, Hants, England
1991; 301 p.

Wong, M. Anthony
Trading and Investing in Bond Options (interest rates)
John Wiley & Sons, Inc.; New York, NY
1991; 262 p.

ADVANCED BOOKS

Brenner, Menachem (editor)
Option Pricing: Theory and Applications (stocks)
Lexington Books; Lexington, MA
1983; 235 p.

Cox, John C.; and Rubenstein, Mark
Options Markets (stocks)
Prentice-Hall; Englewood Heights, NJ
1985; 498 p.

Gibson, Rajna
Option Evaluation: Analyzing and Pricing Standardized Option Contracts
McGraw-Hill, Inc.; New York, NY
1991; 304 p.

Hodges, Stewart (editor)
Options: Recent Advances in Theory and Practice
Manchester University Press; Manchester, England
1990; 181 p.

Hull, John C.
Options, Futures, and Other Derivative Securities
Prentice-Hall, Inc.; Englewood Cliffs, NJ
2nd Edition, 1993; 492 p.

Jarrow, Robert; and Rudd, Andrew
Option Pricing (stocks)
Dow Jones-Irwin; Homewood, IL
1983; 235 p.

Ritchken, Peter
Options: Theory, Strategy and Applications (stocks)
Scott, Foresman and Co.; Glenview, IL
1987; 414 p.

Index

❖ A ❖

Adjustment, 84, 168–169, 193–195
American Stock Exchange, 6n, 303
Assignment, 4–6, 224–225
Arbitrage, 218, 456
ARCH Model, 280
At-the-money. *See* Option, at-the-money

❖ B ❖

Backspread, 138–139, 145, 200, 452
  intermarket, 338
Backwardation, 129
Barone-Adesi, Giovanni, 248, 438n
Beckers, Stan, 66n, 397n, 400n
Binomial tree, 435
Black, Fischer, 40n, 43, 431n, 432n
Bollerslav, T., 281n
Box, 228-231, 254, 456–458
Burghardt, Galen, 275n
Butterfly, 145–148, 235–236, 452, 458
  body of, 145n
  bull and bear, 201
  wings of, 145n
Buy/write, 261

❖ C ❖

Calendar spread. *See* Time spread
Cap, 265
Carrying costs, 38, 41–42, 111, 221–223, 249–250, 436. *See also* Interest rates
Chicago Board of Trade (CBOT), 2, 6n, 128, 129, 134
Chicago Board Options Exchange (CBOE), 2, 43, 120, 197, 231, 323, 329n, 343
Chicago Mercantile Exchange (CME), 2, 120, 133, 272, 323, 324n
Chicago Stock Exchange, 303, 327n
Christmas tree, 157–158
Clearing firm, 8–9
Clearing house, 8–9
Collar, 265
Commodity Exchange, Inc. (COMEX), 105, 128, 131
Condor, 158
Contango relationship, 128
Contingency order, 170
Contract position, 360
Conversion, 217–219, 456
Conversion/reversal market, 219. *See also* Synthetic market
Covered write, 260–262
Cox, John, 248, 400n, 434n
Curvature. *See* Gamma
Cylinder, 264

❖ D ❖

Delta, 82, 99, 359–360
  American vs. European option, 250, 253
  as a condition for early exercise, 246–248
  as a probability, 102
  as a rate of change, 99
  as an equivalent underlying position, 101–102
  characteristics, 118
  dollar ($delta), 332
  effect of price change. *See* Gamma
  effect of volatility change, 106, 110, 210

effect of time passage, 106, 110
implied, 120
of an index futures contract, 311–312
risk, 179, 353
Delta neutral, 82, 106, 110, 137, 159, 199, 227
Diagonal spread, 157, 201n
Diffusion process, 394–395
Distribution, 400–404
high volatility, 55, 56
lognormal, 61–64
low volatility, 54, 56
normal, 52-53, 440
Dividend, 38, 42, 49, 113n, 120, 244n
effect on arbitrage, 228
effect on early exercise, 243–245
effect on index futures, 306–307
Dividend play, 250–251
Dollar delta neutral, 333
Down-tick, 93
Dynamic hedge, 93

❖ E ❖

Edge, 37, 123, 173, 175, 359
Elasticity, 123-124, 126
Engle, R.F., 281n
Execution risk, 224
Exercise, 4-5, 224–225
Exercise price, 1-4, 44–45, 46
Ex-dividend, 48
Expected return, 36-37, 40, 210
Expiration, 1–4, 44–45, 46–47
Exponential function, 446–449

❖ F ❖

Fence, 263-265
Figlewski, Stephen, 40n
Floor, 265
Forced liquidation, 227, 255
Forward price, 42
Front spread. *See* Ratio vertical spread

❖ G ❖

Gamma, 103, 105-106, 160, 360–361
and adjustments, 196
characteristics, 118–119
dollar ($gamma), 346
effect of changing market conditions, 106
implied, 120
of volatility spreads, 160–161
risk, 179, 353
GARCH Model, 281
Garman, Mark B., 66n, 433n
Grabbe, J. Orlin, 433n
Graph
expiration, 23–24
theoretical, 358–363
Guts, 143

❖ H ❖

Haircut, 9n
Heath, David, 393n
Hedge ratio, 45, 82, 101. *See also* Delta
Ho, Thomas, 393n
Horizontal spread. *See* Time spread
Hull, John, 393n

❖ I ❖

In-the-money. *See* Option, in-the-money
Index, 301
capitalization weighted, 302
divisor, 303
implied value, 309
options, early exercise of, 316–320
price weighted, 302
quoted price, 311
replication, 304–305
substitute, 322–326
Interest rates, 38, 45, 47–48, 87, 116, 129, 264–265, 388–389, 445
effect on arbitrage, 223–224
effect on early exercise, 241–242, 245–246, 250n
effect on index futures, 306
Interest play, 252
Investor's Business Daily, 31n
Iron butterfly, 158

❖ J ❖

Jarrow, Robert, 393n
Jelly roll, 231–233, 254, 456–458
Jump-diffusion process, 395, 397
Jump process, 394–395

❖ K ❖

Kappa. *See* Vega
Klass, Michael J., 66n
Kohlhagen, Steven W., 433n
Kuberek, Robert C., 281n
Kurtosis, 402–404, 440–441, 443

❖ L ❖

Ladder. *See* Christmas tree
Lane, Morton, 275n
LEAPS, 388
Lee, Sang-Bin, 393n
Leg, 181n
Leverage value, 124
Liquidity, 181, 196-197, 272
Logarithmic function, 446–449
London International Financial Futures and Options Exchange (LIFFE), 405
Long, 11–12
Long premium, 160
Lot position. *See* Contract position

❖ M ❖

Margin, 9–10, 255
Market
  arbitrage-free, 42
  frictionless, 87, 386
  locked, 87, 386
Mean, 56-57, 59, 60, 440–441
Merton, Robert, 397n
Model, 37–38
  ARCH (autoregressive conditional heteroskedasticity), 280, 281n
  binomial. *See* Model, Cox-Ross-Rubenstein
  Black, 44, 353n, 432–433
  Black-Scholes, 43–44, 48, 81, 248, 315, 352, 353n, 431–432, 446
    assumptions in, 64, 385
  CEV (constant elasticity of variance), 400
  Cox-Ross-Rubenstein, 248–249, 315, 347n, 434–438
  GARCH (generalized autoregressive conditional heteroskedasticity), 281, 281n
  Garman-Kohlhagen, 44, 48, 433
  jump-diffusion, 397
  quadratic. *See* Model, Whaley
  theoretical pricing, 38, 40–41, 132
  Whaley, 248–249, 438–439
Moments, 440
Morton, Andrew, 393n

❖ N ❖

Naked positions, 199
Natural long and short, 257
Nelson, David B., 281n
New York Futures Exchange, 131
New York Mercantile Exchange (NYMEX), 2, 128
New York Stock Exchange, 303, 343
New York Times, 31n
Newton-Raphson search, 446

❖ O ❖

Option
  American, 4, 44, 113, 120n, 148n, 241
  at-the-money, 7-8, 106, 110, 205, 208–209
  call, 1
  European, 6, 44, 113, 204n, 213, 239, 240, 242n
  flex, 2n
  in-the-money, 7–8, 111, 113, 205
  out-of-the-money, 7–8, 205
  on a spread, 351–352
  put, 1
  replication, 94
  serial, 2
  type, 1

value at expiration, 13–19
Outliers, 401
Out-of-the-money. *See* Option, out-of-the-money
Overwrite, 261

❖ **P** ❖

Pacific Stock Exchange, 303
Parity. *See* Value, intrinsic
Parkinson, Michael, 66n
Philadelphia Stock Exchange, 6n, 303
Pin risk, 224–226
Portfolio insurance, 94, 271
Program trading, 310
Pseudo-American Call, 248
Put-Call Parity, 216
Premium, 6
Present value, 222n, 447
Price relative, 443
Protective option, 258–260

❖ **R** ❖

Random walk, 51–52
Range forward, 264
Ratio backspread. *See* Backspread
Ratio spread, 141–142
  bull and bear, 199–200
Ratio vertical spread, 139-141, 145, 200, 452
  intermarket, 339
Ratio write, 266
Reversal. *See* Reverse conversion
Reverse Conversion, 217–219, 456
Riskless hedge, 45
Rho, 116-118, 180
Roll. *See* Jelly roll
Ross, Stephen, 248, 400n, 434n
Rubenstein, Mark, 248, 434n

❖ **S** ❖

Scalping, 127
Scholes, Myron, 43, 431n
Schroeder, Mark, 400n
Scott, Louis D., 393n
Settlement
  cash, 226, 305, 314
  futures-type, 10–11, 220
  of stock index contracts, 315n
  prices, 406n
  risk, 226–228
  stock-type, 10–11, 220
Short, 11–12
Short premium, 160
Short sale, 93, 156–157, 386
Short squeeze, 157
Skewness, 402–403, 440–441, 443
Split-price conversion and reversal, 264
Spread, 127–129
  crack, 335–336
  intermarket, 331
  intramarket, 128, 331
  long and short, 147
  entering an order. 169–171
  NOB, 129
Standard deviation, 56–58, 59, 60–61, 381, 440–443
  daily and weekly, 65–66
  sample, 440n
Stock split, 46n
Straddle, 141–142, 187, 236, 398–399, 452
Strangle, 143–144, 187, 452
Strike price. *See* Exercise price
Synthetics, 213–214, 456
  in futures option markets, 220–221
  in stock option markets, 221–223
  in stock index markets, 320–322
  using in volatility spreads, 233–235
Synthetic market, 216, 457

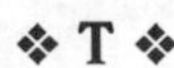

Taxes, 87, 386
Tender offer, 156, 254
Theta, 111, 113, 361–362
  characteristics, 119
  dollar ($theta), 114n, 346
  implied, 120
  of volatility spreads, 160–161

risk, 179, 353
Three-way, 229
Time box, 233
Time decay. *See* Theta
Time premium. *See* Value, time
Time spread, 148–154, 237, 452, 458
bull and bear, 201
effect of dividends, 155
effect of interest rates, 154–155
effect of price change, 150–151
effect of time passage, 149–150
effect of volatility, 151–153, 168
in hedging strategies, 267
in futures option markets, 153–154
Transaction costs, 87, 181, 387
Tunnel, 264

❖ U ❖

Underlying, 1–4, 45
Up-tick, 93

❖ V ❖

Value
extrinsic. *See* Value, time
intrinsic, 6–7, 13
of an underlying contract, 84n
time, 6–7, 261
theoretical, 37–38, 40
Variation, 11, 387n
Vega, 113–115, 361–362
dollar ($vega), 114n, 347
effect of time passage, 115
characteristics, 119–120
implied, 120
of volatility spreads, 160–161, 166
risk, 179–180, 353
Vertical spread, 202–211, 235–236, 252
in hedging strategies, 267
importance of implied volatility, 208
Volatility, 45, 49, 390–393, 399–400
and observed price changes, 67–68
as a standard deviation, 60–61
calculation of historical, 443–446
calculation of implied, 446
cone, 275
effect of changes. *See* Vega
forecast, 70–71
future, 69
historical, 69–70, 71
implied, 72–74, 89, 166, 177, 208, 266, 355
implied versus historical, 290–295
implied versus future, 295–299
mean reverting, 275
of interest rate products, 68–69, 393
realized, 70
relationships, 342–345
seasonal, 76
serial correlation, 280
skew, 407
stochastic, 393
trends, 275
Volume Investors, 105

❖ W ❖

Wall Street Journal, The, 31n
Whaley, Robert, 248, 438n
White, Alan, 393n
Wiggins, J.B., 393n
Wilcox, Darrell, 352, 434